T0234950

Lecture Notes in Computer Science 12242

More information about this series at http://www.springer.com/series/7412

Lucio Tommaso De Paolis ·
Patrick Bourdot (Eds.)

Augmented Reality, Virtual Reality, and Computer Graphics

7th International Conference, AVR 2020
Lecce, Italy, September 7–10, 2020
Proceedings, Part I

Editors
Lucio Tommaso De Paolis ⓘ
University of Salento
Lecce, Italy

Patrick Bourdot
University of Paris-Sud
Orsay, France

ISSN 0302-9743   ISSN 1611-3349 (electronic)
Lecture Notes in Computer Science
ISBN 978-3-030-58464-1   ISBN 978-3-030-58465-8 (eBook)
https://doi.org/10.1007/978-3-030-58465-8

LNCS Sublibrary: SL6 – Image Processing, Computer Vision, Pattern Recognition, and Graphics

This Springer imprint is published by the registered company Springer Nature Switzerland AG
The registered company address is: Gewerbestrasse 11, 6330 Cham, Switzerland

Preface

Virtual Reality (VR) technology permits the creation of realistic-looking worlds where the user inputs are used to modify in real time the digital environment. Interactivity contributes to the feeling of immersion in the virtual world, of being part of the action that the user experiences. It is not only possible to see and manipulate a virtual object, but also perceive them via different sensorimotor channels, such as by using haptic devices and 3D audio rendering.

Augmented Reality (AR) and Mixed Reality (MR) technologies permit the real-time fusion of computer-generated digital contents with the real world and allow the creation of fascinating new types of user interfaces. AR enhances the users' perception and improves their interaction in the real environment. The virtual objects help the user to perform real-world tasks better by displaying information that cannot directly detect with their own senses. Unlike the VR technology that completely immerses users inside a synthetic environment where they cannot see the real world around them, AR technology allows the users to perceive 3D virtual objects superimposed upon the real environment. AR and MR supplement reality rather than completely replacing it, and the user is under the impression that the virtual and real objects coexist in the same space.

This book contains the contributions to the 7th International Conference on Augmented Reality, Virtual Reality and Computer Graphics (SALENTO AVR 2020) organized by the Augmented and Virtual Reality Laboratory (AVR Lab) at University of Salento, Italy, during September 7–10, 2020. This year the event was rescheduled as a virtual conference to ensure the welfare of the community.

The conference series aims to bring together the community of researchers and scientists in order to discuss key issues, approaches, ideas, open problems, innovative applications, and trends on VR and AR, 3D visualization, and computer graphics in the areas of medicine, cultural heritage, arts, education, entertainment, military, and industrial applications. We cordially invite you to visit the SALENTO AVR website (www.salentoavr.it) where you can find all relevant information about this event.

We are very grateful to the Program Committee and Local Organizing Committee members for their support and for the time spent to review and discuss the submitted papers and doing so in a timely and professional manner.

We would like to sincerely thank the keynote speakers who willingly accepted our invitation and shared their expertise through illuminating talks, helping us to fully meet the conference objectives. In this edition of SALENTO AVR, we were honored to have the following invited speakers:

- Massimo Bergamasco – Scuola Superiore Sant'Anna, Italy
- Mariano Alcañiz – Universitat Politècnica de València, Spain
- Emanuele Frontoni – Università Politecnica delle Marche, Italy
- Mariolino De Cecco – Università di Trento, Italy
- Domenico Prattichizzo – Università di Siena, Italy

SALENTO AVR 2020 attracted high-quality paper submissions from many countries. We would like to thank the authors of all accepted papers for submitting and presenting their works, for making SALENTO AVR an excellent forum on VR and AR, facilitating the exchange of ideas, and shaping the future of this exciting research field.

We hope the readers will find in these pages interesting material and fruitful ideas for their future work.

July 2020   Lucio Tommaso De Paolis
                                                                   Patrick Bourdot

Organization

Conference Chairs

Lucio Tommaso De Paolis   University of Salento, Italy
Patrick Bourdot   CNRS/LIMSI, University of Paris-Sud, France
Marco Sacco   CNR-STIIMA, Italy

Scientific Program Committee

Andrea Abate   University of Salerno, Italy
Giovanni Aloisio   University of Salento, Italy
Giuseppe Anastasi   University of Pisa, Italy
Selim Balcisoy   Sabancı University, Turkey
Vitoantonio Bevilacqua   Polytechnic of Bari, Italy
Monica Bordegoni   Politecnico di Milano, Italy
Davide Borra   NoReal.it, Italy
Andrea Bottino   Politecnico di Torino, Italy
Pierre Boulanger   University of Alberta, Canada
Andres Bustillo   University of Burgos, Spain
Massimo Cafaro   University of Salento, Italy
Bruno Carpentieri   University of Salerno, Italy
Sergio Casciaro   IFC-CNR, Italy
Marcello Carrozzino   Scuola Superiore Sant'Anna, Italy
Mario Ciampi   ICAR-CNR, Italy
Pietro Cipresso   IRCCS Istituto Auxologico Italiano, Italy
Arnis Cirulis   Vidzeme University of Applied Sciences, Latvia
Mario Covarrubias   Politecnico di Milano, Italy
Rita Cucchiara   University of Modena, Italy
Yuri Dekhtyar   Riga Technical University, Latvia
Giorgio De Nunzio   University of Salento, Italy
Francisco José Domínguez Mayo   University of Seville, Spain
Aldo Franco Dragoni   Università Politecnica delle Marche, Italy
Italo Epicoco   University of Salento, Italy
Ben Falchuk   Perspecta Labs Inc., USA
Vincenzo Ferrari   EndoCAS Center, Italy
Francesco Ferrise   Politecnico di Milano, Italy
Dimitrios Fotiadis   University of Ioannina, Greece
Emanuele Frontoni   Università Politecnica delle Marche, Italy
Francesco Gabellone   IBAM ITLab, CNR, Italy
Damianos Gavalas   University of the Aegean, Greece
Osvaldo Gervasi   University of Perugia, Italy

Luigi Gallo	ICAR-CNR, Italy
Viktors Gopejenko	ISMA University, Latvia
Mirko Grimaldi	University of Salento, Italy
Heiko Herrmann	Tallinn University of Technology, Estonia
Sara Invitto	University of Salento, Italy
Fabrizio Lamberti	Politecnico di Torino, Italy
Leo Joskowicz	Hebrew University of Jerusalem, Israel
Tomas Krilavičius	Vytautas Magnus University, Lithuania
Salvatore Livatino	University of Hertfordshire, UK
Silvia Mabel Castro	Universidad Nacional del Sur, Argentina
Luca Mainetti	University of Salento, Italy
Eva Savina Malinverni	Università Politecnica delle Marche, Italy
Matija Marolt	University of Ljubljana, Slovenia
Daniel R. Mestre	Aix-Marseille University, CNRS, France
Sven Nomm	Tallinn University of Technology, Estonia
Fabrizio Nunnari	German Research Center for Artificial Intelligence (DFKI), Germany
Roberto Paiano	University of Salento, Italy
Giorgos Papadourakis	Technological Educational Institute (TEI) of Crete, Greece
Gianfranco Parlangeli	University of Salento, Italy
Gianluca Paravati	Politecnico di Torino, Italy
Nikolaos Pellas	University of the Aegean, Greece
Eduard Petlenkov	Tallinn University of Technology, Estonia
Roberto Pierdicca	Università Politecnica delle Marche, Italy
Sofia Pescarin	CNR ITABC, Italy
Paolo Proietti	MIMOS, Italy
Arcadio Reyes Lecuona	Universidad de Malaga, Spain
James Ritchie	Heriot-Watt University, UK
Giuseppe Riva	Università Cattolica del Sacro Cuore, Italy
Andrea Sanna	Politecnico di Torino, Italy
Jaume Segura Garcia	Universitat de València, Spain
Paolo Sernani	Università Politecnica delle Marche, Italy
Danijel Skočaj	University of Ljubljana, Slovenia
Robert Stone	University of Birmingham, UK
João Manuel R. S. Tavares	Universidade do Porto, Portugal
Daniel Thalmann	Nanyang Technological University, Singapore
Nadia Magnenat-Thalmann	University of Geneva, Switzerland
Franco Tecchia	Scuola Superiore Sant'Anna, Italy
Carlos M. Travieso-González	Universidad de Las Palmas de Gran Canaria, Spain
Manolis Tsiknaki	Technological Educational Institute of Crete (TEI), Greece
Oguzhan Topsakal	Florida Polytechnic University, USA
Antonio Emmanuele Uva	Polytechnic of Bari, Italy
Volker Paelke	Bremen University of Applied Sciences, Germany

Aleksei Tepljakov	Tallinn University of Technology, Estonia
Kristina Vassiljeva	Tallinn University of Technology, Estonia
Krzysztof Walczak	Poznań University of Economics and Business, Poland
Anthony Whitehead	Carleton University, Canada

Local Organizing Committee

Ilenia Paladini	University of Salento, Italy
Silke Miss	XRtechnology, Italy

Keynote Speakers

Cognitive Architecture for Virtual Humans and Androids

Massimo Bergamasco

Scuola Superiore Sant'Anna, Italy

The concept of physical space has been recently juxtaposed to other digital entities like Augmented or Mixed Realities. Presumably, such new spaces will be occupied not only by digital objects but also by the digital equivalent of human beings, i.e. virtual humans. How present research in robotics and AI is going to define the behavior of humanoid robots, androids, and virtual humans is something that can be formulated also in terms of ethical and social terms. The class provides a general picture on how the interaction between human beings and artificial entities can be foreseen on the basis of present technology development. An excursus on the different approaches to design cognitive architecture for virtual humans is provided.

Massimo Bergamasco is Professor of Theory of Mechanisms and Machines at the Scuola Superiore Sant'Anna, Italy. At present he is the President of the ARTES 4.0 (Advanced Robotics and enabling digital Technologies & Systems 4.0) Competence Center in the framework of the Industry 4.0 of the Italian Ministry for Economic Development. He has been the founder of the Perceptual Robotics Laboratory. His research activity deals with the study and development of haptic interfaces and wearable robots for the control of the interaction between humans and Virtual Environments. His present research is focused on general aspects of perception and cognitive processes in the field of embodiment and humanoid robotics.

Virtual Reality: New Therapeutic Scenarios to Optimize Neurorehabilitation

Mariano Alcañiz

Universitat Politècnica de València, Spain

Virtual Reality (VR) technologies are demonstrating their clinical utility for neurorehabilitation. In this talk, the scientific and clinical basis of the use of VR in neurorehabilitation as well as current uses and future trends will be presented. The concept of VR-based behavioral biomarkers will be introduced as a convergent concept of areas such as VR, machine learning, and computational psychiatry.

Mariano Alcañiz is Full Professor at the Polytechnic University of Valencia (Spain) and Director of the European Laboratory of Immersive Neurotechnologies (LabLENI). His research interest is to understand human social cognition using emerging technologies end ecologically valid mixed reality-based simulations. He has published more than 300 scientific articles and has coordinated several European projects related to the area. LabLENI focuses its research activity in the integration of Virtual Environments with applied neuroscience techniques to better understand human behavior in fields such as mental health, marketing, human resources, or education.

Artificial Intelligence for Augmented and Virtual Reality Content Creation

Emanuele Frontoni

Università Politecnica delle Marche, Italy

Artificial intelligence (AI) is reshaping the way we manage and create multimedia 2D and 3D contents in AR and VR experiences. The talk will start from modern AI models that have gotten incredibly good at doing many of the things required to build AR experiences. Deep Neural Networks can detect vertical and horizontal planes, estimate depth and segment images and point clouds for realistic occlusion and meaningful content generator, and even infer 3D positions of objects in real time. Because of these abilities, AI models are replacing some of the more traditional computer vision approaches underpinning AR experiences. On the other hand, Generative Adversarial Networks can help on the creation of virtual contents or realistic human behaviors, useful for advanced VR experiences.

Emanuele Frontoni is Professor at the Università Politecnica delle Marche, Engineering Faculty. He received the doctoral degree in electronic engineering from the University of Ancona, Italy, in 2003. He obtained his PhD in 2006 discussing a thesis on Vision Based Robotics. His research focuses on applying computer science, AI, and computer vision techniques to mobile robots and innovative IT applications. He is a member of IEEE and AI*IA, the Italian Association for Artificial Intelligence.

Augmenting the Physician Eye to Optimize Smart Living Environment Settings: Preliminary Outcomes from Ausilia

Mariolino De Cecco

Università di Trento, Italy

The European population is increasingly ageing. The median age in Europe will increase from 37.7 in 2003 to 52 by 2050. The increment in proportion of the retired population is expected to have significant social and economic impacts. In order to keep autonomy and wellbeing a proper configuration (in terms of architecture and technologies) of the elderlies living environment can be very effective. This objective is fundamental in order to reduce the re-hospitalization rate that is part of the societal challenge. On the other end, Mixed Reality (MR) technologies have the potential to augment the human skill in terms of perception and planning. The talk will report on the use of MR technologies that, within Ausilia (Assisted Unit for Simulating Independent LIving Activities), are enabling the augmentation of physician eyes to properly configure the living environment around the user needs/abilities. We will start from the Occupational Therapy context to show Augmented Virtuality and Augmented Reality IoT infrastructures able to accomplish the above goal.

Mariolino De Cecco is Professor of Mechanical and Thermal Measurements and Robotics Perception and Action at the University of Trento. Co-Investigator of OSIRIS (ROSETTA – ESA Cornerstone Mission), he is in the Steering Committee of the project Ausilia, co-founder of Robosense Srl, and participated in several international projects (FP7, H2020, Eureka, ESA, EIT). His research focuses on Measurements, Mobile Robotics, 3D Computer Vision, Action Recognition, and Mixed Reality.

On the Foundations of Wearable Haptics and Applications to VR/AR and Robotics

Domenico Prattichizzo

Università di Siena, Italy

Since 2015, Domenico Prattichizzo is Full Professor at the University of Siena. From 2002 to 2015, he was Associate Professor of Robotics at the University of Siena. Since 2009, he has been the Scientific Consultant at Istituto Italiano di Tecnoloogia, Italy. In 1994, he was the Visiting Scientist at the MIT AI Lab. Professor Prattichizzo obtained his degree in electronics engineering and a PhD degree in Robotics and Automation from the University of Pisa in 1991 and 1995, respectively. His Research interests are in Haptics, Grasping, Visual Servoing, Mobile Robotics, and Geometric Control.

Contents – Part I

Augmented Reality

Mixed Reality

3D Reconstruction and Visualization

Contents – Part II

Applications in Education

Applications in Industry

Virtual Reality

How to Reduce the Effort: Comfortable Watching Techniques for Cinematic Virtual Reality

Sylvia Rothe[✉], Lang Zhao, Arne Fahrenwalde, and Heinrich Hußmann

LMU Munich, Munich, Germany

{sylvia.rothe,hussmann}@ifi.lmu.de, lang.zhao@campus.lmu.de,
arne@fahrenwal.de

Abstract. When watching omnidirectional movies with Head-Mounted Displays, viewers can freely choose the direction of view, and thus the visible section of the movie. However, looking around all the time can be exhausting and having content in the full 360° area can cause the fear to miss something. For making watching more comfortable, we implemented new methods and conducted three experiments: (1) exploring methods to inspect the full omnidirectional area by moving the head, but not the whole body; (2) comparing head, body and movie rotation and (3) studying how the reduction of the 360° area influences the viewing experience. For (3), we compared the user behavior watching a full 360°, a 225° and a 180° movie via HMD. The investigated techniques for inspecting the full 360° area in a fixed sitting position (experiments 1 and 2) perform well and could replace the often-used swivel chair. Reducing the 360° area (experiment 3), 225° movies resulted in a better score than 180° movies.

Keywords: Cinematic virtual reality · User comfort · Rotational gain · Less than 360° · Omnidirectional video

1 Introduction

In Cinematic Virtual Reality (CVR), viewers watch omnidirectional videos (ODV) using Head-Mounted Displays (HMDs). In this way, they are inside the scenery and have the possibility to look around. But turning around all the time can be exhausting, especially for longer movies. Even in normal life, we do not do that so often. Mostly a rotation of the head is sufficient. Additionally, some people are afraid to miss something because the movie continues also in the areas behind them. This Fear of Missing Out (FoMo) can cause negative feelings [13] and can be reduced be guiding methods [15].

Even if the term 360° video is widely used for ODV, it only partially reflects this medium. In addition to the 360° in the horizontal direction, the viewer can look up and down and explore the movie in the vertical direction. Other terms that can be found in the literature are panoramic, spherical, surround, VR and immersive videos. ODV can be watched on desktops by moving the mouse, on mobile devices by moving the device

© Springer Nature Switzerland AG 2020
L. T. De Paolis and P. Bourdot (Eds.): AVR 2020, LNCS 12242, pp. 3–21, 2020.
https://doi.org/10.1007/978-3-030-58465-8_1

or via HMD by moving the head. Using an HMD, the viewer is inside the scenery and can experience the movie in an immersive way. In this paper, we consider the HMD scenario. Since we also investigate the case where the viewing area is reduced in the horizontal angle, we use the terms 180°, 225°, and 360° videos to indicate the horizontal angle of provided movie content. In the following, we use the term CVR generally for videos watched immersively with an HMD, independently of the used viewing angle.

Watching a CVR video in a sitting posture needs methods to turn around. For demonstrations of CVR experiences in public spaces such as film festivals or fairs, swivel chairs are usually used. At home, the viewer often sits on a fixed chair or on a sofa while watching the movie [5]. In this way, it is more difficult to explore the full 360° area without any additional techniques. In this work, we explore methods for enjoying movies in such fixed conditions and compare them with the swivel chair condition. Additionally, we investigate if inspecting the full 360° area is necessary for an immersive CVR experience. For finding the needs to comfortably watch CVR videos in fixed sitting postures, we explore three approaches.

Immobile Techniques: In our first experiment, we compare methods that enable viewers to watch the full 360° of a CVR movie sitting on a sofa or armchair using a controller or rotation gain. The results of experiment 1 show that such techniques can be useful for inspecting the full 360° area in a relaxing sitting posture without additional physical effort for turning around. We explored how the methods influence presence, experience, simulator sickness, and incidental memory.

Rotation Medium: For the second approach, we checked the controller method, which performed best in the first study, against using a swivel chair and a normal armchair without additional methods. The 360° movies for this study were selected so that the action mainly took place in a 180° area. Except for one short scene in one of the movies, there was no relevant content in the other 180° part. Even if the participants of this study inspected the whole 360° area nevertheless, one of the results of this study is, that most of them would prefer a 180° over a 360° movie.

Less than 360°: In the last study, we explored how a limited area influences the viewing experience. For this, we chose two area sizes: 180° and 225°. The size of 225° was determined as the section which can be explored by most persons without changing a sitting posture. We investigated if the full 360° space is necessary for a CVR experience and how a smaller space influences presence, cognitive load, and the viewing experience.

A content area less than 360° would have several advantages: (1) the fear of missing out could be reduced, (2) the production of CVR videos would be easier, since an area for lights and film crew would be available, (3) the image quality could be improved with the same amount of data. In 2017 Google has introduced the VR180 video format which is based on the Spherical Video Metadata V2 standard [25]. This format is supported by YouTube and since 2018 there are several 180° cameras on the market. However, we did not find any research studying whether the reduced area decreases presence or influences the VR experience. In addition, we are interested in whether less reduction over 180° should be preferred.

Humans can rotate their heads horizontally by about 60° in both directions [23]. Comfortable head movements can be performed to 45° for most persons [23]. In an area between 60° and 120° people can recognize colors [23]. Using an HMD with a smaller field of view (FoV) the vision of a person is restricted. In our experiment, we are using a Samsung Gear VR HMD, which has a FoV of 101°. Considering this size and a head movement angle of 120° (60° in both directions), the viewer can inspect an area of about 221° in a fixed sitting posture (Fig. 1).

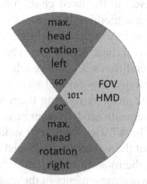

Fig. 1. Area which can be seen in a fixed sitting posture.

Adding a small area for blurring the boundary we investigated if viewers have a similar experience watching 360°, 225° and 180° movies. The results of experiment 3 show that the presence decreases slightly for the 180° movies, even for movies where it is not necessary to look around. However, the experience can be improved using 225° movies instead of 180°.

The results of this works show that other methods besides the swivel chair exist for enjoying CVR movies. These methods need less physical effort and can be used in a fixed sitting posture. Using a controller or rotation gain for seeing the whole 360° area implies a discrepancy between movements in the real and virtual world. However, in our experiments, the participants reported only minor sickness, which could be caused by the fact that the rotation was initiated by themselves. Reducing the 360° area is another valuable approach. All the investigated methods do not replace head and eye movements which are important for natural viewing experiences and immersion.

2 Related Work

2.1 Engagement

Most people watch movies to enjoy and relax in a passive way. In contrast, gaming requires more activity and engagement to achieve goals [2]. With interactive storytelling movies and games get closer to each other [2, 24]. Vosmeer et al. [24] investigated different engagement styles in games and movies. A viewer of a movie is used to *lean back* without any interactivity, while the user of a videogame interacts with the content (*lean forward*). In their paper, the term *lean-in* media was introduced for the engagement style in CVR: the viewer is looking around and chooses the FOV, so there is some sort of interaction.

2.2 Rotation Medium

This engagement of the viewer can be influenced by several aspects. One of them is the chair type. In the experiments by Hong et al. [5] three types of chairs were compared: fixed, half-swivel and full-swivel. For several dependent variables (incidental memory, general engagement, and simulator sickness) there were no significant differences between the chair types. However, in the fixed chair condition, the spatial awareness decreased and the fear of missing something increased for videos where the main characters performed around the viewer. Additionally, the participants explored the scenery more when they used the full-swivel chair. For movies where the content was mainly in a smaller area in front of the viewer differences between the conditions were less obvious.

Gugenheimer et al. [3] developed a motorized swivel chair (SwiVRChair) for supporting the viewers to follow the story by rotating them in the direction of the region of interest. In this way, the participants needed lower head movements for enjoying the VR experience in a more "lean back" way. Simulator sickness in their experiment was very low. A reason for that is that the viewers were turned around and so the rotation in the virtual world matched with the rotation in the real world. One source of simulator sickness is the discrepancy between movements in the real and virtual world [1, 9] and so rotating the VR world in front of the user provokes normally sickness. There is no consistent opinion if rotating a scene causes simulator sickness or not [11]. Lin et al. [11] compared forced rotation (called autopilot) with an arrow which shows in the direction of the region of interest (called visual guidance). The results depend on the type of movie, but there was no generally higher simulator sickness for the forced rotation observed.

Forced methods can be used for guiding the user to the region of interest [3, 11, 22]. There are different ways for that. On the one hand, the user can be rotated, as in SwiVRChair [3]. This has the advantages that the viewer can feel the rotary motion. On the other hand, the VR-world/movie can be rotated [11]. In both cases, the rotation is initiated from outside (e.g. by the filmmaker). In our work, the viewer triggers the rotation. And we investigate how presence and simulator sickness are affected.

2.3 Rotational Gain/Amplified Head Rotation

Rotating the virtual world not completely synchronously to the user's movements is used for redirecting walking [14, 20]. Steinicke et al. [21] explored the thresholds for this technique.

Jaekl et al. [6] introduced amplified head rotation for HMDs. In their experiments, the participants determined the gain factor for which the virtual world is stable in relation to their own head movements. The identified scale factors ranged from 0.88 to 1.33 (yaw), respectively from 0.11 to 1.66 (pitch). These results correspond to the results of Steinicke et al. [21] (yaw: 0.83–1.34). Scaling factors in this range are tolerated as compatible with the perception of moving within a stable world and users are unaware of the manipulation. Jay et al. [7] increased the amount of gain and found significant improvements in performance on visual search tasks. Using a scaling factor of 2, the participants felt comfortable and even preferred the gain method to the baseline without gain implementation.

Amplified head movements work well for watching tasks, however its harder to interact with the virtual environment with body movements which are not amplified in the same way [7]. This problem is not relevant for CVR, but for other VR applications.

Rotational gain can be applied for watching CVR movies [4] in a way that users can enjoy the movies in a chair with less physical movement. Hong et al. [4] compared dynamic and constant rotational gain. For the constant method, a scale factor of 1.3 was used, for the dynamic method between 1.3 and 1.6. The dynamical gain was assigned in a way that gain was higher for fast head movements. Both methods were working and did not influence sickness or usability.

Another dynamic rotation gain method was investigated by Sagunam et al. [17], where the gain in the front area is smaller than in the area further away. With their method, the full virtual 360° area is covered by head movements of 90° to the right and 90° to the left. In their experiments, the amplified methods worked, but participants preferred the standard rotation without any gain.

The gain makes it harder to focus a target exactly. Langbehn et al. [10] explored several dynamic rotation methods aligned to the target. In their experiments, dynamic gain performed best compared to static gain, a scrolling method, and the baseline. Since in our experiments the viewers are looking around without any task, we decided to use a constant gain factor of 2.0 in our first experiment.

2.4 Less Than 360°

In 1996 Pausch et al. [12] examined how the attention of the viewer can be drawn to the desired spot. The position and orientation of the head were logged and conventional histograms were used for illustrating the data. The results show that most people did not turn their head very much, almost all the time in an area from −60° to +60° in the horizontal direction and from −30° to +20° in the vertical direction. These results correspond to the research of Sitzmann et al. [19]. They investigated how people explore virtual environments and showed that viewers tend to fixate the area around the equator.

In our study, we want to investigate if the 360° area can be reduced in the horizontal direction for making watching more comfortable and to reduce the fear to miss something.

3 Experiment 1: Immobile Techniques

Since for most people movie watching is a relaxing activity, techniques are needed to explore the full 360° area of a CVR movie without turning the body around. Such techniques are not only applicable sitting on the sofa but also at the desk, in a train or on other places with limited freedom of movement.

3.1 Methods of Experiment 1

We implemented three methods to watch the movie without turning around, just using head movements or a controller and compared them to each other.

Controller with Constant Speed – const method: With the const method, the user can rotate the image at a constant speed by pressing the controller button to the right or left side. The rotation is only possible in the horizontal direction. For looking up and down, the head should be used. The head movements could also be used for inspecting the scenery without the controller. The initialization speed was set to 45°/s.

Controller with Variable Speed – var method: The *var* method is similar to the *const* method regarding the rotation directions but differs in the speed. The more the participants pressed the button to the right or left side the larger the rotation speed up to a maximum speed of 60°/s.

Rotational Gain – gain method: For the *gain* method amplified head rotation of Jaekl is used [6]. According to this research, a speed factor between 0.88 and 1.33 for rotational gain is accepted as a stable rotation and not perceived by the participants. Taking into account an area of 120° for maximal head movements and a FoV of 101°, a gain factor of 1.33 is not sufficient to cover the full 360° area.

To find the most comfortable rotation gain, six values (1.3, 1.5, 1.7, 1.8, 2, 2.1) were tested in an informal pilot study with 5 participants. As an outcome, we chose 2.0 because of the most natural behavior and least confusion. This result confirms the studies of [7]: a gain factor of 2 is comfortable for viewers, even if the gain is sometimes noticeable. The gain factor of 2.0 has another advantage. Even if people turning around, they will always have the same movie sections in the same position, the movie content is presented exactly twice in a 360° round.

3.2 Material of Experiment 1

Because we were interested in situations of watching movies at home, the experiments were carried out as a field study in a home environment. The viewers watched the movies via Google cardboard and Samsung Galaxy S7, sitting on a couch or chair (not a swivel chair). The cardboard was added with a head strap. It was essential that no cable restricted the movements of the participants.

For implementing the three methods and the recording of the head movements, Unity 2017.2 was used. During watching movies with method *const* and *dyn* the participants used an auvisio mini Bluetooth controller.

Three animated movies with different paces were shown ("Unexpected Guest", "Special Delivery", a fragment of "The dream collector"). Each of them takes approximately 2:30 min. For all three films, the participants had to look around in the full 360° area for following the protagonists. More information about the movies can be found in the supplementary material.

3.3 Measures of Experiment 1

In the beginning, each participant answered questions about age, gender and VR experiences. After each video, the questions of the igroup presence questionnaire (ipq) [18] were answered. For each item, the answers were chosen on a seven-point Likert scale.

For finding out how the viewer experienced the movies with the different methods the following issues were addressed, all of them on a seven-point Likert scale:

Sickness: For investigating if one of the methods causes more simulator sickness than the others, five items of the SSQ questionnaire [8] were used: general discomfort, headache, dizziness, eye strain, difficulty focusing. The answers are given on a four-point Likert scale (0-none to 3-severe).

Comparison: At the end of the study, the participants compared the three methods and answered the following two questions: (C1) Which method did you find the most comfortable? (C2) Which type of methods do you prefer?

For both answers, they should give a brief explanation.

3.4 Participants and Procedure of Experiment 1

18 participants (5 females, 13 males, average age 25.8) took part in the experiment. 33.3% of them had no VR experiences. We used a within-subject test design; every participant used all three methods, each of them with another movie. The order of the methods and the assignments between movie and method was counterbalanced by a Graeco-Latin square as presented in Fig. 2.

A1	B2	C3
B3	C1	A2
C2	A3	B1

Fig. 2. Graeco-Latin square for three methods (A, B, C) and three movies (1, 2, 3).

3.5 Results of Experiment 1

Using the Shapiro-Wilk test, homogeneity of variances was checked which showed that equal variances could not be assumed for all issues. Therefore, the Friedman test was applied to find significant differences between the methods. For determining the significance, an alpha-level 0.05 was chosen. Post-hoc Mann-Whitney tests were used for pairwise comparisons of the methods.

Comparing the methods to each other, some items do not differ significantly between the methods. However, we listed a part of them to show the level of the scores and to offer the opportunity to compare the scores between the experiments.

Presence. The Friedman test did not indicate any significant differences between the methods.

Experience. Three of the experience questions showed significant differences: *EX1*, *EX3*, *EX6*. Regarding *EX1* the score was higher for the *gain* method (M = 5.33, SD = 0.97) than for the *var* method (M = 4.67, SD = 1.08) (p = 0.048). The *const* method (M = 4.0, SD = 1.75) was not so easy to perform (EX3) as the two other methods (p(const/var) = 0.047, p(const/gain) = 0.026). It was easier to keep up with the pace of the content (EX6) for the *gain* method (M = 5.22, SD = 1.11) than for the *const* method (M = 4.0, SD = 1.75) (p = (gain/const) = 0.02). The mean values can be seen in Fig. 3.

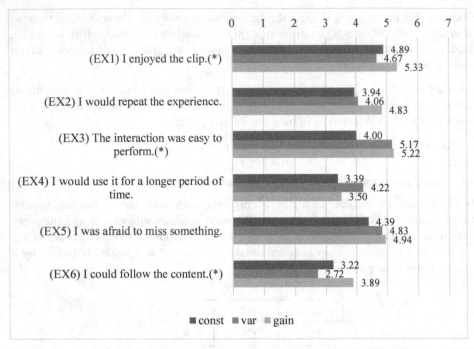

Fig. 3. Means for the experience items, which differed significantly for EX1, EX3, and EX6 indicated by (*).

Simulator Sickness. The scores for the SSQ were generally very low, between 0.11 and 1.11 (Table 1). Significant differences could be found for the dizziness item, the Friedman test resulted in a p-value of 0.009. The gain method indicated the highest values: M(gain) = 1.11, M(const) = 0.61, M(var) = 0.39. Pairwise Mann-Whitney tests showed significant differences between the gain method and the two controller conditions: p(gain/var) = 0.003, p(gain/const) = 0.046.

Table 1. Means for the SSQ items, there are significant differences for dizziness.

	General discomfort	Headache	Dizziness	Eye strain	Difficulty focusing
const	0.78	0.28	0.61 (*)	0.94	1.11
var	0.89	0.11	0.39 (*)	0.67	0.61
gain	0.72	0.33	1.11 (*)	1.11	0.94

Comparison. After all three different methods were applied, the participants compared them to each other. Only 11.1% of the participants scored the *const* method as the most comfortable, 38.9% of the participants the gain and 50% of the participants the *var* method.

The reasons which were given by the participants often concerned easiness, for the *var* method (P3, P5, P10, P11, P14, P18), as well as for the *const* (P6) and the *gain* method (P12).

In contrast to the results of the presence questionnaires, several participants stated as a reason, why they feel most comfortable with the *gain* method, that it is more realistic (P1, P4, P7, P8, P9). Other advantages which were mentioned:

Advantages of controller:

- "convenient" (P13)
- "I don't need to rotate my head" (P4,P18)
- "you can focus on watching and do not have to look around" (P17)

Advantages of Rotation Gain:

- "I could control the angle and speed" (P16)
- "more real" (P1,P4,P7,P8,P9)
- "no dizziness" (P7)
- "could control by head" (P16)

3.6 Discussion of Experiment 1

The results of our study show that the *var* and the *gain* method were accepted by the viewers. The *const* method resulted in the lowest score, especially in the comparison part. There are advantages and disadvantages of the methods. The *gain* method resulted in higher scores for the experience but caused more dizziness.

With the gain method, the full 360° area can be seen just by moving the head in a 180° area. However, it is difficult to realize that things on the left side belong together to things on the right side. This fact was not mentioned by the viewers. In the study of Jay et al. [7], the gain factor of 2.0. was used for a search task and helped the participants a lot. In our study, the participants feel to be inside a movie scenery and without a boundary at the left and right side, it seems as the scene continues there, but it is just a repetition. Over time, the viewers may get used to that fact. The question arises whether the full 360° area is necessary for an immersive CVR movie experience and needs to be recorded. We will explore that in experiment 3.

For the reasons mentioned above (most comfortable, less sickness) we chose the *var* method from this study and compared it with two other methods in the next experiment.

4 Experiment 2: Comparison of Rotation Medium

The goal of this study is to compare the rotation of the movie (experiment 1) with the rotation of the body using a swivel chair or using head rotation only, in a fixed seating position.

4.1   Methods of Experiment 2

We compared the following three methods:

Head Rotation – Fixed: Sitting on a normal chair the participants could look around by moving their heads. They were informed that the action of the movie is in front of them and there were no important story details behind them.

Body Rotation – Swivel Chair: The participants were sitting on a swivel chair and could turn around in all directions. Additionally, they could move the head for looking around.

Movie Rotation – Controller: The controller method with variable speed of experiment 1 (*var*) was reused and compared with the two other methods.

4.2   Material of Experiment 2

For the same reasons as in the first study, we used a Google cardboard and a Samsung Galaxy S7. For the movie rotation, an auvisio mini Bluetooth controller and the script of study 1 was used.

Because we wanted to investigate a lean-back experience, we were looking for a movie where most actions take place in front of the user within a field of 225°. So, the movie could be watched just by turning the head. We chose the movie "Son of Jaguar", directed by Jorge Gutierrez. We did not delete the part behind the viewers. However, the participants were informed about the fact that there are no story-relevant parts in the back. The 9 min movie was divided into three 3 min parts. More information about the movies can be found in the supplementary material.

4.3   Measures of Experiment 2

The questionnaire of study 1 has been revised and adapted to the second study. The attention questions were transformed for the new movie content and the comparison questions were changed to:

(C1) Which method did you find the most comfortable?
(C2) Which type of videos would you prefer? (180°/360°)
(C3) Would you like to turn your head very much?

Again, the participants should justify the answers. Additionally, the head movements of every viewer were recorded.

4.4   Participants and Procedure of Experiment 2

24 participants (10 females, 14 males, average age of 25.25) took part in the experiment. 37.5% of them had no VR experiences. We used a within-subject test design. Each user watched all three parts of the movie, each of them with another method. The order of the movies was equal, corresponding to the whole movie, the order of the methods permuted. All six permutations were used for the same number of participants. Every participant had to view all three parts of the movie: one in a swivel chair, one in a normal chair and one in a normal chair using a controller.

4.5 Results of Experiment 2

As in experiment 1, we used the Friedman test and post-hoc pairwise Mann-Whitney tests for finding significant differences between the methods.

Presence. We could not find significant differences regarding the presence questions.

Experience. Also, for the experience questions, we did not find significant differences between the methods.

Simulator Sickness. Again, there was minor sickness (means between 0.25 and 1.00). The Friedman test did not indicate significant differences between the methods.

Comparison. 45.83% of the participants felt most comfortable with the controller method, 41.67% using the swivel chair and 12.5% the fixed method. Nevertheless, 79.17% of the participants would prefer 180° movies to 360° movies.

The questions if the participants like to turn their head very much (C3) was answered on a 7-point-Likert scale (1 = yes, I liked exploring and seeing new spaces, 7 = No, I don't want to turn the head frequently, I just want to enjoy comfortably) with a mean of 4.9 (SD = 1.8).

Analysis of the Tracking Data. We inspected the head tracking data for all three methods and movies separately to find differences between the test cases. Using the CVR-Analyzer [16], we explored the spatio-temporal data for the whole movie and for parts of the movie.

The patterns for the *swivel* chair and the *fixed* methods were mostly very similar (Fig. 4). The tracks generated by using the *controller* were less concentrated and the heatmap areas smaller. One reason for this could be that it is harder to move around smoothly in a small area. Additionally, it can be more difficult to rediscover an area which was inspected before. For the fixed and even for the swivel method the human orientation system could support returning to an area to continue watching there.

Fig. 4. Heatmaps in equirectangular projection for the 2nd movie: swivel (above), fixed (middle), controller (below)

4.6 Discussion of Experiment 2

The methods did not differ significantly for the presence, experience and sickness items. These results suggest that a swivel chair could be replaced by other methods. Even if 87.5% of the participants considered one of the rotation techniques (*controller* or *swivel*) as most comfortable, most participants would prefer 180° movies. The fact that we did not delete the reverse side of the movie could have influenced this result. Although the action of the movie was mostly visible in front, the viewers wanted to know, what else could be seen. It needs more knowledge about what causes this behavior: is it the awareness that there is more to see or is it the novelty effect of VR medium which arouses this desire.

In the spatio-temporal data, we found similar patterns for the swivel chair and the fixed methods: relatively stable areas around the action. For the controller methods, the patterns were more diffuse and it seems to be more difficult to return to an area, which was inspected before.

5 Experiment 3: Less Than 360°

We compared three methods:

180° (fixed chair): The reduced area of 180° was chosen because this format is already introduced by Google and YouTube. The boundaries of this area were blurred for 4.5°. Looking straight ahead, the participants did not see these boundaries. Horizontal head movements are comfortable for humans in an area of up to 45° degrees in each direction [23]. Taking into account the 101° FoV of the Samsung Gear, the participants could see an area of 191° easily and so the boundaries when moving their heads to the left or right. The participants watched the movie in a fixed sitting position just moving the head.

225° (fixed chair): The 225° area was chosen because of the FoV of the Samsung Gear HMD (101°) and the maximal head rotations of Humans (60° in each direction). The boundaries were blurred at 4.5°. With comfortable head movements (45° in each direction), the boundaries were not visible. However, the boundaries could be seen with extreme head movements. As in the 180° condition, the participants watched the movie in a fixed sitting position just moving the head.

360° (swivel chair): For the third method, the viewers could inspect the full 360° area using a swivel chair.

5.1 Material of Experiment 3

Again, we used the Samsung S7 smartphone, this time with the Samsung Gear headset. Three movies similar in type, length and pace were chosen: professional documentaries where the main action was in a 180° area: "Lions 360° | National Geographic", "Galapagos 360° | National Geographic", "360° Underwater National Park | National Geographic". Two of the three videos were re-edited resulting in similar lengths (around 3 min) and actions always in front of the viewer. For this, some scenes were rotated using Adobe Premiere. More information about the movies can be found in the supplementary material.

5.2 Measures of Experiment 3

The questionnaire was similar to the one in the first two studies. We added four questions of the NASA-TLX for comparing the workload for the different methods.

5.3   Participants and Procedure of Experiment 3

24 participants (12 females, 12 males, average age of 35.79) took part in the experiment. One person had no VR experiences, 17 only la little. We used a within-subject test design. Each user watched three different movies, each of them with one of the methods. Movies and methods were counterbalanced using again a Graeco-Latin square.

5.4   Results of Experiment 3

As in the previous studies, the Shapiro-Wilk test was used for checking the homogencity of variances. It showed that equal variances could not be assumed for all issues. There-fore, the Friedman test and the post-hoc pairwise Mann-Whitney tests were applied for finding significant differences between the methods. For determining the significance, an alpha-level 0.05 was chosen.

Presence. The Friedman test resulted in several significant differences. For the item "I had the sense of being there" (1 = fully disagree, 7 = fully agree), the $360°$ method (M = 5.88, SD = 1.19) resulted in a significantly higher score than the $180°$ method (M = 4.75, SD = 1.39, p < 0.01) and the $225°$ method (M = 5.29, SD = 1.2, p = 0.07). Additionally, more participants "felt that the virtual world surrounded" them in the $360°$ movie (M = 6.21, SD = 1.25) than in the $180°$ movie (M = 3.33, SD = 1.88, p < 0.01) and the $225°$ movie (M = 3.79, SD = 1.93, p < 0.001) (Fig. 5).

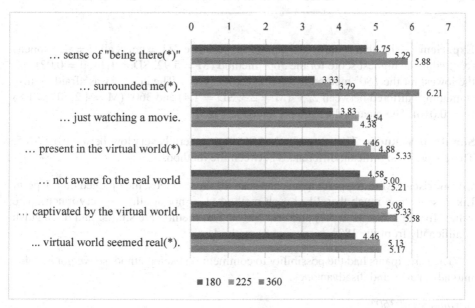

Fig. 5. Means for the presence items. Items with significant differences are indicated by (*).

Workload. The NASA-TLX questions resulted in higher scores for the 360° condition for several items. Physical demand was significantly higher for the *360°* method (M = 4.71, SD = 2.51) than for the *180°* method (M = 2.46, SD = 1.67) (p < 0.01) and the *225°* method (M = 3.08, SD = 1.84, p = 0.02). In addition, the temporal demand was higher for the *360°* method (M = 4.58, SD = 2.75) than for the *180°* method (M = 2.63, SD = 2.28, p < 0.01) and the *225°* method (M = 2.96, SD = 2.2, p = 0.03). The mean values can be seen in Fig. 6.

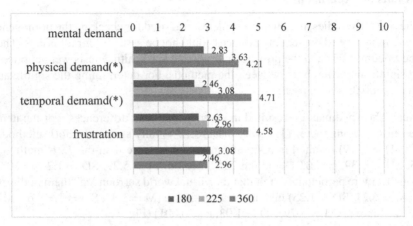

Fig. 6. Means for the task workload items. Items with significant differences are indicated by (*).

Experience. The item "I enjoyed the movie experience." (1 = not at all, 7 = very much) resulted in the highest score for the *360°* method (M = 5.92, SD = 1.14, p = 0.02) and the lowest for the *180°* method (M = 5.17, SD = 1.17). The item "I was afraid to miss something" differed between 225° (M = 2.3, SD = 1.4) and 360° (M = 4.2, SD = 1.8) (p = 0.016). The mean values are presented in Fig. 7.

Simulator Sickness. The scores for the SSQ were generally very low, between 0.17-0.5. There were no significant differences between the methods.

Comparison. After the participants had seen all three videos, they judged on a 7-point Likert scale how much they liked each method (1 = not at all, 7 = very much). The values for the 225° (M = 5.7) and 360° (M = 5.8) method are similar and distinguish significantly from the 180° (mean = 4.8) method.

The participants had the possibility to comment on each method, so we got insights into advantages and disadvantages.

Advantages of 360°:

- "sense of being right in the middle of the scene" (P6)
- "free to look around" (P6)
- "more realistic" (P4)

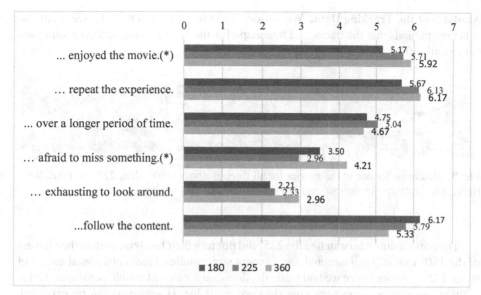

Fig. 7. Means for the experience items. Items with significant differences are indicated by (*).

Disadvantages of 360°:

- "a strong feeling of overwork since much happened around" (P13)
- "you do not know where the main thing is and where to turn" (P15)
- "demanding" (P4), "turning is uncomfortable" (P8)

Advantages of 225°:

- "you are not lost since you know where the main action is" (P15)

Disadvantages of 225°:

- "one was aware that one cannot completely look around" (P15)

Advantages of 180°:
No advantages were mentioned by the participants. However, the remark for 225°, that viewers are less lost, is also true for 180°.

Disadvantages of 180°:

- "feeling to be restricted" (P6)
- "too small field of view" (P15)
- "more like traditional TV" (P1)

Analysis of the Tracking Data. We inspected the tracking data for all three methods. It is conspicuous that the tracks and heatmaps for the 180° and the 225° condition are very similar (Fig. 8).

Fig. 8. Heatmaps for one of the movies for all three methods (180° - left, 225°- middle, 360°- right). The heatmaps for the 180° and 225° conditions are very similar.

The participants who watched the 225° did not turn their heads more than the viewers of the 180° movie. The inspected area (except some outliers) has a horizontal extent of about 145° for both. Since we had made the decision for a comfortable consumer device without any cables, no eye-tracking data are available. However, it can be expected, that in the 180° case the boundaries were more present than in the 225° condition. Surprisingly in both conditions, the viewer rotated the head more than the 120°, which were supposed as the head-only rotation. For seeing more, also the upper body was slightly turned. It also stands out that in the 180° and 225° condition the viewer inspects more the vertical direction, whereas the heatmap area for the 360° movie is flatter.

5.5 Discussion of Experiment 3

Even if viewers were sitting on a fixed chair, where normally the viewing area is not larger than 225° (head and eye) the presence decreased slightly if not the entire 360° range was available. Just the knowledge that there is no content behind, reduces the feeling of presence. On the other hand, the workload was also decreasing.

In our experiment, the Samsung Gear with a FoV of 101° was used. For other HMDs this area is larger and it will increase with technological progress. So, in the future, a 225° movie could be too small for an unrestricted CVR movie experience. Because the maximal FoV of humans' eyes is about 188° [23], and the maximal head movement 120°, a movie of about 308–312° can be necessary. Also, in this case, a small area for the camera operator is remaining. However, reducing the movie content area is not only relevant to improve shooting conditions, but also to avoid overloading the viewer and to decrease the fear of missing something. It needs additional research to find the perfect parameters for all HMDs.

6   Conclusion

In our *first* experiment, we explored new techniques for watching 360° movies sitting on a fixed chair or sofa: rotating the movie via controller and gain rotation. We found out that viewers accept both. However, the speed of the controller method should be dynamic. Even if the full 360° area can be explored by these methods, the natural head movement angle does not correspond with the angles in the virtual world. Using gain rotation with a factor 2, the viewer can see the whole 360° area in a 180° hemisphere. So, things which can be seen on the left side belongs to the things on the right side – things which are close to each other are far away for the viewer. The participants rated the method positively and did not complain about this fact. However, we did not investigate if the participants are aware of it and if the spatial orientation was impaired. Both methods are applicable for movies, where it is important to see easily the whole 360° area and spatial alignment is less important.

In the *second* experiment, where the participants watched a 360° movie on a swivel and on a fixed chair with and without the controller method, the participants preferred the controller and the swivel chair to the fixed chair without a controller. Even if the action of the movies were concentrated in a 225° area and the participants had this knowledge, to know the movie surround them caused a fear to miss something. So, they were looking around even in the fixed chair, which was uncomfortable. However, most participants declared to prefer movies with less than 360°.

Comparing 360°, 220° and 180° movies in the *third* experiment, we found out that the limited viewing area slightly reduces the presence. The viewers were aware of the fact, that there is nothing behind them, even if the content was in front of them and the boundaries in the 225° condition were only visible with extreme head rotations.

6.1 Limitations and Future Work

All three experiments were conducted with consumer devices and no eye tracking was available. The tracked data are head tracking data and we cannot conclude how often the boundaries in the third experiment were seen. Recorded eye-tracks would support in the process to find out more about how people watching CVR videos and support researchers to improve comfortable watching techniques. With the development of new HMD devices, the FoV will increase. It needs more research if a wider FoV entail the need for a larger area than 225°.

The controller, as well as the gain rotation method, were accepted by the viewers, even if the real head rotation was added by other techniques. Further studies are necessary to find out if the spatial orientation suffers from it.

In our study about rotation gain, we amplified the head rotation only in the horizontal direction. However, it is possible to extend it for the vertical movements to compensate for a small field of view and to make it more comfortable to look up and down.

6.2 Summary

We explored several methods for watching CVR videos. Two of them did worse than the others: (1) The controller method with constant speed was difficult to use and reduced enjoyment. (2) The fixed chair for 360° movies where the action was in a limited area so that turning around was not necessary, was uncomfortable for the most participants. For such type of movie (action in limited area), the spatio-temporal data for the fixed chair and the swivel chair condition were very similar: mostly the focus was on the action, but a short inspection of the other parts was done of both groups, however, it needed more effort in the case of the fixed chair. Most participants in this experiment preferred to have an area of less than 360°.

All the other investigated methods were comfortable for the viewers. They neither caused much simulator sickness nor did they reduce the presence considerably. In fixed positions the following methods for watching CVR videos can be used:

- movie rotation with controller – variable speed (360°)
- rotation gain (360°)
- fixed chair (225°)
- fixed chair (180°)

Inspecting the full 360° area, more activity is necessary. Having a reduced area of 225° or 180° is more relaxing. The 225° method was preferred over the 180° method.

7 Contribution

In this work, we investigated new methods for watching movies in a relaxed sitting posture on fixed chairs and compared them with the movie experience on a swivel chair. We found several methods for enjoying CVR movies in a sitting position on a fixed chair which did not cause more sickness and did not reduce the presence compared to watching the movie in a swivel chair. These methods enable a more relaxing posture and more lean-back engagement. Methods based on the reduction of the movie area decrease additionally the fear to miss something. The presented methods are intended to supplement the existing methods and should not replace the active methods where the viewer is turning a lot. Dependent on the movie genre, the content and the desire of the viewer, the most suitable method should be applied.

References

1. Davis, S., Nesbitt, K., Nalivaiko, E.: A Systematic review of cybersickness. In: Proceedings of the 2014 Conference on Interactive Entertainment - IE2014, pp. 1–9. ACM, New York (2014)
2. Dorta, T., Pierini, D., Boudhraâ, S.: Why 360° and VR headsets for movies?: Exploratory study of social VR via Hyve-3D. In: Actes de la 28ième conférence francophone sur l'Interaction Homme-Machine, pp. 211–220. ACM, New York (2016)
3. Gugenheimer, J., Wolf, D., Haas, G., Krebs, S., Rukzio, E.: SwiVRChair: A motorized swivel chair to nudge users' orientation for 360 degree storytelling in virtual reality. In: Proceedings of the 2016 CHI Conference on Human Factors in Computing Systems - CHI 2016, pp. 1996–2000. ACM, New York (2016)
4. Hong, S., Kim, G.J.: Accelerated viewpoint panning with rotational gain in 360 degree videos. In: Proceedings of the 22nd ACM Conference on Virtual Reality Software and Technology - VRST 2016, pp. 303–304. ACM, New York (2016)
5. Hong, Y., MacQuarrie, A., Steed, A.: The effect of chair type on users' viewing experience for 360-degree video. In: Proceedings of the 24th ACM Symposium on Virtual Reality Software and Technology - VRST 2018, pp. 1–11. ACM, New York (2018)

6. Jaekl, P.M., Jenkin, M.R., Harris, L.R.: Perceiving a stable world during active rotational and translational head movements. Exp. Brain Res. **163**, 388–399 (2005)
7. Jay, C., Hubbold, R.: Amplifying head movements with head-mounted displays. Presence Teleoperators Virtual Environ. **12**, 268–276 (2003)
8. Kennedy, R.S., Lane, N.E., Berbaum, K.S., Lilienthal, M.G.: Simulator sickness questionnaire: An enhanced method for quantifying simulator sickness. Int. J. Aviat. Psychol. **3**, 203–220 (1993)
9. Kolasinski, E.M.: Simulator Sickness in Virtual Environments. United States Army Research Institute for the Behavioral and Social Sciences (1995)
10. Langbehn, E., Wittig, J., Katzakis, N., Steinicke, F.: Turn your head half round: VR rotation techniques for situations with physically limited turning angle. In: Proceedings of Mensch und Computer 2019 - MuC 2019, pp. 235–243. ACM, New York (2019)
11. Lin, Y.-C., Chang, Y.-J., Hu, H.-N., Cheng, H.-T., Huang, C.-W., Sun, M.: Tell me where to look: investigating ways for assisting focus in 360° video. In: Proceedings of the 2017 CHI Conference on Human Factors in Computing Systems - CHI 2017, pp. 2535–2545. ACM, New York (2017)
12. Pausch, R., Snoddy, J., Taylor, R., Watson, S., Haseltine, E.: Disney's Aladdin: first steps toward storytelling in virtual reality. In: Proceedings of the 23rd Annual Conference on Computer Graphics and Interactive Techniques - SIGGRAPH 1996, pp. 193–203. ACM, New York (1996)
13. Przybylski, A.K., Murayama, K., DeHaan, C.R., Gladwell, V.: Motivational, emotional, and behavioral correlates of fear of missing out. Comput. Hum. Behav. **29**, 1841–1848 (2013)
14. Razzaque, S., Kohn, Z., Whitton, M.C.: Redirected Walking. In: Eurographics 2001 - Short Presentations, pp. 1-6. Eurographics Association (2001)
15. Rothe, S., Buschek, D., Hußmann, H.: Guidance in cinematic virtual reality-taxonomy. Res. Status Challenges Multimodal Technol. Interact. **3**, 19–42 (2019)
16. Rothe, S., Höllerer, T., Hußmann, H.: CVR-Analyzer: A tool for analyzing cinematic virtual reality viewing patterns. In: Proceedings of the 17th International Conference on Mobile and Ubiquitous Multimedia - MUM 2018, pp. 127–137. ACM Press, New York (2018)
17. Sargunam, S.P., Moghadam, K.R., Suhail, M., Ragan, E.D.: Guided head rotation and amplified head rotation: Evaluating semi-natural travel and viewing techniques in virtual reality. In: 2017 IEEE Virtual Reality Conference - IEEEVR 2017, pp. 19–28. IEEE (2017)
18. Schubert, T., Friedmann, F., Regenbrecht, H.: igroup Presence Questionnaire (IPQ) (2002)
19. Sitzmann, V., Serrano, A., Pavel, A., Agrawala, M., Gutierrez, D., Masia, B., Wetzstein, G.: Saliency in VR: How do people explore virtual environments? IEEE Trans. Visual Comput. Graphics **24**, 1633–1642 (2018)
20. Steinicke, F., Bruder, G., Jerald, J., Frenz, H., Lappe, M.: Analyses of human sensitivity to redirected walking. In: Proceedings of the 2008 ACM Symposium on Virtual Reality Software and Technology - VRST 2008, pp. 149–156. ACM, New York (2008)
21. Steinicke, F., Bruder, G., Jerald, J., Frenz, H., Lappe, M.: Estimation of detection thresholds for redirected walking techniques. IEEE Trans. Visual Comput. Graphics **16**, 17–27 (2010)
22. Stratmann, T.C., Löcken, A., Gruenefeld, U., Heuten, W., Boll, S.: Exploring vibrotactile and peripheral cues for spatial attention guidance. In: Proceedings of the 7th ACM International Symposium on Pervasive Displays - PerDis 2018, pp. 1–8. ACM, New York (2018)
23. Tilley, A.R., Henry Dreyfuss Associates: The Measure of Man and Woman: Human Factors in Design. Wiley, New York (2001)
24. Vosmeer, M., Schouten, B.: Interactive cinema: Engagement and interaction. In: Mitchell, A., Fernández-Vara, C., Thue, D. (eds.) ICIDS 2014. LNCS, vol. 8832, pp. 140–147. Springer, Cham (2014). https://doi.org/10.1007/978-3-319-12337-0_14
25. Whitwam, R.: Google Opens Up VR180 Standard for Virtual Reality Photos and Videos - ExtremeTech (2018)

Asymmetrical Multiplayer Versus Single Player: Effects on Game Experience in a Virtual Reality Edutainment Game

Anders Hansen$^{(\boxtimes)}$, Kirstine Bundgaard Larsen, Helene Høgh Nielsen, Miroslav Kalinov Sokolov, and Martin Kraus

Aalborg University, Rendsburggade 14, 9000 Aalborg, Denmark
{ahans15,kbla15,hhni14,msokol15}@student.aau.dk, martin@create.aau.dk

Abstract. Gamification of learning material is becoming popular within the education field and the possibilities of designing edutainment games are being explored. This project compares a single player and a two-player game experience in a collaborative Virtual Reality (VR) edutainment game. The two versions of the game had exactly the same information, where in the collaborative game the information was divided between the two players in an asymmetrical format, where one player is outside of VR. The evaluation of the two versions compared only the experience of the participants in VR using an independent measures design. The results showed that the two-player version scored higher in questions related to positive game experience with a significant difference to the single player version. Furthermore, participants using the two-player version rated significantly lower on questions related to annoyance. In the setting of an edutainment game the results suggest that incorporating a collaborative aspect through asymmetrical game play in VR increases enjoyment of the experience.

Keywords: Game experience · Edutainment · Virtual Reality · Asymmetrical multiplayer · Single player · Collaborative games

1 Introduction

Well-designed games have clear feedback, well-presented problems and give the players the opportunity to learn through their failures. These aspects can be effective if incorporated into learning. Therefore, gamification of learning content to motivate students has become popular within the education field [30, p. 629]. This concept is related to "edutainment", which has been defined as *"Video games, television programmes, or other material, intended to be both educational and enjoyable"* [22].

In collaboration with the Danish pump manufacturer Grundfos, we created an edutainment game in Virtual Reality (VR) with the objective to create awareness about water and sanitation. In this context, we studied how a single player

L. T. De Paolis and P. Bourdot (Eds.): AVR 2020, LNCS 12242, pp. 22–33, 2020.
https://doi.org/10.1007/978-3-030-58465-8_2

experience compares to a cooperative experience in a game with large amounts of information.

More specifically, the form of the cooperative scenario is an asymmetrical two player game where the players have different roles and skills which they have to use to work together [27], and the research question of our study was whether the asymmetrical two-player collaborative version increases player experience in this edutainment VR puzzle game, when comparing it to a single player version. This is how we got to the following research question:

"In an edutainment VR puzzle game, does an asymmetrical two-player collaborative version increase player experience, when comparing it to a single player version?"

In order to assess the game, we conducted an experiment using an independent measure design. 65 participants took part of the experiment, where they were split into two groups, playing through either the single player or the two-player version of the game. Only the participants using VR were considered when gathering and analysing the data.

The results of the statistical analysis showed that there was a significant difference in answers regarding positive experiences in favour of the two-player version, which suggests that the two-player game was overall a more enjoyable experience for the players. There were also differences in regard to tension/annoyance and challenge in favour of the single player version which suggests that participants playing the single player game felt overall more annoyed and challenged.

2   Background

This section presents and discusses key topics regarding edutainment, specifically for VR, as well as social aspects of gaming and how single player and multiplayer games differ from one another.

2.1   Games as Edutainment

Gamification means applying game elements, e.g., point systems, achievements, quests, challenges and narrative structures [30, p. 629]. Adding these elements to educational content can increase both motivation and engagement, making it at powerful tool for edutainment [8]. "Simulators" are an especially common method of edutainment, where roles and goals, similar to quests and challenges in gamification, provided to players in environments that correlate to real world scenarios [30, p. 629]. Edutainment games should give the players a chance to test whether the knowledge gathered can be applied to different contextualised situations, just like simulators. If a game is well-designed for learning purposes, all the information the player needs should be integrated into the game material [11, p. 86].

Virtual Reality in Edutainment. One way of putting the context into learning is through virtual environments. The benefit of being in the virtual environment while learning is that the experience is more engaging and motivating compared to standard teaching [5,7,17]. The stimulation of the visual senses combined with embodied movements while getting feedback from the environment helps the players to easily remember the performed actions and information [7,10,17,19].

2.2 Sociability in Games

Outside of games, peer tutoring, peer collaboration and cooperative learning have shown to improve learning progress for the people involved. Furthermore, coordination – "the act of making all the people involved in a plan or activity work together in an organised way" [4] – have shown to increase the feelings of mutual liking and connectivity [14].

These social aspects transfer to games as seen from the fact that multiplayer games are played more and preferred, compared to single player games [14,18]. In social games, emotions tend to be contagious and people are able to share emotions by just watching someone act out different emotions while playing [14].

Multiplayer games can be divided based on how players interact with each other and the game - competitive, collaborative or co-operative. Competitive games include playing versus another person/environment. In collaborative game-play, the players attempt to reach a mutual long term goal by working together. While in co-operative play, they work together to reach a short term goal. In this case, the short term goal is part of a process for the player to reach their individual ultimate goal [26].

2.3 Multiplayer and Single Player Experiences

Harteveld and Bekebrede have compared 23 studies of edutainment games [13]. The tendencies they observed were that single player edutainment games are more common (17 to 6 from the 23 in total). Single player games were also found to focus on the player obtaining specific knowledge and skill and are designed to be linear, where the player has little influence over the end results and the rules are formal, pre-configured for the player. These games are also focused on individual learning, with direct transfer of knowledge, where the learning material is pre-compiled. The multiplayer games were found to have widely different outcomes in what the player learned, ranging from attitudes, knowledge, cognitive and interpersonal skills. The correlation that was observed in the multiplayer was only in the aspects of being non-linear, meaning the player has impact on the end result, and orientated towards emergent rules (social rules), rather than defined rules [13].

Wehbe and Nacke attempted to measure game experience by comparing single player and multiplayer experience in Dungeon Duos, a 4 player mini-game within Mario Party 4 (Nintendo, 2002). Using a Self Assessment Manikin (SAM) scale, they were able to observe an increase in pleasure when playing against a human. The scale also revealed a significant difference in social aspects through perceived arousal in both of the two-player conditions compared to playing alone with 3 computer controlled characters [31].

Most VR multiplayer games focus on having players with their own head mounted displays (HMD) in the same environment. However, there are also games that can include co-located multiplayer with a single HMD. That is achieved by giving different tasks/goals/responsibilities to the players outside of VR, creating an asymmetrical multiplayer game [9,15,27]. Examples of these games are Keep Talking and Nobody Explodes [25], VR Diner Duo [32], Sommad [24] and CatEscape [16].

3   Game Development

In order to be able to test our research question, see Sect. 1, we created a game prototype. This section presents the development and implementation of a single player and a two-player version of our VR game.

3.1   Game Content Motivation

In 2015, the United Nations (UN) introduced a long-term plan for improving our planet, which consists of 17 sustainability goals. Some of these goals are directed at the environment, specifically Goal 6, is aimed at clean water and sanitation [28]. Grundfos, a company originating in Denmark, creates water pumps that are used all over the world. The company has become involved in sustainability solutions for energy efficiency and water conservation [12]. they were interested in knowing whether the "life of a water droplet" can be mediated through VR and how users react to this experience.

3.2   Design Considerations

From the background research we see that previous researchers have looked into what learning outcomes single player games and multiplayer games achieve. We also see that their research focuses on comparing different games. In this approach general trends can be observed but a direct comparison between the two genres is impossible. Therefore, we created a VR game where the two-player version and the single player version have the exact same goals, processes and rules. In the two-player version we took inspiration from state-of-the-art VR games on how to divide the information between the two players, introducing a communication element to the game and encouraging them to collaborate. Our VR game aims at direct transfer learning in both versions, for all players involved. The main difference between the single player version and two-player version is whether the learning is individual or social. As the two-player version is a collaborative experience, we cannot rule out that social rules may arise during communication between players.

3.3 Content of the VR Game

In our game, players take the perspective of a body of water coming from the sewers and go through a water treatment facility which is a maze constructed of water pipes. Since the water is coming from the sewers, different contaminants can be found floating in the body of water. These can be grabbed by the player for information on where they might come from and what problems they can cause if not removed. Figure 1 shows a screenshot from the game. The player has to figure out how to navigate through the correct treatment process with the help of a manual and a map.

The manual can be used in order to identify these contaminants as well as getting the information about which filters clean them. The location of the filters and how to get to them through the piping maze can be found in the map. When going through a filter the player gets information about the filter through audio. The aim of the game is to reach the exit and be as clean as possible. At the end they can choose which exit to take based on the condition of the water - dirty or clean.

The game was designed to be played by either one or two players. In the single player version the player has access to all of the information needed to complete the game, this includes the game world and the map and manual which has been put into VR. The two-player version differs, as the player outside of VR has the manual and the map, but cannot see what the VR player sees. This means that the two players need to communicate in order to identify the contaminants and go through the correct water treatment processes.

3.4 Implementation

The prototype for testing was developed using Unity [29] and Steam VR 2.0. 3D models for the prototype, such as the filters and the contaminants, were made using Autodesk Maya [3] while the pipes used for the sewage system was purchased from the asset store [33] and re-textured. Audio for the game was created with the audio manipulation software Audacity version 2.3.1 [2].

4   Game Experience Evaluation

We conducted an experiment using an independent measures design, in which two different test groups played through the game, with each group having a different version in order to test whether a communicative asymmetrical two-player puzzle game improves the game experience of the VR player compared to a single player version of the game. Since one of the versions was two-player we had two participants per test, but only data from the person in VR was gathered to compare it with the single player version.

We used a Game Experience Questionnaire [23] to gather the data, as it consists of four modules, where two of those were of interest for the experiment - the Core Module and the Post-Game Module. The Core Module was relevant for this

Fig. 1. In-game screenshot demonstrating the player standing at a crossroads in the piping system.

experiment as it measures competence, immersion, flow, annoyance, challenge, negative affect, and positive affect. The Post-Game Module was relevant due to the fact that it measures the experience in general, whether positive or negative, how tired the participant was after playing the game, and how hard it was to return to reality after playing through the game.

4.1 Experiment Setup

The test was setup in a meeting room at Aalborg University, with a 290 cm × 250 cm space for navigating in VR. An Oculus Rift was used as the HMD, with a 3 sensors setup in order to get 360° tracking. The computer used for testing had the following specs: Intel i5-8300H CPU running at 2.3 GHz, 8 GB of RAM and a GTX 1050TI graphics card.

A dedicated table was used outside of the tracking space for the researcher. In the two-player version the second participant sat at the table with the needed materials printed on paper.

4.2 Documentation

To document the tests the VR participant's game-play was screen recorded using the Windows 10 in-built Xbox Game Bar [20]. Upon completion of the game the participant was asked to fill out the Game Experience Questionnaire, using the researchers' computer. After that they were interviewed in a semi-structured interview which was audio recorded using the researchers' phones.

4.3 Procedure

In total, 65 people participated in the experiment. Most of the participants were students from Aalborg University and varied in background and experience with VR. 4 participants were from outside the university.

Single Player. Each participant was led into the test room where they signed a consent form. They were then given an introduction to the premise, aim and objectives of the game followed by the controls used in the VR prototype. The participant was placed in the middle of the tracking area and given a VR headset and two controllers. Once equipped with the headset, the game and screen recording were started. When the game was completed the participant would be given the Game Experience Questionnaire to fill out which was followed up with an interview.

Multiplayer. The procedure for the multiplayer version differed from the single player version as there were two participants. The person playing the game in VR was asked to sign a consent form and then both players ware given the introduction to the premise, aim and objectives of the game. The VR player was introduced to the controls, while the other participant was given the paper materials. The VR participant was placed in the middle of the tracking area and given a VR headset and two controllers. The game and screen recording was then started. Upon completion of the game the VR player filled out the Game Experience Questionnaire and was interviewed.

5 Results

This section presents results of the experiment. For the statistical analysis on the data, RStudio [1] was used. Microsoft Excel 365 [21] was used to calculate the questionnaire scores.

5.1 Statistical Analysis Comparing Two-Player and Single Player Data Set

The questionnaire scores for both the single player and two-player data sets were calculated for each participant.

To compare the two sets of scores, we used the Wilcoxon rank-sum test [6, p. 95] since a non-parametric, non-paired test had to be applied to the data set.

Table 1 shows results of one-tailed tests whether the scores for the two-player were either greater or lesser than the single player version. Competence, Positive Affect and Positive Experience showed that the scores for the two-player game data were significantly greater than the single player data ($p < 0.05$) while being significantly less for Tension/Annoyance and Challenge ($p < 0.05$).

Table 1. p-values of the tests that were used on the two-player data set, compared to the single player data set. The two sets include data for the scores of each participant. We checked for differences whether the scores of the two-player version was significantly greater or less than the scores of the single player version

	2-player score < single player	2-player score < single player
Core module:		
Competence	**0.0029**	1.00
Sensory and imaginative immersion	0.82	0.19
Flow	0.86	0.14
Tension/Annoyance	1.00	**0.0026**
Challenge	1.00	**0.0032**
Negative affect	0.92	0.079
Positive affect	**0.0043**	1.00
Post-game module:		
Positive experience	**0.011**	0.99
Negative experience	0.83	0.17
Tiredness	0.53	0.48
Returning to reality	0.21	0.80

5.2 Interview Analysis and General Observations

The players who completed the game in VR were interviewed about the game experience. 80% of the participants found the game enjoyable, while only 53.3% of the single players found it enjoyable.

In the two-player test group, 8% expressed problems with navigating through the pipe system, while 40% of the single player group found it difficult, and 33.3% of them expressed that they needed a pointer on the map to tell them where they were. Of the two-player group, 4% expressed the need for a map pointer. It was observed that navigating around the map appeared to be tedious and time consuming for the single player group. In regard to game-play, we saw that some players used the audio from the different filters to figure out where they were on the map. Others were able to use their surroundings and the water flow in order to find their position on the map when they got lost. However, many of the participants found it difficult to know their exact position and they felt that more landmarks would be a good addition to the experience. The single players often mentioned that a red dot to show where they were would be a good improvement.

40% of the single player group thought they would remember what they learned, while only 8% of the two-player group felt the same. During the two-player experience it appeared that some players were focusing more on the communication aspects of the game, rather than the information being presented.

Sometimes players would speak over the audio or play around with the contaminants circling around them. It was also observed that the participants rarely shared information between each other if they did not consider it to be relevant for solving the problem. For example, the colour of the water droplet was something that was not mentioned often. In other cases, when the participants attempted to identify the contaminants, the person outside VR did not share the name and type of the contaminant with the person in VR. In the two-player version one of the reoccurring themes we saw was that when the player in VR said that they were clean the other one would immediately forget about the cleaning process that was given to them and try to get the VR player out without completing all of the steps that were specified in the manual. Another similar issue was that when the VR player saw that the contaminant along the path was something they were already infected with they would not even mention it to the other player or tell them it does not matter.

6   Discussion

The statistical analysis showed that there was a significant difference in the two-player experience for competence, positive affect and positive experience compared to the single player experience. Since this difference was in favour of the two-player experience, it appears people in the two-player version enjoyed the game more and have an overall better game experience.

The analysis also showed that there was a significant difference in challenge and tension/annoyance between the two versions. As the single players had to figure out everything by themselves, both in regards to the manual, the map and the game, this might have contributed to this difference. Collaboration seemed to help with navigation, indicating that splitting the tasks might help with the overload of information that a player might experience in these sorts of information heavy games. This may also contribute to the two-players feeling more competent playing the game. Another possible reason, relating back to Sect. 2.2, might be that people enjoy games more, when they are played together with others. The majority of people playing the two-player expressed that they found the communication aspect to be what makes the game interesting and fun.

We were made aware that the start of the game was overloaded with information, and there was a lot of text, which brought a halt to the experience until the information had been read through, a possible solution to this could be to gradually introduce the information throughout the game so the initial load is not as heavy. The results indicate that the single player participants felt more often that they had learned something compared to the two-player participants. The two-player participants may have been more focused on the communication and navigation aspect. While it was also observed that some pairs failed to share the information split between them. The single player does have access to all the information by themselves, so this might lead to better learning potential in some cases.

7 Conclusion

The aim of this research was to test how a single player game experience compares to an asymmetrical two-player collaborative game experience in a VR edutainment game. We conducted an experiment using independent measures design on 65 participants. The results of the statistical analysis showed that there was a significant difference in answers regarding competence, positive affect and positive experience in favour of the two-player version, which suggests that this version was overall a more enjoyable experience for the players. There were also differences in regard to tension/annoyance and challenge which suggest that participants playing the single player version felt overall more annoyed and challenged by the game. However, challenge might not be a bad thing for all types of players. Therefore, further testing and commentary from participants should be collected. The interviews and our observations correlate with the statistical analysis, as people had more positive feedback in regards to experience in the two-player scenario. As an edutainment game, the solution needs improvements whether being two-player or single player in regards to features and making the participants share and use knowledge.

Acknowledgements. We would like to thank Christian Carlsson, Loreen Ople Villacorte and Guy Rumsey at Grundfos for their contributions to our background research on water treatment and sanitation.

References

1. Allaire, J.J.: Rstudio: open source and enterprise-ready professional software for R, 15 May 2019. https://www.rstudio.com/. Accessed 15 May 2019
2. Audacity Team: Audacity (2019). https://www.audacityteam.org/. Accessed 23 May 2019
3. Autodesk: Autodesk maya, May 2019. https://www.autodesk.com/products/maya/overview
4. Cambridge Dictionary: Coordination, May 2019. https://dictionary.cambridge.org/dictionary/english/coordination
5. Carruth, D.W.: Virtual reality for education and workforce training. In: 2017 15th International Conference on Emerging eLearning Technologies and Applications (ICETA), pp. 1–6. IEEE (2017)
6. Crawley, M.J.: Statistics: An Introduction Using R, 2nd edn. Wiley, Chichester (2015)
7. Dalgarno, B., Lee, M.J.: What are the learning affordances of 3-D virtual environments? Br. J. Educ. Technol. **41**(1), 10–32 (2010)
8. Deterding, S.: Gamification: designing for motivation. Interactions **19**(4), 14–17 (2012)
9. Game Central: The beauty of asymmetric multiplayer, May 2017. https://metro.co.uk/2017/12/17/the-beauty-of-asymmetric-multiplayer-readers-feature-7159714/
10. Gamlin, A., Breedon, P., Medjdoub, B.: Immersive virtual reality deployment in a lean manufacturing environment. In: 2014 International Conference on Interactive Technologies and Games (iTAG), pp. 51–58. IEEE (2014)

11. Gee, J.P.: What Video Games Have to Teach Us About Learning and Literacy. Palgrave Macmillan, New York and Houndmills (2003)
12. Grundfos: Sustainability, April 2019. https://www.grundfos.com/about-us/sustainability-responsibility.html
13. Harteveld, C., Bekebrede, G.: Learning in single-versus multiplayer games: the more the merrier? Simul. Gaming **42**(1), 43–63 (2011)
14. Isbister, K.: How Games Move Us: Emotion by Design. MIT Press, Cambridge (2016)
15. Kelly, R.: Asymmetric multiplayer horror games are brilliantly reinventing the entire horror genre, May 2019. https://www.gamerevolution.com/features/481181-asymmetric-horror-rise
16. Li, J., Deng, H., Michalatos, P.: Catescape: an asymmetrical multiplatform game connecting virtual, augmented and physical world. In: Extended Abstracts Publication of the Annual Symposium on Computer-Human Interaction in Play, CHI PLAY 2017 Extended Abstracts, pp. 585–590. ACM, New York (2017). https://doi.org/10.1145/3130859.3130860. http://doi.acm.org/10.1145/3130859.3130860
17. Liu, D., Bhagat, K.K., Gao, Y., Chang, T.-W., Huang, R.: The potentials and trends of virtual reality in education. In: Liu, D., Dede, C., Huang, R., Richards, J. (eds.) Virtual, Augmented, and Mixed Realities in Education. SCI, pp. 105–130. Springer, Singapore (2017). https://doi.org/10.1007/978-981-10-5490-7_7
18. Mandryk, R.L., Inkpen, K.M.: Physiological indicators for the evaluation of co-located collaborative play. In: Proceedings of the 2004 ACM Conference on Computer Supported Cooperative Work, pp. 102–111. ACM (2004)
19. Melatti, M., Johnsen, K.: Virtual reality mediated instruction and learning. In: 2017 IEEE Virtual Reality Workshop on K-12 Embodied Learning through Virtual & Augmented Reality (KELVAR), pp. 1–6. IEEE (2017)
20. Microsoft: Xbox game bar. Website (2018). https://www.microsoft.com/en-us/p/xbox-game-bar/9nzkpstsnw4p?activetab=pivot:overviewtab
21. Microsoft: Microsoft excel 365. Website (2019). https://products.office.com/da-dk/excel
22. Oxford Living Dictionaries: Edutainment, April 2019. https://en.oxforddictionaries.com/definition/edutainmentl
23. Poels, K., de Kort, Y., IJsselsteijn, W.: D3.3: Game Experience Questionnaire: development of a self-report measure to assess the psychological impact of digital games. Technische Universiteit Eindhoven (2007)
24. Serubugo, S., Skantarova, D., Evers, N., Kraus, M.: Walkable self-overlapping virtual reality maze and map visualization demo: public virtual reality setup for asymmetric collaboration. In: Proceedings of the 23rd ACM Symposium on Virtual Reality Software and Technology, pp. 91:1–91:2. ACM (2017)
25. Steel Crate Games: Keep talking and nobody explodes. Website (2015). https://keeptalkinggame.com/
26. Stenros, J., Paavilainen, J., Mäyrä, F.: The many faces of sociability and social play in games. In: Proceedings of the 13th International MindTrek Conference: Everyday Life in the Ubiquitous Era, pp. 82–89. ACM (2009)
27. TV Tropes: Asymmetric multiplayer, May 2019. https://tvtropes.org/pmwiki/pmwiki.php/Main/AsymmetricMultiplayer
28. United Nations: 17 goals to transform our world (2019). https://www.un.org/sustainabledevelopment/. Accessed 15 Feb 2019
29. Unity Technologies: Unity3d, May 2019. https://unity.com/
30. Walz, S.P., Deterding, S.: The Gameful World: Approaches, Issues, Applications. MIT Press, Cambridge (2015)

31. Wehbe, R.R., Nacke, L.E.: Towards understanding the importance of co-located gameplay. In: Proceedings of the 2015 Annual Symposium on Computer-Human Interaction in Play, CHI PLAY 2015, pp. 733–738. ACM (2015). http://doi.acm.org/10.1145/2793107.2810312

32. Whirlybird Games: VR the diner duo (2016). http://whirlybirdgames.com/games#vr-the-diner-duo

33. Wiersma, T.: Modular pipes & gauges, May 2017. https://assetstore.unity.com/packages/3d/environments/industrial/modular-pipes-gauges-102134

Procedural Content Generation via Machine Learning in 2D Indoor Scene

Bruno Ježek$^{(\boxtimes)}$ ⓘ, Adam Ouhrabka ⓘ, and Antonin Slabý ⓘ

University of Hradec Králové, Rokitanského 62, 50002 Hradec Králové, Czech Republic
{bruno.jezek,antonin.slaby}@uhk.cz, adam.ouhrabka@gmail.com

Abstract. The article proposes a method of combining multiple deep forward neural networks to generate a distribution of objects in a 2D scene. The main concepts of machine learning, neural networks and procedural content generation concerning this intention are presented here. Additionally, these concepts are put into the context of computer graphics and used in a practical example of generating an indoor 2D scene. A method of vectorization of input datasets for training forward neural networks is proposed. Scene generation is based on the consequent placement of objects of different classes into the free space defining a room of a certain shape. Several evaluate methods have been proposed for testing the correctness of generation.

Keywords: Computer graphics · Machine learning · Procedural content generation (PCG) · Procedural content generation via machine learning (PCGML)

1 Introduction

Machine learning and computer graphics are areas that have seen rapid development in the last two decades. The following reasons for this progress can be identified in the area of machine learning. Machine learning architectures and methods have been developing since the second half of the 20th century, but only sufficient hardware performance in recent years has allowed these methods to be fully utilized and applied in practice. New kinds of more sophisticated models were devised in addition to it. Hardware performance is complemented by software based on high-level programming languages, which makes it easy to implement complex architectures. During the development of the field, data sets have also been created and are advantageously used in training and testing models [1].

There is a significant connection between machine learning and computer graphics. This includes fields such as computer vision or image processing. The core of the theoretical part of the text is the introduction of this connection and a presenting specific sub-area, which is usually called Procedural content generation via machine learning (PCGML).

The article is organized as follows. Section 2 introduces the general features of the machine learning area with an explication of the methods to the problems examined in

L. T. De Paolis and P. Bourdot (Eds.): AVR 2020, LNCS 12242, pp. 34–49, 2020.
https://doi.org/10.1007/978-3-030-58465-8_3

the practical part. The list of applications based on these methods, especially on neural networks, is strictly limited to the area of computer graphics. Selected procedures and methods that are used or discussed in connection with the procedural generation of graphical content are mentioned. First, this area is introduced in general and then the text is focused on applications of selected PCGML techniques. The chapter deals with implementation issues and describes typical technologies and environments that are suitable for the implementation of proposed machine learning methods. These technologies are used in the following practical part of Sect. 3, where the design and implementation of a method that predicts the distribution of objects in a 2D scene based on the learned data is presented using forward neural network architectures. The software implementation of the proposed method is subsequently tested in Sect. 4 and the results are evaluated at the end of the article in Sect. 5, where the findings are summarized and possible extensions of the research are outlined.

2 Applied Approaches and Technologies

2.1 Machine Learning

Machine learning can be differentiated by the way of learning and roughly divided into discriminative and generative models. While discriminatory models are mapping inputs to a particular output, which may be, for example, particular class classification or scalar value regression, a generative approach models probabilistic relations between variables of a given model. The complete associated probability $p(x_1, \ldots, x_n)$ for N variables is typically found in these models. If there exists an expression of the probability distribution, further values of variables can be derived based on this formula, for example using Bayesian rules. Generative models exist in several forms. They include models of deep learning or so-called graphical models of the Bayesian network with directional relations between variables, Markov models, Markov random field and others. More details can be found in [2, 3].

2.2 Generative Adversarial Neural Networks

Generative Adversarial Neural Networks (GAN) are the currently popular generative models introduced by Ian Goodfellow [4]. The basic principle of their functioning is the principle of "maximum probability", i.e. finding parameters for the model to maximize the probability of training data. Goodfellow designed a generative model consisting of two components - a generator and a discriminator. In each learning iteration, both components work in opposite ways and the final learning results from the contradiction created between them. Most of the applied GAN architectures are used to generate image data and apply a convolutional mechanism [5, 6].

2.3 Procedural Content Generation

Procedural content generation (PCG) is a method of creating data algorithmically, typically through a combination of human-generated assets and algorithms coupled with computer-generated randomness and processing power. Traditional PCG approaches create content with a specific reference to the target. However, this reference is not part of the algorithm itself, but it serves merely as an inspiration for the designer. This means that the primary part of the design of such an algorithm is the search for rules, abstractions, and constraints to help approximate the desired content [7].

2.4 Procedural Content Generation via Machine Learning

The same search as in PCG also appears in the context of Procedural Content Generation through Machine Learning (PCGML), but with the essential difference, that the search does not take place by the developer, but computing machine. The model, by which new content can be generated, is created using appropriately tuned machine learning algorithms and suitably processed input data [8]. PCGML models include mainly n-grams, Markov models, generative deep learning models (GAN), and specific architectures of recurrent neural networks.

2.5 Selected PCGML Experiments

Our approach was inspired by selected PCGML applications and methods that motivated the design of the custom solution described in the following part 3. All of these applications had to deal with the problem of a small dataset and the requirement for the functional usability of the generated samples in machine learning.

The variant of the Markov chain together with n-grams was a powerful tool for generating simple content [7]. A more complex alternative to achieve a similar goal is the use of deep neural networks, namely recurrent architectures [8]. Another example is the use of binary coding of the input data set together with the classical autoencoder architecture, which is a neural network with the number of input neurons equal to the number of output [9, 10]. Fisher's attempt to synthesize 3D object arrangements uses a probabilistic model for scenes based on Bayesian networks and Gaussian mixtures for generating these scenes in numerous variations [11]. Other approaches use input data encoding to raster images for generating game levels [12] or terrain [13] using GAN.

3 Design and Implementation

The main aim of the designed algorithm is to generate a new indoor scene of a room, where several objects of defined classes are placed. Placement should respect rules of mutual positional relation of objects. However, these rules are not defined explicitly, but follow from other previously defined scenes. The new scene will be generated by sequentially placing particular objects into their most suitable place.

Our approach effectively combines forward neural network outputs to logically distribution of objects to a defined boundary area, i.e. to the interior of a room. It is based on knowledge and results in the area of PCGML experiments and neural networks and uses selected technologies mentioned in part 2.

The representation of the graphic scene is generally defined by two aspects of the scene. First, along with location, it determines the presence or absence of objects of different classes in the scene. Second, it also defines the type and nature of the scene, which is characterized by the mutual positional relations of objects in the scene space. The algorithm presented here focuses on the second aspect of the scene and place objects gradually in the most likely place concerning the current context of the scene space. The user determines himself whether a particular object of class will be placed in a scene and how many of them will be placed in the scene, the algorithm will only select the appropriate position. A new scene generation is typically carried out sequentially and the current scene and its state acts as an input for the next step of the deploying algorithm.

The common property of the here presented approach is the replication of learned positional relations between existing objects, e.g. between a chair and a table in a 2D scene representing the interior of a room. The set of previously defined scenes are pre-processed and used to achieve encoded rules applied in the machine learning model. The artificial neural network methods require an appropriate encoding of the input and output vector, and for this, a suitable representation of the scene is also required.

The whole designed algorithm consists of three phases.

- Data preprocessing, which prepare input and output vector data for neural network training.
- Neural networks training, several networks are trained, for every object class and every surrounding size.
- Generation method phase, which effectively combines the outputs of neural networks for the final prediction of the location of the object and it is deploying into the scene.

The placement of the furniture in the sample room described below will serve as a model situation for testing the proposed principles. The application of these principles is not limited to this particular case and can generally be applied to other problems. Three phases are described in more detail in the following text.

3.1 Scene Representation

The input data for the algorithm is represented at the highest level, as a list of scenes $S = \{s_1, s_2, \ldots, s_k\}$. Every single scene s_i representing one room is defined as a matrix of $n \times m$ possible object positions $P = (x, z)$, where $x \in \langle 0, n \rangle, z \in \langle 0, m \rangle$. In real scenes, each object placed in the scene is defined by characteristics such as position, rotation, and size. However, we consider only the position in our solution to simplify the task.

Possible object classes are defined as the set $O = \{o_1, o_2, \ldots, o_q\}$, which represents a real object in a room, e.g. a window or a chair. There may be at most one object class o_i at each position P. The allowed classes of objects are given in Table 1 together with the description of mutual positional relation used for placing the objects in the scenes. These data are essential for the description of individual phases and subsequent testing of the generated scenes.

Table 1. Classes of objects presented in the input data and the logic of their location. SS type class represents objects that will not be predicted.

Class ID	Interpretation	Type	Mutual positional relation description
0	Empty space (light blue)	SS	represents the empty interior of the room
1	Wall (dark blue)	SS	is always placed around the perimeter of the scene and forms a boundary of it
2	Table (light green)	O	is located randomly inside the scene, including the at the boundary areas
3	Chair (dark green)	O	is an object with several hypotheses and several special context-based rules are applied. These rules are detailed in Sect. 4
4	Cupboard (pink)	O	is always placed in contact with the wall
5	Free space object (red)	O	is an abstract object that represents empty space within scenes
6	Window (orange)	O	is located inside the wall. Care should be taken not to have a cupboard object in front of it etc.
9	Space behind the wall (magenta)	SS	is an abstract object that simulates an unknown empty outer space. It serves as opposed to object 0 and in predicting spaces with irregular shape

3.2 Scene Preprocessing and Vectorization of Training Data

Preparing data for neural network training is the most demanding step in the process of data transformation. It aims to create vector pairs $(x \rightarrow y)$ expressing the relationship between the input vector and the expected output of the encoded scene. Three array types are used to support the vectorization process and accompanying algorithms. The array types have the following meaning.

The first array S represents the data of all input scenes. The second field C specifies kernels representing "small windows" of the defined size that are used to browse the input scene during the relationship examination process. Typical kernels are usually windows of $C = [(3 \times 3), (4 \times 4), (5 \times 5), (6 \times 6)]$ elements, but irregular windows can also be used. This imaginary window moves systematically through the array of an input scene s_i in rows from left to right and examining them downwards one step at a time (Fig. 1). During this movement, a set of vectors V is generated, consisting of a class of objects located at the corresponding locations of the input scene s_i.

$$s_1 = \begin{pmatrix} 1 & 1 & 1 & 1 & 1 \\ 1 & 0 & 4 & 0 & 0 \\ 1 & 0 & 0 & 0 & 0 \\ 1 & 0 & 2 & 0 & 0 \\ 1 & 4 & 0 & 0 & 0 \end{pmatrix} \tag{1}$$

Fig. 1. Demonstrates first, second and last position of the kernel window of size (3×3) during the movement through the input matrix.

The third array type O stores data of all object classes in the scene, excluding special symbols SS (Table 1). The following framework algorithm is applied for interactive processing of the input data:

```
for each kernel in C do:
  for each scene in S do:
    for each position of kernel in scene:
      create array V
      for each object O located in vector V do:
        for each position of O in V
          create vector x
          create vector y
```

The vectorization operation is illustrated in the following scene arrangement example. Let have the following vector v_1 generated as the part of an input scene of s_i for kernel $c_i = 3 \times 3$.

$$v_1 = \begin{pmatrix} 1 & 1 & 1 \\ 1 & 0 & 4 \\ 1 & 0 & 0 \end{pmatrix} \tag{2}$$

This matrix represents the left-upper corner of a room, where a cupboard is placed next to a wall. The aim is a generation of $(x \to y)$ pairs of vectors for this object with $ID = 4$. For simplicity, now we will consider only three objects in the scene, empty space, wall, and cupboard, represented by the object vector $(0, 1, 4)$. The vectorization process creates an input vector x_1 composed of the object vectors corresponding to individual positions.

$$x_1 = ((0, 1, 0), (0, 1, 0), (0, 1, 0), (0, 1, 0), (1, 0, 0), (0, 0, 1), (0, 1, 0), (1, 0, 0), (1, 0, 0))$$

The x vector without object class $ID = 4$ (cupboard) is needed for neural network training and consequently, vector y is also necessary. So we remove this object class from x_1 vector and place 1 on the corresponding position of vector y.

$$x_1' = ((0, 1, 0), (0, 1, 0), (0, 1, 0), (0, 1, 0), (1, 0, 0), (0, 0, \mathbf{0}), (0, 1, 0), (1, 0, 0), (1, 0, 0))$$

$$f\left(x_1'\right) = y_1 = (0, 0, 0, 0, 0, 1, 0, 0, 0)$$

This process will be repeated for other kernels (3 × 3), (4 × 4), (5 × 5), (6 × 6) and for five next object classes (Table 1). The generated vectors data will be used as a training dataset for 5 × 4 neural networks that can predicate position for the 5 different object classes and the 4 kernels.

Test input data set consisting of 23 manually defined scenes representing the room was used for the here examined testing task, the placement of the furniture in the room. Object scene visualization was done and scenes represented by matrixes were defined. The tested room was square-shaped in 18 cases and irregular with horizontal or vertical edges in further 5 cases. Both room shapes are shown in the Fig. 2.

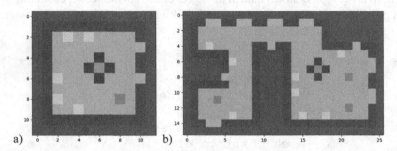

a)   b)

Fig. 2. Examples of defined scenes (two rooms) from the input dataset: a) square-shape room, b) irregular shape. Colors of object classes: Empty space (light blue), Wall (dark blue), Table (light green), Chair (dark green), Cupboard (pink), Free space object (red), Window (orange), Space behind the wall (magenta). (Color figure online)

3.3 Neural Network Training Phase

The forward neural network architecture was used to train all models. All models were defined in the TensorFlow open source platform and Keras framework with GPU support. Specifically, it was a model with the NVIDIA GeForce GTX 970 chip.

Table 2. Statistics of training for selected neural network configurations. The number of neurons in the hidden layers decreases towards the output layer and so the neural network has a pyramid shape with coefficients $0.9 \times K_1$ for L_1 and $0.7 \times K_2$ for L_2.

Id	Batch size	K_1	K_2	K_3	Average success on		Training time [min]
					Training data	Testing data	
1	64	0.9	0.7	0	0.762	0.351	8
2	128	0.9	0.7	0	0.767	0.353	8
3	512	0.9	0.7	0	0.730	0.351	3
4	128	0.9	0.7	0.5	0.766	0.346	10
5	512	0.9	0.7	0.5	0.731	0.346	4
6	512	1	1	0.7	0.739	0.347	4

Several different architectures and network parameters were experimented. Table 2 shows six selected topology and training variants. The input layer dimension L_0 for vector x corresponds to the equation $n_{L_1} = n_V \times n_O$ and depend on the number of elements of V vectors, and consequently is also different for each kernel size. The numbers of neurons in the hidden layers L_1, L_2, L_3 were co-determined by the selected coefficients and correspond always to a product of the respective coefficient with the number of neurons of the input layer L_0. The output layer dimension, L_4 or L_3, is defined by the kernel size for which the neural network is trained. Activation function for hidden layers (L_1, L_2, L_3) is ReLU. Softmax is used, to map the non-normalized output of a network to a probability distribution over predicted output classes. Categorical cross-entropy implemented in the Keras library was selected as an error function.

The test set was created by randomly selecting 20% of the pairs from the training data set. The success of the neural network was evaluated on both training and testing data. The success rate represents the average gained across all twenty neural networks and the learning time of all networks in using 50 epochs of learning.

Based on testing, the topology with two hidden layers L_1 and L_2 was selected as the final neural network, which corresponds to the second row of Table 2. Specifically, the size of a neural network with two hidden layers for 3 classes of objects and the kernel size 3×3 is given by the number of neurons in each layer $L_0 = 27, L_1 = 24, L_2 = 18, L_3 = 9$. The success of training and testing data is summarized in Fig. 3.

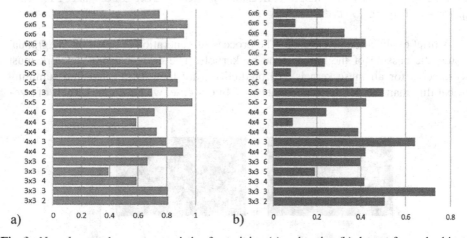

Fig. 3. Neural networks success statistics for training (a) and testing (b) dataset for each object class. For example, identifier $6 \times 6\ 5$ corresponds to the 6×6 kernel in combination with object class ID = 5.

It can be concluded, based on Table 2 and the graphs in Fig. 3, that the average success rate of predictions of individual configurations is higher than 70% and lower than 80%. The figure shows that only object class ID = 5, free space object, were problematic.

3.4 Phase of Scenes Generation

The new scene will be generated by sequentially placing the particular objects in the most suitable place. One object is added to the scene at each generation step. The selection of objects inserted into the scene is determined by the user. The array of kernels C is again used here and determines the way the space of the scene goes through. Each step of scene creation starts with the initial input scene s_0. This scene is user-selected and is usually empty in the first iteration. The input scene in the next iterations is always the output of the previous generation step. The generating procedure can be summarized by the following pseudocode:

```
to place object O to scene S do:
  for each kernel from C do:
    create empty sum matrix MS for scene S and object O
    go through scene S and find all free places
    for each free place do:
      create input vector of actual neighbours
      select the correct neural network from pairs SxO
      use network for prediction
      aggregate prediction into the sum matrix MS
    combine all sum matrices to product matrix MP
  select location with maximum prediction from matrix MP
place object O to space
```

A brief explanation of the code: The process of generation is based on the gradual systematic passing of the initial scene by kernels. The correct neural network must be selected for all these kernels. All predictions are then aggregated into summing probability matrices MS for each kernel size. In our case, we have four kernels of sizes

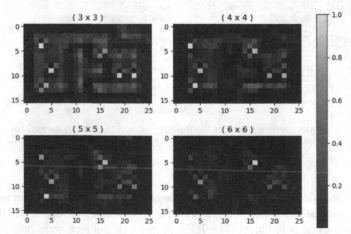

Fig. 4. Example of the four sum predictive matrices MS for kernels $(3 \times 3), (4 \times 4), (5 \times 5), (6 \times 6)$ after the first iteration with the initial scene represented by the matrix M_1, see Fig. 6.

(3×3), (4×4), (5×5), (6×6) and we will obtain four sum predictive matrices MS of the size defined by the default scene s_0 (Fig. 4).

The matrix MP, which is referred to as the final product matrix of the probability of occurrence proved to be best for the final prediction. This product matrix MP is created by successive addition or multiplication of sum predictive matrices MS (Fig. 5).

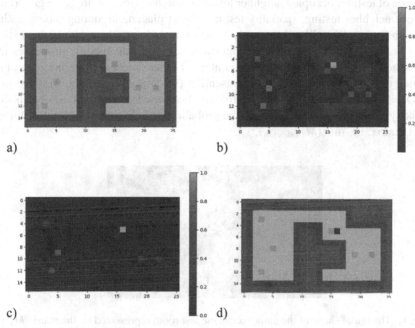

Fig. 5. Example of scene generation a) input space with object class ID = 2, b) visualization of the final product matrix $MP_{addition}$, c) visualization of final product matrix $MP_{multiplication}$, d) application function $\max(MP_{multiplication})$ for placement object class ID = 3.

The selection of the final position of the predicted object can be determined in various ways. The most adequate place was located at the position of the maximum element in matrix MP. This procedure, however, does not produce always the desired content variability within the given starting scene. Therefore, it is possible to choose another sampling technique, for example, a random weighted selection of ordered probabilities MP, etc. The algorithm may be also parameterized. We can experiment with shapes and numbers of kernels, neural network architectures, the methods of selecting the final candidate or method of aggregation into probability matrices of occurrence to achieve better results.

4   Testing and Results

The procedure for measuring the success rate of the proposed algorithms is performed as follows. Within the dataset introduced in the previous section, certain relational rules between objects should be followed, see Table 1. If these relations are found in algorithmically generated data, it is confirmed that the algorithm has learned to follow this logic. It is likely and typical that at the end of each learning process the algorithm may produce different results due to the stochastic nature of neural network initialization. The same applies to the generated scenes when a randomized weighting mode is turned on. The results presented here are based on twenty learned neural networks. We conducted the 8 types of testing: occupied neighbor test, free neighbor test, multiple neighborhood test, close neighbor testing, spatiality testing, object placement among others testing, integration testing. We will mention only some of them due to the scope of the text.

The majority of tests verify if the algorithm can replicate specific properties in a simple space if it is not disturbed by the context of other objects. This space was at the beginning defined as the matrix M_1 representing the empty scene (Fig. 6). Objects of class ID $= 1$, representing wall, define a form of the room. For all predicted objects their most likely position was selected from the probability of maximum of final additional product matrix, i.e. $\max(MP_{addition})$.

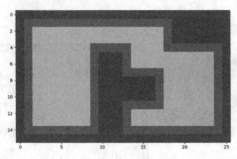

Fig. 6. The initial shape of the empty scene the test room represented by the matrix M_1.

4.1   Occupied Neighbor Test

The neighborhood test monitors the correct location of objects in free space near other objects, such as a table with four chairs. This property is formally expressed by the matrix X_1.

$$X_1 = \begin{pmatrix} 0 & 3 & 0 \\ 3 & 2 & 3 \\ 0 & 3 & 0 \end{pmatrix} \tag{3}$$

All the internal positions of the scene suitable for the table location were tested in space M_1 and the algorithm added gradually four chairs in four iterations concerning the pattern X_1. In all 34 tested cases were chairs placed flawlessly around the tables.

4.2 Free Neighbor Test

In this case, the opposite situation is tested. This rule, for example, determines that if a table is placed one position away from the wall or in a corner, a chair that should be placed there by default rule of the occupied neighbor rule will not be located to that position. The matrices of the patterns used in this test are as follows. During this test, there was generated 50 test positions forming test scene M_1. The results for individual rules are shown in Table 3.

$$X_{2a} = \begin{pmatrix} 0 & 3 & 0 \\ 3 & 2 & 3 \\ 0 & 0 & 0 \\ 1 & 1 & 1 \end{pmatrix}, X_{2b} = \begin{pmatrix} 1 & 0 & 3 & 0 \\ 1 & 0 & 2 & 3 \\ 1 & 0 & 3 & 0 \end{pmatrix}, X_{2c} = \begin{pmatrix} 1 & 0 & 3 & 0 \\ 1 & 0 & 2 & 3 \\ 1 & 0 & 0 & 0 \\ 1 & 1 & 1 & 1 \end{pmatrix} \quad (4)$$

Table 3. The number of errors in all 50 test positions relative to the rules X_{2a}, X_{2b}, X_{2c}.

	Number of errors after			The rule was followed	Number of predictions
	2nd iteration	3rd iteration	4th iteration		
Wall (X_{2a}, X_{2b})	0	3	30	10 times	43
Corner (X_{2c})	0	3	3	Only once	7

Table 3 shows the number of errors across fifty positions after 2nd, 3rd, 4th iteration after applying individual rules. The algorithm did not place a chair around the table within three iterations only in six cases of all 50 tests. In the fourth iteration, the most likely position was usually predicted near the wall following the pattern X_1 (occupied neighbor), which is partly logical, but from the point of view of the free neighbor test X_2 it is a mistake. This phenomenon occurred in 33 cases out of a total of 50. In eleven cases, the result was in accordance with the free neighbor rule even after the fourth iteration, and the algorithm preferred to place the fourth chair in the free space rather than near the wall.

4.3 Close Neighbor Test

The close neighbor test analyzes cases when an object should be placed next to another, for example, the object class ID $= 4$ (cupboard) will be placed correctly next to wall ID $= 1$ (Eq. 5). Fifteen tests with 10 iterations were performed (Fig. 7). The results show that out of the total 150 predictions only 2 did not respect relation rules.

$$X_{3a} = \begin{pmatrix} 1 & 0 & 0 & 0 \\ 1 & 0 & 4 & 0 \\ 1 & 1 & 1 & 1 \end{pmatrix}, X_{3b} = \begin{pmatrix} 1 & 0 & 0 \\ 1 & 4 & 0 \\ 1 & 0 & 0 \\ 1 & 1 & 1 \end{pmatrix} \quad (5)$$

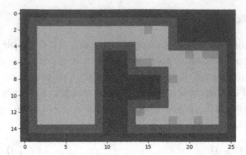

Fig. 7. The result of ten iterations of cupboard placement, all cupboards are generated next to the wall.

4.4 Testing the Object Placement Among Others

The matrices X_{5a} and X_{5b} represent that the object class ID = 6 that symbolizes a window should always replace the object class ID = 1 (wall). At the same time, it is observed that the window will not be placed behind an object that would hypothetically prevent the passage of window light, for example, cupboard object of class ID = 4.

$$X_{5a} = \begin{pmatrix} 1 & 0 & 0 \\ 6 & 0 & 0 \\ 1 & 0 & 0 \\ 1 & 1 & 1 \end{pmatrix}, X_{5b} = \begin{pmatrix} 1 & 0 & 0 \\ 1 & 0 & 0 \\ 1 & 4 & 0 \\ 1 & 1 & 6 \end{pmatrix} \tag{6}$$

The test involved ten runs of the algorithm, each with twenty iterations. First, ten objects class ID = 4 representing cupboards were generated and after that ten objects class ID = 6, which represents windows. Of the total number of hundred iterations, most windows were positioned correctly and only 9 were in the wrong position (Fig. 8). The cupboard stood four times in front of the window, and the window was improperly set in the corner of the room in three cases.

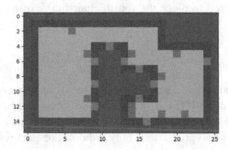

Fig. 8. The result of twenty iterations of cupboard and window placement.

4.5 Integration Testing

The concept of integration tests is taken from the field of traditional software development. It is used here to test the replicability of features and relations followed if greater variability of objects enters the generated space. The resulting 2D matrices were visualized using the Unity3D game engine (Fig. 9). Rotations of objects that are not solved by the algorithm were edited manually with the help of the editor. Object models are taken from a freely available collection [14]. The final placement of the objects was adapted to the geometric properties of the models in this collection two additional objects and

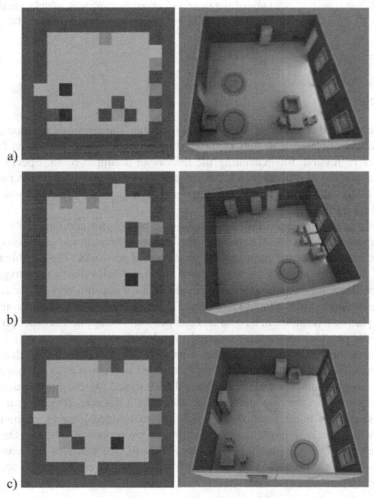

Fig. 9. The example of three resulting scenes and their 3D visualization. Objects were generated in the following order a) window, door, door, window, sofa, sofa, table, chair, chair, carpet, carpet, cupboard, b) table, table, chair, chair, door, sofa, cupboard, cupboard, carpet, window, window, c) table, chair, chair, door, window, window, window, window, carpet, cupboard, cupboard and sofa.

a 7 × 7 kernel were included in the learning algorithms to enrich the variety of scenes generated. These new classes of objects are introduced the following Table 4.

Table 4. Additional classes of objects and their description

Class ID	Interpretation	Type	Mutual positional relation description
7	Door	O	The door is embedded in the wall. Make sure that no object is in front of them
8	Sofa	O	The sofa is primarily located near a wall, but can also be placed at a table. Occasionally, there was an object in the data near its class ID = 5, which was displayed as a carpet (for interpretation)

5 Conclusion

The original method was introduced in the contribution. The proposed solution enables the deployment of classical models of forward neural networks, usually used for classification or regression, for generating the interior of a simple room. Specifically, it is a gradual placing of individual selected objects of predefined classes into the scene according to the rules stored in the neural network. The quality of achieved results was tested and the results were commented.

The core of the presented implementation is a purposeful combination of probabilistic outputs of several neural networks. The proposed suitable vectorization of input knowledge was used for the training of a set of neural networks. The combination of outputs of the trained network creates a matrix of probabilities that is used to generate a new scene. Implemented unit tests confirmed that the algorithm was able to replicate the selected properties of the input knowledge. The application of these principles is not limited to placing a furniture in a room and can generally be applied to other problems.

The order in which objects are inserted into the scene also plays a major role in the success of the algorithm. This aspect, a prediction of the object class that should be conditionally inserted into the scene, was identified as the first essential point of the scene's meaning. Another neural network could be designed for this purpose to improve the success rate. Both the data and new samples have a discrete 2D grid as the basis. Making use of only these aspects, discretion and two-dimensionality, partially limit usability, which partially limits the applicability of the proposed solution. Discretion can be overcome by a suitable transformation of predictive matrices into continuous maps, where the final prediction can take place at the pixel level and scene coordinates correspondingly transformed.

Acknowledgments. This work and the contribution were supported by a project of Students Grant Agency (SPEV 2020) - FIM, University of Hradec Kralove, Czech Republic. The authors of this paper would like to thank Milan Košťák, a PhD student of Applied Informatics at the University of Hradec Kralove, for help with implementation.

References

1. Abadi, M. et al.: TensorFlow: A system for large-scale machine learning. In: Proceedings of the 12th USENIX Symposium on Operating Systems Design and Implementation, pp. 21–28. Savannah USENIX Association, ISBN 978-1-931971-33-1. https://www.usenix.org/system/files/conference/osdi16/osdi16-abadi.pdf (2016). Accessed 20 Feb 2020
2. Goodfellow, I. et al.: Generative adversarial nets. In: Ghahramani, Z., Welling, M. (eds.) Advances in Neural Information Processing Systems, pp. 2672–2680. Curran Associates, http://papers.nips.cc/paper/5423-generative-adversarial-nets.pdf (2016). Accessed 20 Feb 2020
3. Jebara, T.: Machine Learning Discriminative and Generative. Springer, USA (2004)
4. Goodfellow, I.: Tutorial: Generative Adversarial Networks. In: NIPS, http://arxiv.org/abs/1701.00160 (2016). Accessed 20 Feb 2020
5. Suarez, P.L., Sappa, A.D., Victimilla, B.X.: Infrared image colorization based on a triplet DCGAN architecture. In: 2017 IEEE Conference on Computer Vision and Pattern Recognition Workshops (CVPRW), pp. 212–217, Honolulu, HI, USA (2017). ISBN: 978-1-5386-0733-6. https://doi.org/10.1109/cvprw.2017.32
6. Isola, P., Zhou, J.Y., Efros, T.A.: Image-to-image translation with conditional adversarial networks. In: 2017 IEEE Conference on Computer Vision and Pattern Recognition (2016). ISBN: 978-1-5386-0457-1. http://arxiv.org/abs/1611.07004
7. Summerwille, A. et al.: Content Generation via Machine Learning (PCGML). http://arxiv.org/abs/1702.00539 (2017). Accessed 20 Feb 2020
8. Summerwille, A., Mateas, M.: Super Mario as a string: Platformer level generation via LSTMs. http://arxiv.org/abs/1603.00930 (2016). Accessed 20 Feb 2020
9. Jain, R., Isaksen, A., Holmga, C., Togelius, J.: Autoencoders for level generation, repair, and recognition. In: Proceedings of the ICCC Workshop on Computational Creativity and Games, p. 9 (2016)
10. Wick, Christoph: Deep learning. Informatik-Spektrum **40**(1), 103–107 (2016). https://doi.org/10.1007/s00287-016-1013-2
11. Fisher, M. et al.: Example-based synthesis of 3D object arrangements. ACM Trans. Graph. **31**(6), 1-11 (2012)
12. Giacomello, E., Lanzi, P., L., Loiacono, D.: DOOM level generation using generative adversarial networks. In: IEEE Games, Entertainment, Media Conference (GEM) (2018)
13. Beckham, C., Pal, C.: A step towards procedural terrain generation with GANs. http://arxiv.org/abs/1707.03383 (2017). Accessed 15 Mar 2019
14. Kenney: https://www.kenney.nl/assets (2019). Accessed 15 Mar 2019

Keeping It Real!

Investigating Presence in Asymmetric Virtual Reality

Mika P. Nieminen[1]([⊠]) and Markus Kirjonen[2]

[1] Aalto University School of Science, P.O Box 15400, 00076 Aalto, Finland
mika.nieminen@aalto.fi
[2] Aalto University School of Business, P.O Box 15400, 00076 Aalto, Finland
markus.kirjonen@aalto.fi

Abstract. In this paper we discuss the necessity to preserve the sense of presence in virtual reality (VR). A high sense of presence has proven advantages but is also very fragile to interruptions. We outline scenarios where interaction and communication between persons inside and outside virtual environments are necessary and assess challenges for maintaining the immersed user's sense of presence in such cases. We also use existing literature to outline an experiment that allows us to try out different methods of collaboration between immersed users and external facilitators in order to discern their effect on presence.

Keywords: Virtual reality · Sense of presence · Immersion · Collaborative problem-solving · Asymmetric virtual reality

1 Introduction

This paper discussed the concept of presence, or the feeling of being naturally part of an immersive virtual environment (VE). Our goal is to better understand the many uses and challenges of presence. Our goal is to increase the effectiveness of VR in some key tasks in collaborative problem-solving and co-design and to find suitable communication and interaction practices when working in asymmetric VR environments.

Presence, the user's subjective sense of "being there," is a key element of virtual reality [1–3]. It has been shown that when a user experiences a high sense of presence, they respond to the virtual world as they would to the real one, displaying realistic responses such as emotions, reactions, and behaviors [4, 5].

This ability to elicit realistic responses makes VR a promising medium for studying human behavior, and as such, it has seen adoption in the fields of user research, participatory design, co-design, psychology, psychiatry, and more. In many cases, the ability to simulate scenarios and environments at the click of a mouse is a significant advantage over more commonplace methods of immersing users in a desired context. Rather than trying to establish a sense of "being there" through design artifacts and narratives, or having the user physically travel to the environment in question, researchers can anchor them in a context that would otherwise be impossible, impractical, or cost-prohibitive to set up. As long as the user maintains a high sense of presence, they will respond to the virtual environment as if they were actually there in real life.

© Springer Nature Switzerland AG 2020
L. T. De Paolis and P. Bourdot (Eds.): AVR 2020, LNCS 12242, pp. 50–60, 2020.
https://doi.org/10.1007/978-3-030-58465-8_4

Unfortunately, presence in virtual reality is not guaranteed [6, 7]. A user's sense of presence can fluctuate, or even break completely [8], in response to events in both the virtual and real world. One of the most common reasons for this sort of break in presence is interference from the external world; i.e. hearing somebody talking or having them try to get your attention [8, 9]. This is problematic, as interaction between a subject and facilitator is a staple of many design and research approaches. At any point during the experiment, the non-immersed facilitator may want to ask the immersed user to describe their experience, point to something in the virtual environment, or provide guidance if they are unable to proceed with the task at hand. All of these interactions carry with them a significant possibility of shattering the immersed user's sense of presence if not properly integrated into the virtual environment.

This paper makes the case for the search of context-appropriate methods of inter-action and communication between immersed users and external facilitators that are conducive to maintaining the immersed user's sense of presence, thus preserving the virtual environment's ability to elicit realistic behaviors and emotions.

2   The Meaning of Being There

The lately booming interest in VR technology is shared among different variants of augmented reality (AR), mixed reality (MR) or virtual reality. We will concentrate on the right edge of the Milgram and Kishino's [10] virtuality continuum, namely fully immersive virtual environments and augmented virtuality (see Fig. 1).

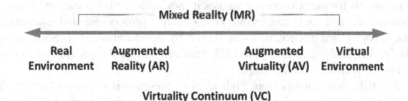

Fig. 1. Virtuality continuum [10].

While we are eagerly waiting for the fully immersive photorealistic massively multi-user environments like the Oasis depicted in the 2011 bestseller Ready Player One [11], we must conclude that the most effective and meaningful VR collaboration requires active participation from parties external to the VR environment. The question of how to facilitate seamless interaction, collaboration and communications between a fully immersed user in the VR and the accompanying users in the real life remains. This kind of setting where users have access to variable levels of immersion is commonly referred to as **asymmetric virtual reality**. Some examples of interactions designed to support such asymmetry in collocated contexts are ShareVR [12] and RoleVR [13]. Peter et al. [14] identified a rich set of conceptual features designed to support interactions between immersed users and external users in such a context (which they dubbed "VR-Guides"). These features were further categorized into four categories:

- View-related features, allowing the VR Guide to observe the virtual scene from multiple perspectives,
- Manipulation features, allowing the VR Guide to control, add, and delete objects in the scene.
- Meta-part features, allowing the VR Guide to control the simulation, e.g. start and end it, trigger a virtual event.
- Monitoring features, allowing the VR Guide to visualize parts of VE that the user has explored or is paying attention to, gather affective computing data (e.g. heart rate or skin conductivity), statistics about the VE experience such as time lapsed.

Presence is often described as the user's subjective psychological response to a virtual environment and the experience of "being there" [1–3]. Presence is needed for eliciting realistic behavior i.e. reactions and emotions in a virtual environment [4, 5], and it has also been shown that the higher the user's sense of presence is, the more realistic their responses are [15].

3   Application Areas that Require Presence

Our hypothesis throughout this paper is that maintaining high level of presence enables seamless collaboration and leads to good flow on interactive activities. VR opens new possibilities for user-centered design, user experience (UX) design, participatory design and **co-design** as long as the necessary interactions between all stakeholders can be kept as natural as possible. Brade et al. [16] concluded that virtual environments can substitute real environments for user experience studies if they achieve high presence. The use of VR environments and tools can enable cost effective prototyping and evaluation of products, services, and environments as shown by Rebelo et al. [17]. Some suitable contexts for VR enabled usability and UX research and co-design are hospitals and ATMs [18] and architectural design [19].

Another field that benefits from high level of presence is exposure therapy. This behavioral therapy technique involves exposing a patient to the source of their phobia, without danger, in an effort to gradually reduce the anxiety they associate with it. As the range of a patient's possible phobias is endlessly broad, one can easily imagine why virtual reality would be useful in this endeavor. With the click of their mouse, a therapist can simulate any stimuli, ranging from spiders to large crowds (given a VE built for such simulations). Indeed, as Koller et al. [20] stated, virtual reality exposure therapy (VRET) is potentially a major improvement over both using real-world stimuli (in-vivo exposure therapy), which may be difficult or cost-prohibitive to procure, and relying on the patient's imagination (in-situ exposure therapy). Of course, VRET requires the virtual environment to elicit realistic reactions and emotions on the part of the patient, and thus, presence has been heavily researched in this context [20–23].

More broadly, virtual reality has seen utilization in psychology for similar reasons; as Diemer et al. [5] describe, it allows us to study human behavior in highly controlled and customizable settings. Examples here include Yee and Bailenson [24] using virtual reality avatars to study the effect of self-presentation on behavior, Peck et al. [25] studying the effect of embodying an avatar representing a minority race in reducing racial bias, and

Slater et al. [26] repeating the infamous Milgram obedience experiment in virtual reality, none of which would be possible without the medium. As before, the usefulness of these experiments depends on the virtual environment's ability to elicit realistic reactions.

4 Presence: On/off

Presence in VR is not guaranteed. The level of presence that a user experiences de-pends on factors relating to hardware, software, and the individual user in question, as discussed below. Nor is it static. The level of presence that a user feels can fluctuate in response to events in both the virtual and real world, and can even break entirely, as discussed by Slater and Steed [8]. This is undesirable, as it reduces the virtual environment's ability to elicit realistic responses.

4.1 Things Making Presence

Presence can be increased by various factors. Some of these relate to the virtual reality hardware itself. Cummings and Bailenson [7] highlight the tracking level, field of view, update rate, and stereoscopy as having a particularly significant effect on the user's sense of presence. These features are important as they allow for a low level of latency between the user's sensory data and sense of self movement, as emphasized by Slater [27]. In other words, it is important for what the user sees to accurately match how they feel their body moving, a dynamic which is heavily dependent on the quality of technology being used. Less impactful features include image quality and resolution [7]. Software-related design choices within the virtual environment are also highly relevant in establishing a high sense of presence. For instance, having the environment appropriately react to the user's actions is important. This includes realistic shadows and lighting [6], having objects that represent living being behaving appropriately in response to the user [27], and the user's ability to participate in and modify the virtual environment [28]. Finally, as presence is a subjective phenomenon, the user in question has a significant effect on the level of presence that is provided by the virtual environment. Samana et al. [29] found that individual traits on the part of the user that affect their level of experienced presence include imagination, empathy, level of anxiety, cognitive style, dissociative tendencies, and more. The user's situational interest is also an important factor in how present the user feels [5, 30], along with their general state of mind and recent history at the time of the experience. [6].

4.2 Things Breaking Presence

Just as some factors can increase a user's sense of presence, others can decrease or even break a user's sense of presence completely. Slater and Steed [8] categorized reasons for breaks in presence into two main categories: external causes (sensory information from the external, real world intruding upon or contradicting what is happening in the virtual world) and internal causes (something is "wrong" in the virtual world, such as improper physics, incorrect or missing sounds, or objects not acting realistically). They also identified other categories, such as experiment-related causes, personal causes, attention-related causes, and spontaneous causes for breaks in presence. In their ranking, external causes such as hearing people talking in the background, or experiencing external touches or forces, were found to be two of the most common reasons for breaks in presence. This seems to be the case for any situation where the user interacts with, or becomes aware of, the external world [9, 31]. This susceptibility to external interruptions presents a problem in virtual reality; while a user is immersed, external people in the real world may want to interact or communicate with them - going as far as nudging them to get their attention before talking [9]. Problems relating to the virtual reality hardware being used have also been shown to be potential causes for breaks in presence. Two common factors here include awareness of the virtual reality equipment and control apparatus [32]. In addition, cybersickness, which can be caused by technology-related factors such as latency in tracking or low refresh rates, has been well-established as a significant source of breaks in presence [33].

5 Measuring Presence

Presence can be conceptually split to two categories: physical and social. IJsselsteijn et al. [34] declare that "The physical category refers to the sense of being physically located somewhere, whereas the social category refers to the feeling of being together (and communicating) with someone." Measuring presence has two main approaches. In subjective measures participants provide a conscious assessment of their psychological state in relation to the mediated environment, while objective measures try to capture person's responses automatically and without conscious deliberation [35]. Van Baren and IJsselsteijn [36] offer a complete compendium of measurements. They list subjective measures which include various questionnaires, continuous assessment, qualitative and psychophysical measures, while objective measures include psychophysical measures, neural correlates and behavioral and task performance measures. While the objective measures sound tempting given the limitations of subjective approaches [33], most researchers have concluded that for now, objective measures are a good addition to asking users to describe their subjective experience, not a replacement [7, 37, 38].

While questionnaires are the most common form of measuring presence, there has been some discussion on their limitations. As Slater [39] points out, by asking about one's sense of presence, you are bringing into question the phenomenon that you're supposed to be measuring, which may affect the phenomenon itself. As questionnaires are usually administered afterwards, they rely on the user's memory of presence, rather than the experience of presence itself [40, 41]. This also means that you must break presence in order to leave the virtual environment and fill out a questionnaire [42]. To circumvent this one can of course implement self-reporting during the experiment, rather than afterwards. One option if to implement questionnaires into the virtual reality environment as explored by Schwind et al. [41, 43].

6 Discussion

Based on the state of the art and our research requirements we were able to outline an experiment consisting of an asymmetric VR environment suited for creative problem solving that is discussed here in further detail. The current design will only fully support the VR experience, while the asymmetric desktop part is used by the experiment facilitator to enforce seamless integration of the various interactivity features in a Wizard of Oz fashion (for examples see [44–46]).

6.1 VR Environment

Our VR test environment is built using the Unity game engine along with Valve Corporation's SteamVR plugin to power our integration with the headset and controllers. Our interactivity features require local networking and VOIP communication, for which we planning to use pre-existing frameworks such as Mirror[1], an open source networking framework for Unity, and WebRTC Video Chat[2], a Unity VOIP plugin with virtual reality support. The hardware used is an off-the-shelf HTC VIVE Pro 2.0 Starter Kit equipped with the VIVE Wireless adapter to enable untethered movement.

Our virtual environment is split into two builds, each featuring a different set of functionality; one is for the immersed user and will run on the VR headset, while the other is for the external user and will run on a nearby desktop PC. The VR build is primarily focused on first-person interactions with the environment to perform the required tasks, while the desktop build is designed for guidance and communication-related features. The non-VR build shows a birds-eye view of the virtual environment and the view of the immersed user. These builds are synchronized in real-time via a local area network. In addition to these two Unity builds, we have also developed a web-based dashboard for preparing upcoming sessions and going through previous session data.

6.2 The Experiment

The experiment design was guided by our requirements to enable seamless yet asymmetric interaction between the fully immersed VR user and their counterpart in the real world. We wanted to support collaborative creative problem solving and be able to test several different kinds of presence preserving interactions.

The whole of the experiment is expected to last no more than an hour including all transitions and putting on and taking off the VR equipment. Upon their departure each participant is given two movie tickets (value 20€) to thank them for their valuable contribution. Selection criteria for the test subjects include equal gender balance, 18–45 years old, no earlier observed or diagnosed VR or motion sickness, and that they do not professionally work with VR technologies.

Chronologically the experiment test setup consists of four parts with expected durations in parenthesis.

Welcoming the participants, pre-task questionnaire and informed consent (10 min)
The test participants are guided into our VR lab, and they fill a short pre-test questionnaire to verify the selection criteria and to collect their informed consent to take part to the test. Each user is informed of the common ethical consideration about the experiment

---

[1] https://github.com/vis2k/Mirror.
[2] http://because-why-not.com.

[47]: we are testing the VR application and not the users, emphasize that the software is not ready and may include errors, tell the users they may stop the test at any time, explain that activities both the VR environment and the lab room are recorded for further analysis, but the results are anonymized and their identities are kept confidential.

Introduction to VR gear and establishing presence baseline (10 min)
In the start of the experiment, the user can try the VR headset and controllers in one of the three different example VR environments, chosen to represent low, medium and high physical presence with a between-subjects design. This will allow the users to learn the basics of selecting and activating objects inside VR environments. Filling a presence questionnaire after this initial trial takes place after removing the headset and before the introduction of our VR environment.

Asymmetric creative problem-solving task (15 min)
We chose to use a virtual escape room as the template for our experiment. Real life escape rooms have become excessively popular lately, so we hope the goals and common practices in them are familiar to our test subjects. This lowers the need to draw detailed instructions for the tasks, which would inevitably hinder the immersion to the actual task.

During the creative problem-solving task, the immersed VR user works through a series of activities with variable difficulty in a single room environment. Some tasks are designed to specifically require external assistance and guidance from the non-immersed party/experiment facilitator. After each task, we will measure the immersed user's sense of presence while they are in the virtual environment using integrated VR presence questionnaires (as seen in [42]). By integrating the questionnaires into virtual reality, we are able to reduce the downtime between each task and avoid having to re-orientate the user to the environment. After filling out the questionnaire, the user is able to move onto the next task, thus starting a new iteration of this task-questionnaire cycle. In addition to the presence questionnaires at the end of each task, the user can also self-report their sense of presence at any point throughout the experiment using a built-in mechanism, a handheld slider, similar to [8].

During the experiment the user must collaborate with the external party to complete some of the tasks. Together with trying out several interaction methods accompanied with an in-VR presence measurement, we can assess the effects of interactions between the virtual and real world on the experienced presence of the immersed user. Among the escape room tasks each immersed user will be reached through two different type of interaction conduits. Some of the conduits are considered highly disruptive to the presence such as shouting instructions to the immersed user while they complete the task. A practice common to current VR use, when a single person is playing a game and others offer their advice in a loud voice to make the VR user to hear them. More subtle conduits aim to enable communication and interactivity in a context-appropriate way and aim to preserve the immersed user's sense of presence by interacting through objects in the VR environment. Example of such presence-preserving methods include talking to the immersed user via an available telephone or walkie-talkie (handheld two-way radio transceiver), or pointing at objects in a way adherent to the laws of that specific virtual environment; for instance, in the case of a fantasy themed setting a sparkling fairy pointing at objects may be appropriate, but it would make less sense in a more realistic environment. Possible interaction methods, with examples of varying levels of integration into the virtual environment, are explored in Table 1.

Table 1. Communication and interaction methods for asymmetric VR environments.

Verbal communication The immersed user and external facilitator interact directly through speech. The effect on presence is presumed to depend on the level of embodiment that is applied to the external user's voice	• Unintegrated voice (the facilitator's voice comes from the real, external world, with no modifications, e.g. person shouting next to you) • Disembodied voice (the facilitator's voice is heard in the virtual reality, with no integration to the VE) • Object-embodied voice (the facilitator's voice is embodied in a dynamic virtual object in the VE, e.g. through a walkie-talkie or a loudspeaker) • Avatar embodied voice (the facilitator exists in the VE as a dynamic avatar or person on a video call, towards which the immersed user feels a sense of social presence)
Spatial communication The facilitator provides spatial directions and calls the user's attention to objects within the virtual environment	• Non-integrated highlighting (highlighting objects in a manner that is not at all context-appropriate, e.g. a big floating arrow or green ring around a virtual object, as commonly seen in video games) • Integrated highlighting (guiding the user's attention in a manner that is a natural part of the VE; e.g. a virtual character appearing and pointing towards the object in question)

Post-task questionnaire and interview (15 min)
After completing all of the tasks and escaping from the escape room, the VR users are shown end credits and are then asked to remove the VR headset. They are invited to fill out a post-task presence questionnaire, after which the experiment facilitator will interview them about the escape room experience in general. We are hoping for the participants to point out interruptions or positive incidents during their collaboration tasks which, with linkage to the in-VR presence measurements, can hopefully validate correlation between pleasant immersive VR experience and high level of presence.

7 Conclusions

In this paper we have outlined the challenges of conducting collaborative problem-solving in an asymmetric virtual environment. We have identified the key elements promoting and hindering the perceived sense of presence in VR. We argue that high sense of presence is a critical ingredient for successful co-design and collaboration. We have described a VR environment and an experiment that will enable us to test different in-VR presence measurement methods for several identified communication and interaction practices in order to study their impact on the immersed user's sense of presence.

Our future work includes developing the described VR environment, preparing a collection of presence measuring instruments and conducting an extended qualitative user experiment based on the constant comparative method described in the grounded theory [48] that enables us to define, model and validate the most suitable methods for collaboration in asymmetric VR environments.

Acknowledgements. We wish to thank the department of Computer Science at Aalto University School of Science for funding this research.

References

1. Heeter, C.: Being there: the subjective experience of presence. presence: Teleoperators and Virtual Environments. 1, 262. (1992) https://doi.org/10.1162/pres.1992.1.2.262
2. Lombard, M., Ditton, T.: At the heart of it all: the concept of presence. J. Comput. Mediat. Commun. 3(2), JCMC321 (1997)
3. Slater, M.: A note on presence terminology. (2003)
4. Slater, M., Khanna, P., Mortensen, J., Yu, I.: Visual realism enhances realistic response in an immersive virtual environment. IEEE Comput. Graph. Appl. **29**, 76–84 (2009). https://doi.org/10.1109/MCG.2009.55
5. Diemer, J., Alpers, G. W., Peperkorn, H. M., et al.: The impact of perception and presence on emotional reactions: a review of research in virtual reality. Front. Psychol. 6, (2015)
6. Bowman, D.A., McMahan, R.P.: Virtual reality: how much immersion is enough? Computer **40**, 36–43 (2007). https://doi.org/10.1109/MC.2007.257
7. Cummings, J.J., Bailenson, J.N.: How immersive is enough? a meta-analysis of the effect of immersive technology on user presence. Media Psychol. **19**, 272–309 (2016). https://doi.org/10.1080/15213269.2015.1015740
8. Slater, M., Steed, A.: A Virtual Presence Counter. Presence **9**, 413–434 (2000). https://doi.org/10.1162/105474600566925
9. Zenner, A., Speicher, M., Klingner, S., et al.: Immersive notification framework: adaptive & plausible notifications in virtual reality. Extended Abstracts of the 2018 CHI Conference on Human Factors in Computing Systems, pp. 1–6. Association for Computing Machinery, Montreal QC, Canada (2018)
10. Milgram, P., Kishino, F.: A taxonomy of mixed reality visual displays. IEICE Trans. Inf. Syst. **77**, 1321–1329 (1994)
11. Cline, E.: Ready Player One, 1st edn. Crown Publishers, New York (2011)
12. Gugenheimer, J., Stemasov, E., Frommel, J., Rukzio, E.: ShareVR: enabling co-located experiences for virtual reality between HMD and non-HMD users. In: Proceedings of the 2017 CHI Conference on Human Factors in Computing Systems - CHI . ACM Press, Denver, Colorado, USA, pp. 4021–4033 (2017)
13. Lee, J., Kim, M., Kim, J.: RoleVR: Multi-experience in immersive virtual reality between co-located HMD and non-HMD users. J. Multimed. Tools Appl. **79**(1-2), 979–1005 (2019). https://doi.org/10.1007/s11042-019-08220-w
14. Peter, M., Horst, R., Dörner, R.: VR-Guide: A Specific User Role for Asymmetric Virtual Reality Setups in Distributed Virtual Reality Applications (2018)
15. Slater, M., Lotto, B., Arnold, M.M.: Sánchez-Vives MV (2009) How we experience immersive virtual environments: the concept of presence and its measurement. Anuario de Psicología **40**, 193–210 (2009)

16. Brade, J., Lorenz, M., Busch, M., et al.: Being there again – presence in real and virtual environments and its relation to usability and user experience using a mobile navigation task. Int. J. Human-Comput. Stud. **101**, 76–87 (2017). https://doi.org/10.1016/j.ijhcs.2017.01.004

17. Rebelo, F., Noriega, P., Duarte, E., Soares, M.: Using virtual reality to assess user experience. Hum. Factors **54**, 964–982 (2012). https://doi.org/10.1177/0018720812465006

18. Tiainen, T., Jouppila, T.: Use of virtual environment and virtual prototypes in co-design: the case of hospital design. Computers **8**, 44 (2019). https://doi.org/10.3390/computers8020044

19. Mobach, M.P.: Do virtual worlds create better real worlds? Virtual Reality **12**, 163–179 (2008). https://doi.org/10.1007/s10055-008-0081-2

20. Koller, M., Schäfer, P., Lochner, D., Meixner, G.: Rich interactions in virtual reality exposure therapy: a pilot-study evaluating a system for presentation training. In: 2019 IEEE International Conference on Healthcare Informatics (ICHI) pp. 1–11 (2019)

21. Ling, Y., Nefs, H.T., Morina, N., et al.: A meta-analysis on the relationship between self-reported presence and anxiety in virtual reality exposure therapy for anxiety disorders. PLoS ONE **9**, e96144 (2014). https://doi.org/10.1371/journal.pone.0096144

22. Price, M., Anderson, P.: The role of presence in virtual reality exposure therapy. J. Anxiety Disord. **21**, 742–751 (2007). https://doi.org/10.1016/j.janxdis.2006.11.002

23. Botella.: Recent Progress in Virtual Reality Exposure Therapy for Phobias: A Systematic Review. - PubMed - NCBI. https://www.ncbi.nlm.nih.gov/pubmed/28540594. Accessed 21 Feb 2020

24. Yee, N., Bailenson, J.: The proteus effect: the effect of transformed self-representation on behavior. Hum. Comm. Res. **33**, 271–290 (2007). https://doi.org/10.1111/j.1468-2958.2007.00299.x

25. Peck, T.C., Seinfeld, S., Aglioti, S.M., Slater, M.: Putting yourself in the skin of a black avatar reduces implicit racial bias. Conscious. Cogn. **22**, 779–787 (2013). https://doi.org/10.1016/j.concog.2013.04.016

26. Slater, M., Antley, A., Davison, A., et al.: A virtual reprise of the stanley milgram obedience experiments. PLoS ONE **1**, e39 (2006). https://doi.org/10.1371/journal.pone.0000039

27. Slater, M.: Place illusion and plausibility can lead to realistic behaviour in immersive virtual environments. Philos. Trans. R. Soc. Lond. B Biol. Sci. **364**, 3549–3557 (2009). https://doi.org/10.1098/rstb.2009.0138

28. Schuemie, M.J., van der Straaten, P., Krijn, M., van der Mast, C.A.: Research on presence in virtual reality: a survey. Cyberpsychol. Behav. **4**, 183–201 (2001). https://doi.org/10.1089/109493101300117884

29. Samana, R., Wallach, H., Safir, M.: The Impact of Personality Traits on the Experience of Presence. pp. 1–7 (2009)

30. Lessiter, J., Freeman, J., Keogh, E., Davidoff, J.: A cross-media presence questionnaire: the itc-sense of presence inventory. Presence **10**, 282–297 (2001). https://doi.org/10.1162/105474601300343612

31. Liszio, S., Masuch, M.: Designing shared virtual reality gaming experiences in local multi-platform games. In: ICEC (2016)

32. Riches, S., Elghany, S., Garety, P., et al.: Factors affecting sense of presence in a virtual reality social environment: a qualitative study. Cyberpsychol. Beh. Social Network. **22**, 288–292 (2019). https://doi.org/10.1089/cyber.2018.0128

33. Weech, S., Kenny, S., Barnett-Cowan, M.: Presence and cybersickness in virtual reality are negatively related: a review. Front. Psychol. **10**, 158 (2019). https://doi.org/10.3389/fpsyg.2019.00158

34. IJsselsteijn, W. A., De Ridder, H., Freeman, J., Avons, S. E.: Presence: concept, determinants, and measurement. In: Human Vision and Electronic Imaging V. International Society for Optics and Photonics, pp. 520–529 (2000)

35. IJsselsteijn, W. A.: Presence in depth. Technische Universiteit Eindhoven (2004)
36. van Baren, J., IJsselsteijn, W.: Measuring Presence A Guide to Current Measurement Approaches (2004)
37. Dillon, C., Keogh, E., Freeman, J., Davidoff, J.: Presence: is your heart in it. In: 4th International Workshop on Presence (2001)
38. Lombard, M., Bolmarcich, T., Weinstein, L.: Measuring Presence: The Temple Presence Inventory (2009)
39. Slater, M.: How colorful was your day? why questionnaires cannot assess presence in virtual environments. Presence **13**, 484–493 (2004). https://doi.org/10.1162/1054746041944849
40. Usoh, M., Catena, E., Arman, S., Slater, M.: Using presence questionnaires in reality. presence: Teleoperators and Virtual Environments 9, (2000). https://doi.org/10.1162/105474600566989
41. Schwind, V., Knierim, P., Tasci, C., et al.: "These are not my hands!": Effect of Gender on the Perception of Avatar Hands in Virtual Reality, pp. 1577–1582 (2017)
42. Schwind, V., Knierim, P., Haas, N., Henze, N.: Using Presence Questionnaires in Virtual Reality (2019)
43. Schwind, V., Knierim, P., Chuang, L., Henze, N.: "Where's Pinky?": The Effects of a Reduced Number of Fingers in Virtual Reality, pp. 507–515 (2017)
44. Dahlbäck, N., Jönsson, A., Ahrenberg, L.: Wizard of Oz studies: why and how. In: Proceedings of the 1st International Conference on Intelligent User Interfaces - IUI . ACM Press, Orlando, Florida, United States, pp 193–200 (1993)
45. Dow, S., Lee, J., Oezbek, C., et al.: Wizard of Oz interfaces for mixed reality applications. CHI Extended Abstracts on Human Factors in Computing Systems, pp. 1339–1342. Association for Computing Machinery, Portland (2005)
46. Klemmer, S. R., Sinha, A. K., Chen, J., et al.: Suede: a Wizard of Oz prototyping tool for speech user interfaces. In: Proceedings of the 13th Annual ACM Symposium on User Interface Software and Technology. Association for Computing Machinery, San Diego, CA, USA, pp. 1–10 (2000)
47. Nielsen, J.: Usability Engineering. Morgan Kaufmann Publishers Inc., San Francisco (1993)
48. Glaser, B.G., Strauss, A.L.: The Discovery Of Grounded Theory: Strategies for Qualitative Research. Aldine de Gruyter, London, UK (1967)

GazeRoomLock: Using Gaze and Head-Pose to Improve the Usability and Observation Resistance of 3D Passwords in Virtual Reality

Ceenu George[1][(✉)], Daniel Buschek[2], Andrea Ngao[1], and Mohamed Khamis[3]

[1] Chair for Media Informatics, LMU Munich, Munich, Germany
ceenu.george@ifi.lmu.de
[2] Research Group HCI + AI, Department of Computer Science,
University of Bayreuth, Bayreuth, Germany
daniel.buschek@uni-bayreuth.de
[3] School of Computing Science, University of Glasgow, Glasgow, Scotland
mohamed.khamis@glasgow.ac.uk

Abstract. Authentication has become an important component of Immersive Virtual Reality (IVR) applications, such as virtual shopping stores, social networks, and games. Recent work showed that compared to traditional graphical and alphanumeric passwords, a more promising form of passwords for IVR is 3D passwords. This work evaluates four multimodal techniques for entering 3D passwords in IVR that consist of multiple virtual objects selected in succession. Namely, we compare eye gaze and head pose for *pointing*, and dwell time and tactile input for *selection*. A comparison of a) usability in terms of entry time, error rate, and memorability, and b) resistance to real world and offline observations, reveals that: multimodal authentication in IVR by pointing at targets using gaze, and selecting them using a handheld controller significantly improves usability and security compared to the other methods and to prior work. We discuss how the choice of pointing and selection methods impacts the usability and security of 3D passwords in IVR.

1 Introduction

Recent advances in immersive virtual reality (IVR) using head mounted displays (HMDs) allow users to shop in virtual stores, visit virtual social networking sites, and experience highly immersive games. These applications demand authentication to confirm users' identity to, for example, perform purchases or log in. At the same time, HMDs are becoming self-contained wireless devices, without external input devices such as keyboards [39]. These trends underline the need for secure and usable authentication that seamlessly integrates into the mobile and ubiquitous IVR experience.

Previous work attempted to transfer authentication concepts from mobile devices to IVR. For example, George et al. [18] experimented with PINs and

© Springer Nature Switzerland AG 2020
L. T. De Paolis and P. Bourdot (Eds.): AVR 2020, LNCS 12242, pp. 61–81, 2020.
https://doi.org/10.1007/978-3-030-58465-8_5

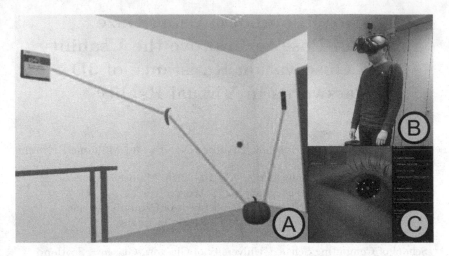

Fig. 1. We compare four input techniques for authentication in IVR by selecting a series of 3D targets. MultimodalGaze and MultimodalHead are the fastest, least error-prone, and most secure against real world observations. MultimodalGaze is even more resilient to video observations.

Android lock patterns in IVR. However, they found that by observing the user during authentication, bystanders in the real world can infer their input [18]. This is a growing threat in the context of IVR with HMDs, in which HMDs are becoming more immersive and users are blindfolded from the real world – making it less likely for users to be aware of bystanders. Additionally, the need to hide IVR users' interactions from bystanders is exacerbated by the affordance of mobile HMDs, such as the Oculus Go [39], which are increasingly used in public settings [19,35] and can be shared across multiple users in the same household. A recent more promising solution for authentication in IVR is by using the handheld controllers to point at virtual 3D objects that make up the password [16]. While that approach's adoption of 3D passwords made it more suitable for IVR, authentication times were relatively long (between 8.58 s and 14.32 s). They also found that the use of HMD controllers while authenticating is prone to observation attacks [16,18]. In the context of 3D authentication for IVR, our research questions summarize as follows:

R1. Do modalities that are hidden from the bystander, such as gaze- and head-based interaction, improve security while maintaining usability?
R2. How does multimodal interaction impact usability and observation resistance in IVR?

To this end, we compare: 1) **UnimodalGaze**: pointing via gaze and selection via dwell time, 2) **MultimodalGaze**: pointing via gaze and selection via tactile input, 3) **UnimodalHead**: pointing via head-pose and selection via dwell time, and 4) **MultimodalHead**: pointing via head-pose and selection via tactile input. Our choice of methods was motivated by the advantages of using gaze to support authentication as outlined by previous work [24]. In two studies, we evaluate the techniques' impact on a) **usability** of the scheme ($N = 48$) in terms of entry time, error rate and memorability, and on b) the **observation resistance** of input ($N = 26$) against real time observations, and offline video attacks. Based on our analysis of usability, memorability and security against two realistic threat models, we recommend **MultimodalGaze** for entering 3D passwords in IVR: We found it to be significantly faster (5.94 s) compared to methods in prior work, significantly less error prone (1.32% error rate), and significantly more resilient to real world observations (18% attack success rate) and offline observations using recordings of the user and the virtual scene (10% attack success rate). We discuss how the choice of pointing and selection methods impacts the usability and security of 3D passwords.

2   Related Work

Authentication in Virtual Reality. 3D virtual environments provide a number of advantages which support the authentication process. Firstly, they offer a limitless space for password creation. Secondly, they aid memorability by utilizing human spatial memory to recall passwords [5]. Alsulaiman et al. [3] proposed an authentication concept, where passwords consist of users' navigation through the virtual space and their interaction with objects; for example, walking to the first room and sitting down. Gurary et al. [20] and George et al. [16] transferred this concept to immersive virtual reality with an HMD. In the latter authentication concept, users could authenticate by pointing at objects in the 3D environment rather than tapping it or interacting with it actively [16]. However, authentication in IVR also has a main drawback, which is users' inability to view the real world while they are interacting with an HMD. In this context, they are unaware of real world bystanders that might be observing their body and/or arm gestures from which they can infer the entered password. Thus, we improve prior work in 3D authentication by utilizing inconspicuous gaze interactions.

Gaze-Supported Authentication. Early work on gaze-based interaction recognized authentication as one of the main domains that can benefit from the subtle nature of eye gaze. For example, EyePassShapes used gaze gestures for authentication [10], while CGP is a graphical scheme that allowed users to gaze and dwell at certain positions on pictures to authenticate [15]. More recently, CueAuth allowed users to authenticate by gazing at on-screen moving targets [30]. These schemes performed well against observations, but were slow with average authentication times ranging from 12.5 s in EyePassShapes [10], 36.7 s in CGP [15], and 26.35 s in CueAuth [30]. Other works employed gaze for multimodal authentication. Kumar et al. [32] proposed EyePassword, in which users gaze at an on-screen digit and press the space bar to select it. Other multimodal schemes include GazeTouchPIN [28], where users authenticated using gaze and touch. Abdrabou et al. [1] compared multiple techniques that used gaze, mid-air gestures or combinations of both for authentication. Their gaze-based scheme

Fig. 2. Pointing Methods. In GazeRoomLock, the area that is pointed at is indicated by a green dot. When using UnimodalGaze and MultimodalGaze, the point follows the user's eye movements (A). While in UnimodalHead and MultimodalHead the point is centered in the middle of the user's view (C). Objects are highlighted once they are pointed at (B and D).

was a replication of EyePassword [32], yet it outperformed the other 5 techniques and even the original version by Kumar et al. The authors underlined the value of replicating prior eye tracking applications in light of the improved hardware and gaze estimation algorithms. The use of several modalities for password entry results splits the observer's attention, which improves security. Multimodal schemes were generally faster than the unimodal counterparts – 9.2 s in EyePassword [32] and 10.8 s in GazeTouchPIN [28]. The aforementioned schemes relied on the knowledge factor. Other schemes leveraged gaze for behavioral biometric authentication [26,31,42,43] and the latest HMDs offer built-in solutions, such as the retina authentication [23,44]. While behavioral biometrics offers continuous authentication and can be fast, they require sharing personal data with third parties, cannot be changed or invalidated if leaked, and are incompatible with many existing backends.

Our work is unique compared to prior work in that it investigates multimodal approaches to enter 3D passwords in IVR. Results show that our Multimodal-Gaze and MultimodalHead methods are faster (5.92 s and 5.51 s) compared to prior work (e.g., 9.2 s [32], 10.8 s [28], 12.5 [10], and 26.35 s [30]). Our work significantly improves over a recently proposed authentication scheme for IVR [16]. Namely, our methods leverage the user's eye gaze for authentication in virtual reality. Instead of pointing at targets, users gaze at the target they want to select as part of their password. This improvement resulted in higher usability: lower entry time (5.92 s–5.51 s vs 8.58 s–14.32 s [16]), and lower error rate (0.46%–1.39% vs 2.78% [16]). Our aim is not to propose a new concept but rather to explore input methods for 3D passwords in IVR: We improve entry time and error rates over prior work (e.g., [16]) despite using the same password space.

3   Concept

We will refer to our authentication concept as GazeRoomLock. In GazeRoomLock, users authenticate by selecting a number of 3D objects in a virtual room. For example, in Fig. 1, the user selects a book, followed by a banana, pumpkin, and then a can of chips. Because the user is wearing an HMD, bystanders

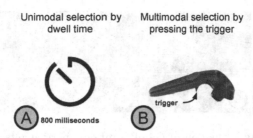

Fig. 3. We experimented with two selections methods in GazeRoomLock. Namely, users can select the object that is pointed at by either a) dwelling at it for 800 ms (Unimodal-Gaze and UnimodalHead) or b) pressing the controller's trigger (MultimodalGaze and MultimodalHead).

cannot see the virtual scene that the user is in[1]. In our current implementation and in our study, 3D passwords are of length 4, and users could choose from 9 selectable objects. While future implementations can allow longer passwords, and integrate more selectable objects, we chose a length of 4 to be comparable to prior work on authentication [16,18,30,47]. Our scheme was influenced by Lock Patterns that are commonly used on Android devices. Lock patterns provide an entropy of 389,112 [6]. Unlike Lock Patterns, our scheme allows selecting the same object multiple times, but not in succession. This means our system has a higher entropy than Lock Patterns.

3.1 Pointing and Selecting

The selection of each target in GazeRoomLock comprises of two steps: *Pointing* at a target, and then (2) *Selecting* it. We studied different approaches for achieving each step.

Pointing. There are two predominant ways for hands-free pointing in virtual reality: 1) users can point using their **eye gaze**, i.e., by looking at the target, or 2) users can adjust their **head pose** such that the target is in the middle of their view. Eye gaze is fast (e.g., faster than pointing [33,41]), and is likely to be very secure due to its subtleness. On the other hand, while changing the head pose can be more obvious to bystanders, it is accurate for pointing [33], does not induce eye fatigue, and was suggested as a proxy for gaze [4,14]. In our study, pointing by gaze was achieved by eye tracking. The gaze point was visualized using a green dot (Fig. 2A). Pointing by head pose was done by moving a point at the center of the user's view to overlay the target (Fig. 2C).

---

[1] Some HMDs show the user's view on a nearby screen. This feature must be automatically disabled during authentication. We expect all HMDs will become untethered.

Fig. 4. In the security evaluation of GazeRoomLock, participants first observed the experimenter as she entered a GazeRoomLock password in VR (A). Participants then put on the HMD and tried providing up to three guesses of the observed password (B). Some participants came up with creative ways to note down their observations. For example, one of the participants folded two sheets of papers to make a replica of the virtual environment (C).

Selection. After successfully pointing at the target, selection can be done in multiple ways. We experimented with the following designs: 1) In **Unimodal selection**, the same modality used for pointing (i.e., eye gaze or head pose) is also used for selection. We realized this using dwell time, which means that users had to fixate at the target for a certain amount of time for the system to distinguish intentional selections from perception of targets. To determine suitable dwell durations, we conducted a pilot study (N = 6) in which we experimented with three different dwell time durations that are based on prior work on gaze-based password and text entry [10,36,38]: 400 ms, 500 ms, and 800 ms. The results indicate that a dwell time of 800 ms is the least error prone, and also the fastest because participants spend less time recovering from errors. Therefore, we used 800 ms in the Unimodal selection condition. In 2) **Multimodal selection**, an additional modality was used to confirm selection of the target that is pointed at [22]. In this version of GazeRoomLock, we chose to confirm the selection of the pointed at target using the handheld controller's trigger button (Fig. 3B). There are other means for selection via eye gaze that leverage gaze behavior rather than fixations. Examples include gaze gestures [12] and Pursuits [13,45]. While these approaches are suitable for selection in IVR , they require either a) arranging targets in a fixed way [12] which is vulnerable to observations, or b) continuously moving the targets in a predefined manner [13,14,29] which requires long authentication times (e.g., 26.35 s [30]).

4   Implementation

We implemented GazeRoomLock using Unity 3D with C#. We designed a virtual room that replicated a real room in our lab, and ten selectable 3D objects using Blender. The virtual objects were selected to cover a range of shapes and colors, and to resemble every day objects so users would relate to them. Their sizes matched the size of their real world equivalents. The selectable objects are: A Pringles can, a lemon, a banana, a pumpkin, a spray bottle, a smartphone, a booklet, a plant, a bottle of water, a soda drink can and a trash can. The HTC Vive was equipped with a binocular eye tracker by Pupil Labs [34] to enable gaze-based selection. We used the built-in calibration of the Pupil labs software.

A green dot represents the area that is pointed at. The point is placed where the user is looking in case of gaze-based pointing (Fig. 2A), or at the center of the user's view in case of head pose selection (Fig. 2C). If this point falls within a predefined area around an object (the "collider"), the object is considered "being pointed at" and is highlighted (see Figs. 2B and 2D).

In case of unimodal selection, we employ the concept of dwell time, i.e., pointing initiates a timer which is reset when the object is no longer being pointed at. If an object is pointed at for 800 ms, it is considered selected. Recall that the 800 ms dwell time threshold was chosen based on the pilot study reported in Sect. 3.1. In case of multimodal selection, an object is considered selected if the user presses the controller's trigger while pointing at the object. Once selected, the object is highlighted (see Figs. 2C and 2D). The objects are highlighted until either a complete password has been entered, or the user undoes the last entry by selecting a virtual trash can. A blue line connects consecutively selected objects. The line turns green if the password is correct, and red otherwise. This feedback design is inspired by Android's pattern locks. While GazeRoomLock is inspired by RoomLock by George et al. [16], this is the first implementation of the aforementioned techniques for authentication using 3D passwords in IVR.

5   Usability Evaluation

We ran a user study to assess the impact of multiple design factors on GazeRoom-Lock. Namely, we evaluate how GazeRoomLock's usability and memorability are influenced by the choice of:

- **UnimodalGaze**: Pointing via gaze, and selecting by dwelling.
- **MultimodalGaze**: Pointing via gaze, and selecting by pressing a controller's trigger button.
- **UnimodalHead**: Pointing via head pose, and selecting by dwelling.
- **MultimodalHead**: Pointing via head pose, and selecting by pressing a controller's trigger button.

5.1   Study Design

The study was split into two parts: 1) a lab study, where we investigated the usability of GazeRoomLock, and 2) a follow up remotely administered questionnaire to gain insights into password memorability. The lab study followed a mixed-subjects design with two independent variables:

- **Pointing method**, a between-subjects variable with two conditions: Gaze vs Head-pose (see Fig. 2). We chose a between-subjects design to avoid potential learning effects which could bias the results.

- **Selection method**, a within-subjects variable being the selection method: Unimodal (dwell time) vs Multimodal (pointing then pressing the controller's trigger). This condition was counter-balanced with a Latin square.

We measured the effect on the following dependent variables:

- **Entry time**, measured from the moment the user pointed at the first object, until the moment the last object was selected. Only correct entries were included in the analysis of entry time to avoid skewing the results towards faster speeds due to including potentially aborted attempts, in line with related work [16,48].
- **Error rate**, measured as the percentage of incorrectly entered passwords.

5.2   Procedure, Apparatus and Particiapnts

First, participants were explained the study and asked to fill a consent form and a demographics questionnaire. They were then asked to stand in the middle of the room and put on the HTC Vive. Participants who used the gaze pointing method underwent a calibration procedure at this point. Participants then had a training session in which they entered a 4-symbol password per condition to become acquainted to the system. Trial attempts were excluded from analysis. Participants examined a virtual board that showed the password they need to enter, and then entered the password three times successfully using the respective selection method. After the trial runs, participants entered three passwords three times each for each condition. The passwords were randomly generated prior to the study, and were displayed on the virtual board for participants to see before they started the authentication procedure. To ensure comparable results, the same set of passwords was used across all participants.

After each condition, we collected subjective feedback using likert-scale questions and a semi-structured interview. To evaluate memorability, participants were asked to define their own password to memorize at the end of the study, and were contacted one week later to fill in a follow-up questionnaire. The experiment complied with the university's ethics regulations.

We recruited 48 participants (14 females) aged between 18 and 57 years ($Mean = 25.23$, $SD = 7.35$) through mailing lists and social networks: 24 participants (4 females) used the gaze-based pointing method, and the other 24 (10 females) used the head pose pointing method. They were compensated with an online shopping voucher, and all had normal or corrected to normal vision.

5.3   Results

In total, we analyzed 864 password entries (3 passwords × 3 repetitions × 2 pointing methods × 2 selection methods × 24 participants per pointing method).

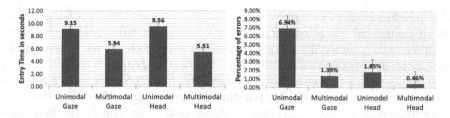

Fig. 5. In GazeRoomLock, multimodal selection is significantly faster than unimodal. We could not confirm that the choice of head or gaze for pointing impacts selection time ($p > 0.05$). Overall, participants performed very few errors using GazeRoomLock; less than 2% of entries using MultimodalGaze, UnimodalHead, and MultimodalGaze are erroneous. However, UnimodalGaze is more error-prone (6.94% error rate).

Entry Time. Figure 5A shows the overall entry time across all three entered passwords for each selection method in seconds. The figure emphasizes that both MultimodalGaze ($Mean = 5.94\,s$, $SD = 2.85\,s$) and MultimodalHead ($Mean = 5.51\,s$, $SD = 2.10\,s$) are faster than UnimodalGaze ($Mean = 9.15\,s$, $SD = 3.75\,s$) and UnimodalHead ($Mean = 9.56\,s$, $SD = 6.51\,s$). Indeed, a repeated measures ANOVA revealed a significant effect of *selection method* on entry time ($F_{1,46} = 35.61$, $p < 0.001$). Post-hoc analysis using Bonferroni corrected t-tests indicated that unimodal selection ($Mean = 9.36\,s$, $SD = 0.56\,s$) is significantly slower than multimodal selection ($Mean = 5.72\,s$, $SD = 0.30\,s$). No significant effects of *pointing method*, or *repetitions* on entry time were found ($p > 0.05$). No interaction was found between pointing and selection method ($p > 0.05$).

This means multimodal selection is significantly faster than unimodal selection. The mean entry time using gaze is slightly faster than that of head-pose, but we have no evidence that one pointing method is significantly faster than the other.

Error per Entry. Out of all 864 entries, only 23 were incorrect. 15 incorrect entries occurred in UnimodalGaze, 4 in UnimodalHead, 3 in MultimodalGaze and 1 in MultimodalHead. Figure 5B shows the average error rate for each *pointing method* (UnimodalGaze: 6.94%, UnimodalHead: 1.85%, Multimodal-Gaze: 1.39% and MultimodalHead: 0.46%). Note that most errors occurred when using UnimodalGaze. The overall error rate is 2.66%, which is lower than that in prior work on multimodal authentication [27] and authentication in IVR [16, 18].

Errors occurred either due to entering the password in a wrong order or switching the objects. The higher error rate in UnimodalGaze is attributed to the shaking of the headset, which leads to imprecise eye tracking.

A repeated measures ANOVA was used to analyze the errors. *Pointing method* was found to have a significant effect on error rate ($F_{1,46} = 8.76$, $p < 0.05$). Post-hoc analysis using Bonferroni corrected t-tests showed that Gaze ($Mean = 0.38$, $SD = 0.07$) is significantly more error prone than Head-pose ($Mean = 0.10$, $SD = 0.07$), ($p < 0.05$). Additionally, the *selection method* had a significant effect on error rate ($F_{1,46} = 8.7$, $p < 0.05$). Post-hoc analysis with Bonferroni corrected t-tests showed significant differences between the modalities, with unimodal selection ($Mean = 0.40$, $SD = 0.01$) being significantly more error prone than multimodal selection ($Mean = 0.08$, $SD = 004$), ($p < 0.05$). No significant effect for *repetitions* was found on error rate ($p > 0.05$). No interaction was found between pointing and selecting method ($p > 0.05$).

In summary, head-pose selections are significantly less error prone than gaze-based selections, and multimodal selection using the controller is significantly less error prone than unimodal selection using dwell time.

Subjective Feedback. Participants preferred multimodal over unimodal approaches (83.3% preferred MultimodalGaze over UnimodalGaze, and 66.7% preferred MultimodalHead over UnimodalHead) due to their faster selection speed and the better control over input. Some unintentionally pointed away from the target before selecting it. Participants suggested using progress bars to show how many objects were selected so far as part of the password.

We used Generalized Estimating Equations (GEE) to analyze the Likert ratings [9]. This allowed us to take into account that we have ordinal dependent variables and both a within-subject factor (selection) and a between-subject factor (pointing). We found significant influences for the two Likert items *comfortable* and *not error-prone*: For the *comfortable* item, *selection* was a significant predictor; the odds of giving a higher *comfortable* rating with multimodal selection were 3.1 times the odds of unimodal selection ($p < 0.05$). Similarly, for the *not error-prone* item, *selection* was a significant predictor; the odds of a higher rating with multimodal selection were 3.4 times the odds of unimodal selection ($p < 0.01$). Moreover, *pointing* was also a significant predictor: The odds of a higher Likert rating on this item with head were 3.9 times the odds with gaze ($p < 0.01$).

Memorability. As mentioned in Sect. 5.2, participants were requested to define their password with a length of four objects at the end of the usability study. Duplicate objects were allowed, albeit not consecutively. To investigate the memorability of GazeRoomLock, 42 of the participants completed a follow-up questionnaire one week afterwards ($Gaze = 21$, $Head = 21$).

First, participants recalled which objects they had selected and entered their self-defined password without any cues. If unsuccessful, they were given pictures of the virtual environment and objects and were allowed to provide a second and third guess. 59.5% (25 participants: 14 Gaze-group, and 11 Head-group) remembered the correct passwords on the first trial. Participants who did not recall their passwords remembered the objects but not their order. After all three trials 83.30% (35 participants: 17 Gaze-group and 18 Head-group) remembered their passwords. There is no evidence that one modality results in better memorability than the other ($p > 0.05$). Participants who recalled their password memorized them in a story-like structure: "First I eat the burger, then chips as a side dish, take a sip of cola, and then eat a cake for dessert". Three participants ordered the objects alphabetically: "banana, burger, book, can". One participant memorized the positions of the objects: "The object on the window, then the one on the table, near the board then again the object on the window". One participant remembered the objects by their colors: "green, blue, green, blue".

6 Observation-Resistance Evaluation

IVR users are unlikely to notice the presence of bystanders either due to the HMD blinding them from seeing the real world, or due to the high immersiveness of the IVR experience. Indeed, George et al. [18] found that bystanders are able to observe passwords entered by IVR users. This underlines the need to evaluate GazeRoomLock against observation attacks.

We conducted two security studies to evaluate the observation resistance of GazeRoomLock. We chose the following two threat models, since they realistically simulate possible observation attacks against our system:

Threat Model 1 – Real World Observations: Here, the adversary is in the real world and observes the user who is wearing the IVR HMD. This closely aligned with prior work which suggests family and friends to be casual attackers [21].

Threat Model 2 – Offline Observations: Here, the attacker has access to two resources that allow them to perform offline observations: 1) A **video** recording that shows the user's movements as they authenticate while wearing the HMD. In a real scenario, this video can be retrieved by recording the user, for example, with a smartphone camera. 2) Additionally, the attacker has access to the **virtual scene** in which the user normally authenticates. This simulates the case where the attacker has full knowledge and access to the virtual environment (e.g., an insider that can use the victim's HMD in their absence), and can exploit this together with the videos to refine the observations. The reason we consider both resources is that in a real scenario, an attacker who has a video recording of the authentication process can revisit the virtual scenes whenever the HMD is unattended.

In both cases, we assume the attacker is able to identify the start and end of the authentication procedure, as confirmed by prior work [17]. After observing it, the attacker then puts on the HMD and tries to enter the password in the user's absence (see Fig. 4).

We evaluated each threat model in a separate study, but they both followed the same study design. The key idea in both studies was to invite participants to observe password entries and try to make 3 guesses. All participants were compensated with online shop vouchers. To encourage high performance, we raffled an additional voucher in each study such that participants who were successful the most in attacking passwords would have higher chances in winning. Both studies complied with the university's ethics regulations.

6.1   Study Design

We followed a within-subjects experiment design with one independent variable: **Input method** with four conditions: UnimodalGaze, UnimodalHead, Multi-modalGaze, and MultimodalHead.

Participants went through 4 blocks (one per input method), in each of which they observed 3 passwords entered using the current block's input method. The order of blocks was counter balanced using a Latin square.

6.2   Security Study 1: Resisting Real World Observations

The first security study focused on real world attacks. We invited 26 participants (7 females) aged between 19 and 33 $(Mean = 23.71, SD = 3.8)$. Participants were invited individually. They first signed a consent form and were explained the study and the reward mechanism. Afterwards, the experimenter put on the HMD and started entering passwords. The participant (i.e., the attacker) first had a training round for each condition, where the experimenter was observed while entering a random password. Attackers then observed the experimenter as she entered 12 passwords (4 input methods × 3 unique passwords) and were provided with pen and paper to take notes. Note that all passwords were unique and predefined by the experimenter, i.e., no passwords were entered more than once in front of the same participant. The attacker was explicitly told when the experimenter started and stopped entering the password. After observing each password, the attacker had the chance to make up to three guesses of the password, and was asked to enter them in IVR, while wearing the HMD. The study was concluded with a semi-structured interview. To avoid priming the participants, we did not reveal their performance until the end.

We analyzed 312 attacks (26 participants × 4 input methods × 3 unique passwords). Participant 3 and participant 10 were the only ones who failed in all their attacks. We believe they did not put enough effort as the rest of the participants who made at least one correct observation, and therefore we excluded

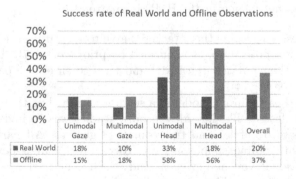

Fig. 6. The gaze-based methods are highly resilient to both types of observations. MultimodalHead is equally resilient to real world observations, but vulnerable to offline ones. UnimodalHead underperforms in both threat models.

their data to avoid skewing the results. Participants were successful in attacking only 20% of GazeRoomLock passwords. They were most successful in attacking UnimodalHead passwords, with a mean success rate of 33.33%, and least successful in attacking MultimodalGaze passwords with a mean success rate of 9.72%. Participants were equally successful in attacking UnimodalGaze and MultimodalHead passwords, with mean success rates of 18.06% for both of them. The results are illustrated in Fig. 6.

6.3   Security Study 2: Resisting Offline Observations

The second security study focused on offline attacks. This study was conducted with a separate set of participants. We invited 26 different participants (7 females) aged between 18 and 31 $(Mean = 22.46, SD = 3.11)$. After being introduced to the study and signing a consent form, participants were provided with a video showing the user entering a password in the real world (see Fig. 4B), and a video of the virtual room without the user present. The user had full control over both videos (e.g., pause, rewind, etc.). For each attack, the participant was able to provide up to three guesses. Similar to the first security study, the attacker was given pen and paper.

We analyzed 312 attacks (26 participants × 4 input methods × 3 unique passwords). Participants were more successful in this threat model, with an overall success rate of 38.86% of GazeRoomLock passwords using offline attacks. Similar to the results of the previous study, participants were most successful in attacking UnimodalHead passwords. However the average success rate is much higher in case of offline attacks compared to real world attacks; offline attacks are successful on average 57.69% of the time in case of UnimodalHead, and almost similarly successful in case of MultimodalHead (56.41%). UnimodalGaze and MultimodalGaze were more resilient to offline attacks, with success rates as low as 15.38% and 17.95% respectively. Participants were most successful in offline attacks against passwords with targets within 90° (40.38%), less successful against passwords with targets within 180° (37.50%), and least successful against passwords with repetitions (32.96%).

Limitations. We chose to investigate authentication using 4-symbols 3D passwords. This makes our results comparable to other works. We acknowledge that usability and security could differ based on the length of the password. For example, we expect that longer 3D passwords will take longer to enter, be more error prone, and be harder to observe. However, the relative results should not differ with different password lengths. This means that, for example, we expect longer passwords to be entered faster using MultimodalHead compared to UnimodalGaze.

7 Discussion

We evaluated the usability of GazeRoomLock in a user study, and we evaluated its observation resistance against real world and offline observations in two separate user studies.

7.1 Gaze-Based Multimodal Authentication Improves Usability

We found that the multimodal selection approach significantly improves usability compared to a) the unimodal methods we evaluated and b) previous work in selecting 3D passwords.

Faster Entry Time. As evidenced by the results, using an additional modality for authentication significantly reduces authentication time. In particular, users authenticated using MultimodalHead and MultimodalGaze in 5.51 s and 5.94 s respectively, but needed 9.56 s and 9.15 s when using UnimodalHead and UnimodalGaze. The reason behind the delay in the unimodal approaches is that users have to precisely point at the targets (i.e., dwell) for a period of time in order to select them. This is done in order to distinguish gaze that is intended for selection from the gaze behavior performed when scanning scenes – this is a challenge in gaze interfaces that is known as the Midas Touch [22]. While the dwell duration we used (800 ms) could theoretically allow selections in $4 \times 800 \, ms = 3.6 \, s$ in addition to the time taken to find the objects, in practice our participants needed more time to maintain the gaze point in the object's collider. This is in part due to the inaccurate nature of gaze estimates [37]. While this can improve in the future by using better sensors and improved calibration algorithms, estimating the exact point of gaze is nearly impossible due to the physiology of the eye – the eye can fixate at 2° at a time, and the user can move attention in this area without any additional eye movements [37]. On the other hand, using an additional modality allows users to make selections as soon as they are pointing at the target, which allows for faster selections in VR.

Similarly, using the controllers only to enter passwords consisting of four 3D objects required 8.58 s and 14.32 s in prior work [16]. This means that entry time using multimodal approaches outperforms previous work on authentication mechanisms by 30.8% to 61.5%. We attribute the improved entry time to the fact that humans move their heads and eyes naturally faster than they point with their arms (see discussion on gaze vs pointing in [41]). Notably, 2D entry schemes, such as patterns, provide a better entry time (3 s) [18,48]. However, this is due to the combined novelty of the device, input technique and password scheme. We are planning to investigate this further in a long-term study.

Lower Error Rate. The multimodal selection methods also outperform the unimodal ones in terms of error rate (0.46% and 1.39% vs 1.85% and 6.94%). We expect that the difficulty of maintaining gaze at the target is the main reason behind the relatively higher error rate in the gaze-based conditions. Kytö et al.

[33], who found similar trends in their results, suggest that their results for gaze-based interaction for AR may be transferred to VR, which we can confirm in the context of 3D password entry. These combined results suggest that authentication concepts are transferable between varying degrees of virtual reality and real world interaction.

Additionally, the multimodal approaches outperform previous work where controllers were used to enter 3D passwords at an error rate of 2.78% [16]. Methods that allow pointing with a controller require eye-hand coordination [8,40], which can be a cognitively demanding process [40], and could thereby be the reason behind making more errors.

7.2 Resilience to Observations

Multimodal authentication offers higher observation resistance because it requires attackers to observe a) the user's pointing, and b) the user's selection. Splitting the attacker's attention is a strategy that overwhelms attackers. Previous work on authentication on mobile devices and public displays employed this strategy to complicate real time observations [11,47]. However this strategy is not effective against video observations [30,47].

Similar to previous work, results from our studies show that MultimodalHead is highly resilient to real world observations (18%) but vulnerable to offline observations (56%). On the other hand, MultimodalGaze is resilient to both real world (10%) and offline video observations (18%). In addition to splitting the attacker's attention, another reason the multimodal methods are resilient to observations is that they are fast; giving attackers less time to observe inputs.

UnimodalGaze is also resilient to both types of observations (online 15% vs real world 18%), but it is not recommended due to its low usability. Gaze-based methods are less vulnerable to video observations because of the subtle nature of eye movements, which are further obscured by the HMDs. On the contrary, head movements are more visible (58%).

7.3 Eye Tracker Calibration

In order to estimate a precise gaze point, users need to calibrate the eye tracker. Calibration is a procedure to map the user's eye movements, which are unique for every user, to points in the environment [37]. Calibration is perceived to be a tedious and time-consuming task [45]. The negative impact of calibration on HMD users was suggested to be negligible [29] because users do it only once, as opposed to desktop settings where it needs to be repeated whenever the setup is changed (e.g., change in user's, eye tracker's, or display's position). Previous work proposed alternative gaze input methods that do not require calibration (e.g., Pursuits [45] and gaze gestures [12]). While promising for calibration-free authentication, these methods typically require longer input times [28,30].

7.4 Story-Like 3D Passwords

Regardless of input method, the majority of participants used story-like structures to memorize their passwords (e.g., *I ate the chips, and then had a cake
for dessert*). Users link objects to tell "stories", facilitating memorability. This
is similar to the concept of PassPhrases, where users attach multiple sentences
[25]. This strategy has implications on usability and security. In terms of usability, it helps participants remember the passwords as shown in the study. On
the other hand, obvious stories could make passwords predictable and result
in easier guessing attacks. For example, knowing that cake is the only object
described as a dessert, an attacker could predict that the last entry is the cake.
A possible approach to counter this is to choose a diverse mix of objects and
object categories to increase the possible options for potential stories.

7.5 Enabling a Choice of Input Modalities

Multimodal interaction methods resulted in better entry times and were found
to be more "comfortable" to use in the presence of others. This confirms prior
work by Alallah et al. [2] who investigated social acceptability of interaction
methods for IVR. Their results show that users prefer controller based input
methods, such as a touchpad, rather than mid-air gestures. Similarly, prior work
on authentication for public displays, where real world bystanders are also a
prominent threat, showed that users find mid-air gestures embarrassing to perform in public [7,30]. These results suggest the need to provide the user with
input modalities that adapt automatically depending on the context of the interaction or that enable the user to choose an appropriate one; for example in the
presence of others vs. alone at home. Our results show that MultimodalGaze
is not only more secure against offline attacks compared to the other methods,
but also almost as highly usable as MultimodalHead. An HMD user in a public
context may prefer using MultimodalGaze or even UnimodalGaze due to the
inconspicuousness of gaze in public, rather than using more visible input methods, such as MultimodalHead. Outside a lab setting it is likely more challenging
to identify the beginning and end of input when gaze is used, thereby grant-
ing even higher observation resistance. Therefore, we recommend that users are
given the option to choose which multimodal method to authenticate with.

7.6 Future Work

In future work, we aim to explore calibration-free techniques for authentication
in IVR. We also plan to investigate gaze input for established 2D authentication
mechanisms, such as PIN and pattern in IVR. Furthermore, we plan to conduct
a field study of GazeRoomLock (e.g., to allow HTC Vive users to log into their
accounts). Field studies are becoming increasingly feasible now that many HMDs
come with integrated eye trackers, such as the HTC Vive pro. Through the field
study, we plan to better understand the effect of object location on password
creation and how this impacts usability and security. We also plan to investigate

strength meters for 3D passwords, and explore modalities beyond the controller's trigger (e.g., feet tapping). Furthermore, there are many ways the tactile input in our implementation can be improved. For example, Yang et al. [46] proposed subtle haptic techniques that can be very difficult to notice by bystanders; these methods can be used to replace the trigger in the multimodal approaches.

8 Conclusion

In this work we investigated multiple methods for pointing and selecting 3D passwords in immersive virtual reality: UnimodalGaze, MultimodalGaze, UnimodalHead, and MultimodalHead. Through three user studies (N = 48, N = 26, N = 26), we investigated the usability of the approaches in terms of entry time, error rate and memorability, and the security in terms of resistance to real world observations and offline observations. We found that the multimodal approaches are significantly faster and significantly less error-prone than the unimodal ones, while memorability does not change significantly depending on the pointing method. MultimodalHead is highly resilient to real world observations, but not offline observations, while MultimodalGaze is highly secure against both. We discussed how multimodal authentication can significantly improve usability and observation resistance over prior work. Rather than exclusively focusing on new authentication mechanisms, our work highlights that there is potential to improve usability and security of existing ones by adapting alternative input modalities for IVR.

Acknowledgements. The contributions from the authors Mohamed Khamis and Daniel Buschek were supported, in part, by the Royal Society of Edinburgh (Award number 65040), and the Bavarian State Ministry of Science and the Arts in the framework of the Centre Digitisation.Bavaria (ZD.B).

References

1. Abdrabou, Y., Khamis, M., Eisa, R.M., Ismail, S., Elmougy, A.: Just gaze and wave: exploring the use of gaze and gestures for shoulder-surfing resilient authentication. In: Proceedings of the 11th ACM Symposium on Eye Tracking Research & Applications. ETRA 2019. ACM, New York (2019). https://doi.org/10.1145/3314111.3319837. http://doi.acm.org/10.1145/3314111.3319837
2. Alallah, F., et al.: Performer vs. observer: whose comfort level should we consider when examining the social acceptability of input modalities for head-worn display? In: Proceedings of the 24th ACM Symposium on Virtual Reality Software and Technology. VRST 2018. ACM, New York (2018). https://doi.org/10.1145/3281505.3281541. http://doi.acm.org.emedien.ub.uni-muenchen.de/10.1145/3281505.3281541
3. Alsulaiman, F., El Saddik, A.: Three-dimensional password for more secure authentication. IEEE Trans. Instrum. Meas. **57**, 1929–1938 (2008). https://doi.org/10.1109/TIM.2008.919905

4. Andrist, S., Gleicher, M., Mutlu, B.: Looking coordinated: bidirectional gaze mechanisms for collaborative interaction with virtual characters. In: Proceedings of the 2017 CHI Conference on Human Factors in Computing Systems. CHI 2017. ACM, New York (2017). https://doi.org/10.1145/3025453.3026033. http://doi.acm.org/10.1145/3025453.3026033

5. Attree, E., Brooks, B., Rose, F., Andrews, T., Leadbetter, A., Clifford, B.: Memory processes and virtual environments: i can't remember what was there, but i can remember how i got there. Implications for people with disabilities. In: ECD-VRAT: 1st European Conference on Disability, Virtual Reality and Associated Technologies, Reading, UK, vol. 118 (1996)

6. Aviv, A.J., Gibson, K., Mossop, E., Blaze, M., Smith, J.M.: Smudge attacks on smartphone touch screens. In: Proceedings of the 4th USENIX Conference on Offensive Technologies. WOOT 2010. USENIX Association, Berkeley (2010). http://dl.acm.org/citation.cfm?id=1925004.1925009

7. Brignull, H., Rogers, Y.: Enticing people to interact with large public displays in public spaces (2003)

8. Chan, L.W., Kao, H.S., Chen, M.Y., Lee, M.S., Hsu, J., Hung, Y.P.: Touching the void: direct-touch interaction for intangible displays. In: Proceedings of the SIGCHI Conference on Human Factors in Computing Systems. CHI 2010. ACM, New York (2010). https://doi.org/10.1145/1753326.1753725. http://doi.acm.org/10.1145/1753326.1753725

9. Clayton, D.: Repeated ordinal measurements: a generalised estimating equation approach (1992)

10. De Luca, A., Denzel, M., Hussmann, H.: Look into my eyes!: can you guess my password? In: Proceedings of the 5th Symposium on Usable Privacy and Security. SOUPS 2009, ACM, New York (2009). https://doi.org/10.1145/1572532.1572542. http://doi.acm.org/10.1145/1572532.1572542

11. De Luca, A., et al.: Now you see me, now you don't: protecting smartphone authentication from shoulder surfers. In: Proceedings of the SIGCHI Conference on Human Factors in Computing Systems. CHI 2014. ACM, New York (2014). https://doi.org/10.1145/2556288.2557097. http://doi.acm.org/10.1145/2556288.2557097

12. Drewes, H., Schmidt, A.: Interacting with the computer using gaze gestures. In: Baranauskas, C., Palanque, P., Abascal, J., Barbosa, S.D.J. (eds.) INTERACT 2007. LNCS, vol. 4663, pp. 475–488. Springer, Heidelberg (2007). https://doi.org/10.1007/978-3-540-74800-7_43

13. Esteves, A., Velloso, E., Bulling, A., Gellersen, H.: Orbits: gaze interaction for smart watches using smooth pursuit eye movements. In: Proceedings of the 28th Annual ACM Symposium on User Interface Software & Technology. UIST 2015. ACM, New York (2015). https://doi.org/10.1145/2807442.2807499. http://doi.acm.org/10.1145/2807442.2807499

14. Esteves, A., Verweij, D., Suraiya, L., Islam, R., Lee, Y., Oakley, I.: Smoothmoves: smooth pursuits head movements for augmented reality. In: Proceedings of the 30th Annual ACM Symposium on User Interface Software and Technology. UIST 2017. ACM, New York (2017). https://doi.org/10.1145/3126594.3126616. http://doi.acm.org/10.1145/3126594.3126616

15. Forget, A., Chiasson, S., Biddle, R.: Shoulder-surfing resistance with eye-gaze entry in cued-recall graphical passwords. In: Proceedings of the SIGCHI Conference on Human Factors in Computing Systems. CHI 2010. ACM, New York (2010). https://doi.org/10.1145/1753326.1753491. http://doi.acm.org/10.1145/1753326.1753491

16. George, C., Buschek, D., Khamis, M., Hussmann, H.: Investigating the third dimension for authentication in immersive virtual reality and in the real world. In: 2019 IEEE Conference on Virtual Reality and 3D User Interfaces (VR) (2019)

17. George, C., Janssen, P., Heuss, D., Alt, F.: Should i interrupt or not?: understanding interruptions in head-mounted display settings. In: Proceedings of the 2019 on Designing Interactive Systems Conference. DIS 2019. ACM, New York (2019). https://doi.org/10.1145/3322276.3322363. http://doi.acm.org/10.1145/3322276.3322363

18. George, C., et al.: Seamless and secure VR: adapting and evaluating established authentication systems for virtual reality. In: Proceedings of the Network and Distributed System Security Symposium (NDSS 2017). USEC 2017. Internet Society (2017). https://doi.org/10.14722/usec.2017.23028. http://dx.doi.org/10.14722/usec.2017.23028

19. Gugenheimer, J., Mai, C., Mcgill, M., Williamson, J.R., Steinicke, F., Perlin, K.: Challenges using head-mounted displays in shared and social spaces. In: Proceedings of the 37th Annual ACM Conference on Human Factors in Computing Systems. CHI EA 2019. ACM, New York (2019)

20. Gurary, J., Zhu, Y., Fu, H.: Leveraging 3D benefits for authentication. Int. J. Commun. Netw. Syst. Sci. **10**, 324–338 (2017). https://doi.org/10.4236/ijcns.2017.108B035

21. Harbach, M., von Zezschwitz, E., Fichtner, A., Luca, A.D., Smith, M.: It's a hard lock life: a field study of smartphone (un)locking behavior and risk perception. In: Symposium On Usable Privacy and Security (SOUPS 2014), pp. 213–230. USENIX Association, Menlo Park (2014). https://www.usenix.org/conference/soups2014/proceedings/presentation/harbach

22. Jacob, R.J.K.: The use of eye movements in human-computer interaction techniques: what you look at is what you get. ACM Trans. Inf. Syst. **9**(2) (1991). https://doi.org/10.1145/123078.128728. http://doi.acm.org/10.1145/123078.128728

23. John, B., Koppal, S., Jain, E.: Eyeveil: degrading iris authentication in eye tracking headsets. In: Proceedings of the 11th ACM Symposium on Eye Tracking Research & Applications. ETRA 2019. ACM, New York (2019). https://doi.org/10.1145/3314111.3319816. http://doi.acm.org/10.1145/3314111.3319816

24. Katsini, C., Abdrabou, Y., Raptis, G.E., Khamis, M., Alt, F.: The role of eye gaze in security and privacy applications: survey and future HCI research directions. In: Proceedings of the 2020 CHI Conference on Human Factors in Computing Systems. CHI 2020, pp. 1–21. Association for Computing Machinery, New York (2020). https://doi.org/10.1145/3313831.3376840. https://doi.org/10.1145/3313831.3376840

25. Keith, M., Shao, B., Steinbart, P.: A behavioral analysis of passphrase design and effectiveness. J. Assoc. Inf. Syst. **10**(2) (2009). https://aisel.aisnet.org/jais/vol10/iss2/2

26. Pfeuffer, K., Geiger, M.J., Prange, S., Mecke, L., Buschek, D., Alt, F.: Behavioural biometrics in VR: identifying people from body motion and relations in virtual reality. In: Proceedings of the 37th Annual ACM Conference on Human Factors in Computing Systems. CHI 2019. ACM, New York (2019). https://doi.org/10.1145/3290605.3300340. https://doi.org/10.1145/3290605.3300340

27. Khamis, M., Alt, F., Hassib, M., von Zezschwitz, E., Hasholzner, R., Bulling, A.: Gazetouchpass: multimodal authentication using gaze and touch on mobile devices. In: Proceedings of the 2016 CHI Conference Extended Abstracts on Human Factors in Computing Systems. CHI EA 2016. ACM, New York (2016). https://doi.org/10.1145/2851581.2892314. http://doi.acm.org/10.1145/2851581.2892314

28. Khamis, M., Hassib, M., Zezschwitz, E.V., Bulling, A., Alt, F.: Gazetouchpin: protecting sensitive data on mobile devices using secure multimodal authentication. In: Proceedings of the 19th ACM International Conference on Multimodal Interaction. ICMI 2017. ACM, New York (2017). https://doi.org/10.1145/3136755.3136809. http://doi.acm.org/10.1145/3136755.3136809

29. Khamis, M., Oechsner, C., Alt, F., Bulling, A.: Vrpursuits: interaction in virtual reality using smooth pursuit eye movements. In: Proceedings of the 2018 International Conference on Advanced Visual Interfaces. AVI 2018. ACM, New York (2018)

30. Khamis, M., et al.: Cueauth: comparing touch, mid-air gestures, and gaze for cue-based authentication on situated displays. Proc. ACM Interact. Mob. Wearable Ubiquitous Technol. **2**(4) (2018). https://doi.org/10.1145/3287052. https://doi.org/10.1145/3287052

31. Kinnunen, T., Sedlak, F., Bednarik, R.: Towards task-independent person authentication using eye movement signals. In: Proceedings of the 2010 Symposium on Eye-Tracking Research & Applications. ETRA 2010, ACM, New York (2010). https://doi.org/10.1145/1743666.1743712. http://doi.acm.org/10.1145/1743666.1743712

32. Kumar, M., Garfinkel, T., Boneh, D., Winograd, T.: Reducing shoulder-surfing by using gaze-based password entry. In: Proceedings of the 3rd Symposium on Usable Privacy and Security. SOUPS 2007. ACM, New York (2007). https://doi.org/10.1145/1280680.1280683. http://doi.acm.org/10.1145/1280680.1280683

33. Kytö, M., Ens, B., Piumsomboon, T., Lee, G.A., Billinghurst, M.: Pinpointing: precise head- and eye-based target selection for augmented reality. In: Proceedings of the 2018 CHI Conference on Human Factors in Computing Systems. CHI 2018. ACM, New York (2018). https://doi.org/10.1145/3173574.3173655. http://doi.acm.org.emedien.ub.uni-muenchen.de/10.1145/3173574.3173655

34. Labs, P.: HTC Vive eye tracking add on (2016). https://pupil-labs.com/blog/2016-08/htc-vive-eye-tracking-add-on/. Accessed 01 Apr 2019

35. Mai, C., Khamis, M.: Public HMDS: modeling and understanding user behavior around public head-mounted displays. In: Proceedings of the 7th ACM International Symposium on Pervasive Displays. PerDis 2018. ACM, New York (2018). https://doi.org/10.1145/3205873.3205879. http://doi.acm.org/10.1145/3205873.3205879

36. Majaranta, P., Aula, A., Räihä, K.J.: Effects of feedback on eye typing with a short dwell time. In: Proceedings of the 2004 Symposium on Eye Tracking Research & Applications. ETRA 2004. ACM, New York (2004). https://doi.org/10.1145/968363.968390. http://doi.acm.org/10.1145/968363.968390

37. Majaranta, P., Bulling, A.: Eye tracking and eye-based human–computer interaction. In: Fairclough, S.H., Gilleade, K. (eds.) Advances in Physiological Computing. HIS, pp. 39–65. Springer, London (2014). https://doi.org/10.1007/978-1-4471-6392-3_3

38. Majaranta, P., Räihä, K.J.: Twenty years of eye typing: systems and design issues. In: Proceedings of the 2002 Symposium on Eye Tracking Research & Applications. ETRA 2002. ACM, New York (2002). https://doi.org/10.1145/507072.507076. http://doi.acm.org/10.1145/507072.507076

39. Rubin, P.: Review: oculus go, January 2018. https://www.wired.com/review/oculus-go/. Accessed 07 Feb 2019

40. Scrocca, M., Ruaro, N., Occhiuto, D., Garzotto, F.: Jazzy: leveraging virtual reality layers for hand-eye coordination in users with amblyopia. In: Extended Abstracts of the 2018 CHI Conference on Human Factors in Computing Systems. CHI EA 2018. ACM, New York (2018). https://doi.org/10.1145/3170427.3188618. http://doi.acm.org/10.1145/3170427.3188618

41. Sibert, L.E., Jacob, R.J.K.: Evaluation of eye gaze interaction. In: Proceedings of the SIGCHI Conference on Human Factors in Computing Systems. CHI 2000. ACM, New York (2000). https://doi.org/10.1145/332040.332445. http://doi.acm.org/10.1145/332040.332445

42. Sluganovic, I., Roeschlin, M., Rasmussen, K.B., Martinovic, I.: Using reflexive eye movements for fast challenge-response authentication. In: Proceedings of the 2016 ACM SIGSAC Conference on Computer and Communications Security. CCS 2016. ACM, New York (2016). https://doi.org/10.1145/2976749.2978311. http://doi.acm.org/10.1145/2976749.2978311

43. Song, C., Wang, A., Ren, K., Xu, W.: eyeveri: a secure and usable approach for smartphone user authentication. In: IEEE International Conference on Computer Communication (INFOCOM 2016), San Francisco, California, pp. 1–9. April 2016

44. Summers, N.: Microsoft's mixed reality hololens 2 headset is official, February 2019. https://www.engadget.com/2019/02/24/microsoft-hololens-2-announced/. Accessed 28 Feb 2019

45. Vidal, M., Bulling, A., Gellersen, H.: Pursuits: spontaneous interaction with displays based on smooth pursuit eye movement and moving targets. In: Proceedings of the 2013 ACM International Joint Conference on Pervasive and Ubiquitous Computing. UbiComp 2013. ACM, New York (2013). https://doi.org/10.1145/2493432.2493477. http://doi.acm.org/10.1145/2493432.2493477

46. Yang, J.J., Horii, H., Thayer, A., Ballagas, R.: VR grabbers: ungrounded haptic retargeting for precision grabbing tools. In: Proceedings of the 31st Annual ACM Symposium on User Interface Software and Technology. UIST 2018. ACM, New York (2018). https://doi.org/10.1145/3242587.3242643. http://doi.acm.org/10.1145/3242587.3242643

47. von Zezschwitz, E., De Luca, A., Brunkow, B., Hussmann, H.: Swipin: fast and secure pin-entry on smartphones. In: Proceedings of the 33rd Annual ACM Conference on Human Factors in Computing Systems. CHI 2015. ACM, New York (2015). https://doi.org/10.1145/2702123.2702212. http://doi.acm.org/10.1145/2702123.2702212

48. von Zezschwitz, E., Dunphy, P., De Luca, A.: Patterns in the wild: a field study of the usability of pattern and pin-based authentication on mobile devices. In: Proceedings of the 15th International Conference on Human-computer Interaction with Mobile Devices and Services. MobileHCI 2013, pp. 261–270. ACM, New York (2013). https://doi.org/10.1145/2493190.2493231. http://doi.acm.org/10.1145/2493190.2493231

Alert Characterization by Non-expert Users in a Cybersecurity Virtual Environment: A Usability Study

Alexandre Kabil[(✉)], Thierry Duval, and Nora Cuppens

Lab-STICC, UMR CNRS 6285, IMT Atlantique, Brest, France
{alexandre.kabil,thierry.duval,nora.cuppens}@imt-atlantique.fr

Abstract. Although cybersecurity is a domain where data analysis and training are considered of the highest importance, few virtual environments for cybersecurity are specifically developed, while they are used efficiently in other domains to tackle these issues.

By taking into account cyber analysts' practices and tasks, we have proposed the 3D Cyber Common Operational Picture model (3D Cyber-COP), that aims at mediating analysts' activities into a Collaborative Virtual Environment (CVE), in which users can perform alert analysis scenarios.

In this article, we present a usability study we have performed with non-expert users. We have proposed three virtual environments (a graph-based, an office-based, and the coupling of the two previous ones) in which users should perform a simplified alert analysis scenario based on the WannaCry ransomware. In these environments, users must switch between three views (alert, cyber and physical ones) which all contain different kinds of data sources. These data have to be used to perform the investigations and to determine if alerts are due to malicious activities or if they are caused by false positives.

We have had 30 users, with no prior knowledge in cybersecurity. They have performed very well at the cybersecurity task and they have managed to interact and navigate easily. SUS usability scores were above 70 for the three environments and users have shown a preference towards the coupled environment, which was considered more practical and useful.

Keywords: Virtual Reality · Cyber security · Usability study

1 Introduction

More and more human activities are digitized and connected in cyberspace. The cyberspace could be defined as Gutzwiller does as a space that 'comprises communications between computing devices, the devices themselves, and the interconnections of machines and networks to the physical world as both sensors and actuators' [5]. In this context cybersecurity grows in importance, as a small security breach in a network can have a huge impact on organizations or countries, as with the WannaCry Attack in 2017. Visual Analytics solutions are now

© Springer Nature Switzerland AG 2020
L. T. De Paolis and P. Bourdot (Eds.): AVR 2020, LNCS 12242, pp. 82–101, 2020.
https://doi.org/10.1007/978-3-030-58465-8_6

provided to analysts to help them to understand cyber situations [20]. These solutions offer efficient 2D visualizations coupled with advanced data processing capabilities, but few 3D visualizations or Immersive Analytics solutions are developed for cybersecurity, even though they can leverage some issues in data analysis and are getting attention in other domains [6].

In the same way, training environments proposed for cybersecurity are still only developed for specific cases with expert tools or serious games for sensitization whereas Virtual Environments for Training have been used for years in the industry for different scenarios or practices [15].

In our opinion, Virtual Environments (VE) for cybersecurity should merge data visualization with contextual scenarios to be useful for both experts and non-experts [10]. Figure 1 shows in a Venn Diagram our position towards the usability of Virtual Reality (VR) for cybersecurity.

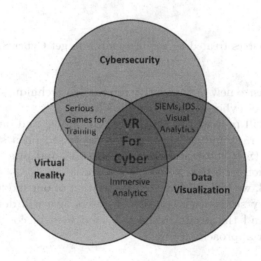

Fig. 1. Venn diagram of our position about the usability of Virtual Reality Applications for cybersecurity, which is at the intersection of three distinct domains, Virtual Reality, Data Visualization and Cybersecurity.

To develop such environments, the analysis of cyber activities, tasks and practices must be performed to model relevant use cases. To face this issue, we have developed a VE instantiation model, the 3D Cyber Common Operational Picture (3D CyberCOP) [8], based on activities and task analysis of Security Operations Centers (SOC) operators. We also have proposed an alert analysis scenario based on the WannaCry ransomware, as a use case of our model.

To assess the effectiveness of a VE for both data visualization and training for cybersecurity, evaluations and exercises should be performed with various users.

In this article, we will present the usability study we have performed with non-expert users, based on an implementation of the 3D CyberCOP model.

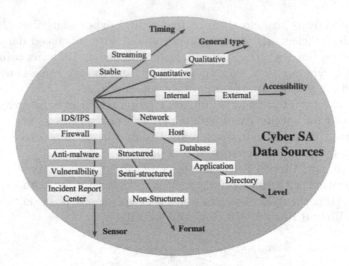

Fig. 2. Data sources treated by a cyber analyst to get Cyber SA, from [22].

We will not emphasize new or innovative interaction techniques but rather more on the adaptation of cyber practices into a VE.

In Sect. 2 we will present the 3D CyberCOP model and our use case based on the WannaCry ransomware. This model was based on a study of Security Operation Center (SOC) operators' activities, tasks and practices and aims at adapting these practices into a VE.

Then in Sect. 3, we will present an instantiation of our model we have developed for a usability study with non-experts users. We will detail our usability study in Sect. 4 and the results in Sect. 5, and we will conclude by showing perspectives of our approach.

2   3D CyberCOP Model and Analysis Scenario

There is a growing interest in human factor field and cognitive science for cybersecurity, which aim at easing the burden of analysts, as they have to deal with a huge number of data sources to develop a mental model of the cyber situation, called the Cyber Situational Awareness (Cyber SA) (Fig. 2).

Defining a cybersecurity operation activity model can facilitate the understanding of operators' activities within organizations and the collaboration between these organizations [19]. We have developed our 3D Cyber Common Operational Picture (3D CyberCOP) model with this in mind. In this section, we will detail our model and the analysis of WannaCry ransomware we have made in order to create alert analysis scenarios.

2.1   Cyber Activity Modeling

Cyber activity studies take often place in Security Operations Centers (SOCs), which are well-defined structures where analysts are monitoring networks round-the-clock, and where they have to investigate alerts for client companies or internal security [7]. There exist anthropological studies in SOC in order to understand the roles and tasks of operators [18], and taxonomies were developed to characterize them [4]. Cognitive Tasks Analysis (CTA) were also performed to assess operator's sense-making capabilities [3] and to help to develop effective visualization tools via the EevI framework, for example [16].

We had the opportunity to visit our industrial partners' SOCs and to perform the following activity analysis described hereafter [9]: after a preliminary visit to understand the context and to get authorizations, we had planned to interview SOC operators and to get information on their practices to develop adapted visualizations.

By using a SOC operator's roles model such as the one proposed by McKenna, Staheli and Meyer in [11] and features from a Computer Supported Cooperative Work (CSCW) model proposed by Casarin, Pacqueriaud, and Bechmann in [2] which are relevant in SOCs, we have defined an activity model which purpose is to adapt cybersecurity practices into a Collaborative VE. In this paper, we will focus only on single-user cyber activities and we are not taking into account collaborative ones. For each feature, we will describe how it is done in SOCs, how we could tailor it for Virtual Environments (VE), and an example of a possible instantiation in an alert analysis scenario, as summarized in Table 1.

Table 1. 3D CyberCOP model allowing the adaptation of SOC features into a Virtual Environment.

Features	Activity model	Design solutions	Example scenario
Roles	- Trade-off between decision and data analysis - Hierarchical interactions	- Users with specific actions - Hierarchical interactions	- Analyst immersed in VR - Coordinator with 2D Dashboard
Tasks	- Ticketing system - Specific tasks from defined roles	- Ticketing system - Simulated interactions or scenarios	- Simulated actions for incident analysis
Visualizations	- Tools for monitoring, correlation and reporting	- 2D, 3D or immersive filtered visualizations - Integration of existing tools	- 2D and immersive visualizations - Physical, Cyber and Alert views
Data	- Aggregated by SIEMs or IDS - From various sources	- Simulated data sets and metrics - Integration with existing tools	- High level events and alerts - Network & Entropy metrics

Roles. Cyber activities are a trade-off between decisions and data analysis [17]. For example, an analyst has to execute the request of a coordinator by investigating alerts and sending reports, and the coordinator must take into account this analysis to make decisions.

To implement roles, we can define specific visualizations and interactions. For example, an analyst role could have a detailed view of an asset from an egocentric point of view whereas the coordinator role could have a global view of all assets of the network from an exocentric point of view (as in the Frame of Reference model from Salzman, Dede, and Loftin [14]). To respect the hierarchies between roles, we could implement hierarchical interactions: analysts are given orders and send reports whereas coordinators give orders and read reports.

Tasks. Cyber analysts have different levels of expertise and they perform tasks with respect to it. To coordinate their actions, they use a ticketing system that tracks their activities and helps them following procedures. Analysts can perform a lot of actions but they can be regrouped into categories such as Asset Analysis, Log Cleaning or File Disassembling. The National Institute of Standards and Technology (NIST) gives global information about tasks in cybersecurity[1].

For our VE, we have modeled and simulated categories of actions such as **inspection** (getting information from a computer or an alert), **analysis** (performing anomaly analysis on a computer), or **reporting** (sending a report on alerts). The ticketing system has been implemented to keep the coordination between users' actions concerning existing procedures.

In an analysis scenario, we want users to perform simple yet relevant tasks by giving them contextual UIs. Tasks are represented by UI buttons and they are related to an incident analysis procedure.

Data. As analysts have to face a lot of heterogeneous data from various sources and sensors [21], aggregation and correlation tools such as Security Information and Event Management systems (SIEMs) or Intrusion Detection Systems (IDS) give them high-level events or alerts that are much more interesting to investigate than raw data [13].

In our VE, we have simulated events or alerts from high-level data sources and we have provided contextual metrics that can give global information about the security state of the system.

In an analysis scenario, we could generate alerts triggered by some metrics provided by the simulated system such as the entropy of filesystems or the network traffic.

Visualizations. Usually, 2D dashboards are used to give general information and status reports to everyone in the SOC. Analysts use a lot of dedicated tools to correlate or monitor data. These tools are tailored for specific cases and

---

[1] https://www.nist.gov/cyberframework.

Visual Analytics solutions are used only if regular ones are not giving enough information [20].

In our VE, we have developed both 2D dashboards and immersive interfaces for different roles and needs. In an analysis scenario, analysts could be immersed while the coordinator will have a holistic point of view from a 2D dashboard (Fig. 3).

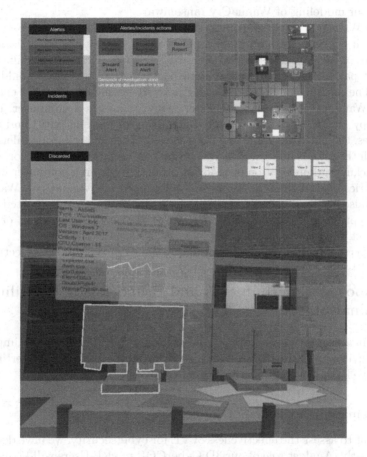

Fig. 3. Examples of visualizations developed from our activity analysis: a 2D monitoring dashboard (TOP) and an immersive interface (BOTTOM).

To limit cognitive load while allowing data correlation [23], we have provided separate views that give complementary information about the monitored systems. For example, one physical view and one cyber view could be provided. These views respectively contain data about the 'physical' environment (device settings, last user logged on the device, geographical position of computers in a building, etc) and the network environment (network flow and topology, IP addresses).

To implement these features, we have designed an alert analysis scenario based on the WannaCry ransomware.

2.2   Ransomware Modeling

We have chosen to model the Wannacry Ransomware[2], as it has caused major troubles in May 2017 and as its behavior could be described simply [12]. Figure 4 sums up our modeling of WannaCry ransomware.

When Wannacry infects a computer (by being downloaded and executed for example), it encrypts data on the computer and it propagates itself through the network by using Windows seven Operating System (OS) vulnerabilities. The user must pay a ransom to get her data back, as the encryption could not be broken. The entropy of filesystems and network traffic metrics are enough to describe Wannacry's high-level behavior: when it infects a computer, it raises the entropy metric (files are encrypted, resulting of high activity) and when it propagates, the network traffic increases as well. These metrics raise alerts when they reach thresholds and these alerts can be true or false positives (for example a data backup and encryption or a download activity from a computer will raise these metrics even if these activities are not caused by WannaCry). WannaCry can also raise only one metric, for example, if the computer is protected against data encryption but not patched (the ransomware can propagate), or if it is patched but not protected.

One specific analysis scenario will be presented in the following section.

3   Proposed Environments and Scenario for Usability Evaluation

To perform a usability evaluation, we have chosen specific features to implement into our environment. In this section, we will detail the VE and the alert analysis scenario we have designed for the evaluation.

3.1   Evaluated Environment

As we want to assess the effectiveness of VE for cybersecurity, we have decided to implement the Analyst role of our 3D CyberCOP model. Users will be immersed in an environment containing a potentially infected network of computers and will have to gather information to characterize alerts.

In order to get information from the environment, we have provided three views, namely the alert, the cyber and the physical view (Fig. 5). Users have to switch between them in order to get relevant information on the situation.

– The alert view contains data regarding the alerts status. If a computer is concerned with an alert, it will be highlighted by a particle system for example.

---

[2] http://cert-mu.govmu.org/English/Documents/White%20Papers/White%20Paper %20-%20The%20WannaCry%20Ransomware%20Attack.pdf.

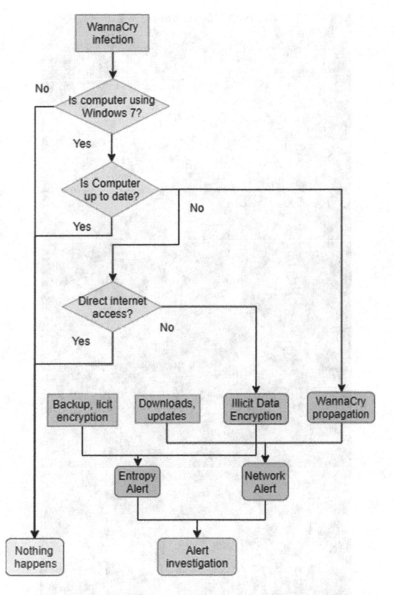

Fig. 4. WannaCry behavioral model used for alert analysis scenario creation.

- The cyber view allows users to get information from the network architecture or network processes.
- The physical view contains data related to the processes of computers, their operating system, and other information.

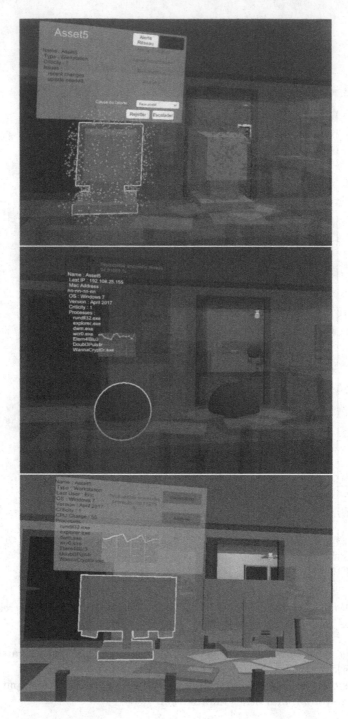

Fig. 5. From top to bottom, the alert view, the cyber view, and the physical view. Views are colocated in the VE, in order to facilitate the switching between them. Users select computer to access data relative to the current view.

Navigation in the Virtual Environment is made by using the teleportation metaphor, but we also have let the possibility to the user to use a joypad to move.

Information is displayed through 2D interfaces that are accessible by selecting computers or relevant 3D objects. Selection is made by using the selecting ray metaphor.

3.2   Analysis Scenario

The alert analysis task has been simplified to be achieved by users with no prior knowledge about cybersecurity: only a few data were available and the procedure was lightened. The analysis scenario was the following (Fig. 6):

- Alerts appear on the alert view, and users have to follow an investigation procedure to resolve the case.
- The investigation is done by switching views to gather relevant information about the alert (an entropy alert should be investigated in the physical view and a network alert in the cyber one). Specific actions will be available for users, such as 'get information from this computer' or 'perform an anomaly analysis' (these actions are simulated according to procedures).
  Once the user thinks she has enough information, she has to characterize the alert by escalating or dismissing it. Once it is done, she has to select another alert and continue the investigation.

This scenario was successfully implemented into a VE, and we have proposed a usability study based on this implementation.

4   Usability Evaluation Protocol

As we wanted to evaluate the usability of a VE for an alert analysis task, we have designed three different environments and an evaluation protocol.

4.1   Virtual Environments for Alert Analysis

Abstract environments, as 3D graph visualization are more and more used for data analysis whereas concrete environments are usually used for training sessions.

We have wanted to see if users would perform better in a classical 3D Graph visualization representing the network topology or in an office-based one where computers, desktops and so on are represented.

To go beyond this comparison, we have also proposed an environment containing both the network topology and the office assets. These environments are represented in the Fig. 7.

Order of the three proposed environment was defined by two conditions: even users begin with the graph-based environment (Abstract-Concrete-Mixed condition) whereas odd users begin with the office-based one (Concrete-Abstract-Mixed condition). The third environment was always the mixed one.

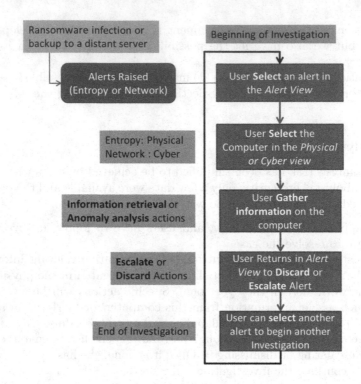

Fig. 6. Alerts investigation simplified scenario.

4.2   Protocol

We thought that users would find the concrete environment more entertaining but that they would also be more efficient in the abstract environment while the mixed one would be considered too complex. We have defined three scenarios presenting similarities so that the tasks were different in each environment to avoid a learning effect. These scenarios contained the same infected assets but positioned differently into the environments.

We had performed the evaluation with an Oculus Rift CV1. VE was developed with the Unity Game Engine and the VRTK toolkit for interaction metaphors. An event-based architecture was used to implement the scenario and to facilitate action logging [9].

Users had to fill a consent form where we explained the purpose of the experiment. Then, they had to perform a tutorial task in order to get familiar with the immersive devices and the VE. Alert analysis tasks lasted fifteen minutes; there were eleven alerts to investigate, and two false positives among them.

In between immersive tasks, we asked users to fill a SUS usability questionnaire [1] and to answer some questions about the task itself.

At the end of the third immersive task, after filling the SUS and task questionnaires, we asked users which interface they had preferred and why. We asked also some questions about the physiological effects of immersive experiments and technology adoption.

Fig. 7. From top to bottom: concrete office environment, abstract graph-based environment, and mixed environment. In these environments, users had to analyze cybersecurity alerts by following specific analysis scenarios.

The experimentation protocol is summed up in the Table 2.

Table 2. Usability experiment protocol

Experimentation step	Duration
Greeting and consent form	15 min
Tutorial and familiarization task	10 min
Three VE experiments in two different orders	10×3 min
Usability and task analysis survey	5×3 min
User experience and preferences survey	10 min

5   Results and Findings

We carried out our experiment for a month and collected the results of thirty users, mostly computer science students. Most users were unfamiliar with immersive technologies and cybersecurity but familiar with video games. The total average duration of a user's evaluation was one hour and thirty minutes, and all users passed the analysis scenarios. In the Figures that we are going to present, the margin of error comes from the standard deviation. The p-values given come from ANOVA-type variance analyzes at 95%.

5.1   Results

The abstract, concrete and mixed environments respectively obtained SUS usability scores of 76.41, 72.42 and 77.33 out of 100 (Fig. 8), which means that they are considered usable (the usability threshold of an interface is set to 70/100 for the SUS test). There were no significant differences in the environmental usability scores between the users who started experimenting with the abstract environment (ACM condition) and users who started with the concrete environment (CAM condition) (Fig. 9).

The results of ANOVA-type variance analysis at 95% between the two conditions and for the abstract, concrete and mixed environments give $p = 0.81$, $p = 0.71$ and $p = 0.69$ respectively.

Users have preferred the mixed environment combining abstract and concrete data representation. The ACM and CAM conditions for passing the experiment (i.e. starting with the abstract or concrete environment) had no effect on user preferences (Fig. 10). Contrary to what we thought, the complexity of this environment was not a limiting factor for most users, but the fact that it was always explored in the third session may have influenced their choice.

The average score for the questions concerning physiological disorders was 3.08/10, which means that users did not experience any discomfort during the experiments (Fig. 11), although we have found that six users (three out of five users older than thirty-five years old, two users under the age of twenty-five and one user between twenty-five and thirty-five years old) felt more dizziness than the others.

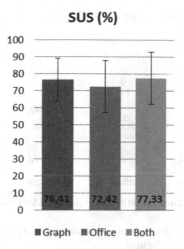

Fig. 8. Mean values (with standard deviation error) of SUS usability score for each environment. All environments gets a score higher than 70, which means that they are usable (from the SUS test perspective).

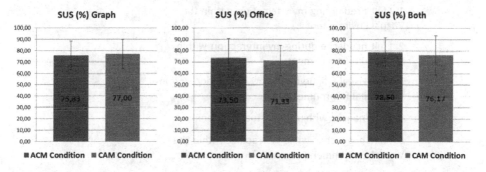

Fig. 9. Mean values of SUS usability score for each environment and for both experimentations' conditions. No significant differences between experimentations' conditions.

Users have considered that they could easily acquire the skills required to use this VE (average score of 8/10), with a significant effect of age (average score of 5.8/10 for those older than thirty-five years old).

Immersive devices were considered pleasant and potentially usable at work. Environments and immersive technology were generally found to be relevant, with scores on questions about technology adoption and user experience above 6 out of 10.

An analysis score was assigned to users based on the accuracy of their alert characterization. A score of eight out of eleven means, for example, that they correctly characterized eight alerts (including false positives) out of the eleven present in the scenarios. On average, users have performed well during the experiments (average score greater than 8.5/11) (Fig. 12 on the left). We found out

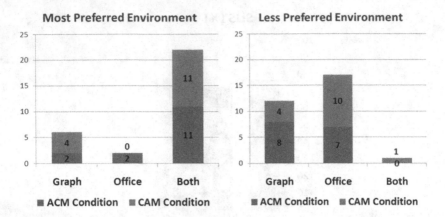

Fig. 10. Users' preferences for proposed environments. No significant differences between experimentations' conditions.

Cybersickness questions	Mean Score
1. I felt tired during my interaction within the Virtual Environment	3,43/10
2. I felt headache during my interaction within the Virtual Environment	3,1/10
3. I felt visual fatigue during my interaction within the Virtual Environment	4,03/10
4. I had nausea within the Virtual Environment	2,8/10
5. I had headaches while interacting within the Virtual Environment	2,66/10
6. I felt dizzy during my interaction within the Virtual Environment	2,5/10

Fig. 11. Cybersickness questionnaire answers. Users have not felt particularly dizzy while performing the experimentation.

that alert analysis time was significantly higher in the concrete environment than in the abstract and mixed environments ($p = 4 \times 10^{-4}$). Users have analyzed alerts more quickly in the mixed environment, although there were no significant differences in analysis times between abstract and mixed environments (p = 0.1).

As the mixed environment was always explored last, adaptation to the experiment as well as familiarity with the task can explain this result (Fig. 12 on the middle). On the other hand, we did not find any differences concerning the distance traveled in different environments (p = 0.59) (Fig. 12 on the right).

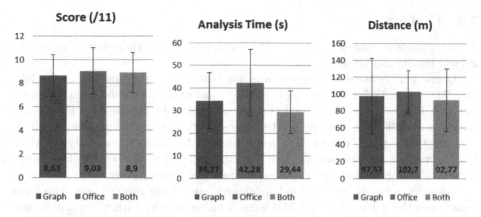

Fig. 12. Mean values of scenario scores, analysis time per alert and distance traveled for each environment.

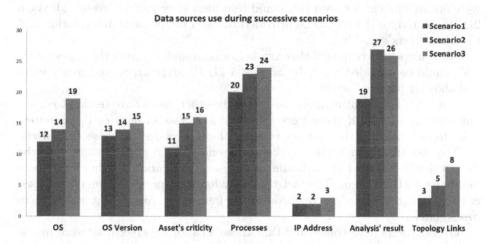

Fig. 13. Data usages for characterizing alerts. We can see a progression of data usages from scenario 1 to scenario 3 (scenarios were always made in the same order).

There was barely any effect of age or familiarity on results, but our sample of users was too small to interpret significant differences between familiarities (for example we had only five users that were more than thirty-five years old).

Some data were available to users to help them to characterize alerts (as the Operating System version or the IP address), and between each experiment, we asked users which data sources were useful. We have noticed that users tended to use more and more data sources to analyze alerts while they were gaining experience during the experiment (Fig. 13).

5.2   Findings

This experiment showed us that a VE for non-experts in cybersecurity is usable, even if results can be discussed.

Users' performance (e.g. score) was not better from the first try to the last one. Maybe the task was too simple so that most of the users had been performing well but have not progressed through experiments. Because we gave users barely any indication (except in the inter-experiment questionnaires in which was mentioned which data source could be used to conduct the analysis), they had sometimes no idea about their performances: they knew that they were correctly characterizing alerts, but sometimes they were having some doubts.

Globally, users did not face cybersickness, even if our five subjects who have more than thirty-five years old and were familiar neither with video games nor with immersive interfaces felt more dizzy according to the questionnaire answers.

The three views were well used by users, but some users pointed out that data were not so different between them, and that alert view was not useful. Maybe a 2D User Interface (UI) could be provided to users to get alerts information and to reduce views switching.

Some users have regretted that any help was available during the experiment. This could be provided easily by adding a 2D UI attached to any user's hand and showing pieces of advice.

Instead of investigating alerts one after the other, users have tended to cross-analyze alerts to see if there were some redundancies in data or if computers close to each other in the network topology have the same processes and alerts.

The fact that users preferred the graph-office mixed environment is maybe due to that it was the last environment they explored, and that they were more familiar with the system. The fact that they have not preferred the office-based environment regardless of condition is an interesting result that we need to investigate.

Overall, users have considered that these VEs for cybersecurity were usable and they were ready to use them, but as they were not cybersecurity experts, we need to perform other studies to analyze this point. Immersive technologies were appreciated by users and they were interested in using them for their work or activities.

6   Conclusion

By studying Security Operations Centers (SOCs) operators' practices, we have designed an activity model, the 3D CyberCOP, which aims at translating cybersecurity activities into a Collaborative Virtual Environment (CVE). This model have allowed us to design a Virtual Environment (VE) in which users could perform cybersecurity alert analysis scenarios based on the WannaCry ransomware. In order to assess the effectiveness of merging both data visualization and training approaches for cybersecurity operators, we have conducted a usability study with non-expert users.

This study has shown that they have succeeded in interacting and navigating through the environments. They have managed to gather data and to understand the cyber situation only after few sessions with great scores, even if the task seemed difficult on the first try. Users have shown a preference to the environment that contained both graph and office visualizations and have found these environments useful for analyzing cyber threats, with a usability score superior to 70.

Further studies should be made to assess the effectiveness of such environments for cybersecurity experts.

In the future we will develop a 2D version of the experimentation, to compare the results between immersive and non-immersive interfaces. The usefulness of view switching will be evaluated maybe in a collaborative experiment. Linking our VE with an existing cyber data analysis tools will bring us more capabilities and more realistic cases, and we will evaluate the reliability of this approach by comparing training with a cyber training tool and with our VE.

Acknowledgments. This work was supported by the Cyber CNI Chair of Institute Mines Télécom, which is held by IMT Atlantique and supported by Airbus Defence and Space, Amossys, BNP Paribas, EDF, Nokia and the Regional Council of Brittany. It has been acknowledged by the Center of excellence in Cyber Security.

References

1. Brooke, J., et al.: SUS-a quick and dirty usability scale. Usability Eval. Ind. **189**(194), 4–7 (1996)
2. Casarin, J., Pacqueriaud, N., Bechmann, D.: UMI3D: a Unity3D toolbox to support CSCW systems properties in generic 3D user interfaces. Proc. ACM Hum.-Comput. Interact. **2**(CSCW), 29:1–29:20 (2018). https://doi.org/10.1145/3274298. http://doi.acm.org/10.1145/3274298
3. D'Amico, A., Buchanan, L., Kirkpatrick, D., Walczak, P.: Cyber operator perspectives on security visualization. In: Nicholson, D. (ed.) Advances in Human Factors in Cybersecurity, pp. 69–81. Springer, Cham (2016). https://doi.org/10.1007/978-3-319-41932-9_7
4. Evesti, A., Kanstrén, T., Frantti, T.: Cybersecurity situational awareness taxonomy. In: 2017 International Conference on Cyber Situational Awareness, Data Analytics And Assessment (Cyber SA), pp. 1–8, June 2017. https://doi.org/10.1109/CyberSA.2017.8073386
5. Gutzwiller, R.: Situation awareness in defensive cyberspace operations: an annotated bibliographic assessment through 2015. Technical report, NIWC Pacific San Diego United States (2019)
6. Hackathorn, R., Margolis, T.: Immersive analytics: building virtual data worlds for collaborative decision support. In: 2016 Workshop on Immersive Analytics (IA), pp. 44–47, March 2016. https://doi.org/10.1109/IMMERSIVE.2016.7932382
7. Hámornik, B.P., Krasznay, C.: Prerequisites of virtual teamwork in security operations centers: knowledge, skills, abilities and other characteristics. Acad. Appl. Res. Mil. Public Manag. Sci. **16**, 73 (2017)

8. Kabil, A., Duval, T., Cuppens, N., Le Comte, G., Halgand, Y., Ponchel, C.: 3D CyberCOP: a collaborative platform for cybersecurity data analysis and training. In: Luo, Y. (ed.) CDVE 2018. LNCS, vol. 11151, pp. 176–183. Springer, Cham (2018). https://doi.org/10.1007/978-3-030-00560-3_24
9. Kabil, A., Duval, T., Cuppens, N., Le Comte, G., Halgand, Y., Ponchel, C.: From cyber security activities to collaborative virtual environments practices through the 3D CyberCOP platform. In: Ganapathy, V., Jaeger, T., Shyamasundar, R.K. (eds.) ICISS 2018. LNCS, vol. 11281, pp. 272–287. Springer, Cham (2018). https://doi.org/10.1007/978-3-030-05171-6_14
10. Kabil, A., Duval, T., Cuppens, N., Le Comte, G., Halgand, Y., Ponchel, C.: Why should we use 3D collaborative virtual environments for cyber security? In: IEEE Fourth VR International Workshop on Collaborative Virtual Environments (IEEEVR 2018), Reutlingen, Germany, March 2018. https://hal.archives-ouvertes.fr/hal-01770064
11. McKenna, S., Staheli, D., Meyer, M.: Unlocking user-centered design methods for building cyber security visualizations. In: 2015 IEEE Symposium on Visualization for Cyber Security (VizSec), pp. 1–8. IEEE (2015)
12. Mohurle, S., Patil, M.: A brief study of wannacry threat: ransomware attack 2017. Int. J. Adv. Res. Comput. Sci. **8**(5) (2017)
13. Pahi, T., Leitner, M., Skopik, F.: Data exploitation at large: your way to adequate cyber common operating pictures. In: Proceedings of the 16th European Conference on Cyber Warfare and Security, pp. 307–315 (2017)
14. Salzman, M.C., Dede, C., Loftin, R.B.: VR's frames of reference: a visualization technique for mastering abstract multidimensional information. In: Proceedings of the SIGCHI Conference on Human Factors in Computing Systems, CHI 1999, pp. 489–495. ACM, New York (1999). https://doi.org/10.1145/302979.303141. http://doi.acm.org/10.1145/302979.303141
15. Sebok, A., Nystad, E., Droivoldsmo, A.: Improving safety and human performance in maintenance and outage planning through virtual reality-based training systems. In: Proceedings of the IEEE 7th Conference on Human Factors and Power Plants, p. 8, September 2002. https://doi.org/10.1109/HFPP.2002.1042867
16. Sethi, A., Wills, G.: Expert-interviews led analysis of EEVi - a model for effective visualization in cyber-security. In: 2017 IEEE Symposium on Visualization for Cyber Security (VizSec), pp. 1–8, October 2017. https://doi.org/10.1109/VIZSEC.2017.8062195
17. Staheli, D., et al.: Collaborative data analysis and discovery for cyber security. In: Twelfth Symposium on Usable Privacy and Security (SOUPS 2016). USENIX Association, Denver (2016). https://www.usenix.org/conference/soups2016/workshop-program/wsiw16/presentation/staheli
18. Sundaramurthy, S.C., McHugh, J., Ou, X., Wesch, M., Bardas, A.G., Rajagopalan, S.R.: Turning contradictions into innovations or: how we learned to stop whining and improve security operations. In: Twelfth Symposium on Usable Privacy and Security (SOUPS 2016), pp. 237–251. USENIX Association, Denver (2016). https://www.usenix.org/conference/soups2016/technical-sessions/presentation/sundaramurthy
19. Takahashi, T., Kadobayashi, Y., Nakao, K.: Toward global cybersecurity collaboration: cybersecurity operation activity model. In: Proceedings of ITU Kaleidoscope 2011: The Fully Networked Human? - Innovations for Future Networks and Services (K-2011), pp. 1–8, December 2011
20. Varga, M., Winkelholz, C., Träber-Burdin, S.: The application of visual analytics to cyber security (2017)

21. Zhang, S., Shi, R., Zhao, J.: A visualization system for multiple heterogeneous network security data and fusion analysis. KSII Trans. Internet Inf. Syst. **10**(6) (2016)

22. Zhong, C., Yen, J., Liu, P., Erbacher, R.F., Garneau, C., Chen, B.: Studying analysts' data triage operations in cyber defense situational analysis. In: Liu, P., Jajodia, S., Wang, C. (eds.) Theory and Models for Cyber Situation Awareness. LNCS, vol. 10030, pp. 128–169. Springer, Cham (2017). https://doi.org/10.1007/978-3-319-61152-5_6

23. Zhong, Z., et al.: A user-centered multi-space collaborative visual analysis for cyber security. Chin. J. Electron. **27**(5), 910–919 (2018). https://doi.org/10.1049/cje.2017.09.021

A Driving Simulator Study Exploring the Effect of Different Mental Models on ADAS System Effectiveness

Riccardo Rossi[1] , Massimiliano Gastaldi[1,2] , Francesco Biondi[3] ,
Federico Orsini[1] , Giulia De Cet[1(✉)] , and Claudio Mulatti[4]

[1] ICEA Department, University of Padova, Padua, Italy
{riccardo.rossi,massimiliano.gastaldi}@unipd.it,
{federico.orsini,giulia.decet}@dicea.unipd.it
[2] DPG Department, University of Padova, Padua, Italy
[3] Faculty of Human Kinetics, University of Windsor, Windsor, ON, Canada
francesco.biondi@uwindsor.ca
[4] Department of Psychology and Cognitive Science, University of Trento, Rovereto, Italy
claudio.mulatti@unitn.it

Abstract. This work investigated the effect of mental models on the effectiveness of an advanced driver assistance system (ADAS). The system tested was a lateral control ADAS, which informed the drivers whether the vehicle was correctly positioned inside the lane or not, with the use of two visual and one auditory stimuli. Three driving simulator experiments were performed, involving three separate groups of subjects, who received different initial exposures to the technology. In Experiment 0 subjects were not exposed to ADAS in order to be able to indicate that no effect of learning affected the results. In Experiment A subjects were not instructed on the ADAS functionalities and they had to learn on their own; in Experiment B they were directly instructed on the functionalities by reading an information booklet. In all experiments drivers performed multiple driving sessions. The mean absolute lateral position (LP) and standard deviation of lateral position (SDLP) for each driver were considered as main dependent variables to measure the effectiveness of the ADAS. Findings from this work showed that the initial mental model had an impact on ADAS effectiveness, since it produced significantly different results in terms of ADAS effectiveness, with those reading the information booklet being able to improve more and faster their lateral control.

Keywords: ADAS · Mental models · Lateral control · Driving simulator

1 Introduction

Advanced driver assistance systems (ADAS) are rapidly penetrating American and European vehicle markets but, as some studies pointed out [1], their road safety benefits may be undermined by how drivers change their behavior as they integrate these new technologies to their driving style, and this depends on the accuracy of their understanding (i.e., their mental model) of these systems' functionalities [1].

© Springer Nature Switzerland AG 2020
L. T. De Paolis and P. Bourdot (Eds.): AVR 2020, LNCS 12242, pp. 102–113, 2020.
https://doi.org/10.1007/978-3-030-58465-8_7

In interacting with the environment, with others, and with technology, persons form internal, mental models of themselves and of the things they are interacting with. These models provide "predictive and explanatory power for understanding the interaction" [2]. In other words, and with respect to a technological system, a mental model is what the user believes about the system; it is based on belief and perception, not on facts. Since it is a model of what the users know (or rather, think they know) about the system, initial information and experience play an important role on its development.

There are only few studies in the literature dealing with drivers' mental models of ADAS, the importance of the initial exposure to these technologies, and the effects that it may produce on ADAS effectiveness. An incorrect driver mental model may compromise the safety benefits of an ADAS, or even produce negative consequences in terms of road safety.

Among these studies, Beggiato and Krems [3] investigated the evolution of mental model, trust and acceptance, in relation to the initial information on an adaptive cruise control system. Three groups of drivers received three different initial set of information, during a driving simulator experiment: a correct description of the system, an incomplete description and an incorrect description. They concluded that initial information forms an initial mental model, which is updated by the real experience with the system and eventually tends to converge to a realistic understanding of system functionalities. However, initial information had an enduring effect on trust and acceptance, as the more cognitive effort was needed to update the mental model the lower were trust and acceptance to the system. In another study, Beggiato et al. [4] analyzed the evolution of the learning process and the development of trust, acceptance and the mental model for interacting with an adaptive cruise control system, by requiring drivers to complete multiple on-road driving sessions. Results showed non-linear trends over time, with a steep improvement in the first sessions, and a subsequent stabilization.

McDonald et al. [5] investigated how drivers' knowledge of a technology is influenced by their initial exposure method to the technology. Two traditional learning methods were tested: reading the owner's manual and through a ride-along demonstration; it was demonstrated that both of them were able to effectively convey information about the ADAS to the user. A subsequent study [6] showed that the two learning methods had different effects on driver perception of usefulness, apprehension and trust.

Correct mental models will be essential in a future of highly automatized mobility, as underlined by Victor et al. [7], who performed three test-track experiments, studying intervention response to conflicts while driving highly automated vehicles. Their study showed the importance of attention reminders to correct the mental model of the drivers.

This study focused on the effect of the driver mental model on the effectiveness of a lateral control ADAS. The ADAS tested in the driving simulator experiment of this work informed the driver about whether the vehicle was correctly positioned inside the lane or not, with the use of two visual and one auditory stimuli. Drivers received two different initial exposures to the technology: they were not instructed on the ADAS functionalities and they had to learn on their own (experiment A); they were directly instructed on the functionalities by reading an information booklet (experiment B). In Experiment 0 subjects were not exposed to ADAS in order to be able to indicate that no effect of learning affected the results. In all experiments drivers performed multiple driving sessions. The mean absolute lateral position (LP) and standard deviation of lateral position (SDLP) for each driver were considered as main dependent variables to measure the effectiveness of the ADAS. The study had the following specific objectives:

- to test how the driver's improvement in lateral control evolves over time;
- to test whether the initial mental model has an effect on this learning process.

The paper is organized as follows: Sect. 2 contains information on the experimental procedure; Sect. 3 presents the results obtained from the experiment; Sect. 4 discusses how these results relate to the objectives declared above, and concludes with some remarks and future research perspectives.

2 Methodology

Three driving simulator experiments were developed and performed. In particular:

1. Experiment 0. Drivers were not exposed to ADAS. The experiment consisted in 4 trials.
2. Experiment A. Drivers formed their mental model of the ADAS without being explicitly informed on its functionalities. The experiment consisted in a control trial (without ADAS), followed 3 trials (with ADAS).
3. Experiment B. Drivers formed their mental model of the ADAS after reading an information booklet. The ADAS and the experiment design were the same of Experiment A.

The following paragraphs present a detailed description of the experiments.

2.1 Participants

Twenty-one subjects were involved in Experiment 0, twenty-eight in Experiment A and twenty-five in Experiment B. Details of participants are presented in Table 1.

Table 1. Participants' gender and age.

Exp	#Part.	Female	Male	Min age	Max age	Avg age
0	21	11	10	20	29	23
A	28	14	14	19	30	23
B	25	10	15	20	30	24

They were students, staff of the University and other persons with the following characteristics:

- at least 1 year of driving experience;
- at least 5,000 km/year of average driving distance;
- no previous experience with the driving simulator.

All of them were volunteers.

2.2 Driving Simulator and Scenarios

The simulation system used in this study is a fixed-base driving simulator produced by STSoftware®, Jentig 60, comprising a cockpit, composed by an adjustable car seat, a gaming dynamic force feedback steering wheel with a 900° turn-angle and gas, brake and clutch pedals. The system also includes three networked computers and five full high-definition (1,920 × 1,080 pixels) screens creating a 330° (horizontal) by 45° (vertical) field of 3 view. It is also equipped with a Dolby Surround® sound system, the whole producing realistic virtual views of the road and the surrounding environment. The simulator was validated in previous multiple conditions [8, 9].

A two-way, two-lane road scenario was built in virtual reality with the 3D software of the driving simulator. The scenario of 10 km in length was composed by a sequence of 28 left and right alternate curves, preceded by a single 200-m straight. Each curve had a radius of 500 m and was 350 m long. Carriageway was composed by one lane per direction (width = 2.95 m). In the opposite direction, low traffic conditions (flow rate of about 300 vehicles/h/lane) were simulated.

An average temperature between 20 °C and 22 °C was maintained in the laboratory; illuminance inside the room was fixed at 4 lx.

2.3 ADAS System

The ADAS monitored vehicle position (centerline) every 10 m following two rules: if the vehicle centerline was out of the admitted area the feedback was negative, otherwise the feedback was positive. The admitted area was defined (see Fig. 1) according to the Italian Highway Code (Art. 143-1), and had a 0.50-m width and its axis was positioned 0.25 m right to the road lane axis.

This ADAS was not developed for on-road applications, but rather for driver training in a simulated environment [10, 11]. Feedback system consists in one auditory and two visual stimuli:

- auditory: two signals, both with a duration of 0.92 s, one with a high frequency (400 Hz) when the vehicle entered the positive feedback zone, and the other one with a low frequency (125 Hz) when it entered the negative feedback zone (see Fig. 1);
- visual 1 (score): a display reporting a numeric score (increasing in the case of positive feedback zone and decreasing in the opposite) (see Fig. 1);
- visual 2 (green bar): a green bar on the windscreen (increasing in the case of positive feedback zone and decreasing in the opposite) (see Fig. 1).

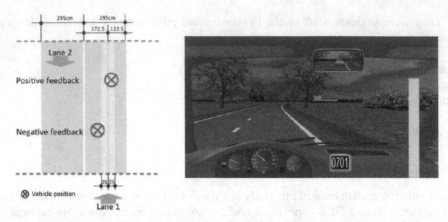

Fig. 1. Positive and negative feedback zones and visual feedback

2.4 Variables

In each experiment and during each trial, a set of variables was recorded at a sampling frequency of 50 Hz.

One of these variables is x_j, which is the lateral position of the vehicle, relative to the axis of the admitted area, at time instant j. $j = 1…T$, where T is the total number of records sampled during the experiment, and the time difference between two successive time instants j and $j + 1$ is 0.02 s. $x_j = 0$ when the centerline of the vehicle is exactly on the axis of the admitted area, $x_j > 0$, when it is on the left and $x_j < 0$ when it is on the right.

In the analysis performed in this work, dependent variables were LP and SDLP, both common parameters used in driving research [12, 13].

LP is the mean absolute lateral position, in meters:

$$LP = \frac{1}{T} \sum_{j=1}^{T} |x_j|$$ (1)

SDLP is the standard deviation of lateral position, in meters:

$$SDLP = \sqrt{\frac{1}{T-1} \sum_{j=1}^{T} \left(x_j - \bar{x}\right)^2}$$ (2)

SDLP allows to evaluate the lateral variability of the vehicle position, and a value of zero indicates a situation in which the vehicle maintains the same value of lateral position throughout the whole trial. LP identifies the position of the vehicle within the lane, with LP equal to zero corresponding to the situation in which vehicle centerline is on the axis of the admitted area.

Taken singularly, SDLP cannot fully describe the quality of a driver's lateral control. For example, it is possible to maintain a constant value of lateral position (therefore with SDLP close to zero), in a completely wrong and dangerous position (e.g., with two wheels in the opposite lane). For this reason, in this study also LP was analyzed. The ADAS may be considered successful in improving driver's lateral control only if it is able to reduce both SDLP and LP.

2.5 Experimental Procedure

In Experiment 0 participants familiarized with the simulator during a training session. During training, subjects performed a ten-minute driving task and completed a Simulator Sickness Questionnaire to ascertain whether they were subject to simulator sickness [14]. Then, each driver had to perform four consecutive trials without ADAS systems.

In Experiment A the initial procedure is the same used in Experiment 0, but after the first trial (control) the ADAS was switched on. Participants were not informed about the meaning of the stimuli, or which driving ability these was correlated to. After the experiment, they were asked to fill out a questionnaire and explain the meaning of the feedback; not all the participants were able to produce a satisfactory response: 9 out 28 participants did not properly understand the ADAS functionalities.

In Experiment B the procedure was similar to that used in experiment A. After control trial, participants were directly instructed on the functionalities by reading an information booklet.

3   Analysis and Results

Data were analyzed using JASP software.

3.1 Experiment 0

In order to evaluate the learning effect on drivers' lateral control, a one-way ANOVA for repeated measures (rANOVA) was performed, considering Experiment 0. The response variables were SDLP and LP, the within-factor was the trial (four levels), and no between-factor was considered. In Experiment 0 no main effects of trial was found for SLDP $F(3,60) = 1.246$, $p = 0.301$ and LP $F(3,60) = 0.161$, $p = 0.922$, as in previews works that showed that the reduction in SDLP and LP values across trials cannot be attributed to the participants becoming more familiar with the driving simulator [10, 11]. Trends of SDLP and LP across trials can be observed in Fig. 2.

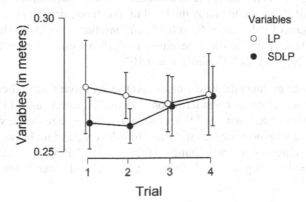

Fig. 2. SDLP and LP (both in meters) across trials 1–4 for Experiment 0 (vertical bars represent 95% confidence intervals).

3.2 Experiment A

All Participants. In order to evaluate the effect of the ADAS on drivers' lateral control, a one-way rANOVA was performed, considering Experiment A. The response variables were SDLP and LP, the within-factor was the trial (four levels), and no between-factor was considered. A significant effect was found on trial for SDLP, $F(3,81) = 8.382$, $p < .001$ and LP, $F(3,81) = 4.012$, $p = 0.010$. Pairwise t-tests revealed a significant improvement in SDLP between trials 1–2, $t(27) = 4.323$, $p < .001$, Cohen's $d = 0.817$, for LP no significant difference between trials 1–2, 2–3 and 3–4. Trends of SDLP and LP across trials can be observed in Fig. 3.

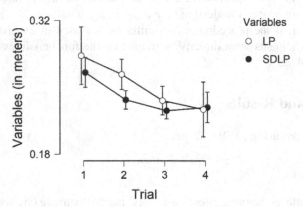

Fig. 3. SDLP and LP (both in meters) across trials 1–4 for Experiment A (vertical bars represent 95% confidence intervals).

In absolute terms SDLP decreases from 0.266 m (baseline) to 0.229 m (last trial), with a reduction of 37 mm; pairwise t-tests revealed a significant improvement between trials 1–4, $t(27) = 2.905$, $p = 0.007$, Cohen's $d = 0.549$, that can be considered significant also from a practical point of view, since previous studies showed that, in fact, even a 20–30 mm variation in SDLP affects significantly the level of risk during driving [15, 16].

In absolute terms LP decreases from 0.283 m (baseline) to 0.233 m (last trial), with a reduction of 50 mm; pairwise t-tests revealed a significant improvement between trials 1–4, $t(27) = 2.129$, $p = 0.042$, Cohen's $d = 0.402$.

Aware. In order to evaluate the effect of the ADAS on drivers' lateral control, a one-way rANOVA was performed, considering only 19 out 28 participants of Experiment A, called "aware", that understand the ADAS functionalities. The response variables were SDLP and LP, the within-factor was the trial (four levels), and no between-factor was considered. A significant effect was found on trial for SDLP, $F(3,54) = 30.944$, $p < .001$ and LP, $F(3,54) = 19.513$, $p < .001$. Pairwise t-tests revealed a significant improvement in SDLP between trials 1–2, t(18) = 4.469, p < .001, Cohen's d = 1.025, trials 2–3, t(18) = 3.718, p = 0.002, Cohen's d = 0.853 and trials 3–4, t(18) = 2.263, p = 0.036, Cohen's d = 0.519. Similar results were found for LP with a significant improvement between trials 1–2, t(18) = 2.761, p = 0.013, Cohen's d = 0.633, trials 2–3 t(18) = 3.812, p = 0.001, Cohen's d = 0.875 and trials 3–4 t(18) = 2.490, p = 0.023, Cohen's d = 0.571. Trends of SDLP and LP across trials can be observed in Fig. 4.

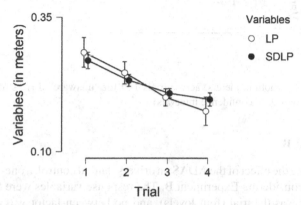

Fig. 4. SDLP and LP (both in meters) across trials 1–4 for "aware" drivers of Experiment A (vertical bars represent 95% confidence intervals).

In absolute terms SDLP decreases from 0.270 m (baseline) to 0.198 m (last trial), with a reduction of 72 mm; pairwise t-tests revealed a significant improvement between trials 1–4, t(18) = 7.109, p < .001, Cohen's d = 1.631.

In absolute terms LP decreases from 0.285 m (baseline) to 0.176 m (last trial), with a reduction of 109 mm; pairwise t-tests revealed a significant improvement between trials 1–4, t(18) = 5.420, p < .001, Cohen's d = 1.243.

Unaware. In order to evaluate the effect of the ADAS on drivers' lateral control, a one-way rANOVA was performed, considering only 9 out 28 participants of Experiment A, called "unaware", that did not properly understand the ADAS functionalities. The response variables were SDLP and LP, the within-factor was the trial (four levels), and no between-factor was considered. A significant effect was found on trial for SDLP, F(3,24) = 8.114, p < .001 and LP, F(3,24) = 4.035, p = 0.019. Pairwise t-tests revealed a significant difference in SDLP between trials 3–4, t(8) = −3.271, p = 0.011, Cohen's d = −1.090, for LP no significant difference between trials 1–2, 2–3 and 3–4. Trends of SDLP and LP across trials can be observed in Fig. 5.

In absolute terms SDLP increases from 0.257 m (baseline) to 0.296 m (last trial), with an increment of 39 mm; pairwise t-tests revealed a significant increasement between trials 1–4, t(8) = −3.484, p = 0.008, Cohen's d = −1.161.

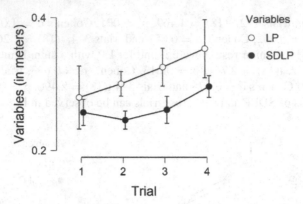

Fig. 5. SDLP and LP (both in meters) across trials 1–4 for "unaware" drivers of Experiment A (vertical bars represent 95% confidence intervals).

3.3 Experiment B

In order to evaluate the effect of the ADAS on drivers' lateral control, a one-way rANOVA was performed, considering Experiment B. The response variables were SDLP and LP, the within-factor was the trial (four levels), and no between-factor was considered. A significant effect was found on trial for SDLP, $F(3,72) = 54.799, p < .001$ and LP, $F(3,72) = 50.744, p < .001$. Pairwise t-tests revealed a significant improvement in SDLP between trials 1–2, $t(24) = 7.781, p < .001$, Cohen's $d = 1.556$, and trials 2–3, $t(24) = 3.490$, $p = 0.002$, Cohen's $d = 0.698$. Similar results were found for LP with a significant improvement between trials 1–2, $t(24) = 6.848, p < .001$, Cohen's $d = 1.370$ and trials 2–3 $t(24) = 3.231, p = 0.004$, Cohen's $d = 0.646$.

In absolute terms SDLP decreases from 0.242 m (baseline) to 0.157 m (last trial), with a reduction of 85 mm, which is a better improvement than in Experiment A; pairwise t-tests revealed a significant improvement between trials 1–4, $t(24) = 8.575, p < .001$, Cohen's $d = 1.714$. Trends of SDLP and LP across trials can be observed in Fig. 6.

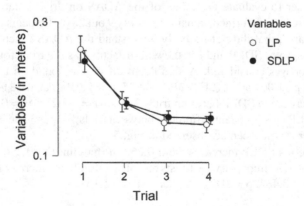

Fig. 6. SDLP and LP (both in meters) across trials 1–4 for Experiment B (vertical bars represent 95% confidence intervals).

In absolute terms LP decreases from 0.259 m (baseline) to 0.147 m (last trial), with a reduction of 112 mm, slightly more than in Experiment A; pairwise t-tests revealed a significant improvement between trials 1–4, t(24) = 9.012, p < .001, Cohen's d = 1.802.

3.4 Experiment A vs Experiment B

Experiments A and B were compared, in order to investigate the effect of different initial mental models on drivers' lateral control; a mixed-factors ANOVA with trial as within factor (four levels) and experiment as between factor (two levels) was performed. 9 out 28 participants did not properly understand the ADAS functionalities and were excluded from this analysis. A significant effect was found on trial for SDLP, F(3,126) = 80.379, p < .001 and experiment, F(1,42) = 13.404, p < .001, but not interaction. A significant effect was found on trial for LP, F(3,126) = 60.424, p < .001 and experiment, F(1,42) = 7.176, p = 0.011, but not interaction.

A main effect of experiment can be observed in Fig. 7, explicitly instructing subjects on ADAS functionalities improved drivers' lateral control, with respect to the SDLP and LP. Values of dependent variables are actually lower, in absolute terms, in Experiment B also during the control trial (i.e., Trial 1). However, as can be observed, the differences between Trials 1 of Experiment A and B are not significant with significance level of α = 0.05.

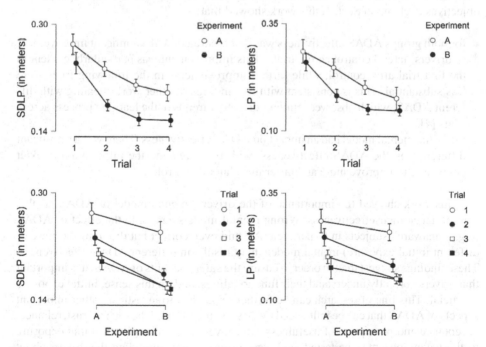

Fig. 7. Comparison between Experiments A and B: trends of SDLP and LP across trials, for each experiment and across experiments, for each trial (vertical bars represent 95% confidence intervals).

On the other hand, it is interesting to notice that, even though both factors, considered separately, had a significant effect, their interaction did not, meaning that in both experiments the rate at which SDLP and LP decreased across trials were similar. The interaction would be significant with a level of $\alpha = 0.10$, and the graphs in Fig. 7 suggest that the improvement between Trials 1 and 2 seems higher in Experiment B. From this analysis it can be observed that informing the participants about the ADAS by making them read an information booklet had a positive impact on their performance and a significant improvement was found. Less conclusive statements can be made about the improvement (in terms of speed) of the learning process, but our analyses suggest a higher reduction of SDLP and LP values between Trials 1 and 2 in Experiment B than in Experiment A.

4 Discussion and Conclusions

In this paper the effect of driver mental model on a lateral position control ADAS was tested with a driving simulation experiment, with particular focus on ADAS effectiveness.

After Experiment 0, drivers were divided into two groups and received two different initial exposures to the system, with the members of former having to learn ADAS functionalities on their own and the members of the latter having to read an information booklet. Both groups performed multiple successive driving trials. With respect to the objectives declared in Sect. 1, this work showed that:

- for both groups ADAS effectiveness was demonstrated, with significant improvement of drivers' lateral control across trials. This improvement was particularly evident in the first trial after control, while further improvements in the following trials were less substantial. This is consistent with the findings of other works dealing with different ADAS, which observed similar non-linear trends in the learning process across trials [4].
- the initial mental model had an impact on ADAS effectiveness. There was a significant difference on the ADAS effectiveness, with those reading the information booklet being able to improve more and faster their lateral control.

This work showed the importance of the drivers' mental model of ADAS, as this can influence their effectiveness. Wrong mental models can undo the effect of ADAS (e.g., "unaware" subjects in Experiment A), and even correct but different (because of different initial exposure) mental models may results in different ADAS effectiveness. These findings suggest that, in order to ensure the safety benefits of ADAS, it is important that drivers correctly understand their functionalities, and, in this sense, initial exposure is crucial. This line of research can be further expanded, to investigate other important aspects of ADAS that can be influenced by drivers' mental models, such as trust, reliance, acceptance and perception of usefulness. Moreover, other strategies of initial exposure to the technology may be tested, and also the impact of reminding the drivers about system functionalities during later trials may be investigated.

Acknowledgment. The authors would like to thank Alberto Sarto, Domenico Pizzorni and Alberto Tosolin for their support in designing the experiment and the students from the course "Human Factors in Transport Systems Safety" of the Master Degree in Safety Engineering for their support during experiment execution and data collection.

References

1. Sullivan, J.M., Flannagan, M.J., Pradhan, A.K., Bao, S.: Literature Review of Behavioral Adaptations to Advanced Driver Assistance Systems (2016)
2. Norman, D.A.: Some observations on mental models. In: Mental Models (1983)
3. Beggiato, M., Krems, J.F.: The evolution of mental model, trust and acceptance of adaptive cruise control in relation to initial information. Transp. Res. Part F Traffic Psychol. Behav. (2013). https://doi.org/10.1016/j.trf.2012.12.006
4. Beggiato, M., Pereira, M., Petzoldt, T., Krems, J.: Learning and development of trust, acceptance and the mental model of ACC. A longitudinal on-road study. Transp. Res. Part F Traffic Psychol. Behav. (2015). https://doi.org/10.1016/j.trf.2015.10.005
5. McDonald, A., Reyes, M., Roe, C., McGehee, D.: Driver understanding of ADAS and evolving consumer education. In: 25th International Technical Conference on the Enhanced Safety of Vehicles (2017)
6. McDonald, A., Reyes, M., Roe, C., McGehee, D.: Impacts on driver perceptions in initial exposure to ADAS technologies. In: 98th Transportation Research Board Meeting, Washington, DC (2019)
7. Victor, T.W., Tivesten, E., Gustavsson, P., Johansson, J., Sangberg, F., Ljung Aust, M.: Automation expectation mismatch: incorrect prediction despite eyes on threat and hands on wheel. Hum. Factors (2018). https://doi.org/10.1177/0018720818788164
8. Rossi, R., Gastaldi, M., Meneguzzer, C.: Headway distribution effect on gap-acceptance behavior at roundabouts: driving simulator experiments in a case study. Adv. Transp. Stud. **46**, 97–110 (2018)
9. Rossi, R., Meneguzzer, C., Orsini, F., Gastaldi, M.: Gap-acceptance behavior at roundabouts: validation of a driving simulator environment using field observations. Transp. Res. Procedia. **47**, 27–34 (2020)
10. Rossi, R., Gecchele, G., Gastaldi, M., Biondi, F., Mulatti, C.: An advanced driver assistance system for improving driver ability. Design and test in virtual environment. In: 5th IEEE International Conference Model. Technologies Intelligent Transportation System MT-ITS 2017 - Proceeding (2017). https://doi.org/10.1109/MTITS.2017.8005725
11. Biondi, F.N., Rossi, R., Gastaldi, M., Orsini, F., Mulatti, C.: Precision teaching to improve drivers' lane maintenance. J. Safety Res. (2020). https://doi.org/10.1016/j.jsr.2019.12.020
12. Zhou, J., Peng, H., Gordon, T.J.: Characterization of the lateral control performance by human drivers on highways. SAE Int. J. Passeng. Cars-Mech. Syst. **1**, 450–458 (2009). https://doi.org/10.4271/2008-01-0561
13. Babaee, S., Shen, Y., Hermans, E., Wets, G., Brijs, T., Ariën, C.: Combining driving performance information in an index score. Transp. Res. Rec. J. Transp. Res. Board. **2434**, 44–51 (2014). https://doi.org/10.3141/2434-06
14. Kennedy, R.S., Lane, N.E., Berbaum, K.S., Lilienthal, M.G.: Simulator sickness questionnaire: an enhanced method for quantifying simulator sickness (questions only). Int. J. Aviat. Psychol. **3**, 203–220 (1993). https://doi.org/10.1207/s15327108ijap0303_3
15. van der Sluiszen, N.N.J.J.M., et al.: On-the-road driving performance after use of the antihistamines mequitazine and l-mequitazine, alone and with alcohol. Psychopharmacology (Berl) (2016). https://doi.org/10.1007/s00213-016-4386-7
16. Hartman, R.L., et al.: Cannabis effects on driving longitudinal control with and without alcohol. J. Appl. Toxicol. (2016). https://doi.org/10.1002/jat.3295

Virtual Reality vs Pancake Environments:
A Comparison of Interaction on Immersive and Traditional Screens

Raymond Holder$^{(\boxtimes)}$, Mark Carey, and Paul Keir

University of the West of Scotland, Paisley PA1 2BE, Scotland, UK
Raymond.Holder@uws.ac.uk

Abstract. Virtual Reality environments provide an immersive experience for the user. Since humans see the real world in 3D, being placed in a virtual environment allows the brain to perceive the virtual world as a real environment. This paper examines the contrasts between two different user interfaces by presenting test subjects with the same 3D environment through a traditional flat screen (pancake) and an immersive virtual reality (VR) system. The participants (n = 31) are computer literate and familiar with computer generated virtual worlds. We recorded each user's interactions while they undertook a short-supervised play session with both hardware options to gathering objective data; with a questionnaire to collect subjective data, to gain an understanding of their interaction in a virtual world. The information provided an opportunity to understand how we can influence future interface implementations used in the technology. Analysis of the data has found that people are open to using VR to explore a virtual space with some unconventional interaction abilities such as using the whole body to interact. Due to modern VR being a young platform very few best practice conventions are known in this space compared to the more established flat screen equivalent.

Keywords: Virtual reality · Immersive · 3D environments · Computer graphics

1 Introduction

Virtual Reality has gained popularity over recent years. With improvements in hardware and software, technology has become affordable to a larger audience [22] and not just the military, industry, and research communities. Affordable systems in the consumer market are opening up opportunities to offer training, entertainment and 3D visualisation in fields such as engineering, healthcare, education, media and gaming. In many of these industries VR is an increasingly important component, enabling innovators to develop advanced prototypes [19], facilitating rapid iteration and testing. Yet there are very few established conventions [31] around implementing the technology at present. Due to the unconventional way the human body is used to interact and control a VR experience, discovering whether the interface offers utility, or is fully accepted by the consumer, is an important step in its evolution.

© Springer Nature Switzerland AG 2020
L. T. De Paolis and P. Bourdot (Eds.): AVR 2020, LNCS 12242, pp. 114–129, 2020.
https://doi.org/10.1007/978-3-030-58465-8_8

"Furthermore, computing power must increase to allow for more photorealistic rendering and complex natural interactions. Researchers will need to better understand how to design specific experiences to teach specific topics, while understanding the capabilities and limitations of learners of varying ages and skills. These and other pragmatic concerns must be addressed to create a robust learning technology." (Bujak, 2013) [2]

The data gathered in the study examined here will be used to build and improve a user interface for Virtual Reality applications being developed for use within computer science education. With our present knowledge there are gaps in the data, which this study aims to fill.

1.1 What Is Virtual Reality?

Virtual Reality has been described as "an artificial environment which is experienced through sensory stimuli (as sights and sounds) provided by a computer and in which one's actions partially determine what happens in the environment" [33].

We are conscious of our immediate surrounding by collecting information from our sensory system – sight, smell, sound, touch and taste. To build a three dimensional spatial awareness of our environments we mainly use our sight and hearing [30]. Virtual Reality recreates a spatial environment in stereoscopic 3D, where high quality visuals and sounds are created in a similar way that computer games are generated. However, in VR, content is then rendered to a head mounted display (HMD) instead of a computer screen. The processing and rendering of the images to the screens in the headset allows the user to perceive the environment in three dimensions [16]. Tracking of the headset's pitch and yaw allows a 360° field of view; with positional tracking allowing the user to move around the environment. The technology can 'fool' the user to accept the 3D environment with a perceived level of realism by implementing; a wide field of view, stereoscopic rendering, binaural sound, head and hand tracking and low latency between the user's movement and visual updates [7].

One of the benefits of VR is that it permits a person to undertake an experience that is 'beyond' reality, negating the need for a hyper-real environment [12]. Such computer generated 'unrealities' can be just as immersive as that we consider natural, yet the experiences undertaken can be highly implausible or impossible [11]. VR is the only media that can present the world in such an immersive way.

Immersive platforms such as VR can be more effective in delivering an experience than any other digital media because the brain perceives the virtual world as a real world; therefore transferring the skills and knowledge learned in the virtual world to the real world with higher retention [28]. This is a progression from non-immersive virtual experiences, as Robertson et al. [27] says, that "places the user in a 3D environment that can be directly manipulated, but it does so with a conventional graphics workstation using a monitor, a keyboard, and a mouse". We will refer to this as desktop 3D.

1.2 The 3D Environment

The virtual environment used for this study is custom built using the game engine Unreal Engine 4 and has been intentionally kept visually simple. The minimalist environment allows the experience to run smoothly and at a high frame rate. A higher frame rate allows the system to negate some of the side effects of motion sickness that some people can experience when using VR motion sickness is experienced by some people when wearing a head mounted display. It is thought this is due to the discrepancies caused by a high latency between actual movement and virtual movement [31]. In addition to the higher performance cost of a VR experience compared to a flat screen experience, using a minimalist approach we ensure both virtual environments are executed at the same quality. Not having a rich environment has also helped the participants focus on the task set out in the study instead of being distracted by the 'wow' factor that can happen when users are put into a virtual reality experience, which could then skew the results. The participants are presented with 4 models on plinths surrounding them to interact with. They are placed at an equal distance from each user's start position.

The 4 objects are: A character model (non-human biped), a motorcycle, a robot and a rifle as shown in Fig. 1.

Fig. 1. Models presented in the virtual environment

The plinths they sit on are translucent and sit around 1 (Unreal Engine) unit in height, which is 1 m in real world measurements. A simple grid-patterned floor is underfoot, and post processing fog prevents the participant from seeing beyond 10 units.

Within the program described, movement in VR can be executed by either physically walking around the play space or using a teleport system that is implemented by the user pressing and releasing a button on the left-hand controller. On the desktop this movement is performed using the mouse: double clicking on a model moves the user's camera to near the model's position, which can then be orbited by moving the mouse. The right-hand controller has a laser pointer attached to it: a model can be picked up in VR by aiming this at the models and depressing the trigger. The user can move the model freely in any axis. The desktop user can move a model in any linear axis (up, down, left, right, back and forth) and rotate it by depressing the right mouse button with the cursor over the model and moving the mouse in the corresponding direction.

On starting the experience in both flat screen and VR the user is presented with a user interface (UI), shown in Fig. 2, that has icons and text describing the control system. This includes how to move and the actions corresponding to each button. In VR the UI is attached to the right controller; and the user can turn this off and on with a button on that controller. A permanent notice of how to pull up the UI is placed in the user's field of view in a head up display, in case users need to access the instructions again. This can also act as a guide for the user to position the headset in the sweet spot when they first put the headset on. The average human field of view is around 180° [25]. The virtual reality headset used in the study has a 105° field of view (FOV) and due to the precise positioning of the Fresnel lenses on the headset, it can take some adjustment to get it right [13]; thus the UI text is used to guide the wearer to see this in focus before tightening the head strap and can help them get the HMD on correctly. On the desktop application the UI is a HUD style element permanently displayed, though fading when the user starts to interact with the 3D scene. The UI can be brought back up again if the user hovers the mouse over the faded element.

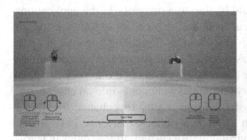 

Fig. 2. Desktop UI (left) Virtual Reality UI (right)

One further interaction has been implemented: the ability to disable texturing and see the wireframe of the models underlying geometry. This feature was included because the majority of participants are students of the creative computing department; studying undergraduate degrees in gaming, animation, or related fields. 3D modelling is part of their education; having the ability to see the wireframe of the models is something these students are interested in. It was taken as an indication that the participants had mastered the basic controls if they then entered the wireframe mode. This also gave the participants more to experience; beyond the basic features of movement and interaction.

1.3 Related Work

We researched prior studies that looked at virtual reality vs traditional content and found some literature undertaking studies within the fields of education, healthcare, and engineering. We expanded our literature review also to incorporate augmented reality (AR). As a sister technology to VR, AR shares many of its key components. However, where VR fully immerses the user in a virtual world, AR takes elements out of the virtual world and overlays them on the real world through either a headset with a see through screen; or a mobile device screen using a pass-through camera system.

In the North study [23] a comparison between an Immersive Visualization Environment (IVE) and a traditional virtual environment was studied to find that a more natural and richer experience had been undertaken while using the immersive system; allowing the participant to become more immersed in the world. They found the feeling of immersion in the environment became increasingly important for users to interact with an application. This feeling of immersion has been described as presence [15] or a 'sense of being there', a game in virtual reality can trick the player's cognitive system into believing the virtual world is real. However, this work discovered that ignoring or breaking the fundamental 'best practices' of VR can cause the user to feel discomfort and experience simulation sickness.

VR can offer more engaging, motivating and better results through experiential learning with students able to learn through practice and repetition [29]. A 3D virtual environment can offer a wealth of experiences and intensity that no other platform can compete with. This richness can be tiring and cause motion sickness in some users. The vibrancy of a virtual environment can also distract a learner [10]. This has led to mixed results between studies regarding whether 3D and virtual environments actively improve or worsen results for the learner [24]. This could be due to a disparity in the applications offered between the different studies; or occur from inconsistencies in how the studies were implemented (e.g. the learning objective, student backgrounds, the specific task performed, and the students' time on task). A superior multi-sensory experience might find an increase in knowledge retention over a less well-provisioned one [20].

The inclusion of emotional, multi-sensory and fantasy elements into an educational interactive and immersive experience by using virtual reality to enhance traditional classroom teaching/learning techniques can provide a richer experience [14]. In the study by Richards [26], using an interactive virtual reality system offered gains in learning outcomes over traditional technology; but the gains in younger adults were more prominent. The greater familiarity with interactive technology for this age demographic could account for the increase. Enjoyment of the experience was recorded for all ages and concludes that the participants engaged more fully in the VR tasks. In other studies when augmented reality was introduced to a learning experience and a comparison to an interactive simulation on a flat screen was made, similar results were found [4]. Students were "deeply engaged" and free of the physical constrictions of the classroom while manipulating physical elements in the augmented world [2]; this added to the learning experience of the participants of the study. However, the research finds that computing power must increase to allow more photo-realistic visuals and complex natural interactions; adding that further research must be undertaken to understand how to design experiences to fully bring the technology in to the education sector.

VR has the potential to create a paradigm shift in education and training [1, 18] yet we find there is very little practical evidence that the learning experiences offer any added value to education beyond that it uses novel technologies. Being 'present' in an experience does not always promote better learning outcomes. Belini [1] concludes that a lab simulation in virtual reality can cause nearly a 50% increase in brain workload compared to the desktop version of the simulation. Further investigation of interaction systems and the immersive environment in VR is needed to better improve the implementation of the technology in an educational setting. Introducing a game-like educational experience could be more engaging to the learners and offer a more attractive application of immersive VR. The serious games industry has years of experience of this, and positive results have been observed with an immersive serious game demonstrating improvements both in the quality of learning, and the retention of learnt concepts [5]. It has been noted that restrictions on the availability of the VR hardware can limit the implementation. While the desktop version may provide an inferior level of immersion, it is open to a far larger user base.

2 Methodology

A 3D virtual gallery with four computer generated models sitting on plinths are presented to the participant to explore in two forms: a computer screen using a keyboard and mouse; and also a virtual reality HMD. Half of the test subjects explored the screen interface first, then the virtual reality interface. The other half explored the environment using the virtual reality interface first, and then the screen interface. Participants used the VR headset and controllers to explore the gallery of 3D models; produced by students from an undergraduate animation degree course. In the virtual environment the user can walk around the play space; teleport to different locations using the controllers; as well as pick up, move and rotate the models. The same virtual gallery was presented on the flat screen experience. The user can move around the play space using the mouse to orbit the viewpoint around each model. A double mouse-click will move between models; a single click will grab and move them. For both modalities, interaction data was recorded using virtual estimation software that records the user's movement; allowing the re-creation of these movement in a game engine. A comparison between the participants' movement data for both interactions was also made side by side using laboratory-controlled analysis. After the participants experienced both interfaces, they were asked to complete a survey consisting of three comparison scale questions and three qualitative questions. Equipment used throughout the testing was as follows: for the pancake deployment, a HP gaming laptop with a dedicated graphics card, 15" LCD screen, keyboard and mouse; for the VR experience, an ASUS gaming laptop with a dedicated graphics card, a HP Windows Mixed Reality VR1000-100nn headset, and controllers for the interactions.

2.1 Testing in VR (Best Practices)

In this section we look at play testing in VR and discuss the best practices we came upon during this study. Play testing is usually undertaken during software development, because of a user's physicality within virtual reality, such testing and observation has a more important role than in traditional game testing. We considered the special requirements needed for virtual reality, such as play space dimensions and took these unique factors into considerations when testing the VR application as opposed to a standard 2D/3D (flat screen) application.

Conducting a play test in Virtual Reality has more elements and conditions to meet than a traditional play test. A player's body can be put under significant strain when using wearable immersive technology in VR. The most recognised comfort issue is motion sickness [3]. To minimise the probability that players will experience simulation sickness in the application we focused upon two main factors:

(i) Technical performance is extremely important for VR applications to maintain a high frame rate and avoid unwelcome rendering artifacts such as screen tear. Today's VR succeeds according to a low delay between the player moving in the real world, and the HMD screen displaying the change in the virtual world; also known as motion to photon latency. If this is low, it will deceive the brain. Poorly optimised applications and hardware issues add to this latency and can break the illusion; with motion sickness being the result for the user [9].

(ii) The second factor is the design of the application. Design can have a great impact regarding motion sickness, design choices to maintain performance and frame rates to make sure they run well are important. If a participant takes the role of a passenger in a moving vehicle, with text to read placed close to them, then a carsickness simulation has been created. Essentially when exposing a player to any type of motion, locomotion, object motion, vehicles or camera, one should consider how this affects comfort [21]. We avoided putting our participant into any scenario that would cause discomfort that could skew the data we gathered.

One of the least researched areas of comfort in VR is eyestrain. Users could experience headaches, nausea or fatigue due to eyestrain while using an HMD [17]. To negate this, during the design process we thought about the scale and position of objects within the virtual environment. We found placing objects half a meter or further away from the user is the best practice. Objects that are too close to the user have been shown to cause vision accommodation [32]. Vision accommodation is used to describe the natural blurring of the background to the foreground when the eye focuses on a particular object. User interface elements that are fixed in place within the user's field of view through the HMD were placed in a comfortable position. Consequently, we ensure users do not strain their eyes; by avoiding them looking to the edge of their vision. Reading text in the headset can also contribute to eyestrain. We focused on size, colour and font of any text that is in the user interface to overcome any problems they may cause by making sure that it was large with an easy to read font, had a good contrast with the environment and is not placed too close in the users field of view.

With VR being a wearable technology, users are often physically moving or at least standing, and hence likely sweating while they play. With a flat screen experience the user is typically seated, and less physically active. It was important for us to consider the intensity and the length of the participants physical activity period. Our application was designed not to push a user's physical ability, by implementing a teleportation and grab & pull function we offered an alternative to room scale movement (Fig. 3). In future testing careful observation will be needed to ensure physical activity is not overdone [8]; looking for the user perspiring, shortness of breath or losing balance as signs that they are over exerted. Similarly, avoiding long load times or periods of inactivity; and minimising the idle time when in the virtual environment. Idle time is also a consideration with flat screen applications but is magnified in VR since the participants are a somewhat captive audience; with a heavy device strapped to their head.

A few other points were considered during our VR testing. We:

- Confirmed HMDs and controllers were sanitised.
- Ensured that all relevant software updates were installed.
- Prepared the play area based on the dimensions needed for the play test.
- Made sure the area was safely clear of clutter or tripping hazards.
- Checked that HMD lenses were clean and clear.
- Checked elements like lighting or other factors would not interfere with tracking.
- Ensured that the VR hardware was ready for immediate use by each test subject.
- Kept spare batteries on hand.

When everything was ready, we pre-briefed the participant before putting on their HMD and handing them a controller. In the pre-brief we set expectations for the test and explained the basics of how the controllers work before putting on the headset while they could see and hear us.

A varied experience level of participants with VR was expected; and some needed help getting the HMD on. To standardise the process with each participant we:

- Loosened all the HMD fittings and had the participant hold the lens assembly close to their face. Some had to shift the lens assembly along their face to find maximum clarity.
- Tightened all the fittings, once they stated the text in the scene was clear.
- Handed over the controllers and secured the wrist straps.

Once the participant had been given all the relevant information and the VR equipment was properly fitted, they were ready to start the experience. We avoided coaching the participant through the experience and avoided creating any type of disturbance that would affect the behavior of the user in VR. Hearing noises outside the virtual environment during the play test can give the tester performance anxiety or break the immersion. Once the play test concluded we assisted the participant with removing the VR equipment.

2.2 Gathering Data

While the VR experience was fresh in the subject's mind we debrief with them. Participants were asked a standard set of questions as per the testing plan; and we gave them a survey to facilitate quantitative analysis. Standardising the procedure to gather data from every participant is essential. We identified the precise conditions of each test as well as listing the actions for the tester. A list of game functions was compiled, as well as any information about the testing environment; the PC specifications, play area size, etc. during play testing. Every effort was made to ensure conditions and tasks were identical for each participant. So too we standardised whatever information we gave to each subject before the play test; as with the questions we asked while we observed the play test. A few questions that we asked ourselves during a play test observation were:

- Does the player understand the objectives?
- What specific oral, visual, or contextual information is missing if they do not understand?
- Are there any visual signs of discomfort such as sweating, flushed skin or the player ending the session early?
- Is there a certain part of the experience that is causing this?
- Are there parts of the experience where players express emotion?
- How does each player spend their time during the play test?
- Do players spend more or less time on a certain interaction? And why?

When the testing was complete a spreadsheet with all the gathered data was compiled. For each of the participants we kept track of the interactions via the virtual estimation software built into Unreal Engine 4, and the answers to a set of standard survey questions that we gave. Once we gathered and organised all the data the next step was to analyse this data.

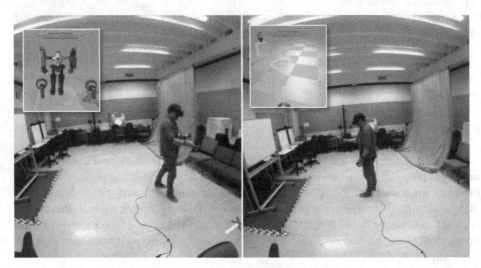

Fig. 3. Participant using room-scale (left) and participant using teleportation (right)

3 Experimental Results

Taking the results from the questionnaires the 31 participants filled in before and after they had completed the two experiences, we compiled the results into spreadsheets and converted the data into easy to read graphs.

3.1 Questionnaire Results

A large percentage of participants had used a virtual reality headset prior to this study with 64.5% of them having previous experience in a VR platform as seen in Fig. 4. However, shown in Fig. 5, a slight majority of the participants described themselves as beginners with 51.6% classifying themselves in this category.

More people found using the VR system very easy compared to the desktop system with 19.4% versus 9.7%. On a scale from 1 to 5, where 1 is easy and is 5 difficult in both experiences more of the participants gave a grade 2 to navigate in the experience; with the desktop gaining the more votes here; 41.9% & compared to 32.3% using VR. Only 1 person found using either system difficult. When asked a question about if they thought that VR gave a better experience over the flat screen interface; 58.1% of the participants thought that it did; 22.6% disagreeing and 19.4% unsure. After undertaking both experiences a large majority of users preferred the VR system over the desktop with 80% versus 20% of all participants liking virtual reality more.

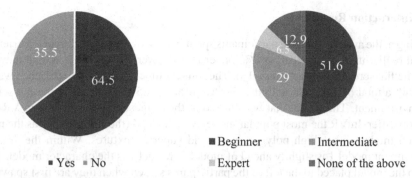

Fig. 4. Have you used Virtual Reality prior to this study?

Fig. 5. What best describes your VR experience level?

The participants were asked three questions regarding their thoughts on both experiences immediately after undertaking the play tests. Here we present the questions and some of the responses.

- Question 1: Based on your previous answer (Which system did you prefer?) what did you like most about the system?

    - "I could bring the model right next to my face and look at it from very specific angles" (VR)
    - "Use of the mouse provides better control" (Desktop)
    - "VR allowed for better object movement to inspect small details that would be hard to check using the desktop version"
    - "I could look around and walk closer to the objects in order to see them better" (VR)
    - "The way that you could interact. It was fun" (VR)
    - "It's easy to leave and I can take my time" (Desktop)
    - "Easy ability to manipulate VR objects" (VR)

- Question 2: What did you dislike, if anything, about the other system?

    - "In the desktop you are not present in the environment" (Desktop)
    - "Visuals not as clear which made it difficult to appreciate" (VR)
    - "How simple and easy it was, it wasn't fun" (Desktop)
    - "I have to be very careful with the system and myself and can't relax and really properly look at the models" (VR)

- Question 3: What suggestions or ideas do you have for improving the system? (Desktop and/or VR)

    - "Have a cinematic resolution for VR so textures can be more clearly seen"
    - "Desktop has no/little sense of scale"

3.2 Interaction Results

Looking at the average time the participants spent in each of the two different experiences virtual reality users spent nearly 10% longer in VR (average 3 min 10 s) than they did with the flat screen (average 2 min 9 s). The longest time spent in an experience was in VR with a total of 7.38 min with the shortest time of 1.51 min spent in the flat screen 3D environment. The model that was looked at the longest amount of time in VR and desktop differ. In VR the most popular model was model 3 (the robot) this was the most detailed model with a high polygon count and superior textures. Within the desktop environment model 1 is slightly ahead of model 3. Model 1 is the character model. This is also the model placed to the left of the participants screen when they are first spawned. The order from high to low of the average time spent looking at the models are shown in Fig. 6:

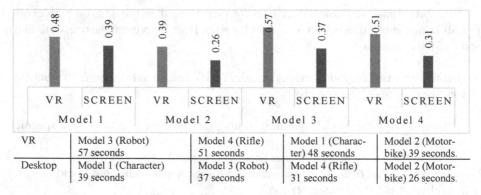

VR	Model 3 (Robot) 57 seconds	Model 4 (Rifle) 51 seconds	Model 1 (Character) 48 seconds	Model 2 (Motorbike) 39 seconds.
Desktop	Model 1 (Character) 39 seconds	Model 3 (Robot) 37 seconds	Model 4 (Rifle) 31 seconds	Model 2 (Motorbike) 26 seconds.

Fig. 6. Time spent looking at the model

Looking to see if the way the participants were spawned into the game affected which model was looked at first. Model 1 (Character) was the prominent model, with 56% of the users in VR and 67% of user on the desktop going to this model first. All the participants in both experiences were spawned into the same location looking in the same direction, with model 1 to the left and model 2 to the right, model 3 & 4 behind them and initially obscured from view. However, within VR the participants could quite easily look around and we observed some users looking in all directions around the environment as soon as they put on the HMD but coming back to the initial direction faced once they settle into VR.

The data collected on how the participants interacted with the models in each of the environments is visible in Fig. 7. We find that all of them picked up all of the four models when in VR; the trend wasn't carried through in the desktop version of the experience with an average of 2.4 of the users picking up a model in the desktop mode.

Studying the statistics on the participants further interactions with the models and whether they took a closer look at a model within the virtual reality experience, can be seen in Fig. 8. This could have been the participant leaning in to look closer at the model by physically moving in the VR's room-scale space (VR/RS) or bring the model closer

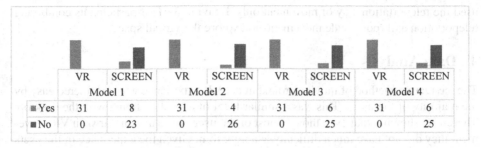

	VR	SCREEN	VR	SCREEN	VR	SCREEN	VR	SCREEN
	Model 1		Model 2		Model 3		Model 4	
■ Yes	31	8	31	4	31	6	31	6
■ No	0	23	0	26	0	25	0	25

Fig. 7. Did the participant pick up the model?

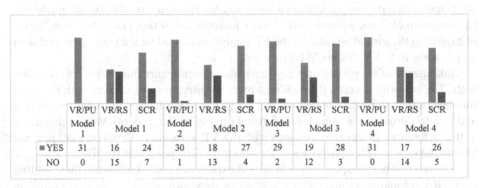

	VR/PU	VR/RS	SCR	VR/PU	VR/RS	SCR	VR/PU	VR/RS	SCR	VR/PU	VR/RS	SCR
	Model 1	Model 1		Model 2	Model 2		Model 3	Model 3		Model 4	Model 4	
■ YES	31	16	24	30	18	27	29	19	28	31	17	26
NO	0	15	7	1	13	4	2	12	3	0	14	5

Fig. 8. Did the participant get a closer look at the model?

to their face by picking it up (VR/PU). In the desktop environment (SCR) this would be done by 'zooming' in on the model.

We find that Model 1 (Character) & 4 (Rifle) were closely examined by all the participants in VR. Only one person did not get closer to Model 2 (Motorcycle) and two people did not examine Model 3 (Robot) closer with the pickup (VR/PU) method. The split is far more even between the participants physical moving closer to look at the models (VR/RS), with Model 3 (Robot) being the most looked at model and 19 people moving to look closer at this model. Generally, all the models had more of the participants moving closer to them although this was slight. In the desktop experience most participants did zoom in to have a closer look at the models with an average of 26 of the participants taking a closer look at the models. Model 3 (Robot) was the most looked at item in this category with 28 of the participants spending time to look at this model in more detail.

Movement of the participants while using virtual reality could be undertaken by either using the controls provided within the app that allowed the user to 'teleport' around the scene or alternatively they could physically walk around the scene. The testing play space was large enough to allow the participants to not only physically walk around each model placed on the virtual plinths but also walk from model to model. Tracking the way that the participants moved around the virtual space we see that around two thirds of users used the teleportation way of movement only. Leaving 34% of participants combining teleportation and room-scale movements to explore the virtual space.

4 Data Analysis

The navigation method of moving around in the VR experience was considered easy by the majority of the users. This was a similar level of ease they found with the desktop. Therefore, showing that even though most of the users were unfamiliar with VR movement they did not have much difficulty adapting to it. Given the experience of the users with a desktop system you might expect that this would have led to a higher percentage of them thinking it provides a better experience. This was not the case; the VR system might have offered these participants a novel way to explore a virtual environment, which has be shown can have a positive effect when learning a new task [15]. The 'wow' factor of exploring the virtual world with the VR equipment could be the cause here and with more exposure to VR this could balance out.

Taking note of the participants answers in the questionnaire that they were presented with. The majority found VR provided a more intuitive way to interact with the environment, although it was pointed out that some found it a less comfortable experience and it didn't provide the same level of visual quality as the desktop. We put this down to the differences in screen resolutions with the VR system (1440 ppi × 1440 ppi) not having the same display properties as the desktop (1920 ppi × 1080 ppi).

The fact that people spent longer in the VR experience could be down to them settling into VR i.e. looking around; seeing how when they move their hands the controllers follow in the virtual world. Investigating further the details of how much time the users looked at each model, we see a similar percentage of time spent here. Therefore, this would back up the data from the subjective questionnaire: participants enjoyed looking at the models in VR more than they did on the desktop.

Model 1 was the prominent model, looked at first by the participants in both experiences, positioned to the left-hand side when the player is first spawned in the virtual world. Readers of European languages are influenced by the left to right reading pattern; suggesting in the western world our attention is drawn to items on the left-hand side of our vision first [6]. This could be observed differently in different cultures.

Examining whether the participants found the VR experience an enhanced way to explore the environment we looked at the data gathered on whether they picked up the models for inspection. Here we find that the participants were more engaged with the models in the VR world, both picked up the models and brought them closer to have a better look, or moved closer in the real world to see the items in better detail.

Teleportation was the most used movement system; this could have been influenced by being told how to use the system during the pre-brief. Therefore, prejudicing the movement ability before they even started the experience. Other factors could also account for the majority of people using this method; (i) They didn't feel safe to walk around in the real world while they could only see the virtual world; (ii) Presumably the user isn't truly immersed (e.g. The Matrix). A controller in hand will certainly remind the user of that. However, the fact that just over a third of the participants also used the room scale movement to explore shows that even though they are aware of the teleportation system they felt comfortable to roam as they would in the real world.

5   Conclusion

A distinct characteristic of virtual reality is the complete immersion of the user into the virtual environment. This allows a person to be physically transported into any conceivable world, and to undertake any task without the physical and financial limitations of the real world. This study compared the influence of immersive and non-immersive platforms on 31 creative computing undergraduate students. It has shown that this demographic is open to the idea of using a virtual reality system to explore virtual environments and use the interface discussed over a more familiar system; 80% preferred the VR interface. While using immersive technology the participant is more engaged and spent 10% longer to undertake a task. Increased engagement is recorded in the virtual reality system with both a greater number of interactions with the models; 100% of the users picked up all the models in VR; and spent longer interacting with the objects; showing that a VR system can deliver a richer experience than a flat screen. Due to VR being relatively early in its development as a platform there are many aspects that still need to be researched in order to make further conclusions. The design of the VR content has a vast impact on the effectiveness of the user's experience, and we noticed that elements placed in the user's initial view are looked at first. Although this is shown to happen in both user interfaces the effect is reduced in VR due to the ability of the user to look around the environment more easily and naturally with the headset.

The main objective of this study was to play test, observe and analyse how the interaction interface influenced the user. We have found it to be essential in undertaking studies like this one to make any informed assertions on how to develop immersive platforms used in virtual reality. As hardware and software develop and improve any such research will need to be updated to reflect these changes. However, we can say with confidence that user comfort while in an immersive experience is greatly important. The design of the interface that a user is put in can affect the level of comfort. This is not as much of a problem when using a traditional 2D computer screen; making it easier to develop and deploy an experience for a pancake system.

References

1. Bellini, H., Chen, W., Sugiyama, M., Shin, M., Alam, S., Takayama, D.: Virtual & Augmented Reality: Understanding the race for the next computing platform. Goldman Sachs report (2016)
2. Bujak, K.R., Radu, I., Catrambone, R., MacIntyre, B., Zheng, R., Golubski, G.: A psychological perspective on augmented reality in the mathematics classroom. Comput. Educ. **68**, 536–544 (2013)
3. Carpenter, B.A., Parks, D., Wilkes, J.: Narrative Storytelling in VR through gaming (2017)
4. Chang, H., Hsu, Y.: A comparison study of augmented reality versus interactive simulation technology to support student learning of a socio-scientific issue (2016)
5. Chittaro, L., Buttussi, F.: Assessing knowledge retention of an immersive serious game vs. a traditional education method in aviation safety. IEEE Trans. Vis. Comput. Graph. **21**(4), 529–538 (2015)
6. Chokron, S., Imbert, M.: Influence of reading habits on line bisection. Cogn. Brain. Res. **1**(4), 219–222 (1993)

7. Cummings, J.J., Bailenson, J.N.: How Immersive Is Enough? A Meta-Analysis of the Effect of Immersive Technology on User Presence. Media Psychology (2016)
8. Farič, N., et al.: P19 thematic analysis of players' reviews of virtual reality exergames, p. A21 (2019)
9. Fernandes, A.S., Feiner, S.K.: Combating VR sickness through subtle dynamic field-of-view modification. In: 2016 IEEE Symposium on 3D User Interfaces (3DUI) (2016)
10. Freina, L., Canessa, A.: Immersive vs. desktop virtual reality in game-based learning. In: European Conference on Games Based Learning (2015)
11. Gavish, N., et al.: Evaluating virtual reality and augmented reality training for industrial maintenance and assembly tasks. Interact. Learn. Environ. 23(6), 778–798 (2015)
12. Graziano, M.S.A., Yap, G.S., Gross, C.G.: Coding of visual space by premotor neurons. Science 266(5187), 1054–1057 (1994)
13. Gu, L., Cheng, D., Wang, Y.: Design of an immersive head mounted display with coaxial catadioptric optics. In: Osten, W., Stolle, H., Kress, B.C. (eds.) Digital Optics for Immersive Displays (2018)
14. Huang, Y.-C., Backman, S.J., Backman, K.F., McGuire, F.A., Moore, D.: An investigation of motivation and experience in virtual learning environments: a self-determination theory. Educ. Inf. Technol. 24(1), 591–611 (2018). https://doi.org/10.1007/s10639-018-9784-5
15. Kateros, S., Georgiou, S., et al.: A comparison of gamified, immersive VR curation methods for enhanced presence and human-computer interaction in digital humanities. J. Herit. 4(2), 221–233 (2015)
16. Kim, G.J.: Designing Virtual Reality Systems: The Structured Approach. Springer, London (2005)
17. Lawson, B.: Motion sickness symptomatology and origins, pp. 531–600 (2014)
18. Makransky, G., Terkildsen, T.S., Mayer, R.E.: Adding immersive virtual reality to a science lab simulation causes more presence but less learning. Learn. Instr. 60(1), 225–236 (2017)
19. Markouzis, D., Fessakis, G.: Interactive storytelling and mobile augmented reality applications for learning and entertainment—a rapid prototyping perspective. In: Interactive Mobile Communication (2015)
20. Matos, A., Rocha, T., Cabral, L., Bessa, M.: Multi-sensory storytelling to support learning for people with intellectual disability: an exploratory didactic study (2015)
21. Marshall, J., Benford, S., Byrne, R., Tennent, P.: Sensory alignment in immersive entertainment. In: Proceedings of the Conference on Human Factors in Computing Systems (2019)
22. Munoz-Arango, J.S., Reiners, D., Cruz-Neira, C.: Design and Architecture of an Affordable Optical Routing - Multi-user VR System with Lenticular Lenses (2019)
23. North, M.: A comparative study of sense of presence of traditional virtual reality and immersive environments (2016)
24. Peterson, D.C., Mlynarczyk, G.S.A.: Analysis of traditional versus three-dimensional augmented curriculum on anatomical learning outcome measures. Anat. Sci. Educ. 9(6), 529–536 (2016)
25. Ragan, E.D., Bowman, D.A., Kopper, R., Stinson, C., Scerbo, S., McMahan, R.P.: Effects of field of view and visual complexity on virtual reality training effectiveness for a visual scanning task. IEEE Trans. Vis. Comput. Graph. 21(7), 794–807 (2015)
26. Richards, D., Taylor, M.A.: Comparison of learning gains when using a 2D simulation tool versus a 3D virtual world: an experiment to find the right representation involving the Marginal Value Theorem. Comput. Educ. 86, 157–171 (2015)
27. Robertson, G., Card, S.K., Mackinlay, J.: Three views of virtual reality: non immersive virtual reality. Computer 26(2), 81 (1993)

28. Rose, F.D., Atree, E.A., Perslow, D.M., Penn, P.R., Ambihaipahan, N.: Training in virtual environments: transfer to real world tasks and equivalence to real task training. Ergonomics **43**(4), 494–511 (2000)
29. Rowe, J.P., Shores, L.R., Mott, B.W., Lester, J.C.: Integrating learning, problem solving, and engagement in narrative-centered learning environments. Int. J. Artif. Intell. Educ. **21**(1–2), 115–133 (2011)
30. Slater, M., Sanchez-Vives, M.V.: Enhancing our lives with immersive virtual reality. Front. Robot. AI **3**, 74 (2016)
31. Vaughan, N., Gabrys, B., Dubey, V.N.: An overview of self-adaptive technologies within virtual reality training. Comput. Sci. Rev. **22**, 65–87 (2016)
32. Vienne, C., Sorin, L., Blondé, L., Huynh-Thu, Q., Mamassian, P.: Effect of the accommodation-vergence conflict on vergence eye movements. Vis. Res. **100**, 124–133 (2014)
33. Merriam Webster: Virtual Reality | Definition of Virtual Reality by Merriam-Webster, pp. 115–118 (2016)

VR Interface for Designing Multi-view-Camera Layout in a Large-Scale Space

Naoto Matsubara[1]($\boxtimes$), Hidehiko Shishido[2], and Itaru Kitahara[2]

[1] Graduated School of Systems and Information Engineering, University of Tsukuba, Tsukuba, Japan
matsubara.naoto@image.iit.tsukuba.ac.jp
[2] Center for Computational Sciences, University of Tsukuba, Tsukuba, Japan
{shishido,kitahara}@ccs.tsukuba.ac.jp

Abstract. Attention has been focused on sports broadcast, which used a free-viewpoint video that integrates multi-viewpoint images inside a computer and reproduces the appearance observed at arbitrary viewpoint. In a multi-view video shooting, it is necessary to arrange multiple cameras to surround the target space. In a large-scale space such a soccer stadium, it is necessary to determine where the cameras can be installed and to understand what kind of multi-view video can be shot. However, it is difficult to get such information in advance so that "location hunting" is needed usually. This paper presents a VR interface for supporting the preliminary consideration of multi-view camera arrangement in large-scale space. This VR interface outputs the multi-view camera layout on the 3D model from the shooting requirements for multi-view camera shooting and the viewing requirements for observation of the generated video. By using our interface, it is expected that the labor and time required to determine the layout of multi-view cameras can be drastically reduced.

Keywords: Free viewpoint video · Multi-view camera · Camera layout · VR simulation

1 Introduction

The application of free-viewpoint video technology, which integrates multi-viewpoint images inside a computer and reproduces the appearance from an arbitrary viewpoint, is progressing, and it is becoming possible to watch sports with a high degree of immersion [1, 2]. In multi-view video shooting, multiple cameras are arranged to surround a shooting space. However, in order to cover the whole of a large-scale space such as a soccer stadium, the number of shooting cameras becomes massive (e.g. over 100). As the result, a great deal of effort, time, and experience are required to determine the optimal camera arrangement that can acquire the visual information (multi-view images), which is necessary to generate high-quality free-viewpoint videos.

In this paper, we propose a VR interface that supports the work of arranging massive cameras in a large space such as a sports stadium as shown in Fig. 1. By using VR space

© Springer Nature Switzerland AG 2020
L. T. De Paolis and P. Bourdot (Eds.): AVR 2020, LNCS 12242, pp. 130–140, 2020.
https://doi.org/10.1007/978-3-030-58465-8_9

constructed from the CG model of the targeted shooting scene, it is possible to calculate camera parameters that satisfy the "shooting requirements" (shooting point, shooting area, spatial resolution of the video) and the "observation requirements" (viewpoint moving range, viewing angle (convergence angle/depression angle)). The validity of the camera arrangement can be confirmed in advance by arranging the calculation result on the VR interface with camera icons and by rendering the appearance from the virtual cameras.

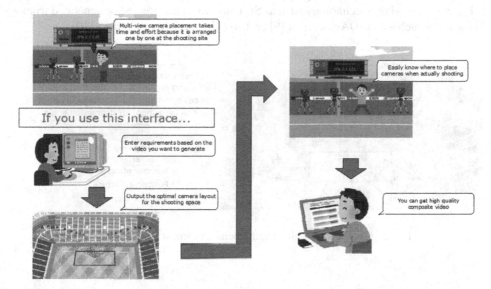

Fig. 1. VR interface for designing multi-view-camera layout.

2 Related Work

Preliminary simulation using VR has been adopted in various fields, and it has also been introduced in the sports field [3–6]. Suzuki [7] proposed a camera placement simulation using a VR environment as a method to support the placement-task of multi-view cameras. It is possible to check the quality of the shot video before actually arranging the camera, by presenting images captured by virtual cameras of an arbitrary number, position, and orientation installed on the stadium CAD model and the spatial resolution of the images, using HMD (Head Mounted Display). However, since the position and angle of all virtual cameras must be set by the user as bottom up approach, the problem of the time and labor required for camera placement has not been solved. In multi-view camera arrangement for free-viewpoint video rendering, it is common to distribute the multi-view cameras uniformly in a certain range, however there is not such reference setting function. We try to solve this problem by developing a VR interface that sets the shooting and viewing requirements that affect the quality of the generated video, and calculates and presents camera parameters that meet those requirements as top down approach.

3   Interface for Multi-view Cameras Layout

3.1   3D Model of Large-Scale Space

In order to consider the camera arrangement, 3D shape information of the shooting scene is required. In this research, we prepare a 3D CAD model of the shooting target scene as shown in Fig. 2 as shooting space information and construct a VR space based on it. If there is no CAD model of the target space, it is possible to use 3D model generated by using computer vision technology such as Structure from Motion [8] or generated from 3D scanner such as a LiDAR scanner [9] or ToF (Time of Flight) camera [10].

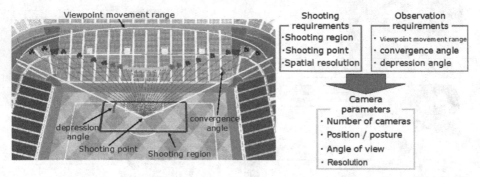

Fig. 2. Overview of setting requirements of camera arrangement.

3.2   Specifications of the Virtual Camera

The specifications (i.e., camera parameters such as the maximum and minimum focal length and the sensor size) of the camera arranged in the VR space are set to be same as those of the actual camera capturing real soccer scene.

3.3   Setting Requirements of Camera Arrangement

It is necessary to set the requirements to be satisfied for arranging the cameras. Specifically, as shown in Fig. 2, our interface requests to input two kind of requirements "shooting requirements" for multi-view camera and "observation requirements" for viewing the generated video.

Shooting Requirements.   "shooting point", "shooting region", and "spatial resolution" are the shooting requirements. Shooting point is the position observed at the center of the screen of all multi-viewpoint images (i.e., the optical axes of all cameras pass through this point). Shooting region on the field is set with a rectangle centered on the shooting point. Spatial resolution is the extent of the 3D space observed by one pixel on the captured video. The smaller this value is, the more detailed will be the resulting visual information.

Observation Requirements. Regarding the observation requirements, "movement range of the observation viewpoint" and observation angles such as "convergence angle" and "depression angle" are set. Movement range is set as the angle between the head and tail around the shooting point as shown in Fig. 2. Convergence angle is a parameter that affects the sense of switching viewpoints in the observed video. An appropriate angle is given by the realization method of the free viewpoint video. When generating bullet-time video, it is possible to generate video in which the viewpoint moves smoothly if multiple viewpoint cameras are arranged on the same plane. In this interface, the requirement of the multi-view camera arrangement is given as the angle (depression angle) between the optical axis of each camera and the field plane.

3.4   Calculation of Multi-view Camera Parameters

Based on the shooting and viewing requirements described above, the parameters of the multi-view camera such as the number of cameras, position and posture, angle of view, and resolution are calculated. The number of cameras is obtained from the observation viewpoint movement range and the convergence angle. A vector (camera posture) from the shooting point to the center of each camera is calculated using the observation viewpoint movement range, convergence angle, and depression angle. The optical axis of each camera is obtained from the shooting point and the camera pose vector, and the intersection of the optical axis and the 3D model is defined as the camera position. The angle of view, focal length, and resolution required for each camera are calculated from the shooting region, spatial resolution, and distance from the camera to the shooting point. As shown in Fig. 3, the calculated number of cameras and the focal length and resolution of each camera are displayed on the console of our developed interface.

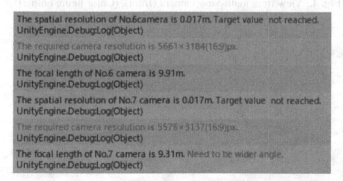

Fig. 3. Displayed information of focal length and resolution.

3.5   Visualization of Multi-view Camera Parameters

As shown in Fig. 2, camera icons are placed on the VR interface using the parameters of each camera calculated in the previous section. By changing the color of the camera icon, it is possible to easily check whether each camera satisfies the setting requirements. When the color is black, all requirements are satisfied. When blue, requirement on spatial resolution is not satisfied. When green, requirement on FoV is not satisfied. When red, the both requirements on spatial resolution and FoV are not satisfied.

A red line is placed as the line of sight from each camera to the shooting point. By visualizing the camera parameters, it is possible to grasp the location of the camera. In addition, as shown in Fig. 4 and Fig. 5, by rendering the appearance from the arranged multi-viewpoint camera based on the calculated camera parameters, it is possible to confirm multi-view images taken at installation; as well as the development of a free viewpoint video generation program using multi-view images without actually performing a shooting experiment on site. Our interface can display the image captured by the virtual camera by setting the position, orientation, and angle of view of the virtual camera to calculated values.

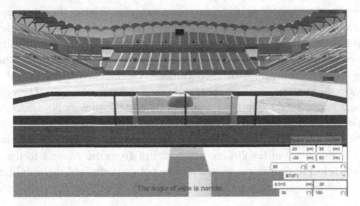

Fig. 4. View from multi-view camera (front). (Color figure online)

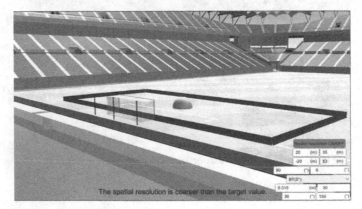

Fig. 5. View from multi-view camera (oblique). (Color figure online)

3.6 Visualization of Spatial Resolution

As shown in Fig. 6, the area where the spatial resolution on the field is high, is visually shown by dyeing in red. First, the field is divided into 0.1 m squares. Spatial resolution of each area is calculated from every camera based on focal length and the distance between the cameras and the divided area. If the area is observed by all cameras and the average spatial resolution of each camera is lower than a threshold, the area is colored in red. The display of the spatial resolution can be switched from the original field plane display by clicking the button on of our developed interface.

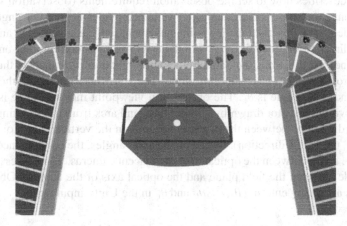

Fig. 6. Visualization of spatial resolution on the field. (Color figure online)

4 Collection of Information Required for Calculation

4.1 Stadium CAD Model

In addition to the CAD models used for stadium design and construction, real stadium models have been published on the web as materials for building VR spaces. In this research, we construct a space where shooting is planned by using these CAD models in the VR world. In this interface, the CAD model of the stadium is imported into Unity, and the horizontal and vertical directions of the stadium are parallel to the Unity coordinate x-axis and z-axis, respectively, and the center point of the field played by the players is arranged to overlap the origin of the xz coordinates.

4.2 Shooting Requirements

This section describes how to set the shooting requirements (shooting points, shooting range, and spatial resolution of the captured video). The shooting range is set as a rectangular area on the field. The size of the rectangular area is given by inputting the x-coordinate range and the z-coordinate range into the input window on the Unity screen.

If the range of x coordinate is x_1 to x_2 and the range of z coordinate is z_1 to z_2, the rectangle whose four vertices are (x_1, z_1), (x_1, z_2), (x_2, z_1) and (x_2, z_2) is the shooting range. The shooting point is the center of this rectangle, and the coordinates on the field are $(\frac{x_1+x_2}{2}, \frac{z_1+z_2}{2})$. For spatial resolution, the required input is the size (length) of a three-dimensional object that fits into one pixel of the captured image at the shooting point in the input window of Unity.

4.3   Observation Requirements

This section describes how to set the observation requirements (observation viewpoint movement range and observation angle (convergence angle/ depression angle) in the generated video). The observation viewpoint movement range is given as an angle when the positive direction of x is 0 degrees with the origin at the shooting point on the field plane (xz plane). At this time, the counterclockwise direction is defined as the positive direction of rotation, similar to the unit circle. The start (head) angle of the range is θ_s, and the end (tail) angle is θ_e. The observation viewpoint moving range is the area drawn by moving the sector drawn by straight lines and arcs from the shooting point in the θ_s and θ_e directions between the positive direction in the vertical direction of the xz plane (that is, the y-axis direction). Of the observation angles, the convergence angle θ_t is given as the angle between the optical axes of adjacent cameras. The depression angle θ_g is the angle between the field plane and the optical axis of the camera. Observation requirements are set by entering θ_s, θ_e, θ_t, and θ_g in the Unity input fields.

5   Calculate Camera Parameters

This section describes how to calculate camera parameters. First, the number of cameras n is obtained from the observation viewpoint movement range and the convergence angle using the following formula.

$$n = \left[\frac{\theta_e - \theta_s}{\theta_t} \right] \tag{1}$$

Next, the position and posture of the multi-view camera are obtained. The direction vector v_k of each camera is expressed by the following equation, assuming that the angle of each camera within the camera arrangement range is θ_k ($k = 1, 2, \ldots, n$).

$$v_k = \begin{pmatrix} \sin(90 - \theta_g) \cos \theta_k \\ \cos(90 - \theta_g) \\ \sin(90 - \theta_g) \sin \theta_k \end{pmatrix} \tag{2}$$

The straight line represented by the shooting point and the vector obtained by the above equation is the line of sight of each camera. The corresponding camera position is found as the intersection of the line of sight and the 3D model. In addition, the posture of the camera is determined by rotating the camera as a rotation matrix that rotates θ_k degrees to the left and tilts θ_g degrees from the ground, with setting the positive direction of x at 0 degree around the shooting point on the xz plane.

Finally, the angle of view and resolution of the camera is determined. The view angle θ_c of the camera is calculated as the smallest view angle in which a rectangular parallelepiped with a height of 5 m with the shooting range (rectangular area specified on the field) as the bottom face fits in the view. Assuming the angle of view θ_c, the specified spatial resolution s, and the distance L from the camera of interest to the shooting point, the resolution r of the camera is calculated by the following equation.

$$r = \frac{\theta_c}{arc \tan \frac{s}{L}} \tag{3}$$

6 Visualization of Spatial Resolution

This section describes a method for visualizing spatial resolution. Let S be one of the 0.1 m squares that divide the field plane. Let the center coordinate of S be (x_c, z_c) and let L be the distance from any camera C_k ($k = 1, 2, ..., n$) to coordinate (x_c, z_c). If the angle of view of C_k is α and the resolution is β; then, the spatial resolution R_k when S is captured from camera C_k is expressed by the following equation.

$$R_k = L \tan \frac{\alpha}{\beta} \tag{4}$$

The condition for coloring S red is expressed by the following equation.

$$\frac{\sum_1^n R_k}{n} < 0.015 \tag{5}$$

7 Implementation of VR Interface

This section describes a pilot system implemented to verify the utility of the proposed interface. The shooting range is specified by two xz coordinates as the shooting requirements. Also, the target spatial resolution is specified by numerical values. The observation viewpoint movement range and observation angle (convergence angle/ depression angle) are specified as observation requirements. The position where the first camera is to be placed is shown in Fig. 7, and the cameras are placed at equal intervals while expanding to the left and right to fit between the observation viewpoint movement ranges. Figure 8 shows an example of the input operation. When both requirements and the number of cameras in possession are set as the input, the camera parameters (camera position and posture) are automatically calculated, and output as camera icons on the 3D model, as shown in Fig. 9. The yellow point on the field indicates the shooting point, the area surrounded by the blue line indicates the shooting range, the red line indicates the line of sight of each camera; the camera icons with four colors indicates camera layout. In addition, as shown in Fig. 10, we can check the video shot from arranged virtual cameras. In this way, by visualizing the camera arrangement based on the input requirements, it is possible to examine the setup and procedures of the installation work in advance, resulting in the possible reduction of the labor and time required for determining the arrangement of multi-view cameras in a large-scale space.

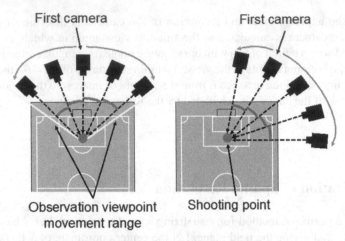

Fig. 7. Camera arrangement order.

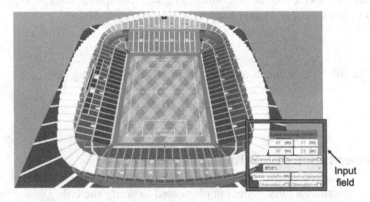

Fig. 8. Input operation on a 3D CG model of a soccer field.

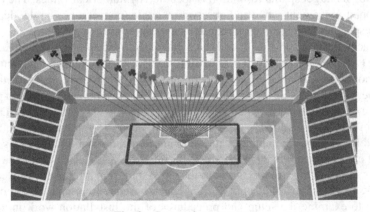

Fig. 9. Camera layout output

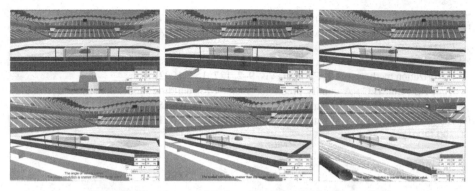

Fig. 10. View from multi-view camera (switching viewpoint)

8 Conclusion

This paper proposed a VR interface to support the preliminary consideration of multi-view camera arrangement in a large-scale space such as a sports stadium. Camera parameters that satisfy the requirements are automatically calculated from the shooting and observation requirements, and the results (camera arrangement) are presented in the VR space. It can be expected that the labor and time required to determine the arrangement of multi-view cameras can be reduced. Although, our proposed system virtually arranges multiple view-points and the captured images by VR cameras in the VR environment, our proposed interface does not well utilize an advantage of VR device such as 3D joystick and a head-mounted display (HMD). We are enhancing our system by using the VR device. For example, we extract shooting and viewing requirements by moving around a VR camera controlled by a 3D joystick. HMD which can display immersive view is also useful to observe the VR shooting environment. This work was supported by Grants-in-Aid for Scientific Research (17H01772).

References

1. Author, F.: Article title. Journal **2**(5), 99–110 (2016). Watanabe, T., Kitahara, I., Kameda, Y., Ota, Y.: Free-viewpoint video interface using both hands for accurate and intuitive camera operation. IEICE Trans. Electron. **DJ95-D**(3), 687–696 (2012)
2. Guillemaut, J.-Y., Hilton, A.: Joint multi-layer segmentation and reconstruction for free-viewpoint video applications. Int. J. Comput. Vis. **93**(1), 73–100 (2011)
3. Zhenhan, L., Shunta, S., Natuska, O., Yuji, I., Yuesong, Z.: Construction of urban design support system using cloud computing type virtual reality and case study. Int. Rev. Spat. Plann. Sustain. Dev. **5**(1), 15–28 (2017)
4. Choi, C., Kim, J., Han, H., Ahn, B., Kim, J.: Graphic and haptic modeling of the oesophagus for VR-Based medical simulation. Int. J. Med. Rob. Comput. Assist. Surg. **5**(3), 257–266 (2009)
5. Takano, et al.: Scenery simulation using VR about display. 3D Video Forum **8**(3), 48–54 (1994)
6. Xu, S., Song, P., Chua, G.G., Chin, C.L., Huang, Z., Rahardja, S.: Tennis space: an interactive and immersive environment for tennis simulation. In: Proceedings of the 5th International Conference on Image and Graphics, Xi'an, China (2009)

7. Suzuki, K., Shishido, H., Kameda, Y., Kitahara, I.: Interface for camerawork consideration for soccer free viewpoint video. In: Proceedings of the IPSJ Annual Conference, pp. 45–46 (2018)
8. Tomasi, C., Kanade, T.: Shape and motion from image streams under orthography: a factorization method. Int. J. Comput. Vis. **9–2**, 137–154 (1992)
9. You, R.J., Lin, B.C.: A quality prediction method for building model reconstruction using lidar data and topographic maps. IEEE Trans. Geosci. Remote Sens. **49**(9), 3471–3480 (2011)
10. Lange, R., Seits, P.: A Solid-state time-of flight range camera. IEEE J. Quantum Electron. **37**, 390 (2001)

Collaboration in Virtual and Augmented Reality: A Systematic Overview

Catlin Pidel[✉] and Philipp Ackermann

Zurich University of Applied Sciences, Zurich, Switzerland
{catlin.pidel,philipp.ackermann}@zhaw.ch

Abstract. This paper offers a systematic overview of collaboration in virtual and augmented reality, including an assessment of advantages and challenges unique to collaborating in these mediums. In an attempt to highlight the current landscape of augmented and virtual reality collaboration (AR and VR, respectively), our selected research is biased towards more recent papers (within the last 5 years), but older work has also been included when particularly relevant. Our findings identify a number of potentially under-explored collaboration types, such as asynchronous collaboration and collaboration that combines AR and VR. We finally provide our key takeaways, including overall trends and opportunities for further research.

Keywords: Augmented reality · Virtual reality · Collaboration

1 Introduction

The idea behind this paper is to better understand the current landscape of collaboration in augmented and virtual reality – to see what is working, what is not, and where further innovations can lead to improvements.

1.1 Types of Collaboration

For the purposes of this paper, collaboration can be broken down along two axes – synchronous versus asynchronous, and remote versus on-site. A task's synchronicity refers to *when* collaborators can make contributions (e.g. simultaneously or separately), whereas its locale (remote versus on-site) refers to *where* the collaborators are.

All possible combinations of these two dichotomies yield four types of collaboration, outlined below.

- **Synchronous and On-Site**: Collaborators are working together in realtime in the same physical space. Examples include social events, university lectures, and in-person meetings.

© Springer Nature Switzerland AG 2020
L. T. De Paolis and P. Bourdot (Eds.): AVR 2020, LNCS 12242, pp. 141–156, 2020.
https://doi.org/10.1007/978-3-030-58465-8_10

- **Synchronous and Remote**: Collaborators work together in real time, but not from the same physical location. Examples include video and phone conferencing, simultaneous document editing (such as with Google Docs), and live chat.
- **Asynchronous and Remote**: This covers many of today's go-to communication tools, such as messaging and email. Collaborators can work when and where is most convenient for them.
- **Asynchronous and On-Site**: A less common type of collaboration where the location itself is important, but collaborators do not need to be present at the same time. More physically focused projects, such as a construction site with workers on different shifts, fit this definition.

Each of these collaboration types come with tradeoffs. Asynchronous and remote tools, such as email, allow for quick and easy dissemination of information. This very characteristic also makes them prone to informational overload and miscommunication [24], however, especially so when users are juggling several accounts [14]. Alternatively, in-person meetings are less prone to distractions and confusion, but finding a time and place can quickly become an intractable problem. Our goal is to understand these types of collaboration through the lens of virtual and augmented reality, as well as any technology-specific tradeoffs.

1.2   Paper Structure

This paper categorizes relevant work into the aforementioned four categories. However, it is important to note that collaboration can transition rather fluidly between these states. Google Docs works as both a synchronous and asynchronous collaboration tool, for example. Similarly, meetings often contain a mixture of co-located and telecommuting participants, thus muddying the waters between "on-site" and "remote". As such, relevant products and research rarely fit neatly into a singular category, so different aspects of papers may be mentioned in multiple sections.

For each section, related work is broken down by whether it applies to VR, AR, or AR/VR-Mixed collaboration. For the purposes of this paper, we define AR to be any computer-generated images overlaid onto the real world, whether a "flat" user interfaces or 3D objects. The latter is sometimes referred to as *mixed reality* (MR). The VR and AR sections cover head-mounted displays (HMDs), as well as mobile and desktop experiences. These experiences may take place entirely in one technology (VR/VR and AR/AR, respectively), or multiple mediums (e.g. AR and video conferencing). Finally, we have a "AR/VR-Mixed" category for collaboration that combines AR and VR.

1.3   Contributions

This paper surveys the current state of collaboration in virtual and augmented realities in both academia and industry.

2   Synchronous and Remote Collaboration

2.1   Synchronous, Remote, VR Collaboration

Cohabiting a virtual space despite physical distance is a classic use case for virtual reality. Of course, the types of interactions that fit these criteria are extremely varied, and the features required for each will vary with the context. Tools like Meetingroom.io [32] are optimized for more professional settings, whereas social collaboration may be more suited to experimental platforms, such as VRChat [56] and AltspaceVR [33]. Virtual reality conferencing affords more social interaction than video conferencing, such as the ability to organically break off into small groups, or interacting with virtual objects in the scene. For example, conducting a design review via VR conferencing allows participants to view and interact with 3D models more intuitively, as well as at real-world scale.

Multiplayer VR games is also a growing industry, with everyone from indie developers to AAA studios releasing titles. For example, "Star Trek: Bridge Crew" [55] and "Space Junkies" [54] are both multiplayer VR games from Ubisoft, an AAA gaming studio. And while many games and social spaces allow for participation via DesktopVR, a growing number require a head-mounted display (HMD), such as the desktop-tethered HTC Vive [22] or standalone Oculus Quest [17]. The market for VR is anticipated to grow even more with the release of 5G [43], so this is a particular area of opportunity.

In terms of research, one of the main factors in creating VR immersion is the idea of *presence* – the feeling of truly being in a space. A variety of metrics have been studied for their corresponding effect on presence, including the method of moving around in a virtual world [48] and the relative realism of a user's own avatar when looking in a virtual mirror [57]. Taking this idea a step further, then, a key component of a collaborative virtual experience is thus *co-presence*.

For example, how does a partner's avatar affect the feeling of connection between two VR collaborators? The feeling of trust? Jo et al. [25] did a number of experiments on how the realism of both an avatar and the surrounding environment affects feelings of co-presence and trust in a teleconference setting. They created cartoonized and photorealistic avatars for participants, and overlaid them onto a backdrop that was similarly cartoonized (3D reconstruction of office) or realistic (actual video feed of office). For clarity, the experimental setup is visually represented in Fig. 1 below. Their experiments showed that a realistic (AR) background created more presence, and a cartoon avatar created stronger co-presence than a realistic one. This is consistent with older work on the topic, showing that hyper-realistic avatars can create a loss of presence through Uncanny Valley [13]. However, when it

Test condition	Avatar type	Form of background
2DV (Baseline)	Conventional 2D video based	Conventional 2D video based
R-AR	Realistically reconstructed avatar	Real environment (video background)
C-AR	Character-like avatar	Real environment (video background)
R-VR	Realistically reconstructed avatar	3D Virtual environment
C-VR	Character-like avatar	3D Virtual environment

Fig. 1. All iterations of Jo et al.'s work to test how avatar realism affects co-presence and trust [25].

came to matters of trust, Jo et al. found realistic avatars to be more trustworthy in the eyes of participants. Given these opposing findings, the type of collaborative task (e.g. social versus professional collaboration) should help determine whether co-presence or trust is more important for the situation.

In fact, co-presence may not even be that important for some collaborative use cases. The context of a task – such as whether it's conversation- or task-based, social or professional, one-on-one or in a large group – will affect the requirements of a tool used for that purpose. As noted by Steed and Schroeder [50], realistic avatar gaze may be important for one-on-one conversations in virtual reality, but avatar distinctiveness is probably more important than realism when it comes to collaborating in large groups. Another study by Roth et al. explored how avatar realism affects performance on a verbal task, ultimately showing that the absence of certain social cues (such as eye contact and facial expressions) shifts the user's attention to other cues (such as tone of voice), and does not impede the task's execution [44]. Other findings have corroborated this, as well as showing that people will adjust their own behavior to compensate for technological limitations [50]. This includes compensations such as narrating movements when a user does not think their collaborator can see them, or exaggerating emotional tone if their avatar does not show facial expressions.

2.2 Synchronous, Remote, AR Collaboration

Augmented Reality (AR) technology using head-mounted displays (HMD) as well as handheld devices has been used as a tool for supporting collaboration, especially spatial problem solving and remote guidance. It allows for expert guidance from afar, such as for remote surgical consults [15] or remote maintenance [1,39]. One paper, by Kim et al. [27], explored how augmented reality markers can increase the efficiency of remote collaborators solving a tangram puzzle. Using SLAM-based tracking, the remote user was able to contribute spatial cues in addition to their voice, which correlated with significantly higher feelings of connectedness and co-presence for both local and remote participants.

2.3 Synchronous, Remote, AR/VR-Mixed Collaboration

A number of studies have found that AR and VR collaboration create better co-presence than traditional video conferencing [25,27], and a number of startups have built products based on this premise. Spatial [49], for example, allows collaboration to join a meeting via AR, VR, or desktop. Their promotional videos promise walls filled with virtual post-it notes and collaborators with photorealistic avatars. Along with these early-adopters, however, there are also critics. Some have argued that augmented or virtual conferencing is most likely unnecessary, even counter-productive, for most use cases, and that the expensiveness of the technology is not worth the purported improvement over traditional methods [16]. That said, Spatial recently announced a $14 million funding round, indicating not everyone shares this viewpoint [52]. There are also a number of enterprise AR solutions, such as Re'Flekt [41], that use desktop or tablet screens to collaborate with on-site AR workers. One opportunity for these tools would be to instead use VR scene reconstructions for remote collaborators. This could allow for more natural and clear collaboration than 2-dimensional arrows and circles.

Another interesting project is CoVAR [40], which experiments with realtime collaboration between a local user in AR and a remote user in a VR reconstruction of the local room. This setup allows for interesting applications, such as allowing the VR participant to drastically change their size relative to the room (e.g. "God Mode" and "Mini Mode"), which could have applications in both games and accessibility. Similarly, Zillner et al. [59] developed a SLAM-based method for incredibly accurate scene reconstruction (up to 1 cm precision) using a specialized headset. This could facilitate remote guidance in VR rather than from a desktop or tablet.

Finally, while not exactly combining AR and VR, Müller et al. [36] conducted a user study comparing performance between AR/AR and VR/VR configurations for distributed (and co-located, discussed in Sect. 5.3) collaboration using mobile devices. Their qualitative results found advantages and drawbacks of both approaches. The AR setup was helpful in avoiding collisions with real-world objects, while VR conversely was more prone to collisions. Some users also mentioned they were easily disoriented when they looked away from the screen during the VR experience (which was necessary to avoid tripping) because there was no visual pairing between the VR and actual worlds. On the other hand, AR struggled where VR excelled – AR collaborators could not reference a virtual object's location relative to their own physical space (despite being visually integrated with the task), but VR users benefitted from seeing the same (virtual) world. Despite these tradeoffs, there was no statistically significant difference between performance or users' mental workload for either condition, and user preference was evenly split between AR and VR. Based on these findings, the authors recommend *transitional interfaces* that go between AR and VR. This could be a compelling way for a single tool to leverage the relative benefits of AR and VR for different contexts.

3   Asynchronous and Remote Collaboration

3.1   Asynchronous, Remote, VR Collaboration

Virtual reality training sessions allow for expert knowledge to be transferred asynchronously and remotely. This has been used quite frequently in both military and medical sectors. Bhagat et al. found that using virtual reality for weapons firing training was more cost-effective, improved learning outcomes, and allowed for more individualized training (since the VR experience could keep track of students' metrics over time) [7]. There have also been multiple studies showing that VR simulations improve operating room performance across a variety of surgery types [45,53].That said, training sessions are only loosely collaborative in that the flow of information is, most often, one-way – one curated experience can disseminate information to a vast number of students, but the student has little to no affect on it.

For asynchronous collaboration between two or more virtual reality users, however, the pool of research is noticeably smaller. A 2013 chapter of Mental Health Informatics discussed the potential of asynchronous psychotherapy, which is currently gaining popularity with text-based therapy apps like BetterHelp [6], as well as VR applications to aid in treatment for a variety of illnesses, such as VR exposure therapy (VRE) for those with post-traumatic stress disorder (PTSD) or a particular phobia [30]. While not mentioned in this paper, a combination of VR-based, asynchronous therapy could be an interesting direction.

Another interesting application is the idea of an asynchronous, virtual classroom, as proposed by Morozov et al. [35]. Their system created a virtual classroom where each student could virtually attend a pre-recorded class, either by observing or re-recording the class with their own input (e.g. to class discussions). This allows for asynchronous class discussions that, though limited, could be an interesting way to encourage collaboration between in-person coursework and remote learners.

3.2 Asynchronous, Remote, AR Collaboration

Similar to virtual reality, there is little work on asynchronous, remote collaboration between multiple AR users. Given that AR is largely location-based, it makes sense that there would be limited use cases for remote (aka location-independent) augmented reality. One interesting example is the Blocks app, which explores co-creation between augmented and virtual reality in a variety of collaboration types, including asynchronous and remote scenarios [20]. While it does fall under the "asynchronous, remote AR" label, it also fits any of the other categories mentioned in this paper – the app allows users to collaboratively build sculptures with virtual blocks, and it's built to work synchronously, asynchronously, on-site, and remote in either AR or VR.

3.3 Asynchronous, Remote, AR/VR-Mixed Collaboration

While there are, again, few papers in this realm, there are use cases that could fit this sort of collaboration. For example, interior design generally requires at-home visits, but using augmented-reality room scanning, designers could design a room in VR that clients could review in their home using AR. This could allow for easier visualization for clients, and to give feedback on designs without needing a scheduled meeting.

4   Asynchronous and On-Site Collaboration

4.1   Asynchronous, On-Site, VR Collaboration

We have been unable to find products or papers that present a use case for this sort of VR collaboration. While some virtual reality experiences are location-dependent, such as in the case of Cave Automatic Virtual Environments (CAVE) experiences, we have found very little current research (since the year 2000) on collaboration in these types of spaces, and virtually nothing asynchronous in nature. While interesting research and use cases could exist outside our knowledge, we still do not find this area to be of very high priority for further research and development.

Applications that combine VR and AR are similarly sparse for this form of collaboration, so that subsection has been excluded from this section.

4.2 Asynchronous, On-Site, AR Collaboration

Augmented reality allows users to place labels to communicate important locations and/or information. This is particularly useful when collaborators need to relay information about a location (e.g. factory floor, shared apartment, construction site), but cannot do so in person. For example, Renevier and Nigay's MAGIC (Mobile Augmented Group Interaction in Context) project shows how AR can be used to label sites in an archaeological dig with important information, thus allowing for teams to work asynchronously [42]. Similarly, multiple papers have discussed various augmented-reality museum guides, allowing for visitors to interact and learn about exhibits at their own pace [18,21]. This is a particularly exciting area, since products like Microsoft's HoloLens [34] and Google's industry-rebranding of Glass [19] are making this sort of technology more accessible to the public.

AR collaboration can also move beyond simply placing markers, however. Irlitti et al. make the distinction between direct and passive interactions, arguing that the latter holds a lot of opportunity, despite the current lack of academic exploration [23]. In their paper, direct interactions are defined as information the user explicitly creates (e.g. markers), whereas passive interactions are information that can be collected by the application itself, such as the time spent at certain locations, or how a user moves through a space.

5 Synchronous and On-Site Collaboration

5.1 Synchronous, On-Site, VR Collaboration

Collocated VR comes with some challenges, such as avoiding collisions between users, and really only makes sense when collaborators need to directly interact with each other in a virtual world. That said, it also has some advantages over remote VR, such as the potential for offline and latency-free collaboration. It also allows the experience to rely on virtually-tracked props, which has been shown to aid in suspension of disbelief (provided the physical props are similar in texture and weight to their virtual representation), a practice sometimes called "substitutional reality" [47]. Seen in Fig. 2 below, this sort of physical/virtual mapping is already being seen on a commercial level with brick-and-mortar virtual reality centers, offering group activities such as VR adventure games and escape rooms designed specifically for the space.

Fig. 2. Example of a physical space mapped to a virtual world, from Simeone et al.'s work on Substitutional Reality [47].

An important research area of co-located VR is avoiding collisions when two or more users are occupying the tracking area. Especially if the virtual world is larger than the physical space, two users can physically collide despite being in different areas of the virtual world. Lacoche et al. experimented with different methods of displaying someone's physical location in VR, including two types of avatars and a "Safe Navigation Floor" (SNF) that highlighted the ground in green or red depending on whether the physical location was occupied or not. Their results showed fewer collisions with avatars relative to the SNF approach, and user sentiment also preferred this setup to the potentially safer approach of separating users into two individual, but smaller, tracking areas [28]. A similar study by Azmandian et al. experimented with redirected walking to prevent user collisions with positive results, though the degree of success was heavily influenced by the size and shape of the physical space [5].

Finally, there are some relevant collaborations that mix virtual reality and actual reality. The video game "Keep Talking and Nobody Explodes", for example, is a cooperative game where a player in VR needs to communicate information to their non-VR counterpart [51]. Another is a paper by Mai et al., which allows for communication between HMD- and non-HMD-wearing users through a shared surface. Cameras above a table allow for the VR participant to see images from the real world without having to remove their HMD, including video overlay of the other participants hands. In a user study using this shared surface, the non-VR participant needed to explain a series of steps to the VR participant, and the presence of hands halved the number of clarifying questions needed to complete the task [31]. While these are not true VR-to-VR collaborations, they are good examples of highly-collaborative interactions that rely heavily on VR.

5.2   Synchronous, On-Site, AR Collaboration

Early research, such as Billinghurst's Shared Space experiment [11], showed the potential for augmented reality to enhance face-to-face communication by combining the task space (such as a computer screen or 3D model) with the collaboration space (face-to-face communication) [9,10]. Today, multi-user AR has become much more common, with popular apps like Pokemon Go [37], and AR development kits from both Google and Apple that simplify the creation of AR apps. Apple's ARKit, for example, makes it quite easy for iOS developers to get realtime, multi-user AR up and running [2]. This technology was featured in the form of a competitive AR slingshot game during the WWDC18 keynote [3].

Augmented reality collaboration has also been used for art exhibitions. Artechouse, a Washington-DC-based experimental art studio, frequently incorporates both phone- and projector-based augmented reality into their exhibits [4].

A particularly interesting example of synchronous AR collaboration is CARS (Collaborative Augmented Reality for Socialization) developed by Zhang et al. [58]. It allows for information to be shared between nearby phones, allowing for lower latency as well as leveraging the computing power of multiple devices to create higher quality AR experiences. While this is a framework rather than an standalone product, it could improve the experience of future AR mobile applications.

5.3   Synchronous, On-Site, AR/VR-Mixed Collaboration

This is another section where research is, perhaps intentionally, sparse. Collaboration between augmented and virtual reality users occupying the same physical space would require a very specific use case. One such use case is the work by Billinghurst et al. to create a "Magic Book" [8]. The book, which looks like a normal children's book, uses image recognition and an HMD to superimpose virtual objects that "pop off" the page. These scenes can then be "entered" and the glasses transition from AR to VR mode for a first-person view of the scene. Multiple readers can enjoy a story together, creating a very interesting collaborative experience – users in VR mode are represented as avatars in the scene and visible by fellow VR collaborators, and also from a "bird's eye view" to those still in AR mode. Other research has explored transitioning between VR and a workstation environment [26], which could aid in collaboration, but the paper was not explicitly collaborative in focus. While fascinating, it's also worth noting that these prior examples were all published at least 10 years ago, so there's room for more research with more current technologies. We have been unable to find research on collaboration in mixed realities, other than the Blocks app mentioned in Sect. 3.2.

That said, there has been research comparing AR/AR and VR/VR configurations for co-located (and distributed, discussed in Sect. 2.3) collaborative tasks [36]. In this paper, Müller et al. conduct an analysis of a turn-based matching game, comparing quantitative performance and qualitative user preferences between the configurations. VR showed a slight, but significant decrease in the number of trials to solve the task, but there was otherwise no significant performance difference between the AR and VR scenarios. Qualitatively, participants' preference was fairly evenly split between AR and VR, but their opinions were strongly held. Those who preferred AR said it was helpful to see their collaborator on the screen, and thus easier to coordinate. Fans of VR found AR distracting, and thought the "tidiness" of VR made it more immersive and easier to focus. One way to address these strong but opposing preferences would be to allow users to switch fluidly AR and VR – a term Müller et al. refer to as *transitional reality*.

6   Additional Research of Note

This section covers related work that does not otherwise fit into one of our predefined categories, but is still relevant to AR/VR collaboration.

Being able to direct a user's attention is incredibly important for collaboration, regardless of the type. Synchronous collaboration requires getting collaborators attention, and asynchronous collaboration needs to represent changes since the last time a user was in a virtual environment. In the realm of AR, Biocca et al. developed an AR "attention funnel" that uses a chain of successively smaller rectangles to direct a user's gaze to a specified point, even if it's outside their current field of view [12]. VR also had a number of papers, especially related to directing attention in 360° video. One study by the BBC showed that a combination of audio and visual cues (in this case, a sound coming from the out-of-frame location, followed by a person in-frame walking towards the sound) was most successful at guiding a user's attention [46]. Another compared a similar situation (a firefly flying toward the target location) with forcibly rotating the video to display the relevant area, but neither showed any significant difference from the control condition (no guidance) [38].

Another interesting question is how to define "remote collaboration". In our research, we define it as two or more parties in separate physical locations. However, distance between collaborators is more than just geographical distance, as illustrated by the Virtual Distance metric developed by Dr. Karen Sobel Lojeski [29]. In addition to physical distance, it also encompasses a wide variety of factors, such as cultural and emotional distance, that can impede productivity between collaborators. While this paper uses the more binary definition of "remote work", it is important to note that not all distance can be bridged by faster computers or better immersive technology.

7   Discussion

Based on this literature review, we have identified four areas with little or no current research, as shown in Table 1.

We have also reflected on the unique tradeoffs to collaborating in augmented and virtual reality, and will outline a number of advantages and disadvantages based on our research and prior experience in augmented and virtual reality.

Benefits of Collaboration in Virtual and Augmented Reality

- Being able to collaborate independently in both time and space gives freedom, but also increases the user's mental load. Similar to multiple versions of a co-edited document, there can be "save points" in AR/VR time, which have potential to be both useful and confusing. This area is currently under explored, and could benefit from further research.
- Visualizations and other immersive experiences make it easier to communicate a concept, meaning less reliance on people's imagination. This is especially helpful in areas like interior design and architecture.

Table 1. Summary of topics discussed in this paper. There are four areas that are currently under explored.

	Synchronous	Asynchronous
Remote	**VR:** Social and gaming experiences [32, 33, 54, 55, 56], 5G facilitating VR [43], presence/co-presence [13, 25, 44, 48, 50, 57], compensating for missing social cues, Blocks app [20].	**VR:** VR training (military, medical) [7, 45, 53], VR exposure therapy and other therapeutic applications [6, 30],"vacademia" virtual classroom [35], Blocks app [20].
	AR: Tangram-puzzle collaboration [27], remote guidance [1, 15, 39], Blocks app [20].	**AR:** Limited existing work (other than Blocks app [20]).
	AR/VR-Mixed: VR/AR have better co-presence than video [25, 27], MR conferencing [16, 41, 49, 52], CoVAR [40], hyper-accurate scene reconstruction for remote guidance [59] , Blocks app [20].	**AR/VR-Mixed:** Limited existing work (other than Blocks app [20]).
On-Site	**VR:** Substitutional reality [47], avoiding collisions [5, 28], "Keep Talking and Nobody Explodes" [51], Shared Surfaces [31], Blocks app [20].	**VR:** Limited existing work (other than Blocks app [20]).
	AR: Shared Space [11], task vs. collaboration space [9, 10], games [3, 37], ARKit [2], art exhibitions [4], CARS framework [58], Blocks app [20].	**AR:** MAGIC (tool for annotating archeological dig sites) [42], AR museum guides [18, 21], collaboration by tracking passive information (e.g. how someone moves through a space) [23].
	AR/VR-Mixed: Magic Book [8], work-space/VR transitional headset [26], Blocks app [20], transitional reality [26].	**AR/VR-Mixed:** Limited existing work (other than Blocks app [20]).

- A truly engaging, immersive AR/VR experience could dramatically improve the quality of remote collaboration, and companies like Spatial are already working towards that end. However, avatar quality is a limiting factor to co-presence. They are often too cartoonish for business purposes, or photorealstic to the point of verging on Uncanny Valley. Commercially available avatars that realistically mimic users' expressions (e.g. gaze, mouth movement) would be a game-changer, though this is reliant on both software and hardware improvements.
- Virtual and augmented reality allow for viewing things from a different user's perspective. For example, being able to see a room through a color blindness filter, or adjusting a user's height to view a space from a child's height. This could be used advantageously for empathy training, as well as a new method of accessibility testing in architecture and design.

Challenges Facing Collaboration in Virtual and Augmented Reality

- Expensive and rapidly evolving technology limits who can participate. This is a problem both from an equality as well as a market size standpoint. Mobile augmented reality with smartphones and consumer-oriented virtual reality headsets are still the most easily accessible.

- Motion sickness and eye fatigue are ongoing problems, further limiting the potential audience for VR and AR applications.
- In teleconferencing settings, the additional complexity of virtual or augmented reality meetings translates to more points for system or user error. There is only so much technical literacy that can be assumed of the average consumer. This will of course increase with time and exposure, but it could lead to lower adoption due to frustration.
- Rapidly changing technology as well as a large variety of platforms (Oculus, Vive, Cardboard, WebVR, mobile, etc) can substantially increase development overhead for a cross-platform application, and focusing on only one platform significantly limits the potential audience.
- A single collaborative task may require several mediums, such as switching between face-to-face discussion, viewing slides or a 3D model, and taking notes. Especially in virtual reality, these sorts of context switches often require taking a bulky headset on and off, which can interrupt the flow of work.
- There's currently no industry standard for drawing someone's attention to something outside their field of vision. This is especially important for asynchronous collaboration – how can we alert the user that something has changed since the last time they were in a virtual/augmented space?

7.1   Conclusions

Virtual and augmented reality collaboration have made some compelling advancements in recent years, but there's still plenty of room for improvement and further exploration. Asynchronous collaboration, for example – whether in augmented or virtual, remote or on-site settings – is particularly under explored. This paper identifies four areas of opportunity, as outlined in Table 1, all of which fall under the asynchronous category. Experiences that combine virtual and augmented reality are also relatively rare, and could benefit from further work.

Based on these findings, the authors propose a number of potential topics for further study. In the vein of asynchronous collaboration, there is relatively little work into how to represent changes to a virtual world – similar to how changes are highlighted in Github, how can changes by one collaborator be represented to another, asynchronous collaborator? While implementation may vary by use case, this seems to be a limiting factor to asynchronous collaborative experiences. For AR/VR-Mixed research, opportunities include applications with both AR and VR participants, as well as transitional interfaces that would allows a single participant to go between virtual and augmented experiences. Ultimately, augmented and virtual collaboration hold a lot of potential, which we hope to explore further in future work.

References

1. Adcock, M., Gunn, C.: Annotating with 'sticky' light for remote guidance. In: ACM SIGGRAPH ASIA 2010 Posters, p. 1 (2010)

2. Apple Inc.: Creating a multiuser AR experience (2020). https://developer.apple.com/documentation/arkit/creating_a_multiuser_ar_experience
3. Apple Inc.: Swiftshot: Creating a game for augmented reality (2020). https://developer.apple.com/documentation/arkit/swiftshot_creating_a_game_for_augmented_reality
4. Artechouse: Artechouse (2019). https://www.artechouse.com/
5. Azmandian, M., Grechkin, T., Rosenberg, E.S.: An evaluation of strategies for two-user redirected walking in shared physical spaces. In: 2017 IEEE Virtual Reality (VR), pp. 91–98. IEEE (2017)
6. BetterHelp: Betterhelp (2020). https://www.betterhelp.com/
7. Bhagat, K.K., Liou, W.K., Chang, C.Y.: A cost-effective interactive 3D virtual reality system applied to military live firing training. Virtual Reality **20**(2), 127–140 (2016)
8. Billinghurst, M., Cambell, S., Poupyrev, I., Kato, K.T.H., Chinthammit, W., Hendrickson, D.: Magic book: exploring transitions in collaborative AR interfaces. In: Proceedings of SIGGRAPH, p. 87 (2000)
9. Billinghurst, M., Belcher, D., Gupta, A., Kiyokawa, K.: Communication behaviors in colocated collaborative AR interfaces. Int. J. Hum.-Comput. Interact. **16**(3), 395–423 (2003)
10. Billinghurst, M., Kato, H.: Collaborative augmented reality. Commun. ACM **45**(7), 64–70 (2002)
11. Billinghurst, M., Weghorst, S., Furness, T.: Shared space: an augmented reality approach for computer supported collaborative work. Virtual Reality **3**(1), 25–36 (1998)
12. Biocca, F., Tang, A., Owen, C., Xiao, F.: Attention funnel: omnidirectional 3D cursor for mobile augmented reality platforms. In: Proceedings of the SIGCHI Conference on Human Factors in Computing Systems, pp. 1115–1122 (2006)
13. Brenton, H., Gillies, M., Ballin, D., Chatting, D.: The uncanny valley: does it exist and is it related to presence. Presence connect (2005)
14. Cecchinato, M.E., Sellen, A., Shokouhi, M., Smyth, G.: Finding email in a multi-account, multi-device world. In: Proceedings of the 2016 CHI Conference on Human Factors in Computing Systems, pp. 1200–1210 (2016)
15. Davis, M.C., Can, D.D., Pindrik, J., Rocque, B.G., Johnston, J.M.: Virtual interactive presence in global surgical education: international collaboration through augmented reality. World Neurosurg. **86**, 103–111 (2016)
16. Dice: Augmented reality collaboration is real. avoid it like the plague (2019). https://insights.dice.com/2019/01/25/augmented-reality-collaboration/
17. Facebook Technologies, LLC: Oculus quest (2020). https://www.oculus.com/quest/?locale=en_US
18. Fenu, C., Pittarello, F.: Svevo tour: the design and the experimentation of an augmented reality application for engaging visitors of a literary museum. Int. J. Hum. Comput. Stud. **114**, 20–35 (2018)
19. Google: Glass (2019). https://www.google.com/glass/
20. Guo, A., Canberk, I., Murphy, H., Monroy-Hernández, A., Vaish, R.: Blocks: collaborative and persistent augmented reality experiences. Proc. ACM Interact. Mob. Wearable Ubiquitous Technol. **3**(3), 1–24 (2019)
21. Hammady, R., Ma, M., Temple, N.: Augmented reality and gamification in heritage museums. In: Marsh, T., Ma, M., Oliveira, M.F., Baalsrud Hauge, J., Göbel, S. (eds.) JCSG 2016. LNCS, vol. 9894, pp. 181–187. Springer, Cham (2016). https://doi.org/10.1007/978-3-319-45841-0_17

22. HTC Corporation: HTC Vive (2020). https://www.vive.com/eu/
23. Irlitti, A., Smith, R.T., Von Itzstein, S., Billinghurst, M., Thomas, B.H.: Challenges for asynchronous collaboration in augmented reality. In: 2016 IEEE International Symposium on Mixed and Augmented Reality (ISMAR-Adjunct), pp. 31–35. IEEE (2016)
24. Jackson, T.W., van den Hooff, B.: Understanding the factors that effect information overload and miscommunication within the workplace. J. Emerg. Trends Comput. Inf. Sci. **3**(8), 1240–1252 (2012)
25. Jo, D., Kim, K.H., Kim, G.J.: Effects of avatar and background types on users' co-presence and trust for mixed reality-based teleconference systems. In: Proceedings the 30th Conference on Computer Animation and Social Agents, pp. 27–36 (2017)
26. Kijima, R., Ojika, T.: Transition between virtual environment and workstation environment with projective head mounted display. In: Proceedings of IEEE 1997 Annual International Symposium on Virtual Reality, pp. 130–137. IEEE (1997)
27. Kim, S., Lee, G., Sakata, N., Billinghurst, M.: Improving co-presence with augmented visual communication cues for sharing experience through video conference. In: 2014 IEEE International Symposium on Mixed and Augmented Reality (ISMAR), pp. 83–92. IEEE (2014)
28. Lacoche, J., Pallamin, N., Boggini, T., Royan, J.: Collaborators awareness for user cohabitation in co-located collaborative virtual environments. In: Proceedings of the 23rd ACM Symposium on Virtual Reality Software and Technology, pp. 1–9 (2017)
29. Lojeski, K.S.: Virtual Distance^{TM}: A proposed model for the study of virtual work. Stevens Institute of Technology (2006)
30. Maghazil, A., Yellowlees, P.: Novel approaches to clinical care in mental health: from asynchronous telepsychiatry to virtual reality. In: Lech, M., Song, I., Yellowlees, P., Diederich, J. (eds.) Mental Health Informatics. SCI, vol. 491, pp. 57–78. Springer, Heidelberg (2014). https://doi.org/10.1007/978-3-642-38550-6_4
31. Mai, C., Bartsch, S.A., Rieger, L.: Evaluating shared surfaces for co-located mixed-presence collaboration. In: Proceedings of the 17th International Conference on Mobile and Ubiquitous Multimedia, pp. 1–5. ACM (2018)
32. meethingRoom.io: Virtual meeting rooms (2019). https://meetingroom.io/the-virtual-meeting-rooms-product/
33. Microsoft: Altspacevr (2020). https://altvr.com/
34. Micrsoft: Hololens 2: A new vision for computing (2020). https://www.microsoft.com/en-us/hololens/
35. Morozov, M., Gerasimov, A., Fominykh, M., Smorkalov, A.: Asynchronous immersive classes in a 3D virtual world: extended description of vAcademia. In: Gavrilova, M.L., Tan, C.J.K., Kuijper, A. (eds.) Transactions on Computational Science XVIII. LNCS, vol. 7848, pp. 81–100. Springer, Heidelberg (2013). https://doi.org/10.1007/978-3-642-38803-3_5
36. Müller, J., Zagermann, J., Wieland, J., Pfeil, U., Reiterer, H.: A qualitative comparison between augmented and virtual reality collaboration with handheld devices. In: Proceedings of Mensch und Computer 2019, pp. 399–410 (2019)
37. Niantic Inc.: Pokemon go (2020). https://pokemongolive.com/en/
38. Nielsen, L.T., et al.: Missing the point: an exploration of how to guide users' attention during cinematic virtual reality. In: Proceedings of the 22nd ACM Conference on Virtual Reality Software and Technology, pp. 229–232 (2016)
39. Palmarini, R., Erkoyuncu, J.A., Roy, R., Torabmostaedi, H.: A systematic review of augmented reality applications in maintenance. Robot. Comput.-Integr. Manuf. **49**, 215–228 (2018)

40. Piumsomboon, T., Lee, Y., Lee, G., Billinghurst, M.: Covar: a collaborative virtual and augmented reality system for remote collaboration. In: SIGGRAPH Asia 2017 Emerging Technologies, pp. 1–2 (2017)
41. Re'flekt GmbH: Re'flekt (2019). https://www.reflekt.com/de/
42. Renevier, P., Nigay, L.: Mobile collaborative augmented reality: the augmented stroll. In: Little, M.R., Nigay, L. (eds.) EHCI 2001. LNCS, vol. 2254, pp. 299–316. Springer, Heidelberg (2001). https://doi.org/10.1007/3-540-45348-2_25
43. Rogers, S.: 2019: The year virtual reality gets real (2019). https://www.forbes.com/sites/solrogers/2019/06/21/2019-the-year-virtual-reality-gets-real/
44. Roth, D., et al.: Avatar realism and social interaction quality in virtual reality. In: 2016 IEEE Virtual Reality (VR), pp. 277–278. IEEE (2016)
45. Seymour, N.E., et al.: Virtual reality training improves operating room performance: results of a randomized, double-blinded study. Ann. Surg. **236**(4), 458 (2002)
46. Sheikh, A., Brown, A., Watson, Z., Evans, M.: Directing attention in 360-degree video (2016)
47. Simeone, A.L., Velloso, E., Gellersen, H.: Substitutional reality: using the physical environment to design virtual reality experiences. In: Proceedings of the 33rd Annual ACM Conference on Human Factors in Computing Systems, pp. 3307–3316 (2015)
48. Slater, M., Usoh, M., Steed, A.: Taking steps: the influence of a walking technique on presence in virtual reality. ACM Trans. Comput.-Hum. Interact. (TOCHI) **2**(3), 201–219 (1995)
49. Spatial Systems Inc: Spatial: Collaborate anywhere in AR (2020). https://spatial.io/
50. Steed, A., Schroeder, R.: Collaboration in immersive and non-immersive virtual environments. In: Lombard, M., Biocca, F., Freeman, J., IJsselsteijn, W., Schaevitz, R.J. (eds.) Immersed in Media, pp. 263–282. Springer, Cham (2015). https://doi.org/10.1007/978-3-319-10190-3_11
51. Steel Crate Games Inc: Keep talking and nobody explodes (2018). https://keeptalkinggame.com/
52. TechCrunch: Spatial raises 14 million more for a holographic 3D workspace app, a VR/AR version of zoom or hangouts (2020). https://techcrunch.com/2020/01/30/spatial-raises-14m-more-for-a-holographic-3d-workspace-app-a-vr-ar-version-of-zoom-or-hangouts/
53. Thomsen, A.S.S.: Operating room performance improves after proficiency-based virtual reality cataract surgery training. Ophthalmology **124**(4), 524–531 (2017)
54. Ubisoft Entertainment: Space junkies (2017). https://www.ubisoft.com/en-us/game/space-junkies/
55. Ubisoft Entertainment: Star trek: Bridge crew puts you and your friends in the heart of a starship (2017). https://www.ubisoft.com/en-us/game/star-trek-bridge-crew/
56. VRChat Inc.: Vrchat (2020). https://www.vrchat.com/

57. Waltemate, T., Gall, D., Roth, D., Botsch, M., Latoschik, M.E.: The impact of avatar personalization and immersion on virtual body ownership, presence, and emotional response. IEEE Trans. Visual Comput. Graphics **24**(4), 1643–1652 (2018)
58. Zhang, W., Han, B., Hui, P., Gopalakrishnan, V., Zavesky, E., Qian, F.: Cars: collaborative augmented reality for socialization. In: Proceedings of the 19th International Workshop on Mobile Computing Systems & Applications, pp. 25–30 (2018)
59. Zillner, J., Mendez, E., Wagner, D.: Augmented reality remote collaboration with dense reconstruction. In: 2018 IEEE International Symposium on Mixed and Augmented Reality Adjunct (ISMAR-Adjunct), pp. 38–39. IEEE (2018)

A User Experience Questionnaire for VR Locomotion: Formulation and Preliminary Evaluation

Costas Boletsis[✉]

SINTEF Digital, Forskningsveien 1, 0373 Oslo, Norway
konstantinos.boletsis@sintef.no

Abstract. When evaluating virtual reality (VR) locomotion techniques, the user experience metrics that are used are usually either focused on specific experiential dimensions or based on non-standardised, subjective reporting. The field would benefit from a standard questionnaire for evaluating the general user experience of VR locomotion techniques. This paper presents a synthesised user experience questionnaire for VR locomotion, which is called the VR Locomotion Experience Questionnaire (VRLEQ). It comprises the Game Experience Questionnaire (GEQ) and the System Usability Scale (SUS) survey. The results of the VRLEQ's application in a comparative, empirical study ($n = 26$) of three prevalent VR locomotion techniques are described. The questionnaire's content validity is assessed at a preliminary level based on the correspondence between the questionnaire items and the qualitative results from the study's semi-structured interviews. VRLEQ's experiential dimensions' scoring corresponded well with the semi-structured interview remarks and effectively captured the experiential qualities of each VR locomotion technique. The VRLEQ results facilitated and quantified comparisons between the techniques and enabled an understanding of how the techniques performed in relation to each other.

Keywords: Locomotion · Questionnaire · User experience · Virtual reality

1 Introduction

Virtual reality (VR) locomotion is an essential interaction component of navigation in VR environments [11,17]. Since the early days of VR, various locomotion techniques have been developed and studied to enable seamless and user-friendly navigation in virtual environments [9,11]. In recent years, major hardware-driven advances have had significant effects on how the users experience and use VR [6,38,46]. The technical and interaction progress in the new era of VR have also marked a new era for VR locomotion [6]. As a result, new locomotion techniques have been developed, and past ones have been significantly updated [6].

VR locomotion techniques are evaluated by testing in different environments that involve a variety of tasks and various user experience (UX) metrics.

© Springer Nature Switzerland AG 2020
L. T. De Paolis and P. Bourdot (Eds.): AVR 2020, LNCS 12242, pp. 157–167, 2020.
https://doi.org/10.1007/978-3-030-58465-8_11

The Locomotion Usability Test Environment (LUTE) [40] addresses the need for a standard testing environment to evaluate different locomotion techniques. It also helps analyse and identify the techniques that work better for different tasks. Regarding UX metrics for VR locomotion, the metrics that are used are either focused on specific experiential dimensions, such as the Presence Questionnaire [50] and the Slater-Usoh-Steed Questionnaire [45] for presence [8, 44], and the Simulator Sickness Questionnaire [19] for motion sickness [14, 32, 44], or based on non-standardised, subjective reporting [22, 23, 32, 36, 43]. A standard questionnaire for evaluating the general UX performance of VR locomotion techniques would help researchers and practitioners produce and communicate UX results within a consistent and shared framework.

This work presents a synthesised UX questionnaire for VR locomotion, consisting of the Game Experience Questionnaire (GEQ) [18] and the System Usability Scale (SUS) survey [12], hereafter called the VR Locomotion Experience Questionnaire (VRLEQ). The results of the VRLEQ's application in a comparative, empirical study of three prevalent VR locomotion techniques are also presented. Finally, a preliminary assessment of the questionnaire's content validity is performed based on the correspondence between the questionnaire items and the qualitative results from the study's semi-structured interviews. Researchers and practitioners in the field of VR and VR locomotion can benefit from this work by being introduced to a new UX metric tool specifically tailored for VR locomotion while getting specific instructions on how to apply it in their projects.

The rest of this paper is organised as follows. Section 2 provides the background relating to VRLEQ components. Section 3 describes VRLEQ, its formulation process (Sect. 3.1) and the results of its application (Sect. 3.2). Section 4 presents a preliminary evaluation of the tool's content validity. Section 5 discusses the results, the study limitations, and the future directions for VRLEQ's development.

2   Background

A paper by Boletsis and Cedergren [7] presented a comparative, empirical evaluation study of three prevalent VR locomotion techniques and their user experiences. They studied the following techniques:

- *Walking-in-place (WIP)*: The user performs virtual locomotion by walking in place, that is, using step-like movements while remaining stationary [6, 23].
- *Controller/joystick*: The user uses a controller to direct their movement in the virtual environment [6, 31].
- *Teleportation*: The user points to where they want to be in the virtual world, and the virtual viewpoint is instantaneously teleported to that position. The visual 'jumps' of teleportation result in virtual motion being non-continuous [6, 10, 11].

Walking-in-place (WIP), controller-based locomotion, and teleportation were used by 26 adults in order to perform a game-like task of locating four specific places (called checkpoints) in a virtual environment. The study employed a mixed-methods approach and used the synthesised VRLEQ questionnaire, consisting of the GEQ and SUS questionnaires, to quantitatively assess UX and semi-structured interviews to assess it qualitatively.

GEQ [18] is a user experience questionnaire that has been used in several domains, such as gaming, augmented reality, and location-based services, because of its ability to cover a wide range of experiential factors with good reliability [24,25,33–35]. The use of GEQ is also established in the VR aspects of navigation and locomotion [28,30], haptic interaction [1], VR learning [4], cyberpsychology [47], and gaming [42]. GEQ is administered after the session and asks the user to indicate how they felt during or after the session with a series of statements. The GEQ comes in different versions depending on the kind of experience the experimenter is trying to document. Apart from the core version (33 statements), there are in-game (14 statements), post-game (17 statements), and social-presence (17 statements) versions of the questionnaire. All GEQ versions cover UX dimensions such as Competence, Sensory and Imaginative Immersion, Flow, Tension, Challenge, Negative Affect, Positive Affect, et al.

SUS [12] allows usability practitioners and researchers to measure the subjective usability of products and services. In the VR domain, SUS has been utilised in several studies on topics such as VR rehabilitation and health services [20,27,29,39,49], VR learning [26], and VR training [16]. SUS is a 10-statement questionnaire that can be administered quickly and easily, and it returns scores ranging from 0 to 100. A SUS score above 68 is considered above average and that below 68 is considered below average [12]. SUS scores can also be translated into adjective ratings, such as 'worst imaginable', 'poor', 'OK', 'good', 'excellent', and 'best imaginable' and into grade scales ranging from A to F [5]. SUS has been demonstrated to be reliable and valid, robust with a small number of participants and to have the distinct advantage of being technology agnostic – meaning it can be used to evaluate a wide range of hardware and software systems [12,13,21,48]. Apart from the original SUS survey, there is also a positively worded version that is equally reliable as the original one [41].

3   VR Locomotion Experience Questionnaire

3.1   Questionnaire Formulation

Statements and Dimensions: The VRLEQ (Table 1) utilises all the dimensions and respective statements of the in-game GEQ version, that is, Competence, Sensory and Imaginative Immersion, Flow, Tension, Challenge, Negative Affect, Positive Affect, along with the dimension of Tiredness and statements relating to it from the post-game GEQ version. For the in-game GEQ statements (i.e., statements 1–14 in Table 1), the VRLEQ asks the user "Please indicate how you felt while navigating in VR". For the Tiredness dimension (i.e., statements 15–16 in Table 1) the VRLEQ asks "Please indicate how you felt after you finished navigating in VR". The in-game GEQ version was chosen because of its brevity compared to the core version (14 versus 33 statements, respectively), the coverage of the same UX dimensions as the core GEQ and its good reliability. Its

Table 1. The VRLEQ statements and the experiential dimensions they address.

#	Statement	Dimension
1.	I was interested in the task	Immersion
2.	I felt successful	Competence
3.	I felt bored	Negative Affect
4.	I found it impressive	Immersion
5.	I forgot everything around me	Flow
6.	I felt frustrated	Tension
7.	I found it tiresome	Negative Affect
8.	I felt irritable	Tension
9.	I felt skilful	Competence
10.	I felt completely absorbed	Flow
11.	I felt content	Positive Affect
12.	I felt challenged	Challenge
13.	I had to put a lot of effort into it	Challenge
14.	I felt good	Positive Affect
15.	I felt exhausted	Tiredness
16.	I felt weary	Tiredness
17.	I think that I would like to use this VR navigation technique frequently	Perceived Usability
18.	I found the VR navigation technique unnecessarily complex	Perceived Usability
19.	I thought the VR navigation technique was easy to use	Perceived Usability
20.	I think that I would need the support of a technical person to be able to use this VR navigation technique	Perceived Usability
21.	I found the various functions in this VR navigation technique were well integrated	Perceived Usability
22.	I thought there was too much inconsistency in this VR navigation technique	Perceived Usability
23.	I would imagine that most people would learn to use this VR navigation technique very quickly	Perceived Usability
24.	I found the VR navigation technique very cumbersome to use	Perceived Usability
25.	I felt very confident using the VR navigation technique	Perceived Usability
26.	I needed to learn a lot of things before I could get going with this VR navigation technique	Perceived Usability

smaller size is preferable so that responders do not get frustrated or exhausted or impatient from a long survey, especially after an immersive VR experience and during a comparative study of VR locomotion techniques where several applications of the VRLEQ (one per technique) would be necessary. Tiredness was considered an appropriate post-session dimension to capture since fatigue is considered a major challenge for VR locomotion [2,37] that would not be fully or clearly covered by the other negative dimensions of the in-game GEQ (e.g. Tension, Negative Affect, Challenge). The original SUS survey adds the dimension of Perceived Usability to the VRLEQ. For the SUS statements (i.e., statements 17–26 in Table 1), the user is asked "Please check the box that reflects your immediate response to each statement." The phrasing of several statements of the GEQ and SUS were modified so that they address VR locomotion and are easily understandable by users with varying knowledge (e.g., "VR navigation" was used instead of "VR locomotion").

Scales and Scoring: VRLEQ uses the scales and the scoring of the original GEQ and SUS questionnaires. The GEQ statements of the VRLEQ (i.e., statements 1–16 in Table 1) were rated on a five-point Likert scale of 0 (not at all), 1 (slightly), 2 (moderately), 3 (fairly), and 4 (extremely). Then, the average score per dimension was calculated and scaled between 0 and 4. The SUS statements of the VRLEQ (i.e., statements 17–26 in Table 1) were also rated on a five-point Likert scale of 0 (strongly disagree), 1 (disagree), 2 (neutral), 3 (agree), and 4 (strongly agree). The scores associated with the negative statements 18, 20, 22, 24, and 26 (in Table 1) should be inverted; therefore, their points were subtracted from 4. The points associated with the positive statements 17, 19, 21, 23, and 25 were not altered. This scaled all values from 0 to 4. Then, all points from the 10 statements were added and multiplied by 2.5, which converted the range of possible values from 0 to 100.

3.2 Application and Results

Twenty-six participants ($n = 26$, mean age: 25.96, SD: 5.04, male/female: 16/10) evaluated the three VR locomotion techniques by filling out the VRLEQ questionnaire and through interviews. The VRLEQ results are shown in Fig. 1. GEQ dimensions' scores are plotted on the same scale as the SUS scores (Perceived Usability), that is, scaled between 0 and 100, for clearer visualisation.

The non-parametric Friedman test was used to detect differences between the techniques' performances. It showed statistically significant differences in the scores of: Competence ($X^2(2) = 16.455, p < 0.001$), Immersion ($X^2(2) = 6.099, p = 0.047$), Challenge ($X^2(2) = 34.587, p < 0.001$), Negative Affect ($X^2(2) = 15.459, p < 0.001$), Tiredness ($X^2(2) = 23.011, p < 0.001$), and Perceived Usability ($X^2(2) = 16.340, p < 0.001$). The Friedman test indicated no statistically significant differences in the Flow, Tension, and Positive Affect components between the three techniques.

4 Evaluation

In this section, the content validity assessment of the synthesised VRLEQ is presented. This helped assess whether the VRLEQ represents all facets of UX for VR locomotion. Content validity can be assessed through literature reviews, expert opinions, population sampling, and qualitative research [3,15], the latter being the case herein. The interview remarks by the VR locomotion users of the three techniques are used as groundtruth. Then, the correspondence between the

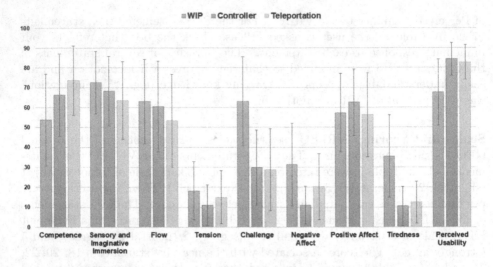

Fig. 1. Mean VRLEQ values (with standard deviation bars) across the experiential dimensions. GEQ values are scaled from 0 to 100 (i.e. values multiplied by 25) for uniform visualisation.

test items (i.e., VRLEQ dimensions) and the interview remarks was examined (Table 2). The VRLEQ and the semi-structured interviews evaluated UX at two different levels. The former provided an overview of UX performance and the latter provided specific insights in addition to a general overview.

During the semi-structured interviews, participants were asked about what they liked and did not like about the evaluated VR locomotion techniques and why. The interviewer followed up on the participants' comments until each topic was covered. In the end, the interview responses were coded by two researchers. The inter-rater reliability showed high agreement.

5   Conclusion

Table 2 shows that the VRLEQ dimensions' scoring corresponded well with the semi-structured interview remarks and captured and reflected the experiential qualities of each VR locomotion technique. In our assessment, VRLEQ documented all facets of the VR locomotion techniques' UX performance and demonstrated satisfactory content validity. Moreover, the VRLEQ results facilitated and quantified the comparisons between the techniques and illuminated how the techniques performed in relation to each other. When these results are combined with the related results from interviews, then the experimenter can potentially pinpoint the interaction strengths and weaknesses of the techniques that impacted the experiential performance, thus collecting valuable information for future improvements. It is suggested that an interview like the one described above should be included following the use of VRLEQ since the interview addresses additional, specific issues of the technical and interaction kinds.

Table 2. Correspondence between the VRLEQ dimensions and the semi-structured interview remarks.

Interview remarks	Dimensions and scoring
–WIP–	
WIP offered high levels of Immersion owing to its natural and realistic way of moving	- Moderate-to-high Immersion - Moderate-to-high Flow
Many participants found that the translation of real body movement to VR motion made the technique tiresome	- Moderate-to-high Challenge - Moderate-to-high Negative Affect - Moderate-to-high Tiredness - "OK" Perceived Usability
Others found that the translation of real body movement to VR motion added a certain level of physical training, fun and entertainment	- Moderate-to-high Positive Affect
WIP caused fear of colliding with physical objects in real life and motion sickness, especially for novice VR users	- Low-to-moderate Tension - Moderate-to-high Challenge - Moderate-to-high Negative Affect - "OK" Perceived Usability
Participants were able to go on with the tasks despite their interaction difficulties	- Moderate Competence - "OK" Perceived Usability
–Controller–	
It was found to be easy-to-use and was characterised as "familiar", "intuitive", and "comfortable"	- Moderate-to-high Competence - Low-to-moderate Challenge - Moderate-to-high Positive Affect - "Excellent" Perceived Usability
It was reported that during the first seconds of use, the technique caused motion sickness. However, after a few seconds, the participants were able to adjust and master the technique	- Moderate-to-high Competence - Low-to-moderate Challenge - Low Tension - Low Negative Affect - Low Tiredness - "Excellent" Perceived Usability
The technique achieved satisfying levels of immersion for participants	- Moderate-to-high Immersion - Moderate-to-high Flow
–Teleportation–	
It was described as the least immersive of the three techniques, owing to its visual "jumps" and non-continuous movement	- Moderate Immersion - Moderate Flow
"Blinking" – the teleporting transition from one place of the virtual environment to another – made the technique tiresome and put extra strain on the participants' vision	- Moderate-to-high Challenge - Low-to-moderate Tension - Low-to-moderate Negative Affect - Low-to-moderate Tiredness
Participants found teleportation to be effective when time was of the essence for the task owing to its fast navigation	- High Competence - Moderate-to-high Positive Affect - Low-to-moderate Challenge - "Good" Perceived Usability
Using the method and mastering its interaction aspects were considered straight-forward and easy; the visual cues, i.e., the direction arc ray and the marker on the virtual ground, were clear and understandable	- High Competence - Moderate-to-high Positive Affect - Low-to-moderate Challenge - "Good" Perceived Usability

A UX questionnaire such as VRLEQ can answer the question "What is the effect that a VR locomotion technique has on UX?". The interview sheds more light on the "why" and reveals the specific factors that together form the UX performance.

Regarding the formulation and evaluation of VRLEQ in this paper, it is important to acknowledge the limitations. The evaluation is of a preliminary nature and based on qualitative comparisons. The small sample size does not assure reliable internal consistency and does not permit the construction of validity measurements. Moreover, the GEQ and SUS dimensions do not operate on the same conceptual UX level. Perceived Usability (SUS) exists at a higher level than the GEQ dimensions, and it contains sub-dimensions or sub-elements that are thematically relevant to those of the GEQ. This issue also arises when examining the relevant questions in both questionnaires (e.g., statements 9 and 25 in Table 1).

Accordingly, the future work on VRLEQ will: 1) include a larger sample size to enable reliable quantitative evaluation (reliability and validity), 2) develop a new UX model describing the relationship between the GEQ and SUS dimensions, 3) develop a shorter version of the VRLEQ by eliminating similar questions that measure the same dimension and 4) assess the reliability and validity of the shorter VRLEQ.

References

1. Ahmed, I., Harjunen, V., Jacucci, G., Hoggan, E., Ravaja, N., Spapé, M.M.: Reach out and touch me: effects of four distinct haptic technologies on affective touch in virtual reality. In: Proceedings of the 18th ACM International Conference on Multimodal Interaction, pp. 341–348. ACM (2016)
2. Albert, J., Sung, K.: User-centric classification of virtual reality locomotion. In: Proceedings of the 24th ACM Symposium on Virtual Reality Software and Technology, pp. 1–2 (2018)
3. Alumran, A., Hou, X.Y., Hurst, C.: Validity and reliability of instruments designed to measure factors influencing the overuse of antibiotics. J. Infection Public Health **5**(3), 221–232 (2012)
4. Apostolellis, P., Bowman, D.A.: Evaluating the effects of orchestrated, game-based learning in virtual environments for informal education. In: Proceedings of the 11th Conference on Advances in Computer Entertainment Technology, p. 4. ACM (2014)
5. Bangor, A., Kortum, P., Miller, J.: Determining what individual SUS scores mean: adding an adjective rating scale. J. Usability Stud. **4**(3), 114–123 (2009)
6. Boletsis, C.: The new era of virtual reality locomotion: a systematic literature review of techniques and a proposed typology. Multimodal Technol. Interact. **1**(4), 24:1–24:17 (2017)
7. Boletsis, C., Cedergren, J.E.: VR locomotion in the new era of virtual reality: an empirical comparison of prevalent techniques. In: Advances in Human-Computer Interaction 2019, pp. 7420781:1–7420781:15 (2019)
8. Borrego, A., Latorre, J., Llorens, R., Alcañiz, M., Noé, E.: Feasibility of a walking virtual reality system for rehabilitation: objective and subjective parameters. J. Neuroeng. Rehabil. **13**(1), 68 (2016)
9. Bowman, D., Kruijff, E., LaViola Jr., J.J., Poupyrev, I.P.: 3D User Interfaces: Theory and Practice, CourseSmart eTextbook. Addison-Wesley (2004)
10. Bozgeyikli, E., Raij, A., Katkoori, S., Dubey, R.: Locomotion in virtual reality for individuals with autism spectrum disorder. In: Proceedings of the Symposium on Spatial User Interaction, pp. 33–42. ACM (2016)
11. Bozgeyikli, E., Raij, A., Katkoori, S., Dubey, R.: Point & teleport locomotion technique for virtual reality. In: Proceedings of the Annual Symposium on Computer-Human Interaction in Play, pp. 205–216. ACM (2016)
12. Brooke, J.: SUS: a retrospective. J. Usability Stud. **8**(2), 29–40 (2013)

13. Brooke, J., et al.: SUS-A quick and dirty usability scale. Usability Eval. Ind. **189**(194), 4–7 (1996)
14. Bruder, G., Lubos, P., Steinicke, F.: Cognitive resource demands of redirected walking. IEEE Trans. Visual Comput. Graphics **21**(4), 539–544 (2015)
15. DeVon, H.A., et al.: A psychometric toolbox for testing validity and reliability. J. Nurs. Scholarsh. **39**(2), 155–164 (2007)
16. Grabowski, A., Jankowski, J.: Virtual reality-based pilot training for underground coal miners. Saf. Sci. **72**, 310–314 (2015)
17. Hale, K.S., Stanney, K.M.: Handbook of Virtual Environments: Design, Implementation, and Applications. CRC Press, Boca Raton (2014)
18. Ijsselsteijn, W., De Kort, Y., Poels, K.: The game experience questionnaire. Technische Universitcit Eindhoven (2013)
19. Kennedy, R.S., Lane, N.E., Berbaum, K.S., Lilienthal, M.G.: Simulator sickness questionnaire: an enhanced method for quantifying simulator sickness. Int. J. Aviat. Psychol. **3**(3), 203–220 (1993)
20. Kizony, R., Weiss, P.L.T., Shahar, M., Rand, D.: Theragame: a home based virtual reality rehabilitation system. Int. J. Disabil. Hum. Dev. **5**(3), 265–270 (2006)
21. Kortum, P., Acemyan, C.Z.: How low can you go?: is the system usability scale range restricted? J. Usability Stud. **9**(1), 14–24 (2013)
22. Kruijff, E., Riecke, B., Trekowski, C., Kitson, A.: Upper body leaning can affect forward self-motion perception in virtual environments. In: Proceedings of the 3rd ACM Symposium on Spatial User Interaction, pp. 103–112 (2015)
23. Langbehn, E., Eichler, T., Ghose, S., von Luck, K., Bruder, G., Steinicke, F.: Evaluation of an omnidirectional walking-in-place user interface with virtual locomotion speed scaled by forward leaning angle. In: Proceedings of the GI Workshop on Virtual and Augmented Reality (GI VR/AR), pp. 149–160 (2015)
24. Lee, G.A., Dünser, A., Kim, S., Billinghurst, M.: CityViewAR: a mobile outdoor AR application for city visualization. In: Proceedings of the IEEE International Symposium on Mixed and Augmented Reality, pp. 57–64. IEEE (2012)
25. Lee, G.A., Dunser, A., Nassani, A., Billinghurst, M.: Antarcticar: an outdoor AR experience of a virtual tour to antarctica. In: Proceedings of the IEEE International Symposium on Mixed and Augmented Reality-Arts, Media, and Humanities, pp. 29–38. IEEE (2013)
26. Lin, H.C.K., Hsieh, M.C., Wang, C.H., Sie, Z.Y., Chang, S.H.: Establishment and usability evaluation of an interactive AR learning system on conservation of fish. Turkish Online J. Educ. Technol. **10**(4), 181–187 (2011)
27. Lloréns, R., Noé, E., Colomer, C., Alcañiz, M.: Effectiveness, usability, and cost-benefit of a virtual reality-based telerehabilitation program for balance recovery after stroke: A randomized controlled trial. Arch. Phys. Med. Rehabil. **96**(3), 418–425 (2015)
28. Meijer, F., Geudeke, B.L., Van den Broek, E.L.: Navigating through virtual environments: Visual realism improves spatial cognition. CyberPsychology Behav. **12**(5), 517–521 (2009)
29. Meldrum, D., Glennon, A., Herdman, S., Murray, D., McConn-Walsh, R.: Virtual reality rehabilitation of balance: assessment of the usability of the nintendo wii® fit plus. Disability Rehabil. Assist. Technol. **7**(3), 205–210 (2012)
30. Nabiyouni, M., Bowman, D.A.: An evaluation of the effects of hyper-natural components of interaction fidelity on locomotion performance in virtual reality. In: Proceedings of the 25th International Conference on Artificial Reality and Telexistence and 20th Eurographics Symposium on Virtual Environments, pp. 167–174. Eurographics Association (2015)

31. Nabiyouni, M., Saktheeswaran, A., Bowman, D.A., Karanth, A.: Comparing the performance of natural, semi-natural, and non-natural locomotion techniques in virtual reality. In: Proceedings of the IEEE Symposium on 3D User Interfaces, pp. 3–10. IEEE (2015)

32. Nabiyouni, M., Scerbo, S., DeVito, V., Smolen, S., Starrin, P., Bowman, D.A.: Design and evaluation of a visual acclimation aid for a semi-natural locomotion device. In: 2015 IEEE Symposium on 3D User Interfaces (3DUI), pp. 11–14. IEEE (2015)

33. Nacke, L., Lindley, C.: Boredom, immersion, flow: a pilot study investigating player experience. In: Proceedings of the IADIS International Conference Gaming 2008: Design for Engaging Experience and Social Interaction, pp. 1–5. IADIS Press (2008)

34. Nacke, L., Lindley, C.A.: Flow and immersion in first-person shooters: measuring the player's gameplay experience. In: Proceedings of the 2008 Conference on Future Play: Research, Play, Share, pp. 81–88. ACM (2008)

35. Nacke, L.E., Grimshaw, M.N., Lindley, C.A.: More than a feeling: measurement of sonic user experience and psychophysiology in a first-person shooter game. Interact. Comput. 22(5), 336–343 (2010)

36. Nilsson, N.C., Serafin, S., Nordahl, R.: A comparison of different methods for reducing the unintended positional drift accompanying walking-in-place locomotion. In: 2014 IEEE Symposium on 3D User Interfaces (3DUI), pp. 103–110. IEEE (2014)

37. Ohshima, T., Shibata, R., Edamoto, H., Tatewaki, N.: Virtual ISU: locomotion interface for immersive VR experience in seated position (1). In: SIGGRAPH ASIA 2016 Posters, pp. 1–2 (2016)

38. Olszewski, K., Lim, J.J., Saito, S., Li, H.: High-fidelity facial and speech animation for VR HMDs. ACM Trans. Graph. 35(6), 221 (2016)

39. Rand, D., Kizony, R., Weiss, P.T.L.: The Sony PlayStation II EyeToy: low-cost virtual reality for use in rehabilitation. J. Neurol. Phys. Therapy 32(4), 155–163 (2008)

40. Sarupuri, B., Hoermann, S., Whitton, M.C., Lindeman, R.W.: Lute: a locomotion usability test environment for virtual reality. In: 2018 10th International Conference on Virtual Worlds and Games for Serious Applications (VS-Games), pp. 1–4. IEEE (2018)

41. Sauro, J., Lewis, J.R.: When designing usability questionnaires, does it hurt to be positive? In: Proceedings of the SIGCHI Conference on Human Factors in Computing Systems, pp. 2215–2224 (2011)

42. Schild, J., LaViola, J., Masuch, M.: Understanding user experience in stereoscopic 3D games. In: Proceedings of the SIGCHI Conference on Human Factors in Computing Systems, pp. 89–98. ACM (2012)

43. Schmidt, D., et al.: Level-ups: motorized stilts that simulate stair steps in virtual reality. In: Proceedings of the 33rd Annual ACM Conference on Human Factors in Computing Systems, pp. 2157–2160 (2015)

44. Skopp, N.A., Smolenski, D.J., Metzger-Abamukong, M.J., Rizzo, A.A., Reger, G.M.: A pilot study of the virtusphere as a virtual reality enhancement. Int. J. Hum.-Comput. Interact. 30(1), 24–31 (2014)

45. Slater, M., Steed, A.: A virtual presence counter. Presence: Teleoper. Virtual Environ. 9(5), 413–434 (2000)

46. Sun, H.M., Li, S.P., Zhu, Y.Q., Hsiao, B.: The effect of user's perceived presence and promotion focus on usability for interacting in virtual environments. Appl. Ergon. 50, 126–132 (2015)

47. Toet, A., van Welie, M., Houtkamp, J.: Is a dark virtual environment scary? CyberPsychology Behav. **12**(4), 363–371 (2009)
48. Tullis, T.S., Stetson, J.N.: A comparison of questionnaires for assessing website usability. In: Proceedings of the Usability Professional Association Conference, pp. 1–12 (2004)
49. Uloziené, I., et al.: Subjective visual vertical assessment with mobile virtual reality system. Medicina **53**(6), 394–402 (2017)
50. Witmer, B.G., Singer, M.J.: Measuring presence in virtual environments: a presence questionnaire. Presence **7**(3), 225–240 (1998)

Virtual Fitness Trail: A Complete Program for Elderlies to Perform Physical Activity at Home

Marta Mondellini[1](✉), Marco Sacco[1], and Luca Greci[2]

[1] Institute of Intelligent Industrial Technologies and Systems for Advanced Manufacturing – STIIMA, Via Previati 1/a, 23900 Lecco, Italy
{marta.mondellini,marco.sacco}@stiima.cnr.it
[2] Institute of Intelligent Industrial Technologies and Systems for Advanced Manufacturing – STIIMA, Via Alfonso Corti 12, 20133 Milan, Italy
luca.greci@stiima.cnr.it

Abstract. This paper presents a Virtual Reality (VR) exergame, Virtual Fitness Trail (VFT), designed to encourage the elderly to regularly exercise in an engaging and safe way staying at home. VFT provides a highly immersive physical activity experiences in first-person perspective and it has been developed to run on Oculus Quest head mounted display. The exergame proposes four activities involving the main muscles of the legs and arms, as well as stabilizing balance and reflexes: monkey bar, side raises, basketball shot and slalom between beams. Each activity has four difficulty level and has been designed to minimize the perception of self-motion so as to reduce the cybersickness arise. The user's performances are saved in .json file and it can be shared, via email, with the caregiver at the end of the exergame session. The application is a prototype and needs to be tested and validated before proposing it for autonomous physical activity at home.

Keywords: Physical activity · Elderlies · Virtual Reality

1   Introduction

"The greying of Europe" is the phenomenon of the aging of the European population due to a combination of factors: a growing average life expectancy, a decrease in mortality rate and a low number of births among Europeans population [1]. In 2015 19.2% of the European population was >65 years of age and projections show that by 2050 the number will almost double, rising to >36% [2]. In this European context, Italy is the country with the highest number of people over 65-years-old [3]. In addition to this, living longer is not necessarily associated with active aging, good health and independence of the elderly population [4]. Rather, the increase in longevity leads to a greater expression of chronic diseases, comorbidities and geriatric syndromes, burdening the economic and health systems with a serious challenge [5]. The concept of active aging [6] is well rooted in the social and economic structure in some countries but it remains less well implemented in many countries [7]. This concept refers to the processes of "healthy

L. T. De Paolis and P. Bourdot (Eds.): AVR 2020, LNCS 12242, pp. 168–176, 2020.
https://doi.org/10.1007/978-3-030-58465-8_12

aging", which translate into reduced rates of chronic diseases, more productive years and greater cognitive and functional skills to perform tasks, participate in and enjoy social and cultural life [6].

Among the factors related to "active aging", physical activity (PA) is crucial [7], as it has a main role in improving the quality of life, reducing chronic physical and cognitive pathologies [8, 9] and promoting people independence [10]. For older adults, the PA consists mainly of activities such as walking and cycling, but also muscle strength and balance training play an important role in promoting health [11].

Although the concept of active aging is now at the heart of European politics, the possibility of participating in activities that promote this lifestyle still depends on strictly personal socio-demographic and socio-economic factors [12]. For this reason, it is necessary to offer low-cost, motivating and engaging solutions to allow and attract as many people as possible to maintain an active lifestyle; these solutions must also take into account the safety aspect, especially important in the case of elderly living alone.

The objective of this article is therefore to propose a series of physical activities to train the elderly users through the support of new low-cost technologies that allow to offer fun and motivating experiences.

2   New Technologies for the Elderly

In a context in which PA becomes necessary for a particular part of the population, often also from a rehabilitative perspective, technological developments have proposed innovative solutions to allow exercise at home, tailoring tasks to the physical and cognitive user's skills [13]. Among the different technologies available, VR has proven to be particularly effective for proposing PA, as Virtual Environments can increase the participants level of engagement and motivation in performing rehabilitation tasks [14], thanks to the ability of Virtual Environments (VEs) to elicit the Sense of Presence [15], and to propose different and fun scenarios [16]. The motivational aspect is crucial since better rehabilitation outcomes have been linked to higher levels of motivation reported by users [17].

However, the elderly users are often not familiar with computer technology [18] although preliminary research has shown that older users have a good acceptability of these technologies [19] as long as they are intuitive and simple to use [20]; in addition, the elderlies need to receive frequent feedback on their performance [21] and to feel supported in the use of the technological system [22].

VR devices such as Head Mounted Display (HMDs), which are capable of transmitting the highest levels of immersion and Sense of Presence [23], are currently available on the market. VR physical activities are generally available in research programs at rehabilitation clinics [24, 25] while less often they are proposed for autonomous use at home [26] probably because wearing an HMD is considered unsafe for autonomous exercising, especially in the elderly. For example, dynamic balance is more perturbed in a VE than in a real environment [27] and moving in a VEs sometimes elicits side-effects such as cyber-sickness or aftereffects [28]. Furthermore, the navigation in VEs is usually performed using a joystick, a keyboard or a wand, and these may difficult to use for people with impairments, as frailty elderlies could be [29].

This article proposes an exercise program, the VFT, to be performed at home wearing an Oculus Quest; the exercises are intended to strengthen the upper limbs, the lower limbs, and the ability to balance so as to elderly can have an adequate level of work out [13, 30].

3 The Virtual Fitness Trail

The VFT has been developed for the Oculus Quest device using the game engine Unity 2019.3.10 and consists of a virtual fitness park with four training stations where the different exercises can be performed.

The Oculus Quest has been chosen because it is an All-in-one VR device. Oculus Insight tracking system instantly reflects user's movements in VR without the need for any external accessories. Oculus Touch controllers precisely recreate user's hands, their gestures and interactions, so every game is real enough to reach out and touch. Oculus Quest works with users' environment, so they can play standing or sitting, in spaces big or small. Moreover, its display features are similar to those of the Oculus Rift S: 1600 × 1440 display per eye with a 72 Hz refresh rate vs 1280 × 1440 display per eye with an 80 Hz refresh rate.

Particular attention has been paid to reduce the arise of cybersickness. The VE respects the limits of 50,000–100,000 triangles or vertices per frame to avoid flickering and/or lag. Most of the interactions with the environment are performed like in the real life, e.g. by pushing virtual buttons, because the elderly encounter difficulties interacting with buttons and/or joysticks. The navigation of the VE is performed using the Physical movements where users use their own body to move around in VR just like they do in real life.

Each exercise starts from a basic level and increases its difficulty level with improving user performance. The complete program allows users to work out the mobility and strength of the upper limbs performing the exercises called "Monkey Bar" and "Side Risers", to strengthen the lower muscles by playing at "Basketball Shot", and to train balance, reflexes and musculature of the lower limbs through the "Slalom between Beams" exercise.

The game begins with a screen showing recommendations on how to setup the real environment so to play safely. Then a screen (main menu) with four training station is shown; the exercise begins by touching the corresponding station. At the end of the exercise, the main menu appears and the user can select another exercise, or s/he choose to exit triggering the "exit" button.

During each session the user's performance are collected and saved in a local repository as .json file and can be shared to caregivers and/or physiotherapists via email.

3.1 Monkey Bar

The exercise consists in overcoming an obstacle formed by pegs, bars and rings, grasping them with hands, therefore using only the upper limbs (Fig. 1). The shoulder muscles, Musculus latissimus dorsi and pectoralis major, are mainly involved in this exercise; in

Fig. 1. The user holds on to the bars and moves his arms to advance along the obstacle.

addition, depending on the difficulty of the exercise, the user must also activate the wrist flexors.

To simulate the player's movement between a peg and next one a transform position is applied to the VE. The translation amount is calculated at each frame and corresponds to the difference between the last position of the controller (previous frame) and the current position of the controller (current frame) if the grabbing condition is true. The grabbing condition becomes true when the virtual hand triggers the peg and the user pushes the controller's trigger button and remains true until the trigger button is released.

The user tries to make as many movements as possible without lowering his arms (and therefore falling from the monkey bar), up to a maximum of 20 movements per arm. At a basic level of difficulty, the bars are at a close distance (10 cm) and they are all placed on the same plane parallel to the floor. Subsequent difficulty levels provide for different bar heights up to a difference of 10 cm in height from each other, increased distance between the bars up to a maximum of 50 cm, use of handholds not in parallel.

3.2 Side Raises

The proposed activity is the classic exercise for training upper limbs. The user is in the middle of the station and two virtual dumbbells are at his feet. The user must grab them and lift his arms sideways (Fig. 2).

To check if the user performs the exercise properly a comparison between the y and z position (the coordinate system is Left-handed Y-up) of virtual hands and head is done: the y axis is used to check if the arms have been raised while the z axis to check if they stay in the frontal plane. A positive sound feedback is provided at each repetition respecting the constraints.

The exercise is designed to be performed until the user's strength is exhausted and it does not provide incremental difficulties but the user is suggested user to wear wristbands if he is sufficiently trained and needs a real weight.

Fig. 2. After grasping the dumbbells, the user lifts them sideways.

3.3 Basketball Shot

The VR station represents a little basketball field, the user is in front of a hoop and a ball is placed at his feet. The user must therefore perform a squatting, take the ball, and try to make basket (Fig. 3). The main leg muscles (quadriceps, hamstrings, adductors and buttocks) intervene in this exercise and the abdominals are used to keep the lumbar area neutral. During the basket shooting, the muscles of the arms also intervene: pectorals, forearm flexors, biceps, triceps, deltoids and trapezius muscles.

Fig. 3. After collecting the ball at his feet, the user has to get it through the hoop.

The throwing ball is simulated by the oculus plugin API while the bouncing effects of the ball is obtained through the use of the Unity's Physic Material. The check of the user posture during the squatting is done by evaluating the knees angle and the head position.

The exercise starts from a basic difficulty in which the user has to perform 5 shots towards a basket from a distance of 2 m. Incremental difficulties involve a more distant basket, a greater repetition of shots, and the variation of the ball's position - not only perpendicular to his barycenter, in front of the user's legs, but to his right and left.

3.4 Slalom Between Beams

The VR consist of a tunnel placed in the park where spawned obstacles (beams) moving towards a virtual model (avatar) of the user forcing it to perform lateral movements and/or crouch to avoid a collision with them. When the avatar of the player is detected as colliding with an obstacle, it triggers the playing of an error sound.

This activity allows the user to exercise the leg muscles that intervene for the squat, the ability to balance and reflexes.

At a basic level of difficulty, the user must bend over his legs and get up to avoid a beam at a height of 1.50. As the difficulty increases, this height can be lowered. Furthermore, the obstacles will force the user to move to the right or left, and they can always present themselves at different heights (Fig. 4). The number of obstacles will also grow according to the user's performance, starting from a minimum of 10 beams.

Fig. 4. The user has to avoid beams that appear in different positions and different heights.

4 Conclusion and Future Works

The presented work shows a series of activities to be carried out, in a virtual environment, by the elderly to maintain a good physical condition both in terms of muscles and of balance and flexibility. The application has been designed for training at home in a safe and engaging way, in complete autonomy, without going to a gym or followed by a doctor or physiotherapist. Therefore, it could be a solution to emergencies involving social isolation, such as COVID-19, which the world is experiencing in these months. In a context where elderly, as the user most at risk, is forced to stay at home as long as possible limiting its movements such as walks, this application can be a motivating way to maintain an active lifestyle.

Before using VFT at home and with the elderly a validation is required. As soon as the COVID-19 emergency will be over the application will be evaluated by a group of healthy elderly users who do not require special precautions in carrying out the exercises. Aim of this trial is the evaluation of the ease of use of the application and the acceptability of the tool, two dimensions that are closely linked to the intention to use [31]. Furthermore, the increase in subjects' motivation to exercise will be evaluated, comparing the involvement and the enjoyment [32] experienced using our system and performing the same exercises in the traditional way. In addition, Sense of Presence [33] and cyber-sickness [34] will also be measured.

The application records user performance, and therefore allows to monitor whether the elderly is performing his exercise routine; this data could be particularly useful for doctors and physiotherapists who cannot follow personally the subjects in the hospital, due to time problems, number of users with the same problems or for health emergencies such as COVID-19, but who want to be sure that the rehabilitation treatment is followed.

In addition, the application will be integrated with sensors suitable for measuring physiological parameters, such as heart rate, oxygen saturation and skin conductance. In this way it will be possible to objectively evaluate the benefits of the application on the person's status of health. In a second moment the activities will be discussed and modified after a comparison with the physiotherapists; adequate levels of difficulty and the precise duration of the exercises will be set according to the needs of the target.

References

1. Carone, G., Costello, D.: Can Europe afford to grow old? Financ. Dev. **43**, 28–31 (2006)
2. Manfredi, G., Midão, L., Paúl, C., Cena, C., Duarte, M., Costa, E.: Prevalence of frailty status among the European elderly population: Findings from the Survey of Health, Aging and Retirement in Europe. Geriatr. Gerontol. Int. **19**, 723–729 (2019). https://doi.org/10.1111/ggi.13689
3. Eurostat - Data Explorer/ http://appsso.eurostat.ec.europa.eu/nui/submitViewTableAction.do
4. Oxley, H.: Policies for healthy ageing: an overview. Oecd heal. Work. Pap. 0_1–4,6-30 (2009). https://doi.org/10.1787/226757488706
5. Divo, M.J., Martinez, C.H., Mannino, D.M.: Ageing and the epidemiology of multimorbidity. Eur. Respir. J. **44**, 1055–1068 (2014). https://doi.org/10.1183/09031936.00059814
6. Kalache, A., Gatti, A.: Active ageing: a policy framework. Adv. Gerontol. **11**, 7–18 (2003)
7. Bauman, A., Merom, D., Bull, F., Buchner, D., Singh, M.: Updating the evidence for physical activity: summative reviews of the epidemiological evidence, prevalence, and interventions to promote "active aging". Gerontologist **56**, 268–280 (2016)
8. Geffken, D.F., Cushman, M., Burke, G.L., Polak, J.F., Sakkinen, P.A., Tracy, R.P.: Association between physical activity and markers of inflammation in a healthy elderly population. Am. J. Epidemiol. **153**, 242–250 (2001). https://doi.org/10.1093/aje/153.3.242
9. Laurin, D., Verreault, R., Lindsay, J., MacPherson, K., Rockwood, K.: Physical activity and risk of cognitive impairment and dementia in elderly persons. Arch. Neurol. **58**, 498–504 (2001). https://doi.org/10.1001/archneur.58.3.498
10. Shephard, R.J.: Exercise and aging: extending independence in older adults (1993)
11. Garber, C.E., et al.: Quantity and quality of exercise for developing and maintaining cardiorespiratory, musculoskeletal, and neuromotor fitness in apparently healthy adults: Guidance for prescribing exercise. Med. Sci. Sports Exerc. **43**, 1334–1359 (2011). https://doi.org/10.1249/MSS.0b013e318213fefb

12. Nilsen, C., Lamura, G., Harper, S.H.: Inequalities in active aging: a european perspective. Innov. Aging **1**, 761–762 (2017). https://doi.org/10.1093/GERONI/IGX004.2758

13. Sá Glauber, B., et al.: Impact of functional home training on postural balance and functional mobility in the elderlies. J. Exerc. Physiol. online. **22**(4), 46–57 (2019)

14. Lourenço, C.B., Azeff, L., Sveistrup, H., Levin, M.F.: Effect of environment on motivation and sense of presence in healthy subjects performing reaching tasks. In: 2008 Virtual Rehabilitation, IWVR, pp. 93–98. IEEE Computer Society (2008)

15. Steuer, J.: Defining virtual reality: dimensions determining telepresence. J. Commun. **42**, 73–93 (1992). https://doi.org/10.1111/j.1460-2466.1992.tb00812.x

16. W, S., A, B.: The Use of Virtual Reality Technologies during Physiotherapy of the Paretic Upper Limb in Patients after Ischemic Stroke. J. Neurol. Neurosci. 06, (2015). https://doi.org/10.21767/2171-6625.100033

17. Maclean, N., Pound, P.: A critical review of the concept of patient motivation in the literature on physical rehabilitation (2000)

18. Rendon, A.A., Lohman, E.B., Thorpe, D., Johnson, E.G., Medina, E., Bradley, B.: The effect of virtual reality gaming on dynamic balance in older adults. Age Ageing **41**, 549–552 (2012). https://doi.org/10.1093/ageing/afs053

19. Colombo, V., Mondellini, M., Gandolfo, A., Fumagalli, A., Sacco, M.: Usability and acceptability of a virtual reality-based system for endurance training in elderly with chronic respiratory diseases. In: Bourdot, P., Interrante, V., Nedel, L., Magnenat-Thalmann, N., Zachmann, G. (eds.) EuroVR 2019. LNCS, vol. 11883, pp. 87–96. Springer, Cham (2019). https://doi.org/10.1007/978-3-030-31908-3_6

20. Anderson, F., Annett, M., Bischof, W.F.: Lean on Wii: Physical rehabilitation with virtua reality Wii peripherals. In: Studies in Health Technology and Informatics, pp. 229–234. IOS Press (2010)

21. Agmon, M., Perry, C.K., Phelan, E., Demiris, G., Nguyen, H.Q.: A pilot study of Wii Fit exergames to improve balance in older adults. J. Geriatr. Phys. Ther. **34**, 161–167 (2011). https://doi.org/10.1519/JPT.0b013e3182191d98

22. Lotan, M., Yalon-Chamovitz, S., Weiss, P.L.T.: Virtual reality as means to improve physical fitness of individuals at a severe level of intellectual and developmental disability. Res. Dev. Disabil. **31**, 869–874 (2010). https://doi.org/10.1016/j.ridd.2010.01.010

23. Schubert, T., Friedmann, F., Regenbrecht, H.: The experience of presence: factor analytic insights. Presence Teleoperators Virtual Environ. **10**, 266–281 (2001). https://doi.org/10.1162/105474601300343603

24. Cano Porras, D., Siemonsma, P., Inzelberg, R., Zeilig, G., Plotnik, M.: Advantages of virtual reality in the rehabilitation of balance and gait: systematic review. Neurology **90**, 1017–1025 (2018). https://doi.org/10.1212/WNL.0000000000005603

25. Arlati, S., et al.: A virtual reality-based physical and cognitive training system aimed at preventing symptoms of dementia. In: Perego, P., Rahmani, A.M., TaheriNejad, N. (eds.) MobiHealth 2017. LNICST, vol. 247, pp. 117–125. Springer, Cham (2018). https://doi.org/10.1007/978-3-319-98551-0_14

26. Kizony, R., Weiss, P.L., Shahar, M.: TheraGame: a home based virtual reality rehabilitation system. Int. J. Disabil. Hum. Dev. **5**, 265–270 (2006). https://doi.org/10.1515/IJDHD.2006.5.3.265

27. Robert, M.T., Ballaz, L., Lemay, M.: The effect of viewing a virtual environment through a head-mounted display on balance. Gait Posture **48**, 261–266 (2016). https://doi.org/10.1016/j.gaitpost.2016.06.010

28. Rizzo, A., Kim, G.J.: A SWOT analysis of the field of virtual reality rehabilitation and therapy. Presence Teleoperators Virtual Environ. **14**, 119–146 (2005). https://doi.org/10.1162/1054746053967094

29. Ferche, O.-M., Moldoveanu, A., Moldoveanu, F., Voinea, A., Asavei, V., Negoi, I.: Challenges and issues for successfully applying virtual reality in medical rehabilitation. eLearning Softw. Educ. **1**, 494–501 (2015)

30. Phungdee, T., Wattanathamrong, V., Sirisopon, N.: The effectiveness of strengthening leg muscles physical exercise promotion program for preventing falls of the elderlies in Thailand. Interdiscip. Res. Rev. **15**, 19–23 (2020)

31. Venkatesh, V., Davis, F.D.: Theoretical extension of the technology acceptance model: four longitudinal field studies. Manage. Sci. **46**, 186–204 (2000). https://doi.org/10.1287/mnsc. 46.2.186.11926

32. Ryan, R.M., Deci, E.L.: Self-determination theory and the facilitation of intrinsic motivation, social development, and well-being. Am. Psychol. **55**, 68–78 (2000). https://doi.org/10.1037/ 0003-066X.55.1.68

33. Steuer, J.: Defining virtual reality: dimensions determining telepresence. J. Commun. **42**, 73–93 (1992). https://doi.org/10.1111/j.1460-2466.1992.tb00812.x

34. Mousavi, M., Jen, Y.H., Musa, S.N.B.: A review on cybersickness and usability in virtual environments. Adv. Eng. Forum **10**, 34–39 (2013). https://doi.org/10.4028/www.scientific. net/AEF.10.34

Exploring Players' Curiosity-Driven Behaviour in Unknown Videogame Environments

Riccardo Galdieri[1](✉)(iD), Mata Haggis-Burridge[2](✉)(iD), Thomas Buijtenweg[2](✉),
and Marcello Carrozzino[1](✉)(iD)

[1] Scuola Superiore Sant'Anna, Piazza Martiri Della Libertà, 33, 56127 Pisa, Italy
{r.galdieri,marcello.carrozzino}@santannapisa.it
[2] Breda University of Applied Sciences, Monseigneur Hopmansstraat 2, 4817 JS Breda,
The Netherlands
haggis.m@ade-buas.nl, Buijtenweg.T@buas.nl

Abstract. Curiosity is a fundamental trait of human nature, and as such, it has been studied and exploited in many aspects of game design. However, curiosity is not a static trigger that can just be activated, and game design needs to be carefully paired with the current state of the game flow to produce significant reactions. In this paper we present the preliminary results of an experiment aimed at understanding how different factors such as perceived narrative, unknown game mechanics, and non-standard controller mapping could influence the evolution of players' behaviour throughout a game session. Data was gathered remotely through a puzzle game we developed and released for free on the internet, and no description on potential narrative was provided before gameplay. Players who downloaded the game did it on their free will and played the same way they would with any other game. Results show that initial curiosity towards both a static and dynamic environment is slowly overcome by the sense of challenge, and that interactions that were initially performed with focus lose accuracy as result of players' attention shift towards the core game mechanics.

Keywords: Curiosity · Game design · Games · Game narrative · Human-computer interaction

1 Introduction

Human beings are curious creatures. They explore, research, observe, and seek knowledge not only for practical reasons but to satisfy a primary need. This fundamental aspect of human nature is exploited in many aspects of modern social dynamics, and gaming is no exception: drawing cards from a deck, opening a door, talking to a character, exploring a region, all these actions are based on a craving for information that players have and that game designers can combine with the game flow to create fulfilling experiences.

In this short paper, we present the results of a preliminary study aimed at understanding how videogame players' curiosity evolves during gameplay. We designed a puzzle game with a linearly growing difficulty and monitored how different curiosity triggers

© Springer Nature Switzerland AG 2020
L. T. De Paolis and P. Bourdot (Eds.): AVR 2020, LNCS 12242, pp. 177–185, 2020.
https://doi.org/10.1007/978-3-030-58465-8_13

were perceived and how they impacted players' behaviour in time. We focused on two main elements: implicit narrative and controller interactions. The evolution of narrative is often designed to follow the concept of flow [1, 2] but, when players approach a game, they tend to have an idea of what the game is about in terms of storytelling and environment. In this game we tested the impact of implicit narrative, elements that may suggest a story beyond what is made explicit by the game, to see how players would naturally be driven towards them. The same applies to button schemes and controllers: when playing a game for the first time, players instinctively know how to interact with it, as they rely on what they consider to be a de-facto standard. We designed a non-intuitive control scheme that could not be associated with any previous knowledge, forcing players to explore button schemes as well as interaction mechanics by themselves.

Instead of relying on pre-existing games, we designed our own product called "EscapeTower", that we released for free on the online platform itch.io. This was the preferred solution for several reasons: it was important, to prevent potential biases that lab experiments could induce, to have a product that people could play at home, just as they would play any other commercial game. Also, it helped us make sure that the game was downloaded by people who had an interest in puzzle games and did not know the game already, and of course it was the only way to satisfy all our criteria: no explicit narrative, a limited number of supported input devices, and randomization of the environments. Data was gathered remotely through the GURaaS platform [3].

2   Previous Literature

The first modern studies on curiosity are dated back to the early fifties, when Berlyne first proposed the differentiation of curiosity in 'perceptual curiosity' (PC), the one that derives from sensory inputs and is shared between all animals – including humans – and 'epistemic curiosity' (EC), the personal desire to obtain new knowledge [4]. Establishing curiosity as a reaction to stimuli, the same author iterated on this categorization a few years later, distinguishing two types of exploratory behaviours that are caused by curiosity [5]: *diversive*, where living creatures seek information as reaction to stimuli, and therefore guided by PC, and *specific*, which is driven not only by the desire to access information, but to gain lasting knowledge, through EC [6]. Believing this subdivision not to be fully exhaustive, in 1994 Loewenstein further expanded on curiosity by defining it as "a form of cognitively induced deprivation that results from the perception of a gap in one's knowledge" [7]. In 2004 a questionnaire to measure curiosity as a feeling of deprivation (CFD) was proposed, where curiosity was defined on the basis of two different possible reactions to uncertainty - interest and deprivation - to include both positive and negative feelings [8].

Given the presented elements, it does not surprise that "curiosity lies deep at the heart of play" [9]. In her four keys to fun, Nicole Lazzaro considered curiosity to be the key trait of what she called "Easy fun", the feeling of engagement created by exploration, role play and creativity. However, as reported by To, this model considers curiosity as a unitary trait, while curiosity has been proven to be a combination of different types. Following this, To proposed to utilise the 5 different types of curiosity presented by Kreiter [10] to game design. In this study we will focus on two of these types: manipulatory curiosity, defined as "the desire to touch and interact with physical game objects, including game controllers", and conceptual curiosity, "the desire to find things out".

3   Setup

EscapeTower is a classic first-person puzzle game, where the player has to solve a series of puzzles to reach the final room and complete the game. The experience is divided in two main areas: the tutorial, where players learn the game's dynamics, and the main tower, where the actual game takes place. Players receive no instruction on how to play the game before the actual gameplay, the tutorial area is therefore designed to gradually introduce the players to the core mechanics, from the button scheme to the interactions with the world around them. All puzzle mechanics are introduced in linear order, each one with a dedicated room, and visual clues to indicate where the player should go next are placed in front of every door. In the tutorial area, there is no window and players are not able to foresee what the external environments will look like. The main area instead has more of a tower structure, every floor has one main corridor that can be used to reach all the surrounding rooms and at least two big windows that the player can use to look outside, one in front of the ladder that is used to reach the floor, and one in a different position [Fig. 1].

Fig. 1. Ground floor corridor. This is the first view that players have when entering the main tower. In this case, the narrative setup has been selected, and the hell-like environment is visible outside the main window.

The whole experience was designed to contain as few references to the real world as possible: the building is composed of white walls and a few dark columns, which were added to reduce the impact on photosensitive subjects. The first-person character is also designed to be as neutral as possible, with the arms being covered so that no age, gender, or skin colour can be assigned to the character.

3.1 Narrative

To understand the impact that implicit narrative could have on the game, two different scenarios were designed. In the first scenario, called "narrative", the main building was surrounded by three different environments, one per floor, each one with unique features and a unique post-processing colour grading on the camera. Every time a player entered a floor, the environment outside and the colour grading switched. The other environment was called "geometry" and featured a series of rotating black geometric shapes with coloured borders, it was the same on all three floors, and did not feature any post-processing effect. At the beginning of each session, players were randomly assigned a specific environment and were not aware that other environments could be potentially available. The game measured the amount of time spent by each player looking outside a window, which window that was, and which environment was displayed.

3.2 Controllers

Both the Itch.io page and the game splash screen clearly stated that the game required and XBOX-style controller, but no indication on how to use it was provided and players were required to learn the button scheme by themselves. Whenever an interaction was available, the game showed the button to press on screen. On the controller, the four buttons on the right were mapped on interactions and the two levers were mapped on movements. The back triggers were not mapped for interactions, but they were still monitored.

From playtesting two possible behaviours have emerged: one where players press all the buttons before getting to the ladder, to see if any interaction is available, and one where they move first, and get to interact with the objects following the UI. We do not expect to see players pressing the back buttons after the first area.

Similar considerations were made for the exit button. To exit the game, players need to press the start button on the controller, move to the "exit game" option, and press any button on the controller. No indication of this mechanic was given anywhere in the game, but if players pressed the escape button on the keyboard the UI displayed the image of an XBOX controller, hinting that to exit the game, the controller should be used. During testing time people simply dropped the controller on the table at the end of the game and no indication on this mechanic was possible.

3.3 Data Gathering

The whole experience was designed like any other game would be, and gameplay data was collected as it would be for similar commercially available games. However, given that the analysis focused on factors related to players' curiosity, no elements were placed in the game to influence players' actions beyond a gameplay purpose: every object in the scene, with the exclusion of windows, was either an interactable object or a visual cue for puzzle solving.

Also, because the goal of this project was to study people's behaviour in their natural environment, data had to be collected remotely, with no input needed from the users to submit their data, and with the least possible distraction from the game. After evaluating all possible options, it was decided to take advantage of GURaaS, an online platform for game-data collection developed at the Breda University of Applied Sciences. By using this approach, we could automatically log every action performed by the player on a remote server. The log includes the player's in-game location, pressed buttons, and game status, without any impact on the user or the gameplay.

4 Results

At the time of writing, the game has been played by 41 unique users, producing 51 gameplay sessions. Considering only meaningful sessions, those where players have spent at least 240 s in the game and have completed the initial tutorial, 26 gameplay sessions have been collected and will be part of this study. 11 of these had the narrative environment assigned to them (with 7 completed games – 63%), while 15 had the geometric one (and 13 completed – 86%).

Out of 26 game sessions, players approached the windows 106 times. However, 61 times they spent less than one second in front of it, 41 times they stayed between 1 and 3 s, and only 4 times spending more than 3 s looking outside. On average players spent 3.3 (σ: 2.8) s watching outside, with 3 sessions with no time in front of a window at all. Only two values are significantly more relevant than the average, with players watching outside for 11 s both times, one in the narrative and one in the geometric setup. Dividing the data by environment, narrative sessions have an average of 3.1 s spent looking outside and no 0-s session, while geometry players have an average of 3.4 s per session, despite having all 3 sessions with no time spent looking outside.

Looking at what windows have been used by the players to look outside, most of them have been used between 1 and 3 times (mean: 3.36, σ: 2.33). The only value that significantly differs from the others is the window at the end of the corridor on the ground floor, the first one that players see when they enter the main tower. Despite being distant and far from any other doors, it has been observed 9 times. Dividing the data by environment, windows from narrative sessions have been watched on average 1.7 times (σ: 1.09) with the same window being the only significant one (watched 4 times), while the geometric environment has an average of 2.1 (σ: 1.44). In this second case, the same window is the most significant one with 5 times, but the window at the end of the second floor has also been watched 4 times.

As it regards the exit menu, despite the advice on the game page, 7 players out of 26 (26.9%) quitted the game without using the menu. All these players completed the tutorial and played for four minutes, which means that they did have a working gamepad and were able to play. It is interesting to notice that in 2 cases, players previously opened the exit menu decided not to use it to quit the game. In total, only 5 sessions did not register any exit menu opening.

Moving to the button analysis, players have pressed a total of 4398 buttons, with 381 (8.6% of the total) of these being inactive buttons that were not shown by the interface at any point, with six game sessions did not register any attempt to press the back buttons at all. The interesting data comes from the distribution of these clicks over gameplay sessions: given the extremely variable length of sessions (going from 7 to 33 min), data has been normalised to a gameplay-length percentage scale. Results show that those clicks are more common towards the end of a gameplay session, with twice as many clicks in the last 20% of the game compared to the first 20%. Full data is shown in Table 1.

Table 1. Where the inactive buttons are pressed, in relation to gameplay length (in percentage)

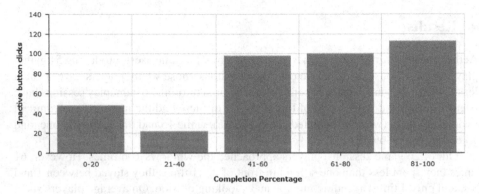

5   Discussion

The first and most obvious result regards players' behaviour towards inactive buttons, with a distribution that goes completely against what emerged from playtesting. Despite knowing that no interaction will result from those clicks, and learning in time that only buttons displayed by the UI will produce an interaction, inactive buttons are being clicked more and more as the game progresses. This discrepancy with playtesting can be motivated in two ways: first, while playtesting the behaviour of the players was observed, but data was not gathered. It was therefore easy to notice that players were testing buttons during the initial phases of the game, but nearly impossible to notice individual clicks during the gameplay. The second reason is a different behaviour that players have while playing the game in a lab environment and at home. Unfortunately there is no way to quantify that with the data at our disposal. Nevertheless, the distribution of inactive button clicks is hard to understand. One possible explanation is that players who got stuck because they could not solve the puzzles then tried to press other buttons, as if they were missing something. Given that no penalty for mis-clicking was given at any point, it is possible that with time, players decided to prioritize speed over accuracy, pressing all buttons at the same time. Alternatively, players may be confident of the correct button, but not the range from which it will have the desired result and so are clicking before, for example, reaching a door to try and use a key on it. In a similar way, they may be holding a key and trying it on multiple locked and incorrect doors because they find that it is faster to try a key than to look for visual feedback that says the key will not work. This optimisation of testing solutions would also result in an increase in mis-clicks. Other unconsidered results of the dynamics of the game may also be producing this behaviour and further experimentation would be necessary to gain further insight into its causes.

A different reasoning seems to apply to the exit menu and the number of people who used it to quit the game. One fourth of the players quit the game without opening that menu, and this is a significant amount. However, there is not enough data to establish any pattern or analyse players' behaviour in this regard. It would be interesting, in future research, to compare how many players use the controller to quit the game when the keyboard option is also available. Also, despite happening in two cases only, it would be interesting to investigate what brought players to quit the game with "brute force" despite being aware of the exit menu.

As it concerns players' curiosity towards perceived narrative, data reflects more or less what was expected. The first window that players see when they enter the main area is also the most viewed, with a statistically significant difference compared with all the others, suggesting that players do notice the outside environment and are intrigued by it. The narrative environment has proven to be of interest for all players at some point, something that cannot be said for the geometric environment and its 3 sessions with no players looking outside. However, despite its variation throughout the experience, the narrative environment does not seem to stimulate the curiosity of players in the long-term run, but quite the opposite: players spent more time watching outside the windows when playing the geometry scenario, not only outside the main window but also while on other floors. There are multiple possible causes of this, such as the geometric environment containing more movement when compared to the relatively stationary narrative environments, and this increased movement holding players' attention for slightly longer. Alternatively, the narrative scenes outside the floors (hell, a dull purgatory, and

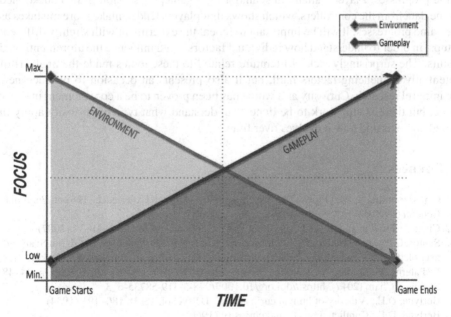

Fig. 2. Players' focus in relation to time. While being extremely receptive and actively curious towards the environment at first, their focus shifts towards the tasks required to complete the game (in our case, puzzle-solving)

a heavenly green landscape) may be highly familiar to experienced video game players and so elicit less interest than moving abstract shapes. In any case, the variation between the two environments is minimal and it has to be expected with a rather small number of playtests.

The general feeling is that players have an initial curiosity towards aspects of the game that they are not familiar with, or that they expect to work in a certain way. However, with no dynamic stimuli as the game progresses, their focus shifts towards gameplay and the surrounding elements are ignored. A very low number of players spent time looking outside the window on the third floor, because as they reach it, they are already in something like a flow-state through being engaged with mechanical and intellectual challenges of the game. This explanation aligns with the results of both implicit narrative, that tends to be ignored as the game progresses, and controller interactions, where precision and accuracy decrease over time. When the challenge increases, players' attention towards those elements that do not add anything to their current mission, solving the puzzles, drops (Fig. 2).

6   Conclusions

In this paper we presented the first preliminary results on understanding what elements can influence players' curiosity in an unknown environment, and how they evolve in time. Results seem to suggest that players are initially interested in the environment around them, especially during the first stages of the game, but tend not to focus on it as the game progresses. Players' attention span during a gameplay session is also questioned by the data from the controllers, which shows that players tend to make more mistakes as the game progresses. It will be important to repeat the experiment with slightly different setups, in order to understand how individual factors could influence the aforementioned results. The surprisingly lack of literature related to these topics made the analysis of potentially influencing factors hard, but it also presents an occasion to produce new meaningful research. Curiosity as a whole has been proven to be a core element in every game, but there is still work to be done to understand what type of curiosity apply in varied contexts and how it evolves over time.

References

1. Csikszentmihalyi, M.: Flow: The Psychology of Optimal Experience. Harper Perennial, London (1990)
2. Chen, J.: Flow in games (and everything else). Commun. ACM **50**(4), 31–34 (2007)
3. Santos, C.P., van de Haterd, J., Hutchinson, K., Khan, V.J., Markopoulos, P.: GURaaS: an end-user platform for embedding research instruments into games. In: Barbosa, S., Markopoulos, P., Paternò, F., Stumpf, S., Valtolina, S. (eds.) IS-EUD 2017. LNCS, vol. 10303, pp. 34–48. Springer, Cham (2017). https://doi.org/10.1007/978-3-319-58735-6_3
4. Berlyne, D.E.: A theory of human curiosity. Br. J. Psychol. **45**(3), 180–191 (1954)
5. Berlyne, D.E.: Conflict, arousal, and curiosity (1960)
6. Berlyne, D.E.: Curiosity and exploration. Science **153**(3731), 25–33 (1966)
7. Loewenstein, G.: The psychology of curiosity: a review and reinterpretation. Psychol. Bull. **116**(1), 75 (1994)

8. Litman, J.A., Jimerson, T.L.: The measurement of curiosity as a feeling of deprivation. J. Pers. Assess. **82**(2), 147–157 (2004)
9. To, A., Ali, S., Kaufman, G .F, Hammer, J.: Integrating Curiosity and Uncertainty in Game Design. In: Digra/fdg (2016)
10. Kreitler, S., Zigler, E., Kreitler, H.: The nature of curiosity in children. J. Sch. Psychol. **13**(3), 185–200 (1975)

Considering User Experience Parameters in the Evaluation of VR Serious Games

Kim Martinez[1], M. Isabel Menéndez-Menéndez[1], and Andres Bustillo[2(✉)]

[1] Department of History, Geography and Communication, University of Burgos, Burgos, Spain
{kmartinez,mimenendez}@ubu.es
[2] Department of Civil Engineering, University of Burgos, Burgos, Spain
abustillo@ubu.es

Abstract. Serious Games for Virtual Reality (SG-VR) is still a new subject that needs to be explored. Achieving the optimal fun and learning results depends on the application of the most suitable metrics. Virtual Reality environments offer great capabilities but at the same time make difficult to record User Experience (UX) to improve it. Moreover, the continuous evolution of Virtual Reality technologies and video game industry tendencies constantly change these metrics. This paper studies the Mechanics, Dynamics and Aesthetic (MDA) framework and User Experience metrics to develop new ones for SG-VR. These new parameters are focused on the intrinsic motivations the players need so they engage with the game. However, the development team budget must be taken into account, since it limits items and interactions but still have to aim to the learning goals. New VR metrics will be 1) UX features: chosen VR headsets, training interactions tutorials to learn control and interactive adaptions to avoid VR inconveniences; and 2) MDA features: exclusive VR aesthetical elements and its interactions.

Keywords: Serious games · Game design · Game evaluation · Virtual reality

1 Introduction

Various types of expertise are required to develop serious games, therefore the design often lacks of structural unification [5]. Different perspectives come from engineers, educators, players or designers when proposing theories and models [3]. This conflict makes challenging the design and development of educational games which get to be a fun and learning experience [4]. This paper collects five of the main theories regarding serious games design since the beginning of the process: the MDA, the DPE, the DDE, the LGDM and the EDG frameworks.

The first framework, Mechanics, Dynamics and Aesthetic (MDA), [6] considers from the designer's point of view to the player's perspective and vice versa, how the game technics should be used. Each of the identified categories influence the others to generate emotional responses in the player which allow to achieve the educational goals. Nevertheless, a few lacks were found in this classification so other works expanded these aspects, as the Design, Play and Experience (DPE) model [5]. This new framework adds

© Springer Nature Switzerland AG 2020
L. T. De Paolis and P. Bourdot (Eds.): AVR 2020, LNCS 12242, pp. 186–193, 2020.
https://doi.org/10.1007/978-3-030-58465-8_14

other layers to the design: storytelling, learning content and User Experience (UX), shown in Fig. 1. DPE model centers on giving users an active role to engage them with the educational process. Additionally, the Design, Dynamics and Experience (DDE) framework [7] encompass every development task since game production and design to the player's experience. Furthermore, DDE model focuses on the mechanics coding more than the dynamics one because distinct type of players and their behaviors are unpredictable. The last framework is the Learning Games Design Model (LGDM) [8, 9] which regards the necessary collaboration between creatives, content specialists and stakeholders during all the development. Figure 1 overviews how DDE and LGDM theories relate to MDA and DPE frameworks. These relations have been adapted to the Educational Digital Games (EDG) framework [3].

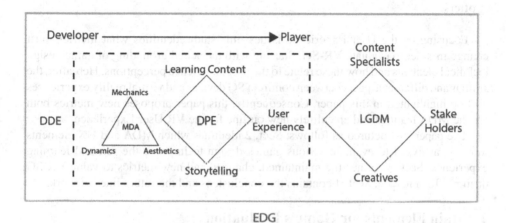

EDG

Fig. 1. Scheme of the game design theories interrelation

To summarize, relevant serious games design frameworks have identified the most important aspects for the development and how the technical characteristics (mechanics, dynamics and aesthetics) are involved with the storytelling and the learning content. Moreover, these theories highlight the development possibilities of the used technology and devices in order to enhance the UX and offer rewarding sensations. Notwithstanding, serious games design has limitations due to the development team structure and profile that must be taken into account.

However, these frameworks have to adapt to Virtual Reality Serious Game (VR-SG) because these are very different experiences. Mechanics, dynamics and aesthetics conceptions affect many gameplay features. In addition, User Experience totally changes due to the special controllers and headset screen. Usual videogames players also find difficult to adjust to VR environment and interactions. Earlier studies of designed VR-SG have found these issues when testing the experiences. Checa and Bustillo [1] made a review of 86 articles in which they identified future research lines regarding the evaluation of these aspects. The followings refer to UX metrics:

- Choosing an interactive experience is preferred because of "its balance between costs, nowadays-technological development, immersion feeling and the possibilities that users have of learning and improving their skills". On the other hand, passive experiences limit the achievement of the aimed learning content and skill improvements.
- Usability and immersion are not commonly considered when assuring the VR-experience success. However, this review highlighted that the user's higher satisfaction promotes higher learning outcomes or skills improvement.
- Most works show that, besides of users enjoying the VR experience, the unknown interface of these devices reduces the capability to learn and train. Accordingly, these VR-SG designs have to incorporate an extensive tutorial stage so users gain confidence, benefitting of all the advantages the interaction with the VR-environment offers.

Focusing on the User Experience issues, this study identifies what metrics must change in order to evaluate VR-SG. Starting with the actual grounding of game design technical elements and how these relate to the user experience perceptions. Hereafter, the similar and different aspects between common SG devices and virtual reality experiences will be highlighted in this paper. Consequently, this paper proposes new metrics both for the MDA features and an entirely new outline for the VR User Experience.

The paper is structured as follows: Sect. 2 identifies which MDA and UX elements must be analyzed to evaluate serious games design to improve the fun and learning experience; Sect. 3 defines the maintained, changed and new metrics to value VR-SG designs. To conclude, Sect. 4 contains the conclusions and the future lines of work.

2 Main Elements for Game's Evaluation

Serious game designs have to be centered on the players intrinsic motivation to motivate them want to finish the experience. In this way, games will have more probabilities to secure the learning aims. Thomas Malone [10] proposed in 1980 for the first time the Key Characteristics of a Learning Game (KCLG): the necessary sensations which allow to have fun playing. Starting with challenge, an emotion defined by the game goals if these are fixed, relevant and clear. The following, curiosity, interpreted by a cognitive and sensory way, and the third one, fantasy, which creates images for the player's imagination. Further on, Malone and Lepper [11] added in 1987 control: the emotion of command and self-determination of the player.

In recent years (2013) the Dynamical Model of Gamification of Learning (DMGL) was developed by Kim and Lee [2]. This theory links each of these sensations with the technical layers from the MDA framework and distinct game elements. The first features, game mechanics, are responsible for establishing the challenge and difficulty the player feels. The elements that build this feeling are mechanics' levels, points, goals and quests. Furthermore, mechanics' virtual items, badges, rewards and feedback allow to generate the game's fantasy. On the other hand, dynamics layer can evoke challenge and curiosity sensations. The reward scheduling system allows the player curiosity to unlock progressively the appointments when playing the game. Moreover, every dynamics pattern or system related to beat time limits and opponents encourage the player to challenge themselves and others. The last aspect encompasses the aesthetics, which generate strong feelings of fantasy through all the features concerning the storytelling. This layer is made up of the audio and visual effects that create love, surprise, delight, beauty and every positive emotion. Besides, aesthetics also increases the user's curiosity by means of thrill, envy, connection and comedy emotions. These DMGL connections are explained in Fig. 2. MDA model embraces the most important game aspects, therefore, DMLG sensations can be used to assess the serious game design. In order to measure the experience, every one of these game elements will be quantified when it appears during the narrative and progress actions. In this manner, serious games can be evaluated by its capability to engage the players to the learning aim through the involvement with the gameplay.

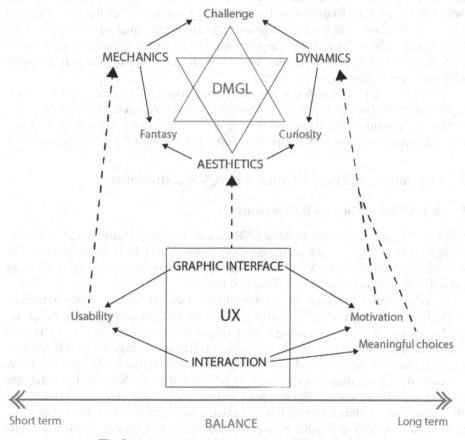

Fig. 2. Scheme of DMGL theory and UX interrelation

Nonetheless, MDA model does not include the features that allow the player interaction and involvement with the fun and learning contents. Schell [12] encompassed these as technology, the hardware and software used to generate the user experience. Likewise, UX is the global effects evoked to the player's insights due to the game interactions. The design of user experience has two important elements: (a) graphic interface, interactive through a device screen and peripherals, and (b) interaction, the player's experience and impact in the game [13]. Both aspects have to be closely planned so the gameplay generates a positive experience that makes the user enjoy and complete the learning task.

Additionally, Ferrara's theory [14] described the following user experience elements: motivation, meaningful choices, usability, aesthetics and the balance between these variables. Each of these must be valued by both long-term and short-term interactions. Motivation is the early user's appeal to experience the gameplay and the available rewards thar keep interesting achieving the goal. Continuing, meaningful choices involves the player's decisions, which change the game results. There are short-term tactics and long-term strategies. The usability layer involves the planning of all interface aspects that allow the player to perceive their own actions and the proposed quests. Interfaces should offer a sense of control since the beginning, besides allowing to master it. Aesthetic UX feature provides a pleasant direct sensory experience, which has to be sustained throughout the game. The last layer is balance, measuring the challenge and fairness the game system offers. The short-term aspect regards how the basic game interactions are quickly learnt and perceived. Besides, long-term elements measure the player's effect while progressing throughout the game.

UX aspects can be quantified as the MDA ones in order to evaluate a serious game capability to involve the player. The importance is equal to mechanics, dynamics and aesthetics elements by the means of creating a fun and learning experience. Figure 2 shows the relation between UX components and MDA elements through its connections.

3   Evaluation of These Elements in a VR Experience

3.1   MDA Evaluation for VR Experiences

MDA metrics are also useful to design VR serious games. Nevertheless, VR devices change considerably how the player interacts, controls and feels the responses [15]. Accordingly, to study future VR serious games designs this paper has to consider every game component and its relation to DMGL emotions.

To begin with, VR-SG use the same mechanics elements (quests, goals and levels) to challenge the players. On the contrary, VR users feel completely different fantasy mechanics aspects [16]. Interacting with items, videos and characters on a screen or being surrounded by these in the virtual environment alters the experience. VR-SG have a greater ability to evoke strong feelings and keep visual information for the player than any other device [4]; thus, a re-evaluation is needed fort these elements. Regarding the dynamics, challenge aspects like progression, patterns and strategies affect just as any other game. By contrast, curiosity features engage quite different with the VR environment. Exploring and interacting with characters, items and venues generate a strong desire in the user to discover and play all the options. As for mechanics, dynamics metrics must be revised. Lastly, the visual and sound effects in VR environment are unlike any other device, constituting a revolutionary aesthetic layer. Players feel stronger the fantasy and curiosity emotions with VR devices than with common games. Hence, aesthetics aspects should be carefully designed to avoid negative sensations and to boost positive ones. The user's involvement is mostly guaranteed if these elements adapt to the VR technology, engaging with the learning content.

3.2 UX Evaluation for VR Experiences

This paper centers on how user experience aspects must change for VR-SG. The most important transformations depend on VR devices, the allowed capacities and the budget so the experiences are passive or active. Furthermore, how the user learns to control the interface, apart from the obtained satisfaction, are essential factors.

The first element to consider is the headset chosen for the game. Some studies highlight [1] how experiences, which allow interaction with game components and follow motivation and meaningful choices UX layers, are preferred by VR users. Consequently, devices with interactive controllers as Oculus Rift or HTC Vive will be a better choice for serious games than, for example, an Oculus Go headset. The review also found a likely problem for future developments due to budget limitations. The high costs of high-visual quality VR-environments and explorative interaction experiences may not allow the choice [1]. Thus, these constraints should be considered during a SG-VR evaluation, not expecting high-quality game effects and interactions. In addition to these matters, the interaction must allow players to enjoy and complete the game avoiding common VR inconveniences. One of them is virtual reality sickness, an issue that must be prevented by adding some interface features. Also, developers should not implement highly complex actions using the controllers or the body movement in the VR-environment. This kind of difficulties may decrease the users' motivation to keep playing and the final perception of the game.

UX possibilities regarding the process to learn the interactions are also relevant. The review pinpoints how important is to design a training tutorial in every SG-VR so players feel comfortable with the controllers and movement in the virtual environment. Taking care of this usability feature will improve the user's perception of its own actions and the game goals. Moreover, UX should be designed to allow the achievement of more difficult interactions following the user's meaningful choices. Lastly, the interface has to be aesthetically pleasant, even when the quality is restricted to the game development possibilities. This feature is indispensable for every user's interaction so this must be

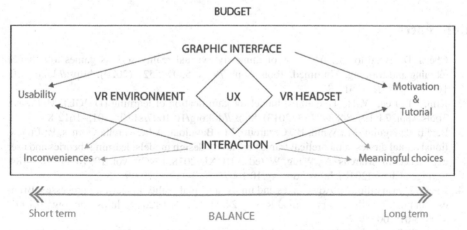

Fig. 3. Scheme of proposed UX metrics for VR

accessible, attractive and easily understood. Every player's action should be complemented by visual or audio effects, no matter if the interface use buttons or movement control. Figure 3 collects these metrics and their connections with VR UX elements.

4 Conclusions and Future Works

This paper defined various elements that different theories have used to evaluate serious games design and propose changes so these can measure VR-SG. The most important alterations are related with the different sensations a VR experience evokes. MDA framework and user experience encompass these new metrics.

The player must be engaged to the game so the learning goal is achieved, thus, the feelings the virtual environment create are essential. Firstly, the VR headset and development team budget limitations must be taken into account. From there, VR-SG designs have to focus on the adaption of virtual items and interactions to avoid the defined VR issues and adjust the narrative to achieve the learning goals. Next essential feature in VR-SG experiences is usability. There must be training interaction tutorials to acquire VR control before starting the game. Avoiding interactive issues will assure VR users perceptions to be optimal. Accordingly, the following step in VR-SG development regards increasing the player's emotions through VR capabilities applied to MDA aspects. Some of these elements will include player's interaction, item's environment integration and audiovisual effects.

Future works will study these features to define which game elements are affecting the intrinsic emotions. This analysis will develop new metrics to apply in the creation of future VR-SG designs. Furthermore, VR experiences implementing these key factors will allow to test its validity so this study could be confirmed or refused.

Acknowledgments. This work was partially supported by the GruaRV project (Reference Number INVESTUN/18/0002) of the Consejería de Empleo of the Junta de Castilla y León (Spain) and the Ministry of Science, Innovation and Universities (FPU18/04688).

References

1. Checa, D., Bustillo, A.: A review of immersive virtual reality serious games to enhance learning and training. Multimed. Tools Appl. **79**(9), 5501–5527 (2020). https://doi.org/10.1007/s11042-013-1612-8
2. Kim, J.T., Lee, W.-H.: Dynamical model for gamification of learning (DMGL). Multimed. Tools Appl. **74**(19), 8483–8493 (2013). https://doi.org/10.1007/s11042-013-1612-8
3. Pereira de Aguiar, M., Winn, B., Cezarotto, M., Battaiola, A.L., Varella Gomes, P.: Educational digital games: a theoretical framework about design models, learning theories and user experience. In: Marcus, A., Wang, W. (eds.) DUXU 2018. LNCS, vol. 10918, pp. 165–184. Springer, Cham (2018). https://doi.org/10.1007/978-3-319-91797-9_13
4. Checa, D., Bustillo, A.: Advantages and limits of virtual reality in learning processes: Briviesca in the fifteenth century. Virtual Reality **24**(1), 151–161 (2019). https://doi.org/10.1007/s10055-019-00389-7
5. Winn, B.: The design, play, and experience framework. In: Handbook of Research on Effective Electronic Gaming in Education, vol. 3, pp. 1010–1024. ISR, New York (2009)

6. Hunicke, R., Leblanc, M., Zubek, R.: MDA: a formal approach to game design and game research. In: Proceedings of the AAAI Workshop on Challenges in Game AI (2004)
7. Walk, W., Görlich, D., Barrett, M.: Design, Dynamics, Experience (DDE): an advancement of the mda framework for game design. In: Korn, O., Lee, N. (eds.) Game Dynamics. LNCS, pp. 27–45. Springer, Cham (2017). https://doi.org/10.1007/978-3-319-53088-8_3
8. Chamberlin, B., Trespalacios, J., Gallagher, R.: The learning games design model: immersion, collaboration, and outcomes-driven development. Int. J. Game-Based Learn. (IJGBL) 2(3), 87–110 (2012)
9. Chamberlin, B., Trespalacios, J., Gallagher, R.: Bridging research and game development: a learning games design model for multi-game projects. In: Gamification in Education: Breakthroughs in Research and Practice, pp. 66–88. IGI Global, Hershey (2018)
10. Malone, T. W.: What makes things fun to learn? A study of intrinsically motivating computer games. Technical report, Xerox Palo Alto Research Center (1980)
11. Malone, T.W., Lepper, M.R.: Making learning fun: a taxonomy of intrinsic motivations for learning. In: Snow, R. E., Farr, M.J., (eds) Aptitude, learning and instruction III (1987)
12. Schell, J.: The Art of Game Design: A Book of Lenses. Elsevier, Burlinton (2008)
13. Menezes, F.M., Silva, I.C.S., Frosi, F.O.: Game user experience (ux): explorando a teoria da diegese. In: SBC, Proceedings of SBGames 2017. XVI SBGames, São Paulo, SP, Brazil, 2–4 November 2017
14. Ferrara, J.: Playful Design: Creating Game Experiences in Everyday Interfaces. Rosenfeld Media, New York (2012)
15. Stapleton, A.J.: Serious games: serious opportunities. In: Australian Game Developers' Conference (2004)
16. De Paolis, L.T., De Luca, V.: The impact of the input interface in a virtual environment: the Vive controller and the Myo armband. Virtual Reality (2019). https://doi.org/10.1007/s10055-019-00409-6

Virtual Reality Technologies as a Tool for Development of Physics Learning Educational Complex

Yevgeniya Daineko[✉], Madina Ipalakova, Dana Tsoy, Aigerim Seitnur,
Daulet Zhenisov, and Zhiger Bolatov

International Information Technology University, Almaty, Kazakhstan
yevgeniyadaineko@gmail.com, m.ipalakova@gmail.com,
danatsoy@gmail.com, aigerim.seitnurova@mail.ru,
zhenisovdk@gmail.com

Abstract. The paper describes the project on physics learning. It was implemented using the Unity game engine, Leap Motion package to provide controlling within the laboratory works, and C# programming language in order to define logic between objects of the app. Also, the survey on the efficiency of similar projects and applications is presented. It was conducted among students of the high school. The observations on using of virtual reality technology are also given. The main purpose of the article is to demonstrate and evaluate use of the application in subject's learning and its efficiency. The paper also raises question on educational tools relevance and modernity.

Keywords: Virtual reality · Virtual physical laboratory · Physics · Unity3d · Education

1 Introduction

Education is one of the most important need of the society. It is a basis of everyone's life that defines the future. That is why it is very important to make learning effective, useful and relevant. One of the features of relevant education is modern tools and approaches. Different companies and educational organizations work on development of specific apps and devices that will improve understanding of the material. The game approach allows presenting information to students in simplified form and at the same time does not ruin its conception. Moreover, it provides better representation of some complex concepts. Another advantage of modern technologies is that contemporary youth are familiar with them. It means that they do not need to be taught in order to work with apps. On the other hand, we can see the poor equipment in some that are not provided with all the necessary physical installations. Thus, the educational applications allow partially solving this problem. In order to gain additional information about other's experience in the field the analysis of existing projects with similar aims and implementation was conducted.

L. T. De Paolis and P. Bourdot (Eds.): AVR 2020, LNCS 12242, pp. 194–202, 2020.
https://doi.org/10.1007/978-3-030-58465-8_15

2 Using of Virtual Reality Technology for Physics Learning

Over the past few years, there has been a sharp increase in the use of virtual reality technology in education, in particular for the study of physics. Sanders et al. present three different virtual environments that were developed using three different technologies [1]. A three-dimensional magnetic field emanating from a magnet in the form of a rod was used as a physical concept. Virtual environments have been developed that allow the interaction, control and study of electromagnetic phenomena. Another project consists of two demonstrations of virtual reality for electro-magnetism, which show electromagnetic fields generated by particles moving along a user-defined trajectory [2]. For this implementation, the Unity game creation engine was used. Testing took place on the headset HTC Vive VR with hand-held controllers. In [3], "measurements" can be carried out to determine various calibration coefficients necessary for correcting the electrometer readings for ion recombination, polarity, temperature/pressure. All of them are conducted within a virtual environment. Morales et al. show a prototype with augmented reality technology [4]. It was developed as a part of the study of mechanics that simulates uniform rectilinear movement and free fall of an object. The result was a prototype with two functions, the first of which allows simulating the movement of the vehicle at a constant speed, the second allows simulating the fall of objects taking into account gravity. In [5], the physics of air bubbles formed in a liquid is considered in detail. With the help of virtual reality, the sounds of drops falling in water were visualized. Sakamoto et al. created a prototype system using virtual reality technology, so that anyone could easily perform scientific experiments in physics and chemistry [6]. Also, the developed system is adapted for mobile devices. The ability of virtual reality technology to provide a sense of immersion and presence with tracking the whole body and receiving feedback allows conducting experiments in laboratories remotely, safely and realistically. Pirker et al. studied the experience of learning in a virtual laboratory within the framework of the scale of an ordinary room [7]. Virtual reality was created using a traditional screen and multi-user settings for virtual reality (mobile VR settings supporting multi-user setups). It is shown that the laboratory of virtual reality has such qualities as immersion, involvement, ease of use and training. Knierim et al. developed an application using virtual and augmented reality technologies to visualize the thermal conductivity of metals [8]. In [9], an interactive visualization of the physics of subatomic particles in virtual reality is presented. This system was developed by an interdisciplinary team as a training tool for the study and investigation of collisions of subatomic particles. The article describes the developed system, discusses solutions for the design of visualization and the process of joint development. Another project presents a multi-user virtual reality environment that allows users to visualize and analyze the structures and dynamics of complex molecular structures "on the fly" with atomic level accuracy, perform complex molecular tasks, and interact with other users in the same virtual environment [10].

3 Results

A software application for physics study with the technology of virtual reality was developed in the International Information Technology University (Almaty, Kazakhstan). As a platform of the application's implementation the Unity game engine was chosen. There were several reasons for this. Unity is a cross-platform engine that supports many additional packages and libraries. Another convenient feature of the engine is the support of the physical characteristics for game objects. Also it lets to extend specifications of the object's behavior and interactions between them using own scripts. For intuitive interaction with the app the Leap Motion controller was used. Its main feature is the ability to work without other additional devices, using only palm of the hands. Thus, it is possible to recreate the closest to real-life interaction between human and objects.

The developed application represents a program that allows studying physics both independently and at a school, together with a teacher. It fully reveals the studied physical laws and concepts thanks to the visual representation. An important aspect is that the software covers all the necessary components of the subject study, as it consists of problem tasks, laboratory works, animations and tests. These modules are the core of the program. Thanks to this structure, students gain new knowledge by doing a laboratory work or observing animation, apply them in practice, solving problem tasks and check their performance using test questions. The modular approach organizes the gradual flow of new information and its active use, thereby simplifying the perception and memorization. Figure 1 shows a component diagram. It reflects the internal structure of the system and demonstrates the relationship between the elements. Based on it, four main components can be identified: tasks, laboratory works, animations and a set of test questions. Their correct operation is ensured by auxiliary components, namely folders with common program objects, models, prefabs, and program codes. There are also separate elements necessary for a specific task, laboratory work, test question or animation exist. The operation of the Leap Motion module is provided by a separate package. Thanks to it, the laboratory works can be controlled with the help of hands.

The diagram presented in Fig. 2 shows the model of interaction between a user and system's components. The actors are the user and the application elements. Use cases are actions that are possible in the program. Thus, the main actor is the user that starts the whole system and initializes the rest of the processes. The user starts the Main launcher by opening the application. Through it, the user can run a laboratory work, a test, a problem task, a tutorial or an animation. Also, through the launcher the user can change the system settings, send feedback, learn about the developers of the application, or close the program. The use case Play allows the user to run the actors Problem, Laboratory work, Tutorial, Test, and Animation. The laboratory works and tasks consist of three precedents: starting a laboratory work/task, changing the values of variables and viewing the conditions of the task/order of laboratory work (Fig. 2).

From the main screen of the application, the user can go to the main elements of the application: laboratory works, tasks, tests, animations and a tutorial that helps to familiarize yourself with the operation of the application.

Figure 3 presents the scene of one of the five developed labs. In this work, the user needs to examine the relationship between voltage, current, and the location of the rheostat slider. The user needs to manage the experiment using the Leap Motion, which allows sliding the virtual rheostat slider manually.

Figure 4 shows a visualization of the problem of a boat and two fishermen of different weights. It is necessary to determine its movement, when the fishermen change their

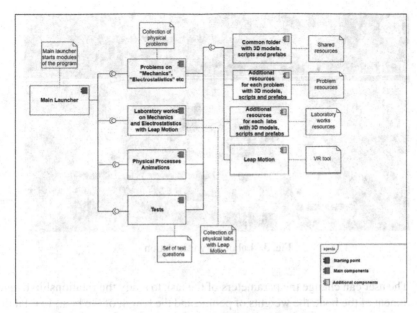

Fig. 1. Component diagram of the application

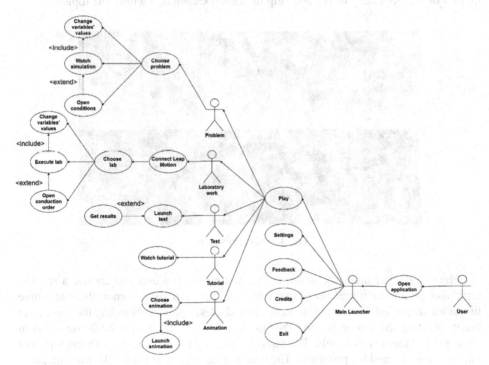

Fig. 2. Use case diagram

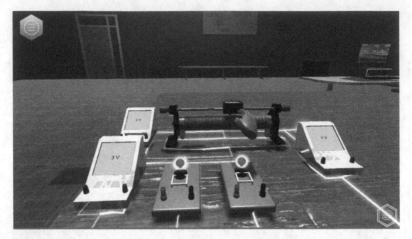

Fig. 3. Laboratory installation

places. The user can change the parameters of the task to study the relationship between the movement of the boat, the weights of people and the length of the boat. In total there are 16 problems on such topics like Mechanics and Electrostatistics. They relate to the themes of the laboratory works and help to deepen knowledge within the topics.

Fig. 4. Problem's scene

Figure 5 demonstrates the program in a test mode. The user can choose a specific topic and get a randomized set of questions. In the upper right corner, there is a time limitation displayed. The test allows checking the level of understanding the topic after the conducting the lab or solving the problem task. It helps to refresh the physical concepts and learned materials. The topics of the questions coincide with the topics of laboratory works and the problems. The total number of questions is 101, they are given to students randomly and have 4 different answers, only one of them is correct.

In Fig. 6 there is an animation scene screenshot. It is provided with the "Launch animation" button. It starts the animation that contains description of specific physical

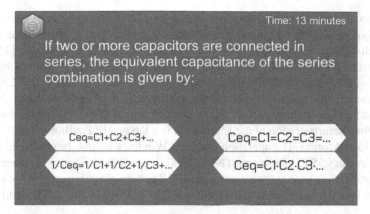

Fig. 5. Screenshot with a test question

process. The animations are dedicated to Dynamics, Kinematics, Statics, Electrostatics. The total amount of the animations is 30.

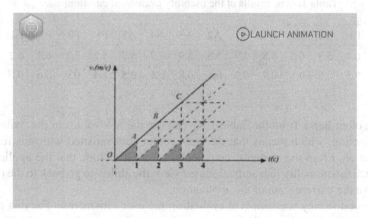

Fig. 6. Screenshot with an animation

Students can choose any of different modules of the application or perform all of them based on their preferences. Such approach improves the level of understanding and perception of information.

4   Evaluation

In order to approve the effectiveness of the application the following surveys were conducted. The participants were students of the 9th grade of the Republican Physics and Mathematical School. The total number of students was 24. The research was performed from September to December in 2019–2020 academic year. The first step of the study consisted of using the virtual laboratory in physics classes. Later in the end of December the students took part in the two types of surveys. The first one was general about evaluation of the usability of the virtual laboratory application. It was estimated based on the well-known method "Practical Heuristics for Usability Evaluation" [11]. This test consists of thirteen questions with the answers within the range from 1 (bad) to 7 (good). They are grouped into three sections: the first four questions relate to "Learning" (L1–L4), the next five questions relate to the quality of "Adapting to the user" (A1–A5), and the last four questions are about "Feedback and errors" (F1–F4). The hardware that was used for a demonstration of the application is a laptop HP Pavilion 15-ab017ur and controller Leap Motion. The operation system is Windows 10 x64, Intel Core i5-5200U, Intel HD Graphics 5500, graphic card NVIDIA GeForce 940 M. To provide correct work of the controller the Orion software was installed. The school equipment did not go under minimal technical requirements of the Oculus Rift HMD, that is why the desktop version was used.

The results of this survey are presented in the Table 1. The high values in each section show that the students are satisfied with the functionality, documentation and feedback provided within the virtual laboratory.

Table 1. The results of the usability evaluation questionnaire

Question	L1	L2	L3	L4	A1	A2	A3	A4	A5	F1	F2	F3	F4	Mean
Mean	6,4	6,3	6,3	5,8	3,9	5,8	5,9	6,2	6,7	5,2	5,8	6,2	6,2	5,9
Std. Dev.	5,5	0,6	0,6	0,7	0,7	0,1	0,8	0,6	0,5	1,4	0,9	0,6	0,6	0,7

On the other hand, from the Table 1 we can see the low values in the "Adapting to the user" section, which means that the students are less satisfied with this feature of the application. From the students' comments we can conclude that the application is missing such functionality like animations preview, the ability to go back to the previous step, or save the current state of the application.

The second survey was aimed at evaluating the user satisfaction. For this purpose, the standard questionnaire for User Interface Satisfaction was chosen [12]. The test is composed of thirty-two questions with answers in the range from 1 (bad) to 7 (good). The questions are grouped into six sections: overall reaction to the software (Impr1–Impr6), representation on the screen (Screen1–Screen4), terminology and system information (TSI1–TSI6), leaning (Learning1–Learning6), system capabilities (SC1–SC5) and usability and user interface (UUI1–UUI5). The original questionnaire was modified by reducing the number of questions to twenty-seven. The section of usability and user interface was removed, since these features were evaluated in the separate survey.

Table 2 presents the results of the answers evaluation. They show the students' positive attitude and the opinion about the laboratory. Separately, in the comments the students made several suggestions. The two most common suggestions were the following. The students would like to have a possibility to register in the system, so they could save the current progress with the practical tasks. Another suggestion was at the same time a disadvantage of the system. The students pointed out that not all visualizations of the practical tasks follow one style. All wishes and shortcomings marked by the students will be taken into account in the development of the next version of the program.

Table 2. The results of the user satisfaction evaluation questionnaire

Question	Mean	Standard deviation	Question	Mean	Standard deviation
Impr1	6,8	0,4	TSI5	4,4	0,5
Impr2	6,6	0,5	TSI6	4,4	0,5
Impr3	6,2	0,7	Learning1	6,6	0,5
Impr4	6,3	0,6	Learning2	6,4	0,5
Impr5	6,3	0,6	Learning3	5,9	0,7
Impr6	6,3	0,6	Learning4	6,7	0,5
Screen1	6,9	0,3	Learning5	6,6	0,5
Screen2	6,3	0,5	Learning6	6,6	0,5
Screen3	6,4	0,5	SC1	6,7	0,5
Screen4	6,4	0,5	SC2	5,5	0,7
TSI1	5,7	1	SC3	7	0
TSI2	6,5	0,5	SC4	5,8	0,7
TSI3	5,9	0,7	SC5	6,4	0,5
TSI4	6,4	0,5	Mean	5,9	0,5

Thus, the results of the conducted surveys indicate that the students are satisfied with the functionality and user interface of the virtual laboratory as an additional learning tool.

5 Conclusion

The paper showed the process of the research on the application of virtual reality technology in education, physics learning specifically. Also, the results of the survey among high school students about the efficiency of the developed software are presented. The process of interaction with the created program is shown and its components are described. The main conclusion of the article is that such type of education increases independent work of students, develop their analytical skills and the used technologies provide the better way of delivering the information.

Acknowledgement. The work was done under the funding of the Ministry of Education and Science of the Republic of Kazakhstan (No. AP05135692).

References

1. Sanders, B., Shen, Y., Vincenzi, D.: Understanding user interface preferences for xr environments when exploring physics and engineering principles. In: Ahram, T. (ed.) AHFE 2019. AISC, vol. 973, pp. 296–304. Springer, Cham (2020). https://doi.org/10.1007/978-3-030-20476-1_30
2. Franklin, J., Ryder, A.: Electromagnetic field visualization in virtual reality. Am. J. Phy. **87**(2), 153–157 (2019). https://doi.org/10.1119/1.5080224
3. Beavis, A.W., Ward, J.W.: Innovation in education: computer simulation in physics training. In: 10th International Conference on 3D Radiation Dosimetry (IC3DDOSE) 1305(UNSP 012057). https://doi.org/10.1088/1742-6596/1305/1/012057
4. Morales, A.D., Sanchez, S.A., Pineda, C.M., Romero, H.J.: Use of augmented reality for the simulation of basic mechanical physics phenomena. Expotecnologia 2018 Research, Innovation and Development in Engineering 519(UNSP 012021) (2019). https://doi.org/10.1088/1757-899x/519/1/012021
5. Bolsee, Q., Bolsee, V.: A Fast water droplet sound simulation. In: 2018 International Conference on 3D Immersion. Brussels, Belgium (2018)
6. Sakamoto, M., et al.: A Study on applications for scientific experiments using the vr technology. In: 2018 International Conference on Information and Communication Technology Robotics (ICT-robot). Busan, South Korea (2018)
7. Pirker, J., Holly, M.S., Hipp, P., Koni, C., Jeitler, D., Gutl, C.: Improving Physics Education Through Different Immersive and Engaging Laboratory Setups. Int. Mobile Commun. Technol. Learn. **725**, 443–454 (2018)
8. Knierim, P., Kiss, F., Schmidt, A.: Look inside: understanding thermal flux through augmented reality. In: Adjunct Proceedings of the 2018 IEEE International Symposium on Mixed and Augmented Reality (2018)
9. Duer, Z., Piilonen, L., Glasson, G.: Belle2VR: A virtual-reality visualization of subatomic particle physics in the belle ii experiment. IEEE Comput. Graph. Appl. **38**(3), 33–43 (2018)
10. O'Connor, M., et al.: Sampling molecular conformations and dynamics in a multiuser virtual reality framework. Science Advances 4(6) (2018)
11. Perlman, G.: Practical Usability Evaluation. CH: Extended Abstracts on Human Factors in Computing Systems, ACM, 168–169 (1997)
12. Chin, J. P., Diehl, V. A., Norman, K. L.: Development of an instrument measuring user satisfaction of the human-computer interface. In: Proceedings of SIGCHI Conference on Human Factors in Computing Systems, pp. 213–218, ACM, New York (1988)

Evaluating the Effect of Reinforcement Haptics on Motor Learning and Cognitive Workload in Driver Training

Thomas G. Simpson[✉] and Karen Rafferty[✉]

Queen's University Belfast, Belfast, UK
{tsimpson07,k.rafferty}@qub.ac.uk

Abstract. Haptic technologies have the capacity to enhance motor learning, potentially improving the safety and quality of operating performance in a variety of applications, yet there is limited research evaluating implementation of these devices in driver training environments. A driving simulator and training scenario were developed to assess the quality of motor learning produced with wrist-attached vibrotactile haptic motors for additional reinforcement feedback. User studies were conducted with 36 participants split into 2 groups based on feedback modality. Throughout the simulation vehicle interactions with the course were recorded, enabling comparisons of pre and post-training performance between the groups to evaluate short-term retention of the steering motor skill. Statistically significant differences were found between the two groups for vehicle position safety violations ($U = 78.50$, $P = 0.008$) where the visual-haptic group improved significantly more than the visual group. The Raw NASA-TLX (RTLX) was completed by participants to examine the cognitive effect of the additional modality, where the visual-haptic group reported greater levels of workload ($U = 90.50$, $P = 0.039$). In conclusion, reinforcement vibrotactile haptics can enhance short-term retention of motor learning with a positive effect on the safety and quality of post-training behaviour, which is likely a result of increased demand and stimulation encouraging the adaptation of sensorimotor transformations.

Keywords: Haptics · Motor learning · Virtual environments · Driver training

1 Introduction

With the advent of AR and VR, virtual training systems are becoming effective educational tools in many applications, including surgery, industrial maintenance, flight simulators, and sports [1]. Haptics have the potential to advance the quality of virtual pedagogical systems with the additional sense of touch, enhancing the bandwidth of communication between the human and the computer with a supplementary channel providing access to haptic and tactile memory, typically ignored by conventional techniques. Advances in haptic technology

© Springer Nature Switzerland AG 2020
L. T. De Paolis and P. Bourdot (Eds.): AVR 2020, LNCS 12242, pp. 203–211, 2020.
https://doi.org/10.1007/978-3-030-58465-8_16

could optimise motor learning by encouraging the adaptation of sensorimotor transformations [2], potentially improving the safety and quality of training in certain driving scenarios; however, limited research has been conducted to assess the practical suitability of haptic implementations in these environments.

A rich corpus of psychology and neuroscience literature describes comprehensive observations of feedback effects on motor learning, yet real-world applications remain limited. Function-specific studies are responsible for maturing the literature further as the success of haptic feedback varies among application [3]. Implementations are typically in the form of haptic guidance, with the motivation to guide individuals to the correct technique in pursuit of reduced errors and improved training quality. Studies have demonstrated negative effects due to a reliance on the feedback and there are many instances where no statistical significance has been found between groups trained with haptic guidance and those without [4].

Poor results from studies regarding haptic guidance have led to the development of progressive haptic guidance, in which the amount of feedback is decreased over the training period, to gradually reduce learners reliance on the stimuli. This process has been applied to a steering task [4], with promising results achieved by integrating a haptic system for a wheelchair driving simulator with an algorithm incorporated to adapt the firmness of guidance relative to on-going error, which was administered through force-feedback in the wheel. Alternative implementations are also being investigated, such as error amplification which provides haptic feedback to increase movement errors during training. These are designed to improve learning practices and have been demonstrated as superior to haptic guidance in some scenarios [5]. This technique has also been applied to a steering task [6], where haptic feedback was delivered through the steering wheel in a virtual environment, commencing with guidance for initial training stages and progressing to error amplification. Insufficient tangible benefits of this approach suggest advancements are required to better exploit cognitive function during driving skill acquisition.

The motor learning literature expresses concern regarding the haptic guidance paradigm as it risks subject dependence on feedback, often compromising post-training performance [7]. Implementations providing error feedback could be beneficial as the motor learning impairment evident in haptic guidance is mitigated. This can be observed in a study [8] that generated seat vibrations when the vehicle travelled further than 0.5 m from the road-centre to promote lane-keeping in a driving simulator task, finding evidence that concurrent error feedback can improve short-term retention of motor behaviour. This study did not isolate modality, giving the haptics group and the control group different levels of information, such that any observed effect may not be due to haptic implementation.

Studies from the literature have not evaluated the potential of reinforcement learning using vibrotactile wrist-attached haptics, where most experiments have elected to use guidance feedback directly from the steering wheel, with varying reported results. The approach presented is a wrist-attached vibrotactile haptic system to promote motor learning by generating increased motivation with concurrent reinforcement feedback during incorrect vehicle positioning. This technique could eliminate the motor learning impairment evident in haptic guidance, due to the feedback style reducing the risk of post-training reliance, as well as increasing the level of challenge by encouraging correct technique. Evaluations of cognitive workload associated with haptic techniques of this nature are critical for understanding how implementations modulate task demands and the effect that has on the motor learning process.

There is a clear research aperture for novel implementations of haptics in vehicle training scenarios; hence, the objective of the presented experiment was to evaluate the suitability of reinforcement vibrotactile haptics for a complex driver training scenario by observing the effect on short-term retention performance and cognitive workload. To accomplish this, 36 participants were divided into 2 groups where 1 group received visual-haptic training feedback and the other visual feedback. Exclusive haptic feedback was not studied as it presents inadequate information regarding impending instructions, limited to immediate reinforcement by concurrent implementation. This arrangement fairly isolated the variable of modality, with comparisons facilitated by simulation based metrics, to measure change in performance, and the RTLX questionnaire, to examine cognitive workload. The remainder of this paper includes descriptions of the system design and experiment procedure, as well as presentation and analysis of the results.

2 System Design

A performance driver training scenario was developed in Unity 3D, a game development engine designed for the production of interactive 3D virtual environments. A driving course was created utilising various components available on the Unity Asset store, such as models of track sections, trees, grass, barriers, and a vehicle; constructed to be demanding to help capture improvement, yet concise to sustain participant concentration levels. The vehicle physics were tuned to be realistic but also punishing for incorrect inputs, so that the error feedback offered significant benefit to the participant. The physical component of the system was comprised of a Playseat racing chair, a G920 wheel and pedals, and a NEC LCD 46 in. monitor with a resolution of 1920×1080 pixels, as seen in Fig. 1a.

An efficient path around the course was devised in conjunction with the Queen's University Racing Team, represented by a white 3-dimensional line visible in Fig. 1d, which participants were instructed to follow and learn. To explore the effect of modality, an Arduino based haptic system was developed to generate vibrations to the relevant sensory input if the projected trajectory was neglected, accomplished via USB serial connection to the Arduino at a communication rate of 9600 baud, with execution instructions transmitted from C# event scripting in Unity. An L298N motor driver board connected to an RS 423D DC PSU, powered two 3V RS PRO DC motors at 1.21 W, one for each wrist. A plastic inertial mass was screwed to the motor shaft to augment generated

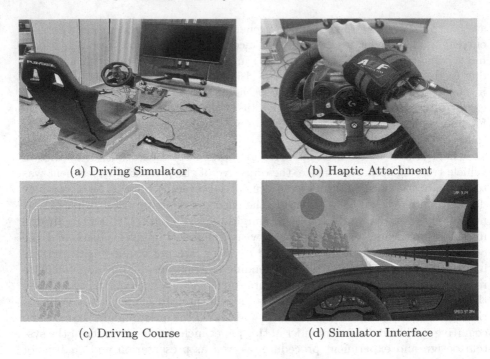

(a) Driving Simulator   (b) Haptic Attachment

(c) Driving Course   (d) Simulator Interface

Fig. 1. Simulator design

vibrations for distribution of haptic feedback. This was then implemented into a small plastic tube with epoxy fixing it firmly in place, creating a haptic module controllable from the computer. This was cable tied to a Velcro wrist strap for human attachment, covered with protective material for increased safety and comfort observed in Fig. 1a, remaining secured to the wrists of visual-haptic participants throughout the study.

Within Unity, a box collider system was created laterally along the vehicle to detect interaction with the instructed trajectory. This was accomplished with four box colliders spaced evenly apart, two inner and two outer colliders. When one of the outer colliders contacted the physical representation of the instruction, the haptics would begin to vibrate on the side that required movement, such that the right haptic motor would vibrate to indicate a right turn. This vibration would continue until the inner box collider contacted the projected path, detecting the participants return to an appropriate position.

3 Experiment

A controlled between-subjects experiment was conducted with 36 participants, with 18 in the visual and visual-haptic groups, where the independent variable being studied was the information type communicated to participants. Both groups were given identical visual instructions to fairly isolate modality.

The visual-haptics group received additional concurrent vibrotactile feedback designed to reinforce the motor learning procedure by promoting the correct steering responses, activated when participants failed to follow instruction. Subjects were required to negotiate the course with the objective of learning to follow the path communicated on screen that represented an optimised route. Each subject experienced the same location of visual instructions regardless of ability or performance, while frequency of haptic feedback was modulated proportionally to time spent in positional error.

3.1 Objectives

The experiment objective was to determine the quality of motor learning with concurrent vibrotactile feedback, through observations of improvements to safety and vehicle positioning, while observing cognitive workload for further analysis. Based on these objectives the following hypothesis was formed: the visual-haptic group would demonstrate improved motor learning because of the additional reinforcement, exhibiting greater cognitive workload due to more demanding stimulation.

3.2 Dependent Variables

There were three dependent variables in the experiment that were utilised to determine the suitability of vibrotactile haptics feedback in this context. The first dependent variable measured the frequency of participants off-road interactions; when the vehicle made physical contact with a component of the course that was not the road. For instance if the vehicle wheel made contact with the grass an error was counted, achieved with object colliders and collision detection in Unity. This dependent variable assesses the efficacy of the training from a safety perspective by quantifying vehicle positioning safety violations.

The second dependent variable measured the frequency with which the vehicle exceeded a distance of $4\,m^1$ from the instructed trajectory. This value was chosen arbitrarily prior to the experiment, based on the width of the driving course. An error was counted for every frame spent more than $4\,m$ from the suggested path, generating a metric for evaluating the short-term retention of motor learning by examining the post-training proximity to the suggested path.

The third dependent variable was the RTLX, a scientifically developed and validated psychological questionnaire that assesses cognitive workload. The raw version was preferred as studies are inconclusive over the benefits of the traditional version which consumes more time and participant effort [9]. This was conducted with 6 different criteria subjectively rated by each participant on a 21-gradation scale to yield a score from 0–100, subsequently averaged for a total score. Individual criteria were also assessed to evaluate any further differences. This variable is important to understand the human-behaviour elicited by the additional haptic modality, supporting interpretations and understanding of the effects observed in the simulation metrics.

---

[1] In simulation metres.

3.3 Participants

Participants were selected via department wide user study invitations. There were 36 participants, of which 2 were left handers and 34 were right handers. There were 16 males and 2 females in each group. The age of participants, in years, ranged from 19 to 63 where the visual-haptic group average age (M = 27.37, SD = 9.97) was similar to the visual group average age (M = 25.79, SD = 11.62).

3.4 Procedure

There were two types of different lap present in the study: a lap with instructions that the participants were required to follow, termed a training lap, and a lap without instructions where the participants were required to replicate what was learned in the training laps, termed a performance assessment lap. The training lap was defined by visual representations of the suggested trajectory for subjects to follow, as well as haptic feedback.

Initially the subjects drove two performance assessment laps, allowing evaluation of baseline performance for comparison with further laps. Subsequently, candidates would complete four training laps, then two performance assessment laps, then four training laps, and a final two performance assessment laps.

4 Results and Discussion

The objective of the presented results is to determine the effect of modality on motor behaviour improvements exhibited in the retention phase, relative to the pre-training phase, according to the dependent variables described. The first and second dependent variables were observed from data recorded to CSV files in the simulation, subsequently analysed in MATLAB and SPSS. Due to the nonparametric characteristics of the data the Mann-Whitney U test was required to compare the medians of the two groups, where all results presented use two-tailed exact significance values. Median and Median Absolute Deviation (MAD) values are displayed where necessary for a robust measure of variability. Results reporting improvement were calculated as percentage decreases by taking the error difference between the initial training phase and final retention phase, and dividing that by the initial training phase errors.

Statistically significant differences were found between the two groups (U = 78.50, P = 0.008) for the improvement between the initial performance assessment phase and the retention phase for the amount of safety errors generated by off-road interaction. The decrease of safety violations in the visual-haptic group (M = 75.96%, MAD = 31.66%) was greater than in the visual only group (M = 43.75%, MAD = 35.80%), displayed in Fig. 2b where the cross is the mean value. The results reveal an observable positive effect on participant motor learning for the visual-haptics group, encouraging appropriate vehicle positioning and path negotiation, which can be detected further in the amount of errors generated by deviations greater than 4 m from the projected trajectory, where statistically significant differences were also observed between the groups (U = 99.00, P = 0.046). The average error decrease in the haptic group (M = 50.12%, MAD = 15.67%) was significantly greater than in the visual group (M = 41.48%, MAD = 18.60%), reaffirming superior short-term motor skill retention in the visual-haptic group.

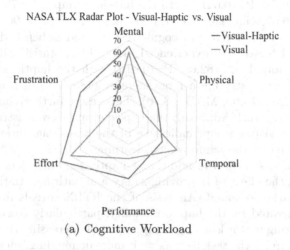

(a) Cognitive Workload

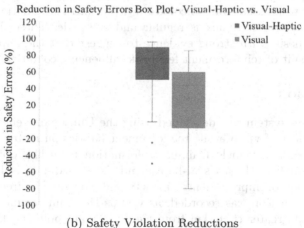

(b) Safety Violation Reductions

Fig. 2. Experiment results

In order to measure cognitive workload the RTLX was completed by the participants, which was scored and uploaded to MATLAB and SPSS for analysis. There were statistically significant differences between the two groups (U = 90.50, P = 0.039) where the haptic group (M = 50.83, MAD = 12.02) reported significantly increased cognitive workload (+32.61%) over the visual group (M = 38.33,

MAD = 11.99). This result is expected due to improved performance, which can be explained by the increase in cognitive workload incited by reinforcement feedback.

Fig. 2a demonstrates the overall results of the RTLX, displaying the elements that were scored differently. Only two sub-elements had statistically significant differences, which were the scores for effort and frustration. For the effort exerted during the task, statistically significant differences were found between the two groups (U = 91.50, P = 0.041), with the haptics group (M = 70.00, MAD = 1.60) reporting a 16.67% increase over the visual group (M = 60.00, MAD = 3.52). A component of the difference in cognitive workload is hence due to effort. For the amount of frustration experienced in the task, statistically significant differences were found (U = 82.00, P = 0.019) with the haptic group (M = 50.00, MAD = 5.63) demonstrating a large increase (185.71%) in frustration over the visual group (M = 15.00, MAD = 3.70). This result further contributes to analysis of the overall task workload; the haptic group were frustrated significantly more than the visual group, indicative of the additional intensity of cognitive response elicited by the reinforcement learning.

Results suggest that the additional haptic modality has promoted motor learning with the effect of improving safety and path negotiation in the vehicle training scenario presented. Analysis of the RTLX reveals increased cognitive workload generated by the haptic modality, particularly frustration and effort levels, suggesting motor learning is supported by increasing the subjects exerted effort to accomplish the task by making it more demanding. Increased frustration levels are likely to be a natural concomitant of the extra stimulation to perform correctly, where error feedback is regular and energetic. These findings align with the hypothesis, with strong evidence to suggest that the improved motor learning is a result of reinforcement feedback influencing cognitive behaviour.

5   Conclusion

A virtual driving system was developed using the Unity game engine, designed to assess the effect of vibrotactile reinforcement haptics on motor learning and cognitive workload in vehicle training. Information regarding optimal vehicle positioning was delivered via visual-haptic and visual mediums, isolating modality for observation of improvements in safety and control. The frequency of off-road vehicle interaction was recorded, as well as the frame count accumulated while positioned greater than 4 m from the immediate point on the suggested trajectory, allowing for objective comparisons of short-term motor skill retention. To further interpret the role of haptics in motor behaviour development, evaluations of cognitive workload were conducted with the RTLX. There was a significant difference in the short-term motor skill retention exhibited by the two groups. The visual-haptics group experienced greater decreases in safety and vehicle positioning errors, as well as higher levels of cognitive workload, particularly effort and frustration.

In conclusion, the additional haptic modality can improve short-term motor skill retention in driver training by increasing the cognitive workload of the task. Analysis of the RTLX indicate this improvement is a result of more efforted responses from participants, likely from increased frustration experienced when committing positioning violations, which has encouraged the adaptation of sensorimotor transformations. Furthermore, the effect of the enhanced motor behaviour exhibited by the haptics trained group is an improvement in vehicle control, where participant negotiation of the course has advanced in safety and quality. It is hence established that vibrotactile reinforcement haptics are suitable for enhancing short-term retention of motor skills in driver training environments which could be adopted in a number of different training scenarios where steering control is involved such as piloting aircraft, emergency response driving, industrial machine operation, and conventional learner driving.

Future works should focus on developing more mature solutions, implementing aspects of artificial intelligence to the feedback based on informed psychological understanding of the motor learning process. Further applications should be researched to determine suitability for haptic feedback, as well as examining effects on long-term retention.

References

1. Jensen, L., Konradsen, F.: A review of the use of virtual reality head-mounted displays in education and training. Educ. Inf. Technol. **23**(4), 1515–1529 (2017). https://doi.org/10.1007/s10639-017-9676-0
2. Wolpert, D.M., Ghahramani, Z., Flanagan, J.R.: Perspectives and problems in motor learning. Trends Cogn. Sci. **5**(11), 487–494 (2001)
3. Morris, D., Tan, H., Barbagli, F., Chang, T., Salisbury, K.: Haptic feedback enhances force skill learning. In: Second Joint EuroHaptics Conference and Symposium on Haptic Interfaces for Virtual Environment and Teleoperator Systems (WHC 2007), pp. 21–26. IEEE (2007)
4. Crespo, L.M., Reinkensmeyer, D.J.: Haptic guidance can enhance motor learning of a steering task. J. Motor Behav. **40**(6), 545–557 (2008)
5. Milot, M.-H., Marchal-Crespo, L., Green, C.S., Cramer, S.C., Reinkensmeyer, D.J.: Comparison of error-amplification and haptic-guidance training techniques for learning of a timing-based motor task by healthy individuals. Exp. Brain Res. **201**(2), 119–131 (2010). https://doi.org/10.1007/s00221-009-2014-z
6. Lee, H., Choi, S.: Combining haptic guidance and haptic disturbance: an initial study of hybrid haptic assistance for virtual steering task. In: 2014 IEEE Haptics Symposium (HAPTICS), pp. 159–165. IEEE (2014)
7. Schmidt, R.A., Lee, T.D., Winstein, C., Wulf, G., Zelaznik, H.N.: Motor Control and Learning: A Behavioral Emphasis. Human Kinetics, Champaign (2018)
8. De Groot, S., De Winter, J.C., García, J.M.L., Mulder, M., Wieringa, P.A.: The effect of concurrent bandwidth feedback on learning the lane-keeping task in a driving simulator. Hum. Factors **53**(1), 50–62 (2011)
9. Hart, S.G.: NASA-task load index (NASA-TLX); 20 years later. In: Proceedings of the Human Factors and Ergonomics Society Annual Meeting, vol. 50, no. 9, pp. 904–908. Sage Publications, Los Angeles (2006)

Augmented Reality

Using Augmented Reality to Train Flow Patterns for Pilot Students - An Explorative Study

Günter Alce[1]([✉])[iD], Karl-Johan Klang[1], Daniel Andersson[1], Stefan Nyström[2], Mattias Wallergård[1][iD], and Diederick C. Niehorster[3][iD]

[1] Department of Design Sciences, Lund University, Lund, Sweden
gunter.alce@design.lth.se
[2] Lund University School of Aviation, Lund University, Lund, Sweden
[3] Lund University Humanities Lab and Department of Psychology, Lund University, Lund, Sweden

Abstract. Today, just as in the early days of flying, much emphasis is put on the pilot student's flight training before flying a real commercial aircraft. In the early stages of a pilot student's education, they must, for example, learn different operating procedures known as flow patterns using very basic tools, such as exhaustive manuals and a so-called *paper tiger*. In this paper, we present a first design of a virtual and interactive *paper tiger* using augmented reality (AR), and perform an evaluation of the developed prototype. We evaluated the prototype on twenty-seven pilot students at the Lund University School of Aviation (LUSA), to explore the possibilities and technical advantages that AR can offer, in particular the procedure that is performed before takeoff. The prototype got positive results on perceived workload, and in remembering the flow pattern. The main contribution of this paper is to elucidate knowledge about the value of using AR for training pilot students.

Keywords: Augmented reality · Interaction design · Flight training · Method

1 Introduction

Already in the late 1920s, there was a great demand for flight instruction and simulators, to help pilots learn to fly in a safe environment without the deadly risks of having beginner pilots take the controls of a real aircraft [3]. Today, just as in the early days of flying, much emphasis is put on the pilot student's flight training and instrument navigation before flying a real commercial aircraft. In the early stages of a pilot student's preparation for the flight simulator of a commercial aircraft, they must learn how to operate an aircraft from the cockpit using nothing but a simulator made out of printed-paper panels also referred to as a *paper tiger* (see Fig. 1) and the aircraft's operation manual. During this stage of their flight training, pilot students are meant to familiarize

© Springer Nature Switzerland AG 2020
L. T. De Paolis and P. Bourdot (Eds.): AVR 2020, LNCS 12242, pp. 215–231, 2020.
https://doi.org/10.1007/978-3-030-58465-8_17

themselves with the procedures to perform in the cockpit before, during and after a flight. Specifically, students learn these procedures partially through the repeated practice of so-called flow patterns, which aim to instill in pilots not only the procedures to be carried out but also the order in which to perform them. During this stage, pilot students also practice working together as a team of captain and copilot by practicing to execute the flow patterns together and cross-checking the other pilot's work to ensure that all steps have been carried out correctly.

Fig. 1. The *paper tiger* at LUSA.

Pilot students spend 40 h or more practicing these skills using paper tigers to prepare themselves for further training sessions in expensive full flight simulators. The aim of these practice sessions is not only to memorize the procedures to perform but also to memorize the location of the different instruments and buttons in the cockpit. Additionally, the aim is to train students' muscle memory to automatize the performance of these procedures [3]. While *paper tigers* offer a cheap and efficient way to train cockpit procedures, their low-fidelity nature also has downsides. For example, the *paper tiger* neither has guidance to help novices find the correct instruments in a complicated cockpit, nor can performance feedback be provided in this setup. Furthermore, *paper tigers* take up significant space, they are limited to certain locations and as such still impose significant resource constraints on student learning. Therefore we decided to build an AR version of the *paper tiger* and use it as a training method with low space requirements, that is portable and allows studying flows at any time and location, while simultaneously offering increased support and feedback through an interactive augmented reality (AR) user interface.

AR is a technology that can superimpose virtual objects on top of the real world. According to Azuma [2], an AR system has the following three characteristics: 1) Combines real and virtual; 2) Interactive in real-time; 3) Registered in 3-D. In the last couple of years, several head-mounted displays have appeared that offer these capabilities, such as Microsoft HoloLens [17] and the Magic Leap [16]. Such glasses-based AR systems open up new opportunities for experimenting with interactive applications for pilot students, in ways that up until now have been too difficult, expensive or time-consuming. Another emerging technology is virtual reality (VR). VR uses computer-generated simulations to create "the illusion of participation in a synthetic environment rather than external observation of such an environment [10]." However, we decided to use AR for the current application since it was the most suitable option allowing the student to simultaneously read the physical manual while interacting with the *paper tiger*, which was needed during the test. Another reason was to let the pilot students have visual contact with their co-pilot.

This paper presents the development of an interactive AR *paper tiger* that can be used to help pilot students to learn particular flow patterns that are done before a takeoff. The application was developed and evaluated using Microsoft HoloLens [17] together with the game engine Unity [20]. The evaluation was conducted at the Lund University School of Aviation (LUSA) in Ljungbyhed, Sweden.

The main contribution of this paper is to elucidate knowledge about the value of using AR for training pilot students.

The next section presents relevant related work that has previously been used to conceptualize an interactive virtual cockpit and the use of AR in the aviation industry. Then the developed AR *paper tiger* is described followed by the evaluation, results, discussion, and conclusions.

2   Related Work

Using AR technology for flight operations with different purposes, such as aircraft design, maintenance development, guidance of the actual flight phase and pilot training, is an area that has been well studied. However, most research has been conducted using AR for maintenance or as guidance of the actual flight phase but less on training for pilot students. This section reviews previous related research in using AR for aviation.

Modern aircrafts are complex machines that require a tremendous amount of manual effort to manufacture, assemble, and maintain. Therefore, mechanics in the hangar are required to use an increasing amount of information in their jobs [5]. However, AR can facilitate these maintenance mechanics' jobs by visualization of the information from maintenance systems and representing how parts should be connected in a safe and interactive way. Caudell and Mizell developed one of the first AR maintenance tools which helped the maintenance workers assemble wires and cables for an aircraft [5]. Macchiarella, and Vincenzi [15] investigated how AR can be used to help the workers to memorize difficult moments of aircraft maintenance tasks. They used AR to develop augmented scenes with which the workers could train a wide variety of flight and maintenance tasks. Macchiarella and Vincenzi [15] followed up their study to see the learning effects on long term memory by testing their participants again after seven days. The results indicate that AR-based learning had positive effects on long term memory and that the participant remembered more information.

AR has also been used to help to guide pilots during the actual flight by providing information from the Primary Flight Display (PFD) regarding speed, altitude and heading [12,13]. Heads-Up-Displays (HUD) are already used in many fighter planes and modern commercial aircrafts such as the Boeing 737 Next Generation [12]. Additionally, "Smart glasses" have been developed for private pilots, for example, Vuzix M3000 [21], Google Glasses [11] and Moverio BT-200 [8] to guide them in a visual traffic pattern. One of the earliest helmet-mounted display (HMD) was developed by Tom Furness for the USA Air Force from 1966 to 1969. It helped the pilot to see a simplified version of reality. Furness continued to improve the helmets and in 1986 he described a virtual crew station concept called the "Super Cockpit" [9]. It discussed how flight information could be portrayed virtually and interactively. However, these applications focus on augmenting information for the pilots via HUD, HMD or "smart glasses" during flight. In this paper, we utilize the potential of AR to see if we can improve learning through procedural training, i.e. the practice and understanding of so-called flows, for pilot students.

3 Building the AR Paper Tiger

The main goal with the presented work was to design and test an interactive *paper tiger* by exploring the possibilities and technical advantages of AR. First, we will explain more details about the background of the *paper tiger*, followed by flow patterns, and limitations of the AR *paper tiger*.

3.1 Background

To obtain a commercial pilot's license (CPL), which is by far the most common training given at flight schools, pilot students need a minimum of 150–200 flying hours in total [7]. However, practice in the simulator of a multi-crew aircraft is significantly less. It consists of approximately 20 h during the Multi-Crew Cooperation Course (MCC) during the final stage of the training. This is aided by approximately 30–40 h of procedure preparation in a *paper tiger*.

The pilot students are trained to use checklists. Checklists are powerful tools; they can increase the precision of a specified behavior and reduce errors. However, when pilots work with a checklist the risk for distraction increases the longer the list is. They may lose concentration and direct their focus towards something else which needs their attention. One result of this is to keep the actual checklists as short as possible. Instead, aircraft manufacturers such as Boeing have set up a working method based on so-called flows. During a flow, you prepare the cockpit for different configurations such as startup, takeoff, descend and landing. Previous research highlights the development and a need for more human-centered interaction design in pilot training [6,19]. One example is during a type-rating course, a course at the end of the pilot's training when he or she learns how to fly a large complex commercial aircraft. Before the course starts, it is good to have as much experience as possible. Due to substantial economic costs for training, approximately 16 000–34 000 EUR for a type-rating [18] and high time pressure in the learning phase, the fresh student can be overloaded with information during a type-rating course. An interactive learning environment may serve as a stepping stone and a more intuitive approach and frame to the content than starting with reading a pure text and exhaustive lists in the initial learning phase of a type-rating.

3.2 Flow Patterns

The instruments and displays in a cockpit are organized in panels and placed in the cockpit according to a specific spatial arrangement. This arrangement is designed with regard to how frequently the instruments and panels are being scanned and monitored and in proportion to their critical value for the flight. To enhance a logical flow during the configuration of the aircraft it is necessary to perform the actions in specific sequences, these sequences or procedures are called flows.

Further enhancement of procedures is obtained by the patterns shaped by the sequences of the flows. Flows follow a logical order and the items, which are to be set up, are organized in chunks within every panel. For example, in the case of the flight control panel, the part-panels on the overhead section build up the "overhead panel" and are scanned in "columns" from top to bottom. Using a top-bottom order for checking the panels and items provides a structure and thereby reduces the work to learn the items. The same spatial technique can be used when verifying items of a checklist. Flows are challenging and a bit mechanic to learn in the beginning but can be rewarding once learned. A comparison can be made to learning a dance. First, you struggle with getting all the steps right and you easily forget what comes next. But after a while, you get into a flow and one move seems to lead into another. When the pattern is recognized one intuitively connects one item to the next. In order to study the flow, pilot students use a paper as guidance which shows the fifteen panels they have to go through (see Fig. 2).

3.3 Flow Patterns with the AR Paper Tiger

The general scanflow is executed before every take off. It consists of 37 items to be set or checked, organized over fifteen panels or locations in the cockpit (see Fig. 2). The correct order of the fifteen panels and locations were reconstructed in the AR *paper tiger* to guide the user's attention to the appropriate area of

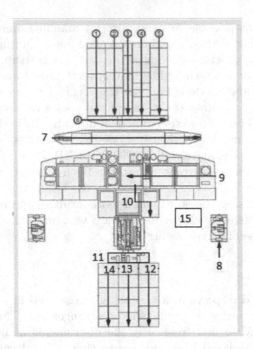

Fig. 2. The paper shows the general scan flow that consists of fifteen steps, borders around the panels are marked and arrows show where the student should start and in which direction to continue.

the items to be set or checked. Green borders are overlaid on top of the virtual *paper tiger* to highlight the specific panels and corresponding arrows similar to those of the paper version were used to tell the student where to start and in which direction to continue (see Fig. 3, left panel). However, in one instance, an additional arrow was added from the end of one section to the start of the next, because these two sections were far apart and otherwise the next section was not discoverable given the limited field of view of the HoloLens. The additional arrow can be seen in the bottom image in Fig. 3.

In order to get the student started, a "Demo" function was implemented that demonstrates the flow sequence. When the "Play Demo" button is pressed, the flow is visualized by sequentially showing a border around each step in the flow sequence together with an arrow corresponding to that step. This function is accessible by interacting with a floating button, in the near vicinity of the virtual cockpit. We chose a location that is not in the line of sight while interacting with the virtual cockpit.

3.4   Limitations

The HoloLens has several hardware and software limitations. For example, because of its narrow field of view, the users cannot use their peripheral vision

Fig. 3. Flow pattern with pointing arrows.

and therefore some sort of guidance must be added to help the user. Another limitation of the HoloLens is the low number of hand gestures available to the user. The pinch movement used for clicking on buttons in a cockpit might not come naturally to a pilot student. The AR *paper tiger* only marks the section of a certain panel. None of the elements on the virtual cockpit's panels were interactive for this first iteration of the cockpit training environment.

4 Evaluation

An evaluation was conducted in order to better understand the perceived workload and usability issues of the AR prototype. The evaluation was conducted at the Lund University School of Aviation (LUSA) in Ljungbyhed, Sweden.

4.1 Setup

One single session involved one participant and four test leaders, where one was in charge of introducing the HoloLens, two conducted the testing and one conducted a post-questionnaire as well as a structured interview (see Fig. 4). All test sessions were recorded and lasted about 20 min. The test session was designed as an assembly line, at certain points we had three pilot students at the same time but in different rooms (see Fig. 4). The technical equipment consisted of:

- Two HoloLenses.
- Two video cameras.
- One computer dedicated to questionnaires.

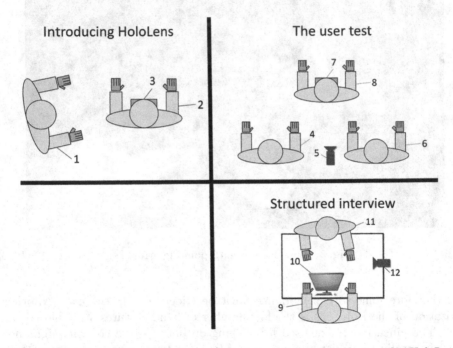

Fig. 4. The setup of the evaluation. 1) Test moderator introducing the HoloLens, 2) Pilotstudent (participant), 3) HoloLens used during introduction, 4) Test moderator leading the main test, 5) Video camera recording, 6) Test moderator responsible to help participant with HoloLens issues, 7) HoloLens running the AR *paper tiger*, 8) Pilotstudent (participant), 9) Pilotstudent (participant), 10) Computer dedicated to questionnaires, 11) Test moderator for the structured-interview, 12) Camera recording the interview.

4.2 Participants

Twenty-seven pilot students (five females) were recruited by their instructor at LUSA (age $M = 23.7$, $SD = 3.06$). Only two of them had previous experience of AR and four of them had less than two hours of experience with the *paper tiger*, while the others had no previous experience.

4.3 Procedure

All participants were given a brief introduction to the project and its purpose. Next, they filled in a short questionnaire together with informed consent regarding their participation and the use of collected data. Thereafter they were introduced to the HoloLens to familiarize them with AR and the mechanics of interacting with AR objects.

Next, they entered the room where the actual test was conducted. Before the test was performed the participant was asked to sit down by the real *paper tiger*, to understand the participant's pre-existing knowledge of the take-off flow. Then the participant got seated in a chair a couple of meters away from the real *paper tiger*, facing an empty wall. Here they opened up the virtual *paper tiger* application and got used to the user interface. The test operators made sure that they noticed all different panels and buttons before continuing with the test by instructing the participant to 1) look up to see the overhead panel, 2) look left to see the thrust and communication panels and 3) look right to see the oxygen mask and asking for a verbal confirmation. In the first step of the test, the Demo was played. The participant stood up and walked a couple of meters behind the chair to get all panels in his/her field of view at the same time. Then the participant played the Demo and observed. When the Demo was done the participant got seated again, handed a paper checklist and started to do the flow. When pilot students normally practice with the real *paper tiger* they pretend they are interacting with buttons and metrics according to a list they have in their hand. This was done in the application as well. The participant pretended to adjust all items of the flow within the outlined green marked area. When the participant was done in one area the "next-button" was clicked, after which the next section of the flow was outlined.

After the testing procedure with the HoloLens, the participant was brought back to the real *paper tiger*. Here the participant was asked to show the flow he/she just practiced with the HoloLens and some spontaneous first thoughts were talked about and noted by the test operators. Their performance in reproducing the flow was scored as number of items correctly recalled.

Last, after the tasks were completed, the participant moved to a third room and filled out the NASA Task Load Index (TLX) [14] and the System Usability Scale (SUS) [4] questionnaires. In an attempt to understand and describe the users' perceived workload NASA TLX was used as an assessment tool. NASA TLX is commonly used to evaluate perceived workload for a specific task. It consists of two parts. The first part is referred to as raw TLX and consists of six subscales (Mental Demand, Physical Demand, Temporal Demand, Performance,

Effort, and Frustration) to measure the total workload. The second part of the NASA TLX creates an individual weighting of the subscales by letting the subjects compare them pairwise based on their perceived importance. However, as reported by Hart [14], using the second part of the NASA TLX might actually decrease experimental validity. For this reason, it was not used in this experiment. A raw NASA TLX score was calculated for each student as the sum of all subscores. Originally each subscore range up to 100, but several researchers use 20 or 10, in this study we used the maximum subscore of 10.

In an attempt to understand and describe the users' cognitive workload, SUS was used. It is often used to get a rapid usability evaluation of the system's human interaction [4]. It attempts to measure cognitive attributes such as learnability and perceived ease of use. Scores for individual items, such as, "I thought the system was easy to use," can be studied and compared, but the main intent is the combined rating (0 to 100) [1]. The questionnaires were followed by a short structured interview. All the structured interviews were video recorded. The video recordings were reviewed to detect recurring themes and to find representative quotes. The procedure is shown in Fig. 5.

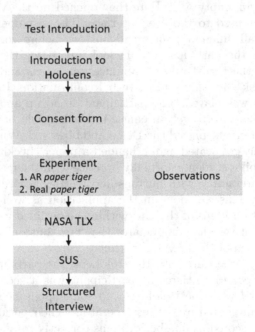

Fig. 5. The procedure of the evaluation.

4.4   Results

In the following section, the results from the NASA TLX, SUS scale, and the structured-interview are presented.

Twenty-two of the twenty-seven participants could see the potential and were positive to the AR *paper tiger*.

NASA TLX. The overall NASA TLX scores were low (see Fig. 6). Participants mean value of $M = 24.6$, $SD = 6.15$.

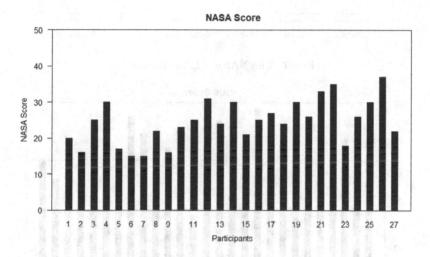

Fig. 6. The NASA TLX scores.

The results obtained from the NASA TLX subscales are illustrated in Fig. 7. All subscale values were relatively low but surprisingly Physical had the lowest median value, then Temporal and Frustration with the same low median value, which is good (Table 1).

Table 1. Median values of the NASA TLX subscore.

Subscale	MD	IQR
Mental	5	3
Physical	2	1.5
Temporal	3	2.5
Performance	7	3
Effort	4	4
Frustration	3	2

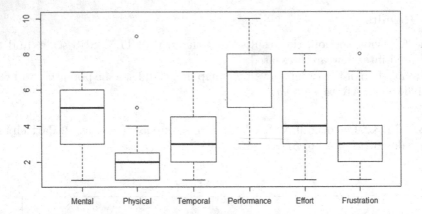

Fig. 7. The NASA TLX subscore.

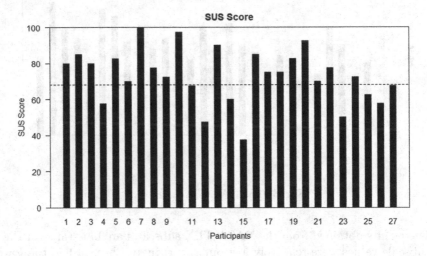

Fig. 8. SUS score for all participants.

SUS Score. The results obtained from the SUS questionnaire for the participants present a mean score of $M = 73.1$, $SD = 15.05$ with a minimum score of 37.5 and a maximum score of 100 (see Fig. 8).

Post Test Check. As described in the procedure section, after the participant used the AR *paper tiger*, the participant did a test on the real *paper tiger* to see how much the participant remembered of the flow, i.e. how many of the fifteen steps were remembered and if they were remembered in the correct order. On average, the participants remembered 73% of the fifteen steps in the correct order.

Structured-Interview. The results obtained from the structured-interviews can be divided into four different topics: 1) The impression of the AR *paper tiger*; 2) If the application managed to fulfill the purpose; 3) Thoughts about having a whole panel highlighted versus having each button highlighted; and 4) Thoughts about using the AR *paper tiger*.

Twenty-two students were positive, one was negative and four were neutral. When they were asked how they found the application, they expressed comments like *"Fun!"*, *"Great learning method!"*, *"different but fun way to learn."* One student expressed it as *"more realistic than the paper tiger."*

All students thought that the application managed to fulfill its purpose. Six of them also mentioned that it will help them to train their muscle memory.

Regarding thoughts about having the whole panel highlighted versus having each button highlighted, fourteen of the students would like to have the whole panel highlighted while thirteen would prefer to have each item highlighted.

Twenty-one of the students would consider using the application as it is and six of them could consider to use it if it was more complete. None of them expressed that this was a bad idea.

5   Discussion

In this section, we will discuss the "take-aways" from the evaluation, developing the AR *paper-tiger*. Finally, we will reflect on the benefits of AR and possible improvements of the AR *paper-tiger*.

5.1   Evaluation

The data from the evaluation suggests that AR could be a valuable tool for learning procedural flows. Overall, the AR *paper tiger* received acceptable scores on both the NASA TLX and the SUS questionnaire, which indicates that the participants were able to complete the experiment reasonably well.

Similar effects as the study by Macchiarella and Vincenzi [15] can be found in our study regarding using AR as a learning tool to recall a task. After using the AR *paper tiger*, the pilot students could recall 73% of the fifteen steps in the correct order.

NASA TLX. Despite the fact that the pilot students had none or very little experience of the real *paper tiger*, the pilot students had very good mean values. This indicates that the idea of using an interactive AR *paper tiger* as a learning tool seems to have good potential. Two interesting values from the NASA TLX subscore are the physical median value which was lowest (see Fig. 1) and the mental median value which was the second-highest value (see Fig. 1). Despite the HoloLens requiring physical movements of the participant's arm when interacting, the perceived mental workload was higher. One reason for this might be the small field of view of the HoloLens, which forced the participants to look around and made it difficult to have an overview of the whole user interface at the same time.

SUS. The AR prototype had a SUS score larger than 68, which is considered to be above average [4]. The SUS score measures cognitive attributes such as learnability and perceived ease of use, the result indicates that the AR *paper tiger* is considered to be easy to use, and easy to learn.

The Structured Interview. All students reacted to the AR *paper tiger* in a positive manner and could see the potential of the application. However, comments that could be considered as negative were mostly directed towards the Microsoft HoloLens. The new version of this headset has been improved in several areas such as the field of view and gestures used for input and may thus alleviate some of the expressed concerns.

5.2   The AR Paper Tiger

In this section, the benefits of AR and improvements are discussed.

Benefits of AR. One major benefit of using AR when training the procedure to prepare for takeoff is the ability to have an interactive paper tiger which augments the panels and helps the pilot students to find the correct panel and perform the actions in the correct order. Another advantage in the HoloLens is the fact that you can see yourself and especially your hand in the AR application. This also enables you to see and communicate with a copilot as well as seeing and working with real physical operation manuals or checklists in your own or your copilot's hand. Moreover, the AR version is mobile and can easily be used in another place. Currently, a pilot student has to use the physical *paper tiger* which is limited to be used at a fixed location for example in the practice room at LUSA which can be seen in Fig. 1. Similarly, the setup could be developed using a VR headset. Current VR headsets have several advantages such as better field of view, more accurate tracking, and a higher display resolution than the HoloLens. However, an important feature which the VR headset cannot offer (at least for now) is the interaction and communication with a copilot and using the physical operation manual or checklists. One can ask how important are these features, maybe using an avatar and virtual operation manuals are good enough but to be sure further studies need to be done. For example, it would be interesting to follow up on this study, with another when which would investigate the pros and cons of the real *paper tiger*, the AR *paper tiger* and a VR *paper tiger*.

The biggest contribution with the developed prototype of an AR *paper tiger* is the ability to choose different scenarios. While using the application you can see a demo of the flow, or interactively receive flow guidance, with the purpose to learn the flow pattern in the cockpit. In our case, we began with a general scan flow to demonstrate the spatial structure of a scanning flow, which you interactively can click your way through. Our solution allows for a potential merge between the source of knowledge - the manual, the practice interface, and the real *paper tiger*. This starting point forms a very good structure for future developments toward even more interactive possibilities for learning.

Further Research. In this section, different improvements or ideas for other projects in the area are described and discussed.

The AR *paper tiger* could be further expanded in many ways to enhance the experience when using the simulator. Panel screens could be animated as well as the surroundings e.g. moving clouds and changing light conditions. Panel lights could be turned on or off, based on what flow the user is training.

Depending on the user's knowledge, different levels of interaction could be added. For example, if the user is a total novice, it could be enough to demo the flow and the user can then be requested to do the flow in a simplified manner, much like the prototype presented in this paper. However, if the user is more advanced, as shown during testing of the prototype, there is a need for more interactive features in the AR *paper tiger*. This could be lights going on and off on the panels and thus allowing the student to follow the flow in a detailed manner.

Having detailed 3D models of the panels would make it possible to use the instruments (knobs) on the panels, thus giving the ability to change values on panel screens in a realistic manner. If the user is able to turn knobs, the AR *paper tiger* can check values against recommended values and then pass or fail a user based on the set values. However, this would not be the same as flow training, this would be more detailed. For a full version of the AR *paper tiger*, there would be a lot more flows available to train on, approximately eighteen, with a menu where the user would be able to choose desired flow.

Another flow which AR is suitable for is the *walk-around flow*. Similar to the flows in the cockpit, are the flows that a pilot does before stepping into the aircraft. The idea is to emulate a plane for a "walk-around", which is an outside check of an aircraft. The pilot checks that everything, for example, control surfaces and tires are as they should. By using a 3D model of an aircraft this could be practiced anywhere using AR, and of course, the model would be able to re-scale and rotate. This can be further developed by adding random variables such as ice or a birds nest in the jet engine that the pilot should notice and handle.

All in all, the improved application could offer a playful and enriching environment and at the same time equip the pilot student with the relevant knowledge needed to be as prepared as possible before the costly and very time-pressured full flight simulator training.

Seen from a broad perspective, the application could potentially be valuable also for Commercial Pilot Licence (CPL) flight training where practice in a real simulator is even less than in the Multi Pilot Licence (MPL) concept, and the time in the paper tiger is shorter. A further developed application could also bridge to the Jet Orientation Course (JOC) or even a type-rating.

6   Conclusion

The contribution of this paper is a novel way of using AR to train pilot students' flow patterns. At the present time, the developed product could be used mainly for early familiarization and introduction to a normal *paper tiger* as well as an introduction to the concept of flows. More development and interactive features are needed for any further applications. All pilot students evaluated the AR *paper tiger* positively and could see the potential of the application. The results indicate that the AR *paper tiger* has the potential to be helpful for pilot students for the process of learning flow patterns.

Acknowledgments. We thank all the pilot students who volunteered to test our application, and the instructors who allowed us to conduct the study and helped to organize. Moreover, we would like to extend our gratitude to Elin Hanstorp, Gustav Lilja and Amar Vrbanjac, who were active contributors to the creation, development and pre-testing of the AR *paper tiger*.

References

1. Albert, W., Tullis, T.: Measuring the User Experience: Collecting, Analyzing, and Presenting Usability Metrics. Newnes, Oxford (2013)
2. Azuma, R., Baillot, Y., Behringer, R., Feiner, S., Julier, S., MacIntyre, B.: Recent advances in augmented reality. IEEE Comput. Graph. Appl. **21**(6), 34–47 (2001)
3. Bailenson, J.: Experience on Demand: What Virtual Reality Is, How It Works, and What It Can Do. WW Norton & Company, New York (2018)
4. Brooke, J., et al.: SUS-a quick and dirty usability scale. In: Usability Evaluation in Industry, vol. 189, no. 194, pp. 4–7 (1996)
5. Caudell, T.P., Mizell, D.W.: Augmented reality: an application of heads-up display technology to manual manufacturing processes. In: Proceedings of the Twenty-Fifth Hawaii International Conference on System Sciences, vol. 2, pp. 659–669. IEEE (1992)
6. Degani, A., Wiener, E.L.: Human factors of flight-deck checklists: the normal checklist (1991)
7. EASA: EASA part FCL (2016). https://www.easa.europa.eu/sites/default/files/dfu/Part-FCL.pdf
8. Epson: Moverio BT-200 (2013). https://www.epson.se/products/see-through-mobile-viewer/moverio-bt-200
9. Furness III, T.A.: The super cockpit and its human factors challenges. In: Proceedings of the Human Factors Society Annual Meeting, vol. 30, pp. 48–52. SAGE Publications, Los Angeles (1986)
10. Gigante, M.A.: Virtual reality: enabling technologies. In: Virtual Reality Systems, pp. 15–25. Elsevier (1993)
11. Google Inc.: Google glass (2013). https://www.google.com/glass/start/
12. Goteman, Ö.: Airborne cognitive systems in search of an appropriate context: studies of the introduction of new technology in aviation using a cognitive systems engineering approach, vol. 24. Lund University (2006)
13. Haiduk, P.M.: Display formats for smart glasses to support pilots in general aviation (2017)

14. Hart, S.G.: NASA-task load index (NASA-TLX); 20 years later. In: Proceedings of the Human Factors and Ergonomics Society Annual Meeting, vol. 50, pp. 904–908. Sage publications, Los Angeles (2006)
15. Macchiarella, N.D., Vincenzi, D.A.: Augmented reality in a learning paradigm for flight aerospace maintenance training. In: The 23rd Digital Avionics Systems Conference (IEEE Cat. No. 04CH37576), vol. 1, pp. 5-D. IEEE (2004)
16. Magic Leap: Magic leap (2018). https://www.magicleap.com/
17. Microsoft: Microsoft hololens (2016). https://www.microsoft.com/en-us/hololens/
18. Mjåtveit, S.: Vad är en type rating? (2018). https://www.osmaviationacademy.com/sv/blogg/vad-ar-en-type-rating
19. Norman, D.: The Design of Everyday Things: Revised and Expanded Edition. Basic Books (2013)
20. Unity Technologies: Unity - game engine (2017). https://unity.com/
21. Vuzix: Jas 39 gripen (2017). https://www.vuzix.com/Products/CES-Products

Scalable Integration of Image and Face Based Augmented Reality

Nahuel A. Mangiarua[1]([✉]) [iD], Jorge S. Ierache[1] [iD], and María J. Abásolo[2,3] [iD]

[1] National University of La Matanza, San Justo, Buenos Aires, Argentina
{nmangiarua,ierache}@unlam.edu.ar
[2] National University of La Plata, La Plata, Buenos Aires, Argentina
mjabasolo@lidi.info.unlp.edu.ar
[3] CICPBA Scientific Research Commission of the Buenos Aires Province, La Plata, Buenos Aires, Argentina

Abstract. In this paper we present a scalable architecture that integrates image based augmented reality (AR) with face recognition and augmentation over a single camera video stream. To achieve the real time performance required and ensure a proper level of scalability, the proposed solution makes use of two different approaches. First, we identify that the main bottleneck of the integrated process is the feature descriptor matching step. Taking into account the particularities of this task in the context of AR, we perform a comparison of different well known Approximate Nearest Neighbour search algorithms. After the empirical evaluation of several performance metrics we conclude that HNSW is the best candidate. The second approach consists on delegating other demanding tasks such as face descriptor computation as asynchronous processes, taking advantage of multi-core processors.

Keywords: Augmented Reality · Face recognition · Approximate Nearest Neighbor Search · Scalability

1 Introduction

Augmented Reality (AR) is a technology that enables us to enhance the real world as it combines virtual content and information with physical elements in real time. We can find many examples and applications on very diverse fields such as arts, education, medicine or engineering, among others. From augmentation based on the geographical location to 3D environment mapping and object registration, the potential of AR to adapt and add value to almost every aspect of our lives is extensive. Image based AR augments the reality by searching the world, over a live stream of video, for exact correspondences of pre configured images. Once such an image is found, any kind of digital element is rendered over the original video to make it appear as if it was part of the physical reality. This particular kind of augmentation has certain limitations in relation to the limited scalability of existing frameworks. Despite this it still provides significant value in the right application contexts.

© Springer Nature Switzerland AG 2020
L. T. De Paolis and P. Bourdot (Eds.): AVR 2020, LNCS 12242, pp. 232–242, 2020.
https://doi.org/10.1007/978-3-030-58465-8_18

Real time face detection has been possible since the methods introduced by Viola and Jones back in 2001. In recent years, face recognition techniques have evolved with the use of deep convolutional neural networks. Such networks, as demonstrated by [24,26,27], can be trained to compute a single multi dimensional descriptor (also called embedding) for a given face with relative robustness to orientation and lightning changes. The integrating face recognition in the context of image based augmented reality for final users without relying on an online service is still a challenging problem, scarcely addressed by the most recent and popular AR libraries like ARCore [2], ARKit [3] or Vuforia [9].

Museum's guided tours, book augmentation or unauthorized person detection are a few concrete examples where a highly scalable image and face based AR framework is needed. The ability to work with thousands of targets in a straightforward and offline architecture enables for simpler and more extensive applications in collaborative augmented environments or even law and public health enforcement systems where network connectivity, latency or costs are a problem. On the other hand, applications like [14] would greatly benefit from the integration of both types of augmentation, allowing them to recognize a wide array of personal identification cards and also an individual's face given a limited context.

The rest of the paper is organized as follows: Sect. 2 presents the proposal of an integrated architecture of image and face based AR. Section 3 presents the parallelization of the tasks presented in the AR pipeline. Section 4 presents the comparison of different Approximate Nearest Neighbor algorithms necessary to achieve a proper level of scalability. Finally, Sect. 5 presents the conclusion and future work.

2 Architectural Proposal

2.1 Image Based AR Pipeline

Image based AR usually relies on architectures that pair pipelines such as [20] and illustrated in Fig. 1 with some authoring tool like Aurasma [6], Aumentaty [5], Augment [4], Zappar [10] or our Virtual Catalogs System [13] among others. A user loads and configures a set of planar images in the authoring tool, associating digital elements that will be inserted as augmentations relative to each. The authoring tool then analyzes each image looking for points of interests (POI) that satisfy certain conditions that will make it able to be easily found again and correctly identified. For each such point the tool computes and stores at least one pseudo invariant descriptor using algorithms such as the popular SIFT [18] as well as ORB [25] or SURF [11].

To produce the effect of augmentation, a usually separate piece of software running on a mobile device captures a frame of a live video stream and searches for points of interest using the exact same algorithm as the authoring tool. The points generated are then described by the same algorithm and the resulting descriptors are matched against all the descriptors previously generated from the loaded images. After further refining a certain number of correct matches,

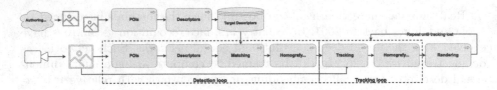

Fig. 1. Conceptual diagram of the image based AR pipeline. The rendering step lies outside of the scope of AR but is included for clarity.

they are used to compute a 3D transformation matrix needed to correctly overlay information over the live video. In order to create a credible and satisfying augmentation, this entire process needs to run on real time, while leaving enough headroom to actually process and render the digital content. Since the amount of descriptors increases with the number of loaded images, this task quickly becomes a bottleneck. The use of fast matching algorithms becomes a requirement to increase the scalability of such systems.

2.2 Face Detection AR Pipeline

New approaches to human face recognition make extensive use of deep convolutional neural networks which can process images with little to no preprocessing in less than a second. In particular, we find as appropriate candidates for an integration, networks trained with the triplet loss term [26]. These networks are trained to maximize the inter-class distance while, at the same time, minimize the intra-class distance to produce a multi dimensional descriptor for each individual that is robust to lightning conditions and small variations. They also ensure a minimum distance at which two or more descriptors belong to the same individual.

Using these techniques, face recognition can be achieved by finding the nearest neighbor of a descriptor in a pool of pre-computed ones generated with the help of the authoring tool. Our proposed pipeline in Fig. 2, also includes the ability to run biometric inference without hindering performance. These inference steps run asynchronously and in parallel to the main thread, implemented with a easily extensible pattern. But as expected, increasing the size of the pool of people able to be recognized by a system, increases the time required to find a single match.

Since the descriptors computed from points of interest used are not perfectly invariant and face descriptors for an individual lie within a given radius, a certain degree of change will always be present and thus exact matching algorithms are not an option. It is here where Approximate Nearest Neighbor (ANN) search algorithms become an important choke point for achieving a satisfactory user experience while maintaining scalability.

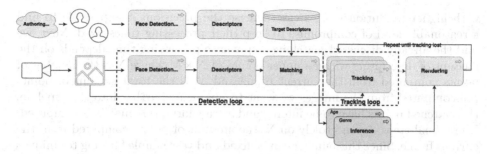

Fig. 2. Conceptual diagram of the face based AR pipeline. The information to infer is not limited to the examples present in the figure. Once again, the rendering step lies outside of the scope of AR but is included for clarity.

2.3   Image Based and Face Detection AR Integration

When face recognition is approached using a pipeline as the one presented above, its similitude to an image based AR pipeline become clear. Such pipelines can be trivially integrated as shown in Fig. 3.

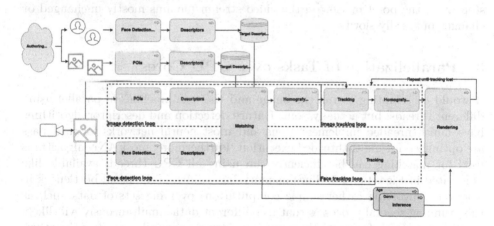

Fig. 3. Both image and face based pipelines integrated by the use of the same descriptor matcher algorithms.

By treating image descriptors and face descriptors the same, both pipelines can be joined at the matching step. Naturally, there's no reason to actually mix both kinds of descriptors in the same pool but algorithms and other data structures can be perfectly shared. With a satisfactory user experience in mind and given a frame of a live video stream, such a system needs to comply with an almost real time processing requirement, but several parts can be actually run in parallel on an async fashion.

On the image processing side, the speed of the algorithms that find and describe the POIs mainly depend on the size of the input image. While working with higher resolution images can increase the precision, it is possible to find a reasonable level of compromise to keep their processing times fixed. Next, we find the already discussed matching step where processing time depends on the amount of descriptors with an upper bound of $N \times M$ where N is the number of points computed from the current frame and M is the total amount of points pre-computed from the images we want to augment. Further into the pipeline, the matched points have to be filtered and a transformation matrix is computed. These final steps depend solely on N, the amount of points computed from the current frame. Since this number can be fixed and very simple filtering techniques apply, their processing time is not a concern.

On the other side, the face augmentation pipeline has to first detect faces present in the current frame. Again, the processing time of these algorithms are usually dependent on the resolution of the image but since neural networks are trained with a fixed input size, we can consider them as constants. Likewise, the neural network used to describe a face runs in a constant time per face but we might have several faces to work with. Once in the matching step, complexity is again upper bounded by $N \times M$ where now N is the number of faces found in the current frame and M is the number of pre processed faces in the application. Finally, both pipelines rely on tracking algorithms to avoid recomputing every step when the point of view in the video stream remains mostly unchanged or changes but really slowly.

3   Parallelization of Tasks over CPU Cores

It would be tempting to run the image and the face pipelines in parallel using different threads, but actually, some feature detection and descriptor algorithms have multi-threaded implementations and most neural networks forward pass are optimized for multi-threaded execution. Furthermore, most ANN algorithms used for matching can be efficiently run using all CPU threads available like illustrated in Figs. 4 and 5. Since memory bandwidth is the usual bottleneck in workloads involving rather simple computations over big sets of data such as this, running several processes that use different data simultaneously will likely result in poorer performance than running them sequentially one after the other.

That being said, the main goal of an AR system is to provide a successful experience by achieving a credible augmentation of the physical reality. But the added running time of both pipelines would in itself be too long. An obvious alternative is to take advantage of the fact that humans don't usually move their heads very fast. This means we can expect very little change from frame to frame of the live video stream most of the time, with some eventual fast changes where the user's eyes won't be able to perceive the details anyway. Since the accuracy of tracking and detection would drop only very slightly if we skip a few of the similar frames, we can perform an interleaving of the pipelines loops, running only one or the other every frame. Even considering the interleaving of the pipelines, we find crucial to relegate some tasks to run asynchronously in the background. Otherwise, their relatively long execution time would cause a noticeable reduction of the augmentation frames per second (FPS). As a widely known fact, less than 30 fps will result in a poor experience. In particular, even the state of the art face descriptor neural networks will take at least a couple hundred milliseconds to run on a desktop computer. Even worse, we can't control the amount of faces present in a video frame, rendering the execution time unpredictable and possibly hindering the user experience. By making the face recognition task run in the background, we can maintain a stable amount of FPS and offer the user feedback about the faces being detected while we wait for the recognition to complete.

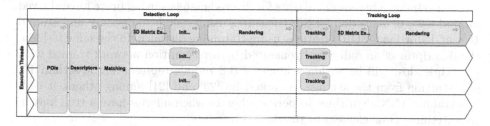

Fig. 4. Conceptual diagram illustrating the relative time each step consumes for the image based loops and if they are sequential, multi-threaded or asynchronous process. The highlighted lane represents the main thread of the application.

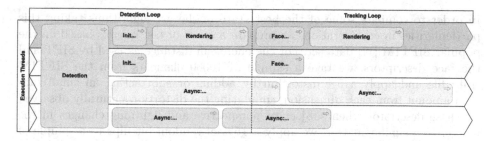

Fig. 5. Conceptual diagram illustrating the relative time each step consumes for the face based loops and if they are sequential, multi-threaded or asynchronous process. The highlighted lane represents the main thread of the application.

The Figs. 4 and 5 illustrate the ideal distribution of tasks over CPU cores. It is worth noting how each pipeline switches from a detection loop to a shorter, faster tracking loop after successfully detecting an augmentation target. On each case the highlighted lane represents the main thread of the application while multi-threaded tasks such as descriptor matching spread across lanes. Information inference tasks, on the other hand, will keep running asynchronously in different threads, crossing the boundary between detection and tracking loops.

4   Comparative Analysis of Approximate Nearest Neighbour Algorithms

As already highlighted, the main bottleneck for both pipelines and thus, for the integrated architecture, lies in the descriptor matching step. Since they depend on the number of images to augment and the number of individuals to recognize, the selection of an ANN algorithm with highly sub linear complexity that maintains its accuracy becomes mandatory to achieve good scalability.

To augment an image, we need to match descriptors pre-computed from it against slightly distorted ones due to perspective and lightning changes present in a video frame. Our empirical tests for filtered matches using brute force showed around a 2% of distortion for SIFT features using euclidean distance and around 15% of distortion for ORB features using Hamming distance. In the same fashion, the descriptor of an individual generated by a recognition network trained with the triplet loss will lie within a circle of 0.6 radius, representing less than 1% of distortion from the average. As noted by [23] and [21] among others, it isn't unusual for ANN algorithms to perform better when queries have a true match, an extremely close element in the data set.

We select ANN algorithms with relative good performance on more general benchmarks and a freely available C++ implementation. In the following section we present a comparative analysis of: ANNG [15], ONNG [16], FLANN [22], HNSW [19] as implemented in [12], ANNOY [1] and KGRAPH [7].

4.1   Comparison Tests

In order to compare some of the best state of the art algorithms taking this particularities in consideration, we prepare a series of test queries based on the popular SIFT1M [17] data set. For the euclidean distance as used by SIFT and the face descriptors, we take a sample of 10000 elements from the SIFT1M train file and apply a 5% distortion by adding or subtracting an small random amount from each dimension, simulating the distortion naturally observed by these descriptor when subject to perspective and lightning changes in the image. In a similar matter, we apply a 15% of random bit flips to a sample of 10000 elements from the SIFT1M train file to use as queries with the Hamming distance.

In all cases the algorithms were wrapped under the DescriptorMatcher interface provided by OpenCV [8]. Time was measured directly over the call to the algorithms, bypassing any possible overhead introduced by the wrapping so test could be replicated without the need to any specific code. Tests were run single threaded in an Ubuntu Linux 19.10 PC equipped with an AMD Ryzen 5 1600X CPU (12Mb L3 cache) and 16Gb of RAM running at 2667Mhz with an approximate memory bandwidth of 20Gbps.

4.2   Results and Metrics

Empirical Complexity. In Fig. 6 we can see the evolution of the execution time per test query when the data set increases its size. The trend observed when the data set grows is more important than the absolute execution time of each algorithm. An algorithm with good scalability must have a sub linear complexity. Stability and predictability are also desirable traits. For all tests, the parameters of the algorithms were auto-tuned when available or empirically selected as to offer the best speed over recall ratio, but avoiding going over 0.2 ms per query whenever possible.

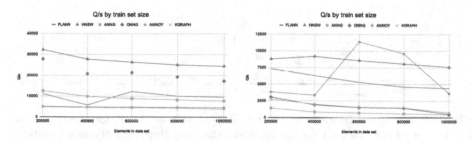

Fig. 6. Queries per second of each algorithm by the amount of elements in the train set for euclidean distance (left) and Hamming distance (right).

Algorithms with auto-tune functionalities and few explicit parameters exhibit a more erratic behavior, especially ANNOY and FLANN. It is important to note these fluctuations in execution time do not always reflect an equivalent increase or decrease in recall. While ANNG results in the more stable algorithm, it is beaten by others when also taking into account the achieved recall as we will discuss in the next paragraphs.

Stability of Recall. Another important aspect we need from a scalable algorithm is stability in its recall (proportion of correct matches) as the data set grows. In Fig. 7 we can appreciate the evolution of the recall for the first and the second nearest neighbors respectively. In general only the first two nearest neighbors (the two most similar pre-computed elements to the query element) are useful for image based AR applications.

Most algorithms achieve a certain degree of stability in their recall when the euclidean distance is used. We attribute this in part to the nature of the test queries created to represent AR workloads. On the other hand, when the Hamming distance is used, only ANNG, HSNW and ONNG remain stable. It is worth mentioning the unexpectedly low 2nd nearest neighbor recall obtained by FLANN and ANNOY. In the case of FLANN, we cross checked results between the latest official release available in Github against the implementation included with the latest OpenCV and the numbers were similar. As for the ANNOY algorithm, we attribute this behavior to the fact the algorithm only performs axis aligned projections for this distance.

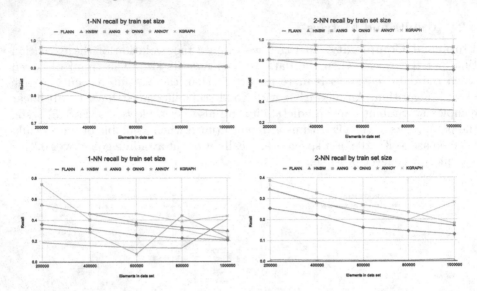

Fig. 7. Recall of the 1st (left) and 2nd (right) nearest neighbors for each algorithm by the size of the train set for the euclidean distance (top) and Hamming distance (bottom).

Performance and Trade Offs. The natural trade off for any ANN algorithm is speed against recall and so all the algorithms tested offer at least one way to alter it. By changing the parameters we build a classic curve characterizing the trade off between speed and recall. For this test the whole SIFT1M data set was used as train set. Recall of the first and second nearest neighbors is measured together as the average rank distance between the nearest neighbors returned by each algorithm and the true ones.

In Fig. 8 we compare the queries per second by the average first and second nearest neighbor index offset of each algorithm. When using the euclidean distance metric HNSW offers considerable better performance at all reasonable offset levels. On the other hand when using the Hamming distance metric, HNSW achieves better performance than ONNG at an average offset of one but ONNG

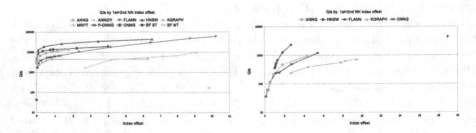

Fig. 8. Amount of queries per second by the index offset for the 1st and 2nd nearest neighbors. Left is euclidean distance while right is Hamming distance.

is capable of achieving significantly lower offsets, albeit at a severe decrease in speed. While several of the algorithms tested display good properties for these AR tuned test sets, we consider HNSW to offer the best balance between recall, stability and raw speed.

The entirety of the algorithms tested need to build some sort of index before being able to process queries. The actual data structure and the amount of processing required for the indices varies with each algorithm. In particular, the best performant algorithms such as HNSW require a long computation time to achieve the best speed versus recall ratios. Since this processing has to be done only once and is usually multi-threaded, we can offload the task to an authoring tool to take advantage of the powerful hardware available in the cloud.

5   Conclusion and Future Work

In this work we presented an architecture that integrates image and face based Augmented Reality over a single camera video stream in real time. By interleaving the face and image pipeline's detection and tracking loops while delegating other more demanding tasks as asynchronous processes the architecture is able to maintain a steady amount of frames per second. To achieve scalability over thousands of augmentation targets, we identify the descriptor matcher step shared by both pipelines as the bottleneck and study several state of the art approximate nearest neighbor algorithms to find the most appropriate ones to solve the problem. By integrating a high performant ANN algorithm such as HNSW, the proposed architecture is able to scale to more than double the augmentation targets than the allowed by other state of the art image based AR systems while also integrating face recognition and augmentation support.

Since the prototype implementation of this integration is currently targeting the x86 architecture, in the following months we will be working to make the necessary adjustments for a cross compilation to the ARM architecture that most mobile devices use. Additionally, an integration of the proposed architecture with [14] is already planned. Such integration will allow the resulting system to recognize a bystander by it's face or id card in a limited environment while offering a hands free experience through the use of voice commands.

References

1. Annoy. https://github.com/spotify/annoy. Accessed 2020
2. Arcore. https://developers.google.com/ar/. Accessed 2020
3. Arkit. https://developer.apple.com/augmented-reality/. Accessed 2020
4. Augment. https://www.augment.com. Accessed 2020
5. Aumentaty. http://www.aumentaty.com. Accessed 2020
6. Aurasma. https://www.aurasma.com. Accessed 2020
7. Kgraph. https://github.com/aaalgo/kgraph. Accessed 2020
8. Opencv. https://opencv.org. Accessed 2020
9. Vuforia. https://developer.vuforia.com/. Accessed 2020

10. Zappar. https://www.zappar.com. Accessed 2020
11. Bay, H., Ess, A., Tuytelaars, T., Gool, L.V.: Speeded-up robust features (SURF). Comput. Vis. Image Underst. **110**(3), 346–359 (2008)
12. Boytsov, L., Naidan, B.: Engineering efficient and effective non-metric space library. In: Brisaboa, N., Pedreira, O., Zezula, P. (eds.) SISAP 2013. LNCS, vol. 8199, pp. 280–293. Springer, Heidelberg (2013). https://doi.org/10.1007/978-3-642-41062-8_28
13. Ierache, J., et al.: Development of a catalogs system for augmented reality applications. World Acad. Sci. Eng. Technol. Int. Sci. Index **9**(1), 1–7 (2015)
14. Ierache, J., et al.: Augmented card system based on knowledge for medical emergency assistance. In: 2016 IEEE Congreso Argentino de Ciencias de La Informática y Desarrollos de Investigación, pp. 1–3 (2016). https://doi.org/10.1109/CACIDI.2016.7785979
15. Iwasaki, M.: Proximity search in metric spaces using approximate k nearest neighbor graph. IPSJ Trans. Database **3**(1), 18–28 (2010). (in Japanese)
16. Iwasaki, M., Miyazaki, D.: Optimization of indexing based on k-nearest neighbor graph for proximity (2018)
17. Jégou, H., Douze, M., Schmid, C.: Product quantization for nearest neighbor search (2011)
18. Lowe, D.: Distinctive image features from scale-invariant keypoints. Int. J. Comput. Vis. **60**, 91–110 (2004). https://doi.org/10.1023/B:VISI.0000029664.99615.94
19. Malkov, Y.A., Yashunin, D.A.: Efficient and robust approximate nearest neighbor search using hierarchical navigable small world graphs. CoRR abs/1603.09320 (2016). http://arxiv.org/abs/1603.09320
20. Mangiarua, N., Ierache, J., Abasolo, M.J.: Implementation of an open source based augmented reality engine for cloud authoring frameworks. J. Comput. Sci. Technol. **19**(2), e16 (2019). https://doi.org/10.24215/16666038.19.e16. http://journal.info.unlp.edu.ar/JCST/article/view/1263
21. Mikolajczyk, K., Matas, J.: Improving descriptors for fast tree matching by optimal linear projection, pp. 1–8 (2007). https://doi.org/10.1109/ICCV.2007.4408871
22. Muja, M., Lowe, D.G.: Fast approximate nearest neighbors with automatic algorithm configuration. In: VISSAPP 2009, International Conference on Computer Vision Theory and Application, pp. 331–340. INSTICC Press (2009)
23. Muja, M., Lowe, D.G.: Scalable nearest neighbor algorithms for high dimensional data. IEEE Trans. Pattern Anal. Mach. Intell. **36**(11), 2227–2240 (2014). https://doi.org/10.1109/TPAMI.2014.2321376
24. Parkhi, O.M., Vedaldi, A., Zisserman, A.: Deep face recognition. In: BMVC (2015)
25. Rublee, E., Rabaud, V., Konolige, K., Bradski, G.: ORB: an efficient alternative to SIFT or SURF. In: Proceedings of the 2011 International Conference on Computer Vision, Washington, DC, USA, pp. 2564–2571 (2011)
26. Schroff, F., Kalenichenko, D., Philbin, J.: FaceNet: a unified embedding for face recognition and clustering. CoRR abs/1503.03832 (2015). http://arxiv.org/abs/1503.03832
27. Taigman, Y., Yang, M., Ranzato, M., Wolf, L.: DeepFace: closing the gap to human-level performance in face verification. In: 2014 IEEE Conference on Computer Vision and Pattern Recognition (CVPR 2014), Columbus, OH, USA, 23–28 June 2014, pp. 1701–1708. IEEE Computer Society (2014). https://doi.org/10.1109/CVPR.2014.220

Usability of an Input Modality for AR

Daniel Brice$^{(\boxtimes)}$, Karen Rafferty, and Seán McLoone

Queen's University Belfast, Belfast, UK
dbrice01@qub.ac.uk

Abstract. The ability to overlay useful information into the physical world has made augmented reality (AR) a popular area of research within industry for maintenance and assembly tasks. However, the current input modalities for state-of-the-art technologies such as the Microsoft HoloLens have been found to be inadequate within the environment. As part of AugmenTech, an AR guidance system for maintenance, we have developed a tactile input module (TIM) with a focus on ease of use in the field of operation. The TIM is formed by 3D printed parts, off-the-shelf electronic components and an ESP-8266 microcontroller. A within-subjects controlled experiment was conducted to evaluate the usability and performance of the module against existing HoloLens input modalities and the Avatar VR glove from NeuroDigital. A System Usability Scale (SUS) score of 81.75 and low error count demonstrated the TIM's suitability for the factory environment.

Keywords: AR input modalities · AR maintenance · HCI

1 Introduction

The use of augmented reality (AR) has been investigated across many industries for its ability to overlay useful information onto the physical world [4,5]. This also holds true for the manufacturing industry, specifically in maintenance and assembly tasks, where it has been shown to reduce training times and increase the skill level of workers [8,14]. Although AR offers great potential in industry, there are still barriers to adoption, such as those caused by the state-of-the-art input modalities such as speech and gesture [15].

Gestures have been known to lead to arm fatigue [12] and when combined with gaze vector lead to the Midas problem for users [6,13]. It has also been found that users can experience difficulties in performing the hand movements necessary for gesture recognition on popular AR devices [19]. Speech is another common modality which brings challenges of its own for users with strong accents. It has also been found to be uncomfortable when used in public settings such as the workplace [1]. Existing issues are amplified in certain environments such as maintenance and assembly tasks where users wear protective gloves and dust masks. In environments such as this alternative modalities are needed.

This paper introduces a module designed to provide a simple to use input modality for the HoloLens, improving its usability within industrial settings.

© Springer Nature Switzerland AG 2020
L. T. De Paolis and P. Bourdot (Eds.): AVR 2020, LNCS 12242, pp. 243–254, 2020.
https://doi.org/10.1007/978-3-030-58465-8_19

The module's 3D printed casing uses a double cantilever design to enable it to be easily connected to the HoloLens strap or used in a detached mode. The module has been integrated with an assistive AR system for the HoloLens, AugmenTech, as a proof of concept.

Developments in the area of virtual reality (VR) have led to state-of-the-art products such as the Avatar VR glove from NeuroDigital arriving on the market. The Avatar VR glove provides functionality for gesture input through use of conductive fabric contact points and tactile feedback through the form of vibrations. The glove has been integrated with the AugmenTech system as an input modality in order to evaluate its usability.

A within-subjects repeated measures experiment was conducted with twenty participants to evaluate the usability of the developed module and Avatar VR glove as input modalities for AR. During the study participants performed input actions when prompted by instructions. Participant performance, using each input modality, was determined through measures for errors and time taken to perform correct actions. The usability of each modality was determined through short interviews with participants and System Usability Scale (SUS) questionnaires.

The key contributions of our work are:

1. The development of a proof of concept solution to provide an easy to use input modality for AR.
2. A user study evaluating different input modalities for AR to determine usability and performance issues.

2 Related Work

There has been a lot of activity in the development of input modalities for AR head mounted displays (HMD). These modalities vary across different application areas and provide different degrees of freedom (DOF) for their specific software applications.

In the work of Yang et al. [18] an input system was formed by combining a mobile phone with the HMD camera. Their system employed the Vuforia software development kit (SDK) to enable the AR system to combine markers displayed on the mobile with gestures performed by the user as inputs. The mobile has also been used as an input modality to enable users to collaboratively perform 3D manipulation on objects in AR by Grandi et al. [9]. In their work they successfully utilise inertial measurement units (IMU) within the mobile to provide 3-DOF analogue input for the HoloLens. Although these systems used novel techniques to facilitate input for AR, use of the mobile in addition to the HMD within an industrial environment would not be ideal.

There has been development of input modalities using the body instead of traditional methods [10,11]. However, these are typically dependant on cumbersome wearables and wouldn't be scalable or suitable in the factory setting. The same principles of skin to skin contact have been investigated by Serrano et al. [16] who utilise infra-red tracking so that AR input can be carried out by performing hand gestures against the user's face. In their work they demonstrate the success users had when performing zooming and panning tasks with the modality.

Some researchers have investigated wearable input devices for AR. Dobbelstein et al. [7] developed a belt embedded with touch sensors for input. A magnetic ring was developed to provide similar input to a system by Ashbrook et al. [2]. During a user study it was demonstrated that the ring was suitable for choice selections. Although use of these devices was shown to be successful in studies, they wouldn't be suitable in an environment requiring personal protective equipment (PPE) gloves to be worn.

Issues regarding vision based gesture and speech modalities for AR were discussed in the work of Tung et al. [17]. In this research a study was performed to evaluate input modalities in public spaces, which the workplace would be considered as. It was discovered many gesture attempts (63%) failed due to problems caused by fatigue and social acceptability. Their findings also indicate that very few AR users choose to use speech input in public, with only 2% of participants choosing to use it. These findings are also supported by Alallah et al. [1] who found participants preferred to use a ring or touch pad over existing modalities. In an analysis of technology issues for AR carried out by J. Peddie [15] input modalities were investigated. It was similarly found that speech and gesture based interactions were flawed. In their summary they recommended constructing a purpose-built controller as a solution to these issues.

3   Concept and Implementation

3.1   The AugmenTech System

AugmenTech is a multi-modal AR guidance system we have developed to assist operators in performing maintenance operations. The guidance is provided to users in the forms of video, image and animated models across all subtasks within a procedure. The user interface (UI) is intentionally simple to ensure acceptability during implementation. Consequently, there are only three input actions required of the user: step task forwards, step task backwards and switch instruction type.

The system input actions are mapped to three keywords for input via the speech modality: "backwards", "forwards" and "type". The Mixed Reality ToolKit (v2) is used with the HoloLens cameras and three virtual buttons containing explanatory text, such as "step forward" and "Type Instruction", as shown in Fig. 1, to enable actions to be performed via gestures. This can be carried out by the user performing the "select" gesture whilst aiming their gaze vector towards one of the three buttons.

3.2   The Tactile Input Module (TIM)

To provide an appropriate solution to the concern regarding technicians' input to the system a module is presented with tactile switches, a battery and an

Fig. 1. UI layout within the AugmenTech system.

ESP-8266 microcontroller in a 3D printed casing, as depicted in Fig. 2. The TIM can be easily attached to either side of the HoloLens to facilitate handedness of the user or removed to operate in a detached mode. This gives the user the option of setting the controller down on a workstation if desired. The module communicates with the HoloLens via message queuing telemetry transport (MQTT) over Wi-Fi. The module is robust and provides an interface for HoloLens usage in an industrial setting. The three buttons on the module are mapped to the three actions, whose order can be reversed if handedness is switched. The TIM box dimensions are 76 mm × 65 mm × 28 mm for height, length and width, respectively. The mass of the TIM is 64 g. This has been found to clip comfortably to the HoloLens without rubbing against the user or HoloLens inner ring.

Fig. 2. The Tactile Input Module (TIM).

3.3 Avatar VR Glove

The AvatarVR glove from Neurodigital was integrated to determine if any additional UI functionality could be provided. The glove utilises capacitive fabrics for gesture recognition and provides tactile feedback to the user on actions via 10 vibrotactile actuators. Although the glove brings multisensorial feedback and additional gesture functionality to the system UI, the level of robustness necessary for maintenance applications limits usability in industrial settings. However, it was decided that as most end users for industrial maintenance AR applications would regularly be wearing gloves it would be worth investigating. Within the AugmenTech system each action was assigned to a different glove gesture. The user receives 30 ms pulse of tactile feedback when the gesture is started by connecting fingertips. Holding the gesture for 700 ms results in another vibrotactile pulse when the input action is registered.

4 Experiment Design

In order to evaluate the TIM and glove as input modalities for the AugmenTech system, a controlled within-subjects experiment was carried out where participants tested them amongst additional modalities.

4.1 Goals

The primary goal of the study was to evaluate the feasibility of using the TIM for user input within the AugmenTech system. The haptic gloves, HoloLens gesture and HoloLen's speech command modalities were also evaluated for comparison.

Additional goals of the study were:

- Comparing the usability of each modality.
- To compare the number of errors incurred for each modality.
- To compare the time taken to correctly perform actions using each modality.

4.2 Hypotheses

Three hypotheses were formed based on the performance of the TIM in comparison to alternative modalities:

- **H1** – We hypothesized that the TIM usability would be scored highly.
- **H2** – We hypothesized that there would be minimal errors incurred whilst using the TIM.
- **H3** – We hypothesized that there would be a short mean input time for the TIM compared to other modalities.

4.3 Independent Variables

The only controlled variable in the study was the input modality. There were four modalities compared: HoloLens speech commands, HoloLens gestures, glove gestures and the TIM. The study was of a repeated measures design, with all modalities being tested by all participants. The order the modalities were tested in was randomised for each participant.

4.4 Dependent Variables

Usability. The subjective usability of the different modalities was quantified using the SUS questionnaire as it had been found to be robust and versatile in the past [3]. The SUS consists of ten questions revolving around usability which can be combined for a benchmark SUS score ranging from 0–100.

Short interviews followed the study to gain qualitative feedback regarding the usability of each modality. Observation of participants during the study also highlighted issues regarding usability.

Errors. Errors within the study are defined as an attempt to perform an action using a modality which did not result in the intended outcome. Participants were asked to orally state, "error" when an attempted action was unsuccessful. The administrator then made a tally of these errors. Ideally these errors would be automatically captured. However, practical constraints were difficult to overcome in determining errors such as under actuated button presses and electronic contact points on glove not making contact.

Time. The duration between the instruction being presented to the user and the correct input being registered was recorded on the HoloLens for each action. There were fifteen actions performed on each device per participant. A mean value for the time taken to perform the correct action on each device was calculated for each participant.

4.5 Participants

There were twenty participants recruited in total. Most of these participants were students and staff from the School of Electronics, Electrical Engineering and Computer Science. Eleven of the participants had tried the HoloLens before. There were sixteen males and four females in the study with an age range of twenty to sixty.

4.6 Apparatus

The first-generation Microsoft HoloLens was used to provide instructions, as well as speech and gesture modalities. A single right-handed Avatar VR glove from NeuroDigital was used for the glove gestures. The TIM was used in a fixed position attached to the HoloLens. A Raspberry Pi 3 was used as an MQTT broker to pass messages between the TIM and HoloLens.

HoloLens development was carried out using Unity 3D (v2018.4.6) using C#. The Mixed Reality ToolKit (v2), M2Mqtt GitHub project (v4.3) and Vuforia SDK (v8.3.8) were also included in the final HoloLens build. The firmware for the ESP-8266 (01-module) within the TIM was compiled in the Arduino IDE (v1.8.9) using embedded C.

4.7 Protocol

Upon arrival each participant was provided consent and information sheets which had been reviewed by the faculty board of ethics. An overview of the AugmenTech system and study protocol was provided orally. Once the system had been explained the participant was able to try the system. The three separate actions, stepping task forwards, stepping task backwards and changing instruction type, were then introduced to each participant.

The process of testing the input modality was repeated four times so that each participant used all modalities. This process began with an explanation on how to perform each of the three actions using the given modality within the AugmenTech system. Next there was a training period of <2 min, followed by the participant successfully performing ten actions in a row. It was during this training period that the participants saw the format for the instructions on which action to perform. The instructions consisted of a sentence stating either, "go next task", "go back task" or "change instruction type" and were displayed in large text via the HoloLens. Once the training period had been completed and the participant had confirmed their readiness the recorded test began. This test consisted of the participant performing fifteen actions in a randomised sequence as instructed. Once these actions were performed the participant was asked to complete a SUS questionnaire. The process was then repeated until each input modality had been tested.

Once all input methods had been undertaken a short interview was carried out with the participant to discuss the usability of the different techniques.

5 Results and Discussion

Box and whisker plots are used throughout this section for graphical comparisons. T-bars indicate 95% confidence interval extents, the edges of the box represent the upper and lower quartiles and the line within the box represents the median. All statistical tests and data plots were carried out using SPSS Statistics software package.

5.1 H1: The TIM Usability Will Be Scored Highly

Results – H1. The SUS questionnaire consists of ten questions based on usability. The format of the questionnaire enables a combined score to be calculated ranging between 0–100.

The mean scores were 66.50 (SD = 22.82), 78.63 (SD = 9.51), 76.63 (SD = 18.25) and 81.75 (SD = 11.98) for the HoloLens gesture, HoloLens speech, glove gesture and TIM modalities, respectively. A one-way repeated measures ANOVA with a Bonferroni adjustment showed there was statistical significance in the difference between SUS scores for at least one pair of modalities, $F(3,57) = 4.63$, $p = 0.002$. Post-hoc tests using the Bonferroni adjustment showed that this difference was between the HoloLens gesture and TIM modalities ($p = 0.022$).

Discussion – H1. Most of the questions on the SUS revolve around ease of use. The TIM was developed with a focus on ease of use for the operator; it was not surprising that it scored highly. Guidance in interpreting the benchmark SUS score is given by Bangor et al. [3] who determined that a system with a score of over 70 is ready for implementation in its use case. They also claim that higher quality systems score high 70s and low 80s.

There were concerns that docking the TIM to the HoloLens, as opposed to using it detached held in the hand, could lead to discomfort for the participants due to the 64 g increase in mass on the headset. However, none of them expressed having any issues with discomfort in using the TIM module on the HoloLens headset when asked.

During discussions many participants reported struggling to perform the HoloLens gesture, which is likely to be the reason for the poor SUS score. The requirement for the participant to move their head to control the gaze vector was also not well received. Some participants reported having better success in gesture recognition when using their non-dominant hands.

Speech input was found to be easy to use for most participants. During observation it was clear there were greater concerns in usability of the speech commands among participants with strong accents. Speech scored highly in the SUS, however during discussions many participants stated they wouldn't be comfortable speaking to the HMD whilst amongst others.

The gloves were found to be easy to use by nearly all participants. There was only one case where a participant with small hands struggled with the poor fit. Many participants expressed satisfaction in receiving haptic feedback during input actions. It was discovered during interviews that one of the most appreciated benefits of using the gloves as an input modality was the ability to perform inputs without needing to move the hand from a comfortable resting position (Fig. 3).

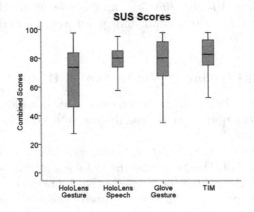

Fig. 3. Box plots for combined SUS scores.

5.2   H2: There Will Be a Low Number of Errors for the TIM

Results – H2. The mean totals of failed attempts whilst performing an action were 2.55 (SD = 2.54), 2.40 (SD = 2.66), 0.95 (SD = 1.00) and 1.40 (SD = 1.50) for the HoloLens gesture, HoloLens speech, glove gesture and TIM modalities, respectively. Across all actions this resulted in success rates of 83%, 84%, 94% and 91% for each modality, respectively.

The distributions of the error counts did not meet the assumptions necessary for a repeated measures one-way ANOVA. Therefore, a non-parametric Friedman test was conducted and showed there to be no statistically significant differences between the modalities, $\chi^2(3) = 3.48$, p = 0.323.

Discussion – H2. The TIM demonstrated the second lowest count of errors in the study, with gloves gestures resulting in the least. Most of the errors reported for the TIM were due to not having sufficiently pressed down on a button.

The gestures on the Avatar VR gloves worked well for most participants, resulting in minimal errors. Users were able to quickly understand how to perform the actions and repeated them with ease. Most of the errors observed whilst using the gloves were due to the gloves being too large for small hands.

The HoloLens' native input modalities had mixed results for errors during trials, resulting in large variance in the data. Participants with strong accents usually struggled with the speech modality, whilst the others typically had no issues. The HoloLens' gesture input success rate was generally poor for most participants, whilst a few participants experienced no problems. The steep learning curve for the HoloLens' gesture makes it difficult for most first time users of the HoloLens. With more training time it is assumed that participants would be able to have much greater success with the modality (Fig. 4).

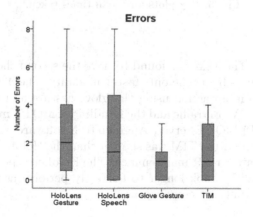

Fig. 4. Box plots for errors counted across 15 actions.

5.3 H3: The Average Input Time for the TIM Will Be Short in Comparison to Other Modalities

Results – H3. The mean durations between the instruction being displayed and the correct input being registered were 4.44 s (SD = 1.44), 3.69 s (SD = 1.14), 2.55 s (SD = 0.79) and 3.03 s (SD = 0.87) for the HoloLens gesture, HoloLens speech, glove and TIM modalities, respectively.

A non-parametric Friedman test showed there was statistical significance in the difference of mean times between modalities, $\chi^2(3) = 24.96$, p < 0.001. Post hoc analysis was performed with Wilcoxon signed-rank tests and showed there was statistical significance in the difference between TIM and each of the other modalities. Between the TIM and HoloLens gesture modality, Z = −2.76, p = 0.006. For the TIM and HoloLens speech modality, Z = −2.28, p = 0.023. Between the TIM and glove gesture modality, Z = −2.165, p = 0.030 (Fig. 5).

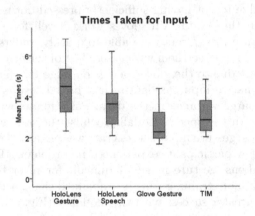

Fig. 5. Box plots for mean times taken.

Discussion – H3. The TIM was found to have the second shortest input time, with the glove gestures being the only faster modality. The 480 ms difference in time taken to perform an action using the glove gesture and using the TIM is believed to be due to Wi-Fi traffic and the handling of MQTT messages occurring on the Raspberry Pi MQTT server, AugmenTech software and ESP firmware. The input time mean for the TIM was shorter than the HoloLens modalities and is more than adequate for AR maintenance. The HoloLens speech and HoloLens gesture input modalities took longer to correctly perform as a consequence of the errors incurred whilst attempting them.

6   Conclusion and Future Work

Issues concerning the use of common AR input modalities in industry were identified and a solution was developed in the form of the TIM. This solution was designed with a focus on usability, which was successfully demonstrated when a score of 81.75 was achieved on the SUS. The TIM performed similarly to HoloLens input modalities in error count, input time and usability when evaluated within an assistive AR system by members of the general population. Recommended future work entails testing of such devices for input in an industrial setting, as opposed to a controlled laboratory. It should also be noted that the scalability of solutions such as the TIM is limited to applications requiring very few exclusive input actions.

The Avatar VR glove was integrated into the AugmenTech system to determine its usability and effectiveness amongst users. The results were positive; the glove gesture modality resulted in the low errors, short input time and received a high SUS score of 76.63. The haptic feedback to input actions was well received by participants. Although the glove provides many functionalities and performed well during testing, its fragile nature limits its usability in an industrial setting. We believe there is a strong case for developing a smart personal protective equipment (PPE) glove with similar capabilities as the Avatar VR glove for the industrial application of AR.

References

1. Alallah, F., et al.: Performer vs. observer: whose comfort level should we consider when examining the social acceptability of input modalities for head-worn display? In: Proceedings of the 24th ACM Symposium on Virtual Reality Software and Technology (VRST 2018), pp. 10:1–10:9. ACM, New York (2018). https://doi.org/10.1145/3281505.3281541
2. Ashbrook, D., Baudisch, P., White, S.: Nenya: subtle and eyes-free mobile input with a magnetically-tracked finger ring, pp. 2043–2046, May 2011. https://doi.org/10.1145/1978942.1979238
3. Bangor, A., Kortum, P.T., Miller, J.T.: An empirical evaluation of the system usability scale. Int. J. Hum.-Comput. Interact. **24**(6), 574–594 (2008). https://doi.org/10.1080/10447310802205776
4. Billinghurst, M., Clark, A., Lee, G.: A survey of augmented reality. Found. Trends® Hum.-Comput. Interact. **8**(2–3), 73–272 (2015). https://doi.org/10.1561/1100000049
5. Bottani, E., Vignali, G.: Augmented reality technology in the manufacturing industry: a review of the last decade. IIE Trans. **51**, 284–310 (2019). https://doi.org/10.1080/24725854.2018.1493244
6. Chen, Y., et al.: Pactolus: a method for mid-air gesture segmentation within EMG. In: Proceedings of the 2016 CHI Conference Extended Abstracts on Human Factors in Computing Systems (CHI EA 2016), pp. 1760–1765. ACM, New York (2016). https://doi.org/10.1145/2851581.2892492. http://doi.acm.org/10.1145/2851581.2892492
7. Dobbelstein, D., Hock, P., Rukzio, E.: Belt: an unobtrusive touch input device for head-worn displays. In: Proceedings of the 33rd Annual ACM Conference on Human Factors in Computing Systems (CHI 2015), pp. 2135–2138. ACM, New York (2015). https://doi.org/10.1145/2702123.2702450. http://doi.acm.org/10.1145/2702123.2702450

8. Gavish, N., et al.: Evaluating virtual reality and augmented reality training for industrial maintenance and assembly tasks. Interact. Learn. Environ. **23**(6), 778–798 (2015). https://doi.org/10.1080/10494820.2013.815221

9. Grandi, J.G., Debarba, H.G., Nedel, L., Maciel, A.: Design and evaluation of a handheld-based 3D user interface for collaborative object manipulation. In: Proceedings of the 2017 CHI Conference on Human Factors in Computing Systems (CHI 2017), pp. 5881–5891. ACM, New York (2017). https://doi.org/10.1145/3025453.3025935. http://doi.acm.org/10.1145/3025453.3025935

10. Harrison, C., Benko, H., Wilson, A.D.: OmniTouch: wearable multitouch interaction everywhere. In: Proceedings of the 24th Annual ACM Symposium on User Interface Software and Technology (UIST 2011), pp. 441–450. ACM, New York (2011). https://doi.org/10.1145/2047196.2047255. http://doi.acm.org/10.1145/2047196.2047255

11. Harrison, C., Tan, D., Morris, D.: Skinput: appropriating the body as an input surface. In: Proceedings of the SIGCHI Conference on Human Factors in Computing Systems (CHI 2010), pp. 453–462. ACM, New York (2010). https://doi.org/10.1145/1753326.1753394. http://doi.acm.org/10.1145/1753326.1753394

12. Hincapié-Ramos, J.D., Guo, X., Moghadasian, P., Irani, P.: Consumed endurance: a metric to quantify arm fatigue of mid-air interactions. In: Proceedings of the SIGCHI Conference on Human Factors in Computing Systems (CHI 2014), pp. 1063–1072. ACM, New York (2014). https://doi.org/10.1145/2556288.2557130. http://doi.acm.org/10.1145/2556288.2557130

13. Istance, H., Bates, R., Hyrskykari, A., Vickers, S.: Snap clutch, a moded approach to solving the midas touch problem. In: Proceedings of the 2008 Symposium on Eye Tracking Research & #38; Applications (ETRA 2008), pp. 221–228. ACM, New York (2008). https://doi.org/10.1145/1344471.1344523. http://doi.acm.org/10.1145/1344471.1344523

14. Palmarini, R., Erkoyuncu, J.A., Roy, R., Torabmostaedi, H.: A systematic review of augmented reality applications in maintenance. Robot. Comput.-Integr. Manuf. **49**, 215–228 (2018). https://doi.org/10.1016/j.rcim.2017.06.002. http://www.sciencedirect.com/science/article/pii/S0736584517300686

15. Peddie, J.: Technology issues. In: Peddie, J. (ed.) Augmented Reality, pp. 183–289. Springer, Cham (2017). https://doi.org/10.1007/978-3-319-54502-8_8

16. Serrano, M., Ens, B., Irani, P.: Exploring the use of hand-to-face input for interacting with head-worn displays, May 2014. https://doi.org/10.1145/2556288.2556984

17. Tung, Y.C., et al.: User-defined game input for smart glasses in public space. In: Proceedings of the 33rd Annual ACM Conference on Human Factors in Computing Systems (CHI 2015), pp. 3327–3336. ACM, New York (2015). https://doi.org/10.1145/2702123.2702214. http://doi.acm.org/10.1145/2702123.2702214

18. Yang, Y., Shim, J., Chae, S., Han, T.: Interactive augmented reality authoring system using mobile device as input method. In: 2016 IEEE International Conference on Systems, Man, and Cybernetics (SMC), pp. 001429–001432, October 2016. https://doi.org/10.1109/SMC.2016.7844437

19. Zimmer, C., Bertram, M., Büntig, F., Drochtert, D., Geiger, C.: Mobile augmented reality illustrations that entertain and inform: design and implementation issues with the hololens. In: SIGGRAPH Asia 2017 Mobile Graphics & Interactive Applications (SA 2017), pp. 23:1–23:7. ACM, New York (2017). https://doi.org/10.1145/3132787.3132804. http://doi.acm.org/10.1145/3132787.3132804

State of the Art of Non-vision-Based Localization Technologies for AR in Facility Management

Dietmar Siegele[1]([⊠]) [iD], Umberto Di Staso[2], Marco Piovano[1], Carmen Marcher[1,3], and Dominik T. Matt[1,3]

[1] Fraunhofer Italia, Via A. Volta 13 A, 39100 Bolzano, Italy
`dietmar.siegele@fraunhofer.it`
[2] Territorium Online Srl, Via B. Buozzi 12, 39100 Bolzano, Italy
[3] Free University of Bozen-Bolzano, Piazza Università 5, 39100 Bolzano, Italy

Abstract. Augmented reality (AR) applications for indoor purpose mostly use vision-based localization systems. However, even with AI-based algorithms, reachable accuracies are quite low. In the field of facility management an important functionality is the possibility to go for a high localization accuracy to display information, warnings or instructions at the correct position, if necessary. Simple vision-based solutions, like QR codes, are widely used. However, they show a high effort during installation and the advantages of using AR are limited. Thus, a state-of-the-art review for non-vision-based indoor localization technologies was carried out. Moreover, an evaluation with respect to usability for augmented reality applications was done. A scenario of the application of AR in the facility management environment is described based on the review results. For use-cases with high accuracy, tracking systems like infrared-based camera systems are a preferable solution. Also, ultrasonic could be a cheap solution for a medium accuracy tracking. For a simple room-based localization Bluetooth beacons and other hybrid indoor position technologies are preferred.

Keywords: Indoor localization · Augmented reality · Facility management

1 Introduction to Indoor Positioning

Indoor positioning technologies (IPT), also known as indoor positioning systems (IPS), are used to track humans or devices in an indoor environment. For outdoor positioning, satellite-based radio navigation technologies are widely used, such as the Global Positioning System (GPS) technology. Thus, satellites equipped with very stable atomic clocks continuously transmit a radio signal containing the current time and data about its position. It works with the so-called transit time methodology (Time of Flight, ToF). Accuracies between 30 cm and 5 m are reachable and with additional base stations and a correction of the received signals, accuracies below 1 cm can be reached (e.g. for surveying and mapping). This system is called Differential Global Positioning System (DGPS). However, a direct line-of-sight to four or more GPS satellites is necessary for a correct positioning. This limits the applicability for indoor positioning. For this reason,

© Springer Nature Switzerland AG 2020
L. T. De Paolis and P. Bourdot (Eds.): AVR 2020, LNCS 12242, pp. 255–272, 2020.
https://doi.org/10.1007/978-3-030-58465-8_20

other technologies were developed for application cases such as indoor navigation, robot navigation and – what we focus on within this paper – augmented reality (AR).

Some extensive literature reviews have been carried out over the last years. One of the most recent was done by Mendoza-Silva et al. 2019. A very comprehensive survey including technologies, mathematics and hybrid IPS was carried out by Oguntala et al. 2018. They focused on the application of IPS working with IoT devices. Liu et al. 2007 did a comprehensive survey of wireless indoor positioning techniques and systems. Alarifi et al. 2016 gave a comprehensive overview about the actual state of the art and technologies, and the UWB technology in particular. Mrindoko and Minga 2016 carried out a review on the performance metrics and the localization techniques in general. Viani et al. 2011 did an extensive review on wireless sensor networks. They identified some key issues: environmental and working conditions are difficult to predict, the accuracy can vary strongly and must be considered, and the overall costs for sensors and calibration are not scalable.

2 Location Detection Techniques and Algorithms

2.1 Proximity

If only presence needs to be recognized, the proximity technology can be used. Depending on the used devices (e.g. RFID or Bluetooth) different 'presence areas' can be defined. Proximity is widely used and very simple to implement. It is only necessary to determine if, e.g., the user is logged into a specific Wi-Fi access point to check its presence. Also, magnetic positioning technologies use this approach. For example, in an industrial area it can be recognized which people are in which building. Moreover, in case of evacuations, proximity can be used to check the absence of single persons. However, if a user is logged into two nodes at the same time, it is unclear in which area it is.

2.2 Trilateration with Received Signal-Strength (RSSI)

In radio-based technologies the received signal strength can be measured very easily. Depending on the signal strength, a distance in meters can be approximated by trilateration. This technology is called Received Signal-Strength Index (RSSI). However, there is not a simple correlation between signal strength and distance, because objects, like walls, furniture and even people have a great impact on the signal strength. Also, temperature and humidity must be considered (density of the air). Depending on the used technology, calibrations can be carried out to improve the accuracy. To get a unique position, at least three stations with known coordinates must be used. The uncertainty strongly depends on the used technology, the calibration and the environment. To achieve an accuracy of less than a meter, various techniques have to be used or combined with trilateration.

2.3 Angle of Arrival (AoA)

Technologies using the Angle of Arrival (AoA) method, determine the direction of the emitted signal and solve mathematically a triangulation problem. It is also called

Direction of arrival (DoA). One common method in IPS is to calculate the AoA measuring the time difference of arrival (TDOA) between individual elements of an antenna array. With the AoA method, accuracies around 10 cm can be reached. The method will play a main role in future indoor positioning technologies, as it can already be seen i.e. in the new Bluetooth 5.1 definition (Suryavanshi et al. 2019).

2.4 Time of Arrival (ToA)

The Time of Arrival method (ToA) – also known as Time of Flight (ToF) – bases on trilateration. However, compared to the RSSI method, all stations must be synchronized in time. GPS is the most-known localization technology that uses ToA. The satellites are equipped with atomic clocks to reach the necessary accuracy. For indoor localization purpose, two-way ranging is used. The position is determined by sending a radio signal, which is mirrored back and received again. This increases the accuracy and an accurately synchronized time is less important. However, for this kind of system a direct line of sight is necessary.

3 Performance Metrics

In Alarifi et al. 2016 six metrics (key performance indicators) have been defined to classify the indoor positioning technologies. Table 1 shows an overview of the results of these metrics.

Table 1. Performance metrics (Alarifi et al. 2016).

Metric	Definition
Accuracy	The closeness of agreement between a measured quantity value and a true quantity value of a measure
Availability	The positioning service availability in terms of time percentage
Coverage area	The area covered by an IPS
Scalability	The degree to which the system ensures the normal positioning function when it scales in one of two dimensions: geography and number of users
Cost	Can be measured in different dimensions; money, time, space, and energy which can be affected at different levels of the system: system installation and maintenance, infrastructure components, and positioning devices
Privacy	Strong access control over how users' personal information is collected and used

4 Indoor Positioning Technologies for AR

4.1 Overview

Table 2 gives an overview about the available technologies and their advantages and disadvantages based on the presented performance metrics. Bartoletti et al. 2019 did a classification on the accuracy and the coverage area, based on the survey of Liu et al. 2007. The privacy is not rated, because it depends strongly on the application case. In the following sections, more detailed descriptions and literature sources are given.

Table 2. Indoor positioning technologies (Farid et al. 2013; Alarifi et al. 2016; Mrindoko and Minga, 2016) (Own sources)

Technology	Algorithms	Accuracy	Availability, Latency	Scalability	Costs	Energy demand
Wireless local area network (Wi-Fi)	Proximity, RSSI	1–15 m	Overloaded frequency band	Very high, because it is building equipment	Low	High
Bluetooth (BLE)	Proximity, RSSI, AoA (BLE 5.1)	1–3 m	Overloaded frequency band, <0.5 s	Middle, new equipment, but quite cheap and battery supplied	High	Very low
Ultra wideband (UWB)	ToA	10–30 cm	Requires LOS, wide frequency range	Very low, very expensive equipment	Very high	Very high
Radio frequency identification (RFID)	Proximity, RSSI, (ToA), (AoA)	Passive: object size Active: 1 m	Requires almost object contact in case of passive RFID	Very low for IPS	Passive: low Active: high	Passive: Very low Active: high
ZigBee	Proximity, RSSI	5–80 cm	Overloaded frequency band	Very high in combination with IoT	Low	Very low
Li-Fi	Proximity	>0.1 m	Requires LOS, no penetration of obstacles, < 0.2 s	Very high, because it is building equipment	Middle	Low
Ultrasonic (Ultrasound)	ToA	1–3 cm	Neglectable penetration of obstacles, 0.1–3.0 s	Low, expensive equipment	High	Middle
Magnetic positioning	Sensors, maps	1–5 m	Magnetic field depends on environmental conditions	Very high, because need no stations, only mapping	Low	Low

(continued)

Table 2. (*continued*)

Technology	Algorithms	Accuracy	Availability, Latency	Scalability	Costs	Energy demand
Infrared (IrDA)	Proximity, ToA	0.1–90 cm	No penetration of obstacles <0.2 s	Low due to limited range and high effort	Medium	Low
GSM based	Proximity, RSSI	20 m	Low to high impact of environmental conditions	Very low, only works on area level	Use of existing stations	High
Dead reckoning (inertial navigation)	Sensors, maps	5–15 m	Re-targeting necessary	High	Very low	Very low
Pseudolites	ToA	10–80 cm	Requires LOS	Low, expensive equipment	Very high	High

4.2 Wireless Local Area Network (WLAN, Wi-Fi)

Utilizing WLAN for indoor positioning was first investigated by Youssef 2004 which proposed the HORUS method, that bases on the RSSI approach.

A lot of research followed to improve the localization accuracy. Mazuelas et al. 2009 applied Wi-Fi RSSI to calculate the distance between a mobile station and an Access Point (AP) by an online estimated propagation model. Yet, the resolution of RSSI-based approaches is not satisfactory. Other metrics were adopted to further improve the localization performance. Gjengset et al. 2014 developed a so-called array phaser, that upgrades a multi-antenna commodity Wi-Fi AP to a phased array signal processing platform for AoA estimation. To avoid using a complicated antenna array, Kumar et al. 2014 proposed *Ubicarse*, that facilitates handhold Wi-Fi devices to emulate large antenna arrays using a synthetic aperture radar (SAR) technique. Vasisht et al. 2015 proposed a very different method by using a frequency mitigation technique to utilize Wi-Fi's 2.4 GHz and 5 GHz spectrums as a whole in combating multipath effect. They achieved sub-nanosecond ToF with commodity Wi-Fi cards. Fingerprint-based approaches compare the current features of ambient signals with those already recorded in a fingerprint database, to correlate the newly collected signals to pre-defined locations. This method is widely used for IPS based on WLAN. Wu et al. 2013 explored the frequency diversity of the subcarriers in OFDM systems and leveraged the Wi-Fi channel state information (CSI) to build a fingerprinting system. Sen et al. 2012 demonstrated PHY layer-based WiFi localization and observed an 89% mean accuracy for a spot-detection of a 1 m/1 m area. Rai et al. 2012 developed a crowdsourcing technique Zee to gather Wi-Fi fingerprints in the area of interest.

Summarizing, WLAN-based IPS can reach accuracies in the range of one meter only in mapped environments, which are frequently updated, and in very optimistic scenarios. Otherwise the accuracy is in the range of 5 to 15 m. For augmented reality cases this accuracy is not sufficient enough.

4.3 Bluetooth, Bluetooth Low Energy (BLE)

Bluetooth Low Energy devices operate in the 2.4 GHz license-free band, and so share the same indoor propagation characteristics as 2.4 GHz Wi-Fi transceivers. The beaconing, or advertising mode, permitted in the BLE standard enables a very short, unsolicited message at very flexible update rates. These messages can be used to allow a device to detect close proximity to a specific location, based on the Received Signal Strength (RSS). In this way, location specific triggers, adverts, vouchers and information can be provided to the user. BLE advertising beacons are particularly attractive to retailers because of the promise of long battery lives of many years, and thus low maintenance requirements. Long battery lives are expected to require low radio power output and/or low beaconing rates. While this does not affect their use for proximity detection, it does affect their usefulness for providing fingerprint-based positioning throughout an entire indoor environment (Faragher and Harle 2014).

Yapeng Wang et al. 2013 demonstrated the principles of using RSSI and triangulation methods first available in the Bluetooth standard 2.1 and stated first results.

Faragher and Harle 2014 investigated as first the impact of Bluetooth Low Energy devices in advertising/beaconing mode on fingerprint-based indoor positioning schemes. They demonstrated that the low bandwidth of BLE signals compared to Wi-Fi, is the cause of significant measurement error when coupled with the use of three BLE advertising channels. They proposed a multipath mitigation scheme and determined, that the optimal positioning performance is provided by 10 Hz beaconing and a one second multipath mitigation processing window size. They investigated that a steady increase in positioning performance with fingerprint size occurs up to 7 ± 1, above this, there is no clear benefit to extra beacon coverage.

Paterna et al. 2017 followed more complex assumptions by considering channel diversity, weighted trilateration and applied Kalman filtering. They stated an improvement in the precision of the system, which goes up to 1.82 m in 90% of the time for a device moving in a middle-size room and 0.70 m for static devices. Furthermore, they have proved that the system is scalable and efficient in terms of cost and power consumption. Castillo-Cara et al. 2017 carried out an empirical study of the transmission power setting for Bluetooth based indoor localization. Following a holistic approach, they started by assessing the capabilities of two Bluetooth sensor/receiver devices. Consequently, they evaluated the relevance of the RSSI fingerprint reported by each BLE beacon operating at various transmission power levels using feature selection techniques. Based on this, they used two classification algorithms in order to improve the setting of the transmission power levels of each of the BLE beacons. With this method, they were able to improve the accuracy by 13% based on a positioning within a 1 m/1 m sector. However, real application of this method seems difficult.

Suryavanshi et al. 2019 described the new direction-finding capability in the Bluetooth 5.1 standard. The Bluetooth Core Specification provided by Bluetooth Special

Interest Group (SIG) added direction finding feature in the Low Energy (LE) standard. This feature enables a tracker to find the target by estimating the relative angle between the tracker and target. It uses either Angle of Arrival (AoA) or Angle of Departure (AoD) method with multiple antennas switching for direction estimation. Lehtimäki 2019 described the new standard from the viewpoint of the software implementation.

The direction-finding capability of Bluetooth 5.1 promises accuracy in the range of 1–3 cm. Until now there is no measurement data available, which could be able to prove this marketing numbers. However, it seems a very promising technology and can have the capability to be a game changer in IPS for augmented reality applications.

4.4 Ultra-Wideband (UWB)

Ultra-Wideband (UWB) technology exploits the diverse interactions between electromagnetic fields and matter, operating on the principle that images, gained from scattering of electromagnetic waves, provide a detailed geometrical dimension of the surrounding environment, since wavelengths are smaller compared to the real size of objects (Sachs 2012). Although, electromagnetic scattering does not reveal detailed information of certain objects, for example, opaque and hidden objects. UWB is designed to operate in the microwave frequency occupying a very large bandwidth of more than 1.5 GHz (Foerster et al. 2001), thereby giving the technology an exceptionally high resolution but low penetrating power especially to most non-metallic materials for easy detection of hidden objects. In addition, the higher bandwidth of microwave frequency enables UWB-based location identification to achieve higher object resolution in the decimeter, centimeter, and millimeter range, and better object recognition capabilities than narrowband technologies (Oppermann et al. 2004; Pinhasi et al. 2004; Sachs 2012). Moreover, since UWB operates by sending ultra-short pulses with low duty cycle across many frequencies (Ingram et al. 2004), this enables the technology to provide accurate ToA positioning information even in the presence of multipath. Other desirable features of UWB include high data rate, that is short-range at very low power density (Rahayu et al. 2008). However, the large bandwidth of UWB causes inevitable interference in the presence of other devices, thereby necessitating a strict low power consumption limit, which makes the technology a conservative approach and impractical for many location identification applications (Radunovic and Le Boudec 2004). Cirulis 2019 investigated the potential of UWB in augmented reality environments.

However, UWB technology is still quite expensive and seems not to be an adequate technology for AR purpose.

4.5 Radio Frequency Identification (RFID)

The RFID technology positioning system usually consists of antennas, tags, readers and positioning algorithms. Each tag is uniquely identifiable and able to transmit stored data, which may be read-only or writable. Active tags are equipped with an inbuilt battery, while passive tags do not have inbuilt batteries, but backscatter the signal received from the base station. Semi-active tags, although they do backscatter the carrier signal received from a base station, also have an inbuilt battery, which powers the circuitry, thereby giving it the flexibility to function in dense environments (Cook et al. 2014).

Research on the applicability of RFID for indoor positioning scenarios was carried out e.g. by Bouet and dos Santos 2008, Chon et al. 2004, Li et al. 2009, Saab and Nakad 2011, Ting et al. 2011. RFID offers other desirable advantages which include high data rate, adaptability to various environment, availability in non-line-of-sight (NLOS), wireless capability, wireless zero-power sensors and low maintainability (Bai et al. 2012; Chen et al. 2011; Khan and Antiwal 2009). RFID technology, however, suffers from several limitations arising from the issue of operating frequency standardization, invasive nature, and requirement of additional infrastructure in location identification techniques like proximity (Kaur et al. 2011). Furthermore, improved accuracy and higher resolution often require the deployment of several tags around the coverage area of interest, which sometimes results in high computational cost.

Latest research was carried out by Xu et al. 2018 or Magnago et al. 2019 using UHF tags and quite large antennas. First authors achieved accuracies below 30 cm in 74% of the cases and below 50 cm in 99% of the cases.

For AR applications RFID can be useful to define an accurate target or anchor, but for a real-time tracking, the technology needs UHF tags and large antennas, which are expensive and do not reach very high accuracies.

4.6 ZigBee

ZigBee is a wireless standard defined by a set of communication protocols designed for wireless personal area networks, thereby making it a short-range technology. Wireless devices using ZigBee operate in the 868 MHz, 915 MHz, and 2.4 GHz ISM band. The effective signal range of ZigBee is up to 100 m in free space, and typically 20 to 30 m in indoor environments (Baronti et al. 2007). The coordinating ZigBee device forms the root of the network by initiating a connection between other networks and nodes of up to 255 nodes, whereas the node receives data from the coordinator (Kanwar and Khazanchi 2012).

ZigBee offers several desirable advantages as described in the literature by several researchers Amutha and Nanmaran 2014, Larranaga et al. 2010, Tadakamadla 2006. However, ZigBee suffers from some drawbacks as well, as the operating frequency of ZigBee, which lies in the unlicensed ISM band, makes the technology prone to interference from signals operating at the same frequency. In addition, since the technology is only suitable for short-range applications with low-data-rate, the range of applications is limited.

However, it could be a feasible (license-free and cheap) solution for augmented reality purposes.

4.7 Li-Fi

Li-Fi is a light communication system that is capable of transmitting data at high speeds over the visible light, ultraviolet, and infrared spectrums. In its present state, only LED lamps can be used for the transmission of visible light. Visible light communications (VLC) works by switching the current to the LEDs off and on at a very high speed, too quick to be noticed by the human eye, thus, it does not present any flickering.

Zhuang et al. 2018 did a literature review on positioning systems using visible LED lights. Islim and Haas 2016 reviewed several modulation techniques, which is one of the main research field right now. The systems should be able to be in operation, even if artificial light is not wished. The high-frequency flickering still needs to be optimized, that human beings are no affected.

The technology is promising for many indoor localization scenarios, but for using it with augmented reality the accuracy is too low, and determination of the orientation is not trivial in many scenarios.

4.8 Ultrasonic (Ultrasound)

Ultrasound is an acoustic sound inaudible for the human ear. Time of flight methods are used; hence high positioning accuracies can be reached.

A literature review specifically on this top was carried out by Ijaz et al. 2013. Yazici et al. 2011 suggested to use Time Difference of Arrival (TDOA) technique and reported of positioning errors of below 20 mm for moving targets. Qi and Liu 2017 suggested a new time domain method to extract the envelope of the ultrasonic signals in order to estimate the ToF. They were able to improve the accuracy below 1 mm for non-moving objects and 10 mm for a moving target. Hazas and Hopper 2006 identified that current ultrasonic location systems suffer from limitations due to their use of narrowband transducers. They investigated the use of broadband ultrasound for indoor positioning systems. They reached a localization accuracy if 2 cm with an increased noise robustness. A. De Angelis et al. 2015 developed a portable ultrasonic positioning system. This could be an interesting solution if a higher localization accuracy is only required in individual cases, e.g. maintenance work.

For the use with augmented reality an advantage is the high accuracy. However, this technology has high investment costs, but portable systems could be used, if higher accuracy is necessary.

4.9 Magnetic Positioning

Due to the presence of large steel components inside building, the geomagnetic field is affected and distorted. Such changes in magnetic field are used for indoor localization. Magnetic positioning can offer pedestrians with smartphones an indoor accuracy of 1–2 m with 90% confidence level, without using the additional wireless infrastructure for positioning. Un-optimized compass chips inside smartphones can sense and record these magnetic variations to map indoor locations.

Lee et al. 2018 proposed a method using deep learning (AMID) to recognizes magnetic sequence patterns using a deep neural network. Features are extracted from magnetic sequences, and then the algorithm is used for classifying the sequences by patterns generated by nearby magnetic landmarks. Locations are estimated by detecting the landmarks. With a probability of 80% they could detect a landmark. Bhattarai et al. 2018 were generating magnetic map to localize the position of a smartphone with built in sensors. They reached a positioning accuracy below 2 m during 70% of the experimental time. G. De Angelis et al. 2015 realized a system using off-the-shelf components based on inductive coupling between resonating coils. They reached an accuracy below 10 cm in a simple room. In complex geometrical conditions they reached accuracies below one meter.

Due to the low accuracies this technology is not recommended using it in augmented reality applications.

4.10   Infrared (IrDA)

Infrared-based indoor localization systems use infrared light pulses to locate signals inside a building. IR receivers are installed in every room, and when the IR tag pulses, it is read by the IR receiver device. Also, CCD or CMOS image sensors are used. They can also be categorized as such systems because they use dedicated markers, even if they use vision-based equipment. One of the largest restrictions is that the infrared spectrum is near to the visible light spectrum. Thus, the accuracy can be greatly influenced by natural light.

Yasir et al. 2016 proposed to use multiple optical receivers and reached an accuracy of 6 cm with a motion speed of 1.3 m/s. Raharijaona et al. 2017 tackled the problem of natural light by using flickering infrared LEDs and reach accuracies around 2 cm for a distance of 2 m. With three sensors they were also able to determine the orientation. Wang et al. 2017 proposed a novel localization-accuracy optical wireless based indoor localization system, based on the use of the mechanism that estimates background light intensity. They reached a localization accuracy of 2.5 cm.

One of the main challenges if the use if infrared is the necessary line of sight and the very small area coverable by one sensor. However, for indoor localization with the purpose of augmented reality, flickering infrared LEDs could be an interesting option. If high accuracy is needed for the use in facility management, such solutions are recommended, also because they could be used as a mobile equipment.

4.11   GSM Based

Using GSM as indoor localization is not wide-spread due to the technical limitations and the low accuracy.

Zhang et al. 2017 reviewed recent literature relating to localization in 5G networks, and emphasizes the prospect for implementing cooperative localization, which exploits the location information from additional measurements between mobile terminals.

Also, 5G is not going to be a recommended technology for indoor positioning purposes. However, low latency and high data rate allow new use cases (e.g. cloud support) for AR applications in the field of facility management.

4.12   Pedestrian Dead Reckoning (Inertial Navigation)

Using data from inertial sensors embedded in smartphones a relative indoor positioning can be carried out called Pedestrian Dead Reckoning (PDR). Kang and Han 2015 proposed a system only based on Smartphone sensors. Li and Ning 2018 showed, that using low-cost sensors in combination with a map and calibration routines can increase the positioning accuracy dramatically. However, a practicable application is not indicated.

Zhang et al. 2018 proposed a novel PDR indoor localization algorithm combined with online sequential extreme learning machine to increase the accuracy. They reached in their experiments a localization error of 1.7 m instead of 5.1 m without an algorithm.

However, for augmented reality applications the errors are still too high, and anchors needs to be used for acceptable results.

4.13 Pseudolites

Pseudolites are ground-based transmitters sending GPS compatible signals. As an independent system for indoor positioning, pseudolites technique can be explored for a wide range of positioning and navigation application where the signal of satellite GNSS can't be received.

Kim et al. 2014 proposed a pseudolite-based positioning system that can be used with unmodified legacy GPS receivers. Wan and Zhan 2011 analyzed the near-far problem in indoor pseudolite positioning systems and the near far ratio. Further, they evaluated different methods of time synchronization based on different structure of pseudolite positioning systems. In combination with PDR Gan et al. 2017 reached a localization accuracy of below 0.5 m. Recently, Li et al. 2019 developed a not algorithm based on a robust estimation and partial ambiguity resolution method to increase the accuracy without need of other IP technologies. They reached a positioning error of almost 0.10 m.

However, for augmented reality applications the necessary technology is quite expensive but could be an alternative in the future.

5   Hybrid Indoor Positioning Technologies

As already mentioned, for certain application cases the combination of different indoor positioning technologies can increase the accuracy significantly. Commonly used methods to fusion the different sensor data are Kalman or particle filters and all kind of machine learning algorithms. This can also be called hybrid IPS. The main technology used is inertial navigation (PDR), in particular because of the cheap sensors and the availability in smartphones. Kuang et al. 2018 proposed using PDR in combination with magnetic field matching and reached an accuracy of 0.64 m in an office environment and 2.34 m in a shopping mall environment. Yucel et al. 2012 proposed a combination of ultrasonic and infrared signals and reached a maximum positioning error of 0.02 cm. However, that could not show how such a system can be scaled up to e.g. building level. House et al. 2011 used passive RFID tags and IMU sensor in the formfactor of a wearable and reached a positioning accuracy of around 50 cm. They used the RFID tags as anchor to reposition the correct absolute position. Januszkiewicz et al. 2016 presented a similar methodology, but used infrared beacons instead of RFID anchors. Ruotsalainen et al. 2011 introduced a visual-aided two-dimensional indoor pedestrian navigation system integrating measurements from GNSS, Bluetooth, WLAN, self-contained sensors, and heading change information obtained from consecutive images. The integration was performed by using an extended Kalman filter. Compared to the indoor positioning without visual-aiding the system reached a 26% higher accuracy. Fu et al. 2018 combined IMU-based indoor navigation with visual-aiding and reached a 90% higher accuracy compared to using only the IMU sensor. Coronel et al. 2008 proposed to use IMU sensors and Bluetooth beacons by applying Kalman filtering. Yu et al. 2019 proposed a Wi-Fi and pedestrian dead reckoning (PDR)-integrated localization approach based on unscented Kalman filters. They showed that their approach may improve traditional approaches in terms of reliability and localization accuracy. Wang et al. 2016 studied map information of a given indoor environment, analyzed variations of Wi-Fi received signal strength (RSS), defined several kinds of indoor landmarks, and then utilized these landmarks to correct accumulated errors derived from PDR. This fusion scheme, called Landmark-aided PDR (LaP), was proved to be light-weight and suitable for real-time implementation. They achieved an average accuracy of 2.17 m.

For AR applications sensor fusion and hybrid indoor positioning technologies are necessary. Not only to achieve higher accuracy, but more important to achieve a higher robustness of the overall system. Combining different technologies can also help to prevent a completely wrong indoor navigation, i.e. if a hardware error occurs.

6 Scenario for Indoor Positioning Systems in AR for Facility Management

Based on this comprehensive literature review a scenario was developed to condense the results and to find the best solutions for the use of AR in facility management scenarios. Figure 1 shows such a feasible scenario in an office environment. Both operators wear AR glasses and can see actual information about the state of e.g. the escalator or a room.

The indoor positioning is carried out on three different levels of detail. This approach has the best scalability and allows to upgrade an existing building with this new system very quickly, easily and with cheap components.

With Bluetooth beacons the actual room is recognized. This means, when the operator enters the room, different states and information can be displayed in its AR glasses. The accuracy than can be reached by using Bluetooth beacons is sufficient for this task. However, using Wi-Fi fingerprint data and a Kalman filter the accuracy and the localization speed could be increased further.

To see specific information, i.e. the next necessary maintenance of a fire-extinguisher, visual markers can be used. A QR code can be mounted to such infrastructure and with image-based technology it can be identified, and information is shown in the glasses, as long as the equipment is in the operators' field of vision.

In more complex rooms, like the plant room or a conference room with many technical equipment, a tracking system based on infrared could be installed. The AR glasses can be equipped with so-called markers (see Fig. 2 for a first prototype).

This system can provide a higher accuracy for detecting the operators position and by using three or more infrared tracking cameras. With five markers on the AR glasses, the position and orientation of the head can be determined. With this information and an accurate 3D B.I.M. model no additional landmarks (like QR codes) are necessary. The information of a specific equipment appears when the operator focuses on it for longer than a specific period of time.

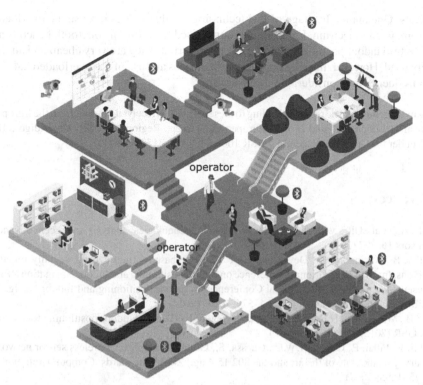

Fig. 1. Scenario for AR in facility management and indoor positioning technology (modified design of macrovector/Freepik)

Fig. 2. AR glasses with markers

7 Conclusion

A huge number of different technologies useable as non-vision-based localization techniques can be identified. For application where a high accuracy is necessary, tracking systems like infrared-based camera systems are a preferable solution. However, this technology is quite expensive, line-of-sight is necessary and natural light has an influence on the accuracy. Such systems are also widely used in the field of robotics, where interesting synergies to the facility management occur. Also, ultrasonic could be a cheap solution for a medium accuracy tracking. This technology is widely used in environments like hospitals. One main advantage of this technology is that it does not use the overloaded electromagnetic spectrum. For a simple room-based localization Bluetooth beacons and other hybrid indoor position technologies are preferred. They are very cheap and already widely used. However, missing opensource standards and use of the overloaded 2.4 GHz radio frequency are considerable disadvantages.

Acknowledgement. The research leading to these results has received funding from the European Regional Development Fund (Fondo Europeo di Sviluppo Regionale FESR Alto Adige 2014–2020) under the Grant Agreement n. FESR 1064 CUP B51B17000850007.

References

Alarifi, A., et al.: Ultra wideband indoor positioning technologies: analysis and recent advances. Sensors **16**, 707 (2016)

Amutha, B., Nanmaran, K.: Development of a ZigBee based virtual eye for visually impaired persons. In: 2014 International Conference on Indoor Positioning and Indoor Navigation (IPIN). Presented at the 2014 International Conference on Indoor Positioning and Indoor Navigation (IPIN), Busan, South Korea, pp. 564–574. IEEE (2014)

Bai, Y.B., Wu, S., Wu, H.R., Zhang, K.: Overview of RFID-based indoor positioning technology. In: GSR (2012)

Baronti, P., Pillai, P., Chook, V.W.C., Chessa, S., Gotta, A., Hu, Y.F.: Wireless sensor networks: a survey on the state of the art and the 802.15.4 and ZigBee standards. Comput. Commun. **30**, 1655–1695 (2007)

Bartoletti, S., Conti, A., Dardari, D., Giorgetti, A.: 5G Localization and Context-Awareness. Whitepaper (2019)

Bhattarai, B., Hwang, S.-S., Pyun, J.-Y.: An efficient geomagnetic indoor positioning system using smartphones. In: 3rd International Conference on Next Generation Computing (ICNGC2017b), Taiwan (2018)

Bouet, M., dos Santos, A.L.: RFID tags: positioning principles and localization techniques. In: 2008 1st IFIP Wireless Days. Presented at the 2008 1st IFIP Wireless Days, pp. 1–5 (2008)

Castillo-Cara, M., Lovón, J., Rocca, G., Orozco-Barbosa, L., García-Varea, I.: An empirical study of the transmission power setting for Bluetooth-based indoor localization mechanisms. Sensors **17**, 1318 (2017)

Chen, X.Q., Alfadhl, Y., Chai, K.K.: An indoor item finder with active RFID tags. In: IET International Conference on Communication Technology and Application (ICCTA 2011), Beijing, China (2011)

Chon, H.D., Jun, S.-B., Jung, H., An, S.W.: Using RFID for accurate positioning. J. Glob. Position. Syst. **3**, 32–39 (2004)

Cirulis, A.: Ultra wideband tracking potential for augmented reality environments. In: De Paolis, L.T., Bourdot, P. (eds.) AVR 2019. LNCS, vol. 11614, pp. 126–136. Springer, Cham (2019). https://doi.org/10.1007/978-3-030-25999-0_11

Cook, B.S., et al.: RFID-based sensors for zero-power autonomous wireless sensor networks. IEEE Sens. J. **14**, 2419–2431 (2014)

Coronel, P., Furrer, S., Schott, W., Weiss, B.: Indoor location tracking using inertial navigation sensors and radio beacons. In: Floerkemeier, C., Langheinrich, M., Fleisch, E., Mattern, F., Sarma, S.E. (eds.) IOT 2008. LNCS, vol. 4952, pp. 325–340. Springer, Heidelberg (2008). https://doi.org/10.1007/978-3-540-78731-0_21

De Angelis, A., et al.: Design and characterization of a portable ultrasonic indoor 3-D positioning system. IEEE Trans. Instrum. Meas. **64**, 2616–2625 (2015a)

De Angelis, G., et al.: An indoor AC magnetic positioning system. IEEE Trans. Instrum. Meas. **64**, 1267–1275 (2015b)

Faragher, R., Harle, R.K.: An analysis of the accuracy of Bluetooth low energy for indoor positioning applications. In: Proceedings of the 27th International Technical Meeting of the Satellite Division of the Institute of Navigation (ION GNSS+ 2014). Presented at the International Technical Meeting of the Satellite Division of the Institute of Navigation, Tampa, Florida, pp. 201–210 (2014)

Farid, Z., Nordin, R., Ismail, M.: Recent advances in wireless indoor localization techniques and system. J. Comput. Netw. Commun. **2013**, 185138:1–185138:12 (2013). [WWW Document]

Foerster, J., Green, E., Somayazulu, S., Leeper, D.: Ultra-wideband technology for short- or medium-range wireless communications. Intel Technol. J. Q2, 11 (2001)

Fu, W., Peng, A., Tang, B., Zheng, L.: Inertial sensor aided visual indoor positioning. In: 2018 International Conference on Electronics Technology (ICET). Presented at the 2018 International Conference on Electronics Technology (ICET), Chengdu, pp. 106–110. IEEE (2018)

Gan, X., Yu, B., Heng, Z., Huang, L.: Indoor positioning technology of Beidou/GPS pseudolites correction PDR. In: International Conference on Indoor Positioning and Indoor Navigation (IPIN), vol. 4 (2017)

Gjengset, J., Xiong, J., McPhillips, G., Jamieson, K.: Phaser: enabling phased array signal processing on commodity WiFi access points. In: Proceedings of the 20th Annual International Conference on Mobile Computing and Networking - MobiCom '14. Presented at the 20th Annual International Conference, Maui, Hawaii, USA, pp. 153–164. ACM Press (2014)

Hazas, M., Hopper, A.: Broadband ultrasonic location systems for improved indoor positioning. IEEE Trans. Mob. Comput. **5**, 536–547 (2006)

House, S., Connell, S., Milligan, I., Austin, D., Hayes, T.L., Chiang, P.: Indoor localization using pedestrian dead reckoning updated with RFID-based fiducials. In: 2011 Annual International Conference of the IEEE Engineering in Medicine and Biology Society (EMBC), pp. 7598–7601 (2011)

Ijaz, F., Yang, H.K., Ahmad, A.W., Lee, C.: Indoor positioning: a review of indoor ultrasonic positioning systems. In: 2013 15th International Conference on Advanced Communications Technology (ICACT). Presented at the 2013 15th International Conference on Advanced Communications Technology (ICACT), pp. 1146–1150 (2013)

Ingram, S.J., Harmer, D., Quinlan, M.: UltraWideBand indoor positioning systems and their use in emergencies. In: Position Location and Navigation Symposium (IEEE Cat. No. 04CH37556), PLANS 2004. Presented at the PLANS 2004. Position Location and Navigation Symposium (IEEE Cat. No.04CH37556), pp. 706–715 (2004)

Islim, M.S., Haas, H.: Modulation techniques for Li-Fi. ZTE Commun. **14**, 29–40 (2016)

Januszkiewicz, Ł., Kawecki, J., Kawecki, R., Oleksy, P.: Wireless indoor positioning system with inertial sensors and infrared beacons. In: 2016 10th European Conference on Antennas and Propagation (EuCAP). Presented at the 2016 10th European Conference on Antennas and Propagation (EuCAP), pp. 1–3 (2016)

Kang, W., Han, Y.: SmartPDR: smartphone-based pedestrian dead reckoning for indoor localization. IEEE Sens. J. **15**, 2906–2916 (2015)

Kanwar, A., Khazanchi, A.: ZigBee the new bluetooth technology. Int. J. Eng. Comput. Sci. **1**(2), 67–74 (2012)

Kaur, M., Sandhu, M., Mohan, N., Sandhu, P.: RFID technology principles, advantages, limitations & its applications. Int. J. Comput. Electr. Eng. **3**, 151–157 (2011)

Khan, M.A., Antiwal, V.K.: Location estimation technique using extended 3-D LANDMARC algorithm for passive RFID tag. In: 2009 IEEE International Advance Computing Conference. Presented at the 2009 IEEE International Advance Computing Conference, pp. 249–253 (2009)

Kim, C., So, H., Lee, T., Kee, C.: A pseudolite-based positioning system for legacy GNSS receivers. Sens. Switz. **14**, 6104–6123 (2014)

Kuang, J., Niu, X., Zhang, P., Chen, X.: Indoor positioning based on pedestrian dead reckoning and magnetic field matching for smartphones. Sensors **18**, 4142 (2018)

Kumar, S., Gil, S., Katabi, D., Rus, D.: Accurate indoor localization with zero start-up cost. In: Proceedings of the 20th Annual International Conference on Mobile Computing and Networking - MobiCom '14. Presented at the 20th Annual International Conference, Maui, Hawaii, USA, pp. 483–494. ACM Press (2014)

Larranaga, J., Muguira, L., Lopez-Garde, J.-M., Vazquez, J.-I.: An environment adaptive ZigBee-based indoor positioning algorithm. In: 2010 International Conference on Indoor Positioning and Indoor Navigation. Presented at the 2010 International Conference on Indoor Positioning and Indoor Navigation (IPIN), Zurich, Switzerland, pp. 1–8. IEEE (2010)

Lee, N., Ahn, S., Han, D.: AMID: accurate magnetic indoor localization using deep learning. Sensors **18**, 1598 (2018)

Lehtimäki, S.: Bluetooth Angle Estimation for Real-Time Locationing. Silicon Labs (2019). [WWW Document]. https://www.silabs.com/whitepapers/bluetooth-angle-estimation-for-real-time-locationing. Accessed 1 July 2020

Li, W., Wu, J., Wang, D.: A novel indoor positioning method based on key reference RFID tags. In: Computing and Telecommunication 2009 IEEE Youth Conference on Information. Presented at the Computing and Telecommunication, pp. 42–45 (2009)

Li, X., Huang, G., Zhang, P., Zhang, Q.: Reliable indoor pseudolite positioning based on a robust estimation and partial ambiguity resolution method. Sensors **19**, 3692 (2019)

Li, Y.-S., Ning, F.-S.: Low-cost indoor positioning application based on map assistance and mobile phone sensors. Sensors **18**, 4285 (2018)

Liu, H., Darabi, H., Banerjee, P., Liu, J.: Survey of wireless indoor positioning techniques and systems. IEEE Trans. Syst. Man Cybern. Part C Appl. Rev. **37**, 1067–1080 (2007)

Magnago, V., et al.: Robot localisation based on phase measures of backscattered UHF-RFID signals. In: 2019 IEEE International Instrumentation and Measurement Technology Conference (I2MTC). Presented at the 2019 IEEE International Instrumentation and Measurement Technology Conference (I2MTC), pp. 1–6 2019

Mazuelas, S., et al.: Robust indoor positioning provided by real-time RSSI values in unmodified WLAN Networks. IEEE J. Sel. Top. Sig. Process. **3**, 821–831 (2009)

Mendoza-Silva, G.M., Torres-Sospedra, J., Huerta, J.: A meta-review of indoor positioning systems. Sensors **19**, 4507 (2019)

Mrindoko, N.R., Minga, D.L.M.: A comparison review of indoor positioning techniques. Int. J. Comput. **21**, 9 (2016)

Oguntala, G., Abd-Alhameed, R., Jones, S., Noras, J., Patwary, M., Rodriguez, J.: Indoor location identification technologies for real-time IoT-based applications: an inclusive survey. Comput. Sci. Rev. **30**, 55–79 (2018)

Oppermann, I., Hämäläinen, M., Iinatti, J.: UWB Theory and Applications UWB Theory and Applications. Wiley, Hoboken (2004)

Paterna, V., Calveras, A., Aspas, J., Bullones, M.: A bluetooth low energy indoor positioning system with channel diversity, weighted trilateration and Kalman filtering. Sensors **17**, 2927 (2017)

Pinhasi, Y., Yahalom, A., Harpaz, O., Vilner, G.: Study of ultrawide-band transmission in the extremely high frequency (EHF) band. IEEE Trans. Antennas Propag. **52**, 2833–2842 (2004)

Qi, J., Liu, G.-P.: A robust high-accuracy ultrasound indoor positioning system based on a wireless sensor network. Sensors **17**, 2554 (2017)

Radunovic, B., Le Boudec, J.-Y.: Optimal power control, scheduling, and routing in UWB networks. IEEE J. Sel. Areas Commun. **22**, 1252–1270 (2004)

Raharijaona, T., et al.: Local positioning system using flickering infrared LEDs. Sensors **17**, 2518 (2017)

Rahayu, Y., Rahman, T.A., Ngah, R., Hall, P.S.: Ultra wideband technology and its applications. In: 2008 5th IFIP International Conference on Wireless and Optical Communications Networks (WOCN '08). Presented at the 2008 IFIP International Conference on Wireless and Optical Communications Networks - (WOCN), Surabaya, Indonesia, pp. 1–5. IEEE (2008)

Rai, A., Chintalapudi, K.K., Padmanabhan, V.N., Sen, R.: Zee: zero-effort crowdsourcing for indoor localization. In: Proceedings of the 18th Annual International Conference on Mobile Computing and Networking - Mobicom '12. Presented at the 18th Annual International Conference, Istanbul, Turkey, p. 293. ACM Press (2012)

Ruotsalainen, L., Kuusniemi, H., Chen, R.: Visual-aided two-dimensional pedestrian indoor navigation with a smartphone. J. Glob. Position. Syst. **10**, 11–18 (2011)

Saab, S.S., Nakad, Z.S.: A standalone RFID indoor positioning system using passive tags. IEEE Trans. Ind. Electron. **58**, 1961–1970 (2011)

Sachs, J.: Handbook of Ultra-Wideband Short-Range Sensing: Theory, Sensors, Applications, pp. 1–30. Wiley, Hoboken (2012)

Sen, S., Radunovic, B., Choudhury, R.R., Minka, T.: You are facing the Mona Lisa: spot localization using PHY layer information. In: Proceedings of the 10th International Conference on Mobile Systems, Applications, and Services - MobiSys '12. Presented at the 10th international Conference, Low Wood Bay, Lake District, UK, p. 183. ACM Press (2012)

Suryavanshi, N.B., Viswavardhan Reddy, K., Chandrika, V.R.: Direction finding capability in Bluetooth 5.1 standard. In: Kumar, N., Venkatesha Prasad, R. (eds.) UBICNET 2019. LNIC-SSITE, vol. 276, pp. 53–65. Springer, Cham (2019). https://doi.org/10.1007/978-3-030-206 15-4_4

Tadakamadla, S.: Indoor Local Positioning System for ZigBee, Based on RSSI. Mid Sweden University, Sundsvall, Sweden (2006)

Ting, S.L., Kwok, S.K., Tsang, A.H.C., Ho, G.T.S.: The study on using passive RFID tags for indoor positioning. Int. J. Eng. Bus. Manag. **3**, 8 (2011)

Vasisht, D., Kumar, S., Katabi, D.: Sub-Nanosecond Time of Flight on Commercial Wi-Fi Cards. arXiv: arXiv:1505.03446 [Cs] (2015)

Viani, F., Rocca, P., Oliveri, G., Trinchero, D., Massa, A.: Localization, tracking, and imaging of targets in wireless sensor networks: an invited review. Radio Sci. **46**, 1–12 (2011)

Wan, X., Zhan, X.: The research of indoor navigation system using pseudolites. Procedia Eng. **15**, 1446–1450 (2011)

Wang, K., Nirmalathas, A., Lim, C., Alameh, K., Li, H., Skafidas, E.: Indoor infrared optical wireless localization system with background light power estimation capability. Opt. Exp. **25**, 22923 (2017)

Wang, X., Jiang, M., Guo, Z., Hu, N., Sun, Z., Liu, J.: An indoor positioning method for smartphones using landmarks and PDR. Sensors **16**, 2135 (2016)

Wu, K., Xiao, J., Yi, Y., Chen, D., Luo, X., Ni, L.M.: CSI-based indoor localization. IEEE Trans. Parallel Distrib. Syst. **24**, 1300–1309 (2013)

Xu, H., Wu, M., Li, P., Zhu, F., Wang, R.: An RFID indoor positioning algorithm based on support vector regression. Sensors **18**, 1504 (2018)

Wang, Y., Yang, X., Zhao, Y., Liu, Y., Cuthbert, L.: Bluetooth positioning using RSSI and triangulation methods. In: 2013 IEEE 10th Consumer Communications and Networking Conference (CCNC). Presented at the 2013 IEEE 10th Consumer Communications and Networking Conference (CCNC), Las Vegas, NV, pp. 837–842. IEEE (2013)

Yasir, M., Ho, S.-W., Vellambi, B.N.: Indoor position tracking using multiple optical receivers. J. Light. Technol. **34**, 1166–1176 (2016)

Yazici, A., Yayan, U., Yücel, H.: An ultrasonic based indoor positioning system. In: 2011 International Symposium on Innovations in Intelligent Systems and Applications. Presented at the 2011 International Symposium on Innovations in Intelligent Systems and Applications, pp. 585–589 (2011)

Youssef, M.: HORUS: A WLAN-based indoor location determination system. Department of Computer Science, University of Maryland (2004)

Yu, J., Na, Z., Liu, X., Deng, Z.: WiFi/PDR-integrated indoor localization using unconstrained smartphones. EURASIP J. Wirel. Commun. Netw. **2019**(1), 1–13 (2019). https://doi.org/10.1186/s13638-019-1365-9

Yucel, H., Edizkan, R., Ozkir, T., Yazici, A.: Development of indoor positioning system with ultrasonic and infrared signals. In: 2012 International Symposium on Innovations in Intelligent Systems and Applications. Presented at the 2012 International Symposium on Innovations in Intelligent Systems and Applications, pp. 1–4 (2012)

Zhang, M., Wen, Y., Chen, J., Yang, X., Gao, R., Zhao, H.: Pedestrian dead-reckoning indoor localization based on OS-ELM. IEEE Access **6**, 6116–6129 (2018)

Zhang, P., Lu, J., Wang, Y., Wang, Q.: Cooperative localization in 5G networks: a survey. ICT Exp. **3**, 27–32 (2017)

Zhuang, Y., et al.: A survey of positioning systems using visible LED lights. IEEE Commun. Surv. Tutor. **20**, 1963–1988 (2018)

AI4AR: An AI-Based Mobile Application for the Automatic Generation of AR Contents

Roberto Pierdicca[1]([✉]), Marina Paolanti[2], Emanuele Frontoni[2], and Lorenzo Baraldi[3]

[1] Department of Civil Engineering, Building and Architecture, Università Politecnica delle Marche, Via Brecce Bianche 12, 60131 Ancona, Italy
r.pierdicca@staff.univpm.it
[2] Department of Information Engineering, Università Politecnica delle Marche, Via Brecce Bianche 12, 60131 Ancona, Italy
{m.paolanti,e.frontoni}@staff.univpm.it
[3] Department of Engineering "Enzo Ferrari", Università degli Studi di Modena e Reggio Emilia, Modena, Italy
lorenzo.baraldi@unimore.it

Abstract. Augmented reality (AR) is the process of using technology to superimpose images, text or sounds on top of what a person can already see. Art galleries and museums started to develop AR applications to increase engagement and provide an entirely new kind of exploration experience. However, the creation of contents results a very time consuming process, thus requiring an ad-hoc development for each painting to be increased. In fact, for the creation of an AR experience on any painting, it is necessary to choose the points of interest, to create digital content and then to develop the application. If this is affordable for the great masterpieces of an art gallery, it would be impracticable for an entire collection. In this context, the idea of this paper is to develop AR applications based on Artificial Intelligence. In particular, automatic captioning techniques are the key core for the implementation of AR application for improving the user experience in front of a painting or an artwork in general. The study has demonstrated the feasibility through a proof of concept application, implemented for hand held devices, and adds to the body of knowledge in mobile AR application as this approach has not been applied in this field before.

Keywords: Augmented reality · Artificial Intelligence · Automatic contents generation · Cultural heritage · Image captioning

1 Introduction

Augmented reality (AR) is a mobile technology that allows to visualize, with the same point of view of the user, virtual content superimposed on a monitor of a device (Hand-held or head-mounted) that is framing a scene with the

© Springer Nature Switzerland AG 2020
L. T. De Paolis and P. Bourdot (Eds.): AVR 2020, LNCS 12242, pp. 273–288, 2020.
https://doi.org/10.1007/978-3-030-58465-8_21

camera. AR applications, together with Virtual and Mixed Reality (VR and MR) in cultural heritage (CH) have proven to be particularly effective, as they allow to discover details that are sometimes invisible to the naked eye. Museums environments are the ones which can benefit the most; particularly effective, in fact, is the adoption of AR to "augment paintings", since it enhances the visitor's knowledge, to magnify hidden details, to interact with the artwork [7, 8, 24]. Broadly speaking, the technological limitations hampering the diffusion of AR applications in the CH domain are going to be overcome, thanks to the growing computational capabilities of smartphones and tablets. The literature assesses the adoption of AR/VR/MR solutions as consolidated ways to convey cultural contents for museum scenario [4]. The term eXtended Reality (XR) embraces the aforementioned methodologies as the cutting edge solutions [3].

Up to few years ago, the exploitation of AR had the main aim of providing the so-called "wow effect" to the public, fascinating the visitors with a novel way of interacting with the exhibition [23]. But the more the technology becomes widespread, the more the expectation increases. Many studies have shown that virtual contents, which are displayed as additional layers, must be conveyed according to both the choices of the domain experts (art historians, exhibition curators, art critics) and according to the preferences of the users [20, 25]. One of the main bottleneck of this process is, however, the creation of contents itself. In fact, it is a very time consuming process, and requires an ad-hoc development for each painting to be increased. In other words, to create an AR experience on any painting, it is necessary to choose the points of interest, to create digital content and then to develop the application. If this is affordable for the great masterpieces of an art gallery, it would be impracticable for an entire collection.

In this direction, Artificial Intelligence (AI) is outperforming conventional approaches in several domains [17, 21, 27] and thanks to the availability of large-scale dataset and faster calculation tools, deep learning approaches have been used in visual recognition tasks [16, 28]. The Deep Convolutional Neural Networks describe a function from an input space to an output space and the parameters are trained using a large collection of labeled images. An important feature is that these models after being trained can be optimized using a different dataset, initializing the parameters from the first training phase and continuing training on a second dataset, improving the final performance. Recently, algorithms for describing images in natural language have proven to be valuable for several applications [10]. Hence, the idea of this research is to exploit automatic captioning approaches towards the automatic generation of AR contents. Having available an AI system that is able to automatically generate labels, it is possible to send a painting's image to the neural network and view what the network has generated in AR.

The task is solved by AI-based automatic captioning techniques for improving the user experience in front of a painting or an artwork in general, thus implementing an AR application. Thanks to this application, when the user wants to view the painting "augmented" must open the app and point the phone or tablet on the painting. Through the active camera, the installed app recognizes the painting. Then, through image captioning and AR salient objects are highlighted and come out and simultaneously an overlapped text describing the painting is automatically generated. Digital contents can be directly displayed upon the device of the user, where computer-generated items co-exist in the real environment. The advantage is that an ad-hoc installation is not necessary, avoiding exhibition obstructions and significantly reducing times, costs and efforts. This research is based on the model proposed by Cornia et al. [9] that presents *SMArT* a fully-attentive captioning algorithm that combines an image encoder and a natural language decoder layer. The application of this method to paintings is more difficult for the presence of the brush strokes, the creativity of the artist, and his style and hand. So this research in a preliminary phase uses the approach proposed by [34], which introduces a method that reduces the visual features gap between realistic and artistic images implementing a translation from paintings to photo-realistic images. The task is to maintain the original content of paintings after the translation in real images. This step is necessary for a preliminary phase of this research considering the complexity of a painting and the consequent effective difficulty of a machine in interpreting a painting.

The paper is organized as follows. Section 2 provides a description of the AR approaches for CH domain. Section 3 describes our innovative solution based on image captioning algorithms. In Sect. 4, we offer a detailed analysis of each component of our approach. Finally, in Sect. 5, we draw conclusions and discuss future directions for this field of research.

2   Related Works

In the museum environment, the use of AR is well known. In the following, just some recent works will be cited, in order to acquaint less experts reader about the possibility offered by such technology in the field. For a more thorough literature review, please refer to [4]. An interesting AR application is installed in San Francisco's Museum of Modern Art that wants to bring the user closer to paintings [30]. The visitors can live an immersive experience with the Magritte's most famous paintings, where the monitors are designed as window frames. An example concerns "Le Blanc Seing" which represents the image of a forest and in front of which visitors are positioned in such a way that sensors and cameras can make them enter the image. Some windows present puzzles that visitors can solve. For example, the images of individuals are not displayed in the opposite windows but in an adjacent one, creating confusion and interaction between visitors to the museum. *AR Weir Type* app is an AR application created by Lieberman and Kuo with the aim to write messages and put them in the air. With *AR Weird Type*, the users can insert words suspended in the real world, choosing choreographically from seven modalities of representations that depend on the touch and movement. The app is intuitive to use, and full of surprises that emerge through exploration. It is possible to draw words in space, sculpt with letters, make a typographic tunnel, etc. Combined techniques of AR and AI can also be used to replace paintings no longer present in museums. One example is the "Hacking the Heist" exhibition at the Isabella Stewart Gardner Museum in Boston, scene of an important theft of works of art never recovered. Using AR and AI techniques the stolen art is can be viewed [1]. In fact, in the empty frames where the stolen paintings were hung, it is possible to see the artworks by pointing the smartphone or tablet towards the original frames. Many different museum have installed BroadcastAR, an application used to transform regular exhibits into AR experiences. BroadcastAR consists of a large customizable and interactive screen that allows you to interact with the digital content displayed [5]. The screen also allows visitors to meet and interact with animated characters and objects. The Tanjung Balau Fishermen Museum in Malaysia has been the subject of a case study for an AR application which, meeting the needs of museum visitors, encourages them to implement a change in terms of interest, knowledge, attitude and skills [31]. The authors developed an application named FishAR that provides the animation combined with information and sounds of four artefacts. Mainly for younger people this is an interesting application since they can learn artefacts no longer available and know the fisherman heritage. Moreover, it also has an educational aspect as it offers students to solve real problems using AR technologies.

AR and AI are disruptive technologies that can, respectively: i) bridge the gap between physical and virtual worlds and ii) change the way machines are able to interpret the world [33]. The challenge, is that, albeit they are two distinct technologies, can be combined to obtain unique and immersive experiences. In augmented reality, a 3D representation of the real world is constructed in which digital objects exist alongside physical ones. To form a digital representation superimposed on the physical one, traditional artificial vision techniques that do not use machine learning make it possible to build a real world map. However, especially in recent decades, AI techniques are widely used for designing immersive AR experiences, replacing some traditional artificial vision approaches that were the basis of AR experiences. AI techniques such as learning based networks are able to perform tasks without explicit instructions. There is a work of synergy between AI and AR in order to create increasingly immersive experiences. Commonly, developers combine AR and AI models by capturing images or audio from a scene, then run data through a model and use the model's output to activate effects within the scene. In the literature, some attempts to combine the two technologies have been made. For example, in the work of [22], AI has been used to improve the scene understanding of the AR application; as it is well known, the main component of an AR system is the tracking phase in which the application recognize the scene and is able to superimpose virtual contents. In this work, the standard image-based tracking system is replaced with a machine learning one. Another noteworthy work is [32], where the authors exploit AI for the object detection task. Instead of focusing only on scientific literature, it is interesting to note that in the latest years, many patents have been proposed, combining AR and AI. The more interesting are [6,11], which leverage machine learning for face recognition. Even it is not the focus of this article, is interesting to note that some more advanced works have been done in the field of VR [29].

This is due to the computational requirements that can be exploited in VR environments and that in AR cannot. Adversarial Networks are very promising in the field [18], as they enable the generation of contents predicting the users behaviours and tasks, possibly in real time [14]. To the best of our knowledge, it is the first time that the combination of AI and AR are proposed for the CH domain. Motivated by such assumption, in the following a prototype of our innovative solution is presented.

3 Materials and Methods

In this section, the overall idea is presented, as summarized in Fig. 1. At a glance, once the user enables the camera of his/her device, the application recognizes the painting and sends it to the Neural network, which computes the image and generates a caption, *i.e.* a textual description of the visual input. Moreover, a proof of concept has been developed, in a very early stage application to demonstrate the feasibility of the proposed approach.

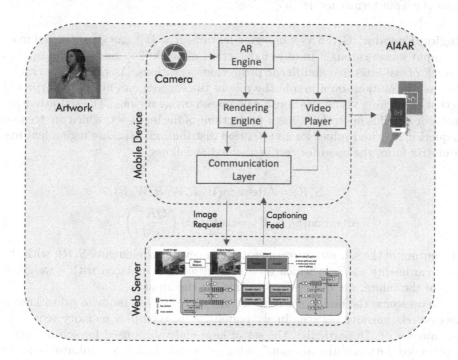

Fig. 1. Workflow of the AI4AR system.

3.1 Automatic Image Captioning

Image captioning is a popular research area of AI that involves computer vision approaches and natural language processing. The task of a system that performs image captioning is to automatically extract the content of the images and generate descriptions of the content in natural language. The automatic description of images can be a support in managing the growing volume of data coming from several sources allowing to reduce human forces and provide people an easy access of many multimedia resources. They can be applied to many areas: commerce, military, education, biomedicine, CH and more [12]. Several tasks must be performed to describe a scene: detecting the objects and localizing them, determining the relationships among objects giving a semantic meaning that indicates how the objects are between them related [19]. To generate sentences of complete meaning, the system must have a syntactic and semantic knowledge of the language [36].

Following recent literature on the topic, we employ a visual encoder based on image regions [26], and a decoder which models the probability of generating one word given previously generated ones. In contrast to the dominant thread of building captioning approaches based on recurrent networks, we employ a fully-attentive model for both the encoding and the decoding stage [9], building upon the Transformer model [35].

Region Encoder. Given a set of region features $R = \{r_1, ..., r_N\}$ extracted from the input image through an object detection network [26], our encoder applies a stack of self-attentive and linear projection operations. As the former can be seen as convolutions on a graph, the role of the encoder can also be interpreted as that of learning visual relationships between image regions. The self-attention operator S builds upon three linear projections of the input set, which are treated as queries, keys and values for an attention distribution. Stacking region features in matrix form, the operator can be defined as follows:

$$S(R) = \mathsf{Attention}(W_q R, W_k R, W_v R),$$
$$\mathsf{Attention}(Q, K, V) = \mathsf{softmax}\left(\frac{QK^T}{\sqrt{d}}\right) V. \tag{1}$$

The output of the self-attention operator is a new set of elements $S(R)$, with the same cardinality as R, in which each element of R is replaced with a weighted sum of the values, *i.e.* of linear projections of the input.

To overcome the limits of self-attention, which cannot model a priori knowledge on relationships between image regions, we also employ memory vectors in our encoder [9]. In particular, the set of keys and values used for self-attention is extended with additional "slots" which can encode a priori information. To stress that a priori information should not depend on the input set R, the additional keys and values are implemented as plain learnable vectors which can be directly updated via SGD. Formally, the operator is defined as:

$$M(R) = \mathsf{Attention}(W_q R, K, V)$$
$$K = [W_k R, M_k]$$
$$V = [W_v R, M_v], \tag{2}$$

where M_k and M_v are learnable matrices with n_m rows, and $[\cdot, \cdot]$ indicates concatenation. Intuitively, by adding learnable keys and values, through attention it will be possible to retrieve learned knowledge which is not already embedded in R. Following the structure of the Transformer model, the memory-augmented operator M is followed by a position-wise feed-forward layer, and each of these two operators is encapsulated within a residual connection and a layer norm operation. Multiple layers of this kind are then applied in a stack fashion to obtain the final encoder.

Language Decoder. The output of the encoder module is a set of region encodings $\tilde{R}$ with the same cardinality of R. We employ a fully-attentive decoder which is conditioned on both previously generated words and region encodings, and is in charge of generating the next tokens of the output caption. The structure of our decoder follows that of the Transformer [35], and thus relies on self-attentive and cross-attentive operations.

Given a partially decoded sequence of words $W = \{w_0, w_1, ..., w_\tau\}$, each represented as a one-hot vector, the decoder applies a self-attention operation in which W is used to build queries, keys and values. To ensure the causality of this sequence encoding process, we purposely mask the attention operator so that each word can only be conditioned to its left-hand sub-sequence, $i.e.$ word w_t is conditioned on $\{w_{t'}\}_{t' \leq t}$ only. Afterwards, a cross-attention operator is applied between W and $\tilde{R}$ to condition words on regions, as follows:

$$C(W, \tilde{R}) = \text{Attention}(W_q W, W_k \tilde{R}, W_v \tilde{R}). \tag{3}$$

As in the Transformer model, after a self-attention and a cross-attention stage, a position-wise feed-forward layer is applied, and each of these operators is encapsulated within a residual connection and a layer norm operation. Finally, our decoder stacks together multiple decoder layers, helping to refine the understanding of the textual input.

Overall, the decoder takes as input word vectors, and the t-th element of its output sequence encodes the prediction of a word at time $t + 1$, conditioned on $\{w_t\}_{\leq t}$. After taking a linear projection and a softmax operation, this encodes a probability over words in the dictionary. During training, the model is trained to predict the next token given previous ground-truth words; during decoding, we iteratively sample a predicted word from the output distribution and feed it back to the model to decode the next one, until the end of the sequence is reached. Following the usual practice in image captioning literature, the model is trained to predict an end-of-sequence token to signal the end of the caption.

Training and Implementation Details. To represent image regions, we use Faster R-CNN [26] finetuned on the Visual Genome dataset [2,15], thus obtaining a 2048-dimensional feature vector for each region. We also employ sinusoidal positional encodings [35] to represent word positions inside the sequence.

The model is trained, following the splits provided by Karpathy $et\ al.$ [13], on the COCO dataset [19] which contains more than 120 000 images, each of them annotated with 5 human-collected captions. Pre-training with cross-entropy loss is done using the learning rate scheduling strategy defined in [35] with a warmup equal to 10 000 iterations. Then, we employ a self-critical CIDEr-D optimization, we use a fixed learning rate equal to $5e^{-6}$. We train the model using the Adam optimizer and a batch size of 50. During CIDEr-D optimization and caption decoding, we use beam search with a beam size equal to 5.

3.2 Mobile Application

The mobile application has been developed extending the existing Vuforia Library, an AR SDK. The main reason is that the tracking functionality is already implemented, and proved to be very robust for image tracking in changing lighting conditions. However, conversely to the well-established markerless AR pipeline, in this case the trackable is not known a-priori by the application, but needs to be recognized after querying the Neural Network endpoint. Thus, once the camera is activated, the application exploits an edge detector developed with openCV to isolate the painting from the background. For this first stage of prototype, tests have been made in convenient condition, i.e. the painting shall be placed with a white background in order to facilitate the extraction of the painting from the camera feed. The resulting rectangle serves as trackable for the AR application, with the aim, for future implementations, to exploit image recognition rather than edge detection. This image is then send to the endpoint as described in the following Subsect. 3.3. After this step, the Neural Network returns the caption, generated automatically, back to the mobile application, that is then shown AR mode. Besides, the system is even designed to fulfill a detection task, pertaining the objects present on each painting. Even in this case, the network is able to return a bounding box with the semantic meaning of such objects, which are then used for the AR mode to highlight the main point of interest of each painting. The application wireframe is depicted in Fig. 2), while the results of the application running are described in the following section.

3.3 Architecture

On the server side, the captioning pipeline is implemented with PyTorch and Speaksee[1], thus running seamlessly on CPU and GPU. On top of this, a web-service has been implemented in Django. The web-service expects POST requests containing an image captured from the mobile device, and replies with a JSON dictionary containing the predicted caption. To assess the computational requirements of the pipeline and its applicability to real-world scenarios, we conducted multiple tests on nodes equipped with NVIDIA P100, 2080Ti and V100 GPUs. On average, the entire server-side pipeline requires 2.5 s on a P100 GPU, while the running time drops down to an average of 1.7 s when running on 2080Ti GPUs and 1.5 s when running on V100 GPUs, thus reducing the overall delay experienced by the final user. The last result is particularly significant considering the reduced market cost of 2080Ti GPUs when compared to V100 s.

---

[1] https://github.com/aimagelab/speaksee.

Fig. 2. Wireframe of the AI4AR app concept. From left to right, the main steps performed by the application.

4   Results and Discussion

In this section, some preliminary results of the application proof of concept are shown. For the experiments, the following paintings have been chosen:

1. Giuseppe Höger Ländliche, Idylle
2. Lucas van Valkenborch, Landscape near Dinant
3. Ryan Brown, Portrait

which returns from the captioning system the following labels:

1. I see a group of people standing on a hill next to an old mountain
2. I see a view of a tree in a field with trees and mountains
3. I see a woman with long hair in a white suit.

The predicted labels can be thus visualized in AR mode, providing the user with additional contents overlaid above the screen; the labels generated automatically are visible in Figs. 3, 4 and 5. Currently, even if the test demonstrates the feasibility of the proposed approach, some remarks are noteworthy; first of all, the latency time is quite high, and require up to 2,5 s before the label can be properly visualized. Moreover, the application requires some specifications to be respected by the user: for instance, the phone should be still as much as possible, in order to allow the camera feed to compute the detection of the painting. Finally, it is fair to note that, due to the specific task of automatic captioning in the CH field, contents are not so informative for the user. This latter aspect has been broadly discussed in the conclusion section.

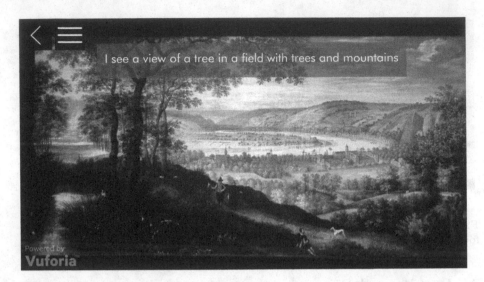

Fig. 3. The mobile application running on painting 1.

Fig. 4. The mobile application running on painting 2.

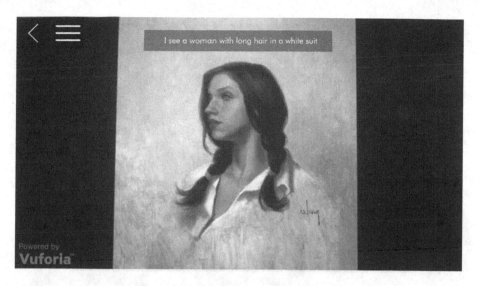

Fig. 5. The mobile application running on painting 3.

Another possibility offered by the application is to visualize the bounding boxes generated thanks to the detection task. In other work, the user is driven to visualize specific Points of Interests of the painting. This is very useful, since it permits the visitor to focus on details that, with a shallow visit might be lost. As demonstrated by the literature [20], driving the user in its augmented visit can help to deepen the knowledge of an artwork. The results of this functionality of the application are depicted in Fig. 6, 7, 8.

Fig. 6. Example of POIs detection in painting 1.

Fig. 7. Example of POIs detection in painting 12

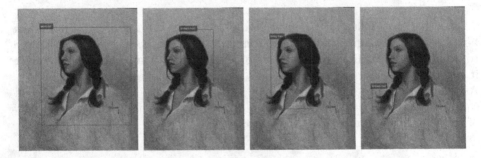

Fig. 8. Example of POIs detection in painting 3. For the sake of completeness, this painting is shown with separated bounding boxes.

While the potential of this second type of visualization are huge, even in this case it is fair to highlight some drawbacks. Confirming the ones stated before about the time of execution, the main concerns is about the position of the bounding box for each focus point. In fact, they are actually positioned with their own coordinates and they are not still implemented with a real tracking system. This aspect is fundamental, since without a robust tracking system, the virtual contents are joined with the camera stream, hence the user experience can be compromised. Concluding remarks and future research directions will be showed in the following section.

5   Conclusion

In this paper, the idea of exploiting AI for the automatic generation of contents for AR application is explored. The study has demonstrated the feasibility through a proof of concept application, implemented for hand held devices, and adds to the body of knowledge in mobile AR application as this approach has not been applied in this field before. The research question that this paper tackles comes from several years of research in the field of Digital Cultural Heritage, and arises from one of the main limitation of AR applications for artworks: the generation of contents is not affordable, especially for large exhibitions where, to experience AR in front of painting, a tidy process of content creation is required. The presented experiments opens up new scenario in which AI can dramatically change the way in which AR applications are developed. For the sake of completeness, and given the very early stage of the research, we faced some issues that deserve the reader attention.

Implementation Issues. The current SoA solution for the implementation of AR experience, at least the ones based on markerless tracking, are entrusted on well established libraries, most of them freely available, which make use of feature tracking for superimposing virtual contents. I.e., there is the necessity of a priory knowledge of both the image to be recognized and the content to be shown. In the case here presented neither the image, nor the contents are known. This make the implementation very tricky, and whether AI partially solves the second, the first one is still an open issue. For this experiment, we bases on edge detection algorithms to create the baseline for the camera feed, but the tracking fare is not enough robust for a commercial release. Even the latency times can represent an impediment for the user, but this issue can be partially solved with a more straightforward internet connection and with a more performing endpoint, reducing the computational times of the Convolutional Neural Network.

Domain Shift Issues. As it has been noted previously, both the visual feature extraction pipeline and the language model employed in our approach have been trained on large datasets consisting of natural images. However, the visual appearance of artworks is often quite different from that of photo-realistic images, due to the presence of brush strokes, the creativity of the artist and the specific artistic style at hand. For this reason, deep learning models are often largely biased towards natural images – and captioning is not an exception in this regards. The final result is the presence of a gap between high-level convolutional features of the two domains, which leads to a decrease in performance on the artistic domain. The issue can be tackled in two fundamental ways: collecting large-scale and annotated datasets with artistic images, and mitigate the effect of the domain shift by employing domain adaptation techniques. While adopting the first solution would require an expensive effort in terms of data collection and annotation, it is worthwhile to mention that some preliminary efforts have been made also in the latter direction [34]. Still, we notice that there is a growing need of research works that address the data shift issue in CH.

References

1. Hacking the heist, ar(t) (2019). https://www.hackingtheheist.com
2. Anderson, P., et al.: Bottom-up and top-down attention for image captioning and visual question answering. In: Proceedings of the IEEE Conference on Computer Vision and Pattern Recognition (2018)
3. Banfi, F., Brumana, R., Stanga, C.: Extended reality and informative models for the architectural heritage: from scan-to-BIM process to virtual and augmented reality (2019)
4. Bekele, M., Pierdocca, R., Frontoni, E., Malinverni, E., Gain, J.: A survey of augmented, mixed and virtual reality for cultural heritage. ACM J. Comput. Cultural Herit. **11**(2), 1–36 (2018)
5. BroadcastAR: 7 great examples of augmented reality in museums (2019). https://www.indestry.com/blog/2018/8/21/augmented-reality-museum-examples. Accessed 7 Feb 2019
6. Chawla, K., Hiranandani, G., Jain, A., Madandas, V.P., Sinha, M.: Augmented reality predictions using machine learning, US Patent App. 15/868,531, 11 July 2019
7. Clini, P., Frontoni, E., Quattrini, R., Pierdicca, R.: Augmented reality experience: from high-resolution acquisition to real time augmented contents. Adv. Multimedia **2014**, 9 (2014)
8. Clini, P., Quattrini, R., Frontoni, E., Pierdicca, R., Nespeca, R.: Real/not real: pseudo-holography and augmented reality applications for cultural heritage. In: Handbook of Research on Emerging Technologies for Digital Preservation and Information Modeling, pp. 201–227. IGI Global (2017)
9. Cornia, M., Baraldi, L., Cucchiara, R.: Smart: training shallow memory-aware transformers for robotic explainability. arXiv preprint arXiv:1910.02974 (2019)
10. Cornia, M., Baraldi, L., Serra, G., Cucchiara, R.: Paying more attention to saliency: image captioning with saliency and context attention. ACM Trans. Multimedia Comput. Commun. Appl. (TOMM) **14**(2), 1–21 (2018)
11. Horie, T., et al.: Creating augmented reality self-portraits using machine learning, US Patent App. 16/177,408, 14 Mar 2019
12. Hossain, M.Z., Sohel, F., Shiratuddin, M.F., Laga, H.: A comprehensive survey of deep learning for image captioning. ACM Comput. Surv. (CSUR) **51**(6), 1–36 (2019)
13. Karpathy, A., Fei-Fei, L.: Deep visual-semantic alignments for generating image descriptions. In: Proceedings of the IEEE Conference on Computer Vision and Pattern Recognition (2015)
14. Kim, H.G., Lim, H.T., Ro, Y.M.: Deep virtual reality image quality assessment with human perception guider for omnidirectional image. IEEE Trans. Circuits Syst. Video Technol. **30**(4), 917–928 (2019)
15. Krishna, R., et al.: Visual genome: connecting language and vision using crowd-sourced dense image annotations. Int. J. Comput. Vis. **123**(1), 32–73 (2017). https://doi.org/10.1007/s11263-016-0981-7
16. Krizhevsky, A., Sutskever, I., Hinton, G.E.: ImageNet classification with deep convolutional neural networks. In: Advances in Neural Information Processing Systems, pp. 1097–1105 (2012)

17. LeCun, Y., Bengio, Y., Hinton, G.: Deep learning. Nature **521**(7553), 436–444 (2015)
18. Lim, H.T., Kim, H.G., Ra, Y.M.: VR IQA Net: deep virtual reality image quality assessment using adversarial learning. In: IEEE International Conference on Acoustics, Speech and Signal Processing (ICASSP), pp. 6737–6741. IEEE (2018)
19. Lin, T.-Y., et al.: Microsoft COCO: common objects in context. In: Fleet, D., Pajdla, T., Schiele, B., Tuytelaars, T. (eds.) ECCV 2014. LNCS, vol. 8693, pp. 740–755. Springer, Cham (2014). https://doi.org/10.1007/978-3-319-10602-1_48
20. Naspetti, S., et al.: Automatic analysis of eye-tracking data for augmented reality applications: a prospective outlook. In: De Paolis, L.T., Mongelli, A. (eds.) AVR 2016. LNCS, vol. 9769, pp. 217–230. Springer, Cham (2016). https://doi.org/10.1007/978-3-319-40651-0_17
21. Paolanti, M., Romeo, L., Martini, M., Mancini, A., Frontoni, E., Zingaretti, P.: Robotic retail surveying by deep learning visual and textual data. Robot. Auton. Syst. **118**, 179–188 (2019)
22. Pauly, O., Diotte, B., Fallavollita, P., Weidert, S., Euler, E., Navab, N.: Machine learning-based augmented reality for improved surgical scene understanding. Comput. Med. Imaging Graph. **41**, 55–60 (2015)
23. Pescarin, S.: Digital heritage into practice. SCIRES IT Sci. Res. Inf. Tech. **6**(1), 1–4 (2016)
24. Pierdicca, R., Frontoni, E., Zingaretti, P., Sturari, M., Clini, P., Quattrini, R.: Advanced interaction with paintings by augmented reality and high resolution visualization: a real case exhibition. In: De Paolis, L.T., Mongelli, A. (eds.) AVR 2015. LNCS, vol. 9254, pp. 38–50. Springer, Cham (2015). https://doi.org/10.1007/978-3-319-22888-4_4
25. Pierdicca, R., Paolanti, M., Naspetti, S., Mandolesi, S., Zanoli, R., Frontoni, E.: User-centered predictive model for improving cultural heritage augmented reality applications: an HMM-based approach for eye-tracking data. J. Imaging **4**(8), 101 (2018)
26. Ren, S., He, K., Girshick, R., Sun, J.: Faster R-CNN: towards real-time object detection with region proposal networks. IEEE Trans. Pattern Anal. Mach. Intell. **39**(6), 1137–1149 (2017)
27. Romeo, L., Loncarski, J., Paolanti, M., Bocchini, G., Mancini, A., Frontoni, E.: Machine learning-based design support system for the prediction of heterogeneous machine parameters in industry 4.0. Expert Syst. Appl. **140**, 112869 (2020)
28. Russakovsky, O., et al.: Imagenet large scale visual recognition challenge. Int. J. Comput. Vis. **115**(3), 211–252 (2015). https://doi.org/10.1007/s11263-015-0816-y
29. Schreiber, A., Bock, M.: Visualization and exploration of deep learning networks in 3D and virtual reality. In: Stephanidis, C. (ed.) HCII 2019. CCIS, vol. 1033, pp. 206–211. Springer, Cham (2019). https://doi.org/10.1007/978-3-030-23528-4_29
30. SFMOMA: Augmented reality meets fine art (2018). https://www.frogdesign.com/work/sf-moma
31. Sulaiman, S., et al.: Museum informatics: a case study on augmented reality at Tanjung Balau fishermen museum. In: IEEE 9th International Conference on System Engineering and Technology (ICSET), pp. 79–83. IEEE (2019)
32. Svensson, J., Atles, J.: Object detection in augmented reality. Master's theses in mathematical sciences (2018)
33. Tanskanen, A., Martinez, A.A., Blasco, D.K., Sipiä, L.: Artificial intelligence, augmented reality and mixed reality in cultural venues. Consolidated Assignments from Spring 2019, p. 80 (2019)

34. Tomei, M., Cornia, M., Baraldi, L., Cucchiara, R.: Art2real: unfolding the reality of artworks via semantically-aware image-to-image translation. In: Proceedings of the IEEE Conference on Computer Vision and Pattern Recognition, pp. 5849–5859 (2019)
35. Vaswani, A., et al.: Attention is all you need. In: Advances in Neural Information Processing Systems (2017)
36. Vinyals, O., Toshev, A., Bengio, S., Erhan, D.: Show and tell: lessons learned from the 2015 MSCOCO image captioning challenge. IEEE Trans. Pattern Anal. Mach. Intell. **39**(4), 652–663 (2016)

AR-Based Visual Aids for sUAS Operations in Security Sensitive Areas

Giulio Avanzini, Valerio De Luca$^{(\boxtimes)}$, and Claudio Pascarelli

Department of Engineering for Innovation, University of Salento, Lecce, Italy
{giulio.avanzini,valerio.deluca,claudio.pascarelli}@unisalento.it

Abstract. The use of UAVs has recently been proposed for services in civil airports and other sensitive areas. Besides specific regulations from authorities, the situation awareness of the UAV operator is a key aspect for a safe coexistence between manned and unmanned traffic. The operator must be provided in real-time with contextually relevant information, in order to take the proper actions promptly based on the notified contingency. Augmented reality can be adopted to superimpose such additional information on the real-world scene. After the definition of an architecture for the integration of drone operations in the airspace, in this paper the interface and the layout of an augmented reality application for the situation awareness of the pilot are designed and discussed.

Keywords: sUAS · Situation awareness · Geofence · Head-up display

1 Introduction

Until a few years ago, drones were being developed and used almost exclusively in the military sector. Their great potential for developing innovative applications, however, is now recognized also in the civil sector, performing a wide variety of tasks and creating new highly specialized jobs. Thousands of drones are already in operation in national airspaces today and their number is forecasted to rise significantly in the next few years. As a consequence, most civil aviation authorities are issuing regulations for prescribing rules that enforce a safe use of drones, dividing vehicles and missions into specific categories. In civil operations, a small unmanned aircraft system (sUAS) is defined as a system consisting of an unmanned aircraft or unmanned aerial vehicle (UAV) weighting less than 25 kg (55 lb). The system includes the vehicle, plus all equipment necessary for its safe and efficient operation [1]. The advancements of miniaturized technologies in all relevant fields, such as digital communications, automatic controls, navigation, and autonomy, at significantly reduced cost and size, enabled fast growing capabilities of sUASs, including model aircraft, that were not even imaginable only a few decades ago. This process sparked an increased access to this class of aerial vehicles by a wider public, which includes professional operators as well as private owners for recreational use [2]. This fact poses several challenges for the integration of this class of aircraft within conventional air traffic. Up to this

© Springer Nature Switzerland AG 2020
L. T. De Paolis and P. Bourdot (Eds.): AVR 2020, LNCS 12242, pp. 289–298, 2020.
https://doi.org/10.1007/978-3-030-58465-8_22

point, civil aviation authorities introduced stringent requirements and limits for the use of unmanned aircraft in order to prevent the risk of possible incidents or even accidents with other flying vehicles, violations of protected areas and risks for the population [3]. This conservative approach is due to the fact that it is not possible to prescribe overall system reliability targets to low-cost, small size flying vehicles, comparable to those imposed on conventional civil aircraft. As a consequence, safety is mainly related to restrictions on admissible operations. Clearly, this approach puts severe constraints on the possibilities of an extensive use of drones in many applicative scenarios. It is thus extremely important and relevant to the community of sUAS operators to design, develop and test technologies that may provide adequate safety margins, while expanding the admissible envelope of practical missions, thus allowing civil aviation authorities to relax at least some of the most stringent constraints. In order to increase sUAS operation airspace access, at least in Very Low Level (VLL) controlled and uncontrolled airspace (where VLL is the portion of the airspace below 500 ft height above ground level) and to fully exploit sUAS market potential, while ensuring safety, some of the main enablers are:

- new mechanisms and traffic management methods for safe and efficient integration of UAS traffic into low altitude airspace (current air traffic management systems need to be thoroughly revised to handle the dense and heterogeneous drones traffic [4]);
- evolution of existing sUAS capabilities and technologies to improve situation awareness during the execution of a task (e.g. an unmanned aircraft should implement technologies and methods to identify intruders on a collision course); in this context, concepts such as sense and avoid represent only a portion of the broader concept of situational awareness, which involves analysing internal and external factors, as part of the decision-making process, acting in accordance with current conditions and goals [5];
- alternative CNS (Communication, Navigation and Surveillance) options, where CNS requirements must be developed in order to establish a CNS architecture supporting integration of Unmanned Aerial Systems in the civil airspace; these requirements must address cybersecurity, future communications, satellite-based navigation and APNT (Alternative Positioning, Navigation, and Timing) [6];
- a risk and performance-based approach regulation for drone operations [7,8], where a careful mission planning is required, in order to enforce adequate safety levels for sUAS operations, especially in (or close to) populated areas.

In this paper the evolution of existing sUAS capabilities and technologies is considered, with a focus on the sUAS operator enhanced situational awareness. Situation awareness can be defined as "the perception of elements in the environment within a volume of time and space, the comprehension of their meaning, and the projection of their status in the near future" [9,10]. This topic has already been addressed in the literature. Most of the papers proposed an enhancement of the video stream, coming from the UAV camera, with artificial elements that provide useful information to the pilot. For this scope Augmented Reality (AR) has been proposed for highlighting some of the elements seen by the user through the camera [11] and/or for fusing video stream data with mission planning information [12]. The optimal representation of occluded elements in an indoor environment through AR was the object of [13]. An AR-based solution for sUAS operators to improve the situational awareness and depth perception is proposed in [14]. AR has also been used to increases the safety during UAV take-off and landing under adverse environmental conditions [15], for implementing a vision-based navigation method [16] and to show the pilot attitude indicators, generally embedded in the ground control station [17]. A set of visual aids for enhancing remote pilot perception of potential violations of allowed flight areas or conflicts with conventional air traffic or other drones operating in the same area was proposed in [3] for the case of constrained airspaces. The present paper aims at providing a contribution in this framework, based on the design of an augmented reality application for enhanced situation awareness of a remote pilot in the form of a head-up display (HUD), to be used for visual line-of-sight (VLOS) operations. A HUD is a transparent display allowing users to view data without the need to look away from the vehicle from their current viewpoint. The development of a head-up display must address usability and user experience issues. While usability describes how a system is easy to use and learn, user experience also includes emotional and aesthetical factors. As defined by ISO 9241-210 [18], user experience encompasses "perceptions and responses that result from the use or anticipated use of a product, system or service". A complete architecture for the AR system will be introduced and a discussion on possible additional features, such as some form of haptic feedback, will also be provided. The AR system and application described in this paper represents a portion of a wider platform developed within the AcrOSS research project (Environment for Safe Operations of Remotely Operated Aerial Systems). The main contents of the AcrOSS project, for a safe, efficient and secure integration of sUAS operations in very low level airspace, and the role of the AR in the project logical and technological framework are described in Sect. 2. Section 3 describes the functional and architectural features of an AR solution under development to support a pilot operating in the AcrOSS operative scenarios. Finally a section of concluding remarks and future work ends the paper.

2   The AcrOSS Project and the Role of Augmented Reality

The AcrOSS research project, funded by the Italian Ministry of University and Research (MIUR), involves two enterprises from the aerospace sector, an IT company and two universities. The project will contribute to the definition of procedures and the identification of technologies for safe, efficient and secure integration of sUAS operations in very low level, with a specific focus on airspace surrounding airports and other sensitive areas, where a specific permission to operate remotely controlled aerial vehicles is required. AcrOSS project is envisioning capabilities and developing technological solutions to pave the way towards increased airspace access and minimization of risks related to sUAS operations. In particular, three high level project objectives are identified:

1. increase airspace access for sUAS operations in low level airspace and enable the implementation of BVLOS operations;
2. ensure safe and efficient integration of sUAS in controlled and uncontrolled airspace, with a specific focus on sensitive areas (e.g. near airports);
3. improve detection and management of unknown/non cooperative drones in airport airspace. Both controlled airspace (i.e. airport airspace) and uncontrolled VLL airspace are within the scope of the AcrOSS project. Project activities and developments aim at evaluating new mechanisms and functionalities that find a practical application and provide an added value to the management of sUAS operations both in airport airspace and within the new U-Space concept, under definition by SESAR JU at a European level. The high level system architecture of the platform developed within the AcrOSS project is shown in Fig. 1.

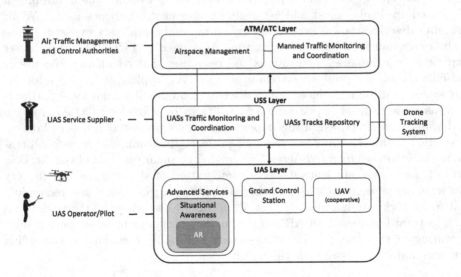

Fig. 1. High level system architecture of the AcrOSS platform.

The architecture consists of three distinct but communicating layers. The first one (ATM/ATC Layer) extends the current systems provided to traditional air traffic managers and controllers, providing an interface with the underlying layer (USS Layer) and a tool for the remodulation of the airspace according to unforeseen events. The second layer, managed by the UAS Service Supplier (USS), represents the interface between the manned and unmanned aviation operations. It receives from ATM/ATC the information on airspace constraints (possibly dynamically evolving, according to specific needs) and on manned air traffic, communicating this information to the concerned UAS operators. At the same time, the USS collects the UAV position data from the operators, in order to coordinate UAS operations and avoid interferences between them. The position data are sent to the system directly by the UAVs, if they are equipped with a tracking device, and through a Drone Tracking System, which identifies all UAVs operating in a certain area. The third layer consists of the UAV, with its Ground Control Station (GCS), and of a ground platform for the provision of advanced services developed within the AcrOSS project. These include services to increase the situational awareness of the pilot, also through Augmented Reality technologies and methods, as described in some detail in the next section.

3   AR-Based Systems for Enhancing Situation Awareness

Situation awareness consists in making the pilot aware not only of aerial space constraints, but also of the main operative UAV parameters. Several methods are available for improving remote pilots situation awareness, which are mainly based on:

1. visual aids, and more specifically
   (a) direct information on relevant flight parameters by means of Head-Up Displays;
   (b) visual aids for improved perception of admissible flight volumes, mission targets and obstacles;
2. haptic feedback, which, in turn can be provided by
   (a) force feedback on joystick controls;
   (b) warnings/alarms based on vibration induced on the controls.

3.1   Visual Aids

Augmented reality can improve user's awareness by enhancing the spatial cognition, the 3D perception of the objects and the level of attention by notifying any dangerous situation in advance. In a similar way, this class of techniques has been employed to guide surgeons in mini-invasive operations [19] by visualizing those organs that are not directly visible, while showing the direction that a surgical tool should follow in the patient's body. Relevant information about distances and visual feedback (such as improved contrast between organs and surgical tool represented in different colours, depending on various situations) can be provided, with audio alerts to draw the surgeon's attention when potential dangers are approaching (such as the risk of cutting a vein). Following an analogous approach, with all due differences for the relevant environment, geofencing techniques define virtual barriers (fences) delimiting geographic areas inside which each agent can move [20]. Geofences depend on static information, dealing with objects having fixed positions in the environment (e.g. fixed obstacles) or limits to admissible flight volumes defined a priori, as well as on dynamic information, concerning other vehicles passing through the aerial space, time-varying limits, and contingencies notified by traffic administrators. For this reason, geofences must be updated dynamically to ensure a safe and efficient exploitation of the aerial space by multiple UAVs [21]. Through augmented reality, geofences can be represented as grids superimposed on the real scene to guide the pilots of UAVs. Their geometric shapes or features (e.g. colour) can be updated according to the vehicle airspeed, altitude or other needs [3]: grids can shrink or enlarge to get closer to the bounds with no-fly zones, depending on the need to increase or decrease the margin needed for the safety of operations. Data collected through inertial sensors and GPS can be used to estimate the future UAV position by means of predictive models based on flight conditions and on velocity and acceleration vectors. In this way, any violation can be announced in advance by changing the colour of geofence grids. Information provided through augmented reality concerns:

- No-fly zones, obstacles, no-landing areas and safety landing areas; their colour depends on how much a violation is imminent and how much the manoeuvre should be aggressive to avoid the collision;
- The presence of other UAVs nearby, which can be represented as a special case of a time-varying no-fly zone by exploiting the communications about the position and the flight conditions of cooperating UAVs and the support of a radar to detect any non cooperating vehicle; moreover, the pilot must be made aware of hidden vehicles with respect to his/her point of view, which can be represented by spheres getting bigger as the other UAVs get closer;
- The maximum altitude to conduct operations, maximum and minimum airspeed and maximum turn radius;
- A representation of the flight attitude and of the 3D orientation of the UAV (since the understanding of the disposition in the space of the UAV components is not trivial, especially when the vehicle is far from the pilot position);
- A cockpit containing a summary of flight parameters (altitude, velocity and direction), the residual battery charge and the distance from the landing point;
- Notifications and instructions coming from other components of the system (such as "go to the (x, y) position and land there").

3.2   Implementation

The augmented reality application will be based on Unity3D [22], a multiplatform game engine for the development of 3D interactive contents: it provides several items, called assets, which can be used in the development of game environments, and allows to import some specific development kits of the used devices. For the AcrOSS augmented reality application an Epson Moverio BT-300 Drone FPV Edition [23] was selected. This piece of equipment is represented by smart glasses designed in the framework of a partnership between Epson and DJI, the latter a world-leading manufacturer of commercial drones. Moverio BT-300 can be connected to the DJI controller via USB or Wi-Fi. They provide an angle of view of about 23° and a 1280 × 720 resolution. They enable a seamless integration of digital content with the outside world through the Si-OLED semi-transparent lens, by combining in optical-see-through mode the drone's video feed with contextual information about flight while keeping the aircraft in sight. Figure 2 depicts the augmented visualization designed to provide the UAV pilot with visual aids. The semitransparent grids represent the geofences delimiting the space the UAV can fly within. The yellow graduated scale in the top centre of the display represents in degrees the current direction followed by the UAV during the flight. The UAV velocity and altitude are represented by the green and the light blue graduated scales on the left and on the right of the screen respectively. The landing point planned for the UAV is highlighted by a semitransparent cylinder: the cylinder colour is red when the UAV is far away, whereas it turns to green when the UAV is inside the vertical cylinder which encompasses the admissible landing spot at its base. The panel at the bottom right of the screen indicates the current distance from the landing spot and the residual battery charge, which is represented by a green bar. The colour turns red when the charge is below a prescribed threshold (e.g. 15%). The user has the possibility to enable a zoom in the bottom left of the screen to have a clear vision of the UAV flight attitude and 3D orientation.

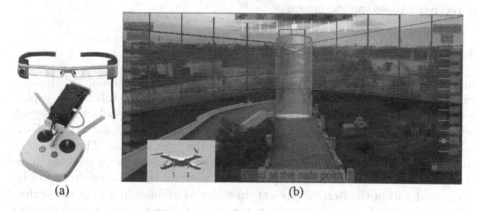

(a)   (b)

Fig. 2. Epson Moverio BT-300 Drone FPV Edition (a); head-up display for the situation awareness of the UAV pilot (b).

3.3 Force Feedback

Besides visual information, the AR-based platform will implement a force feedback to enhance the situation awareness of the pilot by providing him in advance with the perception of imminent collisions and guiding him in the actions to be taken. The aim is to simulate the contact with virtual fences to avoid any collision of the UAV with real objects outside geofence grids. The force feedback will be provided by means of a joystick, the resistance of which is increased in the presence of obstacles and/or other vehicles that should get closer to the vehicle along its current course. A Direct Haptic Aid (DHA) approach can be adopted, which aims at forcing the pilot to take some well-defined actions in place of other ones [24], or an Indirect Haptic Aid (IHA) approach, which generates a haptic feedback requiring an opposite reaction by exploiting the tendency (especially of untrained pilots) to contrast the forces felt on the control device. At a more basic level, warning signals with control vibrations and/or buzzers will also complement the system.

3.4   Communication Protocols

The augmented reality application for situation awareness could receive real-time data on contingency situations through REST services on the HTTP protocol or by means of communication protocols specifically designed for resource constrained devices, such as the Message Queuing Telemetry Transport (MQTT) protocol [25]. This solution would generate a lower message overhead, with a consequent reduction in bandwidth and battery consumption. A notification platform, based on a MQTT broker, can deliver the messages published under some topics by publisher entities to other entities, called subscribers, interested in receiving those specific messages.

4   Conclusions and Future Work

In this paper a platform for safe management of operations conducted through small Unmanned Aerial Systems is introduced. In particular, a head-up display for enhanced situation awareness of the pilot was designed, selecting relevant information and a visualization layout. Two possible models for a force feedback are being considered, that should guide the pilot actions. The possibility to include sounds and vocal commands will be considered as a possible additional feature of the platform. Experimental tests on the whole system will be performed within the AcrOSS project, in order to evaluate not only the performance in terms of responsiveness, but also human factors such as usability and user experience.

References

1. Federal Aviation Administration: Operation and Certification of Small Unmanned Aircraft Systems. Technical report (2016)
2. Ren, L., et al.: Small unmanned aircraft system (sUAS) categorization framework for low altitude traffic services. In: Proceedings of the AIAA/IEEE Digital Avionics Systems Conference, pp. 1–10 (2017)
3. Giulietti, F., Pollini, L., Avanzini, G.: Visual AIDS for safe operation of remotely piloted vehicles in the controlled air space. Proc. Inst. Mech. Eng. Part G J. Aerosp. Eng. **230**(9), 1641–1654 (2016)

4. Kopardekar, P., et al.: Unmanned aircraft system traffic management (UTM) concept of operations. In: 16th AIAA Aviation Technology, Integration, and Operations Conference (2016)
5. Mattei, A.P., et al.: UAV in - flight awareness: a tool to improve safety. In: 5th European Conference for Aerospace Sciences (EUCASS), p. 15 (2013)
6. Templin, F.L., et al.: Requirements for an integrated UAS CNS architecture. In: Integrated Communications, Navigation and Surveillance Conference (ICNS), pp. 2E4-1-2E4-11 (2017)
7. Avanzini, G., Martínez, D.S.: Risk assessment in mission planning of uninhabited aerial vehicles. Proc. Inst. Mech. Eng. Part G J. Aerosp. Eng. **233**(10), 3499–3518 (2019)
8. Rebane, G.: EASA basic regulation: improving the performance of the european aviation safety system. Zeitschrift fur Luft- und Weltraumrecht - German J. Air Space Law **68**, 51 (2019)
9. Endsley, M.R.: Toward a theory of situation awareness in dynamic systems (2017)
10. Endsley, M.R.: Designing for situation awareness in complex systems. In: Second International Workshop on Symbiosis of Humans, Artifacts and Environment, pp. 1–14 (2001)
11. Wither, J., DiVerdi, S., Höllerer, T.: Annotation in outdoor augmented reality. Comput. Graph. (Pergamon) **33**(6), 679–689 (2009)
12. Ruano, S., et al.: Augmented reality tool for the situational awareness improvement of UAV operators. Sensors (Switzerland) **17**(2), 297 (2017)
13. Zollmann, S., et al.: Image-based X-ray visualization techniques for spatial understanding in outdoor augmented reality. In: Proceedings of the 26th Australian Computer-Human Interaction Conference, OzCHI 2014, Sydney, New South Wales, Australia, pp. 194–203 (2014)
14. Zollmann, S., et al.: FlyAR: augmented reality supported micro aerial vehicle navigation. IEEE Trans. Vis. Comput. Graph. **20**(4), 560–568 (2014)
15. Cai, Z., Chen, M., Yang, L.: Multi-source information fusion augmented reality benefited decision-making for unmanned aerial vehicles: a effective way for accurate operation. In: Proceedings of the 6th IEEE Conference on Industrial Electronics and Applications, ICIEA 2011, pp. 174–178 (2011)
16. Wu, H., Cai, Z., Wang, Y.: Vison-based auxiliary navigation method using augmented reality for unmanned aerial vehicles. In: IEEE 10th International Conference on Industrial Informatics (INDIN), pp. 520–525 (2012)
17. Iwaneczko, P., Jędrasiak, K., Nawrat, A.: Augmented reality in UAVs applications. In: Nawrat, A., Jędrasiak, K. (eds.) Innovative Simulation Systems. SSDC, vol. 33, pp. 77–86. Springer, Cham (2016). https://doi.org/10.1007/978-3-319-21118-3_6
18. ISO: Human-centred design for interactive systems. Ergonomics of human system interaction. Part 210. ISO 9241-210 (2010)
19. De Paolis, L.T., De Luca, V.: Augmented visualization with depth perception cues to improve the surgeon's performance in minimally invasive surgery. Med. Biol. Eng. Comput. **57**(5), 995–1013 (2018). https://doi.org/10.1007/s11517-018-1929-6
20. Maiouak, M., Taleb, T.: Dynamic maps for automated driving and UAV geofencing. IEEE Wireless Commun. **26**(4), 54–59 (2019)
21. Zhu, G., Wei, P.: Low-altitude UAS traffic coordination with dynamic geofencing. In: 16th AIAA Aviation Technology, Integration, and Operations Conference (2016)
22. Epson Moverio BT-300 Drone FPV, Edition, June 2020. https://www.epson.eu/products/see-through-mobile-viewer/moverio-bt-300-drone-fpv-edition

23. Unity3D, June 2020. https://unity3d.com/
24. Razzanelli, M., et al.: A visual-haptic display for human and autonomous systems integration. In: Hodicky, J. (ed.) MESAS 2016. LNCS, vol. 9991, pp. 64–80. Springer, Cham (2016). https://doi.org/10.1007/978-3-319-47605-6_6
25. Message Queuing Telemetry Transport, June 2020. http://mqtt.org/

Global-Map-Registered Local Visual Odometry Using On-the-Fly Pose Graph Updates

Masahiro Yamaguchi[1]($\boxtimes$) (iD), Shohei Mori[2] (iD), Hideo Saito[1] (iD), Shoji Yachida[3],
and Takashi Shibata[3] (iD)

[1] Information and Computer Science, Keio University, Yokohama 223-8522, Japan
{yamaguchi,saito}@hvrl.ics.keio.ac.jp
[2] Institute of Computer Graphics and Vision, Graz University of Technology,
8010 Graz, Austria
shohei.mori@icg.tugraz.at
[3] NEC, Kawasaki 211-8666, Japan
s-yachida@nec.com

Abstract. Real-time camera pose estimation is one of the indispensable technologies for Augmented Reality (AR). While a large body of work in Visual Odometry (VO) has been proposed for AR, practical challenges such as scale ambiguities and accumulative errors still remain especially when we apply VO to large-scale scenes due to limited hardware and resources. We propose a camera pose registration method, where a local VO is consecutively optimized with respect to a large-scale scene map on the fly. This framework enables the scale estimation between a VO map and a scene map and reduces accumulative errors by finding corresponding locations in the map to the current frame and by on-the-fly pose graph optimization. The results using public datasets demonstrated that our approach reduces the accumulative errors of naïve VO.

Keywords: Visual Odometry · Graph optimization · Structure from motion · Location-based AR.

1 Introduction

Real-time camera pose estimation is an essential function for Augmented Reality (AR) systems in registering 3D content to the scene. The size of a scene can vary from a desktop to a city scale and depending on the scale, the feasible hardware for camera pose estimation also changes. Since outside-in tracking becomes impractical in wide areas, AR systems with wide scalability rely on inside-out tracking.

Stand-alone inside-out tracking systems, such as Visual Odometry (VO) and Simultaneous Localization and Mapping (SLAM), use vision sensors, i.e., a camera, to achieve pixel-wise registration in the user's view. However, VO accumulates errors over time and drifts from the original location. Although SLAM can

© Springer Nature Switzerland AG 2020
L. T. De Paolis and P. Bourdot (Eds.): AVR 2020, LNCS 12242, pp. 299–311, 2020.
https://doi.org/10.1007/978-3-030-58465-8_23

Fig. 1. Registering a locally growing VO (a) to a globally optimized scene map (b). Since both maps are in individual scales and individual coordinate systems, the proposed method registers the VO to the scene map by reducing such differences at run time (c). This allows the location-based AR system using the VO to retrieve AR contents registered in the scene map.

mitigate this error by detecting re-visits in a scene and attempts to cancel the accumulated errors. Nevertheless, before the loop close detection, SLAM also suffers from the drift. This makes location-based AR error-prone, especially in wider areas, since the drifted position triggers unrelated AR content.

Since VO and SLAM provide only temporal personalized scene tracking to AR, scene registered content can be created only at the runtime and will be paused in the next trial. Therefore, to enable a consistent AR experience on a daily basis, AR developers need to register their content to pre-built common-scene maps, and AR systems are required to match their executing VO or SLAM to the scene map to access pre-built content. Consequently, the scene map creation must be done in a stage earlier than the user's AR experience.

To satisfy these AR-specific needs, we propose a new camera pose registration system using VO in conjunction with a pre-built scene map. Our method enables feeding a pre-built scene map to a VO. In this method, a locally running VO can refer to the preserved scene map's information immediately after the execution. This means that our tracking system can bootstrap the VO within the scene map scale and update the current camera pose with a pose graph optimization without closing the VO's trajectory loop by itself. Figure 1 shows snapshots of a globally optimized scene map (Fig. 1(a)) and a locally growing VO map on different scales (Fig. 1(b)). Our method re-calculates the scale difference of the VO and the scene map on the fly and continues updating the VO map when the scene map is available (Fig. 1(c)). Our contributions are summarized as follows:

- We propose a camera tracking system that automatically registers the local user's VO map to a pre-built scene map relying only on a color camera. With this, the user can receive AR content in the scene map within the adjusted scale immediately after the method finds a matching between the current undergoing VO map and the world map. Additionally, this can mitigate drift errors that would be accumulated over time with solely the VO.

- We present an approach to match the scale between the VO map and a scene map to provide scale-consistent content in the AR space.
- We provide the results of quantitative evaluations, demonstrating the superiority and the limitations of our method.

One can find several similar approaches that combine VO and a pre-built scene map [12,15]. The major difference is that such approaches rely on the inertial measurement unit (IMU), i.e., visual-inertial odometry (VIO) [13], for stability and for the absolute scale factor, whereas ours does not, i.e., VO receives only a video stream.

2   Related Work

Camera pose estimation methods for AR using a color camera are divided into three major approaches: VO, SLAM, and pre-built map-based tracking.

VO and SLAM: VO [3,5] is a camera tracker that gives pixel-wise content registrations in the AR view. As VO is designed to optimize the poses and the map with respect to several of the latest frames, it suffers from drift errors over time. SLAM [4,7,11] is an alternative designed to reduce drift errors with a global optimization process such as Bundle Adjustment (BA) and a loop closure scheme [19].

Regardless of the global optimization process, both approaches use temporally built maps to track the scene. The reason behind this is that VO and SLAM provide different scale factors in every trial depending on how the user moves the camera. This prevents AR applications fetching pre-built content. VIO is one of the choices used to overcome the scale difference issue, as it provides a real-scale map. Several approaches [12,15] have already proposed such methods in the last few years. GPS can also be a tool to obtain a real-scale map in SLAM [21]. Contrary to these sensor-fusion approaches, we solely rely on a monocular camera to minimize the hardware required for AR systems. To this end, we use a pre-built map and estimate a scale from the locally running VO and the pre-built scene map.

Pre-built Map-Based Tracking: Location-based AR applications must have an interface to link the camera pose and the location, to trigger location-specific AR content. One popular approach to achieve this is to register the camera within a preserved scene map to have access to the map registered content. Landmark database-based approaches use maps built with Structure from Motion (SfM) to estimate camera poses in the map by linking observed feature points and those in the database map [9,18,22], therefore, lacking feature point matching results in the tracking failures. Our approach uses VO, with which we continue tracking the camera using its online local map. PTAMM can re-localize the camera in multiple local maps distributed in a scene [2]. This approach is only applicable to room-scale scenes, where no loop closure scheme is required, due to the limited scalability of the core SLAM method. Our method can scale from

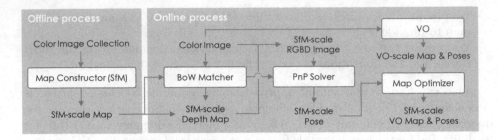

Fig. 2. System overview.

a desktop environment to a city-scale environment with the empowerment of the state-of-the-art VO.

3   Registering Local VO to a Global Scene Map

We propose a method capable of registering and refining a trajectory of a locally running VO using a scene map optimized in advance, potentially with higher accuracy than what naïve VO and SLAM can provide. To this end, we propose a framework that provides an SfM scale in ongoing VO and propose to match and optimize the VO trajectories in an SfM-scale map.

3.1   System Overview

Figure 2 shows an overview of the proposed method. Given a global map of a scene $\mathcal{G}$ that contains frame depth maps in the scale s^{SfM}, poses, and Bags of Binary Words (BoW) database [6], a camera starts exploring the scene, and VO estimates the trajectory in its own scale map s^{VO}. When the system detects the best match of the incoming frame to a frame in $\mathcal{G}$, it calculates the corresponding pose in the SfM scale. Given a collection of such poses, our method optimizes the current VO trajectory through graph optimization. Although this approach best fits VO, we could replace VO with SLAM without losing generality. SLAM is a framework that includes map optimization by itself, so VO is the minimum configuration for the proposed method.

3.2   Global Scene Map Generation Using SfM

Given M images, we construct a map $\mathcal{G}$ using SfM before actual VO tracking starts. As the maps generated by SfM [17] are known to be accurate compared to the ones created by SLAM and VO due to its global optimization nature, we do not update the global map $\mathcal{G}$ during VO tracking. On the other hand, the VO map is optimized at runtime to match the map to the stable global map. Such a global map consists of color frames $\mathcal{I}^{\mathrm{SfM}}$, depth maps at each frame $\mathcal{D}^{\mathrm{SfM}}$, and associated frame poses $\mathcal{T}^{\mathrm{SfM}}$. Hereafter, we denote the $i_{th}(< M)$ color frame, depth frame, and their pose as $I_i^{\mathrm{SfM}} \in \mathcal{I}^{\mathrm{SfM}}$, $D_i^{\mathrm{SfM}} \in \mathcal{D}^{\mathrm{SfM}}$, and $\mathbf{T}_i^{\mathrm{SfM}} \in \mathcal{T}^{\mathrm{SfM}}$, respectively. In addition, we use BoW with ORB features [14], $F_i^{\mathrm{SfM}} \in \mathcal{F}^{\mathrm{SfM}}$, detected at each frame I_m to relate the frames in the global map $\mathcal{I}^{\mathrm{SfM}}$ with the frames given to VO, i.e., we define our global map as $\mathcal{G} \in \{\mathcal{I}^{\mathrm{SfM}}, \mathcal{D}^{\mathrm{SfM}}, \mathcal{T}^{\mathrm{SfM}}, \mathcal{F}^{\mathrm{SfM}}\}$.

3.3 Bootstrapping VO with a Global Scene Map Scale

As the baseline length at the initialization of a monocular VO is unknown in most cases, such a VO randomly estimates a camera trajectory and a corresponding map in an arbitrary scale given at a bootstrapping stage [3]. Although a stereo VO [24] can use a calibrated baseline length between the two cameras to obtain a scale, fitting the scale to that for a global map is another issue, unless these scales are calibrated in the real unit [13,23]. Instead of bootstrapping VO from scratch, we use $\mathcal{D}^{\mathrm{SfM}}$ to feed the scale of $\mathcal{G}$, i.e., s^{SfM}, to VO. Given a VO keyframe $I^{\mathrm{KF}} \subset \mathcal{I}^{\mathrm{VO}}$ and its BoW vector F^{KF}, we search a depth frame D_i^{SfM} that has a frame index, i, satisfying the following condition:

$$\operatorname*{argmin}_{i} |F_i^{\mathrm{SfM}} - F^{\mathrm{KF}}|_2 > t_{\mathrm{BoW}}, \qquad (1)$$

where t_{BoW} is a user-given threshold.

Once such a frame index is found, we unproject the depth map D_i^{SfM} to obtain 3D points. Detecting and matching feature points in I_i^{SfM} and I^{KF} gives their 2D–2D correspondences, and the unprojected 3D points at such feature points in I_i^{SfM} give 3D–2D correspondences between I_i^{SfM} and I^{KF}. Solving the perspective-n-point (PnP) problem with a RANSAC robust estimator gives the pose of the keyframe I^{KF}, T^{KF}, in scale s^{SfM}. Finally, the depth map at the current keyframe D^{KF} is calculated as follows:

$$D^{\mathrm{KF}} = \pi^{-1}(\mathbf{T}^{\mathrm{KF}}(\mathbf{T}^{\mathrm{SfM}})^{-1}\pi(D^{\mathrm{SfM}})), \qquad (2)$$

where $\pi(\cdot)$ is an operator that unprojects a 2D point with depth to 3D space and $\pi(\cdot)^{-1}$ performs the inverse operation. Such a depth map D^{KF} is passed to the bootstrapping procedure in VO. Consequently, VO, after this, estimates the camera poses and the map in s^{SfM}.

3.4 Keyframe Pose Refinement

After bootstrapping VO, our method refines upcoming keyframe poses to fit them to the global map $\mathcal{G}$ using the same strategy as that in bootstrapping. As not all keyframes would receive corresponding frames in $\mathcal{G}$, non-matched keyframes need to be refined using a different approach. For such keyframes, we use pose graph optimization [10]. Figure 3 shows how we establish the pose graph.

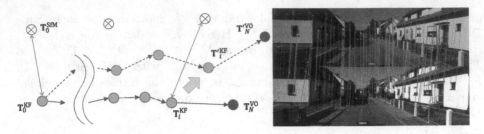

Fig. 3. Pose refinement using graph optimization with pre-registered poses in a global map. The circles with a cross are the camera poses of a global map, and the gray circles are the camera poses of VO ($\mathbf{T}_0, ..., \mathbf{T}_N$). The red arrow shows that the i_{th} frame of VO matches one of the poses in the global map. The right image shows the matching result represented. As a result, the poses of VO are refined to the locations where dotted circles ($\mathbf{T}'_0, ..., \mathbf{T}'_N$) exist. (Color figure online)

For keyframes matched to I^{SfM_i} of $\mathcal{I}^{\text{SfM}}$, we estimate their poses by directly obtaining 3D–2D correspondences and solving the PnP problem in the scale of $\mathcal{G}$, as described in Sect. 3.3. For the other keyframes, we connect them with their previous keyframes. Consequently, we construct an edge, $e_{i,i-1}$, for the i_{th} keyframe, as follows:

$$e_{i,i-1} = ((\mathbf{T}_{i-1}^{\text{KF}})^{-1}\mathbf{T}_i^{\text{KF}})((\hat{\mathbf{T}}_{i-1}^{\text{KF}})^{-1}\hat{\mathbf{T}}_i^{\text{KF}}), \tag{3}$$

where $\hat{\mathbf{T}}_i^{\text{KF}}$ represents the i_{th} estimated pose from the PnP solver and $\mathbf{T}_i^{\text{KF}}$ represents the i_{th} estimated pose from VO.

Every time a new match is detected and the pose estimation by a PnP solver is conducted, our pose graph is renewed by inserting the estimated pose. We optimize the following pose graph by using the g2o algorithm [10]:

$$\mathbf{F}(\mathbf{x}) = \sum_{\langle i \rangle \in N} e_{i,i-1}^{\text{T}} \Omega_{i,i-1} e_{i,i-1}, \tag{4}$$

$$\mathbf{x}^* = \underset{x}{\text{argmin}}\, \mathbf{F}(\mathbf{x}), \tag{5}$$

where N is the last matched keyframe index, $\mathbf{x}^* = (\mathbf{T}'_0, ..., \mathbf{T}'_N)$ is an array of refined poses, and $\Omega_{i,i-1}$ is an information matrix. We optimize Eq. 5 with the Levenberg Marquardt algorithm. Note that the first keyframe pose, i.e., $\mathbf{T}_0$, is fixed, whereas the other poses are not.

3.5 Current Camera Pose Refinement

As only the keyframe poses are refined so far, we need to calculate the current pose as a relative pose from the last keyframe with a given scale $s^{\text{VO}\to\text{SfM}}$ in order to obtain the pose along with the scale s^{SfM}:

$$\mathbf{T}_i^{\prime\text{VO}} := s^{\text{VO}\to\text{SfM}}\mathbf{T}_{ij}^{\text{VO}}\mathbf{T}_j^{\prime\text{KF}} \quad with \quad s^{\text{VO}\to\text{SfM}} = \frac{|\mathbf{t}_i^{\prime\text{KF}} - \mathbf{t}_0^{\text{KF}}|_2}{|\mathbf{t}_i^{\text{KF}} - \mathbf{t}_0^{\text{KF}}|_2}, \tag{6}$$

where $\mathbf{t}_i^{KF}$ is the i_{th} translation vector, $\mathbf{t'}_i^{KF}$ is the i_{th} refined translation vector, and $|.|_2$ is the represented L2 norm. T_{ij}^{VO} is the reference pose from frame j to frame i via VO, and s is the scale-error-resolving factor. The blue circle in Fig. 3 represents this current camera pose refinement step.

4 Evaluations

We validated the proposed method using public dataset of two different kinds, and compared our results to those of state-of-the-art approaches (DSO [3] and ORB-SLAM2 [11]). Through the evaluations, we demonstrate how the proposed approach is capable of mitigating accumulative drift errors in VO with the help of pose updates using a scene map.

4.1 Implementation

We used COLMAP [17] as SfM to generate a global scene map $\mathcal{G}$ consisting of camera poses $\mathcal{T}^{SfM}$ and depth images $\mathcal{D}^{SfM}$. The depth images $\mathcal{D}^{SfM}$ are calculated based on both photometric and geometric consistencies [16]. In addition, we calculated ORB features $\mathcal{F}^{SfM}$ of the input frames and stored them in a DBoW3 database [6]. To mitigate the drift errors for VO in the dataset of sequential images, we took every third frame for SfM.

We used DSO [3] as VO and extended the framework to implement our approach. DSO originally had two threads: a camera pose estimation thread and a visualization thread. In addition to them, we implemented a BoW matching thread and a pose graph optimization thread. The pose graph optimization thread is implemented in a similar way as in the direct sparse odometry with a loop closure (LDSO) [7]. Further, we used g2o [10] for graph optimization.

4.2 Datasets

We evaluated the proposed method using the EuRoC MAV Dataset [1] and the KITTI dataset [8]. The EuRoC MAV dataset provides 11 sequences containing stereo images, synchronized IMU readings, and ground-truth camera trajectories. The sequences are captured in three different scenes consisting of five sequences in Machine Hall, three sequences in a Vehicon Room 1, and three sequences in Vehicon Room 2. In each scene, we used one sequence to generate a global map and the rest for VO. We used the right camera images as an input for both SfM and VO. The KITTI dataset provides 22 stereo sequences of driving cars. In the dataset, 11 sequences (00–10) provide the ground truth trajectories. We utilized left views to generate global scene maps and fed the right views to VO. Further, we used the first 1,000 images for evaluation to exclude frames that could trigger loop closures in SLAM.

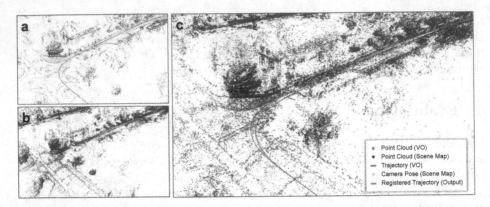

Fig. 4. Registering a VO map (a) to a scene map (b) in the KITTI dataset sequence 05. (c) Both maps are matched regarding the coordinate systems and the scales.

4.3   Evaluation Method

We validated the proposed method by measuring the absolute trajectory error (ATE) in each dataset. We evaluated the ATE only in VO keyframes since such keyframes are the ones we optimize. We should note that we optimized the resultant trajectories with respect to the ground truth using Sim(3)-alignment, i.e., Umeyama Alignment [20]. We discuss this Sim(3)-aligned ATE results in Sect. 4.4. Although Sim(3)-alignment is de-facto-standard post-processing for VO and SLAM evaluations [3,11], such ATE does not represent frame-by-frame errors that the users actually observe in the AR view. Therefore, we conducted another evaluation where we gave an adjusted scale to DSO in the bootstrapping, to evaluate growing ATE over time. We describe this evaluation in Sect. 4.5.

4.4   Results of ATE with Sim(3)-Alignment

Tables 1 and 2 show the results of Machine Hall and Vehicon Rooms 1 and 2, respectively. The cross marks in the tables show there were not enough matching points between the input and global map frames and our method failed to bootstrap our VO. Figure 1 and Fig. 4 show qualitative comparisons of a global scene map, a VO map, and a registered VO map in the global scene map in EuRoC Machine Hall and in KITTI sequence 00–10. Table 3 summarizes ATE in the four scenes in the KITTI dataset and Fig. 5 shows Sim(3)-aligned trajectories of the KITTI dataset.

The proposed method obtained the best RMSE in one sequence of the EuRoC dataset. On the other hand, the proposed method obtained the best RMSE in the eight sequences of the KITTI dataset. In case that the camera could frequently observe revisiting, such as in the EuRoC dataset, we consider that ORB-SLAM2 tends to obtain good BA and loop closure results. Therefore, our refined trajectories could not achieve better scores than ORB-SLAM2 could in such scenes. However, in the KITTI dataset, we could surpass ORB-SLAM2

Table 1. ATE on EuRoC Machine Hall (m)

Sequence	Ours					DSO	ORB-SLAM2
Global map	MH01	MH02	MH03	MH04	MH05	–	–
MH01	–	0.0812	**0.0448**	×	×	0.0532	**0.0448**
MH02	0.0564	–	0.0473	×	×	0.0438	**0.0303**
MH03	0.0845	0.1035	–	0.2014	×	0.1903	**0.0393**
MH04	×	×	0.1562	–	×	0.2043	**0.1160**
MH05	×	×	0.1394	×	–	0.1374	**0.0468**

Table 2. ATE on EuRoC Vehicon Room 1 and 2 (m)

Sequence	Ours			DSO	ORB-SLAM2
Global map	V101	V102	V103	–	–
V101	–	0.0970	×	0.1550	**0.0877**
V102	0.0689	–	×	0.2031	**0.0601**
V103	1.0732	×	–	**0.4356**	×
Global map	V201	V202	V203	–	
V201	–	0.0812	×	0.0678	**0.0623**
V202	0.0970	–	×	0.1084	**0.0557**
V203	×	×	–	1.3888	×

Table 3. ATE on KITTI Training Sequences (m)

Sequence	Ours	DSO	ORB-SLAM2
00	**3.101**	7.165	9.780
01	**5.768**	326.065	518.853
02	**5.926**	93.200	15.100
03	0.824	1.215	**0.810**
04	**0.233**	0.490	1.097
05	**5.797**	16.614	21.103
06	**6.203**	48.641	15.908
07	**4.925**	15.653	16.772
08	**5.994**	13.554	17.375
09	0.104	0.165	**0.090**
10	**2.797**	7.429	3.652

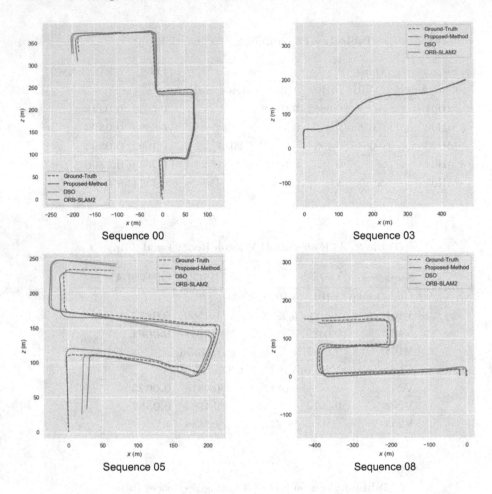

Fig. 5. Sim(3)-aligned trajectories of KITTI sequences 00, 03, 05, and 08

in the scores because most sequences are straight roads, and revisiting does not occur in the sequences. Overall, we observed that our approach achieved a similar level of accuracy as those in ORB-SLAM2 and obtained better scores than DSO in most of the cases. Again, notice that for DSO and ORB-SLAM2, we used Sim(3)-alignment after calculating all the trajectories, while for our approach, we did not proceed such a post-processing at all.

The main limitation in the accuracy of our approach comes from the dependency on BoW. Our pose refinement processing is based on BoW-based feature matching. Therefore, we cannot obtain any benefits from the preserved scene map if the appearance of the scene that the system is currently observing is different from the one in the scene map. This happens when environments change according to various external factors (e.g., weather changes, dynamic

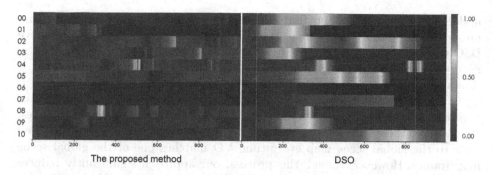

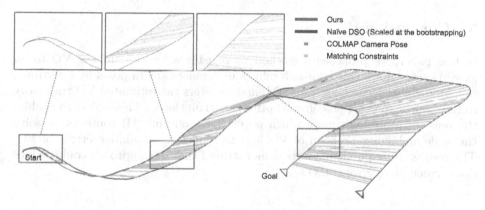

Fig. 6. The error accumulation with the proposed method and DSO in the KITTI dataset. We calculated ATE between the estimated poses and the ground truth poses at runtime. While our approach can keep the ATE significantly lower than the naïve DSO, we see some spikes before the pose updates occur.

Fig. 7. The results of the camera pose plots of COLMAP (scene map), Naïve DSO, and our approach in KITTI sequence 10. Our trajectory keeps the poses next to the COLMAP poses. Naïve DSO travels far from the COLMAP poses even though the scale is initialized in the same manner as our approach.

objects, day-night lighting changes) and prevent applying our approach to outdoor scenes. MH04, MH05, V103, and V203 in the EuRoC dataset are cases such that BoW does not work well due to differences in the illumination between the global maps and test sequences.

4.5 Results of ATE Without Sim(3)-Alignment

One of the advantages of our approach is that it can fit the scale of VO to the global scene map automatically. We finally demonstrate how the trajectory errors accumulate in naïve DSO and how our approach can reduce the errors. VO, in our framework, initializes the scale factor using a SfM depth map and updates it when the systems find a matching between an observed frame and preserved frame in the scene map. For fair comparisons, we bootstrap the naïve DSO with the SfM depth map but do not update the scale in the later frames. Figure 6 shows the frame-by-frame differences in ATE of each tracking and Fig. 7 shows the trajectory results of the proposed approach and the naïve DSO.

One interesting observation from Fig. 6 is that the color gradients of our approach show some spikes even though it achieves lower errors across the frames. We observed these spikes as jumps right after the pose updates when VO is pulled back to the global scene map every time VO matches one of the global scene map frames. However, though this process, our approach significantly reduces the amount of accumulative errors of VO. This should be troublesome for AR applications. For example, annotations registered in the map will always shift in the AR view when the matching happens. Thus, we should design new pose update rules to change these system-oriented pose updates to the user-oriented pose updates to reduce the user's mental load.

5   Conclusion

In this paper, we proposed a method to register a locally running VO to an existing scene map. Our approach refines upcoming camera poses by referring a prepared global scene map from SfM, and registers the estimated VO trajectory to the scene map using pose graph optimization on the fly. This approach enables the reuse of a pre-built map, which potentially contains AR contents, to solve the scale ambiguity problem of VO and to reduce accumulative errors of VO. The results using public datasets demonstrated that our approach could reduce the accumulative errors of VO.

References

1. Burri, M., et al.: The EuRoC micro aerial vehicle datasets. Int. J. Robot. Res. **35**, 1157–1163 (2016)
2. Castle, R., Klein, G., Murray, D.W.: Video-rate localization in multiple maps for wearable augmented reality. In: International Symposium on Wearable Computers, pp. 15–22 (2008)
3. Engel, J., Koltun, V., Cremers, D.: Direct sparse odometry. IEEE Trans. Pattern Anal. Mach. Intell. **40**, 611–625 (2017)
4. Engel, J., Schöps, T., Cremers, D.: LSD-SLAM: large-scale direct monocular SLAM. In: Fleet, D., Pajdla, T., Schiele, B., Tuytelaars, T. (eds.) ECCV 2014. LNCS, vol. 8690, pp. 834–849. Springer, Cham (2014). https://doi.org/10.1007/978-3-319-10605-2_54
5. Forster, C., Pizzoli, M., Scaramuzza, D.: SVO: fast semi-direct monocular visual odometry. In: IEEE International Conference on Robotics and Automation (ICRA), pp. 15–22. IEEE (2014)
6. Gálvez-López, D., Tardos, J.D.: Bags of binary words for fast place recognition in image sequences. IEEE Trans. Robot. **28**, 1188–1197 (2012)

7. Gao, X., Wang, R., Demmel, N., Cremers, D.: LDSO: direct sparse odometry with loop closure. In: 2018 IEEE/RSJ International Conference on Intelligent Robots and Systems (IROS), pp. 2198–2204. IEEE (2018)
8. Geiger, A., Lenz, P., Urtasun, R.: Are we ready for autonomous driving? The KITTI vision benchmark suite. In: IEEE Conference on Computer Vision and Pattern Recognition, pp. 3354–3361. IEEE (2012)
9. Kume, H., Suppé, A., Kanade, T.: Vehicle localization along a previously driven route using an image database. In: IAPR International Conference on Machine Vision Applications (MVA), pp. 177–180 (2013)
10. Kümmerle, R., Grisetti, G., Strasdat, H., Konolige, K., Burgard, W.: g2o: a general framework for graph optimization. In: 2011 IEEE International Conference on Robotics and Automation, pp. 3607–3613. IEEE (2011)
11. Mur-Artal, R., Tardós, J.D.: ORB-SLAM2: an open-source SLAM system for monocular, stereo, and RGB-D cameras. IEEE Trans. Robot. **33**, 1255–1262 (2017)
12. Qin, T., Li, P., Shen, S.: Relocalization, global optimization and map merging for monocular visual-inertial SLAM. In: 2018 IEEE International Conference on Robotics and Automation (ICRA), pp. 1197–1204. IEEE (2018)
13. Qin, T., Li, P., Shen, S.: VINS-Mono: a robust and versatile monocular visual-inertial state estimator. IEEE Trans. Robot. **34**, 1004–1020 (2018)
14. Rublee, E., Rabaud, V., Konolige, K., Bradski, G.R.: ORB: an efficient alternative to SIFT or SURF. In: International Conference on Computer Vision (ICCV), pp. 2564–2571. IEEE (2011)
15. Schneider, T., et al.: Maplab: an open framework for research in visual-inertial mapping and localization. IEEE Robot. Autom. Lett. **3**, 1418–1425 (2018)
16. Schönberger, J.L., Zheng, E., Frahm, J.-M., Pollefeys, M.: Pixelwise view selection for unstructured multi-view stereo. In: Leibe, B., Matas, J., Sebe, N., Welling, M. (eds.) ECCV 2016. LNCS, vol. 9907, pp. 501–518. Springer, Cham (2016). https://doi.org/10.1007/978-3-319-46487-9_31
17. Schönberger, J.L., Frahm, J.M.: Structure-from-motion revisited. In: Conference on Computer Vision and Pattern Recognition (CVPR), pp. 4104–4113. IEEE (2016)
18. Taketomi, T., Sato, T., Yokoya, N.: Real-time and accurate extrinsic camera parameter estimation using feature landmark database for augmented reality. Comput. Graph. **35**, 768–777 (2011)
19. Taketomi, T., Uchiyama, H., Ikeda, S.: Visual SLAM algorithms: a survey from 2010 to 2016. IPSJ Trans. Comput. Vis. Appl. **9**(1), 1–11 (2017). https://doi.org/10.1186/s41074-017-0027-2
20. Umeyama, S.: Least-squares estimation of transformation parameters between two point patterns. IEEE Trans. Pattern Anal. Mach. Intell. **13**(4), 376–380 (1991)
21. Ventura, J., Arth, C., Reitmayr, G., Schmalstieg, D.: Global localization from monocular SLAM on a mobile phone. IEEE Trans. Visual. Comput. Graph. **20**, 531–539 (2014)
22. Ventura, J., Höllerer, T.: Wide-area scene mapping for mobile visual tracking. In: Int. Symp. on Mixed and Augmented Reality (ISMAR), pp. 3–12 (2012)
23. Von Stumberg, L., Usenko, V., Cremers, D.: Direct Sparse Visual-Inertial Odometry using Dynamic Marginalization. In: IEEE International Conference on Robotics and Automation (ICRA), pp. 2510–2517. IEEE (2018)
24. Wang, R., Schworer, M., Cremers, D.: Stereo DSO: large-scale direct sparse visual odometry with stereo cameras. In: Proceedings of the IEEE International Conference on Computer Vision, pp. 3903–3911 (2017)

Mixed Reality

Combining HoloLens and Leap-Motion for Free Hand-Based 3D Interaction in MR Environments

Fakhreddine Ababsa[1](✉), Junhui He[2](✉), and Jean-Remy Chardonnet[1](✉)

[1] Arts et Metiers Institute of Technology, LISPEN, HESAM University,
Chalon-sur-Saône, France
{Fakhreddine.Ababsa,Jean-Remy.Chardonnet}@ensam.eu
[2] ENSEA, Cergy, France
junhui.he@ensea.fr

Abstract. The ability to interact with virtual objects using gestures would allow users to improve their experience in Mixed Reality (MR) environments, especially when they use AR headsets. Today, MR head-mounted displays like the HoloLens integrate hand gesture based interaction allowing users to take actions in MR environments. However, the proposed interactions remain limited. In this paper, we propose to combine a Leap Motion Controller (LMC) with a HoloLens in order to improve gesture interaction with virtual objects. Two main issues are presented: an interactive calibration procedure for the coupled HoloLens-LMC device and an intuitive hand-based interaction approach using LMC data in the HoloLens environment. A set of first experiments was carried out to evaluate the accuracy and the usability of the proposed approach.

Keywords: Mixed reality · Calibration · Natural interaction

1 Introduction

Since a couple of years, both augmented reality (AR) hardware and applications became convincing and widespread in many fields, for example in medicine [1], education, and industry. Microsoft, Facebook and Apple have shown their interest in AR applications, believing in the viability of this technology. Following this trend, the HoloLens head-mounted device, which was released by Microsoft in 2016, is one of the leading MR devices. Features include drawing holograms in the user's field of view and enabling interaction with real-world environments. One of its worthwhile features is its own custom holographic processing unit (HPU), which allows complex calculations to be embedded. However, interaction techniques are limited. It proposes two hand gestures only: air tap and bloom. It cannot track precise information about the position of the hands or identify other hand gestures. On the other hand, the Leap Motion Controller (LMC) is a peripheral device dedicated to high accuracy hand tracking. Originally released in July 2013, its goal was to provide an alternative to the traditional mouse and keyboard by proposing free-hand interaction. Its size is quite small, making it possible to be used in

© Springer Nature Switzerland AG 2020
L. T. De Paolis and P. Bourdot (Eds.): AVR 2020, LNCS 12242, pp. 315–327, 2020.
https://doi.org/10.1007/978-3-030-58465-8_24

combination for example with head-mounted displays in virtual reality. To fill the short-comings of the HoloLens in terms of interaction, we coupled the LMC to the HoloLens to provide hand tracking data to the HoloLens and create enriched gesture-based inter-action in mixed reality. Note that other headsets used for Virtual reality offer already an integration with LMC, such as Oculus. In our case, we developed a communication tool between the two devices to enable data transfer, then we focused on the hand tracking part. As the HoloLens and the LMC have different coordinate systems, it is important to calibrate the coupled device in order to project the 3D points collected by the LMC on the coordinate system of the HoloLens. As long as the spatial configuration of the two devices does not change, the calibration process does not need to be repeated. In this paper, we propose a 3D point based calibration approach in order to achieve more complex and natural 3D interaction. In addition, to collect data, we propose a semi-automatic procedure involving the user without constraining his/her movements. Only the LMC and the HoloLens are used to detect the spatial position of the hand. The entire calibration process uses the user's fingers as a reference and does not require any other instruments. Therefore, the main contribution of this paper is to provide an interactive calibration procedure for the coupled HoloLens-LMC device. Our approach uses the virtual object rendering done by the HoloLens to collect 3D point coordinates from both the HoloLens and the LMC. Based on the calibration results, several demos using free hands to interact with virtual objects are presented. We carried out a set of first experiments to evaluate the accuracy and the usability of the proposed approach.

2 Related Works

Free hand-based 3D interaction is a topic well explored for many years. Lyons [9] proposed camera-based gesture inputs for three dimensional navigation through a virtual reality environment. In [2] the authors showed that the physical interaction between virtual and real objects improves user experience and thus enhances the feeling of the presence of virtual contents in the real world. Ens et al. [5] proposed a mixed-scale gesture interaction technique, which interleaves micro-gestures with larger gestures for computer interaction. Their idea is to create a design space for applying micro-gestures within a greater gestural lexicon in order to adapt the interaction to the task performed by the user. Several input modes are often combined in order to overcome the problems related to the variability of gesture interaction. For instance, using a Leap Motion controller (LMC) allows accurate recognition of natural gestures. Thus, Khademi et al. [7] suggested free-hand interaction to rehabilitate patients with stroke; they modified the Fruit Ninja game to use the LMC hand tracking data, enabling patients with arm and hand weakness to practice rehabilitation. Blaha and Gupta built a virtual reality game displayed on an Oculus Rift head-mounted display and coupled with an LMC to help people with amblyopia restore vision in their amblyopic eye [3].

Most of the developed applications using an LMC are proposed in virtual reality, while MR environments suffer from a lack of applications using an LMC, because of equipment limitations. Furthermore, gesture recognition is almost never used in appli-cations involving the HoloLens. Garon et al. [6] identified the lack of high quality depth data as greatly restricting the HoloLens's potential as a research tool. They mounted a separate depth camera on top of the HoloLens, connected it to a stick computer, which was then used to stream the depth data wirelessly to the HoloLens. Several frameworks propose combining a HoloLens with a Kinect to enable multi-person collaboration on 3D objects in an MR environment. The HoloLens 1 are used so that all participants can view the same 3D objects in real time, while the Kinects are used to expand the available gesture interactions with custom gestures. But still, current research on the HoloLens usually adds a depth sensor on it to get more information. In fact, the LMC can also get data about depth, but it can provide more personalized gestures in mixed reality. In this frame, Köhler proposed a combination of the HoloLens and the LMC [8] which is very close to what we present here. However, the way he manages the data is different from our approach. He used the data collected by the LMC and analyzed the photos taken by the HoloLens to transform the 3D coordinates of the hand into 2D coordinates in the HoloLens screen using Perspective-n-Point, a well-known problem to estimate the distance between a set of n 3D points and their projection on a 2D plane [4]. His work provides the possibility to create new gestures. However, he only gets 2D coordinates of the hand and loses 3D information, therefore 3D interaction cannot be achieved.

3   Communication Between the HoloLens and the LMC

The current version of the LMC needs to be physically connected to a computer using a USB cable to provide enough power to infrared LEDs and to enable fast enough data transfer. For the HoloLens, the only physical ports are a 3.5 mm audio jack and a Micro-USB 2.0 port. Unfortunately, only use the Micro-USB port can currently to install and debug applications, charge, and access the Device Portal. Therefore, the built-in processing unit of the HoloLens cannot be used directly with the LMC and a separate computer is needed to allow the LMC to stream data wirelessly to the HoloLens. As shown in Fig. 1, the LMC was attached on top of the HoloLens using some sticky paste. The LMC was not fixed vertically but with an angle of 45° to enable gesture tracking within the field of view of the HoloLens and to track the hands at the chin or chest level. The inclination of the LMC allows thus better covering this area.

Fig. 1. The LMC is attached on the top of the HoloLens and connected to a computer

To exchange data between the LMC and the HoloLens, the UDP protocol was chosen due to its lightness and high speed. Figure 2 shows the architecture of the developed communication tool, with an external computer as a medium to transfer and process data between the LMC and the HoloLens. In practice, HoloLens works as a server and the PC as a client. Initially, the HoloLens IP address is determined and then used by the client to send its first message to the server. The server in turn retrieves the client's IP address, allowing client-server communication. In our implementation, the LMC SDK is used to capture the fingertips' position at each frame. As long as a new frame is generated, it will be sent to the server (HoloLens). On the client side, the messages are received/sent in different threads. This allows the client to listen to the channel while sending a message. Similarly, on the server side a unity event is invoked to reply to the message sent by the client. This architecture allows synchronized and real-time communication between the LMC and the HoloLens.

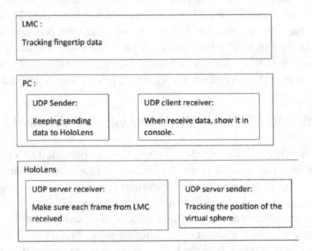

Fig. 2. Communication architecture between the HoloLens and the LMC

4   Calibration Procedure

The main idea of the calibration procedure is to get the coordinates of the same points in different coordinate systems. After careful consideration, we choose fingertips of one hand as the detecting points because fingertips are easy to access from the LMC. The second hand is used to click on the hololens controller once the alignment between the finger and the marker point is completed. This triggers the recording of data. Indeed, fingers can move flexibly and be detected easily by the LMC. The entire calibration process is summarized as follows and will be detailed in the next subsections:

1. Detect the position of a fingertip and get the coordinates from the LMC.
2. Attach a virtual plane to a real plane (either a desk or a wall).
3. Coincide the fingertip with marked points on the plane.
4. The HoloLens records the coordinates of the marked points and the LMC records the fingertip simultaneously. Send the two coordinates to the computer.

5. After collecting a set of points, analyze the data and compute the rigid transformation.
6. Use the computed transformation to change the coordinates of the LMC points in the HoloLens coordinate frame and display in the HoloLens. Compare the error between the virtual and the real points.

4.1 3D Points Collection

As shown in Fig. 3, to collect 3D points, we developed a simple application on Unity3D where we display a calibration plane with six small balls embedded (what we called above the marked points). The data collected from the LMC is displayed in the middle of the plane.

Fig. 3. Calibration plane

The whole plane is attached with a "Taptoplace" function. The HoloLens provides spatial mapping allowing to understand the environment. Users can use the cursor to tap on the plane to move it according to the surroundings (see Fig. 4). The virtual plane must be placed according to the real world, so that it can help users accurately determining the position of their fingertip.

Fig. 4. "Taptoplace" according to the spatial mapping

According to the principle of camera projection, the HoloLens will project three-dimensional objects on a two-dimensional screen in front of the user's eyes. Hence, some points with different 3D coordinates will have the same 2D coordinates on the screen.

We need to use a real object because in this way we can compute the exact spatial coordinate by querying the depth information given by the coordinate in the Z-axis direction. Two buttons are displayed on the plane. The button on the right is a "change button": clicking on it will change the rotation of the calibration plane from horizontal to vertical and vice-versa.

The aim of this button is to make the plane compatible with both vertical and horizontal surfaces in the real world.

Once the user fixes the virtual plane according to the real world as shown in Fig. 5 (in this case we attached it to a computer screen), the HoloLens creates a spatial anchor in the world coordinate frame. Therefore, the user can get the relative position between the HoloLens camera and the virtual plane in real time. The button on the middle is a "send button". Clicking on it will allow the HoloLens to send data for calibration. After the first tap, one marked point (blue ball) will turn red.

Fig. 5. Changing the rotation of the plane and attaching it to a physical surface (Color figure online)

The user positions one fingertip, for example the thumb, on this point (see Fig. 6). If he/she clicks on the send button, both the coordinates of the ball from the HoloLens and the coordinates of the fingertip from the LMC will be sent to the computer. Another ball on the plane will then become red. This operation is done for each point. To help clicking on the buttons, a cursor always appears in the middle of the field of view and can be moved by moving the head. Clicks are performed using the HoloLens built-in clicker, not to affect point collection by the LMC.

Fig. 6. 3D points acquisition from HoloLens and LMC (Color figure online)

4.2 Calibration Approach

Once data collection is complete, we get two points clouds in two different frames (see Fig. 7). The first one is collected by the HoloLens, we name it the "reference point cloud", while the second one is collected by the LMC, we name it the "source point cloud". The relationship between these two point clouds is given by:

$$\begin{pmatrix} H_x \\ H_y \\ H_z \end{pmatrix} = R \cdot \begin{pmatrix} L_x \\ L_y \\ L_z \end{pmatrix} + t \tag{1}$$

The transformation matrix is composed of two parts: a Translation vector (t) and a Rotation matrix (R). The problem is to find the transformation matrix between both point clouds, knowing that the point clouds should be aligned. Several algorithms have been proposed in past work. In our case, we compared two algorithms. We will not focus on specific mathematical calculation, we will only briefly introduce their principle here. Please note that the first paragraph of a section or subsection is not indented. The first paragraphs that follows a table, figure, equation etc. does not have an indent, either. Subsequent paragraphs, however, are indented.

The first method is the Umeyama algorithm [10]. We denote the reference points as $\{H_i\}$ and the source points as $\{L_i\}$, $i = 1, 2, \cdots, n$. The problem is to find the similarity transformation parameters (R and t) giving the minimum value of the mean squared error $\varepsilon^2(R, t)$ of these two point clouds:

$$\varepsilon^2(R, t) = \frac{1}{n} \cdot \sum_{i=1}^{n} ||H_i - (R.L_i + t)||^2 \tag{2}$$

However, we soon discovered that this algorithm causes large errors. In fact, with this method, the result is obtained through many mathematical transformations due to the coordinate matrices $\{H_i\}$ and $\{L_i\}$. This method requires that the point's coordinates be very accurate. It only works when the two coordinate groups can be perfectly matched. Since the coordinates are collected manually, errors obviously occur that must be taken into account in the transformation calculation. Another choice to align two point clouds

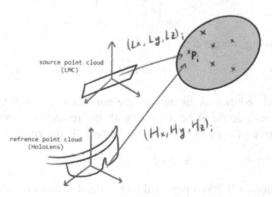

Fig. 7. The points cloud defined in the HoloLens end LMC reference frames

is the Iterative Closest Point (ICP) algorithm [12]. The principle of this algorithm is to find the closest points of the source point cloud in the reference point cloud. The whole algorithm is performed by multiple iterations, in which the points with larger errors are excluded. The algorithm steps are:

1. Find the closest points of the source point cloud (collected by the LMC), match them in the reference cloud (collected by the HoloLens).
2. Use a root mean square metric minimization technique to estimate a transform matrix, which will best align each source point to its match, found in the previous step. This step may also involve rejecting outliers prior to alignment.
3. Transform the source points using the obtained transformation matrix and repeat the steps until a defined threshold is reached.

This algorithm has some limitations. First, in order to match the source cloud to the reference cloud, we should know approximately the position of the reference cloud. Otherwise, finding the nearest point will be impacted. It means that before applying the algorithm, the source cloud should be transformed as close as possible to the reference cloud. Because of the arrangement of the two reference frames as shown in Fig. 8, we have to preprocess the source point coordinates (L_i) so that they are closer to the reference coordinates (H_i). The solution is to apply a rotation matrix:

Fig. 8. HoloLens and LMC coordinate reference systems

$$r = \begin{bmatrix} -1 & 0 & 0 \\ 0 & 0 & -1 \\ 0 & 1 & 0 \end{bmatrix} \tag{3}$$

After preprocessing, we get L_i':

$$L_i' = r \cdot L_i \tag{4}$$

L_i' can be considered then as the new source point cloud, it only needs to be rotated with a relatively small angle to be aligned with the reference point cloud. The new transformation matrix (R', t) can be found using the ICP algorithm, where:

$$H_i = R' \cdot L_i' + t = R' \cdot r.L_i \tag{5}$$

The second limitation of ICP is a practical one. Indeed, when the number of 3D points increases, the probability of errors becomes greater. The best solution is then to limit the number of points and ensure that most of them are on different planes with different depths according to the Z axis. Figure 9 gives an example of twelve reference points, which are located approximately in the same plane.

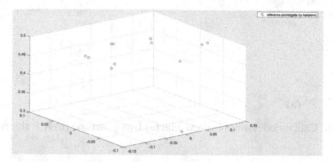

Fig. 9. Example of collected points

One point that is a little bit far from the others is displayed and is considered as wrong. In the current collection process, we can collect multiple points at a fixed distance, then change the distance between the HoloLens and the virtual object (just move the head closer to the virtual plane) to continue collecting points.

4.3 Calibration Results

First, we compared the results of our method with the naïve approach that uses raw LMC data without taking calibration into account. The finger positions provided by the LMC and projected into the HoloLens reference frame are far away and do not match the real hand. This baseline error measurement clearly shows the need of a space coordinates transformation and quantify on the initial mismatch magnitude. Figures (10-a) and (10-b) show the results obtained by the Umeyama and the ICP algorithms when processing the same data set. With Umeyama, we get a mean error of 0.0869 m while with ICP we get a mean error of 0.0189 m. It can be seen that because of some errors while collecting the data, there are two points that have a large deviation. ICP can limit their impact, while Umeyama is easily affected with a larger estimation error.

4.4 Error Analysis

After calibration, we used the obtained transformation matrix to mark the hand position in the HoloLens screen. We represent the fingertips of the index finger and the thumb by two red balls. As shown in Fig. 11, there are misalignment errors, especially when the hand is not parallel to the vertical plane. However, we have improved previous existing works like [8] where the translation error reported by the author is roughly a 4.5 cm along the z-axis; while our approach gives an error of about 1.8 cm. In our case the main factor affecting the registration accuracy is human behavior. All the points are collected manually and using the user's fingertips as reference. During this process, deviations are unavoidable. The spatial mapping provided by the HoloLens also presents deviation

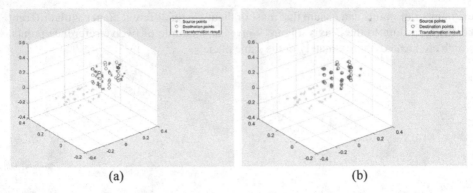

Fig. 10. Calibration results obtained with (a) Umeyama and (b) ICP algorithms

compared to the real environment, especially when the interaction distance is close. This error cannot be ignored. The accuracy limits of the LMC can be another reason. According to past work, the LMC cannot reach a theoretical accuracy of 0.01 mm in real conditions, but a high precision (an overall average accuracy of 0.7 mm) for gesture-based interaction is still possible [11].

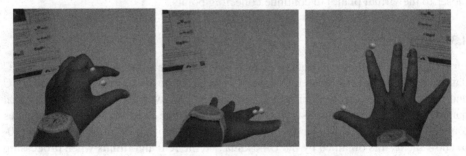

Fig. 11. Registration errors (Color figure online)

5   Free-Hand Interaction

To demonstrate the feasibility of natural interactions in MR environment using LMC data, we implemented intuitive hand-based interaction techniques in the HoloLens environment. These interactions are not proposed for given scenarios, but are chosen to explore simple interaction metaphors allowing virtual object manipulation. The aim is to quickly set up a user evaluation to test the proposed method's ease-of-use. We thus used the 3D coordinates of the fingertips and the center point of the left hand to define three manipulation techniques:

Select by touch: When the index finger collides with the virtual cube in the HoloLens coordinates frame, the cube is selected, and its color changes to green (see Fig. 12).

Fig. 12. Select and move a virtual cube with free hand (Color figure online)

Translate: To move the selected object, the thumb and index finger of the hand must touch each other. To drop the object it simply needs to separate the two fingers.

Rotate: The selected virtual object is rotated according to the 3D rotation of the left hand (Fig. 13). For that, we use the coordinates of the five detected fingertips and the center of the hand to estimate the plane corresponding to the palm of the hand. Finally, the normal to this plane is computed, which defines the 3D rotation applied to the virtual object when the hand rotates.

Fig. 13. Rotate a plane according to the rotation of the hand

In order to evaluate the usability of our free-hand interaction approach, we carried out different pre-experiences. We defined the interaction space above a 120 cm × 80 cm table. The user sat in front of the table wearing a HoloLens. An LMC mounted on the front of the HoloLens, facing down, allows the detection of the user's hands in his vision field.

We showed the user four virtual cubes in the AR scene with different sizes and depths (Fig. 14). The considered sizes are, respectively: 0.1 m, 0.05 m, 0.025 m and 0.01 m. We asked the user to select the different cubes in turn using his index finger, move them around and place them on the table. We found that the interaction with the three largest cubes is done correctly. However, when trying to touch the smallest one, we face difficulties, which is quite normal; as the positioning of the cube in the HoloLens mixed reality environment has a theoretical error in the range between 0.01 m and 0.02 m.

The second experiment consisted in selecting a cube and rotating it in all directions using the Rotate interaction metaphor. We found that the user could rotate the virtual object placed on his hand in a natural and intuitive way. This is explained by the fact that the user performs a physical gesture in accordance with the direct manipulation done on the virtual object. Indeed, the mental load of users is reduced when their gestures reflect real-world metaphors that allow them to use the most intuitive gestures they desire.

Fig. 14. The usability evaluation

Finally, a qualitative evaluation was carried out. Its purpose was to compare the ease and comfort of use between the proposed approaches and the baseline scheme (HoloLens integrated interaction). We have found that overall the interactions that we propose are less tiring and require less effort and concentration, they can be repeated several times over a long period without generating handling errors or hand fatigue. This is not the case with the baseline scheme.

6 Discussion

The HoloLens has its own process without using external devices, which provides a stable and fast AR rendering experience. Its spatial mapping is the basis for our calibration procedure. From the results we got, it can be concluded that the combination of the two devices can provide enhanced results in terms of free-hand interaction in MR environments. However, this study has also allowed us to identify some difficulties:

1. According to the official documentation on the HoloLens, the best distance interval to display AR objects in the HoloLens is between 1.25 m and 5 m. When a user wants to use his/her hand to interact, the operating area is always limited to 1.25 m.
2. The field of view of the HoloLens is not very large. It is hard to show many contents in a close range. In other words, the range of activity of the hand is very small. Moreover, the HoloLens screen consists in two separated screens which are located in front of the left and right eyes. When observing close-range objects, it can be difficult for users to combine the projections of both screens due to the change of the focal length of the eyes, which causes severe ghosting.
3. The performance of the HoloLens spatial mapping at close range is not very stable, misjudgments or instability occur frequently. Although the physical location of the LMC relative to the HoloLens is fixed, due to individual differences of user's 'eyes, calibration needs to be performed for each user.

7 Conclusion

In this study, we introduced free-hand interaction in mixed reality environments combining a HoloLens and an LMC. Two main issues have been solved. The first one concerns the real-time 3D points acquisition from the two devices. For that, we attached a virtual plane with several balls used as reference points to a real object. This idea allowed us to acquire 3D points in the HoloLens reference frame and their corresponding points in the LMC reference frame. The second issue is calibration. We used the ICP algorithm to compute the transformation matrix between both frames. The obtained registration error is about 1 cm, which is quite acceptable to realize basic interaction. Finally, first experiments carried out proved the viability of the proposed free-hand interactions and their interest to improve the sensation of presence in MR environments.

Future work will include improvement of the accuracy of our solution by using additional depth sensors like a Kinect. Another interesting possibility would be to implement the whole 3D model of the hand in the HoloLens environment in order to develop more complex and natural free-hand interactions.

References

1. Aruanno, B., Garzotto, F., Rodriguez, M.C.: Hololens-based mixed reality experiences for subjects with alzheimer's disease. In: Proceedings of the 12th Biannual Conference on Italian SIGCHI Chapter, CHItaly (2017), pp. 15:1–15:9, (2017)
2. Benko, B., Jota, R., Wilson, A.: Miragetable: freehand interaction on a projected augmented reality tabletop. In: Proceedings of the 2012 ACM Annual Conference on Human Factors in Computing Systems, pp. 199–208 (2012)
3. Blaha, J., Gupta, M.: Diplopia: a virtual reality game designed to help amblyopics. In: 2014 IEEE Virtual Reality (VR), pp. 163–164 (2014)
4. Carceroni, R.L., Brown, C.M.: Numerical methods for model-based pose recovery. Technical Report 659, University of Rochester, Computer Science Department (1997)
5. Ens, B., Quigley, A., Yeo, H.-S., Irani, P., Piumsomboon, T., Billinghurst, M.: Counterpoint: exploring mixed-scale gesture interaction for AR applications. In: Proceedings of the 2018, CHI Conference on Human Factors in Computing Systems (2018)
6. Garon, M., Boulet, P., Doironz, J., Beaulieu, L., Lalonde, J.: Real-time high resolution 3d data on the hololens. In: 2016 IEEE International Symposium on Mixed and Augmented Reality (ISMAR-Adjunct), pp. 189–191 (2016)
7. Khademi, M., Mousavi Hondori, H., McKenzie, A., Dodakian, L., Lopes, C.V., Cramer, S.C.: Free-hand interaction with leap motion controller for stroke rehabilitation. In: Proceedings of the Extended Abstracts of the 32nd Annual ACM Conference on Human Factors in Computing Systems, CHI EA 2014, pp. 1663–1668 (2014)
8. Köhler, N.: Integration of a leap motion controller with the hololens to enable improved gesture interactions. Master's thesis, Aalto University (2017)
9. Lyons, D.M.: System and method for permitting three-dimensional navigation through a virtual reality environment using camera-based gesture inputs (2001)
10. Umeyama, S.: Least-squares estimation of transformation parameters between two point patterns. IEEE Trans. Patt. Anal. Mach. Intell. 13(4), 376–380 (1991)
11. Weichert, F., Bachmann, D., Rudak, B., Fisseler, D.: Analysis of the accuracy and robustness of the leap motion controller. Sensors 13(5), 6380–6393 (2013)
12. Zhang, Z.: Iterative point matching for registration of free-form curves and surfaces. Int. J. Comput. Vision 13(2), 119–152 (1994)

Mixed Reality Annotations System for Museum Space Based on the UWB Positioning and Mobile Device

YanXiang Zhang[✉] and Yutong Zi

Department of Communication of Science and Technology,
University of Science and Technology of China, Hefei, Anhui, China
petrel@ustc.edu.cn, yvtongzi@mail.ustc.edu.cn

Abstract. In this research, the authors designed a mixed reality annotations system based on UWB positioning and mobile device, which is a low-cost innovative solution especially for wide range of indoor environments. This design can be targeted to solve the problem of low investment in museums in most parts of the developing country and large visitor flow during holidays. The position of the visitor is obtained through the UWB antenna tag which was attached on smartphones. The gyroscope data and focal length was also used to keep virtual camera and real camera consistent and virtual space's calibration. The system can ensure that when there is a large flow of people, visitors can watch the multimedia annotation of exhibits on their phones during the queuing far away from the exhibits. The types of annotation are mainly video, 3D model and audio. In China, many museums have the function of science education. A rich form of annotation can enhances this functionality. At last, we compare and analyze the localization advantage of this system (to solve the problem of congestion and shortage of funds), and recruited 10 volunteers to experience system. We find that this system can achieve the exact matching standard when the visitors are 0.75 –1 m away from the exhibits, while when the visitors are more than 3 m away from the exhibits, it has the advantages that other systems cannot have, such as playing and watching videos when they cannot get close to the exhibits due to crowding. This system provides a new solution for the application of MR in large indoor area and updated the exhibition of museum.

Keywords: Mixed reality · Wide-area indoor positioning · Ultra-wideband tracking · Multimedia annotations · Museum · Science education

1 Introduction

First of all, we want to clarify the background of this system. China is a country with a long history, rich and diverse folk culture, and great cultural differences between different regions. Therefore, almost every city has its own folk culture museum, and the number of museums in China is very large. These museums have become major tourist destinations during the holidays. As a result, crowds make it necessary for visitors to

© Springer Nature Switzerland AG 2020
L. T. De Paolis and P. Bourdot (Eds.): AVR 2020, LNCS 12242, pp. 328–342, 2020.
https://doi.org/10.1007/978-3-030-58465-8_25

queue for a long time to see the hottest exhibit, some visitors even have no chance to learn about it. So, this is a very urgent and difficult problem. Everyone hopes to enrich his knowledge by visiting the museum. But in developing countries such as China, regional economic development is unbalanced. Not every museum has enough funds to buy expensive equipment, especially when there are a large number of visitors. It is unrealistic to guarantee that every visitor has VR equipment. Every visitor has the right to satisfy their desires and gain knowledge. Therefore, this paper intends to design an MR system that can be used on mobile phones, so that visitors can know about the exhibits in advance when they are far away from them, such as queuing. Or when visitors don't want to wait in line and can't get close to the exhibit, they can watch the multimedia annotations on their phones to make sure they won't miss the knowledge of it. The figure below show what happens during the holiday season. The whole museum is crowded and people are queuing up (Fig. 1).

Fig. 1. Crowds at the museum during holidays

As the "ideal virtual space with [sufficient] reality essential for communication", [1] MR is having both "virtual space" on the one hand and "reality" on the other available within the same visual display environment [2]. In the field of mixed reality, the most commonly used application technologies are HoloLens, SLAM and Magic Leap. HoloLens and Magic Leap is based on depth camera for environmental measurement tracking. HoloLens' scan range is 0.8–3.1 ms, [3] but after walking a long distance from the starting point, space mapping of the original starting position will disappear. Simultaneous localization and mapping (SLAM) allow building point clouds of the building interior with relation to the camera position [1, 4, 5]. It reconstructs the actual environment by acquiring data from the environment based on ground and wall reflections [6, 7]. For large-area space, it will collected for every single facility prior to being able to support AR based indoor navigation during use, which makes it difficult to run for a long time in the case of limited resources because of the huge data [8]. And it is also easier to generate perceptual aliasing problems [9]. All these technologies are more suitable for small areas.

Commonly used positioning technologies for a wide range of spaces are GPS and ultrasound. For example, Jihyun in 2008 proposed a markerless edge tracking AR called UMPC (Ultra Mobile Personal Computer), which integrates cameras, ultrasonic receivers and gyro sensors. This design can realize AR on mobile devices through edge recognition technology [10]. The downside is that it will bring a lot of computation. Francis et al. suggested an AR system for facility management proposed by using image-based indoor localization method, which estimates user's indoor location and direction by comparing user's view and building information modeling (BIM) based on learning calculation [11]. The image retrieval method attempted to find the image closest to the captured image from the database image, and a two-dimensional BIM image was created for the image database in the 3D BIM model of the building [6]. The Streetmuseum APP launched by the London Museum in 2010 uses GPS positioning technology to enable users to see augmented reality scenes in mobile devices [12]. However, the problem of the above research is the GPS positioning accuracy is low and it is easy to appear occlusion problem [13].

Museums are usually large-scale indoor spaces with complex structures [14]. A large number of exhibits will be placed in the pavilion, and the presence of the exhibit will divide the space. For a large-area museum that requires high-precision indoor positioning, we introduced a positioning method using UWB. UWB positioning is suitable for large and medium indoor scenes [15]. Cirulis verified the feasibility of UWB tracking as the solution for AR and VR Systems. He setup a 9×12 m room to test precision and validate the accuracy of the coordinate generator [16]. UWB positioning has high accuracy, which can reach centimeters and transmit position data in real time [17]. The UWB positioning system signal power is distributed over a very wide frequency band, which allows it to coexist with conventional radio without affecting its link quality. Therefore, in the case of multiple devices, the congestion problem of the commonly used frequency band can be effectively solved [18]. Mazhar came up with a design in 2017 called WDMA-UWB, which has been proven to solve the multiple access interference common in indoor precision positioning, such as offices with complex electromagnetic environments [19]. At the same time, UWB positioning has many advantages of low power consumption, security and penetration [20]. For narrow corridors, it has also been proven that it can be adapted with certain modifications [21].

Some researchers use UWB to achieve virtual and real fusion on the stage, but the article is a virtual fusion based on coordinate information on a two-dimensional plane [22].

Among other targeting methods, vision based model tracking is offered by Vuforia and VisionLib [23, 24]. The SDK is also a competitive alternative to the design. At the end of the article, we compared the differences between Vuforia and this system in detail through experiments. First of all, Vuforia is an AR tool, and its outstanding advantage is that it can perfectly display the details of 3D models in a close environment. This advantage is no longer dazzling when the visitors are 1 m away from the exhibits, and even cannot be recognized or works properly when the visitors are more than 3 m away from the exhibits. Vuforia can add to the beauty and richness of an exhibit when viewed up close, but the benefits of Vuforia aren't the right solution to the problem we're trying to solve. Compared with the multimedia annotation including audio and video in this system, Vuforia is only suitable for the 3D model. We want to solve the problem of letting visitors know about the exhibits when the museum is busy and crowded during holidays, and also need the system to enable visitors to view the annotation from a distance. In the face of these problems, Vuforia is not as good as this design [25].

So, this paper proposes a mixed reality technology system which positioning range is up to 300 m. The system uses Unity to establish a 1:1 physical model to deal with the occlusion relationship. UWB measured coordinate parameters, gyroscope angle data and user's mobile phone focal length are used to combine three-dimensional positioning of large indoor space.

2 System Design

The system consists of three modules - user module, positioning module, and scene module. The user module is the beginning and end of the system, because the data is collected and uploaded to the positioning module by the user module, and finally forms a closed loop. The data is processed as location information in the positioning module, and the consistency of the user location information with the virtual camera location information is the basic principle that the MR can be implemented in this design. The following figure shows how the system works (Fig. 2).

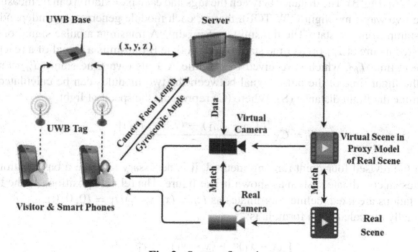

Fig. 2. System flow chart

The position data includes (1) three-dimensional coordinate parameters (x, y, z) provided by UWB (2) gyroscope angle parameters (3) user's mobile phone focal length parameter.

2.1 Principle of Space Ranging

This article uses the UWB Mini3sPlus development board developed by YCHIOT, a company in Wenzhou, Zhejiang, China. The communication distance is up to 300 m.

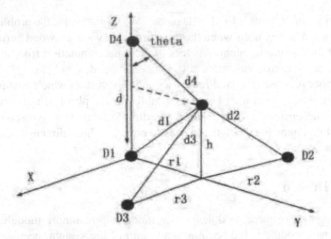

Fig. 3. 3D localization based on RSSI of 4 nodes

The positioning system requires four base stations and multiple tags. Tag coordinate values can be obtained by the two-way time-of-flight method and the modified four-point ranging method in a paper named Approach for 3D Localization Based on RSSI of 4 Nodes [26] (Fig. 3). The distance between the tags and each base station can be measured by the two way-time flight (TW-TOF), that is, each module generates an independent time stamp from the start. The transmitter of module A transmits a pulse signal of the requested nature at T_{a1} on its time stamp, and module B transmits a signal of a reactive nature at time T_{b2}, which is received by module A at its own time stamp T_{a2}. From this, the flight time of the pulse signal between the two modules can be calculated to determine the flight distance (S). Where (C) represents the speed of light.

$$S = C_X \frac{[(T_{a2} - T_{a1}) - (T_{b2} - T_{b1})]}{2} \qquad (1)$$

In the revised four-point ranging method, it is necessary to place a base station in a Cartesian coordinate system as shown in the figure. The relative positions of the four base stations are fixed, define coordinates as $D_i = (x_i, y_i, z_i) D_1 = (0, 0, 0)$.

Finally the calculation formula is:

$$\begin{cases} (x - x_1)^2 + (y - y_1)^2 = r_1^2 \\ (x - x_2)^2 + (y - y_2)^2 = r_2^2 \\ (x - x_3)^2 + (y - y_3)^2 = r_3^2 \end{cases} \qquad (2)$$

$$z = h = d - \frac{d_4^2 - d_1^2 + d^2}{2d} \qquad (3)$$

In the process of solving the triangular centroid method, there are cases where the three circles cannot be crossed by two due to the distance error. At this time, the imaginary solution is ignored and only the real solution with $x \geq 0$ is used as the positioning result.

2.2 Measurement and Positioning of Physical Space

In this design, the physical space we use is an art gallery. The venue faces south and the long side is east-west. The entrance of the venue is set on the south side wall, and the other three walls are adorned with exhibits. This space can be simplified into a cube 771 cm long, 443 cm wide and 277 cm high. The figures below show a photo and a top view of the gallery (Fig. 4).

Fig. 4. Photo of the gallery

According to the actual physical space, we have established a proxy 3D model as shown. We placed the UWB ranging base station at the northernmost end of the east wall, height is 150 cm (D2). The southernmost end of the east wall, height is 150 cm (D3). The middle of the bottom of the west wall, height is 150 cm (D1). And the 1.5 m directly above D1 (D4). Create a Cartesian coordinate system with D1 as the origin. Because the left-handed coordinate system is used in Unity, in order to ensure that the physical space coincides with the virtual space, we also define the coordinate system as the same left-handed coordinate system as Unity when using UWB ranging. The following figures show the mobile phone we use during the experiment, and the positioning of the UWB base station (Fig. 5, Fig. 6 and Fig. 7).

Fig. 5. Tag is pasted on the phone

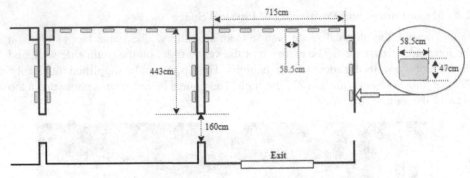

Fig. 6. Top view of the gallery

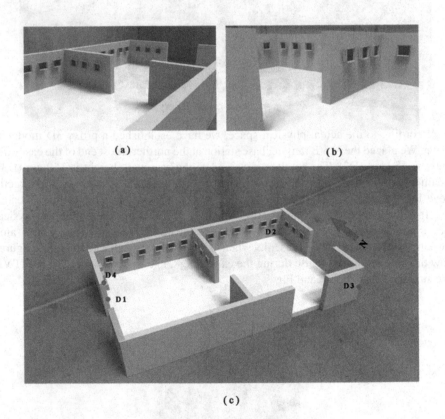

(a)   (b)

(c)

Fig. 7. 3D model of the gallery

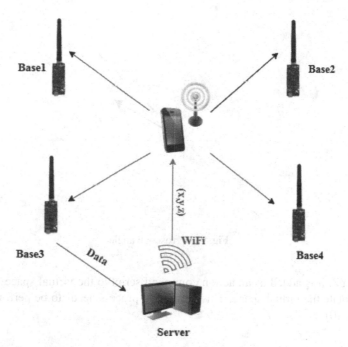

Fig. 8. Location data acquisition model

2.3 Acquisition, Calculation, and Propagation of Positioning Coordinates

As shown in the figure above, in the UWB positioning system, we set up 4 base stations to determine the coordinate position of the tag. We need to connect one of the base stations to the server, and the server can calculate the distance measurement information into position coordinates (x, y, z). In addition to calculating coordinates, the server here also has the function of a location broadcaster. The user's mobile phone can receive the location information data broadcast by the server through Wi-Fi, so that the real-time location data can be transmitted to the mobile phone. This also makes it possible to retrieve location data by writing scripts (Fig. 8).

2.4 Establishment of Low-Resolution Proxy Model and Alignment with Virtual and Real Space

In order to ensure that the MR annotations are not misplaced, the orientation of the virtual space axes needs to be consistent with the direction of the real room. Different from AR which does not reflect the perspective relationship, in order to realize the MR with perspective function, we need to correct the direction of the coordinate axis of the virtual space in the unity system in real time (Fig. 9).

The raw output data format of the gyroscope in the smartphone is AdcGyroXZ, AdcGyroYZ read by the ADC, which represent the corners of the projection of the vector R (actually the direction of the smartphone) in the XZ and YZ planes, respectively. After the two data are retrieved and compensated to obtain the negative value of AdcGyroXZ,

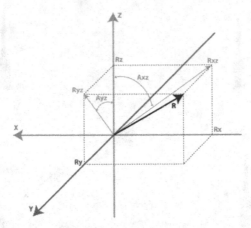

Fig. 9. Gyroscope angle

AdcGyroYZ, it is added as an action command script to the virtual space axis built in unity to rotate the virtual space. This correction process needs to be performed in real time (Fig. 10).

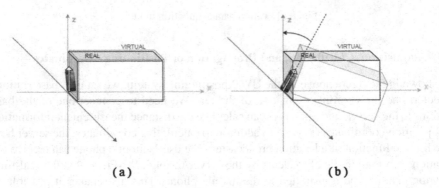

(a)   (b)

Fig. 10. Angle correction

2.5 Keep the Virtual Camera in Sync with the Real Camera

In 2.4, we have achieved the coincidence of real space and virtual space. On the basis of the above, the script is called to transfer the UWB location information transmitted to the phone to the Unity, and bind it as an action command to the virtual camera. At the same time, we also need to retrieve the angle data measured by the gyroscope in real time in the user's mobile phone to understand the orientation of the mobile phone camera. After the user installs it on the phone, it can synchronize the virtual camera with the real camera (Fig. 11).

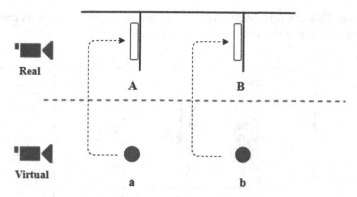

Fig. 11. Keep the virtual camera in sync with the real camera

2.6 Multimedia Annotations

The forms of annotations include text, video, images, and 3D models. In order to ensure that visitors can still learn about the exhibits at a distance, we put a large number of videos in the design. The details of annotation types are 50% for video, 30% for 3D models, 15% for pictures, and 5% for audio and text. When the visitor walks to the exhibit, they can play the video by tapping the play button on the screen. For some ancient artifacts with severe weathering corrosion, authors can reproduce their original form through 3D modeling,this is also a way to revitalize ancient artifacts. Of course, these 3D models are designed to be large to make sure it's easy to see. To ensure that there is no overlap or visual confusion between the 3D models, we will leave each annotation at a distance, or only annotate the popular exhibits that are more prone to congestion, so that people will not miss the knowledge contained in the popular exhibits when they are in line or unable to get close to them.

2.7 Occlusion Relationship Processing and Rendering Synthesis

The establishment of a virtual model in Unity can be used to solve the occlusion relationship. In the museum, the walls will play a role in dividing the space and blocking the view. Therefore, in the actual scene, when the visitor is in position (A), he should only see the annotation of the exhibit on the same side (a), and should not see the annotation (b) of the exhibit on the other side of the wall. The 1:1 modeling for real physical space in Unity can achieve this effect. The (a) can be seen when the visitor is in position (A) because the background of (a) is transparent during rendering (set to alpha channel). This is to combine the annotation (a) with the realistic scene captured by the mobile phone through rendering. At this time, the visitor cannot see (b) on the other side of the wall. This is because during the rendering process, the virtual model (wall) created is set to the alpha channel and acts as a mask to block the virtual camera. Therefore, visitors will not see (a) and (b) at the same time. Which follow the occlusion relationship and the perspective principle in the real space. When the annotation is a video, the play button does not appear when it is occluded. The video can only be placed by clicking the play button when the visitor moves to a position where there is no occlusion relationship with the annotation. This can effectively avoid sound interference, and visitors can actively choose whether to watch the video during the visit (12).

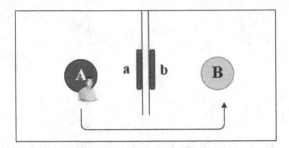

Fig. 12. When visitors are touring

3   Results and Application

When the visitor pastes the tag on the phone and installs the apk, it can synchronize the reality camera with the virtual camera. When visitors walk in the museum and face the camera towards the exhibits, because of the occlusion relationship processing and rendering synthesis, they can see the annotations that are transparent to the background of the same side exhibit, but won't see the annotations on the other side of the wall. This is because authors simulated a virtual model in Unity to describe the spatial barrier relationship. Through mask rendering, you can restore the basic situation that people's vision is obscured by objects in the real world. When visitor walks from one room to another (from A to B), only (b) can be seen. The rendering result of the MR annotation in the real environment conforms to the occlusion relationship of the real physical space. The figure below shows an MR annotation of the exhibit. These multimedia annotations enable the museum to display the scientific knowledge contained in the exhibits more vividly, so as to carry out science education work better (Fig. 13).

Fig. 13. The annotation of exhibit

4 Conclusions and Discussion

This design focus on the MR in special application scenario, which mainly support for wide range of indoor spaces. Especially for the situation as line up to see the museum's popular exhibits during the holiday and the pavilion is too crowded to get close to the exhibits. The UWB-based positioning method can avoid signal occluded often appearing in ultrasound and GPS. At the same time, the positioning accuracy is higher, the cost is lower, and it can support more users. Rich forms of annotation make the introduction of exhibits more comprehensive and enhance the function of museums as places of science education.

Similar comparisons and tests were conducted to ensure that the system could meet the localization function of high visitor flow and low funding for museums in developing countries. First, we compare the cost of the system with other AR/MR equipment. The application scope of this system is up to 300 m, which can be satisfied by arranging 1 or 2 pieces in each museum. The price of a single basic system is about RMB 3,000, the mobile phone is for tourists to bring. The system is relatively simple and maintenance costs are low. Compared with HoloLens (price for each set is 20000–50000 RMB) and Magic Leap (price for each set is about 30000 RMB). This system has a relatively obvious price advantage, thus easy to popularize.

After that, we conducted two sets of experiments to test the accuracy of the system when visitors are close to the exhibits and the advantage degree when visitors are far away from the exhibits. We recruited 10 experiencers to test the tracking accuracy and experience of the system. According to the test1 (Fig. 14), when the distance between the person and the exhibit is more than 1.5 m, the accuracy can reach more than 99.9%. When the distance is 0.75–1.5 m, the accuracy of the system meets the viewing requirements. The following figure shows the feedback of the subjects when they are at different distances from the exhibits. We use green to indicate that the subject feels comfortable and it is the appropriate distance, yellow to indicate that it is the most comfortable and optimal distance, and gray to indicate that it is not comfortable to see at this distance. Different colors can show the optimal distance distribution more intuitively.

	Distance from exhibits					
	<0.50m	0.50m–0.75m	0.76m–1.00m	1.01m–1.50m	1.51m–2.00m	>2.00m
Subject 1	fit	fit	best	fit	fit	fit
Subject 2	fit	best	fit	fit	fit	fit
Subject 3	fit	fit	best	fit	fit	fit
Subject 4	Not fit	fit	fit	best	fit	fit
Subject 5	fit	fit	fit	best	fit	fit
Subject 6	fit	fit	best	fit	fit	fit
Subject 7	fit	fit	best	fit	fit	fit
Subject 8	Not fit	fit	best	fit	fit	fit
Subject 9	fit	fit	best	fit	fit	fit
Subject 10	fit	fit	best	fit	fit	fit

Fig. 14. User test feedback (Color figure online)

In the test2 (Fig. 15), we arranged the 10 subjects to simulate the queuing situation. Use this system to watch a 3-min video annotation of an exhibit when it is more than 3 meters away from it. The following figure shows the feedback of the subjects' viewing experience. In the simulated queue to see the exhibits, all 10 subjects said they saw clear videos. Almost all the subjects were satisfied with the screen size, but Subject5 said he thought it would be better if the phone had a larger screen. All subjects said that they learned about the exhibits by watching the video, and many subjects said that this could relieve anxiety in queuing. To sum up, the feedback is that the system performs well in the sense of experience and adaptability. SDK like Vuforia and VisionLib cannot realize that. This is also the outstanding advantage of the system.

	Whether the video is clear	Whether the screen size is comfort when viewing	Did you learn more about the exhibits by watching the videos?	Whether it alleviates the anxiety of waiting in line
Subject1	Yes	Yes	Yes	Yes
Subject2	Yes	Yes	Yes	Yes
Subject3	Yes	Yes	Yes	Yes
Subject4	Yes	Yes	Yes	Yes
Subject5	Yes	No(Note: Small)	Yes	No(do not help much)
Subject6	Yes	Yes	Yes	Yes
Subject7	Yes	Yes	Yes	No(do not help much)
Subject8	Yes	Yes	Yes	Yes
Subject9	Yes	Yes	Yes	Yes
Subject10	Yes	Yes	Yes	No(do not help much)

Fig. 15. The viewing experience in a distant context

This design supports more multimedia types of annotations. Compared with traditional two-dimensional annotations based on words and pictures in the museum, it has stronger cross-cultural communication ability. The form of higher interactivity can also better stimulate visitors' interest in visiting. Unmarked MR can solve the problems caused by the surge in museum visits during the holidays. In a crowded environment, only visitors close to the exhibit can read the annotated panels or scan the AR markers, while for those who are far away, the annotations on the panels lose their actual communication and annotation value.

There are still some unresolved issues and deficiencies in this design. Initialization needs to be done for specific context, and the UWB positioning system has a certain positional error (less than 5 cm). So this only targeted to solve the problem of crowding in a large area of indoor environment, it is not suitable for small exhibits and super close viewing. When the area is economically developed enough for the museum to increase investment, more expensive equipment can be used to enhance the visiting experience.

Acknowledgements. The work is supported by Ministry of Education (China) Humanities and Social Sciences Research Foundation under Grant No.: 19A10358002.

References

1. Bajura, M., Fuchs, H., Ohbuchi, R.: Merging virtual objects with the real world: seeing ultrasound imagery within the patient. Comput. Graphics **26**(2), 203–210 (1992)
2. Milgram, P., Kishio, F.: A taxonomy of mixed reality visual displays. IEICE Trans. Inf. Syst. **77**(12), 1321–1329 (1994)
3. Adam, T.: Introduction to the HoloLens, Part 2: Spatial Mapping. https://docs.microsoft.com/en-us/archive/msdn-magazine/2017/january/hololens-introduction-to-the-hololens-part-2-spatial-mapping
4. Borrmann, D., et al.: A mobile robot based system for fully automated thermal 3D mapping. Adv. Eng. Inf. **28**(4), 425–440 (2014)
5. Fraundorfer, F., et al.: Vision-based autonomous mapping and expLoRation using a quadrotor MAV. In: Proceedings IROS 2012, pp. 45574564 (2012)
6. Shin, T., Roh, B. H.: Component mapping method for indoor localization system based on mixed reality. In: 2019 Eleventh International Conference on Ubiquitous and Future Networks (ICUFN), pp. 379–383 . IEEE, July 2019
7. Munoz-Montoya, F., Juan, M.C., Mendez-Lopez, M., Fidalgo, C.: Augmented reality based on SLAM to assess spatial short-term memory. IEEE Access **7**, 2453–2466 (2018)
8. Bae, H., Golparvar-Fard, M., White, J.: High-precision vision-based mobile augmented reality system for context-aware architectural engineering construction and facility management (AEC/FM) applications. Visual. Eng. **1**(1), 1–13 (2013)
9. Hashemifar, Z.S., Adhivarahan, C., Balakrishnan, A., Dantu, K.: Augmenting Visual SLAM with Wi-Fi Sensing For Indoor Applications. arXiv preprint arXiv:1903.06687 (2019).
10. Oh, J., Lee, M.H., Park, H., Park, J.I., Kim, J.S., Son, W.: Efficient mobile museum guidance system using augmented reality. In: 2008 IEEE International Symposium on Consumer Electronics, pp. 1–4, IEEE, April 2008
11. Baeka, F., Ha, I., Kim, H.: Augmented reality system for facility management using image-based indoor localization. Autom. Const. **99**, 18–26 (2019)
12. Chun, Qi.: Digital Museum Application Research Based on Mixed Reality Technology (Master's thesis, Tianjin University) (2018). (In Chinese) https://kns.cnki.net/KCMS/detail/detail.aspx?dbcode=CMFD&dbname=CMFD201901&filename=1019702184.nh)
13. White, M., et al.: ARCO-an architecture for digitization, management and presentation of virtual exhibitions. In: Proceedings Computer Graphics International, pp. 622–625. IEEE, July 2004
14. Huan, X.: Research on Construction and Roaming Technology of Mixed Reality Application System in Large-scale Indoor Space (Master's thesis, Shan Dong University) (2019). (In Chinese) https://kns.cnki.net/KCMS/detail/detail.aspx?dbcode=CMFD&dbname=CMFD201902&filename=1019055727.nh
15. Briso, C., Calvo, C., Xu, Y.: UWB propagation measurements and modelling in large indoor environments. IEEE Access **7**, 41913–41920 (2019)
16. Cirulis, A.: Ultra wideband tracking potential for augmented reality environments. In: International Conference on Augmented Reality, Virtual Reality and Computer Graphics, pp. 126–136, Springer, Cham, June 2019
17. Mazhar, F., Khan, M.G., Sällberg, B.: Precise indoor positioning using UWB: a review of methods, algorithms and implementations. Wireless Per. Commun. **97**(3), 4467–4491 (2017)
18. Kopta, V., Enz, C.C.: A 4-GHz low-power, multi-user approximate zero-IF FM-UWB transceiver for IoT. IEEE J. Solid-State Circuits **54**(9), 2462–2474 (2019)
19. Yin, Z., Jiang, X., Yang, Z., Zhao, N., Chen, Y.: WUB-IP: a high-precision UWB positioning scheme for indoor multiuser applications. IEEE Syst. J. **13**(1), 279–288 (2017)

20. Yang, L., Giannakis, G.B.: Ultra-wideband communications: an idea whose time has come. IEEE Signal Process. Mag. **21**(6), 26–54 (2004)
21. Liu, F., Wang, J., Zhang, J., Han, H.: An indoor localization method for pedestrians base on combined UWB/PDR/floor map. Sensors **19**(11), 2578 (2019)
22. Zhang, Y.Z., Shen, Y., Zhang, W.W., Zhu, Z.Q., Ma, P.F.: Interactive spatial augmented reality system for Chinese opera. In: ACM SIGGRAPH 2019 Posters (SIGGRAPH & apos2019). ACM, New York, NY, USA, Article 14, 2 p. (2019)
23. Puljiz, D., Riesterer, K.S., Hein, B., Kröger, T.: Referencing between a Head-Mounted Device and Robotic Manipulators. arXiv preprint arXiv:1904.02480(2019).
24. Puljiz, D., Hein, B.: Concepts for End-to-end Augmented Reality based Human-Robot Interaction Systems. arXiv preprint arXiv:1910.04494(2019).
25. https://vuforia.csdn.net/m/zone/vuforia/resources
26. Dai, C., Song, L., Yan, D.: Three-dimensional spatial localization algorithm based on four-node RSSI. Comput. Measure. Control. 24(1), 229–232. (2016) (In chinese)https://kns.cnki.net/KCMS/detail/detail.aspx?dbcode=CJFQ&dbname=CJFDLAST2016&filename=JZCK201601065)

A Glasses-Based Holographic Tabletop for Collaborative Monitoring of Aerial Missions

Bogdan Sikorski, Paolo Leoncini$^{(\boxtimes)}$, and Carlo Luongo

CIRA Italian Aerospace Research Centre, Capua, Italy
{b.sikorski,p.leoncini,c.luongo}@cira.it

Abstract. This paper describes the development of a HoloLens application for experimenting the ability to collaboratively monitor flight tests by a shared holographic-like tabletop approach. The situational awareness arising from a high sense of presence deriving from the glasses-based holographic representation of the flying scenario leads to effective decision making. Moreover, the optical see-through MR approach to in-site collaboration makes inter-person communication as easy as in the reality. Finally, the shared holographic representation virtually recreated in the in-between space among participants promises a visually coherent basis for "look here" collaboration style.

A flexible architecture is proposed for this application separating the core app from the data feeds for a slimmer development-deployment process, and technologies and data source to be used for the realization are reviewed.

Finally, the paper reports the results of experimental use of the system collected in a couple of flight tests held in our Center, and allows readers to draw a perspective pathway to future MR developments.

Keywords: Holographic immersive visualization · Collaboration · Shared mixed reality · Automatic Dependent Surveillance - Broadcast (ADS-B) · Air Traffic Control (ATC) · Air Traffic Management (ATM) · HoloLens · Open Sound Control (OSC)

1 Introduction

Tactical planning is a top-level, top-down strategic planning which requires a big-picture situational awareness of the complexity to manage. The strategic-tactical one constitutes the highest level of planning for a mission involving forces in the field (air, naval, ground vehicles, and humans) cooperating with a common goal under a central coordination.

Widely figurable in the military for high-level strategic situational awareness and issuing decisions down to field forces, this model could be applied in the civilian domain as well; to name a few, in firefighting [1] which is actually a war against the fire, and in Air Traffic Management. Strategic/tactical planning usually involves multiple persons, each with own specialization and authority, leveraging a key common understanding of the situation for taking the right decisions.

A representation in three-dimensional computer graphics of the territory and the arrangement of forces in the field, along with other graphic symbols representing relevant

© Springer Nature Switzerland AG 2020
L. T. De Paolis and P. Bourdot (Eds.): AVR 2020, LNCS 12242, pp. 343–360, 2020.
https://doi.org/10.1007/978-3-030-58465-8_26

data such as the weather conditions, visually summarize situations to decision makers in a complete and effective way, giving the possibility of in-depth detailed exploration by arbitrarily moving the point of view around the scene.

An effective approach to the big picture-style monitoring of air traffic around an airport could take advantage of modern see-through technology for holographic-style visualization. With this approach, one or more persons acting in the ATM/ATC decision process with maybe different roles or authority can look at a 3D terrain model of the area surrounding an airport and see geo-located representations of flying aircrafts, along with relevant aircraft info. Additionally, spatial graphics representations of meteorological conditions (turbulence, wind, etc.), relevant 3D ground obstacles, and additional info such e.g. as 4D agreed trajectories of the aircrafts might be added under users' specification to the 3D representation which is visualized in view-dependent way through the glasses displays in stereoscopic form (hologram). A synchronization mechanism ensures that participants view the same scene each in his/her own point of view, with the ability to freely move around it, zoom to reveal details, to command changes in the representations (e.g. zoom in/out, add or remove features) and to forward changes to the other participants. Vocal commands and finger pointing further contribute to raise the naturalness of the interaction.

Such a hologram-based collaborative, multi-user, big-picture approach enriches the situational awareness of the ATC team as it collects all relevant data into one single actively-updated representation, presented in a very intuitive way, and is shared among them. The several eyes looking at a common representation, with fluid non-mutually interfering intra-team communication, can more easily detect critical evolutions and conflicts of the managed situation. Last, yet not least important, such a system favors a rapid perception of the needed awareness of personnel in the current situation in case of "manual" management of critical situations, which, by anticipating the human role in the future automated ATM/ATC, might take a bit of time to tune in to the traffic situation.

Modern eXtended Reality technologies (Virtual Reality, Augmented Reality, and their mixed combination) allow the fruition of these three-dimensional graphic representations in an intuitive and natural way thanks to visual immersion, stereoscopic visualization and point of view tracking, as well as the possibility of sharing the experience among several people - even geographically distant. The immersive visualization in Virtual Reality (VR) provides a wide field of view but prevents collaborating people from seeing each other in the reality e.g. sharing gestural indications and other visual communication that cannot be easily represented in the simulated graphic environment. Conversely, Mixed Reality (MR) combines three-dimensional view-dependent representations in the user's visual space with the real view and the related communication possibilities with collaborators at the price of a less extensive graphic window compared to VR. Thus, the MR-style approach of holographic glasses exploits two key features:

- 6-DoF inside-out head tracking with respect to environment features (furniture, walls, desks, etc.) which resembles AR's pose estimation – e.g. two of more participants can look at the same hologram each by a different point of view;
- keeping the communication between the participating persons as natural as in the reality (they are able to see each other through the optical see-through screens, and

they can communicate verbally or gesturally, including the possibility to point out a feature in the 3D scene and the others can look at it).

The objective of the described research and related experimentation was to create a collaborative Mixed Reality environment, that we called Holographic Shared Tactical Tabletop (HSTT). The aim is to use it for monitoring an aircraft flight mission along with other active actors (e.g. other cooperating aircrafts or non-collaborative intruders) and passive constraints (no-fly zones, obstacles) of the mission within a three-dimensional graphic representation of the scenario. In the purposes of our aimed experience, we want to keep the user interface as simple as possible, so that for naturalness the recreated scenario occupies the holographic 3D space by alone. A limited number of voice command will suffice for users to interact with scenario content (show/hide features, zoom in/out the terrain tile extent, etc.).

2 Related Work

In recent years, other pilot and research experiences have been underway in the world both in military and civil areas on the topic of shared three-dimensional relief maps used as tactical tabletop scale model.

Su et al. [2] dealt with 3D holographic object registration for a shared augmented reality application with Microsoft HoloLens, and set up a sensor data-fusion framework for improving function's accuracy leveraging external sensors; based on this, they developed a shared augmented reality application supporting a mission-planning scenario using multiple holographic displays to illustrate details of a mission.

Chusetthagarn et al. [3] used the concept of Microsoft's HoloLens spatial anchors to create a collaborative AR environment that can work through the server in Holo-toolkits running under the Unity platform, and demonstrated collaborative AR in shared application for disaster management.

In [4], Kase and her co-authors developed a survey instrument, *Shared Augmented Reality Experience* (SARE), for conducting a user-based experiment collecting performance data. The assessment compared a HoloLens device to a traditional 2D flat screen display against performance metrics regarding an intelligence mission-planning task.

Croft et al. [5] developed a Command and Control display system using the Microsoft HoloLens and the Intelligent Multi-UxV Planner with Adaptive Collaborative Control Technologies (IMPACT) as a demonstration of a new advanced user interface. This allows human-to-human-to-machine collaboration for situational awareness, decision-making, and C2 planning and execution of simulated multi, unmanned and autonomous heterogeneous vehicles.

On the non-research side, Saab Australia was one of the first developers invited by Microsoft into their Mixed Reality partner program, and they were among the first to create HoloLens-based shared applications used for the defense and resources management decision-making (Fig. 1).

A pre-holographic experience to simulate air traffic control by means of a prototype tabletop interface has been done in 2007 by the VR Lab research group led by Francesca De Crescenzio at University of Bologna-Forlì, Italy [7, 8]. Their TABO prototype was

Fig. 1. Mixed Reality-based collaborative operational environment visualization (source: [6]).

a rear (under)-projected tabletop with a glass plate acting as display screen in which an ATC scenery was visualized in a stereoscopic form. Two or more persons looking from the same side could, thus, effectively share a 3D representation of the decision-making scenario. More recently, in the HoloLens era, they applied glasses-based holographic representations to augment the real view out of the ATC tower windows in the SESAR 2020 *RETINA* project [9], so that aircrafts approaching an airport can be easily located in the sky by an air traffic controller wearing a HoloLens. By subjective view approach, RETINA only shows flying aircrafts falling within the user glasses' field of view, while a tabletop approach such as ours put users from a God's eye point of view, which instead encompasses all the air traffic within the selected territory tile.

Lastly, in a recent work, Han et al. [10] at Sejong University, Seoul, Korea, started from International Civil Aviation Organization (ICAO) forecasts of air traffic controllers' increase in workload due to future air traffic expansion, and its recommendations of stronger controllers' simulator education. Thus, authors first carried out and reported deep surveys of air traffic controllers' current habits and quests for a future operational environment. Then, they propose a 4D mixed reality system using both visual and voice interaction through a HoloLens, with interaction mechanisms to control traffic in the air as well as on the ground. Users can switch between multiple interfaces within a single holographic display by 3D menus or voice commands. Moreover, controllers can give plain voice commands to endpoint pilots, and 3D spatial audio was used to make them to interpret the location of airplanes in the holographic space. This is a comprehensive system and represents a reference milestone for any further work in the field.

3 Survey of Applicable Technologies

The following chapters describe a series of technologies (electronic, IT) and data and related sources emerging as applicable and a common factor for the implementation of the HSTT application.

3.1 Glasses-Based Holographic-Like Visualization

In the present state of technology, in order to see a hologram, or, rather, a virtual three-dimensional representation that seems to materialize in the space in front of and surrounding an observer, it is necessary to combine a series of techniques and technologies such as:

- Stereoscopic visualization, to recreate the perception of the depth of the scene and therefore of its three-dimensionality;
- Optical see-through MR glasses, with semi-transparent displays;
- A set of sensors attached to the glasses that support the 3D pose estimation function - or inside-out tracking with six degrees of freedom (6-DoF - position and orientation).

The first function combined with the second gives rise to the latest generation of stereoscopic MR holographic glasses with semi-transparent displays. The integration of the sensors referred to in the last point allows a user who wears these glasses to see the virtual three-dimensional representation steadily anchored in the space in front of him and allowing panning around or move closer to away from it as if in front of an equivalent physical representation, albeit immaterial.

The forerunner of this new technological sector was Microsoft with its HoloLens. Microsoft recently announced an upgraded and improved second version that went on sale in the United States, Japan, China, Germany, Canada, United Kingdom, Ireland, France, Australia and New Zealand on the 7th of November 2019 Subsequently, the Magic Leap One became available - more compact than HoloLens and maybe more practical to wear, albeit with the same annular band for the head rather than a helmet for immersive Virtual Reality as the HoloLens. The Magic Leap One model has a belt-attached computer whereas the HoloLens has it totally integrated into the structure instead.

The availability in our Virtual Reality Laboratory of a pair of HoloLens units determined the choice of the MR-holographic glasses technology as the base for HSTT development, at least for the presented 2019 version (Fig. 2).

Fig. 2. Holographic AR glasses: Microsoft HoloLens (left), HoloLens 2 (center), Magic Leap One (right).

3.2 The MixedRealityToolkit.Sharing Client-Server Software Library

"The *MixedRealityToolkit.Sharing* library allows applications based on Microsoft's Mixed Reality Toolkit to span multiple devices and enable collaboration on a holographic basis. Originally developed for OnSight, a collaboration between SOTA (a Microsoft study) and NASA to improve their current Mars rover planning tool with HoloLens, MixedRealityToolkit.Sharing allows users to use multiple devices for a collaborative activity by allowing apps running on each device to communicate and stay synchronized in real time. Users in the same room or remote locations can collaborate with each other (who also use multiple devices)."[1]

The MixedRealityToolkit.Sharing library is distributed in source code through the Github platform [12].

3.3 The OSC General-Purpose Protocol

OSC - Open Sound Control [19] is a structured-typed general-purpose protocol based on the creation and sending of messages identified by an address string and a series of parameters that constitute the topics of the message. The address, despite the misleading name used in the definition of the standard, is an ASCII string conventionally preceded by the/(slash) symbol that identifies a message. Sub-addresses can be arbitrarily defined to follow the former with the aim of addressing specific functions within the family of messages with the same address.

Arguments in an OSC message are typed, that is, they are packed into the message while keeping information about their type. OSC supports the most common types used in programming such as 32-bit integers (int32), 32-bit floating point (float32), character strings, unsigned 64-bit integers for transmission e.g. of time, and a blob type - generic byte array for exchanging unstructured binary data.

Messages can be sent both individually and as a bundle, that is, in a group for "all together" processing upon receipt. This may be the case when updating a graphic scene following a simulation step where the multiple changes in the scene make sense only if applied all together to avoid partial misleading updates.

The OSC communication layer is deliberately left unspecified because this is actually an instrument for transporting information "packed" by OSC and has no type constraints (serial connection, MIDI, IP socket) nor implementation. Typically, in the use for message exchange between applications on the local network OSC is based on an IP socket, and in particular on UDP transport protocol.

We have chosen the OSC protocol with respect to other middleware framework/protocol because it is lightweight, available for many programming languages and not needing any server part for message distribution. We already have used it numerous times in other laboratory applications that without any code change or recompilation can already exchange data with our HSTT system.

3.4 ADS-B Air Surveillance Technology: Receivers and *Dump1090* Software

Automatic Dependent Surveillance - Broadcast (ADS-B) [13] is an air traffic monitoring technology by which an aircraft after determining its position through satellite navigation broadcasts this position (ADS-B Out), allowing tracking by others (other aircrafts and/or Air Traffic Control) that are equipped with the corresponding receivers (ADS-B In). *Automatic* stands for non-requiring voluntary human intervention, while *Dependent* is

---

[1] Description of *MixedRealityToolkit.Sharing* from the Github webpage [12].

to represent the dependence on the data of the plane's navigation system (typically GPS or other global terrestrial positioning system). The signals are unencrypted and transmission takes place in the 1090 MHz reserved band through transmission equipment called the Universal Access Transceiver (UAT).

Although not yet mandatory by international regulations, practically all commercial aviation aircrafts, as well as more and more general aviation aircraft are already equipped with ADS-B.

For amateur purposes, ground ADS-B reception *dump1090* is an open-source software for receiving ADS-B signals by means of a Software-Defined Radio (SDR) dongle. Cheap hardware (Fig. 3) and free software such as dump1090 can be used to display the speed, route, altitude, name and identification of an aircraft equipped with an ADS-B transponder within 200+ nautical miles from the receiver as far as it is placed in a position favorable to radio reception and equipped with a good gain antenna (Fig. 3).

Fig. 3. USB SDR dongle for receiving ADS-B signals [20] (left), and related 9 dBi antenna [21] (right) - objects not in the same scale.

Appropriately modified to send OSC messages, the dump1090 software constitutes a solid basis for the implementation of a client app for reading the surrounding air traffic using an ADS-B receiver of the cheap USB dongle class and sending this data to the geographical holographic 3D representation of the HSTT.

In order to be detected by dump1090 on our server's Windows 10 laptop, the SDR ADS-B dongle in Fig. 3 required the installation of a special USB driver with the help of the *Zadig* utility [22] as showed in Fig. 4.

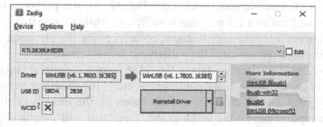

Fig. 4. The Zadig utility window showing the WinUSB driver to install for our ADS-B receiver dongle.

4 Survey of Usable Data Sources

Data sources referred to in the proposed HSTT consist in those of digital cartography and digital terrain, in order to feed the three-dimensional holographic representation of the terrain in support of the specific thematic views of the tactical tabletop application.

4.1 3D Digital Terrain: ESRI ArcGIS REST Services

ESRI ArcGIS WorldElevation3D/Terrain3D (ImageServer) [14] provides global elevation data for use in 3D applications. You can use this data to view 3D maps and layers. Terrain heights are based on several sources. The heights are orthometric (sea level = 0) and the water bodies that are above the sea level have the approximate nominal water heights. This layer includes data from multiple sources ranging from a resolution of one point every 1000 m to one every 3 m, including USGS NED (1/9, 1/3, 1 and 2 arc seconds) covering North America, SRTM (3 arc seconds) covering 60 north and 56 south and USGS GMTED (7.5, 15 and 30 arc seconds) covering global terrestrial data contributors and other members of the GIS community including Europe.

A code asset for Unity is provided by ESRI of a sample integration of 3D terrain functionality in applications such as our HSTT (see Sect. 6).

4.2 The OpenStreetMap Open Digital Cartography and the OSM2World Data Converter

OpenStreetMap [15] is a world map created by enthusiasts, ordinary people not affiliated with any commercial activity in providing maps software, and free to use under an open license. The map repository is fed by a community of mappers who contribute and keep data updated about roads, buildings, public service lines and more, from all over the world.

The OpenStreetMap website offers, in addition to a viewer for interactive exploration of the cartographic map, the possibility to download data relating to an area by interactively highlighting its rectangular geographical area. One of the file formats, the OSM, is in clear documented XML format and easily decodable.

OpenStreetMap data are essentially two-dimensional and georeferenced (that is, defined in longitude-latitude geographic coordinates). For the purposes of interactive consultation in the form of a 2D map this is sufficient, while to map it as a cartographic layer on a 3D terrain it is necessary to know, point by point, the elevation of the terrain in order to make three-dimensional the underlying digital terrain.

Furthermore, the cartographic data in the OSM format is defined "by type" (roads, buildings, power lines, railway lines, public green, etc.) [16], therefore to be transformed into a 3D polygonal model, an interpretation based on the models of the features is needed. An example could be the width of the "tape" that will graphically represent a road will be wide according to the type of road in the OpenStreetMap classification to distinguish a highway from a cycle way and dozens of other sub-types.

OSM2World [17] is a converter that creates a three-dimensional model of the world based on OpenStreetMap data exported in XML OSM format. The 3D model produced can be exported in different formats including the Wavefront OBJ, whose direct import is supported by Unity. OSM2World can be used both in batches, for long conversions of medium-large data sets, and interactively through a practical GUI.

For the three-dimensional conformation of the map data to OSM2World, the terrain elevation files of the area to which the map data refer must be supplied separately from the distribution of the software package. SRTM elevation data in HGT format can be downloaded interactively e.g. from the Viewfinderpanoramas.org website [18].

The developers warned users that the support for the elevation of the ground by OSM2World was unstable and inefficient (long lasting conversion, and unusual core memory occupation) for the conversion of medium-large areas (e.g. of the order of magnitude of a large city center). For these reasons, it was only possible to convert the rural area surrounding our Research Center where we tested the HSTT (Fig. 5).

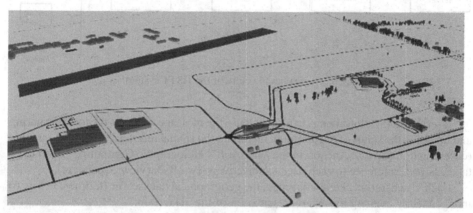

Fig. 5. 3D georeferenced model of the area surrounding our Research Center output of OSM2World, including the airport grass runway (green strip) (Color figure online).

5   HSTT Architecture Design

The main objective of the architectural design proposed for the HSTT system is to make the client application for HoloLens as light and generic as possible with respect to the various client applications and the related external data sources. In this way, as long as the implemented functionalities are general enough, the impact of additions or changes on the HoloLens client is minimal or null. Another goal of keeping application-specific parts external is that its compilation does not depend on application-specific libraries e.g. for reading from devices or from particular formats of data files or databases. In the proposed architectural design, this objective is pursued by ensuring that HoloLens clients, based on the Unity development environment, perform functions, essentially graphical, in response to the reception of structured messages from client applications (see Sect. 3.4).

The logical architecture represented in Fig. 6 formalizes the client-server approach chosen for the architecture of the HSTT. The set of message server and display user customers (center and left in the figure) offer client applications (right in the figure) a series of services, which, for the most part, will be reflected in a change (additions, removals, changes) of the holographic representation. And, for other usage, they will provide specific information to the applications such as, for example, the geographical delimitation of the 3D terrain displayed at that time.

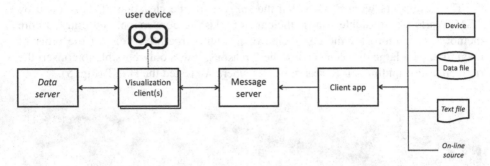

Fig. 6. Logical architecture of the HSTT system.

Users' visualization clients, in turn, will use the message server as the tool for sharing and updating the status of the program, including the spatial reference of the holographic representation (Spatial Anchor, in the Microsoft's Holographic Computing SDK) to be taken as base reference to each user's subjective view offset (view dependent).

Each visualization client will access the geographical data server (leftmost in Fig. 6) independently creating its own representation of the 3D terrain.

In Fig. 7 the logical architecture has been translated into a physical correspondent where the functions, modules and devices take on specific names, roles and locations.

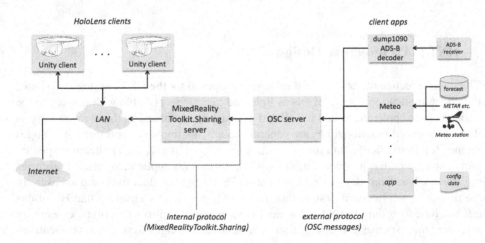

Fig. 7. Physical architecture proposed for the HSTT system.

From an IT point of view, the core of the HSTT application consists of two server programs, the MixedRealityToolkit.Sharing and the OSC Server, the latter developed specifically for the HSTT. These can also be run on the same computer, as small amount of resources are required. Key parts of the software scenario include one or more instances of the client programs for HoloLens, which must be deployed on the device (via direct USB connection or via local network or the Internet). Each client application (rightmost in Fig. 6) can be run separately and if necessary, possibly on the same computer as the two servers, by mapping their destination addresses and ports in accordance with the reception of the UDP packets of OSC messages by the OSC Server. The two servers and the client applications can all be hosted on a single laptop computer to which the USB SDR dongle for the reception of the ADS-B and the relative antenna can be attached, for a compact and energetically autonomous, deployable anywhere, setup.

The role of the external protocol of the HSTT, based on the structured-typed OSC protocol introduced in 3.3, is described later in 5.1.

As mentioned earlier, each display client accesses the geographic data server independently. Although this architectural choice appeared as an unnecessary duplication of the function and which leads to the doubling - in the case of two participants - of the network bandwidth used, the possibilities offered by the message server used internally did not include data caching. To move access functions to ArcGIS terrain mapping data from clients to the internal server is, now, too expensive as development effort and will be considered as enhancement for future developments.

The recognition of voice commands is a functional software addition to the hardware of the HoloLens, which is simply programmed in terms of voice-command correspondence - a function performed on board each device.

5.1 The OSC-Based External Application Protocol

As mentioned at the beginning of Sect. 5, the basic architectural choice was to keep the client application running on board the HoloLens as light and general as possible, which offers, with the possibility of activation from the outside, a set of functions usable by client applications. The applications using the HSTT services are made up of programs external to the core of the HSTT, actually communicating with it by means of messages in a defined protocol based on OSC.

The main OSC messages are messages from the ADS-B client regarding detected aircrafts and their parameters: identifier, aircraft type, geographical position, altitude and heading.

An example of the generality with which the external HSTT protocol was designed is the *Cone* function. The cone is a graphic primitive that can be drawn by the graphic client for the HoloLens developed in the HSTT project which, suitably parameterized (top and bottom diameter, height, orientation, georeferenced position, material/transparency/color/texture and other parameters), can be used to draw e.g. a windsock for the *Meteo* application client. Another cone example is a conical volume of air space that has − or has not − to be crossed by an aircraft, or even to represent the lobe of a tracking antenna that moves in pursuit of an aircraft in flight. The on-terrain 3D red ring marker underneath the volume cone in Fig. 10 is also designed using cones; three to be exact.

We wanted to avoid the internal transcoding of the messages from the external protocol of the HSTT, based on OSC, to the internal one based on the message server MixedRealityToolkit.Sharing. In fact, this hasn't any functional advantage, and would have only been done in order to make the external protocol messages to reach the HoloLens clients. Thus, in the OSC Server module, OSC messages from external client apps are "transferred" sic-et-simpliciter for internal transport to clients - without interpretation or transcoding - in a MixedRealityToolkit.Sharing message internally classified as "OSC message". As such, they arrive at HoloLens clients where they are eventually put back in the form of OSC messages, and finally interpreted. With this approach, the burden of their interpretation occurs just once instead of the two that would be required by doing it also in the OSC Server. In this way, the internal protocol of the MixedRealityToolkit.Sharing server is transparent to the external OSC-based protocol allowing HoloLens clients to be reached by the external protocol of the HSTT and to keep up to date with each other towards the requests of the client apps.

6   Implementation

The prototype HSTT system has been developed in Unity utilizing the integration of the Microsoft Mixed Reality Toolkit (MRTK) [23] and the MixedRealityToolkit.Sharing library (see 3.2). During our development timeframe, Microsoft has released a new version of the MRTK, the 2.0, to address the newly coming HoloLens 2 yet retro-compatible with HoloLens 1. In MRTK 2.0 Spatial Anchors are shared via the Microsoft Azure cloud platform instead of the server core memory. Because we did not want to switch completely to a new platform, Azure, for the sharing part we have tried to utilize the last version of MRTK just before v2.0 (the Dev_Working_Branch on Github), but the porting effort has been not so trivial. There were numerous changes, with newly introduced registrations of assets, but with no improvement in the stability of Spatial Anchor sharing as we hoped, so we reverted to the initial MRTK version that we started to work with.

The HoloLens Terrain Viewer, an experimental mapping application for HoloLens developed by ERSI's Prototype Lab [24], has been the basis for a tile-based terrain visualization in our prototype app. The sample app constructs Unity terrains at runtime in the form of Splat Maps from imagery and elevation data, dynamically sourced from ArcGIS Online (see 4.1). Unfortunately, a Unity Terrain Object has the limitation that it cannot be rotated, and this conflicts with the approach of sharing a HoloLens's Spatial Anchor among multiple participants by not allowing an offset transformation to their own local pose. Thus, we rewrote the terrain visualization subsystem of the HoloLens Terrain Viewer substituting the Terrain Object by transformable textured graphics primitives (meshes), with no apparent loss of performance for the tile size of our prototype (256 x 256).

7   Results

The HSTT prototype system has been finalized in September 2019, and an example MR screenshot is reported in Fig. 8. Then it has been experimented with in two flight campaigns held at CIRA in the October-December 2019 timeframe. The Italian Aerospace

Research Centre site is adjoining to the Capua airport, which is used by general aviation and ultralight-class aircraft manufacturers for flight testing, and by our center's experimental aircraft FLARE (Fig. 9). The latter has been the main flying actor of our experimental campaigns and is equipped with an ADS-B Out transmitter for signaling its position to the surrounding air traffic.

Fig. 8. A user-captured picture of the HSTT with 3D terrain populated by flying aircrafts (Color figure online).

Fig. 9. The CIRA FLARE flight testbed (TECNAM P92-S Echo) and its 2500-triangle virtual counterpart in the HSTT application.

The SESAR 2020 *GRADE* project – *GNSS Solutions for Increased GA and Rotorcraft Airport Accessibility Demonstration* – gave our HSTT the first opportunity to be experimented in a real flight context. In its flight trial scenario, the subject aircraft has to execute GNSS-based departures and approaches around the airport area, which were monitored by people in and outside the FLARE Ground Station even through our MR prototype setup. Since this trial has been held in the country field or our Center, our autonomous setup included a laptop connected to Internet via a 4G smartphone–shared Wi-Fi connection. The single HoloLens used in this trial was connected in Wi-Fi to the laptop, with the Hotspot function enabled on the latter in order to make the HoloLens to access the Internet.

A second opportunity of experimenting the HSTT prototype was in December 2019 in a flight trial campaign for the ENAC accreditation of our Center's Environmental

Acoustic Lab. A ground microphone was registering an acoustic signature from the ground. Its "useful" space volume, defined by predetermined tolerance levels, was represented as "listening" to within a truncated conical air space (the mid-air truncated cone in Fig. 10). The experimental aircraft FLARE had to fly above the ground microphone within specified parameters for the flight to be valid for the pursued certification – its flight path must have flown through the predetermined air volume. Due to safety reasons the use of our HSTT application by the pilot on board was excluded, he was helped nevertheless to cross the conical air space by radio indications from a ground operator wearing the HoloLens glasses with the HSTT running. In fact, both the aircraft's flight traces (on ground – red, in air – yellow) gave the operator the confidence on whether the aircraft could fly and effectively did, into the cone or not (Fig. 10). When the ground help wearing the HoloLens was realizing that the aircraft would have flown outside of the cone, he was able to suggest via radio the on-board pilot corrective maneuvers in order to meet the goal. A post-processing analysis of the actual aircraft trajectories has validated what has been seen by the HSTT-equipped operator.

Fig. 10. Uncropped 3D georeferenced objects laid over the digital terrain and left extending beyond the terrain tile.

The experimental setup included a laptop computer, which acted as an Internet hotspot and hosted all the necessary programs, namely the OSC message server, the MixedRealityToolkit.Sharing-based server, and the dump1090 ADS-B decoder. A single or pair of HoloLens accessed Internet through the laptop for downloading terrain data from the ESRI ArcGIS server, and for communicating with the sharing server and, thus, between them.

In our experience, the sharing capability that we implemented in the HSTT based on the MixedRealityToolkit.Sharing library has revealed to be not reliable enough for collaboration experiment sessions. The sharing of Spatial Anchors had an intermittent, unpredictable behavior, and their exchange from a HoloLens unit to another participant's one was not easily traceable along the various levels of libraries they crossed. Hence, the completion callbacks were the only usable debugging mechanism, and only when

Fig. 11. One of the participants in a two-person collaborative session indicating the other participant where he actually sees the two flying aircrafts in his hologram space.

running in the emulator. Figure 11 depicts a situation of correct working of the view sharing mechanism.

Performances of the HoloLens clients with a limited-complexity scenario (the 256 x 256 terrain tile, and an air traffic of 1–2 aircrafts) were very good and the app run fluidly. Overlaying the quite complex cartographic data set onto the terrain representation (Fig. 10), and/or complicating the air traffic scenario to 10+ aircrafts, significantly downgraded app performances as largely expected, supposedly due to the limited 3D graphics capabilities of the device (Microsoft recommendations in this aspect are clear, though). The negative effect is more evident on the motion-to-view latency than on the update of the flying scenario, which may occur at an unpredictable rate of the ADS-B messages reception.

The HoloLens tracking when a user moved around a holographic representation in the real space has proven rock-solid in all circumstances as expected, even in outdoor use. The HoloLens vocal command recognition has proven both solid and flexible in being quite tolerant to non-mother-tongue English speakers.

The usability of the HoloLens outdoor with sun exposure has been revealed as critical, with too much light limiting the correct perception of the displayed graphics. For mitigating such a problem, we have put a sunglass filter in front of each display.

The ADS-B reception has sometime revealed difficult, especially when the line of sight between the transmitting aircraft and the receiving antenna is occluded by some artifacts, such as when an aircraft flies low on the horizon (e.g. when landing) and the receiving station is on the ground as well. Paradoxically, the airlines hi-route air traffic was usually captured clearly; instead, it was not the low altitude one around the receiver when in presence of hard obstacles.

Although the implemented possibility to change the scale of the visualized terrain tile (zoom in or out) is discreet and not arbitrary (follows the guidelines of multi-resolution image pyramids implemented by top Tile Map Service providers like ArcGIS, Google and Microsoft) it was proven to be a very desirable feature. For instance, vocalizing the "decrease level", even a few times, allowed to pinpoint the location of actors (like our FLARE testbed aircraft) especially when they were out of the focus region while preparing for the fly-over events. As soon as they began approaching the focus region, in our ENAC accreditation experiment it was the location of the cone-shaped space volume, we could once again increase resolution of the visualized terrain and surroundings by issuing the "increase level" vocal command.

Introduction of vocal commands to change the visual perception of the scene like "show/hide features" and changing the scale of the visualized region of interest allowed a true hands-free experience of the HSTT application. Speech synthesis was added as an aural confirmation of given speech commands, since voice recognition is not always 100% reliable. Synthesized speech feedback was also useful to acknowledge commands that require some time before they are visually apparent, like the download from Internet servers of the 3D terrain data and creation of the graphical representation of the terrain.

The currently implemented voice commands are:

- *Help* – recites currently recognized voice commands
- *Information* – recites some current visualization parameters (tile zoom level etc.)
- *Reset Placement* – reactivates the procedure for world tile placement
- *Increase/Decrease Level* – increases/decreases the tile level (zoom)
- *Show/Hide features* – toggles visualization of terrain features
- *Reset Annotations* – deletes all annotations.

No test of application usability has been performed yet, neither in absolute nor in comparison to a "standard" application of the same type, which, in this case, could be a 3D visualization of the live tactical scenario on an either conventional or stereoscopic display/projection system.

8 Conclusions and Perspectives

The attractiveness of a holographic-like tabletop fully sharable from multiple points of view for collaborative strategic-tactical monitoring and decision making, along the maturity of the HoloLens MR solution, has pushed our VR Lab to develop a prototype application for an hands-on experience with this concept. Our experiments 'till now have been held with few real aircrafts flying concurrently in the holographic scenario, yet with additional features on the territory which customized each application to the flight trial scopes. Sharing sessions has not been convincing concerning the reliability of the solution implemented, and we aim to get back on it with a MRTK 2.0-based setup soon.

On the usage field side, an attractive perspective is to see MR techniques and technologies to experimentally enter in the air traffic control tower, with the aim of testing MR solutions for big-picture situational awareness by air traffic controllers and to prove their effectiveness in their perspective way to operate in the Future Sky ATM concepts.

On the technical side, an attractive opportunity for future developments of MR apps is to switch to OpenXR. OpenXR [25] is a new Khronos standard API enabling cross-platform applications for the wide interoperability of apps and devices aiming at preventing XR market fragmentation. Along with the multi-platform nature of app development environments such as Unity and Unreal, OpenXR is the answer to the *write once, deploy everywhere* quest of both XR hardware and software developers. Engine/development IDEs have to support the *Application Interface* level of OpenXR, while VR/AR/MR hardware manufacturers have to support it at the *Device Plugin Interface* level in order to make their devices visible at runtime in OpenXR-capable engines.

In apps such as our HSTT, interfacing the OpenXR API e.g. in Unity would result in transparent deployability of the app in a variety of MR-capable glasses, and a collaboration scenario with a heterogeneous set of glasses in the same session (e.g. using HoloLens and Magic Leap One alongside).

Acknowledgments. The activity described in the present work has been partially supported by the PRORA UAV National research program. In particular, the experimental activity has been carried out by flight test campaigns held in the second half of 2019 in the airspace around the Capua airport, based on the FLARE flight testbed. The authors wish to acknowledge Pier Paolo de Matteis, Attilio Rispoli and all the FLARE team at CIRA for their technical and management support.

References

1. Boeing drones and Microsoft holograms to fight wildfires. Commercial UAV News web site. [www.commercialuavnews.com/public-safety/boeing-drones-microsoft-holograms-fight-wildfires]
2. Su, S., Perry, V., Guan, Q., Durkee, A., Neigel, A.R., Kase, S.: Sensor data fusion framework to improve holographic object registration accuracy for a shared augmented reality mission planning scenario. In: Chen, J.Y.C., Fragomeni, G. (eds.) VAMR 2018. LNCS, vol. 10909, pp. 202–214. Springer, Cham (2018). https://doi.org/10.1007/978-3-319-91581-4_15
3. Chusetthagarn, D., Visoottiviseth, V., Haga, J.: A prototype of collaborative augmented reality environment for hololens. In: 2018 22nd International Computer Science and Engineering Conference (ICSEC), pp. 1–5 Chiang Mai, Thailand, (2018)
4. Kase, S., Su, S., Perry, V., Roy, H., Gamble, K.: An augmented reality shared mission planning scenario: observations on shared experience. In: Chen, J.Y.C., Fragomeni, G. (eds.) HCII 2019. LNCS, vol. 11575, pp. 490–503. Springer, Cham (2019). https://doi.org/10.1007/978-3-030-21565-1_33
5. Croft, B.L., et al.: Command and Control Collaboration Sand Table (C2-CST). In: Chen, J.Y.C., Fragomeni, G. (eds.) VAMR 2018. LNCS, vol. 10910, pp. 249–259. Springer, Cham (2018). https://doi.org/10.1007/978-3-319-91584-5_20
6. Saab Australia Mixed Reality web site. [saab.com/region/saab-australia/mixed-reality]
7. Persiani, F., De Crescenzio, F., Fantini, M., Bagassi, S.: A tabletop-based interface to simulate air traffic control in a distributed virtual environment. In: Proceedings of the XVI ADM Congress and XIX Ingegraf Congress. June 6–8, Perugia, Italy (2007)
8. Bagassi, S., De Crescenzio, F., Persiani, F.: Design and development of an ATC distributed training system. In: Proceedings of the 26th Congress of the International Council of Aeronautical. Sciences (ICAS 2008)/8th AIAA Aviation, Technology, Integration and Operations. September 14–19, Anchorage, Alaska (2008)
9. Masotti, N., Bagassi, S., De Crescenzio, F.: Augmented Reality for the Control Tower: The RETINA Concept. In: De Paolis, L.T., Mongelli, A. (eds.) AVR 2016. LNCS, vol. 9768, pp. 444–452. Springer, Cham (2016). https://doi.org/10.1007/978-3-319-40621-3_32

10. Han, K., Hammad, H.S.S., Weon Lee, J.: Holographic mixed reality system for air traffic control and management. Appl. Sci. 9, 3370 (2019). https://doi.org/10.3390/app9163370
11. Unity. [unity.com]
12. Microsoft-NASA   MixedRealityToolkit.Sharing   [github.com/microsoft/MixedRealityToolkit/tree/master/Sharing]
13. Automatic Dependent Surveillance - Broadcast ADS-B [en.wikipedia.org/wiki/Automatic_dependent_surveillance_%E2%80%93_broadcast]
14. ESRI ArcGIS WorldElevation3D/Terrain3D ImageServer [elevation3d.arcgis.com/arcgis/rest/services/WorldElevation3D/Terrain3D/ImageServer]
15. OpenStreetMap.[www.openstreetmap.org]
16. OpenStreetMap map features. [wiki.openstreetmap.org/wiki/Map_Features]
17. OSM2World Create 3D models from OpenStreetMap. [osm2world.org/,wiki.openstreetmap.org/wiki/OSM2World]
18. Digital Elevation Data.[www.viewfinderpanoramas.org]
19. OpenSoundControl: an Enabling Encoding for Media Applications [opensoundcontrol.org]
20. ADS-B Flightaware Pro Stick Plus USB SDR receiver
21. ADS-B omnidirectional antenna Yilianduo EUOL-2957 9dBi 1090 MHz
22. Zadig: USB driver installation made easy. [zadig.akeo.ie]
23. MRTK-Unity [github.com/microsoft/MixedRealityToolkit-Unity]
24. HoloLens Terrain Viewer. ESRI Prototype Lab. [github.com/Esri/hololens-terrain-viewer]
25. OpenXR. Khronos Group. [www.khronos.org/openxr/]

3D Reconstruction and Visualization

A Comparative Study of the Influence of the Screen Size of Mobile Devices on the Experience Effect of 3D Content in the Form of AR/VR Technology

YanXiang Zhang[✉] and Zhenxing Zhang

Department of Communication of Science and Technology,
University of Science and Technology of China, Hefei, Anhui, China
petrel@ustc.edu.cn, zysman@mail.ustc.edu.cn

Abstract. Differences in screen size of mobile devices can affect users' experience of products, but very few researches have confirmed that differences in screen size of mobile devices can affect users' experience of VR/AR content are few, or even affect the choice of VR/AR content form by 3D content creators. The authors use the AR and VR forms of the same 3D content to evaluate the participants' convenience, intuitive feedback and comfort of VR/AR interactive experience on mobile devices with different screen sizes, in order to explore whether the difference of screen size affects the experience effect of 3D content AR/VR. Research has shown that participants tend to use larger screen mobile devices for interactive experiences, but not the larger the screen of the mobile device used, the stronger the willingness of participants are. We found that participants tend to use mobile devices with moderate screen size for VR/AR interaction.

Keywords: VR/AR · Screen size · User selection

1 Introduction

In recent years, the size of digital content components is an important factor affecting user experience. For example, in recent years, the screen size of mobile electronic devices is increasing, and the design of notebook products also reduces the volume and size of products as much as possible to ensure high portability. In the field of AR/VR, there are researches on the influence of avatar size on user experience in a virtual environment [1] and the influence of hand size on user experience in a virtual environment [2]. At present, many users experience VR/AR through mobile devices. However, no re-search has been found on the influence of the screen size of mobile devices on users' AR VR experience.

Research on the effect of screen size on video-based mobile learning shows that participants using mobile devices with "medium" and "large" screens rated screen quality significantly higher and learned significantly more than participants using mobile devices with "small" screens [3]. However, there was no significant difference between

L. T. De Paolis and P. Bourdot (Eds.): AVR 2020, LNCS 12242, pp. 363–374, 2020.
https://doi.org/10.1007/978-3-030-58465-8_27

the result screens of participants using the medium and large screens. Some studies have confirmed the mobile screen size limits the multimode synergistic effect [4]. The authors hope to explore whether the conclusions can be applied to VR/AR scenarios through experiments. At present, no studies have correlated screen size with the VR/AR interactive experience. Some studies have shown that the differences in operation caused by the changes in the screen size of mobile phones affect the efficiency and accuracy of mobile phone operation in a certain extent [5]. However, the difference of screen size is not related to the experience effect of VR/AR interaction. Our research evaluates the VR/AR interaction experience of users between mobile devices with different screen sizes.

Research related to 3D games has confirmed that perspective and physical screen size affect the existence and emotional response of players [6]. But such re-search has not evaluated the behavior of players. Therefore, our research focuses on mobile device screen size and the experience of user's interaction. In our experiment, we used the VR/AR technology form of the same 3D content and took the physical screen as an independent variable to evaluate the interaction experience of the participants. To prove the screen size difference of the mobile device will affect the user's experience of VR/AR through the effect of the interaction experience of the participants. In addition, we will evaluate the VR/AR experience of users on the same device separately, and such comparative study can provide a reference for the selection of technical form (VR/AR) when 3D content creators publish content. Research on the audience's immersion shows very small screen could reduce the immersion, but in a certain size, the effect is not that obvious [7]. Immersion is the most important performance measure of VR system, which means that users immerse themselves in a virtual environment from the perspective of protagonist during the VR experience. Hoffman and Novak (1996) proposed an immersive experience model for online users, suggesting that immersive experience can enhance consumers' exploration tendency and positive subjective experience [8]. The comfortable senses of operation will not necessarily improve the efficiency and accuracy of operation, but the uncomfortable sense of operation caused by the change of size will inevitably affect the performance of users operating mobile phones. Some studies have shown that the larger the size of mobile phone, the more obvious the action trend of wrong click. Therefore, the authors hope to explore whether participants' experience of VR/AR interaction with different screen sizes of mobile devices is consistent [5].

2   Experiment

2.1   Overview and Design

The purpose of our experiment was to investigate whether the screen size is relevant to the user's choice of VR/AR by evaluating and comparing the 3D content-based VR/AR interactive experience of the participant using a screen-sized mobile device. The screen size is an independent variable. In addition, we also assessed the convenience of participants operating mobile devices with different screen sizes, intuitive feedback and comfort of interactive experience, including screen brightness, accuracy and operational efficiency in VR/AR interaction. Participants experience VR/AR interaction on devices with different screen sizes but the same display effect, the same screen size but different display effect. Participants' experience is not to explore the virtual environment by holding the device and walking around, such as watching 360 videos, but to play games in the 3D virtual environment through mobile devices. Whether it is smart phone, tablet computer, notebook, display or LCD TV, screen display effect is always the core existence in the process of interaction with users, so we control some variables in the experiment:

(1) Unified gamut

Color gamut determines the color expressiveness, the larger it is, and the more colors can be displayed, so that users have the opportunity to see more and more real colors. Therefore, we have the same color gamut of mobile devices, as far as possible to provide users with the same experimental conditions for VR/AR interactive experience.

(2) Unified screen brightness, uniformity and contrast

A picture with uneven back lighting is like a picture with black spots, and if the brightness is not enough, the dim picture will lack the sense of permeability. The larger the dynamic range of brightness is, the better the detail performance is in extreme cases such as over bright and over dark. Research shows that the perception of screen brightness is related to the physical size and distance [9]. To ensure the scientific nature of the experiment, we controlled the brightness of the screen, and chose mobile devices with uniform screen and contrast.

(3) Unified operating interface

Different operating interfaces will affect the use of users. In order to reduce the adaptation time of participants to experience different devices, we used the IOS system of the mobile devices to unify the user's operating experience of the device interface.

The effectiveness of a virtual environment is usually related to the sense of presence reported by users of the virtual environment. The researchers developed an immersion tendency questionnaire (ITQT) to measure the difference of individual experience tendency. The results show that individual tendencies as measured by the ITQ predict presence as measured by the presence questionnaire [10]. Therefore, before the experiment, we conducted pretests in the laboratory. After analyzing the data and making assumptions, we obtained the relevant variables that affect the user's choices. We integrated these variables into the questions in the questionnaire, and after the participants completed the questionnaire, we evaluated the results of the questionnaire. Evaluation typically takes one of three forms: (1) smaller lab studies with real users; (2) batch tests with offline collections, judgments, and measures; (3) controlled experiments (e.g. A/B tests) looking at implicit feedback. But it is rare for the first to inform and influence the latter two; in particular, implicit feedback metrics often have to be continuously revised and updated as assumptions are found to be poorly supported [11]. So we used a hybrid approach to assess participants' propensity.

2.2 Experimental Setup

2.2.1 Interactive Content

The authors used VR/AR data based on 3D technology as the content of interactive experience, and used VR/AR technology in the scene of science education. Because the participants have enough knowledge of the revolution and rotation of the earth, it is difficult to arouse their thirst for knowledge. The authors improve the enthusiasm of participants through this form of scientific education. In addition, in order to let the participants have a more macro experience. The authors also produced a spacecraft to grab the satellite VR/AR material. Participants will be watching the VR/AR version of the interactive material and fill in the questionnaire after the end of the experience (Fig. 1).

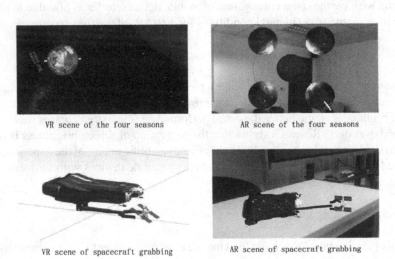

VR scene of the four seasons   AR scene of the four seasons

VR scene of spacecraft grabbing   AR scene of spacecraft grabbing

Fig. 1. Interactive scene

2.2.2 Mobile Devices

The authors provided five mobile devices with different screen sizes to participants, and they experimented with every device. Research on the effect of the screen size of mobile phone on user perceived usability, effectiveness and efficiency shows that users with screens larger than 4.3 in. interacted more efficiently [12]. But in order to compare participants' experience of using mobile devices with different screen sizes, we set the 10.8-in. screen as the maximum size of the user experience. Although the increase of device size leads to the decrease of thumb mobility, users can usually perform localized mobility well, even for large devices [13]. To improve participants' overall experience, we chose a 10.8-in. tablet (surface), a 9.7-in. tablet (IPad 5), a 7.9-in. tablet (IPad mini4), a 5.8-in. mobile phone (iPhone X) and a 4.7-in. mobile phone (iPhone 6S).

2.3 Participants

All 24 participants (12 male, 12 female; aged 20 to 30 years old) were postgraduates, and none of them had serious visual impairment (no color blindness, no color weakness and the visual acuity of both eyes after correction shall not be less than 0.8), and all participants participated in the experiment voluntarily. The participants we selected were adults with mature hands to ensure the same dimension of user experience. This is due to a considerable correlation between the size of the hand and all aspects of tactile interaction [14].

After completing a preliminary demographic questionnaire, participants used a 12.9-in. tablet, a 9.7-in. tablet, a 7.9-in. tablet, a 5.8-in. phone and a 4.7-in. phone to experience VR/AR interaction. Relevant research has proved that it is most difficult for users to interact in the left and right lower corners of the screen, so we designed the interaction content in the middle of the VR/AR scene [15]. In the AR interaction, participants need to experience with the recognition tag, they need to interact with the camera of mobile devices against the recognition tag. After the VR/AR interactive experience of mobile devices with different screen sizes, participants filled in the questionnaire of this experiment.

2.4 Questionnaire

Firstly, the questionnaire includes basic demographic questions; secondly, We considered whether differences in screen size affect user comfort, including whether the weight of the mobile device affects the participant's experience, whether the participant's field of vision is limited and can see details in the scene, and participants' assessment of the accuracy and efficiency of mobile device operation during interaction, and used these dimensions as comfort criteria; in terms of attitude, we evaluated which experience users are most satisfied with in the same size; finally, we considered the interaction experience of AR/VR, user satisfaction with the experience of mobile devices of different screen sizes.

3 Results

3.1 Questionnaire

Although some studies have shown that children can adapt effectively to different devices without major problems, we still want to know whether overweight devices will affect users' choices. Participants used different screen sizes of devices for VR/AR experience and filled out questionnaires for data statistics. We assess which devices or sizes are suitable for VR/AR scenes by observing whether participants could see details in VR/AR scenes; in terms of user experience, we evaluate whether any participants experience vertigo in VR/AR experiences to design products and scene content; in addition, we evaluate the correlation between screen size differences and field of view limitations generated in scenes; and we evaluate the correlation between screen size differences and field of view limitations; In terms of portability, we correlated the weight of devices with different screen sizes with the participants' sense of experience; finally, We conducted horizontal and vertical comparisons to evaluate the best experience of participants using the same size screen device, and the best device in the same experience (VR/AR).

3.2 Data Collection

(1) Scene details

Participants in the VR experience were able to see details using a larger screen, but not the larger screen, all participants could see details at 7.9 in. and above, and the larger the screen of a device below 7.9 in. is, the more details could be seen. In the AR scene, with 7.9 in. as the limit, the clarity of details of devices below 7.9 in. was proportional to the screen size, and there was no significant difference between devices above 7.9 in. Participants with devices 5.8 in. and above had greater detail clarity in VR than AR, but more participants believed that AR details were better than VR on mobile devices with 4.7-in. screens (Fig. 2).

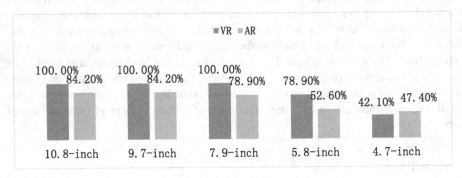

Fig. 2. Whether the details in the scene are clear

(2) Vertigo

Vertigo is one of the factors that affect the sense of existence in a virtual reality social environment [16]. In the VR experience, none of the participants felt dizzy when they were using the 5.8-in. device, and the larger the screen is, the more people felt vertigo. But when using a small screen device to experience, some participants also felt vertigo. In the AR scene experience of various screen size devices, all experienced vertigo, and the largest size (10.8 in.) device was used by the largest number of participants. More participants experienced VR vertigo with larger screens than with AR; more participants experienced AR vertigo with medium screens than with VR (Fig. 3).

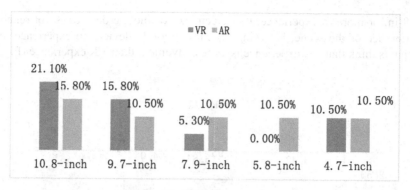

Fig. 3. Vertigo in the experience

(3) Vision

Taking 9.7-in. device as the limit, the smaller the screen of the device is, the more limitation of the visual field the participants feel in the VR scene, and no participants feel the limitation of visual field when using the screen size of 9.7-in. and above. In AR scene experience, taking 9.7-in. device as the limit, the smaller the screen of the device is, the more participants feel the limitation of visual field, and no participants feel the limitation of visual field when using screen size of the 9.7-in. and above. The number of participants using 5.8 in. or more for VR experience is less limited by visual field than that of VR experience, and a considerable number of participants feel the visual limitation in both VR and AR scenes (Fig. 4).

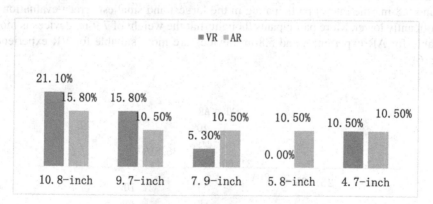

Fig. 4. Limited vision in the scene

(4) Convenience

Participants in the VR scene experience, with 5.8-in. as the limit, the larger the screen is, the more inconvenient the participants feel; in the AR scene, also with 5.8-in. as the limit, the larger the screen is, the more inconvenient the participants feel. Participants use 5.8-in. or more to experience, the screen size of mobile devices is not related to the difference of the scene, but using 4.7-in. of mobile devices to experience, more participants think that AR experience is more convenient than VR experience (Fig. 5).

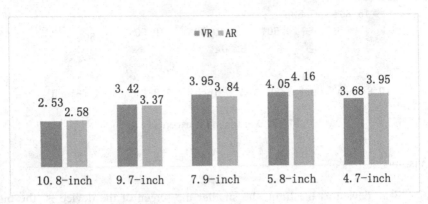

Fig. 5. User experience convenience (5-point system)

(5) Weight

Participants in the VR scene experience of 7.9-in. for the best, followed by 5.8-in. and 9.7-in., the evaluation of the largest and smallest screen size of the device evaluation is significantly lower. For AR experience, 7.9-in. evaluation is the best, followed by 9.7-in. and 5.8-in., the rate of participating in the largest and smallest screen evaluation is significantly lower. More participants thought that the weight of 7.9-in. devices is more suitable for AR experience, and 5.8-in. devices are more suitable for VR experience (Fig. 6).

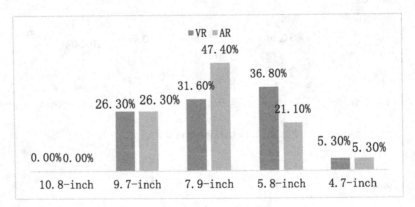

Fig. 6. The most suitable device for the experience

(6) The same screen size devices

More participants used 7.9-in. or larger devices and thought VR experience was better than AR, There was little differences in the participants' experience with the 5.8-in. device. But more participants had a better AR experience with the small device (4.7-in.) than VR (Fig. 7).

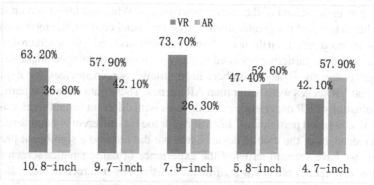

Fig. 7. The best content in the same scene

(7) Experience the same scene

In the VR experience, the number of participants who thought the 9.7-in. screen had the best experience was significantly higher than that of other devices. Few participants thought that too large or too small devices had the best VR experience. Similarly, more participants thought that the mobile device with 9.7-in. screen had the best AR experience, followed by 7.9-in. and 5.8-in. Few participants thought that too large or too small devices had the best AR experience. Whether it is VR or AR experience, more participants believe that the experience of 9.7-in. screen devices is the best, and few participants believe that too large or too small devices have the best experience (Fig. 8).

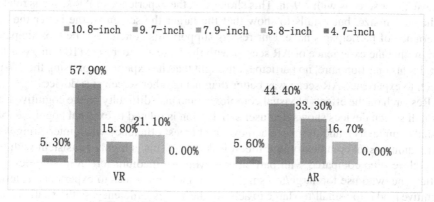

Fig. 8. The best experience in the same scene

4 Discussion

4.1 Content and Form

This study found that more participants tended to experience VR with 10.8-in., 9.7-in., and 7.9-in. screens than with 5.8-in. and 4.7-in. screens. For 5.8-in. and 4.7-in. devices with smaller screens, participants are more inclined to choose AR scenes for experience. The results showed that larger screens were more attractive to participants, but not the bigger the screen is, the more attractive it is. While the larger screen size may be preferable in terms of the greater display area for visual content, the increased screen weight also induced fatigue on the user's hand. Participants used 7.9-in. screen devices for experience, and more participants tended to choose VR scenes, but a considerable number of participants (nearly 50% in number) used smaller screen devices for experience, believing that VR scenes were better than AR scenes. These data show that participants' overall evaluation of VR experience using devices with different screen sizes was higher than AR. We compared participants' intentions for the two different content formats with the five screen sizes of the mobile devices, and we did not find a significant preference for AR. As we have seen, in terms of the experience of using smaller screen devices, participants' differences are not as significant as using larger screen devices. But it also shows that with smaller screens, participants are more likely to experience AR than VR.

4.2 Sense of Experience

Although the vast majority of participants tend to use 7.9-in. screen devices to experience VR scenes (a small number of participants tend to experience AR scenarios), more participants rated a 9.7-in. screen as the best way to experience a VR scene compared to other screen size devices, especially the 9.7-in. screen. The VR scene experience of more participants using 5.8-in. screen devices is better than that of 7.9-in. screen devices. No participant rated the 4.7-in. (the smallest) device as the best VR experience, but participants rated the AR experience differently from the VR experience, even though more participants rated the 9.7-in. device as the best choice for AR experience than any other screen size of device. The VR experience was opposite to the AR experience, when participants used 7.9-in. and 5.8-in. devices to experience. In fact, more participants tend to have larger screens with 7.9-in. This shows that the experience of AR scene is related to the screen size, but it fails to show that the larger the screen is, the better the AR experience of participants have. Our results support this conclusion: Few participants thought that the experience of AR scenes with the largest screen size (10.8 in.) was the best. In this questionnaire, no participant thought that the experience of using the 4.7-in. screen to experience AR scene was better than using other screen size devices.

Research on the effects of visual complexity and task difficulty on the cognitive load of small screen devices shows that user satisfaction is related to external cognitive load (visual complexity), and users can achieve the highest efficiency when interacting with the medium visual complexity in difficult tasks [17]. This is highly consistent with our research results: compared with participants who use medium screen mobile devices, participants who use too large/too small screen mobile devices to experience external cognitive load is too small/too large to achieve the highest efficiency, so their satisfaction is low. Participants who use medium screen mobile devices achieve the highest efficiency, so they are most satisfied.

5 Conclusion

This research draws a conclusion that can be provided as a reference for 3D content creators, promotes the renewal of VR/AR interactive mobile device products and innovation of design concept, and provides opinions for consumers to choose VR/AR scenes. In the process of participants' experience, the authors can clearly feel that they are interested in the way of science education combined with virtual reality technology. Although the participants in our study were all college students, they provided evidence that users are more likely to choose larger and lighter mobile devices for VR/AR experience. We found that participants tended to use 9.7-in. screen mobile devices for both VR and AR scenes. The 9.7-in. screen device is the best choice for users to experience VR/AR scenes.

Acknowledgements. The work is supported by Ministry of Education (China) Humanities and Social Sciences Research Foundation under Grant No. : 19A10358002.

References

1. Walker, M.E., Szafir, D., Rae, I.: The influence of size in augmented reality telepresence avatars. In: 2019 IEEE Conference on Virtual Reality and 3D User Interfaces (VR), pp. 538–546, IEEE, March 2019
2. Lin, L., et al.: The effect of hand size and interaction modality on the virtual hand illusion. In: 2019 IEEE Conference on Virtual Reality and 3D User Interfaces (VR), pp. 510–518 IEEE, March 2019
3. Maniar, N., Bennett, E., Gal, D.: The effect that screen size has on video-based m-learning. In: Fifth Annual IEEE International Conference on Pervasive Computing and Communications Workshops (PerComW 2007), pp. 145–148, IEEE, March 2007
4. van der Sluis, F., van den Broek, E.L., van Drunen, A., Beerends, J.G.: Mobile screen size limits multimodal synergy. In: Proceedings of the 36th European Conference on Cognitive Ergonomics. p. 16, ACM, September 2018
5. Hai Ling, Z.: Study on the influence of screen size of touch screen mobile phone on user's operation behavior and comfort (Master's thesis, Zhejiang University) (2013)
6. Wu, Z., Lin, T., Tang, N.: How do visual angle and physical screen size affect presence and emotional responses of game players? In: 2011 International Conference on Consumer Electronics, Communications and Networks (CECNet), pp. 4128–4131, IEEE April 2011
7. Rigby, J.M., Gould, S.J.J., Brumby, D.P., Cox, A.L.: Watching movies on netflix: investigating the effect of screen size on viewer immersion. In: Proceedings of the 18th International Conference on Human-Computer Interaction with Mobile Devices and Services Adjunct, MobileHCI 2016, pp. 714–721, ACM (2016)
8. Hoffman, D.L., Novak, T.P.: Marketing in hypermedia computer-mediated environments: conceptual foundations. J. Mark. **60**(3), 50–68 (1996)
9. Chapiro, A., Kunkel, T., Atkins, R., Daly, S.: Influence of screen size and field of view on perceived brightness. ACM Trans. Appl. Percept. **15**(3), 18 (2018)
10. Witmer, B.G., Singer, M.J.: Measuring presence in virtual environments: a presence questionnaire. Presence **7**(3), 225–240 (1998)

11. Garcia-Gathright, J., Hosey, C., Thomas, B.S., Carterette, B., Diaz, F.: Mixed methods for evaluating user satisfaction. In: Proceedings of the 12th ACM Conference on Recommender Systems. pp. 541–542, ACM, September 2018
12. Raptis, D., Tselios, N., Kjeldskov, J., Skov, M.B.: Does size matter?: Investigating the impact of mobile phone screen size on users' perceived usability, effectiveness and efficiency. In: Proceedings of the 15th International Conference on Human-Computer Interaction With Mobile Devices And Services, pp. 127–136 ACM, August 2013
13. Karlson, A.K., Bederson, B.B., Contreras-Vidal, J.L.: Studies in one-handed mobile design: Habit, desire and agility. In: Proceedings 4th ERCIM Workshop User Interfaces All (UI4ALL), pp. 1–10, (2006)
14. Prange, S., Buschek, D., Alt, F.: An exploratory study on correlations of hand size and mobile touch interactions. In: Proceedings of the 17th International Conference on Mobile and Ubiquitous Multimedia. pp. 279–283 ACM, November 2018
15. Parhi, P., Karlson, A.K., Bederson, B.B.: Target size study for one-handed thumb use on small touchscreen devices. In: Proceedings of the 8th conference on Human-computer interaction with mobile devices and services, pp. 203–210, ACM, September 2006
16. Riches, S., Elghany, S., Garety, P., Rus-Calafell, M., Valmaggia, L.: Factors affecting sense of presence in a virtual reality social environment: a qualitative study. Cyberpsychol. Behav. Soc. Netw. 22(4), 288–292 (2019)
17. Jinghua, H., Zhenb, C., Mingc, A.: The effect of visual complexity and task difficulty on human cognitive load of small screen devices (2019)

Photogrammetric 3D Reconstruction of Small Objects for a Real-Time Fruition

Lucio Tommaso De Paolis[1], Valerio De Luca[1]([✉]), Carola Gatto[2],
Giovanni D'Errico[1], and Giovanna Ilenia Paladini[1]

[1] Department of Engineering for Innovation, University of Salento, Lecce, Italy
{lucio.depaolis,valerio.deluca,giovanni.derrico,
ilenia.paladini}@unisalento.it
[2] Department of Cultural Heritage, University of Salento, Lecce, Italy
carola.gatto@unisalento.it

Abstract. Among the techniques for digitalization and 3D modeling of real objects, photogrammetry is assuming an increasing importance due to easy procedures and low costs of hardware and software equipment. Thanks to the advances of the last years in computer vision, photogrammetry software can reconstruct the geometric 3D shape of an object from a series of pictures taken from different viewpoints. In particular, close-range photogrammetry for the reconstruction of small objects allows performing image acquisition around the target object almost automatically. In this paper we present a brief survey of the hardware setup, algorithms and software tools for photogrammetric acquisition and reconstruction applied to small objects, aimed at achieving a good photorealism level without an excessive computational load.

Keywords: Close-range photogrammetry · Image-based modelling · Textures · Real-time rendering · Photorealistic rendering

1 Introduction

The 3D reconstruction of small objects is becoming more and more popular in various fields including forensic investigations, archaeological documentation, medical reconstruction and virtual prototyping.

Modern photogrammetry is emerging as a more affordable alternative to laser scanning techniques, which require expensive and cumbersome tools, specialized operators and sophisticated software. Photogrammetry exploits several pictures taken from different viewpoints to build a digital 3D model of the object: it detects several feature points in each 2D image based on shape and colour discontinuities and then associates homologous points among different pictures to reconstruct the object position, orientation and shape in the 3D space.

Besides the reconstruction of single objects, photogrammetry allows the construction of immersive virtual environments from panoramic images [1]: both consumer and professional 360° cameras can be employed to acquire in a single

© Springer Nature Switzerland AG 2020
L. T. De Paolis and P. Bourdot (Eds.): AVR 2020, LNCS 12242, pp. 375–394, 2020.
https://doi.org/10.1007/978-3-030-58465-8_28

shot several pictures of the whole scene around a standpoint. Other important applications can be found in cultural heritage [2] and deal with the modeling of facades [3], buildings and monuments, for which Unmanned Aerial Vehicles (UAVs) are often employed for image acquisition [4–6].

Compared to the architectural photo-modeling and the reconstruction of archaeological sites, photogrammetry for 3D modeling of small objects has to cope with different challenges. Beyond the obvious difference in terms of focus depth, there are other important differences between photogrammetry for the reconstruction of buildings and close range photogrammetry. First of all, close range photogrammetry has no limitation in image acquisition, whereas the presence of neighboring buildings or other obstacles in the urban environment often prevents from collecting images from arbitrary points of view around the object of interest. For this reason, close range photogrammetry can take advantage of automated systems designed to take pictures from all the angles needed for an accurate 3D reconstruction, despite some difficulties deriving from shadows, occlusions, changes in lighting conditions and lack of feature points [7].

Starting from the requirements of cultural heritage and e-commerce applications, described in Sects. 2 and 3, in this paper we present a survey on the photogrammetric modelling of small objects, covering all phases of image acquisition, 3D reconstruction and texture extraction. In particular, cultural heritage applications have more strict requirements on morphological details, which should emphasize the relevant aspects from the historical point of view, while e-commerce requires a special focus on visual appearance, which should emphasize the objects' quality.

The rest of the paper is structured in this way: Sect. 4 deals with the typical camera settings for a good photogrammetric acquisition, which is described in Sect. 5; Sect. 6 describes the camera calibration process; Sect. 7 gives some suggestions to build automatic systems for image acquisition; Sects. 8 and 9 presents the most common algorithms and software tools for 3D reconstruction; Sect. 10 deals with the texture extraction process by suggesting also some techniques to improve the visual appearance of the target object; Sect. 11 concludes the paper.

2   Photogrammetry for Cultural Heritage

In Cultural Heritage (CH), photogrammetry is one of the most important techniques since it gives effective possibilities for recording, analysing and operating with very small objects of great interest: it can be typically used in archaeological researches, but it is also very common in restoration, analysis of materials, museum digital archiving, non-destructive investigations.

This technology allows to create 3D models with a high level of detail, with accuracies in the order of tenth of a millimetre, or in any case sub-millimetres, capable of expressing at best all the geometric information content in relation to the size of the object same [8].

Even if the survey in this sector is often associated with a restricted operating field in the space, called "close range", we often see interventions that need different scales at the same time. It means a survey campaign can require distinct instruments that operate with non-homogeneous precision and different reference systems, but that, in the end, must dialogue to each other [9]. Basically, it must be considered that the principles to be applied in close-range photogrammetry are in part the same as for larger objects, but some of the equipment and techniques that can be used will vary. The main factors to consider are related to the size and shape of the object and to the reflective properties of the light on its surface (whether it is opaque, glossy or translucent). Turntables can be typically used with small objects to allow the camera to remain relatively static while the subject is revolved between each exposure, generating the effect of circling the subject with the camera [10].

Before starting a survey campaign, the aims and scope must be carefully evaluated, since the final result can be closely related to them. In an archaeological or museum context, photogrammetric acquisitions can have documentary or divulgation value (different to the commercial advertising purpose). In the first case, photogrammetry constitutes a powerful tool for recording and analysing the objects, in support of scientific research, archiving activities and restoration. The level of detail must be very high, in order to provide a document as accurate as possible. In the second case, photogrammetric acquisitions are carried out to build 3D models for Virtual Reality environments, available through head-mounted displays (HMDs), or 3D web pages, accessible via desktop. In this case, the operator has to balance the level of accuracy with performance and usability requirements. Therefore, close-range photogrammetry in CH must comply with the basic rules of photogrammetry that apply to all the application areas, but in addition a survey campaign must be planned by taking into account the features of that single manufact and the intended use of the same, guaranteeing in each case a good level of loyalty to the original and very high safety standards.

Photogrammetry and laser scannning can be considered as equivalent for some use cases, although it is evident that the direct use of laser scanning on site is not realistic in archaeological campaigns, for the high cost of the instruments and for the logistical and practical constraints of archaeological sites [11].

3 Photogrammetry for E-Commerce

In e-commerce applications, the 3D visualization of items for sale can allow the customers to inspect and appreciate them directly at home from a web portal, provided that the morphological details, the material properties and the overall visual appearance are faithfully and reliably rendered to enhance the value of the object. Online shopping can benefit from the 3D visualization of digital replicas of real objects, which allows customers to zoom, move and rotate items for sale and inspect them from several viewpoints [12].

The adoption of 3D scanners in this field is partially hampered by the dense data points of the generated 3D model, which are not suitable for web visualization, and by the limitations of some devices that do not provide the object's images needed for the reconstruction of the colour model [13].

In particular, when jewelry and valuables are sold through an e-commerce portal, a very important role is played by photorealism, which is intended as a very accurate rendering of the visual appearance aimed at emphasizing those details that are more representative of value or authenticity. It does not require a sub-millimetre precision as in the investigation on historical artefacts. On the contrary, it focuses mainly on reproducing accurately optical and visual effects, such as light reflections, glitters, gradations of colour and material properties, which will allow customers to appreciate the items as if they were exposed in real shop windows. Photorealism does not require an extremely detailed 3D mesh, since many details can be represented by textures. This allows to save a significant amount of time in the mesh construction and to improve the performance of the rendering process. On the other hand, more sophisticated techniques, such as bump mapping and texture baking, employed to convey photorealistic details in textures, bring additional time in the overall workflow.

4   Camera Settings

Before the acquisition process, some camera settings should be carefully adjusted to make pictures suitable for an optimal 3D reconstruction in the later phases.

A medium focal length (50 mm for a full frame camera) is the best choice to reduce any perspective distortion. If a wide-angle lens is used, a larger overlap between adjacent images should be chosen to improve the reconstruction accuracy near the frame edges [14].

A reduced depth of focus can bring important limitations in image acquisition [15]: in this case only a limited portion of images appears sharp enough to be used for 3D reconstruction. To address this problem we can combine a series of optical sections of the object acquired from various focus planes (by moving the camera on a micrometric rail or adjusting the optical parameters).

As an alternative, depth of focus could be extended by increasing the f-number, which is the ratio of the focal length to the diameter of the entrance pupil. However, a smaller aperture greatly reduces the resolution, since it produces diffraction, and requires longer exposure times, with a higher risk of blur caused by vibrations.

Three parameters should be tuned to minimize the noise at the maximum sharpness and focus on the object surfaces: aperture, shutter speed and ISO. Unfortunately, low-end consumer devices do not allow an adequate control of such parameters and produce visible artefacts in JPEG compression [14]. A possible camera setup could be based on [16]:

- An ISO value not greater than 100 (suitable for good lighting conditions and reduced enough to avoid introducing noise in images);
- Moderate aperture values, between f/2.4 and f/13, that could provide a depth of focus suitable for small objects;

– A medium value of shutter speed, between 0.01 and 1 second, that considers light conditions and assures sharp images.

Multiple pictures taken at different focus distances can be combined into a single image with a higher depth of field by means of the focus stacking technique [17,18] available in Helicon Focus[1] based on one of the following three methods:

1. it assigns each pixel a weight depending on its contrast and computes the weighted mean among pixels in all the images;
2. it chooses the source image having the sharpest pixel and creating a depth map from it;
3. it employs a pyramidal approach to represent the image.

The radius parameter defines the number of pixels around a given pixel used to compute its contrast. The smoothing parameter defines the highest contrast regions should be combined within the image set. In the considered scenario we should choose the second method, since we aim at preserving original contrast and colours for a realistic reproduction of the object, and low values for radius (3 pixels) and smoothing (4).

5   Image Acquisition

Image acquisition should be carried out under homogeneous light conditions to avoid colour discontinuities in the textures that will be extracted in the later phases. At the same time, contrast should be set up to avoid harsh shadows or overexposed regions that could hamper the identification of feature points in the pictures.

An optimal photographic session consists in taking several pictures at the same distance around the vertical axis passing through the centre of the target object. The camera can be mounted on a device able to perform a 360° rotation by a step of maximum 20°. It could be necessary to carry out multiple (2 or 3) acquisition cycles setting the camera at different heights. Then the operations should be repeated by changing the object position to take pictures of the parts that were previously in contact with the table.

A scale bar of known length should be included in some pictures to allow an easy scale detection during the 3D reconstruction phase.

Diffuse lighting should be preferred to avoid both light overexposure and harsh shadows that could hide significant details of the object. Polarized filters can be used to reduce any effect deriving from specular reflections of artificial lights.

After camera calibration, settings should not be modified during all the acquisition process since any change to optical parameters could modify the internal geometry of the camera. Even though algorithms allow performing camera calibration and image orientation simultaneously, it is worth keeping the two procedures separated to achieve a better accuracy.

---

[1] https://www.heliconsoft.com/heliconsoft-products/helicon-focus/.

Images should neither be altered geometrically (by means of crop, resize or stabilization operations) nor compressed. For a good texture quality High Dynamic Range (HDR) acquisition mode should be preferred to reproduce a luminance range comparable to the one perceived by the human visual system. White light led strips moving jointly with the table rotation can be used to face with internal shadows produced by the object shape [19].

Projection systems based on laser diodes [20] can be employed during the acquisition phase to create artificial patterns on an object with uniform surfaces to allow the recognition of reference points during the later feature extraction phase. However, such technique is feasible only for highly reflective surfaces that allow the detection of the projected targets.

In general, pictures should have between 50 and 70% of common regions to allow an accurate reconstruction of the hidden parts of the object.

Then a software application can be employed to carry out the feature extraction from each image and identify common points among pictures in a triangulation process.

6   Camera Calibration

A reliable 3D reconstruction requires an accurate camera calibration aimed at estimating internal parameters, to reduce lens distortion effect, and external parameters, to describe the object orientation in the space and the camera-object mutual positions [21].

Structure from Motion (SfM) algorithms are able to estimate internal parameters automatically without the need for artificial targets or calibration grids, provided that the object structure contains a sufficient number of characteristic points that could be recognized in the pictures. In the considered scenario, which deals with small objects, the camera introduces only minor distortions that can be fixed with the radial and tangential model [21].

Some targets with well-defined coordinates and distances can be applied around the object or on its surface to determine a reference system, which is necessary to compute the scale factor. Such a solution is not suitable when the object is too small or when small details should be reproduced accurately.

Another solution consists in using 2D or 3D reference targets containing patterns with a known geometry. They are used as calibrators to compute the external orientation with the scale factor for each camera position. Camera positions identified in 3D space can be used for the 3D reconstruction of the considered object. The same acquisition strategy should be used for the reference target and the object to be modelled: this means the same focus settings, camera-object reciprocal positions and number of photos. This condition is assured by the use of automatic systems to control the rotation of the object table and the camera shots.

A possible 2D target is depicted on the left hand of Fig. 1: it contains 12 patterns with a known geometric shape [19].

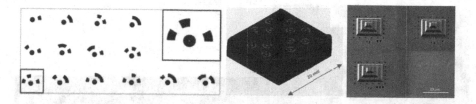

Fig. 1. 2D, 3D and pyramidal targets for calibration

However, 2D targets are not suitable for low tilt angles of the camera ($30°$) and reduced number of photos. On the contrary, 3D targets greatly ease the first step of point recognition and make the procedure more reliable even for low tilt angles. A possible 3D target, reproducing a staircase (shown in the middle of Fig. 1), is described in [22]: 12 targets with an internal diameter of 0.7 mm have been engraved on its surface through laser ablation technology. As an alternative, the pyramidal calibrator described in [23] could be used too (shown on the right hand of Fig. 1).

7   Automatic Acquisition

For close-range photogrammetry, the acquisition process can be carried out automatically by means of motorized systems [24, 25] based on cartesian or polar settings. The polar configuration is usually preferred due to the minor required space. It exploits a camera mounted on an arm inclined with respect to a rotating table [19] (Fig. 2). The choice of the proper distance of the camera from the object is fundamental for an optimal usage of the camera depth of field. Other important parameters, which depend on the object shape and geometry, are the tilt angle of the camera and the rotation step, which determines the number of shots and the overlap between two images.

An Arduino Mega microcontroller can be used to implement an automatic system for photogrammetric acquisition. Some stepper motors can be used to handle the rotation of the object table and some stepper drivers can be employed to protect the mechanical and electronic components from overheating and power/voltage surges. Camera is mounted on an arm with a certain tilt angle, which should be increased or reduced if horizontal or vertical surfaces are predominant respectively.

By reducing the rotation step we can obtain a higher number of shots and a higher percentage of common regions among the pictures. This improves the reconstruction accuracy, but it increases the time needed for both image acquisition and processing. However, a high number of pictures does not provide substantial benefits, while the tilt angle seems the most influencing parameter on the overall quality of the final result.

The acquisition process can be totally automatic and remotely controlled through a computer. At every rotation step a signal is sent to the camera to take a picture. The process is repeated until a 360° rotation is completed.

Fig. 2. Rotation tables for automatic acquisition

8   Algorithms for 3D Reconstruction

Structure-from-Motion (SfM) is the most common algorithm for reconstructing the 3D structure of the object from several pictures taken from different viewpoints [26]. As a first step, SfM extracts a set of features from each image. Thanks to their perspective invariance, features in pictures taken from different viewpoints can be compared according to a similarity metric. In this way, SfM can find out correspondences among features in multiple images (feature matches). Then it performs a geometric verification by estimating a perspective transformation that relates features among different images: in this way it can discard outliers among matching features by means of robust methods such as RANSAC [27]. The remaining image pairs become the edges of a scene graph, which is the input to an incremental reconstruction made up of image registration and triangulation. The former iteratively estimates the pose and the camera intrinsic parameters for each image by solving the Perspective-n-Point problem on the basis of already registered images. The latter tries to extend the scene coverage with points from every newly registered image. A global or local bundle adjustment process refines camera and point parameters to minimize the reprojection error. Global bundle adjustment aims at finding the parameters of the camera view and the 3D points that minimize the mean squared distances between the reprojected points and the observed points. On the other hand, local bundle adjustment, which is typically faster than global bundle adjustment, is performed after the processing of a new image to refine the projection matrix and the reconstructed 3D points.

Multi-View Stereo (MVS) transforms the sparse point cloud produced by SfM into a dense scene representation that includes depth and normal information [28]. Thanks to the information retrieved from multiple views, MVS can solve occlusion problems that typically affect two-view approaches. An important factor is the optimal selection of the views. Depth maps are combined into a unified scene representation, where any inconsistency among single estimates is mitigated.

Shape from photoconsistency (SfP) methods, based on texture and silhouette data retrieved from multiple images, are generally suitable to reconstruct 3D models of hand-made sculptures, but they are affected by colour noise and low accuracy in camera calibration [13]. Shape from silhouette (SfS) methods reconstruct the object geometry from the intersection of infinite polygons corresponding to silhouettes of 2D images taken from different views. Irregular distributions of mesh sizes, consisting in low mesh densities over flat regions and high densities to represent real object features, seem the best approach in terms of result quality, model complexity and computational requirements [13]. However, traditional SfS techniques are not able to handle object concavities and occlusions. For this reason, space carving techniques are often employed to make the reconstruction closer to the real object volume.

9 Software for 3D Reconstruction

Software tools for photogrammetric reconstruction are able to detect automatically the spatial orientation of each image and the camera position with respect to the centre of the snapshots, by performing an automatic calibration of the radial distortion parameters. They automatically detect those points that are stable in pictures taken from different viewpoints and generate a descriptor for each of them [29]. The collimation of homologous points identifies accurately the projection beam with respect to the centre, generating a point cloud that takes into account the metric proportions, composition and shape of the target object. Depth data are retrieved from the camera pose estimated for each picture. Cloud points are seen as mesh vertices on which textures will be applied.

The polygon density can be adjusted according to the desired quality and the scale requirements. In particular, in Agisoft Photoscan/Metashape[2], two important parameters are quality and depth filtering: they establish the level of quality and the level of detail respectively, which determine the required processing time. In general, it is not necessary to build extremely detailed meshes, since the visual rendering of many details will be demanded to textures.

Table 1 reports the time (in minutes) spent by some reconstruction software in the benchmark described in [30]: the test was run on a 4.2 GHz quad core processor and involved 199 photographs taken by a 16 MP camera with 2.2 aperture, focal length 31 mm, sensor size 1/2.6", pixel size 1.12 μm.

In the following subsections, after a survey on commercial and open source software for photogrammetry, we will describe in detail the workflow of 3D reconstruction from images in Agisoft Metashape and in ColMap[3] (Fig. 3).

---

[2] https://www.agisoft.com/pdf/metashape-pro_1_5_en.pdf.
[3] https://colmap.github.io/tutorial.html.

Table 1. Time (in minutes) spent by some reconstruction software

	Photoscan metashape	Reality Capture	3DF Zephyr	Meshroom
Camera matching	4	3	10	481
Dense point cloud generation	201	49	13	
Mesh reconstruction	8		15	
Texture creation (8K medium quality)	3	9	4	
Total 3D reconstruction	216	61	42	481

9.1   Commercial Software

RealityCapture[4] with default settings is able to extract more points than any other software and generates very big files, but it does not assure a higher quality of the 3D model. The model surfaces are affected by noise and do not reproduce accurately the appearance of the physical object.

Photoscan and 3DF Zephyr[5] provide the best results in terms of model resolution, model file size, reconstruction time, texture file size and visual quality. 3DF Zephyr is able to reconstruct 3D models from the minimum number of points in the shortest time (about 40 min), but the resulting surfaces have a poor detail level. Therefore Photoscan seems the most versatile software for photogrammetric reconstruction. Agisoft has recently replaced Photoscan with Metashape, which also provides the possibility of a cloud-based processing that allows saving on hardware costs.

The more expensive Autodesk Recap[6] provides features for mesh correction, such as fixing holes and gaps, polygon and topology optimization, and takes a time between 2 and 5 h to process the model [31]. It can exploit both local CPU/GPU and cloud facilities provided by Autodesk servers.

Agisoft Photoscan provides more features and the possibility to operate at every stage of the work, from photo alignment to texture extraction. After photo upload, Recap carries out a background process and can rebuild the polygonal model automatically, though providing also correction tools for the post-production step.

9.2   Open Source Software

VisualSfM[7] and Regard3D[8] are two easy and immediate open source solutions. The former has faster processing times than Photoscan, but it produces incomplete models. The latter provides a good accuracy, but it still generates incomplete models [32].

The Meshroom[9] open source software processes more than 1.3 millions of points in 8 hours, but it seems not able to generate accurate 3D models [30].

---

[4] https://www.capturingreality.com/.
[5] https://www.3dflow.net/3df-zephyr-pro-3d-models-from-photos/.
[6] https://www.autodesk.com/products/recap/overview.
[7] http://ccwu.me/vsfm/.
[8] https://www.regard3d.org/.
[9] https://alicevision.org/.

Another open source software, OpenDroneMap[10], was originally designed for processing UAV imagery, but it can be used also for close-range photogrammetry.

Among open source solutions, ColMap is able to produce very detailed and accurate 3D models by supporting the entire photogrammetric reconstruction from image matching to mesh production. It exploits the GPU CUDA environment to optimize image matching and dense reconstruction, which are the most computationally intensive tasks.

9.3   Metashape Workflow

Metashape provides a tool for an automatic evaluation of image quality to allow discarding photos with focus issues. It suggests to leave out from the reconstruction process those images with a score lower than 0.5, provided that the remaining photos could assure a good coverage for the target object. The score value expresses the sharpness level of the region with the best focus within the image.

The alignment process detects the camera position and orientation for each photo and generates a sparse point cloud. The final result can be visualized to remove or realign any not properly positioned photo. We can realign a group of images by selecting at least 4 points in each photo and indicating their projections at least on two of the already aligned photos.

The level of accuracy is one of the parameters in the alignment process. The "high accuracy" setting provides a high level of accuracy by processing photos in their original size. On the other hand, "medium accuracy", "low accuracy" and "lowest accuracy" options enable a downscaling along each image dimension by a factor of 2, 4 and 8 respectively. With the "highest accuracy" option a 2 factor upscale is applied along each image dimension to improve the accuracy in the localization of anchor points. However, in most cases this setting does not assure consistent benefits (since it assumes a very high image sharpness) and requires a very long processing time.

Since the sparse point cloud generated by SfM is not enough to describe the object surface accurately, a dense point cloud should be created: it includes depth data computed from the camera positions estimated in the previous step. The "ultra high quality" option, which requires the longest processing time, works on original images, whereas lower quality options imply image downscaling. Noisy or blurry images can generate outliers among detected points, which can be filtered by the algorithms provided by Metashape. If some small details of the target object should be preserved, the "Mild" option under "depth filtering mode" should be selected. If there is no significant detail to be rendered, the "Aggressive" mode can be chosen to discard most of outliers. The "Moderate" option is a trade-off between the two modalities.

Before 3D mesh construction, a bounding box is automatically generated. In the considered scenario, which deals with close-range small objects, the "Arbitrary" option should be selected under the "Surface type" setting to make no assumption on the object morphology.

---

[10] https://www.opendronemap.org/.

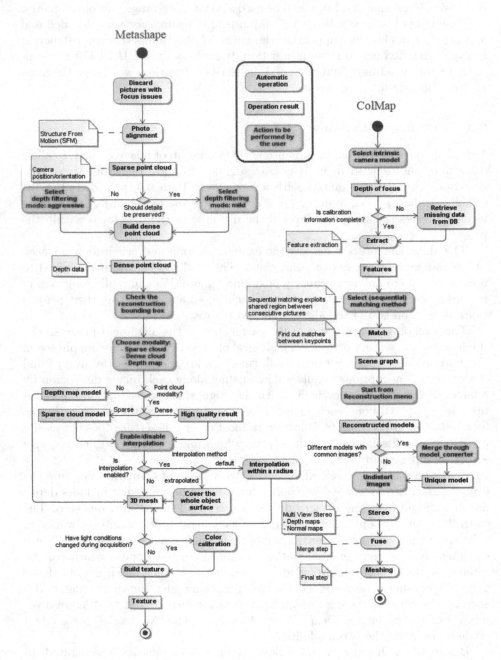

Fig. 3. UML activity diagrams for Metashape and ColMap workflows

The "Source data" option allows to choose among "Sparse cloud", "Dense cloud" and "Depth maps". The first option quickly generates a model based only on the sparse point cloud. The second option provides a high quality result, but it requires a long processing time. The third option should be preferred when the "Arbitrary" surface type has been chosen: it makes the reconstruction process less demanding than the "Dense cloud" mode thanks to a better exploitation of the information retrieved from input images. On the other hand, if we select a modality based on a point cloud we can choose whether an interpolation procedure should be disabled or not. By enabling interpolation, we can choose between a default mode, which interpolates around each point within a certain coverage radius, and an "Extrapolated" mode, which generates a model covering the whole object surface. If interpolation is disabled, the process reconstructs only dense point cloud areas leaving holes that should be filled in a manual post processing step.

Before launching the texture extraction process through the "build texture" command, if light conditions have changed during the acquisition process, a colour calibration should be carried out, even though it could be a time demanding job.

For a good visual quality of the model, a generic texture mapping should be performed based on default settings to make textures as uniform as possible without any particular assumption on the object geometry. Among texture generation parameters, the "Mosaic" option should be chosen under the "Blending mode" setting. In this way, for the low frequency component a weighted average will be computed among pixels in images with common regions, while the high frequency component, representing details, will be taken from the image having the best resolution in the area of interest.

9.4 ColMap Workflow

In the first step ColMap carries out feature extraction, which consists in detecting key points distributed in the loaded pictures. This processing step can be run on either GPU or CPU: the first mode provides a better result for high contrast images, but it requires a display connected to the PC. By choosing "Extract features" from the "Processing" menu an intrinsic camera model can be selected: it is possible to retrieve depth of focus information automatically from data in images or to specify intrinsic parameters manually. If calibration information encoded into images is incomplete, ColMap tries to retrieve missing data from a database. The "Extract" command can be given to launch the process.

The second step aims at finding out matches between keypoints in different images. After selecting "Match features", the matching mode can be chosen from the "Processing" menu among the following options: exhaustive, sequential, vocabulary tree, spatial, transitive and custom. The "Sequential matching" method is the most suitable for the considered scenario, characterized by a sequence where only consecutive pictures have shared regions. For this reason, we do not need to compare each image with all the other ones, as the "Exhaustive matching" method would do at the cost of a longer processing time. The "Match" command should be given to launch the process, which requires a CUDA-enabled GPU.

After the generation of the scene graph, the reconstruction process can be launched by choosing "Start" from the "Reconstruction" menu: the scene is extended incrementally through point triangulation and results are shown in real-time. ColMap tries to reconstruct multiple models if not all the pictures are registered within the same model. If different models have common images, the *model_converter* executable can be launched to merge them into a unique reconstruction.

Then the reconstructed model should be selected and the "Multi-view stereo" command can be chosen from the "Reconstruction" menu. After the "undistort" command on the images, depth maps and normal maps are computed through the "stereo" command. Then a merge step and a final step are performed through the "fuse" command and the "meshing" command respectively.

Reconstructed normals for the point cloud cannot be directly visualized in ColMap but only by means of external software, such as in Blender by enabling "Show Normal/Curvature" from the "Render" menu.

10   Texture Extraction and Visual Rendering

Texture extraction consists in isolating those image regions related to the 3D model entities by detecting matches for each region and dividing the image according to the object geometry. The next step is the UV unwrapping process, which represents the polygonal faces of the 3D mesh in an ordinary image called UV texture map: it transforms every point (X, Y, Z) of the 3D model space into a point (U, V) on the image plane through a surface parametrization called UV mapping.

The picture to be preferred for texture extraction is the one with the largest space taken by the projection (to achieve a higher level of detail) and where the axis of sight of the camera tends to be orthogonal to the 3D model (to obtain a better distribution of the texture pixels in the image). Some software solutions are able to execute this process automatically by selecting the images according to these two criteria. However, manual intervention could be necessary because the automatic procedure does not consider hidden details and cannot fill information gaps caused by shaded areas.

The mapping of the extracted textures requires the identification of groups of adjacent faces belonging to connected regions on the object surface.

A photo editing software could be used to remove visual discontinuities caused by light variations and shaded areas, for instance by cloning pixels in the neighbouring regions. Moreover, filters could be employed to adjust the level of tones or saturation and light parameters of a colour component or all the colours.

For a photorealistic rendering not only the object geometry but also the material properties should be simulated by reproducing also ambient lighting accurately. To this end, an important factor is the rendering of all the articulations of the model shapes through the reproduction of reflections and contact shadows among the object fissures.

Since ambient light would tend to flatten the rendering of different surface regions, it should be replaced by a set of diffuse lights. Ambient occlusion [33,34] can be employed to avoid that such expedient makes processing times significantly longer: it provides an approximation to full global illumination by considering the amount of ambient light every surface point can receive from the outside. Computing times can be furtherly reduced by adopting texture baking [35], described in the following section, to register rendering features as textures.

Bump mapping allows to improve the level of detail of textures without changing the geometrical complexity of the model. A perturbation of the surface normal is associated with each pixel according to a depth map, that is an image where relief elements are represented by a greyscale of 255 levels: each UV coordinate is associated with an elevation value that will warp the texture. In the rendering phase the light will transform the U and V normals of the texture pixels according to the direction vectors in the depth map to determine a brightness value.

Among the rendering platforms where the 3D model can be imported, Unreal Engine offers levels of photorealism very close to those achievable with precomputed rendering. It exploits Ray Traced Distance and Field Ambient Occlusion techniques, which allow to soften net shadows and simulate wide and close light sources, and Lightmass Bake Texturing, which allows reducing computation time to face with hardware performance issues [31].

During the "Shadowing" step, only surfaces intercepted by light beams are considered, while the processing of all the other regions of the model is omitted. Unfortunately, this technique can generate visible artifacts if the mesh is tasseled or not uniform.

The ray tracing hardware support recently introduced by NVIDIA RTX[11] enables real-time processing for global illumination effects (such as refraction, order-independent transparency and complex shadows), for which only approximations were employed in previous implementations.

10.1 Texture Baking

Texture baking [35] is a good compromise for a realistic reproduction of spatial details on systems with low rendering capabilities or not able to deal with dense and complex geometric meshes.

Firstly, a continuous triangle mesh can be generated from a non structured dense point cloud. Beside representing morphological details accurately, such mesh should have no artifact or hole, it should have a uniform distribution and it should be two-manifold. Mesh defects could be fixed by means of Graphite[12] free software.

Then decimation and reconstruction processes should be carried out to simplify the mesh complexity and optimize the topology. The aim of the decimation process is to reduce the number of faces, edges and vertices by preserving the

---

[11] https://devblogs.nvidia.com/introduction-nvidia-rtx-directx-ray-tracing/.

[12] http://alice.loria.fr/index.php/software/3-platform/22-graphite.html.

general morphology without changing the coordinates of textures and the boundaries of materials. Atangeo Balancer nPro[13] can perform decimation by taking care of visual appearance of details on the mesh surfaces. The aim of topological reconstruction is to render the general morphology of the model by omitting details that will be rendered through texture baking. Many semi-automatic tools allow the user to draw guiding curves on the surface to determine the edges of the final mesh.

The Instant Meshes free software computes the parameters describing the face orientation and the border alignment. Then it optimizes position data to distribute the faces on the new polymesh uniformly and splits the edges to get sharp features. It is worth generating triangular meshes to avoid any shadow inconsistency caused by the use of different rendering engines. Moreover, this allows to perform a further mesh repairing step.

While bump maps simply encode height information by means of grayscale values, normal maps represent the orientation of surface normals through Red-Green-Blue (RGB) values. Therefore, they describe three depth dimensions: red shades represent the height for the X-axis, while green and blue shades describe values for the Y- and Z- axis respectively.

The impact of the light on a surface region can be determined from surface normal data and from the light source angle in the virtual environment. Even though faces in the low-poly mesh may have the same orientation, the interaction of the light with the normal orientation (retrieved from the high-poly faces) gives a realistic visual appearance of morphological details.

The next step is UV unwrapping, which consists in dividing the object geometry in correspondence of well known seams and grouping polygons optimally. To this aim we can use the tools in 3DCoat[14], a software package providing better results than many other solutions.

The next normal baking process can be carried out with the Knald[15] software, which exploits GPU computing to generate high quality textures in a short time from meshes containing up to 350 millions of triangles. Knalds builds up a tangent space normal map, which defines the normals to the low-poly mesh surface. This normal map must be converted to grayscale. The level of adherence in visual appearance obtained after the topological reconstruction directly influences the amount of details represented by the normal map.

To create standard photo textures we can import the topologically reconstructed mesh and its UV components in Photoscan or Metashape by selecting "Keep uv" as texture mapping mode to use existing UV parameterization.

Then the standard colour texture map (diffuse map) and the greyscale normal map can be merged. In the GIMP[16] image processing software we can carry out this operation by choosing the "Overlay blending" mode: according to dark tones in diffuse texture and contrast enhancement in grayscale normal map, changing

---

[13] https://www.atangeo.com/buy/nPro.

[14] https://3dcoat.com/.

[15] https://www.knaldtech.com/knald/.

[16] https://www.gimp.org/.

the opacity/alpha values of the base and top layers can improve the desired effect. The obtained texture can be applied to the low-poly mesh by means of Photoscan or Metashape.

10.2 Improving Texture Mapping with Artificial Markers

The accuracy and reliability of texture mapping can be improved by surrounding the target with artificial markers used as control points and integrating partial 3D data acquired through laser scanning [36]. The marker coordinates, the parameters of texture camera and the pose parameters of texture images are optimized through a global bundle adjustment method. Marker registration and Iterative Closest Point algorithms are employed to detect the rigid transformations from the coordinate system of the scanner to that of the object and from the coordinate system of the 3D model to that of the scanner.

10.3 Surface Reflectance

Traditional photogrammetry pipelines assume the object to be reconstructed has only Lambertian surfaces: this unrealistic assumption is often the main cause of a poor visual appearance of the 3D model. Lambertian surfaces are characterized by an isotropic luminance, which makes them uniformly bright from any direction of view. Unfortunately, many real-world surfaces of glossy materials like metals, plastics or ceramics are typical examples of non-Lambertian surfaces. In these cases, a Bidirectional Reflectance Distribution Function (BRDF) is estimated to represent the surface reflectance. The spatially varying BRDF model proposed in [37] exploits light-field cameras, which are able to detect light direction, for depth and reflectance estimation by assuming a known distant light source.

Since the typical assumption of an infinite light distance is not valid for close-range photogrammetry, another spatially varying BRDF model [38] jointly estimates the position of light sources, albedo and BRDF parameters. Besides images used for mesh reconstruction, it requires a High-Dynamic-Range environment map as input data. While low luminosity samples contain the diffuse albedo, high luminosity samples represent specular highlights and can be used to triangulate the light sources. Based on this consideration, an alternating optimization is iterated until convergence, which consists of a step estimating the optimal reflectance and light setup from high luminosity samples, given the current diffuse albedo, and a step estimating the optimal diffuse albedo from low luminosity samples, given the current light.

Another work [39] showed the BRDF reconstruction accuracy can be improved by a preliminary selection of reliable regions based on three assumptions:

1. the estimation error is higher for regions with higher curvature;
2. the reflectance distribution increases with the dot product of the surface normal and the half vector between the light direction and the view direction;
3. for distant light images, the region of highest intensity represents the peak of specular reflection.

11   Conclusions

Photogrammetry can build 3D replicas of real objects by reconstructing their position, orientation and shape from several pictures taken from different viewpoints. Nowadays it is emerging as a more affordable alternative to laser scanning techniques, which require complex acquisition procedures. For the reconstruction of a small object, pictures can be taken by performing a complete rotation around it without the obstacles that usually hamper such operation in outdoor environments. We have described the typical hardware setup for an automatic and accurate image acquisition. Then, we have presented a survey on algorithms and tools for 3D reconstruction and for the enhancement of visual appearance, which is important to emphasize the object quality.

Contribution

The author Carola Gatto wrote Sect. 2 of the paper, entitled "Photogrammetry for cultural heritage".

References

1. Barazzetti, L., Gianinetto, M., Scaioni, M.: Automatic processing of many images for 2D/3D modelling. In: Daniotti, B., Gianinetto, M., Della Torre, S. (eds.) Digital Transformation of the Design, Construction and Management Processes of the Built Environment. RD, pp. 355–365. Springer, Cham (2020). https://doi.org/10.1007/978-3-030-33570-0_32
2. Hanan, H., et al.: Batak Toba cultural heritage and close-range photogrammetry. Procedia - Soc. Behav. Sci. **184**, 187–195 (2015)
3. Fritsch, D., et al.: Modeling Façade structures using point clouds from dense image matching. In: International Conference on Advances in Civil, Structural and Mechanical Engineering, pp. 57–64 (2013)
4. Alidoost, F., Arefi, H.: An image-based technique for 3D building reconstruction using multi-view UAV images. In: International Archives of the Photogrammetry, Remote Sensing and Spatial Information Sciences - ISPRS Archives, vol. XL-1-W5, pp. 43–46. Copernicus GmbH. December 2015
5. Murtiyoso, A., Grussenmeyer, P.: Documentation of heritage buildings using close-range UAV images: dense matching issues, comparison and case studies. Photogram. Rec. **32**(159), 206–229 (2017)
6. Adamek, M., et al.: The possibilities of using drones in the 3D object modelling field. In: MATEC Web of Conferences, vol. 210 (2018)
7. Granshaw, S.I.: Structure from motion: origins and originality. Photogram. Rec. **33**(161), 6–10 (2018)
8. Girardi, F.: Rilevamento e modellazione tridimensionale per oggetti di piccole dimensioni. Ph.D. thesis, University of Bologna, May 2011
9. Bitelli, G.: Moderne tecniche e strumentazioni per il rilievo dei beni culturali. In: Atti della VI Conferenza Nazionale ASITA, Perugia, 5–8 Novembre (2002)
10. England, H.: Photogrammetric applications for cultural heritage. Guidance Good Pract. **8**(2), 383–388 (2017)

11. Bitelli, G., et al.: The potential of 3D techniques for cultural heritage object documentation. In: Videometrics IX, vol. 6491, p. 64910S. International Society for Optics and Photonics, January 2007
12. Kaewrat, C., Boonbrahm, P.: Identify the object's shape using augmented reality marker-based technique. Int. J. Adv. Sci. Eng. Inf. Technol. 9(6), 2193–2200 (2019)
13. Phothong, W., et al.: Quality improvement of 3D models reconstructed from silhouettes of multiple images. Comput.-Aided Des. Appl. 15(3), 288–299 (2018)
14. Remondino, F., et al.: Design and implement a reality-based 3D digitisation and modelling project. Dig. Heritage Int. Congr. 1, 137–144 (2013)
15. Gallo, A., et al.: 3D reconstruction of small sized objects from a sequence of multi-focused images. J. Cult. Heritage 15(2), 173–182 (2014)
16. Lastilla, L., et al.: 3D high-quality modeling of small and complex archaeological inscribed objects: rele vant issues and proposed methodology. In: ISPRS Annals of the Photogrammetry, Remote Sensing and Spatial Information Sciences, vol. XLII-2-W11, pp. 699–706. Copernicus GmbH, May 2019
17. Clini, P., et al.: SFM technique and focus stacking for digital documentation of archaeological artifacts. In: International Archives of the Photogrammetry, Remote Sensing and Spatial Information Sciences - ISPRS Archives, vol. XLI-B5, pp. 229–236. Copernicus GmbH, June 2016
18. Kontogianni, G., et al.: Enhancing close-up image based 3D digitisation with focus stacking. In: International Archives of the Photogrammetry, Remote Sensing and Spatial Information Sciences - ISPRS Archives, vol. XLII-2-W5, pp. 421–425. Copernicus GmbH, August 2017
19. Galantucci, L.M., et al.: A stereo photogrammetry scanning methodology, for precise and accurate 3D digitization of small parts with sub-millimeter sized features. CIRP Ann. - Manuf. Technol. 64(1), 507–510 (2015)
20. Sims-Waterhouse, D., et al.: Verification of micro-scale photogrammetry for smooth three-dimensional object measurement. Meas. Sci. Technol. 28(5), 055010 (2017)
21. Galantucci, L.M., Guerra, M.G., Lavecchia, F.: Photogrammetry applied to small and micro scaled objects: a review. In: Ni, J., Majstorovic, V.D., Djurdjanovic, D. (eds.) AMP 2018. LNME, pp. 57–77. Springer, Cham (2018). https://doi.org/10.1007/978-3-319-89563-5_4
22. Lavecchia, F., et al.: Performance verification of a photogrammetric scanning system for micro-parts using a three-dimensional artifact: adjustment and calibration. Int. J. Adv. Manuf. Technol. 96(9), 4267–4279 (2018)
23. Ritter, M., et al.: A landmark-based 3D calibration strategy for SPM. Meas. Sci. Technol. 18, 404–414 (2007)
24. Barbieri, G., da Silva, F.P.: Acquisition of 3D models with submillimeter-sized features from SEM images by use of photogrammetry: a dimensional comparison to microtomography. Micron 121, 26–32 (2019)
25. Marshall, M.E., et al.: Automatic photogrammetry for the 3D digitisation of small artefact collections. In: International Archives of the Photogrammetry, Remote Sensing and Spatial Information Sciences - ISPRS Archives, pp. 355–365. Research for Development (2019)
26. Schönberger, J.L., Frahm, J.M.: Structure-from-motion revisited. In: Conference on Computer Vision and Pattern Recognition (CVPR) (2016)
27. Fischler, M.A., Bolles, R.C.: Random sample consensus: a paradigm for model fitting with applications to image analysis and automated cartography. Commun. ACM 24(6), 381–395 (1981)

28. Schönberger, J.L., Zheng, E., Frahm, J.-M., Pollefeys, M.: Pixelwise view selection for unstructured multi-view stereo. In: Leibe, B., Matas, J., Sebe, N., Welling, M. (eds.) ECCV 2016. LNCS, vol. 9907, pp. 501–518. Springer, Cham (2016). https://doi.org/10.1007/978-3-319-46487-9_31

29. Bocanet, V., et al.: Low-cost industrial photogrammetry for rapid prototyping. In: MATEC Web of Conferences, vol. 137, p. 06001 (2017)

30. Reljić, I., et al.: Photogrammetric 3D scanning of physical objects: tools and work-flow. TEM J. 8(2), 383–388 (2019)

31. Palestini, C., Basso, A.: The photogrammetric survey methodologies applied to low cost 3D virtual exploration in multidisciplinary field. In: International Archives of the Photogrammetry, Remote Sensing and Spatial Information Sciences - ISPRS Archives. vol. XLII-2-W8, pp. 195–202. Copernicus GmbH, November 2017

32. Vacca, G.: Overview of open source software for close range photogrammetry. In: International Archives of the Photogrammetry, Remote Sensing and Spatial Information Sciences - ISPRS Archives, vol. XLII-4-W14, pp. 239–245. Copernicus GmbH, August 2019

33. Le, B.H., et al.: High-quality object-space dynamic ambient occlusion for characters using bi-level regression. In: I3D 2019: ACM SIGGRAPH Symposium on Interactive 3D Graphics and Games, I3D 2019, pp. 1–10. Association for Computing Machinery, May 2019

34. Campagnolo, L.Q., Celes, W.: Interactive directional ambient occlusion and shadow computations for volume ray casting. Comput. Graph. (Pergamon) 84, 66–76 (2019)

35. Verhoeven, G.J.: Computer graphics meets image fusion: the power of texture baking to simultaneously visualise 3D surface features and colour. In: ISPRS Annals of the Photogrammetry, Remote Sensing and Spatial Information Sciences, vol. IV-2-W2, pp. 295–302. Copernicus GmbH, August 2017

36. Yin, Y., et al.: Texture mapping based on photogrammetric reconstruction of the coded markers. Appl. Opt. 58(5), A48–A54 (2019)

37. Wang, T.C., et al.: SVBRDF-invariant shape and reflectance estimation from a light-field camera. IEEE Trans. Pattern Anal. Mach. Intell. 40(3), 740–754 (2018)

38. Innmann, M., et al.: BRDF-reconstruction in photogrammetry studio setups. In: IEEE Winter Conference on Applications of Computer Vision (WACV), pp. 3346–3354, March 2020

39. Ono, T., et al.: Practical BRDF reconstruction using reliable geometric regions from multi-view stereo. Comput. Vis. Media 5(4), 325–336 (2019)

Adaptive Detection of Single-Color Marker with WebGL

Milan Košťák(✉) ⓘ, Bruno Ježek ⓘ, and Antonín Slabý ⓘ

Faculty of Informatics and Management, University of Hradec Králové, Rokitanského 62, 50003 Hradec Králové, Czechia
{milan.kostak,bruno.jezek,antonin.slaby}@uhk.cz

Abstract. This paper presents a method for real-time single-color marker detection. The algorithm is based on our previous work, and the goal of this paper is to investigate and test possible enhancements that can be done, namely color weighting, hue calculation, and modified versions of dilatation and erosion operations. The paper also explains a solution for dynamic color selection, which makes the system more robust to varying lighting conditions by detecting the color hue, saturation, and value under the current conditions. The designed methods are implemented in WebGL, which allows running the developed application on any platform with any operating system, given WebGL is supported by the web browser. Testing of all described and implemented improvements was conducted, and it revealed that using hue weighting has a good effect on the resulting detection. On the other hand, dynamic thresholding of saturation and value components of the HSV color model does not give good results. Therefore, testing for finding the right threshold for these components had to be done. The erosion operation improves the detection significantly while dilatation does not have almost any impact on the result.

Keywords: Marker detection · WebGL · GPGPU · Augmented reality

1 Introduction

Marker detection is a process of finding the area in the given image that possesses a unique character, sign, or color. There are many ways and many existing systems that try to solve this problem.

A broad spectrum of applications can use such markers. The most typical example is reading QR codes, which are usually used as a way of storing textual information in the real world in a form that is easily and quickly readable by machines. Other examples of these systems include ARTag [1], ARToolKit [2], ARToolKit Plus [3], AprilTag [4], and CALTag [4]. More sophisticated augmented reality (AR) applications need to obtain information about the surrounding environment. These applications combine the real world with artificial elements. The typical AR system uses a camera to capture information about the real world. One of the ways to obtain this information is to use a marker, defined by a pattern that the application has to detect in the image (e.g. [5–7]).

L. T. De Paolis and P. Bourdot (Eds.): AVR 2020, LNCS 12242, pp. 395–410, 2020.
https://doi.org/10.1007/978-3-030-58465-8_29

On the other side of the spectrum, there are marker-less systems that extract information from the real scene only (e.g. [8, 9]). This process is usually more complicated and requires more computational time than a situation where the marker is present. Several studies focused on the comparison of marker-based and marker-less systems have been conducted in [10–12].

The authors focus their research on the area of single-color marker detection over a longer period. Previous works include two implemented algorithms for color marker detection [13, 14]. Even though the algorithms were functional, detection problems appeared in some cases. Their common problem is the detection of a fixed color marker only. Our current goal is to develop an improved version of the algorithm that works for any color without editing the application code. Modifying source code is usually cumbersome for programmers and other IT specialists and impossible for everyone else. The color should be selected by the user in an interactive way without using any color pickers and other similar approaches. Another improvement is adapting the selected color to the current lighting conditions that can change the way the camera perceives the color.

The paper is structured as follows. Section 2 presents related works. Section 3 describes in detail the algorithm we propose. Section 4 gives details about the implementation in the WebGL environment. Section 5 presents the results we achieved, explains the testing methodology, and contains tests and comparisons that we made. Finally, Sect. 6 includes conclusions and outlines future research.

2 Related Work

Markers represent a popular system for camera localization, and many publications on this topic can be found. The following summary focuses on the most related works to our work.

Lai and Wang [15] present an interactive AR system using adaptive marker tracking. The system's target domain is entertaining education. The authors used ARToolKit [2] for marker detection. The adaptivity of the system was achieved by having a cube, the faces of which were all covered with different markers. This method always leads to a situation when at least three markers are visible.

Smith et al. [16, 17] demonstrate the system for adaptive color marker detection with visual feedback. The system uses the color light sensor to capture the surrounding light of the scene environment. The sampled color information is used to select the optimal tracking color. Using the HSV color model, they select the hue color component of the marker color gained by moving 180° from the environmental color to find the opposite color. This approach achieves the maximum contrast between the surrounding light and the marker color.

Rasmussen et al. [18] deal with the tracking object by color alone. The work focuses on tracking one or multiple objects in space based on user-selected sample pixels. They also introduce a loss recovery procedure.

Romero-Ramirez et al. [19] focused on possible approaches in speeding up the process of detection of squared fiducial markers. They claim that their method processes over 1000 frames per second in 4K resolution images. The main idea of their solution lies in detecting multiple scales because markers can usually be detected in smaller versions of the image. This approach is maintaining precision while speeding up the process.

Marker detection is not restricted just for AR games and other similar applications. Other applications can be found in the medical tracking domain. Saaidon et al. [20] investigated a color marker-based navigation system for image-guided surgery. They deal with problems like unintended patient moving. They admit that the accuracy and performance of these systems still need some improvements.

Our previous publications [13, 14] were focused on this area – and both present different solutions for real-time color marker detection. The first one [13] describes a GPU algorithm that divides the image into rectangular sub-areas of the same size in which a marker is localized. The main problems have appeared in cases where the marker was split between two or more regions, and it consequently may be difficult to detect. Such situations did not often occur in the test environment, but it was not appropriate to ignore the problem. The second version [14] of the algorithm eliminated this problem by the horizontal and vertical projection of the segmented area of color marker. The image pixels are scanned in all columns and rows, and the number of pixels with the marker color is summed. Afterward, the coordinate at which the center of the marker is most likely to be located was obtained using the weighted arithmetic mean. Both algorithms are parallelized and were implemented using GPU shaders.

3 Marker Detection

Our proposed solution consists of several algorithms, each implementing a part of the functionality. Apart from the main detection, there is an algorithm for initial color selection and a separate algorithm for detection testing. The solution uses mainly the hue-saturation-value component color model (HSV) through its algorithms.

The main detection itself includes several partial improvements that enhance the precision of marker location detection. The first improvement is hue weighting and color component thresholding. The second one uses a raster processing of a color image that is similar to binary morphological operations dilation and erosion.

3.1 Introduction of the Main Algorithm

All implemented improvements were incorporated in the main detection algorithm that is based on the algorithm that we already published in [14]. This paper focuses on its possible improvements and color adaptability algorithm. The base algorithm summary follows.

The main algorithm consists of two steps implemented on GPU (Fig. 1). During the first step, pixels with the correct color are horizontally and vertically projected and summed for every column and every row. During the second step, the weighted arithmetic means of pixel counts and pixel coordinates is calculated. The horizontal and vertical means represent the (x, y) coordinate of the detected marker.

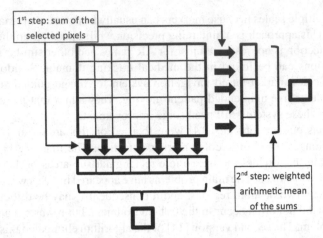

Fig. 1. Illustration of the two steps of the main detection algorithm

3.2 Target Color Selection

The detection of single-color markers is based on correct target color selection, and it is the first processing task. The manual setting of the target color is cumbersome, and it could be imprecise. Also, the problem is that many colors look different outside on a sunny day or inside under artificial lighting. For instance, our testing showed that green color (RGB 0,255,0) looks like green under daylight, but the camera perceived it almost like a cyan color (RGB 0,255,255) under artificial light. We decided to overcome this problem by implementing an algorithm that selects the color under the current lighting conditions.

One frame of the camera feed is taken with the marker in an exact predefined area. This means that the area should contain only the color of that marker. The area is processed only for 10×10 pixels output resolution regardless of the input size. Each unit is processing a hundredth of the area, which means that 100 groups are present. The mean value for every RGB component is calculated, and all pixels inside the group are processed. As the last step, the final mean RGB color is converted to the HSV color model, which is the output of every group. Those one hundred colors in the HSV color model are copied from the GPU memory to the CPU memory. The mean value of the hue component of all obtained color values is calculated. Mean calculation is a problematic operation because the range of hue values is mapped to the circle in the HSV model. Conversion to another space allowing the correct mean calculation of the circular hue component must be made according to the following formula (1). It must be noted that the result of this calculation is not the same as the arithmetic mean, and the result becomes less precise when the values are far from each other.

$$huemean = atan2\left(\sum_{i=1}^{100} \sin(h_i), \sum_{i=1}^{100} \cos(h_i)\right) \tag{1}$$

Saturation and value components of the HSV model do not have this problem. Both components are processed separately but in the same way. Firstly, they are normalized and sorted. The lowest ten values and highest ten values are ignored. Minimum and maximum value from the remaining values is used for thresholding of the marker saturation and value. If the difference between the minimum and maximum is lower than 0.1, they are edited equally to make the difference between them at least 0.1.

The final output of the target color calibration is five specific values – one for hue, two for saturation, and two for value. All of them are used as color marker etalon for detection until the user changes it to a different one with the same steps.

3.3 HSV Color Model and Hue Weighting

The algorithm is supposed to work more dynamically with the color space. HSV color model provides the advantage of working with color through only one value instead of three as in the RGB color model. Saturation and value components are depending on the color that was detected.

The target hue is always fixed beforehand, but a whole range of colors with similar hues needs to be considered. The less the color is similar to the selected target color, the lower is the weight the pixel coordinates will have. The calculation we propose is nonlinear. The pixel coordinates weight is calculated as a difference from the target hue and the actual pixel hue. The absolute value of this value is converted to the range, and finally, square root operation is performed to achieve nonlinearity. The threshold divergence is currently fixed to 20° in the (0°, 360°) interval. In cases where the target hue and the actual hue are both close to 0°, a problem can occur when one of these values is lower and will appear as a number close to but lower than 360°. This situation must be dealt with, too.

$$pixel\ coordinates\ weight = \sqrt{\frac{thresholddivergence - abs(targethue - actualhue)}{thresholddivergence}}$$

$$(2)$$

HSV saturation and value components are also used in the detection, but only for thresholding permitted values. The threshold is partially dynamic; it is calculated during the step of target color selection from minimum and maximum detected values.

3.4 Improving Results by Morphological Dilatation and Erosion

Our proposed algorithm does not implement the dilatation and erosion operations fully, but their principle is used when calculating the pixel weight. As described earlier, the pixel coordinate weight is calculated as a difference of its hue from the target color hue. However, the input image usually contains many failures like small holes inside a marker region and small areas of the right colored pixels, which are not part of the marker. These operations are performed to smoothen possible holes in the marker and to penalize individual pixels of a similar hue. To save computation time, we do not perform them on the whole image in a separate pass. They are merged with the first step of the algorithm. Both operations are tested separately, and combined testing is performed too.

Dilatation-Like Operation

If the pixel weight is nonzero, then its value is returned without performing the dilatation operation. When pixel weight is zero, the algorithm looks on all eight neighboring pixels, and it takes the mean value of the weights of the pixels that are nonzero.

$$weight = \begin{cases} weight; \ if \ weight \neq 0 \\ \frac{\sum_{k=1}^{8} w_k}{\sum_{k:w_k \neq 0}^{8} 1}; \ if \ weight == 0 \end{cases} \tag{3}$$

Erosion-Like Operation

If the pixel weight is zero, then this value is returned. When pixel weight is nonzero, the algorithm looks at all eight neighboring pixels. If the sum of weights of all these pixel weights is less than a threshold value X, then the previous weight is discarded, and zero is returned. This operation helps to discard separate groups of pixels that have similar colors to the selected target color.

$$weight = \begin{cases} 0; \ if \ weight == 0 \\ 0; \ if \ weight \neq 0 \ and \ \frac{\sum_{k=1}^{8} w_k}{\sum_{k:w_k \neq 0}^{8} 1} < X \\ weight; \ if \ weight \neq 0 \ and \ \frac{\sum_{k=1}^{8} w_k}{\sum_{k:w_k \neq 0}^{8} 1} \geq X \end{cases} \tag{4}$$

3.5 Possible Future Improvements

Currently, the system adaptability is achieved by dynamically selecting the color of the marker when the user starts the application and is asked to scan the marker. This approach can easily overcome different lighting conditions that can have a substantial impact on how the camera perceives colors. This adaptability could be further improved. In the current situation, when the user selects the color, this color is fixed unless he decides to select a new one manually.

A detected marker is usually an integral area without any gaps. Our algorithm works by scanning all rows and columns of the image. These projections could be used to detect if multiple integral areas were detected by using Otsu's method for automatic image thresholding. The original Otsu's method [21] is very time consuming, but computationally efficient implementations have since been proposed [22, 23].

Artificial neural networks are a different approach to detection. Nowadays, they are a popular tool in the field of computer vision. They should be capable of enough generalization to be able to detect single-color markers. Works in this area have already been conducted (e.g. [24, 25]).

4 Implementation

The algorithms were implemented using WebGL in the web browser environment. Web browsers are available on both desktop and mobile devices. That is a significant advantage in comparison to native applications. The development of the native application depends on the target operating system and whether the target platform will be a desktop or mobile device. WebGL is a standard JavaScript API for GPU accelerated 3D rendering. The designed algorithm works heavily with images in real-time, and therefore using GPU acceleration is a necessity.

4.1 Main Algorithm

The main algorithm is based on the same principle as in our previous work [14]. It is a two-pass algorithm where each pass is processed by the classical visualization pipeline that is composed of vertex and fragment shaders. The summary of the algorithm is presented in Sect. 3.1.

The current implementation uses the same algorithm only with a few improvements that do not influence the algorithm's principle. The main algorithm was improved in several ways to achieve more precise detection, namely, hue weighting, dynamic calibration of hue, saturation, and value components of the HSV color model, and operations similar to erosion and dilatation.

4.2 Target Color Selection (Calibration)

Target color selection is implemented in a single fragment shader. Postprocessing of the values is done in JavaScript code. Before the main detection algorithm is executed, the user is required to present the marker he is planning to use. This marker must fit in a specific rectangular region of the input camera image. The GPU pipeline processes this image. Namely, the fragment shader is reducing the resolution for consequent faster reading to CPU operating memory. The fragment shader is invoked only for 10×10 pixels resolution regardless of the input size. Each unit is processing a hundredth of the area that is supposed to contain the marker color. Following snippet of JavaScript code shows the algorithm for the calculation of mean of circular quantity, which in our case is the hue component of the HSV model.

```
let sumSin = 0;
let sumCos = 0;
hues.forEach(val => {
    sumSin += Math.sin(toRadians(val));
    sumCos += Math.cos(toRadians(val));
});
let atan = toDegrees(Math.atan2(sumSin, sumCos));
if (atan < 0) atan += 360;
hueMean = Float32Array.from([atan]);
```

4.3 Hue Weighting

Hue weighting is achieved by this minimalistic GLSL (OpenGL Shading Language) function inside a fragment shader.

```
float hueWeight(float targetHue, float currentHue) {
    float diff = abs(targetHue - currentHue);
    float weight = pow((hueThreshold - diff) /
hueThreshold, 0.5);
    return weight;// in range <0;1>
}
```

4.4 Dilatation and Erosion

Dilation and erosion are implemented inside the first step of the algorithm. They are separate functions implemented in GLSL in the fragment shader. Dilatation is only performed when the pixel hue weight is zero. Erosion is done only when pixel hue weight is not zero.

```
float weight = getPixelWeight(texCoords);
// do dilatation operation
if (weight == 0.0) {
    float weights[8];
    readNeighborPixels(texCoords, weights);
    float sum = 0.0;
    float count = 0.0;
    for (int i = 0; i < 8; i++) {
        if (weights[i] != 0.0) {
            sum += weights[i];
            count++;
        }
    }
    weight = count == 0.0 ? 0.0 : sum / count;
}
// do erosion operation
if (weight != 0.0) {
    float weights[8];
    readNeighborPixels(texCoords, weights);
    float sum = 0.0;
    for (int i = 0; i < 8; i++) sum += weights[i];
    if (sum < 6.5) weight = 0.0;
}
sum += weight;
```

4.5   Source Code

The source code of the implementation is publicly available in this GitHub repository:
https://github.com/milankostak/Marker-detection/tree/v3.0.

5   Results and Testing

The implemented algorithm was tested on various images grabbed by a mobile phone camera. Selected results of calibration and detection are shown in the form of the following mobile phone screenshots (Fig. 2–3).

Fig. 2. These figures present the process of aligning the marker inside the box in the middle to select the marker color during the calibration process before starting its detection.

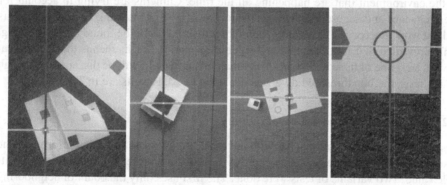

Fig. 3. These figures display the correct detection of different markers (pink, red, blue, blue circle) in a real environment where there are other markers of different colors, which are correctly ignored. The first two (pink, red) detected markers were drawn manually by hand. The third one (blue) was printed. The last figure shows the detection of a shape with a hole in it. Our algorithm allows such detections due to its nature of summing pixels for every row and every column. (Color figure online)

Testing is an essential part of examining whether the algorithm is working as intended. It is also crucial for comparing with other solutions. As this is not our first attempt to develop an algorithm for single-color marker detection, we needed to have a reliable way of testing the performance of those detectors.

The testing methodology that we implemented consists of having a set of images. These images were created as frames from captured videos. All these snapshots were tagged with the right center of the marker. There were 140 images from 8 different videos. Out of those 140 images, 66 images did not contain any marker, and 74 images contained exactly one marker. The color of the marker in each recorded video was calibrated beforehand and inserted into the test program automatically from a previously manually created file. The testing images sometimes contained an object of a similar color as the marker color to test the limits of the algorithm. That is one of the reasons why false positive counts are sometimes high.

A separate testing algorithm was implemented to compare detected results with the expected correct results. This algorithm counts true positive, true negative, false positive, and false negative cases. True positive is each case where the marker was detected with the distance from the ground truth that is lower than 50 pixels. False positive is a situation where there was a detected marker, but there was no marker in the image, or the distance from it is greater than 50 pixels. The mean and median of the deviation from the correct marker are calculated for true positive cases, and lower results mean a better outcome. The accuracy is a sum of true positive and true negative cases divided by the total number of images.

5.1 Saturation and Value Threshold Finding

Preliminary testing showed that using the dynamic values for saturation and value components of the HSV color model often breaks the detection. That is probably due to changes in the environment that are happening all the time. Cameras are trying to account for these changes and accordingly change the image in a way that using those components did not work as expected. Therefore, the right threshold had to be found through testing, which revealed that for saturation and value is around 0.3. This means that colors that have at least one of the components lower than this threshold will be discarded. Through all the tests, the hue threshold divergence is fixed to 20. Results are in Table 1.

5.2 Testing the Erosion-Like Operation

Testing with the same settings but with the erosion-like operation was performed. The results show that this operation can improve the detection if the threshold is set to a suitable value. Two variants of tests were done. The first uses only the count of neighboring pixels that have the hue in the threshold divergence range (Table 2). This method did not have as good effect as using the sum of the weighted hues of the neighboring pixels (Table 3). That is probably because the count is including pixels which hue can be less similar to the target hue while using the sum ensures that only pixels that have neighboring pixels with similar hue are used. Best results were achieved with 0.35 threshold for saturation and value, and with 6.5 threshold for the weight of neighboring pixels (Table 3). This setting achieved the best result among all the tests that we performed.

Table 1. The table contains the results of testing of different threshold for saturation and value components of the HSV color model. The results show that the threshold around 0.3 is providing the best detection.

Threshold for saturation and value components of the HSV color model	Accuracy	Mean of true positive	Median of true positive	False positive count	False negative count
0.20	48.6%	4.08	1.65	72	0
0.25	56.4%	3.83	1.76	61	0
0.30	56.4%	4.11	1.81	60	1
0.35	56.4%	5.37	2.16	59	2
0.40	52.1%	5.99	2.64	58	9
0.45	46.4%	5.72	2.43	55	20
0.50	51.4%	5.87	3.33	30	38

Table 2. The table contains the results of testing of a different threshold for erosion-like operation. The erosion is performed in the variant where only the count of neighboring pixels is considered.

Threshold for saturation and value components of the HSV color model	Erosion threshold count	Accuracy	Mean of true positive	Median of true positive	False positive count	False negative count
0.3	8	57.8%	5.78	1.95	58	1
	7	57.1%	4.92	1.83	59	1
	6	57.1%	5.14	1.81	59	1
	5	56.4%	3.98	1.83	60	1
0.4	8	50.7%	5.11	2.43	58	11
	7	51.4%	5.36	2.57	58	10
	6	52.1%	5.63	2.60	58	9
	5	52.1%	5.72	2.59	58	9
0.5	8	55.0%	7.18	4.00	25	38
	7	55.0%	7.19	4.07	25	38
	6	55.0%	7.19	3.95	25	38
	5	52.9%	5.13	3.37	28	38

Table 3. The table contains the results of testing of a different threshold for erosion-like operation. Erosion is performed in the variant where the weight of neighboring pixels is considered. The table shows that this operation improves the results significantly over the situation where it is not used in Table 1.

Threshold for saturation and value components of the HSV color model	Erosion threshold	Accuracy	Mean of true positive	Median of true positive	False positive count	False negative count
0.30	7	74.3%	5.42	1.79	22	14
	6.5	75.0%	5.40	2.13	33	2
	6	70.7%	4.28	1.74	40	1
	5	69.3%	4.35	1.66	42	1
0.35	7	75.7%	5.78	1.82	20	14
	6.5	**79.3%**	**4.85**	**2.13**	**25**	**4**
	6	72.1%	5.34	1.93	37	2
	5	68.6%	4.21	1.85	42	2
0.40	7	72.9%	6.78	2.96	19	19
	6,5	76.4%	5.49	3.45	22	11
	6	67.9%	3.91	2.41	35	10
	5	64.3%	4.97	3.18	9	9
0.45	7	67.1%	10.55	5.99	12	34
	6,5	65.7%	4.74	3.93	17	31
	6	60.0%	4.13	3.01	28	28
	5	58.6%	6.95	4.08	34	24

5.3 Testing Dilatation-Like Operation

This testing was done with the same parameters as in Table 1, but the dilatation-like operation was performed. Two variants of the test were done (Table 4). Dilatation is executed only when the pixel weight is zero. The first variant looks at the neighboring pixels and returns their mean weight. The second variant returns the largest weight.

Testing of the combination of erosion-like and dilatation-like operation was also done. All the results did not show any significant changes compared to the situation where dilatation was not used.

5.4 Testing Previously Implemented Algorithms

The algorithms published in [13, 14] were also included in the testing. The same methodology and the same dataset were used. Both algorithms were using fixed color, and a

Table 4. The table contains the results of testing of the dilatation-like operation. Both versions of outputs are presented in the table. The table shows that dilatation operation does not improve the results in either variant compared to the situation when the operation is not used in Table 1.

Threshold for saturation and value components of the HSV color model	Dilatation output	Accuracy	Mean of true positive	Median of true positive	False positive count	False negative count
0.3	mean	56.4%	4.48	1.82	60	1
	max	55.7%	3.29	1.79	61	1
0.4	mean	51.4%	6.80	3.00	59	9
	max	51.4%	6.84	2.99	59	9
0.5	mean	50.0%	3.70	2.57	32	38
	max	50.0%	3.70	2.57	32	38

Table 5. This table contains the testing of the first detection algorithm [13].

Threshold for components of the RGB color model	Accuracy	Mean of true positive	Median of true positive	False positive count	False negative count
0.10	55.0%	21.81	15.86	16	47
0.15	**57.1%**	**18.07**	**14.32**	**24**	**36**
0.20	52.9%	17.05	16.43	42	24
0.25	25.0%	18.89	13.02	94	11

change implementing support for dynamic color was necessary. These algorithms use the RGB color model and testing for a different threshold from the selected target color components was performed. The testing was conducted for comparison purposes. The results of the first algorithm (Table 5) [13] are slightly better in the detection than the second algorithm (Table 6) [14], but the actual precision is significantly worse. Both results are worse than the new investigated improvements.

5.5 Performance

The performance of the main GPU algorithm is still the same as the original. Rendering time for one full pass through the pipeline takes around 2 ms for laptop version of Nvidia GTX 1060 [14].

Table 6. This table contains the testing of the second detection algorithm [14].

Threshold for components of the RGB color model	Accuracy	Mean of true positive	Median of true positive	False positive count	False negative count
0.10	**55.0%**	**5.20**	**2.18**	**16**	**47**
0.15	52.9%	4.49	2.90	30	36
0.20	37.9%	14.28	7.37	63	24
0.25	11.4%	4.86	2.43	113	11

While running, the web application is using between 5 to 6 MB in JavaScript heap space. The whole browser tab is taking around 90 MB of memory. CPU usage is oscillating between 30 to 40% for Intel Core i5-8300H.

These measurements mean that our algorithm is not only precise but also has great performance allowing real-time experience.

5.6 Summary

The best results were achieved with the algorithm that uses hue weighting and includes erosion operation in the variant that uses the weight of the neighboring pixels. The best version was using an erosion weight threshold of 6.5. The most suitable threshold for saturation and value components of the HSV model was 0.35.

Table 7. Summary of all tested algorithms, its improvements, and other used methods.

Previous marker detection implementations	Worse results, especially precision
Using Hue in HSV instead of RGB	An issue with calculating mean
Using weighted hue instead of a fixed threshold as in the previous implementations	Better results
Using calculated saturation and value components of the HSV model	Not usable; the environment changes a lot; using a fixed low threshold of around 0.3 works well
Erosion-like operation with count	Small improvement
Erosion-like operation with weight	Significant improvement
Dilatation-like operation with mean or max	Almost no change

6 Conclusion and Future Work

In the paper, we present several ideas for marker detection improvements, namely, hue weighting, dynamic calibration of hue, saturation, and value components of the HSV color model, and operations similar to erosion and dilatation. Several of these ideas work, but some of them did not make any change to the detection.

Using hue weighting improves the results significantly. The erosion-like operation improves detection in a great way, too. These enhancements improve the precision of the detection but also help to reduce false positive and false negative cases.

On the other side, things that did not work as expected include using dynamic saturation and value. The main problem seems to be the way cameras handle environment changes, which has a major impact on saturation and brightness. Dilatation-like operation was also among those ideas that did not change the results of the detection.

Our future work will probably focus on the possibility of using machine learning and artificial neural networks. These are popular and powerful tools in computer vision, and we suppose it should be possible to achieve satisfying results.

Acknowledgement. This work and the contribution were supported by a project of Students Grant Agency (SPEV) - FIM, University of Hradec Kralove, Czech Republic.

References

1. Fiala, M.: ARTag, a fiducial marker system using digital techniques. In: 2005 IEEE Computer Society Conference on Computer Vision and Pattern Recognition (CVPR 2005). pp. 590–596. IEEE, San Diego (2005). https://doi.org/10.1109/CVPR.2005.74
2. KATO, H.: ARToolKit : Library for vision-based augmented reality. Tech. Rep. IEICE PRMU. 101, pp. 79 86 (2002)
3. Fiala, M.: Comparing ARTag and ARToolkit Plus fiducial marker systems. In: IEEE International Workshop on Haptic Audio Visual Environments and their Applications. p. 6 (2005). https://doi.org/10.1109/HAVE.2005.1545669
4. Shabalina, K., Sagitov, A., Sabirova, L., Li, H., Magid, E.: ARTag, AprilTag and CALTag fiducial systems comparison in a presence of partial rotation: manual and automated approaches. In: Gusikhin, O., Madani, K. (eds.) ICINCO 2017. LNEE, vol. 495, pp. 536–558. Springer, Cham (2020). https://doi.org/10.1007/978-3-030-11292-9_27
5. Hirzer, M.: Marker detection for augmented reality applications. (2008)
6. Xiang, Z., Fronz, S., Navab, N.: Visual marker detection and decoding in AR systems: a comparative study. In: Proceedings International Symposium on Mixed and Augmented Reality. pp. 97–106. IEEE Computer Social Darmstadt, Germany (2002). https://doi.org/10.1109/ISMAR.2002.1115078
7. Susan, S., Tandon, S., Seth, S., Mudassir, Chaudhary, R., Baisoya, N.: Kullback-Leibler divergence based marker detection in augmented reality. In: 2018 4th International Conference on Computing Communication and Automation (ICCCA). pp. 1–5 (2018). https://doi.org/10.1109/CCAA.2018.8777570
8. Gao, Q.H., Wan, T.R., Tang, W., Chen, L.: A stable and accurate marker-less augmented reality registration method. In: 2017 International Conference on Cyberworlds (CW). pp. 41–47 (2017). https://doi.org/10.1109/CW.2017.44
9. Chen, C.-W., Chen, W.-Z., Peng, J.-W., Cheng, B.-X., Pan, T.-Y., Kuo, H.-C.: A real-time markerless augmented reality framework based on slam technique. In: 2017 14th International Symposium on Pervasive Systems, Algorithms and Networks 2017 11th International Conference on Frontier of Computer Science and Technology 2017 Third International Symposium of Creative Computing (ISPAN-FCST-ISCC). pp. 127–132 (2017). https://doi.org/10.1109/ISPAN-FCST-ISCC.2017.87

10. Gupta, A., Bhatia, K., Gupta, K., Vardhan, M.: A comparative study of marker-based and marker-less indoor navigation in augmented reality. Int. Res. J. Eng. Technol. (IRJET) **5**, 1–4 (2018)
11. Cheng, J.C.P., Chen, K., Chen, W.: Comparison of marker-based and markerless Ar: a case study of an indoor decoration system. In: Lean and Computing in Construction Congress - Volume 1: Proceedings of the Joint Conference on Computing in Construction. pp. 483–490, Greece (2017). https://doi.org/10.24928/JC3-2017/0231
12. Stridbar, L., Henriksson, E.: Subjective evaluation of marker-based and marker-less ar for an exhibition of a digitally recreated swedish warship. (2019)
13. Košť'ák, M., Ježek, B.: Mobile phone as an interactive device in augmented reality system. In: DIVAI 2018 (2018)
14. Košťák, M., Ježek, B., Slabý, A.: Color marker detection with webgl for mobile augmented reality systems. In: Awan, I., Younas, M., Ünal, P., Aleksy, M. (eds.) MobiWIS 2019. LNCS, vol. 11673, pp. 71–84. Springer, Cham (2019). https://doi.org/10.1007/978-3-030-27192-3_6
15. Lai, C.-L., Wang, C.-L.: Mobile edutainment with interactive augmented reality using adaptive marker tracking. In: 2012 IEEE 18th International Conference on Parallel and Distributed Systems. pp. 124–131. IEEE, Singapore (2012). https://doi.org/10.1109/ICPADS.2012.27
16. Smith, R.T., Marner, M.R., Thomas, B.H.: An adaptive color marker for Spatial Augmented Reality environments and visual feedback. In: 2011 IEEE Virtual Reality Conference. pp. 269–270. IEEE, Singapore (2011). https://doi.org/10.1109/VR.2011.5759502
17. Smith, R.T., Marner, M.R., Thomas, B.H.: Adaptive color marker for SAR environments. In: 2011 IEEE Symposium on 3D User Interfaces (3DUI). pp. 119–120 (2011). https://doi.org/10.1109/3DUI.2011.5759234
18. Rasmussen, C., Toyama, K., Hager, G.D.: Tracking Objects By Color Alone. (1996)
19. Romero-Ramirez, F.J., Muñoz-Salinas, R., Medina-Carnicer, R.: Speeded up detection of squared fiducial markers. Image Vis. Comput. **76**, 38–47 (2018). https://doi.org/10.1016/j.imavis.2018.05.004
20. Saaidon, N., Sediono, W., Sophian, A.: Altitude Tracking Using Colour Marker Based Navigation System for Image Guided Surgery. In: 2016 International Conference on Computer and Communication Engineering (ICCCE). pp. 465–469. IEEE, Kuala Lumpur, Malaysia (2016). https://doi.org/10.1109/ICCCE.2016.103
21. Otsu, N.: A Threshold Selection Method from Gray-Level Histograms. IEEE T. Syst. Man. Cy. B. **9**(1), 62–66 (1979)
22. Liao, P.-S., Chen, T.-S., Chung, P.-C.: A Fast Algorithm for Multilevel Thresholding. (2001)
23. Huang, D.-Y., Wang, C.-H.: Optimal multi-level thresholding using a two-stage Otsu optimization approach. Pattern Recognit. Lett. **30**, 275–284 (2009). https://doi.org/10.1016/j.patrec.2008.10.003
24. Kim, G., Petriu, E.M.: Fiducial marker indoor localization with artificial neural network. In: 2010 IEEE/ASME International Conference on Advanced Intelligent Mechatronics. pp. 961–966. IEEE, Montreal, QC, Canada (2010). https://doi.org/10.1109/AIM.2010.5695801
25. Dash, A.K., Behera, S.K., Dogra, D.P., Roy, P.P.: Designing of marker-based augmented reality learning environment for kids using convolutional neural network architecture. Displays **55**, 46–54 (2018). https://doi.org/10.1016/j.displa.2018.10.003

Users' Adaptation to Non-standard Controller Schemes in 3D Gaming Experiences

Riccardo Galdieri[1] (✉) (iD), Mata Haggis-Burridge[2] (✉) (iD), Thomas Buijtenweg[2], and Marcello Carrozzino[1] (✉) (iD)

[1] Scuola Superiore Sant'Anna, Piazza Martiri della Libertà, 33, 56127 Pisa, Italy
{r.galdieri,marcello.carrozzino}@santannapisa.it
[2] Breda University of Applied Sciences, Monseigneur Hopmansstraat 2, 4817 JS Breda,
The Netherlands
haggis.m@ade-buas.nl, Buijtenweg.T@buas.nl

Abstract. With hundreds of new games being released every week, designers rely on existing knowledge to design control schemes for their products. However, in the case of games with new game mechanics, designers struggle to implement new button schemes due to the lack of research on players' adaptation to new and non-standard controls. In this study we investigated PC players habits when playing a game they have no knowledge of, and how they adapt to its non-standard control scheme. Data was collected by using a specifically designed game instead of relying on pre-existing ones, allowing us to design specific game mechanics to exploit users' habits and monitor players' behaviour in their home environments. Preliminary results seem to indicate that PC players do pay attention to control schemes and are able to quickly learn new ones, but they also prefer to make mistakes in favour of execution speed.

Keywords: Game studies · Game design · Human-Computer interaction · Player-video game interaction · Game peripherals · Subconscious behaviour

1 Introduction

Every aspect of the interaction between a user and a videogame has been subject of analysis for as long as game existed, with many different disciplines working together to produce a significant amount of valuable literature to guide the design of new experiences. It is surprising that, of all the elements that contribute to the creation of a digital game, there is a fundamental one that seems to receive very little attention: users' relationship with input devices. Game peripherals - often called controllers or gamepads - tend to share similar features and ergonomics, which led to the creation of de-facto standards that are more based on intuitions or historical choices than on real studies. This creates a problem when a new type of game emerges and a new control scheme is required: there is no previous knowledge on how to design the experience so that players can quickly adapt to the control scheme, or what players' behaviour would be in with different mechanics. Finding a solution has become a priority in later years,

© Springer Nature Switzerland AG 2020
L. T. De Paolis and P. Bourdot (Eds.): AVR 2020, LNCS 12242, pp. 411–419, 2020.
https://doi.org/10.1007/978-3-030-58465-8_30

especially with new technologies such as Virtual Reality (VR) and Augmented Reality (AR) struggling to find the best way to make players adapt to completely new types of games.

In this project we aim to investigate how players adapt to non-standard button schemes while playing in unsupervised environments. A game was specifically designed for this purpose, and it was released on an online platform where players could download and play the way they would play any other game. This paper introduces the first preliminary results of our study, obtained by analysing the first game sessions, and aims to introduce the first observations regarding players' behaviour. A follow-up study is currently being planned and will be published as soon as more conclusive data will be gathered and analysed.

Current literature is based on in-lab experiments, where players are asked to play in conditions that are not familiar to them. The bias that these experiments inherently have is hard to quantify, and verifying this data against similar experiments in players' natural gaming environment has proven to be a challenge. Our approach solves this problem, but introduced many more variables to be taken into account to prevent potential data contamination. By building a game that was as close as possible to a commercial product we hope that the results would contribute to building a literature that would be helpful in the design of new experiences.

2   Previous Literature

As cliché as this may sound, game peripherals have been studied for as long as videogame existed. By definition, games require a series of inputs by the user, and in digital worlds this happens through external hardware. From the first "pong" in 1958, played on an oscilloscope through a small joystick [1], to the modern consoles with ergonomic controllers, hardware has always been part of the game experience itself. Of course in recent years different inputs have successfully been tested, but historically speaking, as reported in the survey presented in [2], standard controllers are still the most common way to interact with a digital experience.

A comprehensive study on the relationship between game peripherals and performance has been published in 2019 [3], where the authors evaluated the influence of game controllers on experience and perceived performance. A similar study was conducted in [4], where they evaluated the self-perceived emotional response (frustration, boredom, flow) of players using different controllers to play the same FPS game, showing initial evidence that what is perceived as "natural" interaction, as defined in [5], may not be as natural for videogame players. FPS games were also the core element of the study proposed by [6], where the authors evaluated players' overall performances with two different hardware configurations, comparing a non-standard device with players' preferred ones.

A first study to actively research how different control schemes could influence players enjoyment was conducted in [7], where university students were asked to play the same sports game on different consoles with radically different control schemes, reporting a significant difference between the groups. A similar experiment was conducted in [8], where a group of FIFA 12 players were asked to play two matches with two different control schemes, the first one familiar to them, and the second one being slightly

Fig. 1. End of the tutorial area. All tutorial rooms have an arrow that point the player to the right directions

different. No significant variation in subjective or objective measures indicated any preference for any control scheme, even though several potentially influencing factors were highlighted by the authors and more research should be conducted on the matter (Fig.1).

At the best of our knowledge, all the aforementioned experiments were conducted in a lab environment and were conducted through pre-existing games.

3   The Experiment

The game, called "EscapeTower", was built with the use of Unreal Engine and distributed through Itch.Io store, while the data was collected through GuraaS, an online platform for remote gameplay data collection. Players were not aware of the purpose of the study during their experience to preserve their natural behaviour throughout the experience. "EscapeTower" is a classic first-person puzzle game, where the player has to solve a series of puzzles to reach the end. Two main areas constitute the "tower": a tutorial area, that is also used to collect players' demographics, and the actual puzzle area, divided on three floors connected by ladders. The whole experience is structured to have a linear progression in terms of interactions and difficulty, and there is no loading time between the two areas.

It was important for the study to profile players' basic demographics, but it was also preferable not to use a questionnaire to keep the game experience intact. Making a digital questionnaire would have been challenging in terms of interaction, and was likely to introduce some unwanted biases on controller mapping. It was first thought that a questionnaire could be set up through mouse and keyboard, but being these disabled in the game, it would have been misleading for the user. Using the controller was also not an option, as it would give players interaction indications that will not represent actual gameplay interactions. For these reasons, it was decided to use the tutorial section to introduce all interaction before the actual game. All mechanics that players will use in the main area – with the only exception of invisible walls – are introduced in this first section.

Unlike the tutorial area, the main tower has more of a labyrinth-structure. Each floor has a main corridor through which players can enter all rooms (if unlocked). Floors are connected through ladders, some of which are freely accessible and some others that must be unlocked by pressing a button. The game also features hidden doors, that can be unlocked just by pressing a button, and levers that are associated with certain doors. Every time a lever was pressed, all doors linked to it were switched from close to open or vice versa, depending on their current status.

3.1 Interaction Design

Before the game even starts players are notified that the only way to interact with the game is through a standard XBOX controller (Fig. 2), and no instruction is provided nor any possible combination of buttons was somehow presented or introduced before the game itself. Players are required to understand by themselves how the game works and how to interact with the environment.

Fig. 2. Standard XBOX controller for PC. On the right, the four buttons that can be used to interact in the game

Given the absence of literature on the matter, it was assumed that the most common button, the lowest one in a gamepad, would be the most common to press if players already had a background in gaming. It was therefore decided not to assign A – the button in the bottom position on XBOX controllers – to any common interaction. Back buttons such as L1, L2, R1 and R2 were also tracked, but no interaction has been assigned to them. The final scheme can be found in Table 1.

The interaction dynamic is the same for each object. When a player gets close to an object and looks approximately in its direction, the UI shows the expected button, and the player can interact by pressing it on their controllers (Players could interact only when its button is visible). Some objects, such as doors and buttons, have big colliders and are easy to interact with. Other objects, such as grabbables and ladders, are much harder to interact with.

By having small objects that are harder to grab, it was possible to measure if players assimilate the action required to grab a key and automatically perform it, and if players wait for the UI to show before performing an action or they press regardless of that and adjust their aim. No vibration feedback was provided.

Table 1. Map of all actions that can be performed in the game

ID	Interaction	Button	Min Interactions*
0	PressButton	A	3
1	InvisibleDoor	A	3
2	JumpFromLadder	A	3
3	Unscrew	B	8
4	GrabObject	B	2
5	PlaceObject	B	1
6	EnterLadder	B	3
7	OpenDoor	X	7
8	SwitchLever	X	2
9	UnlockDoor	Y	3
10	GrabKey	Y	7
11	UnlockCage	Y	3
		TOTAL	45

* Excluding tutorial

3.2 Potential Biases and Data Contamination

Being the audience unknown, the scenario was designed to be as neutral as possible, with no clear cultural references presented anywhere. The walls were painted in white with minimal ambient occlusion, and some simple decorations were added around the main corridors to reduce the impact that the game could have on photosensitive subjects. Different decorations had been tested, but some of them seemed to guide players' eyes towards certain elements that were being monitored and were therefore discarded. Hands and arms were covered by gloves and sleeves so that it would not be possible for players to assign gender, skin colour or age to it.

The main problem emerges in terms of interactions. The game clearly states that the game requires an XBOX-style controller, and an icon showing a similar controller was displayed every time a keyboard or mouse button was pressed. However, due to technical limitations, different peripherals (such as PlayStation controllers) were also able to play the game. Regardless of the used controllers, the game always showed an icon representing an XBOX controller when an interaction was available.

4 Results

At the time of writing, the game has been downloaded 128 times from the official Itch.io page, with 51 game sessions played by 41 unique users. Out of 51 sessions, only 26 are meaningful, where a meaningful session is defined as one where the player has stayed within the game more than 240 s and has entered the main area. These 26 sessions have been completed by 22 unique players, which means that 4 sessions have been conducted and completed by players who have previously played the game. It is not possible however, to know whether if the same person has played the game twice or if a second person has played instead, as the tutorial is only played the first time the game is started.

In terms of users' profiling, data shows that the game was played by 19 people who identify as male, 1 who identify as female, and 2 who would rather not say. 16 players were playing from Europe, 4 from North America, 1 from South America and 1 from Africa. 21 out of 22 users play games "Every day" or "often". The only diversifier is the age, with one person younger than 14, 1 between 15 and 20, 9 from 21 to 26, 5 from 27 to 32, 4 from 33 to 38, and 2 older than 50. In terms of experience, 12 people have been playing for over 20 years, 2 have played between 15 and 20 years, and the remaining between 6 and 15 years.

In terms of interactions, adding together all the interactions from meaningful sessions we obtained 4017 button clicks (average of 154.4 per session), plus 381 button clicks from the controllers' back buttons (14.65 per session). On average, the A button has been clicked 19.7 times per sessions, B has been pressed 49.2 times, X has been pressed 37.5 times, and Y has been pressed 48.0 times.

Out of these 4017 clicks, 669 (16.5%) resulted in a missed interaction, meaning that the click was done when no interaction was possible, and 538 (13.4%) were wrong interactions, meaning that the player clicked the wrong button when an interaction was available. It is worth noticing that out of 538 wrong interactions, 76 of them (15%) were done on objects that previously had an interaction and was no longer active, such as an open door or a button. Looking at how the wrong interaction distributes, X is the button that is mostly pressed as substitute of another (166 times), while A and B are used as substitute significantly fewer times (117 and 101 respectively). Y is not often used as substitute, being wrongly pressed only 78 times. Giving it a different perspective, it is possible to evidence that mistakes do not happen with the same frequency: for instance, X is often used as substitute of Y (93 times out of 166) while Y is used instead of A only 4 times out of 78. It is interesting to see the data from a different perspective: if we consider the expected interaction first, we notice that Y is the button that most often not pressed when expected, with 158 mistakes, while only 48 times players have pressed a different button when A was expected. Full data is shown in Fig. 3. The majority of a missed hits, 388 out of 669 (58%), is followed by another missed hit, making series of multiple hits more likely than one simple missed hit. Of the remaining 281 missing hits, 82 were grab actions (12% of the total), 45 were ladder climbs (6.7%), 31 lever press (4.6%) and 21 an exit menu opening (3.1%). The remaining 15.3% is constituted by a mix of all other possible interactions.

If we ignore the sequence of missed hits, and look for the next meaningful interaction following each one of them, data shows a completely different scenario. 175 times it

```
'A': {'X': 43, 'Y': 17, 'B': 57, 'Tot': 117}   'A': {'X': 26, 'Y': 4, 'B': 18, 'Tot': 48}
'B': {'X': 35, 'Y': 48, 'A': 18, 'Tot': 101}   'B': {'X': 47, 'Y': 21, 'A': 57, 'Tot': 125}
'X': {'A': 26, 'Y': 93, 'B': 47, 'Tot': 166}   'X': {'A': 43, 'Y': 53, 'B': 35, 'Tot': 131}
'Y': {'X': 53, 'A': 4, 'B': 21, 'Tot': 78}     'Y': {'X': 93, 'A': 17, 'B': 48, 'Tot': 158}
```

Fig. 3. Each error was logged as "Used button 1 on object @, 2 was expected". On the left, mistakes are grouped by 1, with the expected buttons between brackets. On the right, buttons are grouped by 2, with the used buttons between brackets.

was an object grab (26%), 109 exit menu (16.3%), 101 were a ladder climb (15.1%) 78 were lever press (11.6%) and 65 were interactions with a door (9.8%). The remaining 21.2% is constituted by a mix of all other possible interactions.

5 Discussion

Looking at players' demographics, the majority of players were European males who play games on a daily basis. They have all played games for at least 5 years, with the majority of them with more than 15 years of experience. The logical conclusion is that the gathered data will be representative of experienced players only.

Putting together missed and wrong interactions results in 30% buttons being pressed with no consequence. Given that the game does not require any action to be performed within any time range, this shows that players have a general tendency to ignore accuracy to perform the action as fast as possible. The long series of missed hits also support this intuition, suggesting that they would rather press a button as quicktly as possible and make a mistake, rather than aim with precision and wait for the action to be available.

It is surprising, given the initial considerations, that missed interactions appear more often – even though just by a small margin – than wrong interactions. This seems to suggest that for experienced players, it is more important to perform a quick action than to get the right button to interact. This interpretation of data is supported by the type of interaction that follows a missed interaction: excluding the 109 times people opened the exit menu after missed hits, out of 560 missed interactions, 300 of these (53.5%) were either an object grab or an interaction with a ladder, the two that were most difficult by design. The collider size here presents a significant role: object grabs and ladder interactions are the most common action that follows a missing hit regardless of counting single or multiple missing hits, but they also show a significant increment from the first to the second group, suggesting that these objects were hard to grab and caused many missing hits in a row. Big objects such as button to press and doors had big colliders, were easy to interact with, and were therefore subject of less missed interactions.

An interesting consideration can be done by looking at how many times buttons have been pressed on average in each game. A is pressed 2.1 times more than needed, B 3.5 times, X 3.1 times, and Y 4.8 times. These results are mostly in line with what was expected, as Y is used by most of the main key mechanics, B and X are used for some of them, and A is used only for things that are supposed to happen once, such as activating a button or unlocking an invisible door.

A is also the button that players get right most of the time (with only 48 substitutions out of 482, 10%), because every object that can be interacted with by pressing that button is a "one click only", meaning that players cannot get it wrong multiple times. Other things such as key grabbing happen more often, and errors can therefore happen multiple times. The initial intuition would be that A, being the button in the easiest position to press, would be intuitively be pressed as substitute of others, but this does not happen as often as it does with X, which is used as substitute of other buttons 166 times against the 117 of A.

Looking at the whole picture, the behaviour that emerges seems to indicate that players do focus on the button scheme, getting the right interaction 70% of the times. However, It also seems that expert players would rather try to complete an action as quickly as possible rather than complete it without making a mistake. This is understandable as there is no penalty for misclicking a button, but it also suggests that, given the high amount of correct interactions, they either learned the control schemes fairly quickly, or that they did pay attention to the required button most of the times. Further analysis of the distribution of missed hits during a game session will give a more definitive answer.

It also surprises that the role of A, considered to be the button that most players would likely press, has not been supported by the data. On the contrary, X has often been the substitute for other actions, despite not being the button that is pressed the most on average. In other words, when an interaction is possible and players do not know what to press, they are most likely to go for X instead of A. This is confirmed by the distribution of Y: despite being pressed more than the other buttons, because of the key swapping, it is not often used as substitute for other interactions.

6   Conclusions

In this paper we have introduced a preliminary study aimed at understanding how players' interact with non-standard button schemes. From our preliminary data it seems that players actively focus on learning a new button scheme if they have not seen a game before, getting the pressed button right most of the time. However, speed seems to be an important variable that plays a role during gameplay, with more missed interactions than wrong ones, and with a significant amount of missed interactions following one another.

There is a huge gap in literature when it comes to the relationship between controllers, players' adaptation and gameplay, and there is little knowledge of how environmental factors could have influenced the data. It is way too early to make conclusive assumptions, and it is our hope that this initial study will raise more question than it answers. Replication studies will be needed to rule out potentially influential factors that have not been foreseen in the design of the experience.

References

1. Kent, S. L.: The Ultimate History of Video Games: Volume Two: from Pong to Pokemon and beyond. the story behind the craze that touched our li ves and changed the world. Three Rivers Press, New York, USA (2010)

2. Cummings, A. H.: The evolution of game controllers and control schemes and their effect on their games. In: The 17th annual university of southampton multimedia systems conference (Vol. 21). (2007)
3. Ke, X., Wagner, C.: The Impact of Game Peripherals on the Gamer Experience and Performance. In: International Conference on Human Computer Interaction (pp. 256–272). Springer, Cham. (2019)
4. Rogers, R., Bowman, N.D., Oliver, M.B.: It's not the model that doesn't fit, it's the controller! The role of cognitive skills in understanding the links between natural mapping, performance, and enjoyment of console video games. Comput. Human Behav. **49**, 588–596 (2015)
5. Biocca, F.: The cyborg's dilemma: Progressive embodiment in virtual environments. Journal of computer-mediated communication, 3(2), JCMC324. (1997)
6. Gerling, K. M., Klauser, M., Niesenhaus, J.: Measuring the impact of game controllers on player experience in FPS games. In: Proceedings of the 15th International Academic MindTrek Conference: Envisioning Future Media Environments, pp. 83–86 (2011)
7. Limperos, A.M., Schmierbach, M.G., Kegerise, A.D., Dardis, F.E.: Gaming across different consoles: exploring the influence of control scheme on game-player enjoyment. Cyberpsychol. Behav. Soc. Netw. **14**(6), 345–350 (2011)
8. Ellick, W., Mirza-Babaei, P., Wood, S., Smith, D., Nacke, L. E.: Assessing user preference of video game controller button settings. In: CHI'13 Extended Abstracts on Human Factors in Computing Systems, pp. 1107–1112 (2013)

3D Dynamic Hand Gestures Recognition Using the Leap Motion Sensor and Convolutional Neural Networks

Katia Lupinetti(✉) , Andrea Ranieri , Franca Giannini ,
and Marina Monti

Istituto di Matematica Applicata e Tecnologie Informatiche "Enrico Magenes", CNR,
Via De Marini 6, 16149 Genova, Italy
{katia.lupinetti,andrea.ranieri,franca.giannini,marina.monti}@cnr.it

Abstract. Defining methods for the automatic understanding of gestures is of paramount importance in many application contexts and in Virtual Reality applications for creating more natural and easy-to-use human-computer interaction methods. In this paper, we present a method for the recognition of a set of non-static gestures acquired through the Leap Motion sensor. The acquired gesture information is converted in color images, where the variation of hand joint positions during the gesture are projected on a plane and temporal information is represented with color intensity of the projected points. The classification of the gestures is performed using a deep Convolutional Neural Network (CNN). A modified version of the popular ResNet-50 architecture is adopted, obtained by removing the last fully connected layer and adding a new layer with as many neurons as the considered gesture classes. The method has been successfully applied to the existing reference dataset and preliminary tests have already been performed for the real-time recognition of dynamic gestures performed by users.

Keywords: 3D dynamic hand gesture recognition · Deep learning · Temporal information representation · 3D pattern recognition · Real-time interaction

1 Introduction

Gesture recognition is an interesting and active research area whose applications are numerous and various, including, for instance, robotics, training systems, virtual prototyping, video surveillance, physical rehabilitation, and computer games. This wide interest is due to the fact that hands and fingers are used to communicate and to interact with the physical world [2]; then, by analyzing human gestures it is possible to improve the understanding of the non-verbal human interaction. This understanding poses the basis for the creation of more

---

K. Lupinetti and A. Ranieri—Contributed equally to this work.

© Springer Nature Switzerland AG 2020
L. T. De Paolis and P. Bourdot (Eds.): AVR 2020, LNCS 12242, pp. 420–439, 2020.
https://doi.org/10.1007/978-3-030-58465-8_31

natural human-computer interaction, which is fundamental for the creation of immersive virtual environments with a high sense of presence. Despite this popularity and interest, until a few years ago, finger movements were difficult to acquire and characterize, especially without the use of sophisticated wearable tracking devices, which usually turn to be quite unnatural. Indeed, there exist many methods trying to solve hand gesture recognition by using wearable devices [10,13,21]. With the recent technology improvement, fingers' tracks can be digitally obtained relying only on RGB cameras eventually enhanced with depth information. In this manner, it is possible to abstract human hands by adopting two main representations: 3D model-based and appearance-based [35]. Generally, 3D model-based representations are deduced by exploiting depth information, but there are methods trying to reconstruct 3D hand representations using only RGB-data.

Hand gestures can be classified as *static*, i.e. if no change occurs over time, or *dynamic*, i.e. if several hand poses contribute to the final semantics of the gesture within an arbitrary time interval. So far, several works address static gestures, focusing on pre-defined gesture vocabularies, such as the recognition of the sign language of different countries [20,25–27,30,36]. On the contrary, very few works address the detection and classification of dynamic hand gestures in a realistic real-time environment [11], even if dynamic gestures are recognized to be more natural and intuitive than the static ones.

To allow a user experience as much natural as possible, we decide to track hands without gloves or invasive controllers preferring contact-free sensors. Among the different tracking systems, we decided to adopt the Leap Motion sensor due to its easy availability and affordability. For this reasons, in this paper we aim at defining a method for dynamic gesture recognition based on 3D hand representation reconstructed from the Leap Motion sensor tracking. Our method relies on deep learning techniques applied to the images obtained by plotting the positions of the hands acquired over time on a specific 2D plane, condensing the temporal information uniquely as traces left by the fingertips that fade towards a value of transparency (the alpha value) equal to zero as time passes. Compared to also drawing the traces of the other edges that make up the hand, we have found that this approach maximizes the information that can be condensed into a single image while keeping it understandable for humans.

For the training, a public available dataset presenting 1134 gestures [8,9] has been used. The first stage of the evaluation of the deep neural network has been carried out on a subset of the 30% of the available gestures, maintaining the split as presented in the original paper [8] and reaching an overall accuracy of the 91.83%. We also propose our own dataset with about 2000 new dynamic gesture samples, created following considerations on the balance, number of samples and noise of the original dataset reaching an accuracy of over 98%. Finally, we will briefly talk about the real-time setup and how it has already been successfully used to acquire the new dataset proposed in this paper and to perform some preliminary user tests.

The rest of the paper is organized as follows. Section 2 reviews the most pertinent related works. Section 3 and 4 detail the proposed method and show the results of the experimentation carried out respectively. Finally, Sect. 5 ends the paper providing conclusions and future steps.

2   Related Works

The ability to recognize hand gestures, or more in general understanding the interaction between humans and the surrounding environment, has arisen interests in numerous fields and has been tackled in several studies consequently. So far, several commercial sensors for capturing full hand and finger action are available on the market, generally they can be divided into *wearable* (such as data gloves) and *external* devices (such as video cameras). Wearable sensors can address different purposes, for instance VR Glove by Manus[1], Cyber Glove System[2], Noitom Hi5 VR[3] are designed mainly for VR training; while the Myo Gesture Control Armband is especially used in medical applications [4]. This kind of technology is very accurate and with fast reaction speed. However, using gloves requires a calibration phase every time a different user starts and not always allows natural hand gestures and intuitive interaction because the device itself could constrain fingers motion [1,16,28,40]. Therefore, research on hand motion tracking has begun investigating vision-based techniques relying on external devices with the purpose of allowing a natural and direct interaction [2].

In the following sections, we review methods registering hands from RGB cameras (both monocular or stereo) and RGB-D cameras and interacting through markerless visual observations.

2.1   Methods Based on RGB Sensors

The use of simple RGB cameras for the hand tracking, and consequently for their gesture recognition, is a challenging problem in computer vision. So far, works using markerless RGB-images mainly aim to the simple tracking of the motion, as the body movement [7,22,32] or the hand skeleton [33,37,41]; while the motion recognition and interpretation has still big room for improvement. Considering the method proposed in [33], which presents an approach for real-time hand tracking from monocular RGB-images, it allows the reconstruction of the 3D hand skeleton even if occlusions occur. As a matter of principle, this methodology could be used as input for a future gesture recognition. Anyhow, it outperforms the RGB-methods but not the RGB-D ones presenting some difficulties when the background has similar appearance as the hand and when multiple hands are close in the input image.

---

[1] https://manus-vr.com/.
[2] http://www.cyberglovesystems.com/.
[3] https://hi5vrglove.com/.

Focusing on hand gesture recognition, Barros et al. [5] propose a deep neural model to recognize dynamic gestures with minimal image pre-processing and real time recognition. Despite the encouraging results obtained by the authors, the recognized gestures are significantly different from each other, so the classes are well divided, which usually greatly simplifies the recognition of the gestures.

Recently, [39] proposes a system for the 3D dynamic hand gesture recognition by a deep learning architecture that uses a Convolutional Neural Network (CNN) applied on Discrete Fourier Transform on the artificial images. The main limitation of this approach is represented by the acquisition setup, i.e. it must be used in an environment where the cameras are static or where the relative movement between the background and the person is minimal.

2.2   Methods Based on Depth Sensors

To avoid many issues related to the use of simple RGB-images, depth cameras are widely used for hand tracking and gesture recognition purposes. Generally, the most commonly used depth cameras are the Microsoft Kinect[4] and the Leap Motion (LM) sensor[5].

The Kinect sensor includes a QVGA (320 × 240) depth camera and a VGA (640 × 480) video camera, both of which produce image streams at 30 frames per seconds (fps). The sensor is limited by near and far thresholds for depth estimation and it is able to track the full-body [43]. The LM is a compact sensor that exploits two CMOS cameras capturing images with a frame rate of 50 up to 200 fps [3]. It is very suitable for hand gesture recognition because it is explicitly targeted to hand and finger tracking. Another type of sensor that is adopted sometimes is the Time-of-Flight camera, which measures distance between the camera and the subject for each point of the image by using an artificial light signal provided by a laser or an LED. This type of sensor has a low resolution (176 × 144) and it is generally paired with a higher resolution RGB camera [6].

Using one of the above mentioned sensors, there are several works that address the recognition of *static* hand gestures. Mapari and Kharat [30] proposed a method to recognize the American Sign Language (ASL). Using the data extracted from the LMC, they compute 48 features (18 positional values, 15 distance values and 15 angle values) for 4672 collected signs (146 users for 32 signs) feeding an artificial neural network by using a Multilayer Perceptron (MLP). Filho et al. [42] use the normalized positions of the five finger tips and the four angles between adjacent fingers as features for different classifiers (K-Nearest Neighbors, Support Vector Machines and Decision Trees). They compare the effectiveness of the proposed classifiers over a dataset of 1200 samples (6 uses for 10 gestures) discovering that the Decision Trees is the method that better performs. Still among the methods to recognize static postures, Kumar et al. [26] apply an Independent Bayesian Classification Combination (IBCC)

---

[4] https://developer.microsoft.com/en-us/windows/kinect/.
[5] https://developer.leapmotion.com.

approach. Their idea is to combine hand features extracted by LM (3D fingertip positions and 3D palm center) with face features acquired by Kinect sensor (71 facial 3D points) in order to improve the meaning associated with a certain movement. One challenge performing this combination relies on fusion of the features, indeed pre-processing techniques are necessary to synchronize the frames since the two devices are not comparable.

A more challenging task, which increases the engagement by a more natural and intuitive interaction, is the recognition of *dynamic* gestures. In this case, it is crucial preserving spatial and temporal information associated with the user movement. Ameur et al. [3] present an approach for the dynamic hand gesture recognition extracting spatial features through the 3D data provided by a Leap Motion sensor and feeding a Support Vector Machine (SVM) classifier based on the one-against-one approach. With the aim of exploiting also the temporal information, Gatto et al. [15] propose a representation for hand gestures exploiting the Hankel matrix to combine gesture images generating a sub-space that preserves the time information. Then, gestures are recognized supposing that if the distance between two sub-spaces is small enough, then these sub-spaces are similar to each other. Mathe et al. [31] create artificial images that encode the movement in the 3D spaces of skeletal joints tracked by a Kinect sensor. Then, a deep learning architecture that uses a CNN is applied on the Discrete Fourier Transformation of the artificial images. With this work, authors demonstrate that is possible to recognize hand gestures without the need of a feature extraction phase. Boulahia et al. [8] extract features on the hands trajectories, which describe *local information*, for instance describing the starting and ending 3D coordinates of the 3D pattern resulting from trajectories assembling, and *global information*, such as the convex hull based feature. Temporal information is considered by extracting features on overlapping sub-sequences resulting from a temporal split of the global gesture sequence. In this way, the authors collect a vector of 356 elements used to feed a SVM classifier.

In general, the use of complex and sophisticated techniques to extract ad-hoc features and manage temporal information requires more human intervention and does not scale well when the dictionary of gestures to be classified has to be expanded. Furthermore, the extraction of hundreds of features at different time scales may even take more CPU time than a single forward pass on a standard CNN already optimized against modern GPU architectures, thus not guaranteeing real-time performance in classification.

3   Overview of the Proposed Approach

Based on the assumption that natural human-computer interaction should be able to recognize not only predefined postures but also dynamic gestures, here we propose a method for the automatic recognition of gestures using images obtained from LM data. Our method uses state-of-the-art deep learning techniques, both in terms of the CNN architectures and the training and gradient descent methods employed.

In the following sub-sections, first we describe the problem of dynamic gesture recognition from images (Sect. 3.1), then we illustrate the pipeline to create the required images and how we feed them to the neural network model (Sect. 3.2). Finally, we introduce the LMHGD dataset adopted and the rationale that led us to use it (Sect. 3.3).

3.1 Problem Formulation

Let $S = \{C_h\}_{h=1}^{N}$ be a set of gesture classes, where N identifies the number of classified gestures. The variation of a dynamic gesture over time can be defined as:

$$g_i = \left\{ \mathcal{G}_i^\tau \right\}_{\tau=1}^{T_i}, \tag{1}$$

where $\tau \in [1, T_i]$ defines a certain instant in a temporal window of size T_i and $\mathcal{G}_i^\tau$ represents the frame of g_i at the time τ. Note that a gesture can be performed over a variable temporal window (depending on the gesture itself or on the user aptitude). The dynamic hand gesture classification problem can be defined as finding the class C_h where g_i *most likely* belongs to, i.e. finding the pair (g_i, C_h) whose probability distribution $\mathbb{P}(g_i, C_h)$ has the maximum value $\forall h$.

Let Φ be a mapping that transforms the space and the temporal information associated with a gesture g_i resulting into a single image defined as:

$$I_i = \Phi(g_i) = \sum_{\tau=1}^{T_i} \Phi(\mathcal{G}_i). \tag{2}$$

With this representation, there exists a single I_i for each gesture g_i regardless of the temporal window size T_i. This new representation encodes in a more compact manner the different instants τ of each gesture and represents the new data to be recognized and classified. Then, the classification task can be redefined in finding whether an image I_i belongs to a certain gesture class C_h, i.e. finding the pair (I_i, C_h) whose probability distribution $\mathbb{P}(I_i, C_h)$ has the maximum value $\forall h$.

3.2 Hand Gesture Recognition Pipeline

We propose a view-based approach able to describe the performed movement over time whose pipeline is illustrated in Fig. 1. As input, a user performs different gestures recorded as depth images by using a Leap Motion sensor (blue box). A 3D gesture visualization containing temporal information is created by using the joint positions of the 3D skeleton of the hands (magenta box) as obtained from the Leap Motion sensor. From the 3D environment, we create a 2D image projecting the obtained 3D points on a view plane (green box). The created image is fed to the pre-trained convolutional neural network (yellow box), to whose output neurons (14 such as the gesture classes to be classified) a softmax function is applied which generates a probability distribution which finally represents the predicted classes (purple box). Finally, the gesture is labeled with the class that obtains the maximum probability value (orange box). In the following the two main steps are described.

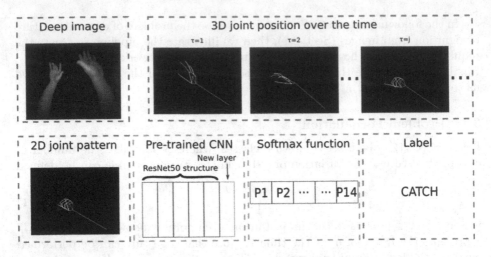

Fig. 1. Pipeline of the proposed hand gesture recognition

The 3D Visualizer. We used the VisPy[6] library to visualize the 3D data of the hands in a programmable 3D environment. The visualizer is able to acquire the skeleton data both from the files belonging to the LMHGD dataset (through the Pandas[7] library), and in real time using the Leap Motion SDK wrapped through the popular framework ROS (Robot Operating System) [34] which provides a convenient publish/subscribe environment as well as numerous other utility packages.

A 3D hand skeleton is created by exploiting the tracking data about each finger of the hand, the palm center, the wrist and the elbow positions. If at a certain time the whole or a part of a finger is not visible, the Leap Motion APIs allows to estimate the finger positions relying on the previous observations and on the anatomical model of the hand.

Once the 3D joint positions are acquired, spatial and temporal information of each gesture movement are encoded by creating a 3D joint gesture image, where 3D points and edges are depicted in the virtual space for each finger. Here, the color intensity of the joints representing the fingertips changes at different time instants; specifically, recent positions ($\tau \sim T_i$) have more intense colors, while earlier positions ($\tau \sim 0$) have more transparent colors. Finally, we create a 2D image by projecting the 3D points obtained at the last instant of the gesture on a view plane. In particular, we project the 3D fingertips of the hands on a plane corresponding to the top view, which represents hands in a "natural" way as a human usually see them. Figure 2 shows an examples of the 2D hand gesture patterns obtained for four different gestures. Although this view does not contain all the information available in the 3D representation of the hands, we

---

[6] http://vispy.org.

[7] https://pandas.pydata.org.

have found that it is sufficient for a CNN to classify the set of dynamic gestures under study very accurately.

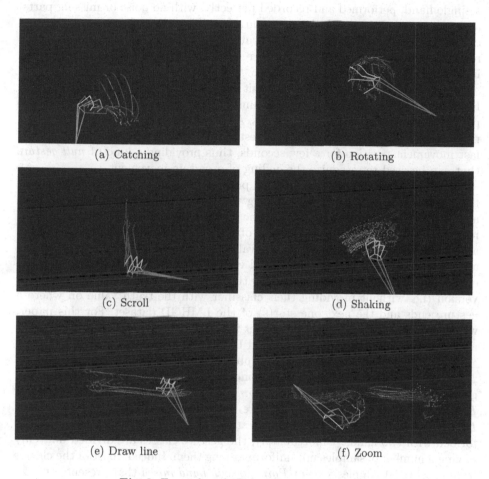

Fig. 2. Examples of 2D hand gesture patterns

Classification Method. The proposed method leverages a pre-trained ResNet-50 [18], a state-of-the-art 2D CNN that has been modified and fine-tuned to classify the images produced by our 3D visualizer. We decided to use a ResNet-50 because this kind of architecture is pre-trained on ImageNet [38] and it is one of the fastest at making inference on new images, having one of the lowest FLOPS count among all the architectures available today [17]. Unfortunately, given the modest size of the original LMDHG dataset, it would not have been possible to train from scratch a 3D CNN model capable of classifying all the available information coming from the LM sensor.

3.3   The LMHGD Gestures Dataset

Most of the reviewed gesture datasets are composed of gestures executed with a single hand, performed and recorded perfectly, with no noise or missing parts, and segmented always with the same duration. These hypotheses ensure a good class separation improving the classification results but they are far from the reality. For instance, it is not unusual to record hand trembles during the gestures including a significant amount of noise.

To improve the evaluation of different methods over a more realistic dataset, Boulahia et al. [8] define a dataset of unsegmented sequences of hand gestures performed both with one and two hands. At the end of each gesture, the involved participants were asked to perform a "rest" gesture, i.e. keeping the hands in the last movement position for a few seconds, thus providing a kind of *null gesture* that can be used to recognize the ending of a certain movement.

We chose their dataset as a starting point to test our method because it was the most realistic dataset created using the Leap Motion sensor that we were able to identify. It is our opinion that the original LMHGD paper provides three major contributions: i) the evaluation of the method proposed by the authors against the DHG dataset [12], ii) the evaluation of the method proposed by the authors against the properly segmented version of the LMHGD dataset, iii) the evaluation of the method proposed by the authors against the non-segmented version (i.e. without providing their classifier with the truth value on where a gesture ends and the next one starts) of the LMHGD dataset. For this paper, we decided to apply our method in order to replicate and improve only point ii), namely, against the properly segmented LMHGD dataset.

This dataset contains 608 "active" plus 526 "inactive" (i.e. classified as the *Rest* gesture) gesture samples, corresponding to a total of 1134 gestures. These gesture instances fall into 14 classes, *Point to, Catch, Shake down, Shake, Scroll, Draw Line, Slice, Rotate, Draw C, Shake with two hands, Catch with two hands, Point to with two hands, Zoom* and *Rest*, of which the last 5 gestures are performed with two hands. Unfortunately, the gesture classes are divided unevenly having a number of samples not uniform among them. Indeed, most of the classes have roughly 50 samples, except *Point to with hand raised* that presents only 24 samples and *Rest*, as previously said, that presents 526 samples.

4   Experiments

In this section, we present the experimental results obtained by processing the LMHGD dataset, represented in form of images from our 3D visualizer. The main obtained results concern the training of three distinct models through (i) images depicting a single view of the hands from above (see Subsect. 4.2); (ii) images obtained by stitching two views together (from the top and from the right) to provide further information to the classifier (see Subsect. 4.3); and (iii) a new dataset that we publicly release at this URL[8] containing about 2000 new

---

[8] https://imaticloud.ge.imati.cnr.it/index.php/s/YNRymAvZkndzpU1.

gestures performed more homogeneously with each other, with less noise and with fewer mislabeling occurrences than in the LMHGD dataset (see Subsect. 4.4). Indeed, we deem this dataset is richer and more suitable for the initial stages of training of CNN models when there are few samples available and it is important that the signal-to-noise ratio of the information used for training is high.

4.1 Training of the Models

The training took place using Jupyter Notebook and the popular deep learning library, Fast.ai [19], based on PyTorch. The hardware used was a GPU node of the new high-performance EOS cluster located within the University of Pavia. This node has a dual Intel Xeon Gold 6130 processor (16 cores, 32 threads each) with 128 GB RAM and 2 Nvidia V100 GPUs with 32 GB RAM.

The training was performed on 1920×1080 resolution images rendered by our 3D visualizer, properly classified in directories according to the original LMHGD dataset and divided into training and validation sets, again following the indications of the original paper [8].

As previously mentioned, the model chosen for training is a pre-trained version of a ResNet-50 architecture. Fast.ai convenient APIs, allow to download pre-trained architecture and weights in a very simple and automatic way. Fast.ai also automatically modifies the architecture so that the number of neurons in the output layer corresponds to the number of classes of the current problem, initializing the new layer with random weights.

The training has performed using the progressive resizing technique, i.e. performing several rounds of training using the images of the dataset at increasing resolutions to speed up the early training phases, have immediate feedback on the potential of the approach, and to make the model resistant to images at different resolutions (i.e. the model generalizes better on the problem). The specific section in [14] explains very well the concept of progressive resizing. For our particular problem, we have chosen the resolutions of 192, 384, 576, 960, 1536 and 1920 px (i.e. 1, 2, 3, 5, 8 and 10/10 of the original 1920×1080 px resolution).

Each training round at a given image resolution is divided into two phases (a = frozen, b = unfrozen), each consisting of 10 training epochs. In phase a, the weights of all the layers of the neural network except those of the new output layer are frozen and therefore are not trained (they are used only in the forward pass). In phase b, performed with a lower learning rate (LR), typically of one or two orders of magnitude less[9], all layers, even the convolutional ones, are trained to improve the network globally.

As neural network model optimizer, we chose Ranger as it combines two of the best state-of-the-art optimizers, RAdam [29] (Rectified Adam) and Lookahead [44], in a single optimizer. Ranger corrects some inefficiencies of Adam [23], such as the need for an initial warm-up phase, and adds new features regarding

---

[9] Fast.ai's *Learner* class has a convenient *lr_find()* method that allows to find the best learning rate with which to train a model in its current state.

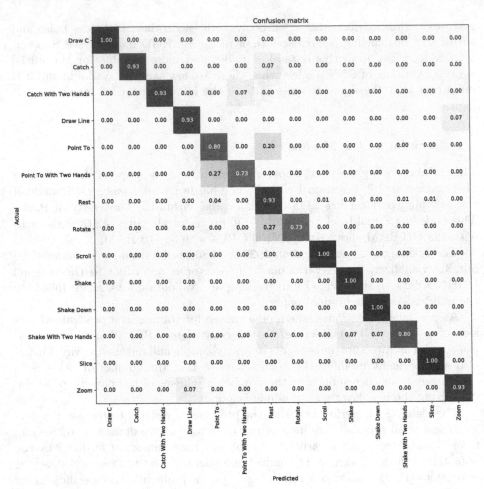

Fig. 3. Confusion matrix obtained using a single view.

the exploration of the loss landscape, keeping two sets of weights, one updated faster and one updated more slowly, and interpolating between them to improve the convergence speed of the gradient descent algorithm. Once all the training rounds were completed, the model with the best accuracy was selected for the validation phase. At the same accuracy between checkpoints at different training rounds, the model generated by the lowest round (i.e. trained with lower image resolution) was selected and reloaded for validation. This has a substantial advantage in the inference phase since smaller images are classified faster.

All the code and jupyter notebooks described in this section are available at the following URL[10].

---

[10] https://github.com/aviogit/dynamic-hand-gesture-classification.

Prediction/Actual/Loss/Probability

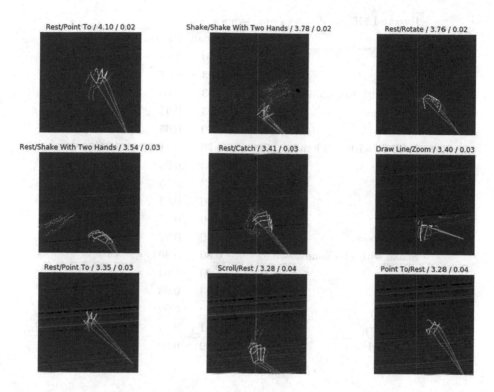

Fig. 4. Top losses plot obtained using a single view.

4.2 Evaluation on the LMHGD Gesture Dataset - Single View

To allow a further comparison with the method provided by Boulahia et al. [8], we split the dataset according to their experiments, i.e. by using sequences from 1 to 35 of the dataset to train the model (779 samples representing ~70% of the dataset) and sequences from 35 to 50 to test it (355 samples representing ~30% of the dataset).

With this partition, our approach reaches an accuracy of 91.83% outperforming the 84.78% performed by Boulahia et al. From the confusion matrix illustrated in Fig. 3, we can notice that most of the classes are well recognized with an accuracy over 93%. Misclassifications occur when the paired actions are quite similar. For example, the gestures *Point to* and *Rotate*, which are recognized with an accuracy of 80% and 73% respectively, are confused with the nosiest class *Rest*; *Point to with two hands*, recognized with an accuracy of 73%, is confused with the close class *Point to*; while *Shake with two hands*, recognized with an accuracy of 80%, is reasonably confused with the two close classes *Shake*, *Shake down*. Table 1 shows the detailed F-Score values for each class.

Table 1. F-score values for our classifier (single view) trained on the LMDHG Dataset.

F-score LMDHG dataset (single view)				
	Precision	Recall	F1-score	Support
Draw C	1.00	1.00	1.00	15
Catching	1.00	0.93	0.97	15
Catch with two hands	1.00	0.93	0.96	14
Draw line	0.93	0.93	0.93	15
Point to	0.55	0.80	0.65	15
Point to with two hands	0.92	0.73	0.81	15
Rest	0.94	0.93	0.94	162
Rotate	1.00	0.73	0.85	15
Scroll	0.88	1.00	0.93	14
Shake	0.94	1.00	0.97	15
Shake down	0.94	1.00	0.97	15
Shake with two hands	0.92	0.80	0.86	15
Slice	0.88	1.00	0.94	15
Zoom	0.93	0.93	0.93	15
Accuracy			0.92	355
Macro avg	0.92	0.91	0.91	355
Weighted avg	0.93	0.92	0.92	355

For a comprehensive evaluation, in Fig. 4 we show the top losses for our model. The top losses plot shows the incorrectly classified images on which our classifier errs with the highest loss. In addition to the most misclassified classes deduced also from the confusion matrix analysis (i.e. *Point to*, *Rotate* and *Shake with two hands*), from the analysis of the top losses plot, we can pinpoint a few mislabeled samples. For example, in Fig. 4 it can be seen that the third sample (prediction: *Rest*, label: *Rotate*) does not actually represent a *Rotate* at all. The same is valid for *Draw Line/Zoom*, *Scroll/Rest* and *Point to/Rest* samples, and having so few samples in the dataset, these incorrectly labeled samples lower the final accuracy of the model and prevent it from converging towards the global optimum.

4.3   Evaluation on the LMHGD Gesture Dataset - Double View

To reduce these misclassifications, we trained a new model by increasing the amount of information available in each individual image: in this case, in addition to the top view, we stitch the final image by adding a view from the right. This approach allows the classifier (exactly like a human being) to disambiguate between gestures that have a strong informative content on the spatial dimension implicit in the top view (such as the *Scroll* gesture, for example). Some example

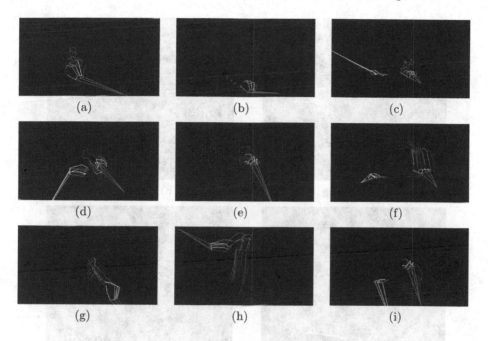

Fig. 5. Examples of *point* patterns present in the training set.

images are shown in Fig. 6. Using this pattern representation, the accuracy of our method reaches 92.11%. This model performs better than the one trained only with top view images, but the improvement is not as significant as we expected. The main reason is that the LMHGD dataset is challenging both in terms of noise, mislabeled samples and for the various semantic interpretations of the gestures which are collected from different users. Figure 5 shows different examples of the *Point to* gesture performed by several persons and used to feed the neural network. As we can see, it is objectively difficult, even for a human being, to distinguish shared characteristics among all the images that univocally indicate that they all belong to the *Point to* class.

4.4 Evaluation on Our New Dataset - Single View

With the aim of reducing this type of occurrence, we decided to create a new, more balanced dataset[11], with more samples per class, and with gestures performed in a more homogeneous and less noisy way. The dataset has around 2000 gesture images sampled every 5 seconds and each class has around 100 samples. The *Rest* class now contains only images of hands that are mostly still. Two further classes have been added: the *Blank* class which contains only traces of

---

[11] The images obtained from our new dataset and the ones for the LMHGD dataset are available at this URL: https://github.com/aviogit/dynamic-hand-gesture-classification-datasets.

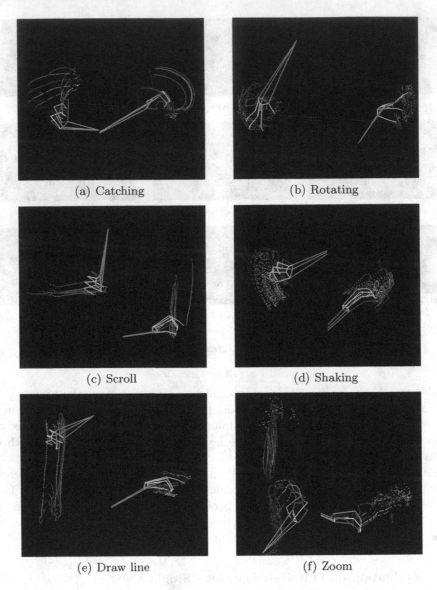

(a) Catching

(b) Rotating

(c) Scroll

(d) Shaking

(e) Draw line

(f) Zoom

Fig. 6. Examples of 2D hand gesture patterns obtained using a double view.

gestures that are distant in time (or no gesture at all) and the *Noise* class, which represents all the gestures not belonging to any other class. The dataset is provided both in the form of images and ROS *bags*. The latter can be replayed (in a very similar way to a "digital tape" of the acquisition) through ROS' *rosbag play* command and this will re-publish all the messages captured during the acquisition (skeleton + depth images) allowing to rerun the pipeline, possibly

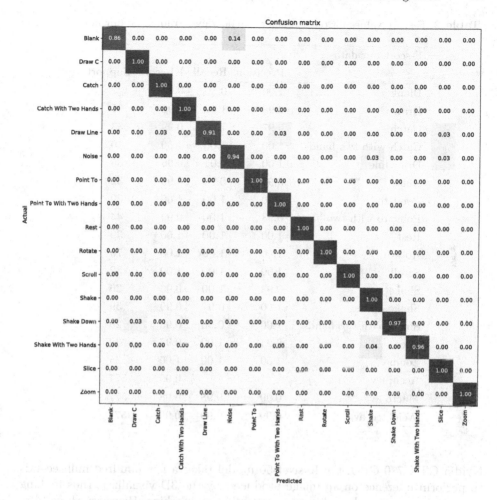

Fig. 7. Confusion matrix obtained using the new dataset.

by changing the processing parameters (e.g. displaying the gestures in a different way or changing the sampling window to improve the real-time acquisition).

Using this new dataset, we then trained a new model, using a 70%/30% random split (1348 images for the training set, 577 images for the validation set). The overall accuracy of the model is 98.78%. We report in Fig. 7 the confusion matrix obtained from this model. Table 2 shows the detailed F-Score values for each class.

4.5   Real-Time Application

The real-time acquisition, visualization and classification pipeline has already been used extensively to acquire the new dataset proposed in this paper and for qualitative user tests, again with a sampling window set to 5 s. On a PC with an

Table 2. F-score values for our classifier (single view) trained on our new Dataset.

F-score our dataset	Precision	Recall	F1-score	Support
Blank	1.00	0.86	0.92	7
Draw C	0.98	1.00	0.99	51
Catch	0.97	1.00	0.99	33
Catch with two hands	1.00	1.00	1.00	40
Draw line	1.00	0.91	0.96	35
Noise	0.97	0.94	0.95	32
Point to	1.00	1.00	1.00	30
Point to with two hands	0.98	1.00	0.99	44
Rest	1.00	1.00	1.00	39
Rotate	1.00	1.00	1.00	79
Scroll	1.00	1.00	1.00	32
Shake	0.93	1.00	0.96	26
Shake down	1.00	0.97	0.99	39
Shake with two hands	1.00	0.96	0.98	26
Slice	0.94	1.00	0.97	30
Zoom	1.00	1.00	1.00	34
Accuracy			0.99	577
Macro avg	0.99	0.98	0.98	577
Weighted avg	0.99	0.99	0.99	577

Nvidia GTX 770 GPU, the ResNet-50 model takes a few hundred milliseconds to perform inference on an image produced by the 3D visualizer, thus making the real-time approach usable on practically any machine. However, these tests do not yet have sufficient statistical significance and must therefore be extended to several participants before they can be published. This part will be a subject of future works.

5   Conclusions

In this paper, we have proposed a visual approach for the recognition of dynamic 3D hand gestures through the use of convolutional neural network models. The pipeline that we propose acquires data (on file or in real-time) from a Leap Motion sensor, it performs a representation in a 3D virtual space from which one or more 2D views are extracted. These images, which condense the temporal information in the form of traces of the fingertips with varying color intensity, are then fed to a CNN model, first in the training phase, then in real-time for the inference phase. The two models trained on the LMHGD dataset achieved an accuracy of above the 91% and 92% respectively, while the model trained on the new dataset proposed in this paper reaches an accuracy above the 98%.

Future work will have the primary objective of enriching the new dataset, both in terms of the number of images, possibly by joining it with the LMHGD dataset after making the appropriate modifications and re-labeling, and in terms of the number of recognized gestures. In addition, the performance of the real-time pipeline will be validated with a benchmark extended to the largest possible number of users.

References

1. Abraham, L., Urru, A., Normani, N., Wilk, M., Walsh, M., O'Flynn, B.: Hand tracking and gesture recognition using lensless smart sensors. Sensors 18(9), 2834 (2018)
2. Ahmad, A., Migniot, C., Dipanda, A.: Hand pose estimation and tracking in real and virtual interaction: a review. Image Vis. Comput. 89, 35–49 (2019)
3. Ameur, S., Khalifa, A.B., Bouhlel, M.S.: A comprehensive leap motion database for hand gesture recognition. In: 2016 7th International Conference on Sciences of Electronics, Technologies of Information and Telecommunications (SETIT), pp. 514–519. IEEE (2016)
4. Bachmann, D., Weichert, F., Rinkenauer, G.: Review of three-dimensional human-computer interaction with focus on the leap motion controller. Sensors 18(7), 2194 (2018)
5. Barros, P., Parisi, G.I., Jirak, D., Wermter, S.: Real-time gesture recognition using a humanoid robot with a deep neural architecture. In: 2014 IEEE-RAS International Conference on Humanoid Robots, pp. 646–651. IEEE (2014)
6. Van den Bergh, M., Van Gool, L.: Combining RGB and TOF cameras for real-time 3D hand gesture interaction. In: 2011 IEEE Workshop on Applications of Computer Vision (WACV), pp. 66–72. IEEE (2011)
7. Bobick, A.F., Davis, J.W.: The recognition of human movement using temporal templates. IEEE Trans. Pattern Anal. Mach. Intell. 23(3), 257–267 (2001)
8. Boulahia, S.Y., Anquetil, E., Multon, F., Kulpa, R.: Dynamic hand gesture recognition based on 3D pattern assembled trajectories. In: 2017 Seventh International Conference on Image Processing Theory, Tools and Applications (IPTA), pp. 1–6. IEEE (2017)
9. Boulahia, S.Y., Anquetil, E., Multon, F., Kulpa, R.: Leap motion dynamic hand gesture (lmdhg) database (2017). https://www-intuidoc.irisa.fr/english-leap-motion-dynamic-hand-gesture-lmdhg-database/
10. Bourke, A., Obrien, J., Lyons, G.: Evaluation of a threshold-based tri-axial accelerometer fall detection algorithm. Gait Posture 26(2), 194–199 (2007)
11. Caputo, F.M., et al.: Online gesture recognition. In: Eurographics Workshop on 3D Object Retrieval. The Eurographics Association (2019)
12. De Smedt, Q., Wannous, H., Vandeborre, J.P.: Skeleton-based dynamic hand gesture recognition. In: Proceedings of the IEEE Conference on Computer Vision and Pattern Recognition Workshops, pp. 1–9 (2016)
13. Dipietro, L., Sabatini, A.M., Dario, P.: A survey of glove-based systems and their applications. IEEE Trans. Syst. Man Cybern. Part C (Appl. Rev.) 38(4), 461–482 (2008)

14. Fang, L., et al.: Deep learning-based point-scanning super-resolution imaging. bioRxiv (2019). DOIhttps://doi.org/10.1101/740548. https://www.biorxiv.org/content/early/2019/10/24/740548

15. Gatto, B.B., dos Santos, E.M., Da Silva, W.S.: Orthogonal hankel subspaces for applications in gesture recognition. In: 2017 30th SIBGRAPI Conference on Graphics, Patterns and Images (SIBGRAPI), pp. 429–435. IEEE (2017)

16. Gunawardane, P., Medagedara, N.T.: Comparison of hand gesture inputs of leap motion controller & data glove in to a soft finger. In: 2017 IEEE International Symposium on Robotics and Intelligent Sensors (IRIS), pp. 62–68. IEEE (2017)

17. HasanPour, S.H., Rouhani, M., Fayyaz, M., Sabokrou, M.: Lets keep it simple, using simple architectures to outperform deeper and more complex architectures. CoRR abs/1608.06037 (2016). http://arxiv.org/abs/1608.06037

18. He, K., Zhang, X., Ren, S., Sun, J.: Deep residual learning for image recognition. CoRR abs/1512.03385 (2015). http://arxiv.org/abs/1512.03385

19. Howard, J., Gugger, S.: Fastai: a layered API for deep learning. Information **11**(2), 108 (2020). http://dx.doi.org/10.3390/info11020108

20. Kaluri, R., CH, P.R.: Optimized feature extraction for precise sign gesture recognition using self-improved genetic algorithm. Int. J. Eng. Technol. Innov. **8**(1), 25–37 (2018)

21. Kevin, N.Y.Y., Ranganath, S., Ghosh, D.: Trajectory modeling in gesture recognition using cybergloves/sup/spl reg//and magnetic trackers. In: 2004 IEEE Region 10 Conference TENCON 2004, pp. 571–574. IEEE (2004)

22. Khokhlova, M., Migniot, C., Dipanda, A.: 3D point cloud descriptor for posture recognition. In: VISIGRAPP (5: VISAPP), pp. 161–168 (2018)

23. Kingma, D.P., Ba, J.: Adam: a method for stochastic optimization (2014)

24. Kruusamäe, K., Pryor, M.: High-precision telerobot with human-centered variable perspective and scalable gestural interface. In: 2016 9th International Conference on Human System Interactions (HSI), pp. 190–196. IEEE (2016)

25. Kumar, E.K., Kishore, P., Kumar, M.T.K., Kumar, D.A.: 3D sign language recognition with joint distance and angular coded color topographical descriptor on a 2-stream CNN. Neurocomputing **372**, 40–54 (2020)

26. Kumar, P., Roy, P.P., Dogra, D.P.: Independent bayesian classifier combination based sign language recognition using facial expression. Inf. Sci. **428**, 30–48 (2018)

27. Kuznetsova, A., Leal-Taixé, L., Rosenhahn, B.: Real-time sign language recognition using a consumer depth camera. In: Proceedings of the IEEE International Conference on Computer Vision Workshops, pp. 83–90 (2013)

28. Lawson, G., Salanitri, D., Waterfield, B.: Future directions for the development of virtual reality within an automotive manufacturer. Appl. Ergon. **53**, 323–330 (2016)

29. Liu, L., et al.: On the variance of the adaptive learning rate and beyond (2019)

30. Mapari, R.B., Kharat, G.: American static signs recognition using leap motion sensor. In: Proceedings of the Second International Conference on Information and Communication Technology for Competitive Strategies, p. 67. ACM (2016)

31. Mathe, E., Mitsou, A., Spyrou, E., Mylonas, P.: Hand gesture recognition using a convolutional neural network. In: 2018 13th International Workshop on Semantic and Social Media Adaptation and Personalization (SMAP), pp. 37–42. IEEE (2018)

32. Mehta, D., Sridhar, S., Sotnychenko, O., Rhodin, H., Shafiei, M., Seidel, H.P., Xu, W., Casas, D., Theobalt, C.: Vnect: real-time 3D human pose estimation with a single RGB camera. ACM Trans. Graph. (TOG) **36**(4), 1–14 (2017)

33. Mueller, F., Bernard, F., Sotnychenko, O., Mehta, D., Sridhar, S., Casas, D., Theobalt, C.: Ganerated hands for real-time 3D hand tracking from monocular rgb. In: Proceedings of Computer Vision and Pattern Recognition (CVPR), June 2018. https://handtracker.mpi-inf.mpg.de/projects/GANeratedHands/

34. Quigley, M., et al.: Ros: an open-source robot operating system. In: ICRA Workshop on Open Source Software (2009)

35. Rautaray, S.S., Agrawal, A.: Vision based hand gesture recognition for human computer interaction: a survey. Artif. Intell. Rev. **43**(1), 1–54 (2012). https://doi.org/10.1007/s10462-012-9356-9

36. Ravi, S., Suman, M., Kishore, P., Kumar, K., Kumar, A., et al.: Multi modal spatio temporal co-trained cnns with single modal testing on RGB-D based sign language gesture recognition. J. Comput. Lang. **52**, 88–102 (2019)

37. Romero, J., Kjellström, H., Kragic, D.: Hands in action: real-time 3D reconstruction of hands in interaction with objects. In: 2010 IEEE International Conference on Robotics and Automation, pp. 458–463. IEEE (2010)

38. Russakovsky, O., et al.: ImageNet large scale visual recognition challenge. Int. J. Comput. Vis. **115**(3), 211–252 (2015). https://doi.org/10.1007/s11263-015-0816-y

39. Santos, C.C.d., Samatelo, J.L.A., Vassallo, R.F.: Dynamic gesture recognition by using CNNs and star RGB: a temporal information condensation. arXiv preprint arXiv:1904.08505 (2019)

40. Sharp, T., et al.: Accurate, robust, and flexible real-time hand tracking. In: Proceedings of the 33rd Annual ACM Conference on Human Factors in Computing Systems, pp. 3633–3642 (2015)

41. Stenger, B., Thayananthan, A., Torr, P.H., Cipolla, R.: Model-based hand tracking using a hierarchical bayesian filter. IEEE Trans. Pattern Anal. Mach. Intell. **28**(9), 1372–1384 (2006)

42. Stinghen Filho, I.A., Gatto, B.B., Pio, J., Chen, E.N., Junior, J.M., Barboza, R.: Gesture recognition using leap motion: a machine learning-based controller interface. In: 2016 7th International Conference Sciences of Electronics, Technologies of Information and Telecommunications (SETIT). IEEE (2016)

43. Suarez, J., Murphy, R.R.: Hand gesture recognition with depth images: a review. In: 2012 IEEE RO-MAN: the 21st IEEE International Symposium on Robot and Human Interactive Communication, pp. 411–417. IEEE (2012)

44. Zhang, M.R., Lucas, J., Hinton, G., Ba, J.: Lookahead optimizer: k steps forward, 1 step back (2019)

RGB-D Image Inpainting
Using Generative Adversarial Network
with a Late Fusion Approach

Ryo Fujii[✉] [ID], Ryo Hachiuma[ID], and Hideo Saito[ID]

Keio University, Yokohama, Japan
{ryo.fujii0112,ryo-hachiuma,hs}@keio.jp

Abstract. Diminished reality is a technology that aims to remove objects from video images and fills in the missing region with plausible pixels. Most conventional methods utilize the different cameras that capture the same scene from different viewpoints to allow regions to be removed and restored. In this paper, we propose an RGB-D image inpainting method using generative adversarial network, which does not require multiple cameras. Recently, an RGB image inpainting method has achieved outstanding results by employing a generative adversarial network. However, RGB inpainting methods aim to restore only the texture of the missing region and, therefore, does not recover geometric information (i.e, 3D structure of the scene). We expand conventional image inpainting method to RGB-D image inpainting to jointly restore the texture and geometry of missing regions from a pair of RGB and depth images. Inspired by other tasks that use RGB and depth images (e.g., semantic segmentation and object detection), we propose late fusion approach that exploits the advantage of RGB and depth information each other. The experimental results verify the effectiveness of our proposed method.

Keywords: Image inpainting · Generative adversarial network · Mixed reality

1 Introduction

Diminished Reality (DR), which allows removing objects from images and filling in the missing regions with plausible textures, plays an important role in many mixed and augmented reality applications. Previous methods for DR can be divided into two groups. The first group takes advantage of multi-view observations to obtain actual background pixels. Pre-observation [4], active self-observation [7], and real-time observation with multiple cameras [16] are representative of this group of methods.

They can provide accurate restoration since multi-view-based methods utilize pixels directly observed from other views. Mori *et al.* [13] presented 3D PixMix,

Supported by JST (JPMJMI19B2).

which addresses non-planar scenes by using both color and depth information in the inpainting process. However, if the background of the target object is also occluded in other views, a multi-view based method does not work. In the second group, inpainting-based methods can handle this problem, because they use pixels in the image to replace pixels that have been removed. Therefore, they do not require multiple cameras and pre-recorded observation.

Image inpainting is the task of synthesizing alternative content in missing regions. It can be used for many applications, such as photo editing, image-based rendering, and computational photography. Inpainting of RGB image can restore the region's texture, but it cannot restore the geometric structure of missing regions. In this paper, we aim to perform texture and geometry restoration of the missing region.

Traditional image inpainting works make use of low-level features from surrounding images. They work well on background inpainting tasks. However, they are unable to create novel image content not found in the source image. They often fail to restore complex missing regions and objects (e.g., faces) with none-repetitive structures. Moreover, they cannot consider high-level semantics.

Thanks to the rapid development of deep convolutional neural networks (CNNs) and generative adversarial networks (GANs) [8], convolutional encoder-decoder architectures jointly trained with adversarial networks have been used for inpainting tasks. Iizuka et al. [10] improved the consistency of image inpainting results by introducing a global and local discriminator. In this paper, we employ this global and local discriminator.

While GANs-based works show promising visually realistic images, it is quite difficult to make the training of GANs stable. Many methods are proposed on this subject, but stable training of GANs remains unresolved. Arjovsky et al. [1] proposed WGAN to handle this problem and prevent model collapse. Gulrajani et al. improved WGAN and proposed an alternative way of clipping weight seeking for a more stable training method [9]. WGAN-GP has been used for image generation tasks. On this type of task, it is well known that WGAN-GP exceeds the performance of existing GAN losses and works well when combined with l_1 reconstruction loss. Yu et al. [18] proposed to utilize WGAN-GP loss for both outputs of the global and local discriminator. We employ WGAN-GP to make training stable.

One simple solution that restores both the texture and geometry of missing regions is to train two networks independently; one restores textures with an input of RGB image and the other restores geometry with an input from an depth image. We call the no fusion approach. Another possible solution is to train one network which input is RGB-D four-channel image. We call the early fusion approach. Inspired by a recent object recognition method [17], we aim to construct an inpainting network that exploits the complementary relationship between RGB and depth information for RGB-D inpainting. Wang et al. [17] showed that the late fusion approach, which combines extracted features from RGB and depth images, improves the classification accuracy of objects in the images. Therefore, we also employ the late fusion approach using RGB and depth information.

We propose a method to jointly restore texture and geometry information in an image. Our method is based on GAN with the input of a pair of RGB. We employ the late fusion approach to fuse RGB and depth information. The experimental results show that our method successfully restored the missing regions of both RGB and depth images.

Our contributions are as follows:

- We propose deep learning architecture that jointly restores the texture and geometry of scenes from RGB and depth images.
- We employ the late fusion approach to fuse RGB and depth information and show late fusion approach is nicer than early and no fusion approach.

The rest of this paper are organized as follows. We first provide preliminaries of our work in Sect. 2. Section 3 reviews related work on image inpainting. The proposed RGB-D inpainting method is presented in Sect. 4. Section 5 describes the experiment setting and evaluate results and performance comparisons. This paper is concluded in Sect. 6. Finally, we discuss the future work in Sect. 7.

2   Preliminaries

2.1   Generative Adversarial Networks

The concept of generative adversarial networks was introduced by Goodfellow *et al.* [8]. Two networks, a discriminator (D) and generator (G), are jointly trained in the GAN learning process. The generator network learns to map a source of noise to the data space. First, the generator samples input variables from a simple noise distribution such the uniform distribution or spherical Gaussian distribution $P_{z(z)}$, then maps the input variables z to data space $G(z)$. On the other hand, the discriminator network aims to distinguish a generated sample or a true data sample $D(x)$. This relationship can be considered as a minimax two-player game in which G and D compete. The generative and discriminator can be trained jointly by solving the following loss function:

$$\min_G \max_D \mathbb{E}_{x \sim P_{data(x)}}[\log D(x)] + \mathbb{E}_{z \sim P_{z(z)}}[\log(1 - D(G(z)))] \tag{1}$$

2.2   Wasserstein GANs

Minimizing the objective function of GAN is equal to minimizing the Jensen-Shannon divergence between the data and model distributions. GANs are known for their ability to generate high-quality samples, however, training the original version of GANs suffers from many problems (e.g., model collapse and vanishing gradients). To address these problems, Arjovsky *et al.* [1] proposed using the earth-mover (also called Wasserstein-1) distance $W(\mathbb{P}_g, \mathbb{P}_g)$ for comparing the generated and real data distributions as follows:

$$W(\mathbb{P}_g, \mathbb{P}_g) = \inf_{\gamma \in \prod(\mathbb{P}_g, \mathbb{P}_g)} \mathbb{E}_{(\mathbf{x},\mathbf{y}) \sim \gamma}[\|\mathbf{x} - \mathbf{y}\|], \tag{2}$$

where $\prod(\mathbb{P}_g, \mathbb{P}_g)$ denotes the set of all joint distributions $\gamma(\mathbf{x}, \mathbf{y})$ whose marginals are, respectively, $\mathbb{P}_g$ and $\mathbb{P}_g$.

Its objective function is constructed by applying the Kantorovich-Rubinstein duality:

$$\min_{G} \max_{D \in \mathcal{D}} \mathbb{E}_{\tilde{\mathbf{x}} \sim \mathbb{P}_g} [\log(D(\tilde{\mathbf{x}}))] - \mathbb{E}_{\mathbf{x} \sim \mathbb{P}_r} [\log D(\mathbf{x})], \tag{3}$$

where $\mathcal{D}$ is the set of 1-Lipschitz functions, and $\mathbb{P}_g$ is the model distribution, defined by $\tilde{\mathbf{x}} = G(z)$, $z \sim P_z(z)$.

To enforce the Lipschitz constraint in WGAN, Arjovsky *et al.* added weight clipping to $[-c, c]$. However, recent works suggest that weight clipping reduces the capacity of the discriminator model. Gulrajani *et al.* proposed an improved version of WGAN adds a gradient penalty term:

$$\lambda \mathbb{E}_{\hat{\mathbf{x}} \sim \mathbb{P}_{\hat{\mathbf{x}}}} [(\|\nabla_{\hat{\mathbf{x}}} D(\hat{\mathbf{x}})\|_2 - 1)^2], \tag{4}$$

where $\hat{\mathbf{x}}$ is sampled from straight lines between pairs of points sampled from the data distribution $\mathbb{P}_r$ and the generator distribution $\mathbb{P}_g$.

3   Related Work

3.1   Image Inpainting

In early works, two broad approaches to image inpainting exist. Traditional diffusion-based and patch-based methods belong to the first approach. The diffusion-based method [2] propagates pixel information from around the target missing region in an image. Diffusion-based methods can only fill plain and small or narrow holes. However, the patch-based method, which searches for the closest matching patch and pastes it into the missing region, works well on more complicated images. PatchMatch [3], which represents this method, has shown compelling results in practical image editing applications. However, as these methods are heavily based on low-level features (e.g., the sum of squared differences of patch pixel values) and do not consider the global structure, they often cause semantically inconsistent inpainting results. Moreover, they are unable to generate novel objects not found in the existing image.

The second approach is learning-based methods, which train CNNs to predict pixels for missing regions. At the beginning, CNN-based image inpainting approaches can only deal with very small and thin holes and often generate images with artifacts, resulting in blurry and distorted images. To handle these problems, Pathak *et al.* [14] introduced Context Encoder (CE), which is firstly trained with both Mean Square Error (MSE) loss and generative adversarial loss [8] as the objective function. This method allows larger mask (64×64 mask in a 128×128 image) to be restored. Iizuka *et al.* [10] improves this work by introducing global and local discriminators. The global discriminator judge whether

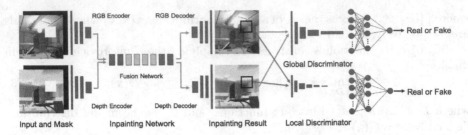

Fig. 1. Illustration of the RGB-D image inpainting network. The network takes the input of RGB and depth images with missing regions, and it jointly outputs restored RGB and depth images.

the restored section is consistent with the whole image, and the local discriminator focuses on the inpainted region to distinguish local texture coherency. Furthermore, Iizuka *et al.* employed dilated convolutions, which allow each layer to increase the area of an input. Yu *et al.* [18] proposed an end-to-end image inpainting model consisting of two networks: a coarse network and a refinement network, which ensures the color and texture coherency of generated regions with surroundings. They also introduced a context attention module that allows networks to use information from distant spatial locations and applied a modified version of WGAN-GP loss [9] instead of existing GAN loss to ensure global and local consistency and make training stable. We also employ this WGAN-GP in the proposed method.

3.2 Learning-Based RGB-D Inpainting

Only one prior work [5], which discussed RGB-D image restoration. It focused on predicting depth map and foreground separation mask for hallucinating plausible colors and depths in the occluded area. In this work, they use the independent completion network, a discriminator for RGB and depth images and a pair discriminator for RGB-D image. We employ the idea of pair discriminator in our proposed method.

4   Approach

Our proposed method predicts both missing RGB and depth pixels jointly. This approach restores not only the textures but also the geometries of a scene We propose using the GAN-based late fusion architecture to utilize each feature as complementary information. Our network consists of two parts, a completion network and a discriminator network.

4.1   The Network Architecture

RGB-D Inpainting Network. In Fig. 1, our inpainting network is depicted. Our inpainting network is basically based on the architecture proposed upon the Iizuka *et al.* [10]. It consists of an RGB encoder-decoder, a depth encoder-decoder, and a fusion network. The inpainting network is applied to images with a rectangle-shaped region with missing pixel. Hole region is implied with white pixels filled in the holes and a binary mask. The hole size and location are randomly selected during training. RGB and depth features, which are extracted from individual encoders, are used as the input of the fusion network. We adopt dilated convolution layers with different dilation rates in the four convolution layers of the fusion part to increase receptive fields.

Discriminator Network. We employ a discriminator network architecture proposed by Iizuka *et al.* [10]. It consists of two networks: a local discriminator and a global discriminator. The global discriminator judges scene consistency, and the local discriminator assesses the quality of the small completed area. Following Dhamo *et al.* [5] method, to encourage inter-domain consistency between RGB and depth, we set the discriminator's input as RGB-D data, four channels.

4.2   Loss Function

We combine content loss and generative adversarial loss for training. Unlike using the standard version of GAN loss, we adopt WGAN-GP, which makes training stable. We use l_1 reconstruction loss of RGB and depth images for content loss. WGAN-GP works well when combined with l_1 reconstruction as $Wasserstein$-1 distance in the WGAN is based on l_1 distance.

$$\mathcal{L}_{content} = \mathcal{L}_c + \alpha \mathcal{L}_d \tag{5}$$

where $\mathcal{L}_c$ and $\mathcal{L}_d$ denote RGB and depth l_1 reconstruction loss, respectively. We set α as 1.

Given a raw RGB image $\mathbf{x}_c$ and depth image $\mathbf{x}_d$, we choose a random size and location for the binary image mask. We make holes by pixel-wise multiplication of the image and mask ($\mathbf{z}_c = \mathbf{x}_c \odot \mathbf{m}$, $\mathbf{z}_d = \mathbf{x}_d \odot \mathbf{m}$). The RGB encoder and depth encoder takes concatenation of each image and binary mask. Therefore, the input of the RGB encoder and depth encoder are four channels (R, G, B color channels and the binary mask) and two channels (D, depth channels, and the binary mask), respectively. We utilize $[-1, 1]$ normalized image pixels as an input image of the network, and generate an output image with the same resolution $G(\mathbf{z}_c, \mathbf{z}_d, \mathbf{m})$. The details of training procedure are shown in Algorithm 1.

5   Experiments

5.1   Dataset

We evaluate our network with the SceneNet RGB-D dataset [12], which consists of five million rendered RGB-D images from over $15,000$ trajectories in

Algorithm 1. The training algorithm of our proposed method

---

while G has not converged **do**

    for $i = 1$ to 5 **do**

        Sample batch images $\mathbf{x}_c$, $\mathbf{x}_d$ from training data;

        Generate random masks $\mathbf{m}$ for $\mathbf{x}_c$, $\mathbf{x}_d$;

        Construct inputs $\mathbf{z}_c \leftarrow \mathbf{x}_c \odot \mathbf{m}$, $\mathbf{z}_d \leftarrow \mathbf{z}_d \odot \mathbf{m}$;

        Get predictions

$$\tilde{\mathbf{x}}_c \leftarrow \quad \mathbf{z}_c + G(\mathbf{z}_c, \mathbf{z}_d, \mathbf{m})_c \odot (1 - \mathbf{m});$$

$$\tilde{\mathbf{x}}_d \leftarrow \quad \mathbf{z}_d + G(\mathbf{z}_c, \mathbf{z}_d \mathbf{m})_d \odot (1 - \mathbf{m});$$

        Sample $t \sim U[0, 1]$ and $\hat{\mathbf{x}}_{cd} \leftarrow (1 - t)\mathbf{x}_{cd} + t\tilde{\mathbf{x}}_{cd}$;

        Update two critics with $\mathbf{x}_{cd}, \tilde{\mathbf{x}}_{cd}$ and $\hat{\mathbf{x}}_{cd}$;

    end for

    Sample batch images $\mathbf{x}_c$, $\mathbf{x}_d$ from training data;

    Generate random masks $\mathbf{m}$ for $\mathbf{x}_c$, $\mathbf{x}_d$;

    Update inpainting network G with RGB and depth $l1$ reconstruction loss and two adversarial losses;

end while

---

synthetic layouts. The poses of objects are randomly arranged and physically simulated with random lighting, camera trajectories, and textures. We train our model using about two million images taken from the SceneNet RGB-D dataset. Following the image inpainting task, we use images of size 256×256. We also conduct tests on $10,000$ images from the test data.

5.2 Implementation Details

The input of the completion network is an RGB image, depth image, and a binary channel. The outputs are inpainted RGB and depth images. The models are implemented by Pytorch 1.2.0.

5.3 Baseline Methods

To evaluate our late fusion approach, we also trained two baseline models using no fusion and early fusion approaches. In the no fusion approach, RGB and depth images are compensated via two individual networks. Therefore, one network uses the RGB image, and the other network uses the depth image as input. While the late fusion network has encoder-decoder architecture for RGB and depth, respectively, the early fusion approach only has encoder-decoder architecture for RGB-D data. For both the no fusion and early fusion approaches, other configurations are the same as that of late fusion.

5.4 Training Procedure

The sizes of holes are between 1/8 and 1/2 of the size of the image. We train the inpainting network for $900,000$ iterations using a batch size of 32 images on

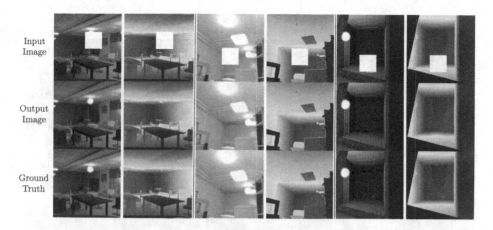

Fig. 2. The results of the proposed inpainting network. Missing regions in the images of the first row are colored in white. The pixels with large depth values are colored in red and the pixels with small depth values are colored in blue. (Color figure online)

an NVIDIA Titan GV 100 GPU. The total training time is roughly one week, and the inference is in real-time. We train our model with Adam optimizer [11] with the learning rate of 0.001.

5.5 Performance Evaluation

Qualitative Comparison. In Fig. 2, we show the inpainting result of three images from the dataset. We confirmed that our network restores the missing region of both RGB and depth images. This shows that the late fusion approach formed the edge of each restored region clearly.

We compare the qualitative performance of our late fusion approach with early and no fusion approaches. As shown in Fig. 3, compared to baseline methods, late fusion successfully merges the depth clue into RGB results to enhance sharp edges. However, early fusion sometimes provides a discontinuous result. The no fusion approach shows obvious visual artifacts, including blurred or distorted images in the masked region in both RGB and the depth of the masked region.

Moreover, we use the RGB-D image masked to the object as the input of our proposed network. As depicted in Fig. 4, our method generates a plausible depth inpainted image, while the RGB outcome includes some blurs. This result shows the possibility of applying our method to diminished reality (DR) applications.

5.6 Quantitative Comparison

RGB Inpainting Result. Table 1 shows the quantitative results of the RGB restoration of our proposed method. We present a comparison with baseline methods to verify the effectiveness of our proposed method. Since many possible

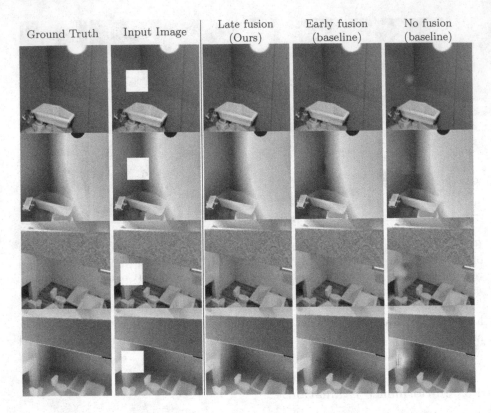

Fig. 3. Qualitative comparisons of our proposed method with two baselines.

solutions different from the original image content exist, image inpainting task does not have perfect metrics. Nevertheless, we evaluate our proposed method by measuring $l1$ loss, signal-to-noise ratio (PSNR) and the structural similarity (SSIM) following the RGB inapainting task [10]. Our proposed method slightly outperforms two baseline methods.

Depth Inpainting Result. Table 2 illustrates the quantitative evaluation of the depth inpainting result. We compute the absolute relative error (Abs rel), squared relative error (Sq rel), root mean square error (RMSE), and logged root mean square error (RMSE log) following the monocular depth estimation task [6]. From the table, our proposed method significantly improves the accuracy of the depth inpainting.

Input Image   Output   Ground
                         Image   Truth

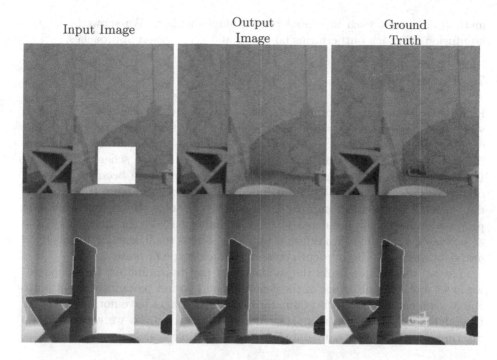

Fig. 4. The result of the proposed method with the input of the object mask.

Table 1. RGB quantitative result.

Method	$l_1\downarrow$	PSNR↑	SSIM↑
Early fusion	4.27×10^{-3}	$\mathbf{3.94 \times 10^{-3}}$	0.985
No fusion	6.33×10^{-3}	2.75×10^{-3}	0.980
Late fusion (Ours)	$\mathbf{3.38 \times 10^{-3}}$	2.61×10^{-3}	**0.987**

Table 2. Depth quantitative result.

Method	$l_1 \downarrow$	Abs Rel↓	Sq Rel↓	RMSE↓	RMSE log↓
Early fusion	11.0	4.29×10^{-3}	10.1	77.2	2.02×10^{-2}
No fusion	14.3	4.06×10^{-3}	5.45	93.4	2.28×10^{-2}
Late fusion (Ours)	**6.83**	$\mathbf{2.06 \times 10^{-3}}$	**2.21**	**52.2**	$\mathbf{1.29 \times 10^{-2}}$

6 Conclusion

In this work, we proposed a GAN-based RGB-D encoder-decoder inpainting network and evaluated late fusion on a synthetic dataset. Our network jointly restored the missing region of RGB and depth images. We discussed the fusion method enhancing each inpainted result complementary. We showed that the late fusion approach outperforms no fusion and early fusion approaches.

7   Future Work

First, we will compare our proposed method with [5], which also uses NYU depth v2 (real) for evaluation, in addition to SceneNet [12] (synthetic). Second, we will explore the fusion method. In this method, we show the advantage of the late fusion approach, of which fusion way is very simple. Fusion schemes for RGB-D image inpainting have not been proposed, but they have been explored for other tasks. Zeng *et al.* [15] focused on surface normal estimation from RGB-D data using a hierarchical network with adaptive feature re-writing, which are proposed to fuse color and depth features at multiple scales. In their work, Zeng *et al.* stated that single-scale fusion (our method) is inefficient for fusing RGB and depth when RGB and depth contain different type of noise.

Lastly, we will also study the validation of the discriminator. In this paper, we focus on the architecture of the generator and do not pay much attention to the discriminator model. Discriminators for depth images have not been studied thoroughly. Following the monocular depth estimation task, we will propose a discriminator that judges inpainted depth at multiple scales.

References

1. Arjovsky, M., Chintala, S., Bottou, L.: Wasserstein generative adversarial networks. In: ICML, pp. 214–223 (2017)
2. Ballester, C., Bertalmi, M., Caselles, V.: Filling-in by joint interpolation of vector fields and gray levels. IEEE Trans. Image Process. **10**, 1200–11 (2001)
3. Barnes, C., Shechtman, E., Finkelstein, A., Goldman, D.B.: PatchMatch: a randomized correspondence algorithm for structural image editing. ACM SIGGRAPH (2009)
4. Cosco, F.I., Garre, C., Bruno, F., Muzzupappa, M., Otaduy, M.A.: Augmented touch without visual obtrusion. In: ISMAR, pp. 99–102 (2009). https://doi.org/10.1109/ISMAR.2009.5336492
5. Dhamo, H., Tateno, K., Laina, I., Navab, N., Tombari, F.: Peeking behind objects: layered depth prediction from a single image. Pattern Recogn. Lett. **125**, 333–340 (2019)
6. Eigen, D., Puhrsch, C., Fergus, R.: Depth map prediction from a single image using a multi-scale deep network. In: NIPS (2014)
7. Flores, A., Belongie, S.: Removing pedestrians from google street view images. In: CVPR - Workshops, pp. 53–58 (2010). https://doi.org/10.1109/CVPRW.2010.5543255
8. Goodfellow, I., et al.: Generative adversarial nets. In: NIPS, pp. 2672–2680 (2014). http://papers.nips.cc/paper/5423-generative-adversarial-nets.pdf
9. Gulrajani, I., Ahmed, F., Arjovsky, M., Dumoulin, V., Courville, A.C.: Improved training of Wasserstein GANs. In: NIPS, pp. 5767–5777 (2017)
10. Iizuka, S., Simo-Serra, E., Ishikawa, H.: Globally and locally consistent image completion. ACM SIGGRAPH **36**, 107:1–107:14 (2017)

11. Kingma, D.P., Ba, J.: Adam: a method for stochastic optimization (2014)
12. McCormac, J., Handa, A., Leutenegger, S., Davison, A.J.: Scenenet RGB-D: can 5M synthetic images beat generic imagenet pre-training on indoor segmentation? In: ICCV, pp. 2697–2706 (2017)
13. Mori, S., et al.: 3D PixMix: image-inpainting in 3D environments. In: ISMAR, pp. 1–2 (2018)
14. Pathak, D., Krähenbühl, P., Donahue, J., Darrell, T., Efros, A.: Context encoders: feature learning by inpainting. In: CVPR, vol. 28 (2016)
15. Qiu, J., et al.: DeepLiDAR: deep surface normal guided depth prediction for outdoor scene from sparse LiDAR data and single color image. In: CVPR (2019)
16. Siavash, Z., Julien, E., Yakup, G., Nassir, N.: Multiview paraperspective projection model for diminished reality. In: ISMAR, pp. 217–226 (2003). https://doi.org/10.1109/ISMAR.2003.1240705
17. Wang, A., Lu, J., Cai, J., Cham, T.J., Wang, G.: Large-margin multi-modal deep learning for RGB-D object recognition. IEEE Trans. Multimed. **17**, 1887–1898 (2015)
18. Yu, J., Lin, Z.L., Yang, J., Shen, X., Lu, X., Huang, T.S.: Generative image inpainting with contextual attention. In: CVPR (2018)

3D Radial Layout for Centrality Visualization in Graphs

Piriziwè Kobina(✉), Thierry Duval(✉), and Laurent Brisson(✉)

IMT Atlantique, Lab-STICC, UMR CNRS 6285, 29238 Brest, France
{piriziwe.kobina,thierry.duval,laurent.brisson}@imt-atlantique.fr
http://www.imt-atlantique.fr

Abstract. This paper presents new methods of 3D visualization of graphs that allow to highlight nodes structural centrality. These methods consist in projecting, along the vertical axis, 2D graph representations on three 3D surfaces: 1) a half-sphere; 2) a cone and 3) a torus portion. The transition to 3D allows to better handle the visualization of complex and large data that 2D techniques are generally unable to provide. The 3D radial layout techniques reduce nodes and edges overlap and improve, in some cases, the perception of nodes connectivity by exploiting differently or better the display space.

Keywords: Radial layout · Immersive graph visualization · Centrality visualization

1 Introduction

Social network analysis is defined as a methodology that studies relationships between social actors [10]. It allows to model and visualize these networks of actors using graphs. Thus, within a network, we can often find groups actors according to a certain affinity [12] and isolated actors. However, the interpretation of this sociogram of affinities and/or rejections is sometimes not easy [8,11]. Indeed, to interpret the affinities and rejections that can be observed in a network, one should take into account, on the one hand, personal and social factors which determine the form and content of relationships, and on the other hand, processes of the interaction between different actors.

Thus, it is common to determine metrics, in the field of graphs, that characterize the affinities or the rejections that can be observed or the importance of each actor in the network, and find a visualization technique that allows to highlight these metrics.

For this, many 2D graph visualization techniques are useful to visualize affinities in networks or to visualize the importance or the role that each actor plays in the network. However, when faced with large and complex data, these techniques are generally unable to provide appropriate visualization due to a lack of display space for example.

© Springer Nature Switzerland AG 2020
L. T. De Paolis and P. Bourdot (Eds.): AVR 2020, LNCS 12242, pp. 452–460, 2020.
https://doi.org/10.1007/978-3-030-58465-8_33

Therefore the analysis becomes complicated. It is then necessary to increase the data display space, and for this it is possible to adapt certain 2D techniques to 3D [4,6], which still remains a vast area to explore [13].

In this paper, we illustrate our contributions to the transition to 3D from a 2D technique which allows to highlight the importance of nodes in the graph by their centrality.

2 Community Management and Graphs

Community management is an approach that consists in monitoring, controlling, influencing and defending the interests of a personality, a company or a brand on social networks. Thus, when analyzing a given social network, a community manager would need to understand the structure of this network; to identify different types of actors; to understand the nature of links of the neighborhood of certain actors; etc.

It is a business perspective that must be analyzed and transformed into a technical problem [5]. The network to be analyzed would therefore be a graph where each member would be represented by a node and where the edges between nodes could, for example, be friendship relations. In this graph, we would need to find the most important nodes, that is to say nodes which make bridge between others or the most central nodes, etc.

So, the importance of a node in a graph depends on the business interest and it can be characterized by a number of metrics such as centrality measures. In this paper, we are interested in two of them: the betweenness centrality and the closeness centrality [9]. The betweenness centrality is based on the frequency at which a node is between pairs of other nodes on their shortest paths. The closeness centrality shows, for its part, how close a node is to all the others in the graph.

3 2D Visualization of Centrality

The early work of [2], on graphs visualization, show the highlighting of betweenness and closeness centralities. [3] then propose a 2D radial approach by materializing the notion of centrality by concentric circles to illustrate the importance of nodes in the graph. This approach is based on an extension of stress minimization algorithm (MDS) [1,7] by including radii of circles determined from the centrality values of nodes. So, nodes having a strong value of centrality are in the center and those of weak value to the periphery. They also propose to emphasize the center of the network or else its periphery. The central emphasis is to make more distinctive nodes that are in the center of circles, which concentrates all the other nodes on the periphery. On the other hand, the peripheral emphasis spreads nodes of the periphery.

Thus, Fig. 1 shows the highlighting of closeness and betweenness centralities with a famous social network studied by Zachary [14]. This network describes friendship relations between 34 members of the karate club of a U.S. university

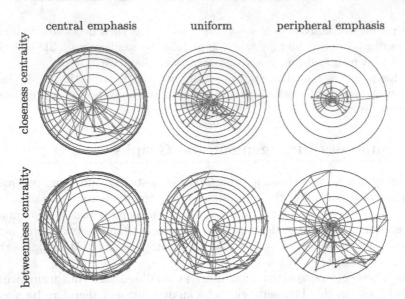

Fig. 1. Radial visualization of the karate club (34 nodes and 78 edges) [14]

in the 1970s. It is therefore represented by a graph of 34 nodes and 78 edges and its 2D visualization makes it possible to clearly and unambiguously distinguish all the nodes and edges thanks to the uniform radial visualization, to the central emphasis and to the peripheral emphasis. Indeed, «center and periphery are emphasized using transformed radii $r_i' = 1 - (1 - r_i)^3$ and $r_i' = r_i^3$ ($0 \le r_i \le 1$ and $0 \le r_i' \le 1$), respectively» [3].

However, faced with data comprising a few hundred nodes and edges, it will be impossible to distinguish certain nodes and edges. As an example, we have considered a larger graph of 419 nodes and 695 edges. This graph represents a network of actors who fund projects together. Thus, one actor is in relation with another if they fund all together the same project or a set of projects.

Figure 2 shows the highlighting of closeness and betweenness centralities of our example. The result of this graph shows the inability to see the connectivity of some nodes, because some edges hide others, which makes the network analysis a little more difficult.

4   3D Extension of Graphs Radial Visualization

To extend these radial representations to the 3D domain, we propose to project them, along the vertical axis, on three different 3D surfaces so as to always keep the radial 2D view in top view. The three projection surfaces are: 1) a half-sphere, 2) a cone and 3) a torus portion. Each projection constitutes a 3D object with which one can interact. Thus, adding a third dimension to 2D radial representations allows to better distinguish the nodes connectivity.

central emphasis   uniform   peripheral emphasis

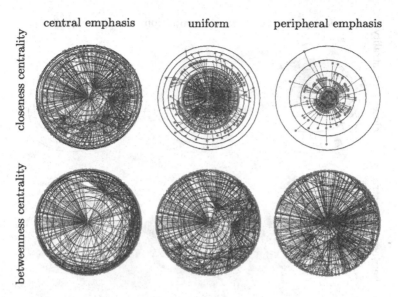

Fig. 2. Radial visualization of a larger graph (419 nodes and 695 edges)

In this paper, we are only interested in nodes placement and we will denote by *central nodes* the nodes that have a normalized centrality value equal to *1*, *intermediate nodes* those with a normalized value belonging to *]0; 1[* and *peripheral nodes* those that have a normalized centrality value equal to *0*.

4.1   3D Extension of the Uniform View

From the point of view of nodes distribution along the vertical axis, the spherical projection spreads out less the central nodes compared to the peripheral nodes. So the more nodes are on the periphery, the more they are spread out, which increases the visibility of gaps between them. The conical projection distributes nodes uniformly while the one on the torus portion spreads out less peripheral nodes. Figure 3 shows the result of uniform projections based on closeness and betweenness centralities.

When one changes the angle of view of the uniform spherical projection, one perceives much better the position differences of the peripheral nodes. So a uniform elevation over a half-sphere can provide both the benefits of uniform 2D representation and the peripheral emphasis. However it does not improve much the way of visually dissociating the central nodes from each other, since they are on top of the half-sphere. Moreover, edges between the center and the periphery are inside of the projection surface and some are hidden in dense areas.

The projection on the torus portion allows to better distinguish the central nodes. Moreover, we have an excellent view of edges between the center and the periphery, compared to the spherical projection, for with this approach, edges are outside the projection surface but some can also hide certain intermediate

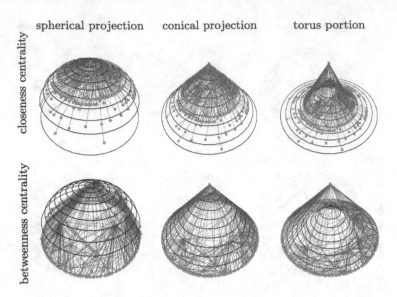

Fig. 3. Uniform 3D radial visualization (419 nodes and 695 edges)

nodes. However, there are edge overlaps in dense areas, but less significant than those observed with the spherical projection.

The conical projection is an intermediate version of spherical and the torus portion approaches with a particular property for edges. Indeed, when one changes the angle of view, it moderately provides a visualization of the central and peripheral nodes. With this approach, edges are mainly on the projection surface and are very visible, compared to the spherical approach.

Thus, an elevation on the half-sphere, on the cone and on the torus portion of the 2D uniform view provides, in addition, the benefits of the 2D representations emphasizing the center and the periphery.

4.2   3D Extension of the Central Emphasis

Figure 4 shows the result of the projection of the 2D views that emphasize the center. The spherical elevation of the central emphasis evenly distributes the intermediate nodes on the lower part of the half-sphere. Compared to the 2D representation, the combination of the spherical elevation and the central emphasis helps to mitigate the crushing of the intermediate and peripheral nodes. Thus, thanks to 3D, we reduce the crushing of the 2D radial view that emphasizes the center. Unlike the uniform elevation, the elevation of the central emphasis gives good visibility of edges between the center and the periphery. However, certain edges of the central nodes are hidden towards the periphery by the edges of the intermediate nodes, because they are much more inside the projection surface.

However, by combining the conical projection and the central emphasis, we reduce a little nodes crushing on the periphery and we improve the visibility of edges between the center and the periphery. So, thanks to the cone, we reduce a little the crushing of the 2D radial view that emphasizes the center, compared to the spherical approach where the crushing reduction is more important.

The projection on the torus portion of the central emphasis crushes all the intermediate and peripheral nodes and only highlights the central nodes. Also, it provides a better view of the edges between the center and the periphery, compared to the conical elevation of the central emphasis. However, it is much more complex to identify the edges of the peripheral nodes, unlike the spherical and conical projections that emphasize the center.

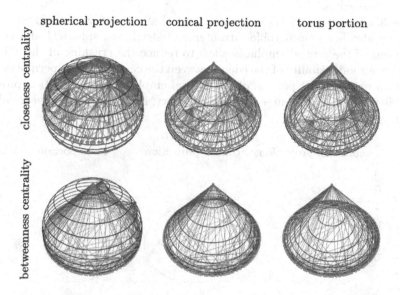

Fig. 4. 3D radial visualization that emphasizes the center (419 nodes and 695 edges)

4.3 3D Extension of the Peripheral Emphasis

Figure 5 shows that the combination of the peripheral emphasis and elevations on a half-sphere, on a cone and on a torus portion gather the central nodes on the upper part of the projection surface and spread out the peripheral nodes.

For the spherical and conical elevations of the peripheral emphasis, the intermediate nodes can still be seen even if they are grouped together. On the other hand, with the elevation on the torus portion of the peripheral emphasis, some intermediate nodes are hidden by the edges of the central nodes. Unlike the spherical and conical elevations that emphasize the periphery, the elevation on the torus portion of the peripheral emphasis always gives a view of the center and the periphery but with sometimes a little overlap.

4.4   Discussion

A uniform spherical elevation provides the same benefits as the uniform 2D view and the one emphasizing the periphery from different angles of view. With uniform conical projection, we have a good view of the edges between the center and the periphery. The projection on the torus portion provides an excellent view of the center and the periphery. Thus, the uniform spherical projection gives the same advantages as the peripheral emphasis, the uniform projection on the torus portion the same advantages as the central and peripheral emphases, and the uniform conical projection is an intermediate version of the spherical and torus portion approaches.

The 3D transition of 2D representations that emphasize the center or the periphery also has considerable advantages. Indeed, the spherical and conical projections of the central emphasis allow to reduce the crushing of the 2D view and to have good visibility of the edges between the center and the periphery. The projection on the torus portion of the central emphasis representation provides an excellent view of the center and the periphery, compared to the spherical and conical approaches.

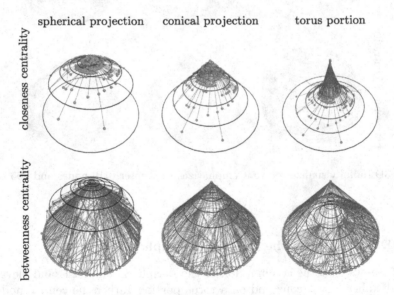

Fig. 5. 3D radial visualization that emphasizes the periphery (419 nodes and 695 edges)

The projection on different 3D surfaces of the peripheral emphasis allows to spread the peripheral nodes to improve the visibility of their edges. So, the elevation on the torus portion of the peripheral emphasis provides the same benefits as the central and peripheral emphases thanks to 2D and 3D respectively, unlike the spherical elevation of the peripheral emphasis which only provides the benefits of the peripheral emphasis. The conical elevation of the peripheral emphasis also provides, but moderately, the same benefits as the peripheral and central emphases. A summary of the pros and cons of each approach is presented in Table 1.

However, some nodes and edges are less visible in dense areas according to the projection surface. Indeed, with the spherical projection, the edges are inside the surface and some edges hidden, and there are others that cross the half-sphere. On the other hand, with projections on the cone and on the torus portion, the majority of the edges are respectively on the projection surface and outside the surface and there is less overlap compared to the spherical approach. With the combination of the peripheral emphasis and the projection on the torus portion, some intermediate nodes are less visible due to the edges of the central nodes, unlike the spherical and conical projections.

Table 1. Summary table of the different approaches.

	Uniform view	Central emphasis	Peripheral emphasis
2D approach	+ uniform nodes distribution according to their centrality value − too much node and edge coverings	+ central nodes spreading − covering of nodes and edges	+ peripheral nodes spreading − covering of nodes and edges
Spherical projection	+ good visibility of peripheral nodes − some edges are less visible	+ highlighting of the periphery and the center thanks to 3D and 2D respectively − covering of certain edges	+ double spreading of the peripheral nodes thanks to 2D and 3D spreads − loss of visibility of the center because of the surface type
Conical projection	+ good visibility of the center and the periphery − some edges are less visible	+ uniform 3D spreading of nodes thanks to the cone − some edges in periphery are less visible because of 2D	+ highlighting of the periphery and the center thanks to 2D and 3D respectively − some edges are less visible due to 2D
Projection on the torus portion	+ excellent visibility of the center and the periphery − some intermediate nodes are less visible	+ better visibility of edges between the center and the periphery − some nodes are less visible due to 2D	+ highlighting of the periphery and the center thanks to 2D and 3D respectively − some nodes are less visible due to 3D

5   Conclusion and Outlooks

We described three new methods of 3D graph visualization which consist in projecting on three different surfaces, according to the vertical axis, the 2D radial representations [3] highlighting the notion of centrality. These methods are a first transition to 3D of the concept of 2D "radial layout". The results of this work show, while preserving the characteristics of the 2D radial view (which can always be perceived in "top view"): 1) that a uniform spherical elevation gives a peripheral emphasis; 2) that a uniform elevation on a torus portion gives a central emphasis; 3) that an elevation on a cone provides the same benefits as the central and peripheral emphases, but less pronounced than elevations on the half-sphere and on the torus portion. These elevations also improve, in some cases, the perception of edges. In addition, the 3D transition of 2D representations that emphasize the center or the periphery allows to mitigate the crushing of 2D radial views according to the projection surface and to reduce the overlap of nodes and edges that can be observed with the 2D representations.

In the future, we will also study in detail the results obtained during the visualization of large data in terms of number of nodes and edges in order to identify the right approach to be used to visualize them. Moreover, we will work on improving the edges representation: either 1) by projecting them onto the surface in order to reduce the overlap of nodes or 2) by using the edge bundling algorithm to reduce the overlap of edges. We will also study other types of 3D surfaces and types of projections in order to identify the most appropriate approach or combination of approaches that could be used to visualize large and complex data.

References

1. Borg, I., Groenen, P.J.F.: Modern Multidimensional Scaling. Springer, New York (2005). https://doi.org/10.1007/0-387-28981-X
2. Brandes, U., Kenis, P., Wagner, D.: Communicating centrality in policy network drawings. IEEE Trans. Visual Comput. Graph. **9**, 241–253 (2003)
3. Brandes, U., Pich, C.: More flexible radial layout. J. Graph Algorithms Appl. **15**, 151–173 (2011)
4. Brisson, L., Duval, T., Sahl, R.: Visualisation immersive de graphes en 3D pour explorer des graphes de communautés. EGC-VIF (2018)
5. Chapman, P., et al.: CRISP-DM 1.0 - step-by-step data mining guide (1999)
6. Cliquet, G., Perreira, M., Picarougne, F., Prié, Y., Vigier, T.: Towards HMD-based immersive analytics. In: Immersive Analytics workshop of IEEE VIS 2017 (2017)
7. Cox, T.F., Cox, M.A.A.: Multidimensional Scaling. CRC/Chapman and Hall, Boca Raton (2001)
8. Dao, V.-L., Bothorel, C., Lenca, P.: Community structures evaluation in complex networks: a descriptive approach. In: Shmueli, E., Barzel, B., Puzis, R. (eds.) NetSci-X 2017. SPC, pp. 11–19. Springer, Cham (2017). https://doi.org/10.1007/978-3-319-55471-6_2
9. Freeman, L.C.: Centrality in social networks conceptual clarification. Soc. Netw. **1**, 215–239 (1978)
10. Freeman, L.C.: The development of social network analysis (2004)
11. Lancichinetti, A., Kivelä, M., Saramäki, J., Fortunato, S.: Characterizing the community structure of complex networks. PLoS ONE **5**, e11976 (2010)
12. Moreno, J.L.: Who Shall Survive? Foundations of Sociometry, Group Psychotherapy and Socio-Drama, 2nd edn. Beacon House, Oxford (1953)
13. Spritzer, A., Freitas, C.: Navigation and interaction in graph visualizations. Rev. Informática Teórica e Apl. **15**, 111–136 (2008)
14. Zachary, W.W.: An information flow model for conflict and fission in small groups. J. Anthropol. Res. **33**, 452–473 (1977)

A Preliminary Study on Full-Body Haptic Stimulation on Modulating Self-motion Perception in Virtual Reality

Francesco Soave[✉], Nick Bryan-Kinns, and Ildar Farkhatdinov

School of Electronic Engineering and Computer Science,
Queen Mary University of London, London E1 4NS, UK
f.soave@qmul.ac.uk

Abstract. We introduce a novel experimental system to explore the role of vibrotactile haptic feedback in Virtual Reality (VR) to induce the self-motion illusion. Self-motion (also called vection) has been mostly studied through visual and auditory stimuli and a little is known how the illusion can be modulated by the addition of vibrotactile feedback. Our study focuses on whole-body haptic feedback in which the vibration is dynamically generated from the sound signal of the Virtual Environment (VE). We performed a preliminary study and found that audio and haptic modalities generally increase the intensity of vection over a visual only stimulus. We observe higher ratings of self-motion intensity when the vibrotactile stimulus is added to the virtual scene. We also analyzed data obtained with the igroup presence questionnaire (IPQ) which shows that haptic feedback has a general positive effect of presence in the virtual environment and a qualitative survey that revealed interesting and often overlooked aspects such as the implications of using a joystick to collect data in perception studies and in the concept of vection in relation to people's experience and cognitive interpretation of self-motion.

Keywords: Haptic feedback · Virtual reality · Self motion · Sound

1 Introduction

Vection is a condition for which a visual stimulus can induce a strong and embodied sensation of locomotion relative to the fixed surrounding environment, even when the body is not physically moving [15]. The traditional real-life example used to describe vection is the sensation of motion that arises when observing a departing train on a neighbouring railway track. Although visual stimulus is traditionally the one that elicits the strongest self-motion, Keshavarz [4] found that auditory stimuli increase compellingness of visual vection and confirmed that self-reported auditory vection happens in about 25–60% of participants. The literature on auditorily and haptically induced vection is rather scarce and highly heterogeneous in terms of settings and setups. For instance, some studies on auditory-haptic vection do not have a visual component and participants are

© Springer Nature Switzerland AG 2020
L. T. De Paolis and P. Bourdot (Eds.): AVR 2020, LNCS 12242, pp. 461–469, 2020.
https://doi.org/10.1007/978-3-030-58465-8_34

simply blindfolded [5,10]. Notably Valjamae [14] did not find haptic feedback to facilitate or increase the intensity of self-reported vection, while Riecke did [10]. Furthermore, the role of vibrotactile stimuli often seems to be just a marginal addition to auditory and/or visual cues. Some researchers [2,8] explored the influence of haptic feedback applied to the feet of a person. However these studies are hard to compare. Riecke [10] haptic feedback was generated by adding a small USB fan to a hanging hammock chair to produce "barely noticeable" vibrations at 7 Hz. Participants were blindfolded and the study focused on circular vection. On the other hand, Farkhatdinov et al. [2] designed a visual optical flow, while Nilsson [8] had standing participants in a realistic visual context (e.g. a train and a lift).

Our experimental setup is concerned with producing a so called "whole-body" vibration. Research on full body haptics often focuses on audio-haptic cross modal mappings and multisensorial integration, which is regarded as a key point on building consistent VR experiences [1]. For example, Lindeman et al. [6] designed and implemented a wearable suit made of multiple individually addressable vibrotactile actuators placed on the upper body of a user. Recently, Merchel and Altinsoy [7], used vertical vibrations to explore vibrotactile feedback influence on music perception and enjoyment.

Vection has often been linked to presence (the feeling of "being there") in virtual environments [13]. A number of studies, [5,12,14] explored correlations between self motion and presence in virtual environment, and how understanding vection can be fundamental to improve the user experience of a VE. Most results show correlation between vection intensity and onset times with ratings of spatial presence and involvement [11].

In this paper we describe our hardware setup for whole-body haptic vibration and a user study to investigate the role of haptic feedback on linear forward vection in VEs under normal viewing conditions (e.g. no fixation point) and specifically when the vibrotactile signal is dynamically produced by the sound. We hypothesize that:

H1 Every condition (visual, audio and haptic) produces at least a minimum amount of vection, as found in previous research; [8]
H2 The addition of fully body haptic feedback, produces the highest vection intensity, similarly to how visual and auditory vection has been shown to be stronger than visual-only conditions [4];
H3 Full body haptic feedback increases ratings of presence similarly to how Larsson [5] reported higher presence by adding sound to visual stimulus.

2   Methods

2.1   Experimental Setup

We designed a virtual scene of a person sitting on a train and moving linearly at constant speed inside a tunnel. The idea of the train was used by other

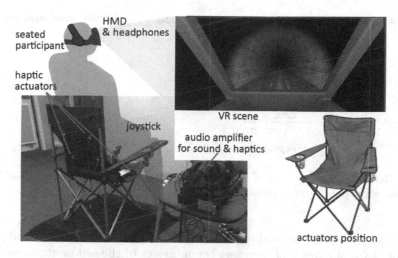

Fig. 1. Experimental setup for studying self-motion perception in virtual reality with visual, audio and haptic feedback modalities.

researchers before and intuitively it is correlated with the traditional paradigm used to explain vection in the previous chapter, that is the train departing from the platform. The VE was implemented in Unity3D (www.unity.com) and played through an HTC Vive headset. The audio is processed in Pure Data (pure-data.info) which triggers the sound at the start of the trials and applying a fifth order Butterworth Low Pass filter (cutoff 120 Hz) and sends the signal to the actuators. We used a Motu 828 Mk3 and Behringer Powerplay Pro XL to output the audio signals. The haptic feedback is produced by eight Lofelt L5 (www.lofelt.com) actuators (frequency range 35–1000 Hz). We designed and 3D printed a custom holder for each of them to ease the placement of the actuators which were then sewed to the back and seat of the chair in 4 × 2 design similar to [3].

2.2 Procedure

Twelve unpaid postgraduate students (6 males; age 29 ± 4.2) participated each in one session of 45 min. Eight of them rated their experience with VR applications at level 3 on a scale 1 to 5. In a mixed experimental design, each participant was exposed to three conditions (*visual* V, *visual-audio* VA, *visual-audio-haptic* VAH). The between factor was the ordering of conditions therefore each participant was randomly assigned to one of three sets, based on Latin Square design. The experimental sets were 1) V, VA, VAH; 2) VA, VAH, V; 3) VAH, V, VA. Each participant experienced 15 trials of 60 s duration each (5 trials per stimuli type). The task was described as "rate the intensity of your sensation of self-motion". We stressed our interest in their honest report and to only move the joystick if vection was perceived. They were made believe the platform on which the chair was mounted, could slightly move during the trials. This was done in

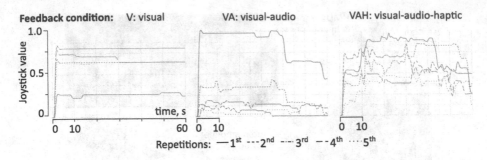

Fig. 2. Recorded joystick data of a typical participant for three different conditions. Each line corresponds to one repetition.

accordance with previous studies [5,9] that demonstrated how the actual possibility of physical movement increases the intensity of the self-motion sensation. An initial test scene was designed so participants could get used to the joystick range of motion. There was a 5 s pause between each repetition to avoid stimuli carryover effect. The study was approved by the University Research Ethics Committee (ref. 2207).

2.3 Measurements

Participants were asked to use a joystick (Logitech Extreme 3D Pro) to rate the intensity of vection, while immersed in the VE. After each set of conditions (V, VA, VAH) they were asked to fill the standard IPQ presence questionnaire. At the end of the study the participants were also asked to fill a qualitative survey with questions on their experience and on the task itself.

3 Results

3.1 Self-motion Intensity Reported with Joystick

Figure 2 shows the joystick data recorded for a typical participant. Variability across conditions and repetitions is easily observed.

In Fig. 3(left) we compared the joystick values for self-motion intensity across the three conditions for all subjects. The highest self-motion intensity is reported in condition VAH with the highest mean (0.49) across conditions. The lowest variation and mean (0.19) is reported in condition V.

Figure 3(right) shows the results reported with joystick across all subjects for each experimental set. It is important to consider these results as we were interested in exploring potential ordering and learning effects. Figure 3(right) highlights that the greatest difference between V and VAH happens in the experimental set 3 when VAH is presented first and followed by condition V.

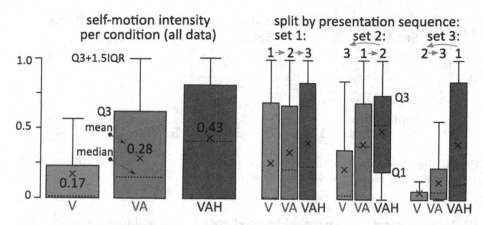

Fig. 3. Full joystick recordings of reported self-motion intensity across all participants for visual (V), Visual-Audio (VA) and Visual-Audio-Haptics (VAH) feedback modalities (left panel). Right panel demonstrates the results split by three presentations sets (order sets). Notations for mean, median second and third quartiles (Q2 and Q3) and 1.5 interquartiles range (IQR) limit are indicated in the left panel.

The interaction plots in Fig. 4 show the VAH condition points are always above the others (except for the *4th* repetition in Set 1). There is a visible positive trend, especially for conditions VA and VAH, particularly in Set 3, where the V condition also shows a negative slope. Additionally, the Set 3 plot shows highest and lowest absolute means for VAH and V respectively.

3.2 Haptic Effect on Presence

The standard iGroup Presence Questionnaire was presented three times to each participant, once after each type of condition (V, VA, VAH). The questions are grouped in four areas: Involvement, sense of Being There, Spatial Presence and Realism. Figure 5 shows the results for each area. Three out of four subgroups benefited from haptic feedback: "Being there", "Involvement", "Spatial Presence". "Being There" is the subgroup with the largest difference in median between VAH (M = 4.67) and V/VA (M = 2.33). The "Realism" subgroup instead reports unexpected result in which the VAH condition seems to be less consistent with the corresponding real-world experience, compared to condition V. This subgroup has opposite medians to those of "Being There" (M(V) = 4.67, M(VA/VAH) = 2.33).

3.3 Qualitative Survey

Due to a technical issue two responses had to be excluded. We summarize the main findings in four key-points:

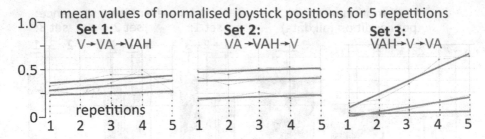

Fig. 4. Regression lines for each condition, in relations to sets and repetitions. Each data point is the mean of joystick values in a repetition.

P1 Vection is not a uniquely understood concept. Most literature on vection seem confident in the fact that people understand and interpret the expressions "self-motion", "illusion of motion", "vection", "sensation of motion", "speed" interchangeably. In our case, we found that most participant do not find these wording to be the same at all, actually some reported how the traditional description of vection (the train motion illusion) does not seem coherent with the description of "sensation of self-motion".

P2 Seven participants reported how the full congruency between sound and haptics was fundamental to the experience. However, six participants reported that the sound did not appear to be correlated with the visual and how this affected realism of the VE. Three participants questioned whether their sensation of motion was due to the additional modalities or just the duration of the visual animation.

P3 The usage of joystick to report self-motion intensity introduces a series of questions that should be considered. One participant reported how using a joystick automatically made him feel as if he "had to" or "was" controlling the animation. Four people reported they were not aware of the current position of the joystick and that it was hard to tell if they were pulling the lever or not and how precise it was.

P4 Every participant stated that haptic stimuli increased the realism of the VE and it made the experience unique and engaging (*"the haptic experience was quite visceral, I felt like having a 2D screen on my legs"*). Those who first experienced the VAH condition reported being "bored" by the others. This might confirm the order effect visible in the Set 3 of the other measures.

4   Discussion

All the conditions used in the study seem to have elicited self-motion confirming hypothesis H1. Comparing the means and maximum values of the whiskers in our joystick data, it is visible how the haptic seem to confirm our second hypothesis (H2) that haptic feedback enhances the intensity of self-motion perception. This is true both for the comparison between V and VAH and also between VA and

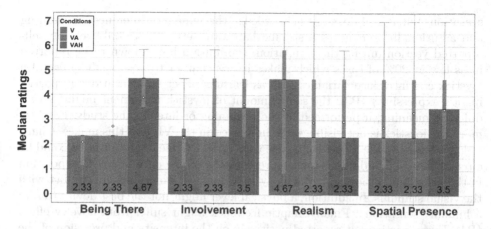

Fig. 5. Questionnaire subgroups. Every question was answered on a 0–7 Likert scale. Each subgroup is divided by the 3 conditions. Each bar represents 1 condition of the subgroup. The median value of each condition is shown at the bottom of each bar. White squares are the means. Whiskers are the min/max values $-/+1.5$ * interquartile range.

VAH conditions. The interaction plots show the regression line of VAH condition being constantly above the others. Figure 3 reveals how the difference between conditions V and VAH seem to be much stronger when multisensorial stimuli is experienced before a plain visual condition. A similar result was previously found by Riecke [10] and Nilsson [8].

The effect of haptic addition on presence is reported through the IPQ questionnaires which confirm that vibrotactile stimulus indeed increases sense of presence, involvement and spatial presence. Unexpectedly, the data reports low ratings of realism (e.g. "how real did the virtual world feel to you") which is in contrast with previous studies [5,12]. One possible explanation might come from the qualitative survey (P2): while every participant felt sound and vibration to be crossmodally congruent, this did not always happen with the visual stimulus. Some participants reported that the vision did not seem to necessarily match the audio. One hypothesis might be that haptic feedback increased the incongruities between visual and auditory stimuli, which produced a "less realistic" simulation when compared to the V and VA condition.

The qualitative survey also reports interesting findings. First, it is very hard to discern between participants who experience vection as in the "train illusion" example, from those who just focused on the speed or intensity of movement (P1). This is mostly because it seems not trivial to convey the idea of vection, especially in studies under normal viewing conditions, in that vection might be harder to induce. Some studies report how they initially have the participants experience real vection. Riecke [9] was able to physically rotate their own chair thus inducing real motion illusion in the participant before the study. This of course provides a safe method to ensure participants can later refer to the sensation, but it still does not acknowledge the semantic differences in wording and additionally it requires a specific hardware setup. If we only rely on self-reported vection during the simulation, the illusion it is known to be reported in as low at 20% of cases which makes it even harder to observe. The use of a joystick can introduce variables such as learning effect and variations in participant's expressivity (P3): the same amount of joystick movement might have a different meaning, if performed at the beginning or later in the study. Furthermore the joystick is not visible while immersed in the VE and this makes it hard to know where in the movement range you "are". On one hand this issue could be circumvented by adding a visual representation of the current joystick position in the visual animation, but it is likely that doing so would heavily conflict with the visual stimulus. In addition, a physical lever might not the best device to rate a human "sensation". Finally, haptic feedback might suffer from novelty effect (P4). Every participant reported positively on the intensity and precision of the vibratory stimulus. Although this is a positive feedback towards our hardware, it might also influence the data produced by a study. This condition might have induced participants to do or rate "more" no matter the "what".

5   Conclusion

Self-motion has been traditionally explored by means of quantitative analysis of self-reported and joystick values. Our participants reported some insights on how we frame the study of the illusion of self-motion that has not been often acknowledged in literature. We argue that if self-motion perception has to play a major role in the User Experience design of VEs then it is fundamental to include a qualitative perspective in the topic. Future research will engage with an in-depth statistical analysis, investigate the semantic relations of congruency between sound as visual in our context and focus on alternatives to joystick or self-reported measures.

Acknowledgements. The authors thank Lorenzo Picinali for fruitful discussions. This work is supported by the EPSRC and AHRC Centre for Doctoral Training in Media and Arts Technology (EP/L01632X/1). I. Farkhatdinov was partially supported by the UK EPSRC grant NCNR EP/R02572X/1.

References

1. Covaci, A., Zou, L., Tal, I., Muntean, G.M., Ghinea, G.: Is multimedia multisensorial? - a review of mulsemedia systems. ACM Comput. Surv. **51**(5), 1–35 (2018)
2. Farkhatdinov, I., Ouarti, N., Hayward, V.: Vibrotactile inputs to the feet can modulate vection. In: 2013 World Haptics Conference (WHC), Daejeon, pp. 677–681. IEEE, April 2013
3. Karam, M., Branje, C., Nespoli, G., Thompson, N., Russo, F.A., Fels, D.I.: The emoti-chair: an interactive tactile music exhibit. In: Proceedings of the 28th of the International Conference Extended Abstracts on Human Factors in Computing Systems - CHI EA 2010, Atlanta, Georgia, USA. p. 3069. ACM Press (2010)

4. Keshavarz, B., Hettinger, L.J., Vena, D., Campos, J.L.: Combined effects of auditory and visual cues on the perception of vection. Exp. Brain Res. **232**(3), 827–836 (2014). https://doi.org/10.1007/s00221-013-3793-9
5. Larsson, P., Västfjäll, D., Kleiner, M.: Perception of self-motion and presence in auditory virtual environments. In: Proceedings of Seventh Annual Workshop Presence 2004, pp. 252–258 (2004)
6. Lindeman, R.W., Page, R., Yanagida, Y., Sibert, J.L.: Towards full-body haptic feedback: the design and deployment of a spatialized vibrotactile feedback system. In: Proceedings of the ACM Symposium on Virtual Reality Software and Technology - VRST 2004, Hong Kong, p. 146. ACM Press (2004)
7. Merchel, S., Altinsoy, M.E.: The influence of vibrations on musical experience. J. Audio Eng. Soc. **62**(4), 220–234 (2014)
8. Nilsson, N.C., Nordahl, R., Sikström, E., Turchet, L., Serafin, S.: Haptically induced illusory self-motion and the influence of context of motion. In: Isokoski, P., Springare, J. (eds.) EuroHaptics 2012. LNCS, vol. 7282, pp. 349–360. Springer, Heidelberg (2012). https://doi.org/10.1007/978-3-642-31401-8_32
9. Riecke, B., Schulte-Peikum, J., Caniard, F., Bulthoff, H.: Towards lean and elegant self-motion simulation in virtual reality. In: IEEE Proceedings. VR 2005. Virtual Reality, Bonn, Germany, 2005, pp. 131–138. IEEE (2005)
10. Riecke, B.E., Feuereissen, D., Rieser, J.J.: Auditory self-motion simulation is facilitated by haptic and vibrational cues suggesting the possibility of actual motion. ACM Trans. Appl. Percept. **6**(3), 1–22 (2009)
11. Riecke, B.E., Feuereissen, D., Rieser, J.J., McNamara, T.P.: More than a cool illusion? Functional significance of self-motion illusion (circular vection) for perspective switches. Frontiers Psychol. **6**, 1174 (2015)
12. Riecke, B.E., Schulte-Pelkum, J., Avraamides, M.N., von der Heyde, M., Bülthoff, H.H.: Scene consistency and spatial presence increase the sensation of self-motion in virtual reality. In: Proceedings of the 2nd symposium on Appied perception in graphics and visualization - APGV 2005, A Coroña, Spain, p. 111. ACM Press (2005)
13. Sanchez-Vives, M.V., Slater, M.: From presence to consciousness through virtual reality. Nat. Rev. Neurosci. **6**(4), 332–339 (2005)
14. Väljamäe, A., Larsson, P., Västfjäll, D., Kleiner, M.: Vibrotactile enhancement of auditory-induced self-motion and spatial presence. J. Audio Eng. Soc. **54**(10), 954–963 (2006)
15. Väljamäe, A., Larsson, P., Västfjäll, D., Kleiner, M.: Sound representing self-motion in virtual environments enhances linear vection. Presence Teleoperators Virtual Environ. **17**(1), 43–56 (2008)

Author Index

Printed in the United States
By Bookmasters